A Century of Anarchy?

THE HISTORY AND THEORY OF INTERNATIONAL LAW

General Editors
NEHAL BHUTA
Chair in International Law, University of Edinburgh

ANTHONY PAGDEN
Distinguished Professor, University of California Los Angeles

BENJAMIN STRAUMANN
ERC Professor of History, University of Zurich

In the past few decades the understanding of the relationship between nations has undergone a radical transformation. The role of the traditional nation-state is diminishing, along with many of the traditional vocabularies that were once used to describe what has been called, ever since Jeremy Bentham coined the phrase in 1780, 'international law'. The older boundaries between states are growing ever more fluid, new conceptions and new languages have emerged that are slowly coming to replace the image of a world of sovereign independent nation-states that has dominated the study of international relations since the early nineteenth century. This redefinition of the international arena demands a new understanding of classical and contemporary questions in international and legal theory. It is the editors' conviction that the best way to achieve this is by bridging the traditional divide between international legal theory, intellectual history, and legal and political history. The aim of the series, therefore, is to provide a forum for historical studies, from classical antiquity to the twenty-first century, that are theoretically informed and for philosophical work that is historically conscious, in the hope that a new vision of the rapidly evolving international world, its past and its possible future, may emerge.

PREVIOUSLY PUBLISHED IN THIS SERIES

Sepúlveda on the Spanish Invasion of the Americas
Defending Empire, Debating Las Casas
Luke Glanville, David Lupher, and Maya Feile Tomes

The World Bank's Lawyers
The Life of International Law as Institutional Practice
Dimitri Van Den Meerssche

Preparing for War
The Making of the Geneva Conventions
Boyd van Dijk

The Invention of Custom
Natural Law and the Law of Nations, ca. 1550–1750
Francesca Iurlaro

The Right of Sovereignty
Jean Bodin on the Sovereign State and the Law of Nations
Daniel Lee

Jews, Sovereignty, and International Law
Ideology and Ambivalence in Early Israeli Legal Diplomacy
Rotem Giladi

Crafting the International Order
Practitioners and Practices of International Law since c. 1800
Marcus M. Payk, Kim Christian Priemel

A Century of Anarchy?

War, Normativity, and the Birth of Modern International Order

HENDRIK SIMON

Researcher, Peace Research Institute Frankfurt (PRIF) and Lecturer, Goethe University Frankfurt

OXFORD
UNIVERSITY PRESS

Great Clarendon Street, Oxford, OX2 6DP,
United Kingdom

Oxford University Press is a department of the University of Oxford.
It furthers the University's objective of excellence in research, scholarship,
and education by publishing worldwide. Oxford is a registered trade mark of
Oxford University Press in the UK and in certain other countries

© Hendrik Simon 2024

The moral rights of the author have been asserted

All rights reserved. No part of this publication may be reproduced, stored in
a retrieval system, or transmitted, in any form or by any means, without the
prior permission in writing of Oxford University Press, or as expressly permitted
by law, by licence or under terms agreed with the appropriate reprographics
rights organization. Enquiries concerning reproduction outside the scope of the
above should be sent to the Rights Department, Oxford University Press, at the
address above

You must not circulate this work in any other form
and you must impose this same condition on any acquirer

Public sector information reproduced under Open Government Licence v3.0
(http://www.nationalarchives.gov.uk/doc/open-government-licence/open-government-licence.htm)

Published in the United States of America by Oxford University Press
198 Madison Avenue, New York, NY 10016, United States of America

British Library Cataloguing in Publication Data
Data available

Library of Congress Control Number: 2023946431

ISBN 978–0–19–285550–3

DOI: 10.1093/oso/9780192855503.001.0001

Printed and bound by
CPI Group (UK) Ltd, Croydon, CR0 4YY

Links to third party websites are provided by Oxford in good faith and
for information only. Oxford disclaims any responsibility for the materials
contained in any third party website referenced in this work.

The Book's Main Argument: The Old in the New and the Newness of the Old

In the beginning there was anarchy—but was there? Anarchy stands for the absence of a common authority. A 'war of all against all'. While Thomas Hobbes's concept of a 'state of nature' is known to be hypothetical, for most scholars in the field of international relations and international law it seems to have found its historical realization in the nineteenth century. To this day, when it comes to the use of international force, the nineteenth century is (mis)understood as a century of international anarchy. Beyond binding international norms and regulations, it is said, states could wage war against each other whenever they deemed it politically necessary. Accordingly, it was not until the League of Nations, the Kellogg-Briand Pact, and the UN Charter that this 'free right to go to war' (*liberum ius ad bellum*) was gradually outlawed, and the prohibition of the use of force became a kind of *Grundnorm* in modern international order. The dark times of anarchy were over. Lighter times dawned—and, with them, radical transformations of international law and politics.

This, at least, is the established story of progress on war and international order that still prevails across the disciplines today. Yet this story is surprising, for a 'free right to go to war' in the nineteenth century has never been empirically proven. It has hardly been problematized either. So, what if *liberum ius ad bellum* never existed? What would be the implications of this finding for the historiography of the international order and its black-and-white images of anarchy and progress? And how could the emergence of this myth so central to the history of the international order be explained?

This book offers answers to these questions: by outlining a genealogy of modern war justifications, I argue that a 'free right to go to war' existed neither in the nineteenth century nor prior to it. It was largely an invention of Imperial German scholars, who wrote in a realist, militarist tradition against the international order of their time. Together with military and political leaders, they pursued a German *Sonderweg* ('special path') of judging war that subordinated law to military and political necessities as being in the spirit of a 'free right to go to war'. Paradoxically, this *Sonderweg* reading was then universalized in international historiographies after the World Wars. The characterization of nineteenth-century international relations as anarchic has prevailed to this day. But this characterization is as inaccurate as it is widespread: the nineteenth century is not to be understood as an anarchic photo-negative of the modern international order governing the use of force. It was in fact the era of its birth.

Understanding the Link between War, Order, and Peace: Hendrik Simon's Great Contribution to this Endeavour

Foreword by Lothar Brock

More than a century after the League of Nations was founded to contain war, followed by the signing of the Kellogg-Briand Pact to prohibit it, and by the creation of the United Nations to abolish it, cities are being bombed again (also) in the midst of Europe, civilians are fleeing in large numbers to escape the violence, and soldiers are creeping through muddy ditches risking and losing their lives in a sustained military struggle across international borders—a struggle driven by a crude mixture of imperial ambition and security claims on the one hand, and military self-assertion on the other. Is what we got used to call the international community sliding back into anarchy as it prevailed in the era preceding the League, the Kellogg-Briand Pact, and the establishment of the UN? In his impressive study, Hendrik Simon demonstrates that this would be a wrong conclusion, both with a view to our understanding of 'the long nineteenth century' and of what perhaps may be called the dialectical trinity of war, order, and peace in general.

I.

As to the first aspect, in 2018, Joseph H.H. Weiler, editor-in-chief of *The European Journal of International Law* (EJIL), introduced an article by Hendrik Simon by stating that it dealt with 'one of the most prominent and provocative doctrines in the history of international law'. With this, Weiler referred to the assumption that the nineteenth century was an era of anarchy characterized by the freedom of states to use force as they pleased (*liberum ius ad bellum*), or at least by the toleration of the respective behaviour by international law (Michael Bothe). Simon demonstrates that this perception of the nineteenth century continues to be quite popular in academic and non-academic writings. In most cases, reference to it constitutes a conscious claim; sometimes it merely echoes what is perceived to be a common understanding of the issue.

What makes the image of the nineteenth century as an era of anarchy so attractive? Simon's provocative but well-founded answer is that the 'anarchy thesis' fits well with both realist as well as with liberal images of what makes the world go round: realists can refer to the presumed anarchy of the nineteenth century when they want to underline their credo that with a view to peace and war, nothing much is changing in international relations. This implies that all efforts to move towards a lasting peace amount to mere episodes of ephemeral importance when dealing with the hard facts of inter-state politics. In contrast, those who follow a more Kantian approach to peace and war can claim that the League, the Kellogg-Briand Pact, and the UN, when read against the assumed anarchy prevailing in the nineteenth century, all point to a fundamental change in international relations from an 'old' to a 'new' world order. The idea of such a change is attractive to those who question that war (in the absence of a world state) is God-given: the darker the nineteenth century appears to be, the brighter the light that radiates from the subsequent era as a time of collective efforts to move closer to a lasting peace, or to what may be called the normative containment of war.

The distinction between an 'old' and a 'new' order is, of course, at the centre of the widely discussed 2017 study by Hathaway and Shapiro, *The Internationalists*. The authors stress that with the Kellogg-Briand Pact, for the first time in human history war was prohibited in a legal treaty. Simon's book does not take issue with this statement. It rather explains that the prohibition of wars of aggression after the First World War does not mean that the use of force was unrestricted in the nineteenth century. Simon's point is that the modern normative order designed to govern the use of force in international relations did not emerge with a 'big bang' in response to the preceding anarchy. According to Simon, the roots of the normative innovations of the twentieth century lie in the nineteenth century, more specifically, in the nineteenth-century European discourse on the normativity of war. Therefore, the nineteenth century should not be regarded as the negative counterpart of the later efforts to regulate international relations, but rather as the era of their birth. This is the central thesis of Simon's book. It opens up a productive way forward in observing the nineteenth century even when we concede that this century is no longer as understudied as it appeared to be a few years ago.

II.

As already hinted, Simon's study also opens up a new way of looking at the history of, and the issues at stake in, more recent aspirations to come to grips with the interplay between war and order. In the words of the author: 'The way we remember the nineteenth-century discourse on war and international order touches on essential questions of the emerging modern legal theory and its sources in the so-called "positivist" nineteenth century.' However, if the assumption of a free right to go to war in the nineteenth century plays an important role in structuring narratives on the reality of war and the feasibility of peace up to the present, it is all the more puzzling that the existence of a *liberum ius ad bellum* in the nineteenth century has for so long been undisputed in research. It is also unclear where this thesis actually came from. Hendrik Simon's book fills this gap. The way he does that fully lives up to the magnitude of the task. Simon uses discourse analysis as his methodological tool. His presentation of how he understands discourse analysis and how he works with it pays tribute to the high degree of methodological (and theoretical) reflexivity which permeates Simon's entire work. The author is a historian and a political scientist who is in constant dialogue with international law, and also works in this academic arena. This combination of expertise comes fully to bear in this book, and makes for enlightening reading not only for readers with an academic background in the three disciplines but also far beyond.

Hendrik Simon's ambition is not to debunk the idea of substantive change in international relations. Rather, his aim is to gain a better understanding of the historical pathways which it travelled in the complex interaction between politics and law in the nineteenth century. But why concentrate on the nineteenth century and not on early modernity *in toto* as the focus of the study? Besides reasonable arguments referring to the feasibility of his project, Simon substantiates the notion (already to be found in the pertinent literature) that as an era of multilaterally concerted politics, the nineteenth century is closer to the twentieth century than to the preceding ones. That may still sound a bit arbitrary, depending on the reader's understanding of historical periodization. However, Simon addresses this issue quite cautiously. On the one hand he includes new debates coming to the fore in early modernity (for instance on sovereignty and the idea of a mutually just war), on the other hand he uses the concept of a 'long' nineteenth century, reaching from the French Revolution to the First World War. This way he extends the period under observation (which from a historian's viewpoint remains risky business, of course) and at the same time softens the lines of distinction along which the different time periods are constructed.

For instance, as Simon observes, the French Revolution is often marginalized in legal histories of the nineteenth century in spite of the fact that the French Revolution and its political and academic aftermath produced a modern vocabulary for the justification and critique of war which permeate the entire nineteenth century. Consequently, the French Revolution features as a substantial point of reference in his analysis of war and order in the nineteenth century.

Opening up the focus on the beginning of the nineteenth century is matched by Simon's argument that the image of the nineteenth century as an era of anarchy results from a focus on 'the last five minutes' of the century (David Kennedy). In these 'five minutes' the public debate on the right to use force and on its normative limitations (which climaxed in the two Peace Conferences at the turn of the century) was overshadowed by the revisionist German ambition to attain a *'Platz an der Sonne'* that is, to cash in on the successful, if late wars of unification in the form of a stronger standing of Germany in the Concert of Great Powers. This leads Simon to the conclusion that the anarchical image of the nineteenth century at least in part reflects the unwillingness of the German government (assisted by the scholars of Clausewitz) to balance power political ambitions with the principle of restraint in the mutual relations among the great powers on which the Vienna Order was built. From this it follows that the image of the nineteenth century as an era of anarchy paradoxically resulted from the 'universalization' of the late German power politics as standing in for the typical behaviour of states in the entire nineteenth century. That this was by no means the case is spelled out by Hendrik Simon in an extremely rich analysis of the twists and turns in nineteenth-century discourse on the normativity of war. His reconstruction of this discourse offers an impressive contribution to the historiography of international relations in the nineteenth century.

III.

What do we know when we know that the widely assumed anarchy of the nineteenth century is a myth? Simon's analysis could be interpreted as strengthening realist readings of history, according to which all attempts to achieve peace beyond a mere truce are futile in a world of sovereign states. In contrast, Simon's analysis invites the reader to focus on the persistence of efforts to achieve a normative containment of war in the context of conflict. It invites us to understand the limitations of such efforts, their seriousness, the fragility of normative orders, and their power. This is important to grasp, in times of major upheavals and disruption such as the present.

The persistence of efforts to achieve a normative order spanning the ambitions of sovereign states comes to the fore in the fact that beyond Europe and the nineteenth century, the history of war is a history of its justification. The justification of war logically is tied to its critique. You cannot have one without the other. And this creates a basic dilemma for states as international actors. Their authority depends not only on their military power but also on their ability to justify the use of force with reference to existing (and changing) norms. In justifying their behaviour in terms of these norms, they are tempted to make the norms available to themselves, whereas the authority of the respective norms depends on their unavailability to any manipulation. It is this dilemma which comes to bear in the present struggle over a new world order in which colliding claims are justified in terms of the normative achievements of the past 200 years. Hendrik Simon's book is a fascinating contribution to understanding the resulting 'dialectical trinity of war, order, and peace' (Simon) which is at the centre of his observations.

Lothar Brock
Frankfurt
May 2023

The Multinormative Nineteenth Century on the Legitimacy of War

Foreword by Miloš Vec

It says a lot about societies what attitudes towards violence they practise and accept. This also applies to inter-state relations. Numerous testimonies in early human history attest to the existence of war and massacres going back a long way. With the emergence of writing and the condensation of administration, it is possible to reconstruct normative ideas and claims that accompanied such use of violence. To this day, justifications of war or the absence thereof remain a central object of research in all disciplines that have an interest in norms.

International Law, International Relations, and International History, in particular, have always studied the emergence and evolution of such justifications of violence. The questions that have arisen in these three (sub-)disciplines are also central concerns of the present important study: has the use of force between states been justified at all—and if so, under what circumstances? What justifications were given by the actors perpetrating violence for their actions? Were they accepted by the various publica that were addressed?

The nineteenth century has a special role to play here. In historiography, various attributions to this epoch oscillate. They range—at least for Europe—from the epoch of a 'Hundred Years' Peace', which is said to have successfully tamed war, at least in practice, to an age of glorious state sovereignty, in which war was as permissible as it was natural for the European powers. The latter position culminated in the notion of a 'free right to war', which has been ascribed to the actors of European states also in legal terms. And if even law characterizes war as permitted at all times and as an eminent outlet of state sovereignty, then of course the consequences for the coexistence of states and peoples are considerable.

Hendrik Simon's book takes a very Frankfurtian, critical stance towards such a perspective. He argues that war has historically required justification in principle. In doing so, he links theory and practice of inter-state relations. He looks a long way back in time and begins with a locus classicus, the Melian Dialogue. Here, opposing positions are articulated in nuce that still characterize any discourse on war today: the belief that power alone is sufficient meets the belief that violence requires justification.

According to our modern understanding, the strongest justification code lies in law, or more precisely, in international law. International law provides a canon of binding reasons for war. Wherever force is to be used, international law must be explicitly or implicitly invoked. Otherwise, this use of force is illegitimate and unlawful. Hendrik Simon's work is devoted to the genesis of this notion, and he reconstructs the various elements that led to this conviction in the course of the long nineteenth century. Justifications of force in classical European international law collide with the new normative ideas of the French Revolution. The Congress of Vienna establishes an inter-state order and limits the legitimate grounds for war. It is a history of the increasing juridification of international violence.

Yet, by no means is this nineteenth-century discourse on the legitimacy of war a purely historical discourse, nor is it conducted solely in the language of law. On the contrary, in the multinormative nineteenth century, legal arguments are deployed, but they are complexly interrelated with moral, political, and theological ideas. Constitutional law, constitutional theory, and political science focus on notions of sovereignty; other disciplines contribute competing normative spheres of reference. This interrelationship of discourses on war legitimacy is characterized by tensions and contradictions. In the various conflicts and wars of the nineteenth century, these normative notions are made explicit, and they are met in part with approval and in part with rejection. Observing this discourse provides a deep insight into the normative beliefs of historical actors. In this context, they interact with each other: 'war justifications and the international orders surrounding them co-constitute each other in discourse' (Simon in this book at 52).

These discourses on the legitimacy of war are with us to this day. Ideas about the rightness of political action are deeply imbued with narratives that have a historical dimension. Positive international law must be interpreted; it is subject to attack, reform, and fundamental criticism. Historical arguments have always had a special function in this field of law. It is therefore all the more important to make that century before the emergence of the prohibition of the use of force in the UN Charter and the Kellogg-Briand-Pact the subject of attentive readings of sources. What was the assumed need for legitimacy of war? What was the customary international law and positive treaty law of the time? What reasons for war were accepted as legitimate here? What attempts were there at international legislation on the *ius ad bellum/ius contra bellum*? How were argumentation patterns of religion, security, and counter-revolution dealt with? Can majority opinions be identified among the various voices? How did the various academic disciplines relate to each other? And are there particular preferences in this discourse that can be identified more strongly in some nations than in others?

This attempt at analysis is all the more important because it involves the century during which, on the one hand, the Kantian peace project was controversially debated and legal pacifist voices grew stronger, while on the other hand, interstate tensions eventually increased to the point of culminating in a First World War at the beginning of the violent twentieth century. Since then, too, every use of international force—even by autocrats and totalitarian systems—has been accompanied by its justification. Breaches of international law are made to appear legal.

Hendrik Simon's book helps to understand this paradox and the ambivalent role of arguments of humanity, religion, and civilization. It opens a view into the plurality of normative and political legitimation claims of interstate violence with unprecedented analytical acuity. Hendrik Simon's impressive study at the intersection of law, politics, and history serves to enlighten our society.

Miloš Vec
Vienna
March 2023

Series Editors' Preface

It has long been argued that the right to wage war (*ius ad bellum*), although an ancient notion widely evoked by Roman jurists, only became normative within modern international law and international relations after the end of the First World War. The decisive moment came with the signing of the Paris Peace Pact (or Kellogg-Briand Pact) of 1928, which declared that henceforth the 'recourse to war' would not be a solution to 'international controversies between states', nor 'an instrument of national policy in their relations with one another'. Hitherto the positive 'international law' that had emerged in the nineteenth century had imposed no restrictions upon states, which believed themselves to exist in an Hobbesian state of 'war of all against all' and that, as a consequence, they enjoyed a universal 'free right to go to war' (*liberum ius ad bellum*) to be exercised wholly at the sovereign's discretion. War was viewed in Carl von Clausewitz's famous—or infamous—words as merely 'a continuation of politics by other means'.

A Century of Anarchy? tells a very different story. This powerful new book provides a detailed historical account of the origins of the doctrine of *liberum ius ad bellum*, and of its discursive authority in the nineteenth century and beyond. It argues that the 'free right to go to war' was, in effect, not a norm supposedly shared by all European states, but rather a neologism that emerged in the context of the new German Empire, after the Franco-Prussian war of 1870–71. The ideologues of the *Kaiserreich*, from Heinrich Rettich—probably the first to assert *liberum ius ad bellum* as a positive legal norm—through to the neo-Hegelian nationalist historians and philosophers such as Heinrich von Treitschke and Adolf Lasson, all pursued a distinctly German *Sonderweg* ('special path'), which saw war and the unhindered right to wage war as crucial to the creation of the modern state. It was this *Sonderweg*, Hendrik Simon argues, that was subsequently universalized and further developed by the most influential of what he calls 'the proponents of the myth of *liberum ius ad bellum*', Carl Schmitt and Wilhelm G. Grewe, to the extent that it has today become commonplace in the history of international law and international relations.

Far from being a 'century of anarchy', however, the 'long nineteenth century' (1789–1918) saw the birth of the first sustained European discourse on the legislation of war. The Congress of Vienna, 1814/15, which brought the Napoleonic Wars to an end, may not quite have been, as Friedrich von Gentz, Prussian *littérateur* and former pupil of Kant, enthusiastically declared it to be, the 'Areopagus' of Europe, but, in Hendrik Simon's words, it 'sounded the bell for the emergence of a complex—and often paradoxical—European discourse on the international legitimacy of war.' It was complex and paradoxical, not least of all because the debates over the normativity of war and the new international law required to bring war to an end were accompanied by a number of wars of national liberation, driven by a new ideology: nationalism. From the point of view of the formation of modern international law, the most significant of these were the Italian *Risorgimento* and the unification of Germany. 'We are still under the influence of the reaction against the Napoleonic world-empire,' wrote von Treitschke in 1897. 'Both Italy and Germany offered the imposing spectacle of two great peoples rising to the attainment of a political unity.' But Italy and Germany were not alone. Between 1830 and the end of World War I, at least ten new states came into existence in Europe, all, in part or wholly, the creation of the new nationalism: Greece (1830), Belgium (1830–39), Romania (1856), Serbia (1867–68), Bulgaria (1878), Norway (1905), Albania (1912), and Finland (1917). Ireland, after a prolonged war of independence, followed in 1922. The 'Century of Vienna' was also the century in which, if the European powers had indeed ceased to fight amongst themselves, they had done so, at least in part, by shifting their attention to the world beyond Europe. 'For ten years,' observed the highly influential political economist Paul Leroy-Beaulieu in 1874, 'colonization has become the condition of peace within Europe ... It has quenched the desire for conquest and the restlessness of peoples: their eyes fixed on the immense spoils to be had in distant lands, they have forgotten their mean quarrels with their neighbours.' These two forces, the need to explain (and legitimate) the new empires of the nineteenth century, and the need to create what would eventually become the (human) right to self-determination, resulted in the emergence of a wholly new conception of the laws of war, which, as Hendrik Simon argues, drew its inspiration in part from Immanuel Kant's attempt to recast the older discourse of the 'law of nature and nations' into a positive international *right*. It is little wonder that in 1903 the most powerfully influential legal body of the day, the *Institut de droit international*, was awarded the Noble Peace Prize.

As Simon argues forcefully, the new international law that emerged after the settlement of 1815 was not, however, the sole factor in limiting and legitimating (or de-legitimating) future war. For the 'discourse of war' was always 'multinormative' and, when convenient, lawyers and policymakers could refer to earlier natural-law, moral, or religious arguments, as the Russians did to justify their war against the Ottoman Empire in 1877, or even—as in the case of the French invasion of Algeria in 1830—appeals to national honour. All of this may not have resulted, as Frank Kellogg and Aristide Briand predicted it would, in a more peaceful more balanced world. But it has created what Hendrik Simon calls 'a communicative practice of ordering the international', a new normative order that was born in the course of the nationalist and imperial struggles of the nineteenth century, and in which no state can claim with impunity, even to its own people, to possess the right to decide on grounds of its own security and self-interest whether or not to make war upon another. True Kantian peace may still be, as Kant himself had insisted that it could only ever be, a condition of future time, but the international order that alone could make it a possibility had, as this book demonstrates, come into being with the Congress of Vienna and continues, unbroken, to this day.

Anthony Pagden
Los Angeles
January 2024

Acknowledgements

The very first idea for this book arose during an undergraduate research internship at the Max Planck Institute for European Legal History (now Max Planck Institute for Legal History and Legal Theory) in Frankfurt am Main. I was stunned by the widespread claim that states had a 'free right to go to war' (*liberum ius ad bellum*) before the First World War. The question of whether this was true has accompanied me ever since, as a background to other research projects. Expanding the scope of this work was encouraged by the publication of some of my initial findings, most notably in the *European Journal of International Law* in 2018. Since then, new questions have been added to the project, such as: where and when did the claim of a 'free right to go to war' emerge? Why was it so successful in academic and public discourse? Why was there so little academic research on the normativity of war in nineteenth-century theory and political practice when, at the same time, the 'anarchy' claim was central to highlighting normative change in the twentieth century? This book offers a systematic approach to answering these question, by reconstructing the politics of justifying and mitigating collective violence in the nineteenth century.

The fact that the book is now published is due to so many people that I cannot possibly name them all. But to make a start: first and foremost, I thank Lothar Brock and Miloš Vec, who have accompanied my work as PhD supervisors from the very beginning with great vigour and enthusiasm. Lothar became my teacher in International Relations/Peace and Conflict Studies in my first semester in Frankfurt. I remember well the always-crowded lecture halls of 'Brock Seminars' in the old (now demolished) AfE University Tower in Frankfurt Bockenheim. For me, these years were formative in many ways. When I received an offer from Lothar to work with him after graduation, I didn't hesitate for a second. Much joint work followed (among others a volume in the same series as the present book), numerous seminars, articles, lectures—and discussions about the book at hand of course, often over a good cappuccino or espresso.

Miloš I also met back then, during my aforementioned internship at the MPI, where he led the research group of the Normative Orders cluster of excellence on 'International Law and its Science, 1789–1914'. It was here that the legal-historical topic of the present book was formed. Multiple discussions, collaborations, and joint research trips followed. Miloš became a professor at the University of Vienna, giving me the opportunity to present the progress of my work during several visiting research stays there. These fellowships have remained in my memory as particularly rewarding and stimulating. It is undoubtedly a great privilege in today's fast-moving academic system to find a supervisor who is seriously interested not only in a PhD thesis but also in the person behind it. The fact that I found two such supervisors for my work was a stroke of luck.

I was also fortunate to have further encounters which helped me a lot with producing this book. I thank Nicole Deitelhoff, who wrote the third opinion, as well as Rainer Forst as head of the doctoral committee, along with Hanna Pfeifer and Thomas Scheffer as members of my doctoral committee (in addition to the three thesis reviewers). The composition of this committee highlights the importance of Frankfurt University, the Peace Research Institute Frankfurt (PRIF), and the Normative Orders research cluster (and now ConTrust) as contexts for the emergence of this book and as points of reference for its theoretical foundation. In addition to these institutions, I would particularly like to thank Anuschka Tischer, who, as a pioneer in the study of early modern war legitimation, was available from the very beginning as a highly competent and encouraging interlocutor, for example on methodological questions or on the tension between theory and practice in the History of International Relations and International Law. The same applies to Beate Jahn and Benno Teschke, who showed interest in my work not only during my guest stay at the Centre for Advanced International Theory at the University of Sussex (Brighton, UK), but far beyond. I also thank Andreas Fahrmeir who was supportive from the very beginning during my studies of international history. Many thanks to Stephan Nitz, long-time scientific librarian at PRIF, with whom I have had a remarkable exchange about modern writings on war, law, and peace.

I have also had the opportunity to present and discuss my thoughts not only in Frankfurt, Vienna, and Brighton, but also at numerous conferences and meetings as well as in personal conversations (in Covid times often digitally as well). For content-related comments, other advice, and/or comradeship along the way, I thank, inter alia, Mathias Albert, Michael Bothe, Anny Bremner, Raphaël Cahen, Tony Carty, León Castellanos-Jankiewicz, Christopher Daase, Michael Erhardt, Bardo Fassbender, Patrick Flamm, Anna Geis, Andreas Heinemann, Rainer Hofmann, Martti Koskenniemi, Gert Krell, Stefan Kroll, Phil Langer, Carmen Ludwig, Siddharth Mallavarapu, Thilo Marauhn, Kamran Matin, Mary Ellen O'Connell, Stefan Oeter, Anne Peters, Christian Pogies, Justin Rosenberg, Elvira Rosert, Bruno Schoch, Sebastian Spitra, Alexander Wagner, Andreas Wagner, J.H.H. Weiler, Irene Weipert-Fenner, Tobias Wille, Jonas Wolff, the authors of our edited volume *The Justification of War and International Order* (OUP 2021), and all my colleagues and students at Frankfurt University, TU Darmstadt, PRIF, and the *Völkerrechtsblog*. Special thanks go to the two anonymous reviewers who helped me to sharpen the argument of this book. With all this support, it remains, of course, that all errors are mine.

With a view to the finalization of the text, I am very grateful to Carla Welch for her great language editing, which the Peace Research Institute Frankfurt generously funded as part of my post-doc work. The same goes for Christopher Long as well as the Newgen team for the final linguistic and formal polish. Furthermore, I thank the Hans Böckler Foundation for support. I would also like to express my gratitude to Nehal Bhuta, Anthony Pagden, and Benjamin Straumann to suggest the project for inclusion in Oxford University Press's *History and Theory of International Law* Series. I thank the OUP team, especially Merel Alstein and Jacqueline Larabee, for another great collaboration and their helpful support in the publication process.

Finally, in addition to academic thanks, I am especially grateful to my friends and family for encouragement, distraction, and love. I thank my mother Regine Simon for always providing unconditional support. The biggest thanks go to Sabrina, for much patience and reminding me that there is a world beyond writing. I dedicate this book to Regine, Sabrina, and Antonia.

Hendrik Simon
Frankfurt
May 2023

Editorial Note

Unless otherwise noted, all translations in this book are mine. This work partly contains elements from the following preliminary works: Simon, 'Über das "freie Recht zum Krieg" in Politik und Völkerrecht des 19. Jahrhunderts', *Research Paper/ Max Planck Institute for European Legal History* (2012); Simon, 'The Myth of Liberum Ius ad Bellum. Justifying War in 19th-Century Legal Theory and Political Practice', 29 *European Journal of International Law* (2018) 113; Simon, 'Theorising Order in the Shadow of War. The Politics of International Legal Knowledge and the Justification of Force in Modernity', 22 *Journal of the History of International Law* (2020) 218; Simon, 'Anarchy over Law? Towards a Genealogy of Modern War Justifications (1789–1918)', in L. Brock and H. Simon (eds), *The Justification of War and International Order: From Past to Present* (2021) 147; H. Simon, *Der Mythos vom 'freien Recht zum Krieg'. Zu einer Genealogie der modernen Kriegslegitimation* (2022).

Contents

List of Illustrations   xxxi

SETTING THE SCENE

1. Introduction: A Century of Anarchy, a Right to War?   3
   1.1 Problematizing the Past of an Omnipresent Doctrine   3
   1.2 Force—Normativity—History: Deciphering the Grammar of the Modern Discourse of Justifying War   9
   1.3 Bridging the Gap: A Note on Discourse Levels, Sources, and Disciplines   13
   1.4 Reordering the Modern Discourse of War: The Structure of the Book   18

2. Thesis and Antithesis: Why States Justify War   22
   2.1 Introduction: Anarchy, War, and Normative Order(s)   22
   2.2 Narratives of 'Anarchy' and 'Progress': Reconstructing a Myth   22
          Transformation of the European War Discourse: From *Bellum Iustum* to *Liberum Ius ad Bellum*?   23
          'Right' without Legal Regulation: A Narrative of 'Anarchy'   25
          Beyond Anarchy: The Discursive Construction of Legal Progress   31
          Disenchantment: Ordering War as a Modern Discourse of Rationalization?   36
   2.3 The Discursive Power of Normativity: Towards a Genealogy of Modern War Justifications   38
          Discourses Remembered—Discourses Forgotten   39
          War and Order: The Dialectics of a Normative Dichotomy   46
          A Constructivist Argument: The Discursive Co-constitution of the Justification of War and International Order   49
          Continuity, Contingency, and Change: The Nineteenth Century as the Era of Birth of Modern International Order   53
          Legalization, Moralization, Politicization: A Discourse of Multinormativity   56
   2.4 Conclusion: On the Front Stages of Diplomacy   57

PART I: JUSTIFYING WAR IN THE NINETEENTH CENTURY: A EUROPEAN DISCOURSE

3. On the Threshold of Modernity: From Revolutionizing to Reordering War   63
   3.1 Introduction: The Change of an Epoch   63
   3.2 Justifying Revolutionary War—Revolutionizing War Justifications?   64
          '*Au nom de la nation*': The Revolution as the Birth of Modern War Discourse   65

		Paradoxes of Popular Sovereignty: From Limitation to Legitimation of Violence	67
		Emperor of the Revolution: Rise, Decline, and Justification of Napoléon's Hegemony	72
		Between 'Old' and 'New': Europe's Reactions to Revolutionary Violence	76
		The Battle of the 'Nations': The Birth of Modern Mass War and its Justification	81
	3.3	Kant versus Clausewitz: Law, Politics, and the Formation of the Modern Discourse of Justifying War	85
		Revolutionizing Reform? The 'Positivist Turn(s)' in International Legal Thought: British Edition (Bentham)	86
		Revolutionizing Reform? The 'Positivist Turn(s)' in International Legal Thought: German Edition (Martens)	89
		Peace through Legalization: Towards a Modern Prohibition of War (Kant)	92
		War as an Instrument of Politics: On the Realist Discourse of Modern Warfare (Clausewitz)	99
	3.4	Conclusion: 'In the Beginning was Napoléon'	106
4.	Birth of an International Order		109
	4.1	Introduction: Peace and Coercion after an Epoch of War	109
	4.2	Towards a Modern Order of International Violence	111
		The Emergence of the Concert between Revolution and Reform	112
		Against War: Political and Normative Contours of a Modern Order of International Violence	118
		Hybrid Normativity: Two Paths to the Prohibition of War Beyond International Treaty Law	122
		'Positivists' without Positivism: A Methodological Tragedy	128
		From the Trauma of War to the Institutionalization of Peace	130
	4.3	Peace through Coercion: Limitation as Legitimization of Violence	133
		An Order Built on Normativity and Power	134
		Inventing Intervention: War in the Name of Peace	136
		Debating Intervention beyond Positive Law	141
		Ungentle Civilizers: Violence in the Name of Humanity?	143
		Violence as a Herald of Legal Progress?	147
	4.4	Conclusion: The Janus Face of the Vienna Order	150
5.	Between Might and Right: Justified Wars and Multiple Normativities		153
	5.1	Introduction: Normativity in Times of War	153
	5.2	Europeanizing the Eastern Question: The Struggle for Law at its 'Semi-periphery'	154
		The 'Last Crusade'? From the 'Monks' Quarrel' to the Ottoman Declaration of War	155
		Law vs Religion? War Justifications in 1853/54	158

Norm Emergence in Conflict: The Treaty of Paris as an International Suborder	162
Submission: Law as an Imperial Project	165
The Abolition of Privateering: Towards Universal International Law	167
'A Vague Promise' as 'a First Step in the Right Direction'? The Mediation of Mediation	168
New Conflicts—New Principles: The Rise of the Nationality Principle	170
5.3 'Viva l'Italia'—e Viva l'Ordine Internazionale? The Justification of War in the *Risorgimento*	171
Revolution from Above: The Justification of the First War of Independence	172
David against Goliath: Cavour's Strategy of Justifying War against Austria	173
Liberation of Italy—Sardinian Rule: A Contradiction of the International Order?	179
5.4 Blood, Iron—and Law?! Justifying German Unification	181
'Blood and Iron': Laying the Foundations of Bismarck's Realpolitik	181
1864: Bismarck Turns Law against Law	183
1866: An Austro-Prussian Duel?	186
1870/71: An 'Unprovoked Attack'?	188
5.5 Conclusion: Law and Realpolitik—a Mid-century Crisis of the International Norm of Peace?	198
6. The Promise of 'Peace through Law' in the Shadow of War	201
6.1 Introduction: Plans to Outlaw War and Their Antinomies	201
6.2 Pacification Through Professionalization? Liberal International Legal Doctrine as the '*Conscience Juridique du Monde Civilisé*'	203
6.3 Mere Continuity? Liberal Legal Theory between Limiting and Outlawing War	207
Liberal Legal Theory between Grotius and Kant	211
Organizing Peace	217
6.4 Antinomies of the 'Gentle Civilizers': Liberal Justifications of War	220
Liberal Justifications of Illiberal Violence	227
Justifying Liberal Empires	231
6.5 'The Right Path': Toward Reflexive Legal Peace (Schücking)	233
6.6 Conclusion: Politicized Depoliticizers between Utopias of Peace and Apologies of Violence	236

PART II: EMERGENCE OF A MYTH: A GERMAN *SONDERWEG*?

7. *Recht zum Krieg*: A Clausewitzian Tradition	241
7.1 Introduction: German Realism and the 'Right to War'	241
7.2 A Positivist Polemic	243

7.3	War in the Name of the *Machtstaat*: The Formation of the 'Right of the Strongest' in German Historicism	253
	From Freedom to Power (Ranke)	254
	'Positive law is the only law that has real existence'—Immoral Realism (Treitschke)	257
	'A people that cannot hate the foreign is a wretched people' (Lasson)	261
7.4	A Clausewitzian 'Legal' Tradition	264
	War—Always Factual and Very Often Political Violence (Lueder)	264
	Military Necessity: A German Cult	267
	War, 'a true necessary bearer of culture' (Lueder; Meurer)	271
	Towards Perpetual War (Stengel)	273
7.5	Varieties of Realism: Between Positivism and Bellicism	276
	Two Variations of a Thesis	276
	Radical Positivism beyond Germany: A Glimpse at Europe	278
7.6	Conclusion: A Counter-Movement Against Liberalism	280

8. A Hegemonic Discourse? On Mainstream(s) and Myth(s) — 282

8.1	Introduction: The Exception to the Rule(s)	282
8.2	A 'First Great Debate' between Realism and Liberalism	283
	Un Dialogue de Sourds? From the Excavation Sketches of a Buried Debate (Bluntschli vs Moltke)	285
	Against 'Prussian Ethics' (Pfau)	289
	Plea for a Public Science Beyond Realism (Lucas)	290
	Peace through Law—or through 'Holy War' (Saripolos)	292
	'A Prism without Colours and Shapes' (Beauharnais and Martens)	293
8.3	Defending Law against War—Defending War against Law	295
	Defending War against Law (Lueder vs the Liberal Mainstream)	295
	Defending Law against War (the Liberal Mainstream vs Lueder)	296
	'Objections that are Easy to Refute': Peace through Polemics (Novicow vs Stengel)	298
	Anarchy vs Pacifism	301
8.4	Conclusion: Bifurcation—The Ruling Doctrine vs the Doctrine of the Rulers	303

9. Antinomianism: The *Kaiserreich*'s Politics of Justifying War — 306

9.1	Introduction: Breaking and Confirming the Law	306
9.2	International Legalization and Its Circumvention	307
	Peace at the Hague? An Unconventional Conference	308
	'And shit on all the resolutions': German Anti-Legalism at the Hague Conference	312
9.3	The End of an Era: Justifying the Great War	316
	Caught in Lies: Justifying the Unjustifiable	317
	Speaking Right and Wrong: The First World War as another Struggle for Law	321
	'Necessities' of War: Elements of a German 'Special Path'	325
9.4	Conclusion: A German *Sonderweg*	331

10. Old Order, New Order: Historiography between Anarchy and
    Progress   333
    10.1 Introduction: Beyond Black and White   333
    10.2 Beyond Anarchy and War: The Narrative of Progress   334
    10.3 Beyond Law and Order: Constructing the Narrative of Anarchy   342
    10.4 Two Halves of a Whole: The Discursive Robustness of a Myth   348
    10.5 Conclusion: Towards a New Historiography of War and
         International Order   354

CONCLUSION

11. War, Normativity, and the Birth of Modern International Order   359

Select Bibliography   369
Index   381

List of Illustrations

7.1	Frontispiece to Rettich's *Zur Theorie und Geschichte des Rechts zum Kriege* (1888)	243
8.1	A First Debate between Liberalism and Realism	284

SETTING THE SCENE

1
Introduction

A Century of Anarchy, a Right to War?

'One cannot conceive of international right as a right to war...'
Immanuel Kant
'War is merely the continuation of policy by other means.'
Carl von Clausewitz

1.1 Problematizing the Past of an Omnipresent Doctrine

This book deals with discourses on war and normativity in the formation of modern international order. It engages with the old yet insufficiently researched question of whether, according to which norms, and—most importantly—since when the use of force by states has been regulated under international law in modern history. In this analytical context, the study develops the argument that a state's decision to wage war (*ius ad bellum*) has been constrained by international norms not just since the mid-twentieth century, as historiographies of international order usually hold. Rather, it points to the special significance of the 'long nineteenth century' (1789–1918). My main argument is that the modern normative order governing the use of force in international relations did not simply emerge with a 'big bang' after the First World War, as is generally assumed.[1] Rather, its roots lie in the nineteenth-century European discourse on the normativity of war (including Europe's confrontation with non-European political entities).

This argument is in obvious contradiction to prevailing tenets: to this day, most academic publications on the history and theory of war and international order contain the thesis that prior to the early twentieth century, sovereign states held a 'free right to go to war' (*liberum ius ad bellum*).[2] The latter has aptly been called 'one

---

[1] The idea of 'radical' progress from an 'old world order' before 1928 (Kellogg-Briand Pact) to a 'new world order' afterwards has most recently and particularly prominently been put forward by O.A. Hathaway and S.J. Shapiro, *The Internationalists: How a Radical Plan to Outlaw War Remade the World* (2017); for the narrative of 'progress' in historiographies of war and international order, see Chapter 2.2.

[2] From the overwhelming number of texts across the relevant academic disciplines affirming the thesis of *liberum ius ad bellum*, see e.g. C. Schmitt, *Die Wendung zum diskriminierenden Kriegsbegriff*

of the most prominent and provocative doctrines in the history of international law'.[3] But this doctrine can mean many things. Frequently, it also appears without any substantive explanation.

However, if it *is* elaborated further, the thesis of *liberum ius ad bellum* goes broadly as follows: until its legal prohibition in the twentieth century, a state's resort to war was not regulated by any international legal norms or general principles. The

---

(1938), at 49; Wehberg, 'Universales oder Europäisches Völkerrecht? Eine Auseinandersetzung mit Professor Carl Schmitt', 41 *Die Friedens-Warte* (1941) 157, at 162; Kunz, 'Bellum Justum and Bellum Legale', 45 *American Journal of International Law* (1951) 528, at 528; R. Koselleck, *Kritik und Krise. Eine Studie zur Pathogenese der bürgerlichen Welt* (13th edn, 2017 [1954]), at 33 ff.; I. Brownlie, *International Law and the Use of Force by States* (1963), at 19; Q. Wright, *A Study of War* (2nd edn, 1965), at 685 ff.; Kimminich, 'Das Problem der Friedenssicherung im Völkerrecht des 20. Jahrhunderts, in C. Eisenhart and G. Picht (eds), *Frieden und Völkerrecht* (1973) 295; W. Preiser, *Macht und Norm in der Völkerrechtsgeschichte: Kleine Schriften zur Entwicklung der internationalen Rechtsordnung und ihrer Grundlegung* (1978), at 22; Koskenniemi, 'The Politics of International Law', 1 *European Journal of International Law* (1990) 4, at 6; K.H. Ziegler, *Völkerrechtsgeschichte* (1994), at 230 ff.; E.-O. Czempiel, *Friedensstrategien. Eine systematische Darstellung außenpolitischer Theorien von Machiavelli bis Madariaga* (2nd edn, 1998), at 89; W.G. Grewe, *The Epochs of International Law*, translated and revised by M. Byers (2000), at 531; M. Koskenniemi, *The Gentle Civilizer of Nations. The Rise and Fall of International Law 1870–1960* (2002), at 85 ff.; Walzer, 'The Triumph of Just War Theory (and the Dangers of Success)', 69 *Social Research* (2002) 925, at 927; G. Dahm, R. Wolfrum, and J. Delbrück, *Völkerrecht/Die Formen des völkerrechtlichen Handelns* (2nd edn, 2002), at 818; Stolleis, 'Zur Ideengeschichte des Völkerrechts 1870–1939', in L. Raphael and H.-E. Tenorth (eds), *Ideen als gesellschaftliche Gestaltungskraft im Europa der Neuzeit. Beiträge für eine erneuerte Geistesgeschichte* (2006), at 162; J. Habermas, *The Divided West*, edited and translated by C. Cronin (2006), at 118; J. Black, *European International Relations, 1648–1815* (2008), at 50; S.C. Neff, *War and the Law of Nations: A General History* (2005), at 197; W. Baumgart, *Europäisches Konzert und nationale Bewegung. Internationale Beziehungen 1830–1878* (2nd edn, 2007), at 82; M. Schulz, *Normen und Praxis. Das europäische Konzert der Großmächte als Sicherheitsrat, 1815–1860* (2009), at 16, 633; Peters, 'Membership in the Global Constitutional Community', in J. Klabbers, A. Peters, and G. Ulfstein (eds), *The Constitutionalization of International Law* (2009) 153, at 183; J. von Bernstorff, *The Public International Law Theory of Hans Kelsen. Believing in Universal Law* (2010), at 88; Lutz-Bachmann, '"Peace" and "Justice" in the Tradition of "Just War-Theories"', in G. Hellmann (ed.), *Justice and Peace. Interdisciplinary Perspectives on a Contested Relationship* (2013) 90, at 93–5; M. Kaldor, *New and Old Wars. Organized Violence in a Global Era* (3rd edn, 2012), at 19; Ungern-Sternberg, 'Religion and Religious Intervention', in B. Fassbender and A. Peters (eds), *The Oxford Handbook of the History of International Law* (2nd edn, 2014) 294, at 303; M. Abbenhuis, *An Age of Neutrals. Great Power Politics, 1815–1914* (2014), at 193; B. Buzan and G. Lawson, *The Global Transformation: History, Modernity and the Making of International Relations* (2015), at 86; N. Deitelhoff and M. Zürn, *Lehrbuch der Internationalen Beziehungen: Per Anhalter durch die IB-Galaxis* (2016), at 19; R. Voigt, *Staatliche Souveränität* (2016), at 11; C. Chinkin and M. Kaldor, *International Law and New Wars* (2017), at 133; Hathaway and Shapiro (n. 1), at xv; Kreß, 'Introduction: The Crime of Aggression and the International Legal Order', in C. Kreß and S. Barriga (eds), *The Crime of Aggression: A Commentary* (2017), at 1; M.M. Payk, *Frieden durch Recht? Der Aufstieg des modernen Völkerrechts und der Friedensschluss nach dem Ersten Weltkrieg* (2018), at 2, 112, 147, 498; Anghie, 'Wo der Imperialismus noch wirkt', *Frankfurter Rundschau* (27 January 2018); M. Herdegen, *Völkerrecht* (18th edn, 2018), at 1; Heintze, 'Frieden und Völkerrecht', in H.-J. Gießmann and B. Rinke (eds), *Handbuch Frieden* (2nd edn, 2019) 753, at 754; Brown, 'Justified: Just War and the Ethics of Violence and World Order', in L. Brock and H. Simon (eds), *The Justification of War and International Order: From Past to Present* (2021) 435, at 436; B. Heuser, *War: A Genealogy of Western Ideas and Practices* (2022), at 189.

[3] Weiler, 'Editorial', 29 *European Journal of International Law* (2018) 1, at 6, commenting on Simon, 'The Myth of *Liberum Ius ad Bellum*. Justifying War in 19th-Century Legal Theory and Political Practice', 29 *European Journal of International Law* (2018) 113.

decision to wage war in the nineteenth century is said to have required no international justification. It depended solely on the political will of the sovereign: given the absence of a common international or supranational authority, states found themselves in a Hobbesian state of nature, an anarchic 'war of all against all' (*bellum omnium contra omnes*). Accordingly, states could wage war whenever they deemed it politically necessary. If one follows the prevailing transdisciplinary research consensus, states were virtually 'entitled' to go to war at any time[4]—international law, at least, did not stand in their way.[5]

So, is it true that in the nineteenth century, if 'states wanted to go to war, they could'?[6] Judging from a cursory glance at the research literature, it would indeed appear so. There is broad consensus confirming the proposition of *liberum ius ad bellum*. And this consensus has a long tradition. In a 1941 article for the journal *Die Friedens-Warte*, German lawyer and legal pacifist Hans Wehberg referred to the nineteenth century as a century of international anarchy.[7] This was a fundamental critique of nineteenth-century international law. According to Wehberg, states had made no serious attempt in this era to do away with the 'anarchic right'[8] to arbitrarily use war as a political tool. Wehberg's polemic reference to the nineteenth century reverberates to this day. Even recently published standard books in the History and Theory of International Law and International Relations characterize the nineteenth century as a '*laissez-faire* era for warmakers',[9] in which war was simply, in the famous words of Carl von Clausewitz, a 'political procedure among others'[10]—'a continuation of politics by other means'.[11] As a corollary, it is assumed that law did not rule over sovereigns or the relationships between them, but that the political will of the sovereign ruled over law.[12] Anarchy prevailed.

On closer inspection, however, a weakness in the line of argument of these strong assumptions becomes apparent: although—or perhaps precisely because—the thesis of *liberum ius ad bellum* is virtually omnipresent in a variety

---

[4] See n 2.
[5] Bothe, 'Friedenssicherung und Kriegsrecht', in W. Graf Vitzthum (ed.), *Völkerrecht* (4th edn, 2014) 642, at 643; see also Bilfinger, 'Vollendete Tatsache und Völkerrecht', 15 *Zeitschrift für ausländisches öffentliches Recht und Völkerrecht: ZaöRV* (1953/54) 453.
[6] Buzan and Lawson (n. 2), at 50.
[7] Wehberg (n. 2), at 162.
[8] *Ibid.*, at 162.
[9] Neff (n. 2), at 161, 168.
[10] Koskenniemi, 'Politics of International Law' (n. 2), at 6; see also Koskenniemi, *Gentle Civilizer* (n. 2), at 85 ff.
[11] Hathaway and Shapiro (n. 1), at xv.
[12] Fassbender, 'Die souveräne Gleichheit der Staaten – ein angefochtenes Grundprinzip des Völkerrechts', 43 *Aus Politik und Zeitgeschichte* (2004) 7, at 9; for a closer definition of *liberum ius ad bellum*, see Chapter 2.2.

of corresponding scientific,[13] political,[14] and public[15] discourses, an extensive examination of its historical validity and genesis has not yet been carried out. This finding is puzzling: the claim that states had a 'free right to go to war' in 'anarchic' nineteenth-century international relations is central for the periodization of modern historiographies of war and international order. Both realist and liberal grand narratives in modern international thought are structured around it. For political realists, the alleged free right to the use of force in the nineteenth century expresses the eternal 'law of the strongest' in international relations in an almost ideal-typical way. For liberals, in contrast, the nineteenth-century 'free right to go to war' represents the pre-modern antithesis to their narrative of international legal progress in the twentieth century.[16] However, since the existence of an alleged 'free right to go to war' in the nineteenth century has not yet been scientifically proven, its widespread and uncritical affirmation is as problematic as it is puzzling.

The present volume takes up this puzzle. It offers an in-depth historical examination of the doctrine of *liberum ius ad bellum*, its genesis, and its discursive authority in the nineteenth century and beyond. For this, I develop three arguments with regard to the normative status of war in the nineteenth century: *first*, I reject the prevailing view that there was a 'free right to go to war' in the 'long nineteenth

---

[13] See n. 2.
[14] Commenting on the illegal annexation of Crimea by the Russian Federation, German Chancellor Angela Merkel stated in March 2014 that the 'law of the strong is being pitted against the strength of the law.... Actions modelled on those of the 19th and 20th century are thus being carried out in the 21st century.' A. Merkel, *Policy statement by Federal Chancellor Angela Merkel on the situation in Ukraine 2014* (13 April 2014), available at: https://www.bundesregierung.de/breg-en/chancellor/pol icy-statement-by-federal-chancellor-angela-merkel-on-the-situation-in-ukraine-443796 (last visited 1 December 2022). The thesis of *liberum ius ad bellum* can also be found in non-governmental discourses, see the website of the International Committee of the Red Cross: 'Until the end of the First World War, resorting to the use of armed force was regarded not as an illegal act but as an acceptable way of settling disputes. In 1919, the Covenant of the League of Nations and, in 1928, the Treaty of Paris (the Briand-Kellogg Pact) sought to outlaw war.' International Committee of the Red Cross, *What are jus ad bellum and jus in bello?* (22 January 2015), available at: https://www.icrc.org/en/document/what-are-jus-ad-bellum-and-jus-bello-0 (last visited 1 December 2022).
[15] The German Federal Agency for Civic Education (*Bundeszentrale für politische Bildung*) claimed in an editorial that war was 'long regarded as a natural means of enforcing foreign policy interests'; see *Aus Politik und Zeitgeschichte: Moderne Kriegsführung* (2016), at 3. See also *Die Zeit* of 6 December 2012: 'It was only after the Second World War that the UN, international law, and the EU—slowly and only selectively—developed norms, procedures, and institutions which restrict the sovereignty of nation states', available at: https://www.zeit.de/2012/50/Europaeische-Union-300-Jahre-Abbe-de-Saint-Pierre/komplettansicht (last visited 1 December 2022). In this same vein, Aurèle Jacquot and Matthieu Putzolu's ARTE production 'Is the UN in its Death Throes?' entails the assurance that while the 'UN was founded in 1945 with the idea that cooperation trumped conflict', before 'WWI, people thought differently: states faced off on the international scene and war was seen as necessary', available at: https:// www.arte.tv/en/videos/087070-003-A/is-the-un-in-its-death-throes/, at 00:57 (last visited 1 December 2022). The thesis of a 'free right to go to war' can also be found in political art: Thomas Bellinck's 'House of European History in Exile: Domo de Eŭropa Historio en Ekzilo', which I visited during the Wiesbaden *Biennale* in 2016, started with a poster arguing that 'the project of Europe was born of disaster and total exhaustion. Until the middle of the twentieth century, Europe was governed by the law of the strongest'.
[16] These two grand narratives of 'anarchy' and 'progress' are discussed in more depth in Chapter 2.2.

century' (1789–1918).[17] By analysing international legal and political discourse[18] on the justification of war, I argue that *liberum ius ad bellum* was neither accepted in nineteenth-century state practice nor by the majority of international legal scholars. Instead, throughout the century, war and other forms of military violence were regarded as in need of justification: after the Napoleonic Wars, the Vienna Congress of 1814/15 sounded the bell for the emergence of a complex—and often paradoxical—European discourse on the international legitimacy of war. The genealogy of this international discourse will be the focus of Part I, in which I emphasize the importance of discursive practices in a relatively poorly formalized 'order of justification'.[19]

Second, I reconstruct the historical roots of the proposition of *liberum ius ad bellum* from a history of science perspective (*Wissenschaftsgeschichte*).[20] To this day, it remains unclear in which historical context this proposition emerged—and how it became dominant in scientific discourse. In Part II, I argue that the concept of *liberum ius ad bellum* was indeed developed in the (late) nineteenth century. Although there are many precursors of the claim of an international 'right of the strongest'[21] in the history of realist political ideas, the era in which the myth of *liberum ius ad bellum* was born, according to political, military, historical, and legal debates, was in the German *Kaiserreich* between 1871 and 1918.

The book therefore combines a genuinely European perspective on nineteenth-century war discourses in Part I with a strong contextualization of the war discourses in the German Empire in Part II. After the failed revolution of 1848 and the Wars of German Unification in 1864, 1866, and 1870/71, militarism and nationalism had a particularly powerful impact, and not only on civil political decision-making. Parts of legal scholarship,[22] which I describe as *Clausewitzian*, were also affected. The historical genealogy and provenance of the thesis of *liberum ius ad bellum* is therefore linked to the important question of a German *Sonderweg* ('special path') in nineteenth-century politics of international law. Political and military primacy in the assessment of war led to a hostility to international law in the *Kaiserreich* that was unique in Europe. Only by bringing this forgotten episode of nineteenth-century war discourse back into the analytical focus, can it be explained why the myth of *liberum ius ad bellum* prevailed in the legal historical discourse of the twentieth century and to this very day.[23]

---

[17] On this term, see E. Hobsbawm, *The Age of Empire: 1875–1914* (1989).
[18] On this gap, see Chapter 1.3.
[19] R. Forst, *Normativity and Power. Analyzing Social Orders of Justification* (2017), at 15.
[20] For a classic definition of *Wissenschaftsgeschichte* of public law as a 'history of the literature of the scientific gathering, the dogmatic permeation and systematization of public law', see M. Stolleis, *Geschichte des öffentlichen Rechts in Deutschland*, vol. 1 (1988), at 43; see also Hueck, 'The Discipline of the History of International Law', 3 *Journal of the History of International Law* (2001) 194.
[21] R.N. Lebow, *The Tragic Vision of Politics* (2003), Chapters 2 and 3.
[22] I first used the term '*Clausewitzians*' in Simon (n. 3).
[23] See n. 2, which, however, only is the tip of the iceberg.

8 INTRODUCTION

Third and finally, I reposition the normative status of war in the nineteenth century in modern historiographies of war and international order. A critical reassessment of the thesis of *liberum ius ad bellum* invites us to critically reflect on the emergence and continuity of realist and liberal narratives of 'anarchy' and 'progress' in these modern historiographies. The way we remember the nineteenth-century discourse on war and international order touches on essential questions of the emerging modern legal theory and its sources in the so-called 'positive century'.[24] This discourse was shaped by 'multinormativity', i.e. multiple forms of normativity, despite positivism.[25] In accord with this finding, I argue that the myth of *liberum ius ad bellum* mirrors the way in which modern historiographies of war and international order have been structured around false dichotomies of 'old' and 'new', 'classical' and 'modern international law'. To reflect the complex and multi-faceted genesis of the modern international order, the book provides a genealogy of the nineteenth-century war discourse in sequence. Consequently, the analytical focus shifts to the justification and critique of war as a communicative practice of ordering the international.[26]

Taking these three research foci together, the central concern of this book is manifest: by reconstructing the long-neglected nineteenth-century political and legal discourse on the legitimacy of waging war, it aims to deconstruct *liberum ius ad bellum* as a myth in modern historiographies of war and international order. Given the increasing normative limitation of the *ius ad bellum* in the nineteenth century, the roots of the modern international legal order and the 'radical plan to outlaw war'[27] cannot be found at the beginning of the twentieth century. They began to emerge in nineteenth-century discourse on war and international order. Accordingly, the nineteenth century is not to be understood as the anarchic antithesis of the modern international order governing the use of force, but as its era of birth.

---

[24] S.C. Neff, *Justice among Nations. A History of International Law* (2014), at 215; Critically Vec, 'Sources in the 19th Century European Tradition: The Myth of Positivism', in S. Besson and J. d'Aspremont (eds), *The Oxford Handbook of the Sources of International Law* (2017) 121.

[25] On the concept of 'multinormativity', see Vec, 'Multinormativität in der Rechtsgeschichte', in Berlin-Brandenburgische Akademie der Wissenschaften (vormals Preußische Akademie der Wissenschaften) *Jahrbuch 2008* (2009) 155, at 162–5. M. Stolleis, *Geschichte des öffentlichen Rechts in Deutschland. Staats- und Verwaltungsrechtswissenschaft in West und Ost 1945–1990*, vol. 4 (2017), at 684, 696; Duve, 'Was ist "Multinormativität"? – Einführende Bemerkungen', 25 *Rechtsgeschichte – Legal History* (2017) 88; see also Vec's Preface to this book.

[26] L. Brock and H. Simon (eds), *The Justification of War and International Order: From Past to Present* (2021).

[27] Hathaway and Shapiro (n. 1).

1.2 Force—Normativity—History: Deciphering the Grammar of the Modern Discourse of Justifying War

Before deconstructing *liberum ius ad bellum* in the following chapters, this introductory chapter contains some reflections on the (discourse-)theoretical (Chapter 1.2) and methodological (Chapter 1.3) foundations of the book as well as a brief outline of the structure of the book and its individual chapters (Chapter 1.4).

This study departs from a basic theoretical assumption: the justification of war is to be understood as a communicative practice of 'normatively ordering'[28] the international. That is to say that the way in which the use of force is justified or criticized reveals much about the role of international norms within a certain period in this most politicized field of international relations.[29] Hence, the nineteenth-century discourse on international war and international order is at the analytical centre of the present book's examination of the thesis of the 'free right to wage war'.

The premise of any historical discourse analysis is, obviously, that a discourse is a truly historical phenomenon.[30] A discourse is not an ideal-typical, timeless, or even metaphysical unit. Rather, it appears as a 'fragment of history, a unity and discontinuity in history itself'.[31] It has been 'fabricated in a piecemeal fashion'[32] via human interaction, as cultural and constructivist turns and 'paradigm shifts'[33] in the humanities and social sciences have rightly reminded us.[34] When I use the term 'discourse' in the context of this book, I refer to a socio-political practice of knowledge production: the sum of written, spoken, or symbolic statements describing, defining, (re)interpreting, and ordering the appropriateness of military force in a specific historical context.[35]

Understanding a discourse as a thoroughly historical phenomenon includes rejecting the assumption that it develops in a linear way. As Michel Foucault has rightly pointed out in his writings on 'genealogy',[36] the claims and norms that gain

---

[28] R. Forst and K. Günther, *Die Herausbildung normativer Ordnungen. Interdisziplinäre Perspektiven* (2011); Forst (n. 19).
[29] For a more detailed presentation of this theoretical assumption, see Chapter 2.3.
[30] Schöttler, 'Historians and Discourse Analysis', 27 *History Workshop Journal* (1989) 37; A. Landwehr, *Historische Diskursanalyse* (2008); Brinton, 'Historical Discourse Analysis', in D. Tannen, H.E. Hamilton, and D. Schiffrin (eds), *The Handbook of Discourse Analysis* (2015) 222.
[31] M. Foucault, *The Archaeology of Knowledge* (1972), at 117.
[32] Foucault, 'Nietzsche, Genealogy, History', in M. Foucault, *Language, Counter-Memory, Practice: Selected Essays and Interviews*, edited by D.F. Bouchard (1977), at 142; see also the use of 'genealogy' in J. Habermas, *Auch eine Geschichte der Philosophie*, vol. 1 (2019), at 72; for a combination of Foucault and Habermas in discourse analyses on justification and order, see Forst (n. 19), at 28.
[33] T.S. Kuhn, *The Structure of Scientific Revolutions* (1962); for paradigm shifts in International Relations see Deitelhoff and Zürn (n. 2).
[34] M. Koskenniemi, *From Apology to Utopia. The Structure of International Legal Argument. Reissue with a New Epilogue* (2005); Guzzini, 'A Reconstruction of Constructivism in International Relations', 6 *European Journal of International Relations* (2000) 147; B. Stollberg-Rilinger, *Rituale* (2013).
[35] For other social- or cultural-theoretical approaches to war discourses, see B. Hüppauf, *Was ist Krieg? Zur Grundlegung einer Kulturgeschichte des Kriegs* (2013), at 106; J. Bartelson, *War in International Thought* (2017).
[36] M. Foucault, *L'Ordre du discours* (1977); see also M. Saar, *Genealogie als Kritik. Geschichte und Theorie des Subjekts nach Nietzsche und Foucault* (2007).

authority in discourse do not arise in the sense of a philosophical teleology. They are products of historical debates[37] (even if teleological arguments can play a role in these debates, as we shall see below). Very much in this vein, international norms in discourses on the justification of force are continuously the object of social and political disputes: they may be declared valid in one moment and challenged in another.

The historical constellations of discursive disputes are decisive for my understanding of a war discourse as a discourse on ordering the international through the practice of justification. Here, a reciprocal relationship between political agents and normative structures[38] can be identified: when states' political agents, like diplomats, refer to international norms in their speech acts, they do so not only to portray their own violence as legitimate, i.e. 'appropriate behaviour'[39] according to the norms of the international order. Rather, by selecting, (re)interpreting and prioritizing certain norms instead of others, they also try to shape what is deemed appropriate and 'sayable'[40] in a specific historical context.

The political leeway in shaping the international order, however, has limits. By referring to the international norms in their justifications of war, states become, to a certain degree, 'entrapped'[41] in the normative language of the international order.[42] Both are true: norms of the international order shape the justification practices of states, and the practice of justification shapes the general normative order. Thus, the international normative order has a double function: it entraps but also enables political actors 'to do things'[43] with norms. It limits but also legitimates the use of force.[44]

Given this *discursive co-constitution of war justifications and international order*,[45] it is clear that is insufficient to analyse (the genealogy of) the normative order regulating the international use of force based only on formal codifications.

---

[37] Foucault (n. 36).

[38] On the so-called *agent-structure problem*, see Wendt, 'Anarchy is What States Make of It: The Social Construction of Power Politics', 46 *International Organization* (1992) 391.

[39] Finnemore and Sikkink, 'International Norm Dynamics and Political Change', 52 *International Organization* (1998) 887, at 891; Jepperson, Wendt, and Katzenstein, 'Norms, Identity, and Culture in National Security', in P.J. Katzenstein (ed.), *The Culture of National Security: Norms and Identity in World Politics* (1995) 33, at 54.

[40] Foucault (n. 36).

[41] Risse, 'Let's Argue! Persuasion and Deliberation in International Relations', 54 *International Organization* (2000) 1; Schimmelfennig, 'The Community Trap: Liberal Norms, Rhetorical Action, and the Eastern Enlargement of the European Union', 55 *International Organization* (2001) 47; Deitelhoff and Müller, 'Theoretical Paradise – Empirically Lost? Arguing with Habermas', 31 *Review of International Studies*, Special Section 'Habermas and IR-Theory' (2005) 167.

[42] Schachter, 'In Defense of International Rules on the Use of Force', 53 *University of Chicago Law Review* (1986) 113; critically on this point C. Peevers, *The Politics of Justifying Force. The Suez Crisis, the Iraq War, and International Law* (2013), and T.M. Fazal, *Wars of Law: Unintended Consequences in the Regulation of Armed Conflict* (2018).

[43] I. Hurd, *How to Do Things with International Law* (2017).

[44] Simon and Brock, 'The Justification of War and International Order: From Past to Present', in L. Brock and H. Simon, *The Justification of War and International Order: From Past to Present* (2021) 3.

[45] Chapter 2.3, and Simon and Brock (n. 44).

This applies in particular (but not only[46]) to the time before the twentieth century, when international law was relatively poorly codified—especially in what is arguably the most important field of public international normativity, the regulation of armed force.[47] But even in fields with more legal codification, it remains true that the 'texts of international law cannot talk—they are talked about.'[48] As with any sphere of international normativity, international law evolves as 'an argumentative practice'.[49] Accordingly, the focus of the present study is on the role of plural norms in political and legal discourse. In free adaptation of a formulation by Randall Lesaffer: the focus is on multiple normativities 'in action'.[50]

In this vein, the historical discourse analysis will identify patterns of the justification of war by examining:

first, how and in what contexts wars were justified in nineteenth-century Europe,
second, whether, by whom and in what context *liberum ius ad bellum* was claimed, and
third, how war justifications were commented by other members of the discourse community.

The organization of the book in two main parts reflects the dual focus of the historical discourse analysis applied here: Part I deals with the 'long nineteenth-century' discourse on war and international order from a genuinely European perspective (including its '[semi-]periphery'[51]). The broad historical perspective in Part I makes it possible to reconstruct the emergence of the nineteenth-century international normative order governing the use of force and to identify change and continuity in reference to certain normative arguments, subjects, objects, and sources.

My analytical approach is based on two arguments: *first,* I argue that norms—like all rites and dogmas—depend on repeatability in discourse. Without the latter, according to Reinhart Koselleck, 'order and justice—however endangered—are

---

[46] Peevers (n. 42); see also Parts V, VI and VII in Brock and Simon (n. 26).
[47] Janssen, *Die Anfänge des modernen Völkerrechts und der neuzeitlichen Diplomatie. Ein Forschungsbericht* (1965), at 20; O'Connell, 'Peace and War', in B. Fassbender and A. Peters (eds), *Oxford Handbook of the History of International Law* (2nd edn, 2014) 272; Bartelson (n. 35).
[48] I. Venzke, *How Interpretation Makes International Law. On Semantic Change and Normative Twists* (2012).
[49] Koskenniemi, 'Methodology of International Law', in R. Wolfrum (ed.), *Max Planck Encyclopedia of Public International Law* (2007); Koskenniemi (n. 34).
[50] Lesaffer, 'Introductory Note', in R. Kubben, *Regeneration and Hegemony. Franco-Batavian Relations in the Revolutionary Era, 1795–1803* (2011) xi, at xii; see also E.J. Kolla, *Sovereignty, International Law and the French Revolution* (2017).
[51] For an explanation of the term of 'semi-periphery' in international legal history, see A. Becker Lorca, *Mestizo International Law. A Global Intellectual History 1842–1933* (2014). On the Ottoman Empire as European 'semi-periphery', see Chapters 4–6.

unavailable'.[52] In order to be accepted and, thus, valid, norms depend on being communicatively practised—being spoken—as arguments in discourse. *Second*, I claim that due to the contingency of discourses, the authority of a political or normative argument may change significantly in the course of time. Justifications of war as an expression of failed diplomatic efforts are particularly interesting in this context: they often appear in discursive moments in which an established political and/or normative vocabulary of international justification is questioned by individual actors and may become contested or blurred by other vocabularies.

Delineating a *genealogy of modern war justifications* as proposed in the present study therefore amounts to a research project on discursive conflicts. It analyses moments of discontinuity,[53] in which the plurality of political and normative claims in nineteenth-century war discourse can be observed particularly clearly. Here, transformations of beliefs, values, and interests may gradually and quietly come to the surface, old and formerly stable concepts of order may be questioned, and new ones propagated. This may lead 'to discontinuities, ruptures, gaps, entirely new forms of positivity, and [to] sudden redistributions'[54] of accepted narratives and arguments in a discourse. In the development of the nineteenth-century discourse on war and international order, the German and Italian Wars of Unification as well as the Russo-Turkish Wars in the context of the Eastern Question were of central importance. By focusing on discursive conflicts and disputes, it is also possible to identify those claims and narratives that did not gain acceptance, let alone acquire authority in mainstream discourse.

One such claim, which was clearly denied authority in the European discourse, was the one of *liberum ius ad bellum*. Nevertheless, it is not totally anachronistic to talk about a 'free right to wage war' as a feature of nineteenth-century war discourse: while not accepted in the European discourse, this thesis was indeed popular in political, military, historical, and also legal debates in the German Empire. Thus, the discourse analysis in Part II of the book describes for the first time how the thesis of *liberum ius ad bellum* emerged in the *Kaiserreich* at the end of the nineteenth century and—unlike in the European war discourse—gained broader discursive acceptance. Following on from more recent studies on international law and 'military culture'[55] in the German Empire, Part II therefore focuses on the

---

[52] R. Koselleck, *Zeitschichten. Studien zur Historik* (2000), at 14 (my translation); see also Osterhammel, 'Über die Periodisierung der neueren Geschichte', 10 *Berichte und Abhandlungen der Berlin Brandenburgischen Akademie der Wissenschaften* (2006) 45.

[53] On crises as opportunities for discursive transformation, see N. Luhmann, 'Kommunikation über Recht in Interaktionssystemen', in E. Blankenburg, E. Klausa, and H. Rottleuthner (eds), *Alternative Rechtsformen und Alternativen zum Recht* (1980) 99, at 101; Schulz (n. 2), at 17.

[54] M. Foucault, *The Archaeology of Knowledge* (2002 [1969]), at 187.

[55] Messerschmidt, 'Völkerrecht und "Kriegsnotwendigkeit" in der deutschen militärischen Tradition seit den Einigungskriegen', 6 *German Studies Review* (1983) 237; Hull, '"Military Necessity" and the Laws of War in Imperial Germany', in S.N. Kalyvas, I. Shapiro, and T. Masoud (eds), *Order, Conflict, and Violence* (2008) 352; Vec, 'All's Fair In Love and War or The Limits of the Limitations. Juridification of Warfare and its Revocation by Military Necessity', in M. Killingsworth (ed.), *Who do the Laws of War Protect? Civility, Barbarity and IHL* (forthcoming).

German discourse on law, politics, and war in the late nineteenth century to highlight the deviation from the European norm(s).[56] However, discontinuities and alternative voices are also to be observed and heard in the German discourse: the thesis of *liberum ius ad bellum* was by no means shared by all German international legal scholars.

The juxtaposition of European (Part I) and German (Part II) war discourses is crucial in order to clarify whether there was a German *Sonderweg* in the nineteenth-century war discourse: in a way, Europe and Germany represented thesis and antithesis with regard to the justification of war and the proposition of *liberum ius ad bellum*. The vocabulary of (de)legitimizing war and the role of norms in these discursive contexts deserve a closer look, since it is in this analytical synthesis that the nineteenth-century discourse on war and international order can be adequately reconstructed, and the myth of the 'free right to go to war' deconstructed.

1.3 Bridging the Gap: A Note on Discourse Levels, Sources, and Disciplines

This is, of course, not the first book dealing with the justification of war. Quite the contrary, the study of war (de)legitimizations has a long tradition across disciplines. Normative judgments in the shadow of ever new wars were virtually constitutive for the emergence of International Law and International Relations as academic disciplines. After all, the regulation of war is the 'core problem' of both international law[57] and international relations.[58] However, despite its long

---

[56] On the war discourse in the *Kaiserreich*, see e.g. J. Dülffer, *Regeln gegen den Krieg? Die Haager Friedenskonferenzen von 1899 und 1907 in der internationalen Politik* (1981); I.V. Hull, *Absolute Destruction: Military Culture and the Practices of War in Imperial Germany* (2005); I.V. Hull, *A Scrap of Paper: Breaking and Making International Law during the Great War* (2014); Carty, 'The Evolution of International Legal Scholarship in Germany during the Kaiserreich and the Weimarer Republik (1871–1933)', 50 *German Yearbook of International Law* (2007/2008) 29; A. Toppe, *Militär und Kriegsvölkerrecht. Rechtsnorm, Fachdiskurs und Kriegspraxis in Deutschland 1899–1940* (2008); generally on public law in the *Kaiserreich*, see M. Stolleis, *Public Law in Germany, 1800–1914* (2001), Chapters 8–10; Koskenniemi, *Gentle Civilizer* (n. 2), Chapter 3; Wiegeshoff, 'Nationale Macht und Internationales Recht. Völkerrecht und Politik im Deutschen Reich (1870/71–1890)', 18 *Historische Mitteilungen* (2005) 199; K. Nies, 'Die Geschichte ist weiter als wir': Zur Entwicklung des politischen und völkerrechtlichen Denkens Josef Kohlers in der Wilhelminischen Ära (2009); Bernstorff, 'Innen und Außen in der Staats- und Völkerrechtswissenschaft des deutschen Kaiserreiches', in G. Schneider and Th. Simon (eds), *Verfassung und Völkerrecht in der Verfassungsgeschichte: Interdependenzen zwischen internationaler Ordnung und Verfassungsordnung* (2015) 138; S. Wiederhold, *Die Lehren vom Monismus mit Primat staatlichen Rechts. Sonderwege deutschen Völkerrechtsdenkens im Kaiserreich und deren Bewahrung durch die Bonner Schule* (2018); Payk (n. 2), Chapter 5.
[57] Janssen (n. 47), at 20; see also R. Tuck, *The Rights of War and Peace: Political Thought and the International Order from Grotius to Kant* (1999); Neff (n. 2); O'Connell (n. 47).
[58] A. Linklater, *The Problem of Harm in World Politics: Theoretical Investigations* (2011); Bartelson (n. 35); Brock and Simon (n. 26); for an analysis of the 'problem of war' in early twentieth-century IR, see Andrä, 'Problematising War: Towards a Reconstructive Critique of War as a Problem of Deviance', 48 *Review of International Studies* (2022) 705; on the nineteenth-century tradition see Chapters 4, 6, 8, and 10 in this book.

tradition, the scientific analysis of war discourses suffers from a serious methodological gap: while studies on theoretical and conceptual issues, such as the 'just war' theory, fill entire shelves—or even entire libraries[59]—there is a lack of analysis on the actual political practice of justifying war and the role of norms in that practice. This is particularly evident in the blatant paucity of studies that bridge the gap between theory and practice. An analytical link is missing here.[60]

Perhaps surprisingly, however, this finding is not new at all. For the dominance of doctrine and the simultaneous ignorance of political practice in analyses on war discourses was criticized early on by legal and political historians:[61] in his article *Kriegslegitimationen in Alteuropa* published in 1985, German historian Konrad Repgen examined early modern war manifestos. Repgen suggested investigating 'the specific reasons given by the warring parties for the legitimacy of their use of force' in these manifestos in order 'to construct a pattern which would enable us to discover and describe the particular as it relates to the general'.[62] Repgen explained to a sceptical American colleague that the true motives of the warring parties were mostly irrelevant to his analysis of patterns of justification: to the German historian, only the warring parties' justifications were of interest, regardless of whether the claimed reasons for war were true or feigned.[63] Despite his euphoria over the sources he had discovered, Repgen complained that he could find nobody who had examined this early modern political discourse on justifying war.[64] There was a lack of research.

And there still is. Konrad Repgen's finding is as astonishing as it is topical. As Lothar Brock and I have argued elsewhere, a historically oriented body of research on the role of norms in the political practices of justifying war has just recently started to emerge.[65] In 2012, Repgen's plea for an analytical turn to early modern war manifestos was responded to by Anuschka Tischer's pioneering study examining more than 300 war manifestos published between 1492 and 1792.[66] Starting in Chapter 3 with the French declaration of war on 20 April 1792, the present

---

[59] See only the extensive bibliography in M. Farrell, *Modern Just War Theory: A Guide to Research* (2013).
[60] Simon, 'Theorising Order in the Shadow of War. The Politics of International Legal Knowledge and the Justification of Force in Modernity', 22 *Journal of the History of International Law* (2020) 218.
[61] W. Preiser, *Die Völkerrechtsgeschichte, ihre Aufgaben und ihre Methode* (1964); Janssen (n. 47).
[62] K. Repgen, *Kriegslegitimationen in Alteuropa. Entwurf einer historischen Typologie* (1985), at 19 f.
[63] *Ibid.*, at 19. Very much in this vein, Hathaway and Shapiro have argued that early modern manifestos mattered 'precisely because they are propaganda. The function of propaganda is to persuade. We can therefore tell what reasons people usually found persuasive by examining the reasons that propaganda offered to persuade them', Hathaway and Shapiro (n. 1), at 42.
[64] Repgen (n. 62), at 18.
[65] See, for instance, Lesaffer, 'Defensive Warfare, Prevention and Hegemony: The Justifications for the Franco-Spanish War of 1635', 8 *Journal of the History of International Law* (2006) 91; Peevers (n. 42); Kolla (n. 50); Fazal (n. 42); Hathaway et al., 'War Manifestos', 85 *University of Chicago Law Review* (2018) 1139; Simon (n. 3). Brock and Simon (n. 26) offer a first compilation of studies on this issue from early modernity to the present.
[66] A. Tischer, *Offizielle Kriegsbegründungen in der Frühen Neuzeit. Herrscherkommunikation in Europa zwischen Souveränität und korporativem Selbstverständnis* (2012).

study ties in chronologically with Tischer's work. In contrast to its frequent marginalization in the History of International Law and International Relations,[67] the era of the French Revolution is thus integrated in this book's analysis of the 'long nineteenth century' war discourse. Both in political practice as well as in political theory (Clausewitz) and legal theory (Kant), a modern vocabulary for the justification—and critique—of war was formed here which was to remain central for the entire nineteenth century. Only by including these neglected narratives and arguments as well as those of the early and mid-nineteenth century in the analysis, can the genesis of the modern international order be adequately reconstructed. What is more, only against this background can the myth of *liberum ius ad bellum* be deconstructed. Focusing on the nineteenth century's 'last five minutes',[68] as has so often been the practice in the History of International Law, is not enough.

With a broader historical framework, there is clearly a need to select discourse levels, actors/speakers, and sources to be examined in the analysis. On the discourse level of political practice, the study focuses on the international war discourse of the European Great Powers between 1792/1815 and 1918, but also includes the critical voices of smaller powers involved in the respective conflicts. Of primary interest is the *international* discourse, since it is here that states justify their use of force before the international 'communication community' (*Kommunikationsgemeinschaft*).[69]

Correspondingly, some key sources for this study's analysis of the political discourse of war and international order are official war declarations and counter-declarations, public political speeches, official documentations, protocols, acts of international congresses and conferences, as well as legal treaties. These documents were examined in published editions, or, if unpublished, in libraries and archives with a view to evaluating them for the first time in light of the book's research questions. As explained by Konrad Repgen, motives are less central to the analysis of the discursive authority of international norms in war discourse.[70] Where it seemed helpful for contextualization, however, war motives are selectively analysed by referring to research literature or documents, such as internal writings by state leaders (e.g. political memoirs).

---

[67] For an analysis of this marginalization, see Lesaffer, 'In the Embrace of France. An Introduction', in B. Jacobs, R. Kubben, and R. Lesaffer (eds): *In the Embrace of France. The Law of Nations and Constitutional Law in the French Satellite States of the Revolutionary and Napoleonic Age (1789–1815)* (2008) 7; and Kolla (n. 50).

[68] David Kennedy refers to the period between about 1900 and 1914—see Kennedy, 'International Law and the Nineteenth Century: History of an Illusion', 65 *Nordic Journal of International Law* (1996) 385, at 391.

[69] Tischer (n. 66), at 22, 220 f.; see also Tischer, 'Princes' Justifications of War in Early Modern Europe: the Constitution of an International Community by Communication', in L. Brock and H. Simon (eds), *The Justification of War and International Order: From Past to Present* (2021) 65; for the concept of '*Kommunikationsgemeinschaften*' as a philosophical concept of discourse ethics, see K.-O. Apel, *Transformation der Philosophie – Band II: Das Apriori der Kommunikationsgemeinschaft* (1999).

[70] Repgen (n. 62).

To avoid misunderstandings, while the present text emphasizes the historical analyses of political practice in war discourses, the intention is not at all to relegate normative theories to second place. This is all the more pertinent since international legal scholars gained an important role in the formulation, ordering, and systematization of international political discourses in the nineteenth century.[71] Their decisive role in 'crafting the international order'[72] was accepted and even increasingly demanded by politicians. Accordingly, key debates on the political or normative justification of war and its valid sources were conducted in international legal doctrine. In the present study, particularly interesting sources pertaining to the level of scientific discourse include academic handbooks and treaties, public commentaries on military conflicts and their justifications, as well as private letters and memoirs (some of which are unpublished) of well-known and less well-known nineteenth-century legal scholars.

It should also be emphasized here that international legal scholars of the nineteenth century (or of other eras) are not to be misunderstood as apolitical commentators. A strict separation of law and politics, in the sense of Hans Kelsen's ideal type of an 'objective' international legal scholarship, seems highly doubtful in many respects: legal scholars often had close professional or personal relationships to political elites. Some of them were diplomats or even parliamentarians themselves. Furthermore, besides this dual role of lawyers, 'constructing international law' as a modern academic discipline in the nineteenth century by no means meant a complete depoliticization of academic discourse.[73]

This is particularly true of the discourse on the normative assessment of force:[74] lawyers were not only the main authors of scientific analyses of the legitimacy of war. Since as early as the early seventeenth century, when Grotius commissioned work for the Dutch East India Company,[75] legal scholars have regularly published private writings or commentaries in which they justified the use of force by states or empires as being in accordance with the norms of the international order. Hence, again and again, international lawyers provided 'the "objectivity" that no politics is able to generate on its own',[76] as Kelsen would later concede when he expressed scepticism concerning his own ideal type of an 'objective' legal scholar. In doing so, Kelsen anticipated a core statement of

---

[71] Koskenniemi, *Gentle Civilizer* (n. 2); L. Nuzzo and M. Vec (eds), *Constructing International Law. The Birth of a Discipline* (2012); Payk (n. 2).
[72] M.M. Payk and K.C. Priemel (eds), *Crafting the International Order* (2021).
[73] Nuzzo and Vec (n. 71).
[74] Simon (n. 60).
[75] Ittersum, 'The Long Goodbye: Hugo Grotius' Justification of Dutch Expansion Overseas, 1615–1645', 36 *History of European Ideas* (2010) 386; Hathaway and Shapiro (n. 1), Chapter 1.
[76] Kelsen, 'Juristischer Formalismus und Reine Rechtslehre', 58 *Juristische Wochenschrift* (1929) 1723, at 1723; see also Bernstorff, 'International Legal Scholarship as a Cooling Medium in International Law and Politics', 25 *European Journal of International Law* (2014) 977, at 977.

current critical (international) legal studies,[77] which, of course, also applies to the nineteenth-century discourse of war and international order: that law—and lawyers—'both justify and enable the critique of established practices'.[78] Legal scholars' academic *and* politicized constructions of 'state practice'[79] are thus of interest as historical sources. Their analysis helps to identify which claims in international discourse were recognized, contested, or at least debated as valid norms. Furthermore, the inclusion of international legal theory as a historical source in the present study is also important, since if current proponents of *liberum ius ad bellum* further substantiate this proposition, they almost exclusively refer to nineteenth-century international legal doctrine. The reconstruction of dissenting voices in contemporary legal doctrine would thus challenge the proposition of *liberum ius ad bellum* particularly clearly.

To sum up this section: even if, as Heinhard Steiger suspected, it might be 'the most difficult problem of the scholarly treatment of the history of international law',[80] the effort to combine perspectives from normative theory and political practice seems worthwhile. Both are needed: histories of international law as well as analyses of 'international law in history'.[81] These two approaches are not contradictory, but rather complement each other. In a similar vein, bridging the analytical gap between legal doctrine and political practice in analysing war discourses should open the way to dealing critically with the proposition of *liberum ius ad bellum* beyond what are sometimes artificial disciplinary boundaries. How this is to be done in the present book will be outlined in the following section.

---

[77] Carty, 'Critical International Law: Recent Trends in the Theory of International Law', 2 *European Journal of International Law* (1991) 1; P. Singh and B. Mayer (eds), *Critical International Law. Postrealism, Postcolonialism, and Transnationalism* (2014).

[78] Koskenniemi. 'What is Critical Research in International Law? Celebrating Structuralism', 29 *Leiden Journal of International Law* (2016) 727, at 731.

[79] Carty, 'Doctrine Versus State Practice', in B. Fassbender and A. Peters (eds), *The Oxford Handbook of the History of International Law* (2nd edn, 2014) 972.

[80] Steiger, 'Ius belli in der Völkerrechtsgeschichte – universelle Geltung oder Beschränkung auf "anerkannte Kulturvölker"?' in T. Marauhn, S. Heselhaus, and T. Bruha (eds), *Legalität, Legitimität und Moral. Können Gerechtigkeitspostulate Kriege rechtfertigen?* (2008) 59.

[81] This argument has been convincingly put forward by Payk, 'The History of International Law – or International Law in History? A Reply to Alexandra Kemmerer and Jochen von Bernstorff', *EJIL Talk!* (8 January 2015), https://www.ejiltalk.org/the-history-of-international-law-or-international-law-in-history-a-reply-to-alexandra-kemmerer-and-jochen-von-bernstorff/ (last visited 1 December 2022); for a more in-depth account of the debate between lawyers and historians on the 'historical turn of international law', see also Benton, 'Beyond Anachronism: Histories of International Law and Global Legal Politics', 21 *Journal of the History of International Law* (2019) 7; Cogan, 'A History of International Law in the Vernacular', 22 *Journal of the History of International Law* (2020) 205; for an opposing position see A. Orford, *International Law and the Politics of History* (2021).

1.4 Reordering the Modern Discourse of War: The Structure of the Book

Before I turn to the two main parts of this study to deconstruct *liberum ius ad bellum* as a modern myth, the subsequent Chapter 2 first *re*constructs this omnipresent, but rarely substantiated proposition. Furthermore, I develop the antithesis of the necessity of a constant normative need for the justification of war to challenge the two standard narratives in historiographies of war and international order: the realist narrative of perpetual 'anarchy' and the liberal narrative of teleological 'progress'.

This juxtaposition of thesis and antithesis is followed by the four chapters of Part I: *Justifying War in the Nineteenth Century: A European Tradition*. The main aim of these chapters is to underline the constant need for justifying war in the nineteenth-century discourse on war and international order. Chapter 3 reconstructs the great transformations in the discourse of war and international order that were triggered at the 'threshold of modernity'.[82] I argue that the modern discourse on war and peace emerged in the context of the French Revolutionary and Napoleonic Wars. While modern narratives such as nationalism and popular sovereignty entered the political practice of justifying war (Chapter 3.2), two political theorists were to become constitutive for the modern discourse on the legitimacy of war: Immanuel Kant and Carl von Clausewitz (Chapter 3.3).

Dialectically, the French Revolution was a violent catalyst for the emergence of the nineteenth-century international order. Following Paul W. Schroeder, I identify the Vienna Congress of 1814/15 as a 'decisive turning point'.[83] My central argument in Chapter 4 is that the modern international order governing the use of force was born in 'Vienna 1814/15'. In response to the trauma of the Revolution, the European Great Powers created a new normative framework for the (de)legitimation of war, with the prohibition of war as a yet uncodified emerging norm[84] at its centre (Chapter 4.2). The chapter then addresses the Vienna Order's highly paradoxical normative regulation of collective force, with a special focus on so-called 'measures short of war', and, more specifically, on anti-revolutionary and 'humanitarian' interventions in the first half of the nineteenth century (Chapter 4.3).

Chapter 5 deals with political, public, and legal debates that accompanied the crises and interstate wars between 1853 and 1878. The chapter's focus is on the international debates on the legitimacy of war in the context of the Crimean War

---

[82] R. Koselleck, *Vergangene Zukunft. Zur Semantik geschichtlicher Zeiten* (1988).
[83] P.W. Schroeder, *The Transformation of European Politics, 1763–1848* (1994), at v.
[84] For more on the concept of 'emerging norms', see Finnemore and Sikkink (n. 39); Deitelhoff, 'The Discursive Process of Legalization: Charting Islands of Persuasion in the ICC Case', 63 *International Organization* (2009) 33; Forst and Günther (n. 28); Forst (n. 19); and Eaton, 'An Emerging Norm? Determining the Meaning and Legal Status of the Responsibility to Protect', 32 *Michigan Journal of International Law* (2011) 765.

of 1853–56 (Chapter 5.2) as well as on the Italian (Chapter 5.3) and German Wars of Unification (Chapter 5.4). As can be observed in these Great Power debates on justifying war, the multilateral diplomacy that followed the 1814/15 Congress of Vienna had given rise to stable normative expectations. The proposition that war could be waged without an internationally accepted 'just cause', as the thesis of *liberum ius ad bellum* claims, can be falsified in this chapter with reference to the discourse between 1815 and 1878. Even after the Crimean War, many wars between the Great Powers were prevented through diplomacy.[85] I therefore agree with the research opinion that the institution of the Concert of Europe only ceased to operate with the First World War.[86]

But the mid-nineteenth century, wars *did* change the international normative order: while the Treaty of Paris (1856) generated an international subsystem for the Eastern Question, the Franco-Prussian War (1870/71) arguably marked the most important historical caesura in the European legal discourse. In Chapter 6, I first refer to the professionalization of international legal scholarship around the 1870s (Chapter 6.2) before discussing the continuities and changes in liberal thinking about war and peace (Chapter 6.3). Liberal international legal scholars not only referred to Kant's plan of an 'outlawry of war', but also to 'old' narratives of morality and natural law. The liberal legal scholars thus fluctuated in their thinking somewhere between Grotius and Kant. At the same time, liberal legal thinking on peace was not free of ambivalences. While they were in favour of *peace through law*, some liberal scholars developed justifications for wars of national unification (Chapter 6.4). This is a particularly clear example of the nineteenth-century paradoxes of nationalism and internationalism.[87] But liberal legal discourse was also strongly influenced by colonialist, racist, chauvinist, and antisemitic narratives. One exception was a particularly progressive Kantian—Walther Schücking. In his reflexive approach to the ambivalences of liberal legal thought, Schücking consistently strove for *ius contra bellum* (Chapter 6.5) and thus underlined the importance that this legal political demand had gained at the end of the nineteenth century. A clear rejection of a 'free right to go to war'!

In Part II: *Emergence of a Myth: A German Sonderweg?*, the Franco-Prussian War of 1870/71 is once again the historical starting point. To this day, it remains unclear where the thesis of the 'free right to war' came from. In Part II, I argue that the German Empire, as the new European central power, provided extraordinarily

---

[85] J. Dülffer, M. Kröger, and R.-H. Wippich, *Vermiedene Kriege: Deeskalation von Konflikten der Großmächte zwischen Krimkrieg und Erstem Weltkrieg, 1865–1914* (1997).

[86] Schulz (n. 2), at 28; R.J. Evans, *The Pursuit of Power: Europe, 1815–1914* (2017); J. Paulmann, *Globale Vorherrschaft und Fortschrittsglaube. Europa 1850–1914* (2019), at 356 ff.

[87] For more on these paradoxes, see M.H. Geyer and J. Paulmann (eds), *The Mechanics of Internationalism* (2001); Osterhammel, 'Nationalism and Globalization', in J. Breuilly (ed.), *The Oxford Handbook of the History of Nationalism* (2016) 694.

favourable socio-political as well as 'military-cultural'[88] conditions for a realist reorientation in legal discourse. The myth of *liberum ius ad bellum* is not a twentieth-century ex-post construction. It began to emerge in the context of the German Empire.

To develop this argument, Chapter 7 reconstructs how a *Clausewitzian* school gained in importance in the *Kaiserreich*'s legal discourse during the Wilhelminian era (1890–1918). In 1888, German lawyer Heinrich Rettich published a treatise entitled *Zur Theorie und Geschichte des Rechts zum Kriege*, probably the first legal work of the nineteenth century to assert *liberum ius ad bellum* as a positive legal norm (Chapter 7.2).[89] Rettich introduced realist viewpoints, developed by German nationalist historians and philosophers such as Heinrich von Treitschke and Adolf Lasson, into legal discourse (Chapter 7.3). While Rettich had some reservations about openly acknowledging the primacy of politics in his text, numerous influential German lawyers after him, such as Christian Meurer or Karl Lueder, strictly dissociated themselves from the internationalism of their liberal contemporaries (Chapter 7.4). They developed a second, bellicist variant of the thesis of the 'free right to go to war' (Chapter 7.5). Both variants—the positivist and the bellicist—were largely of German origin.

This raises the question of whether the thesis of *liberum ius ad bellum* was in fact influential beyond Germany. Chapters 8 and 9 will answer this question. In Chapter 8, I first show that the mainstream of legal scholars in Europe clearly opposed the German 'outsiders'. I argue that, in the last third of the nineteenth century, the first major debate between realist and liberal scholars in Europe emerged, anticipating the First Great Debate in International Relations, usually dated to the mid-twentieth century. What is striking is how, in this transdisciplinary debate, the arguments between the primates of law and politics, and the military, were exchanged and related to each other in an antithetical manner.

Chapter 9 turns to the German politics of justifying military force between 1870/71 and 1918. The chapter's focus is on the genesis of *Notstand* ('necessity') as a narrative of justification. While studies on the necessity of war have mainly focused on *ius in bello*,[90] I point to Germany's reservations regarding efforts to foster *ius contra bellum*, as discussed in the context of the Hague Peace Conferences (Chapter 9.2). Subsequently, I address the *Kaiserreich*'s war justifications in the context of the First World War (Chapter 9.3). While Germany did not explicitly claim a 'free right to wage war', it justified blatant violations of the norms of *ius contra bellum* and *ius in bello* with reference to *Notwehr* ('self-defence') and broad interpretations of *Notstand* ('necessity'). In its eclectic use of both the *Clausewitzian* legal theory of

---

[88] Hull (n. 55).
[89] H. Rettich, *Zur Theorie und Geschichte des Rechts zum Kriege. Völkerrechtliche Untersuchungen* (1888), at xiii.
[90] Messerschmidt (n. 55); Hull (n. 55), Chapter 5; Vec (n. 55).

liberum ius ad bellum and elements of the European war discourse, the *Kaiserreich* attempted to create alternative normative facts. As I show in reference to European reactions, Germany pursued a 'special path' in its politics of justifying war—one which was not accepted by the international legal community.

Chapter 10 refers to another German 'special path'. It reconstructs why the German thesis of *liberum ius ad bellum* prevailed in the broader academic research discourse after the First World War. To this end, the chapter takes up the debates in the interwar and post-war periods and examines the influence of proponents of the myth of *liberum ius ad bellum*, such as Carl Schmitt and Wilhelm G. Grewe, on the further development of the History of International Law and International Relations.

Finally, the concluding chapter brings together the findings of Part I and Part II. In view of the nineteenth-century normative order regulating the use of force in international relations, the thesis of *liberum ius ad bellum* must be rejected as a myth. Here, the question of continuity and change is posed once again. Although positive international law became increasingly important in political debates in the second half of the nineteenth century, the discourse on war and international order remained characterized by multiple normative narratives throughout the entire century. Based on this finding, I develop two final arguments: *first*, as 'multinormativity'[91] is still with us, it seems worthwhile to examine the role of norms in more recent war discourses beyond the vocabulary of legal positivism. *Second*, and this will be shown throughout the study, the results clearly indicate that there is a need for a more systematic historical engagement with discourses of justifying war in the past and present. After all, the emergence of the myth of *liberum ius ad bellum* was only possible because historical accounts of nineteenth-century normative war discourses were long neglected and ignored.

As the present study aims to illustrate, such historical analyses on the role of norms in international relations are worthwhile and can lead to unexpected results. This is particularly evident when we consider another nineteenth-century phenomenon long obscured by the myth of the 'free right to wage war': the birth of the modern international order governing the use of force.

---

[91] Vec (n. 25); Stolleis (n. 25); Duve (n. 25).

2
Thesis and Antithesis
Why States Justify War

2.1 Introduction: Anarchy, War, and Normative Order(s)

Proponents of *liberum ius ad bellum* usually cite this provocative proposition very briefly—as if it needs no further explanation. The present chapter, in contrast, investigates the substantiation of this thesis in greater detail. To this end, the proposition of *liberum ius ad bellum* has to be critically reconstructed *first* in order to show that it emanated not only from the realist narrative of 'anarchy', but also from a liberal teleological narrative of 'progress' (Chapter 2.2). *Second*, against these oversimplifying narratives, I will develop the counter-thesis that, throughout history, war has always required normative justification (Chapter 2.3). Contrasting thesis and antithesis, the book's theoretical premise will become apparent: the justification of war constitutes a political discourse on normatively ordering the international.

2.2 Narratives of 'Anarchy' and 'Progress': Reconstructing a Myth

To begin with the reconstruction of what makes the proposition of *liberum ius ad bellum*, I refer to the main assumptions and narratives attached to it. The most fundamental of these is the following: modern historiographies of war and international order usually proceed from the notion of a 'radical transformation' of the European war discourse between early modernity and the nineteenth century. In this 'radical transformation', it is said, the basic concepts, vocabulary, and sources for the justification of war underwent a transition.[1] It is claimed that the oldest and probably most influential set of criteria for the justification of war (at least) in the European tradition—'just war' (*bellum iustum*)—was gradually eradicated in this alleged process.[2] The first question to be asked here is: how is this assertion justified by its proponents?

---

[1] See this book's introductory chapter.
[2] From the vast amount of literature on 'just war', see A. Lang Jr., C. O'Driscoll, and J. Williams (eds), *Just War: Authority, Tradition, and Practice* (2013); N. Rengger, *Just War and International Order. The*

Transformation of the European War Discourse:
From *Bellum Iustum* to *Liberum Ius ad Bellum*?

Rooted in Greek and Roman antiquity[3] and moulded into 'its classical form'[4] in the thirteenth century, the moral theological theory (and practice)[5] of 'just war' could be regarded as the 'crowning achievement of *ius gentium* in the Middle Ages'.[6] Drawing from eternal law, divine law, natural law, and positive, human law, the 'just war' theory bound a prince's right to wage war to higher principles and to specific criteria: most importantly to 'just cause' (*causa iusta*), 'right intention' (*intentio recta*), and 'legitimate authority' (*auctoritas principis*).[7] By distinguishing between 'just' and 'unjust' wars, the normative order under *bellum iustum* was designed to fulfil a double task: it limited the use of arbitrary violence (*violentia*) while at the same time legitimizing the use of force (*potestas*) which conformed to the normative order of *res publica Christiana*.[8] Hence, warring parties had to justify their use of force publicly to locate it in the common normative frame of reference. With *bellum iustum*, the justification of war became a central political communication practice for distinguishing between legitimate and illegitimate force.

Despite its major discursive importance over the centuries, however, the doctrinal architecture of 'just war' suffered from two fundamental construction flaws. *First*, the concept of 'just cause'—the normative core of the 'just war' doctrine—was only vaguely defined. It remained largely undecided among ancient, medieval, and early modern theorists, such as Aristoteles, Cicero, Augustine, Thomas, Vladimiri, Vitoria, Grotius, Pufendorf, or Vattel, as to what actually constituted an 'injustice' to be sanctioned by war in specific cases.[9] Clear legal norms for a 'just cause' were missing in political practice, too. Rather, the acceptance of a justification as 'just'

Uncivil Condition in World Politics (2013), and M. Farrell, *Modern Just War Theory: A Guide to Research* (2013).

[3] For an analysis of the ancient tradition, see e.g. Keller, 'Cicero: Just War in Classical Antiquity', in H.-G. Justenhoven and W.A. Barbieri, Jr. (eds), *From Just War to Modern Peace Ethics* (2012) 9.
[4] Lesaffer, 'Too Much History: From War as Sanction to the Sanctioning of War', in M. Weller (ed.), *The Oxford Handbook of the Use of Force in International Law* (2015) 35, at 37.
[5] Brown, 'Justified: Just War and the Ethics of Violence and World Order', in L. Brock and H. Simon (eds), *The Justification of War and International Order: From Past to Present* (2021) 435.
[6] S.C. Neff, *Justice among Nations. A History of International Law* (2014), at 67.
[7] M.E. O'Connell, *The Power and Purpose of International Law: Insights from the Theory and Practice of Enforcement* (2008), at 22 ff.; see also Elbe, 'The Evolution of the Concept of the Just War in International Law', 33 *American Journal of International Law* (1939) 665.
[8] See also Brock and Simon, 'Die Selbstbehauptung und Selbstgefährdung des Friedens als Herrschaft des Rechts. Eine endlose Karussellfahrt?', 59 *Politische Vierteljahresschrift* (2018) 269. For the justification of early modern colonialism with recourse to 'just war', see A. Anghie, *Imperialism, Sovereignty and the Making of International Law* (2004), Chapter 1; and Becker Lorca, 'The Legal Mechanics of Spanish Conquest: War and Peace in Early Colonial Peru', in L. Brock and H. Simon (eds), *The Justification of War and International Order: From Past to Present* (2021) 81.
[9] See also the critique by Lang, Jr., 'Politics, Ethics and History in Just War', in L. Brock and H. Simon (eds), *The Justification of War and International Order: From Past to Present* (2021) 29.

depended on the respective higher political authority, with pope and emperor being at the top of the medieval feudal hierarchy.

Second, the doctrine of *bellum iustum* was principally 'lacking in any idea of moral equivalence, or equality of rights' between a 'just' and an 'unjust' enemy.[10] For it was assumed that the 'unjust enemy' had violated not only the rights of his war opponent, but those of the entire normative order of *res publica Christiana*. It was therefore difficult to remain neutral when war had broken out between a 'just' and an 'unjust' enemy.[11] Indeed, Neff argues that the 'logic of the just-war outlook clearly had no room for neutrality'[12] at all. Nevertheless, the doctrine's actual practicability depended on a central authority that could distinguish between 'just' and 'unjust' causes for war on a case-by-case basis. As the impact of the medieval dual 'source of all legitimacy'[13]—pope and emperor—was waning in early modernity, such central authority was missing.[14]

Alongside the 'just war' theory, new approaches and languages of justification and critique of military force now emerged. The reasons for this discursive diversification were manifold: on the one hand, the discourse of war and international order was affected by tendencies of de-theologization as a consequence of the Reformation (1517) and the ensuing division of the church;[15] on the other, these developments were intertwined with state-building processes and a corresponding early modern 'bellicosity'.[16] In the History of International Relations and International Law, these developments have led to the widespread assumption that in early modernity, increasingly if not entirely, political interests and '[l]aw, instead of theology or philosophy, explained the reality of a fragmenting world'.[17]

It is indeed correct that, beyond the 'just war' doctrine, notions of *raison d'état* and positive law acquired discursive significance. Yet, by no means did theology become obsolete in this process. It has remained alive as a discursive argument in

---

[10] S.C. Neff, *War and the Law of Nations: A General History* (2005), at 62; J. Bartelson, *War in International Thought* (2017).

[11] M. Abbenhuis, *The Hague Conferences and International Politics, 1898–1915* (2018), at 1; Vec, 'Neutralität', in A. Cordes, H. Lück, and D. Werkmüller (eds), *Handwörterbuch zur Deutschen Rechtsgeschichte*, vol. 3 (2nd edn, 2016) 1892.

[12] Neff (n. 10), at 75.

[13] B. Stollberg-Rilinger, *Des Kaisers alte Kleider: Verfassungsgeschichte und Symbolsprache des Alten Reiches* (2012), at 93; on medieval hierarchies and multinormativity see also Steiger, 'Zwischen-Mächte-Recht im Frühmittelalter', in M. Jucker, M. Kintzinger, and R.C. Schwinges (eds), *Rechtsformen internationaler Politik. Theorie, Norm und Praxis vom 12. bis 18. Jahrhundert* (2011) 47, at 73.

[14] See also A. Tischer, *Offizielle Kriegsbegründungen in der Frühen Neuzeit. Herrscherkommunikation in Europa zwischen Souveränität und korporativem Selbstverständnis* (2012), at 52.

[15] M. Stolleis, *Geschichte des öffentlichen Rechts in Deutschland*, vol. 1 (1988), at 172–4; Roth-Isigkeit, 'Niccolò Machiavelli's International Legal Thought – Culture, Contingency and Construction', in S. Kadelbach, Th. Kleinlein, and D. Roth-Isigkeit (eds), *System, Order, and International Law. The Early History of International Legal Thought from Machiavelli to Hegel* (2017) 19.

[16] Burkhardt, 'Die Friedlosigkeit der Frühen Neuzeit. Grundlegung einer Theorie der Bellizität Europas', 24 *Zeitschrift für historische Forschung: ZHF* (1997) 509.

[17] Koskenniemi, 'Georg Friedrich von Martens (1756–1821) and the Origins of Modern International Law', 1 *IILJ Working Paper* (2006) 3, referring to early modern German public law.

(early) modernity.[18] Quite in contrast to the argument of a narrowing of the vocabulary used in early modern war discourse, political and normative languages multiplied. Inter alia, arguments relating to the prince's will to seize power, natural law, and secular concepts of positive law, were available for passing judgement on violent coercion.[19] This wide variety of political and normative arguments entered complex, not always uniform discursive relationships with one another: they would cooperate, coexist, or compete for discursive authority.

The emergence of this plurality of arguments for the justification and critique of war may, of course, indicate *some* change in the architecture of early modern war discourse. The crucial question here, however, is a different one: did this argumentative differentiation also lead to a genuine transformation of the European war discourse, as a result of which the 'just war' doctrine had lost its discursive authority by the nineteenth century? In other words: was *bellum iustum* gradually replaced by *liberum ius ad bellum* in this process?

'Right' without Legal Regulation: A Narrative of 'Anarchy'

Hardly surprisingly, for the proponents of the thesis of *liberum ius ad bellum*, the answer to this question seems clear. They argue, with reference to political and legal theorists such as Machiavelli, Bodin, Ayala, Gentili, Hobbes, Zouch, Vattel, and Clausewitz, that in the period leading up to the nineteenth century, the concept of 'just cause' increasingly lost its persuasiveness in political and legal scholars' discourses.[20] Accordingly, it was eventually deemed obsolete.

In the interwar period of the twentieth century, this argument was put forward by a German lawyer who was to become not only the 'Crown lawyer of the Third Reich'[21] but also the main exponent of the *liberum ius ad bellum* proposition: Carl Schmitt. Tellingly, in his *Der Nomos der Erde* (1950), Schmitt titled a chapter 'The Transformation of Medieval Wars (Duels or Feuds) into Non-Discriminatory State Wars: From Ayala to Vattel'.[22] As is well known, Schmitt understood the history of international law as 'a history of the concept of war'.[23] Thus, he associated

---

[18] M. Koskenniemi, M. García-Salmones Rovira, and P. Amorosa (eds), *International Law and Religion. Historical and Contemporary Perspectives* (2017).
[19] See Tischer's (n. 14) study on early modern war manifestos; see also Hathaway et al., 'War Manifestos', 85 *University of Chicago Law Review* (2018) 1139, and Steiger (n. 13), at 73.
[20] See, for instance, C. Schmitt, *The Nomos of the Earth in the International Law of the Jus Publicum Europaeum*, translated by G.L. Ulmen (2006 [1950]) 152; W.G. Grewe, *The Epochs of International Law*, translated and revised by M. Byers (2000), at 210; for critical accounts, see below.
[21] Weiler, 'Editorial: Cancelling Carl Schmitt?', 32 *European Journal of International Law* (2021) 389, available at: *EJIL Talk!* (13 August 2021): https://www.ejiltalk.org/cancelling-carl-schmitt/ (last visited 1 December 2022).
[22] Schmitt (n. 20), at 152.
[23] Schmitt, 'The Turn to the Discriminating Concept of War (1937)', in C. Schmitt, *Writings on War*, translated by T. Nunan (2011) 30, at 31.

the slowly changing nature of war, from medieval princely to modern national,[24] with a parallel fundamental change in its legal structure. According to Schmitt, between the sixteenth and nineteenth centuries, war was 'transformed into a relation between mutually equal and sovereign states'.[25] Being a strong opponent to the doctrine of 'just war' and, more generally, the 'criminalization of war' in his own time,[26] Schmitt claimed that this 'new', modern, war was no longer seen as a discriminating instrument of 'justice'. Instead, he claimed that in the run up to the nineteenth century, war gradually became a duel over conflicting political interests between sovereign states. In Schmitt's understanding, these legally equal states accepted each other as 'just enemies' (*iusti hostes*) and, thus, agreed to certain legal rules in war (*ius in bello*), regardless of a war's 'just cause'. Furthermore, the legal institute of neutrality is said to have emerged as part of this alleged *Hegung des Krieges* (legal 'hedging', or 'bracketing', of war).[27]

Schmitt understood the latter as marking the beginning of modern international law as he conceived it—the *Ius Publicum Europaeum*: a purely territorial order of European sovereign states.[28] Accordingly, Schmitt named Alberico Gentili (who was influenced by Bodin's theory of sovereignty) and Richard Zouch, rather than Vitoria or Grotius, 'the true founders of European international law'.[29] Gentili and Zouch are said to have been the legal theoretical pioneers of the concept of *iustus hostis*. In Schmitt's interpretation, Gentili and Zouch had not only done away with the concept of the 'unjust enemy', but in so doing they had also contested the discriminatory concept of war enshrined in *bellum iustum*. Schmitt's reading of early modern legal theory is problematic, however, and I will provide a critique of this reading below.[30]

Schmitt praised a non-discriminatory concept of war as the precondition for the legal 'bracketing of war'.[31] However, his concept of *Ius Publicum Europaeum* was not at all averse to war. Instead, according to Schmitt, the legal limitation of force was itself strictly limited in three respects: *first*, Schmitt understood *ius in bello* to be applicable only to land war between European sovereign states. Schmitt's law was

---

[24] On this issue, see H. Strachan and S. Scheipers (eds), *The Changing Character of War* (2014).
[25] Schmitt (n. 20), at 309.
[26] Schmitt (n. 23); see also Slomp, 'Carl Schmitt's Five Arguments against the Idea of Just War', 19 *Cambridge Review of International Affairs* (2006) 435.
[27] Schmitt (n. 20), at 309; W.G. Grewe, *The Epochs of International Law*, translated and revised by M. Byers (2000), at 209.
[28] For critical discussions, see Teschke, 'Carl Schmitt's Concepts of War: A Categorical Failure', in J. Meierhenrich and O. Simons (eds), *The Oxford Handbook of Carl Schmitt* (2016) 367; and Bogdandy and Hinghofer-Szalkay, 'Das etwas unheimliche *Ius Publicum Europaeum*. Begriffsgeschichtliche Analysen im Spannungsfeld von europäischem Rechtsraum, *droit public de l'Europe* und Carl Schmitt', 73 *ZaöRV* (2013) 209.
[29] Schmitt (n. 20), at 309. Referring to Vitoria, Schmitt wrote: 'By no means should he [Vitoria, HS] be associated intellectually with the likes of Balthasar Ayala, Alberico Gentili, or Richard Zouch, all of whom, being jurists of international law, eschewed theological arguments.' *Ibid.*, at 110.
[30] Chapter 2.3.
[31] Schmitt (n. 20), at 309.

a purely Eurocentric and anti-universalist notion, according to which European sovereigns were not bound by norms of *ius in bello* in civil wars or in colonial warfare.[32] Rather, in Schmitt's view, 'by limiting war to a military relation between states', the 'rationalization, humanization, and legalization—a bracketing—of war was achieved against this background of global lines'.[33] Beyond the lines, 'for want of any legal limits to war, only the law of the stronger applied'.[34]

Second, adopting a particularly wide and increasingly totalitarian[35] interpretation of the tradition of military necessity, Schmitt argued that the laws of war could be overridden by sovereign decision in cases of 'emergency'. As will be shown in Part II of this book, for this concept of justification, Schmitt could build on an exceptionally strong tradition of military necessity ('*Kriegsnotwendigkeit*') that had its origins in the German Empire's 'military culture'[36] and—to tie it to Schmitt's first argument presented here—to German colonial warfare.

Third, and most importantly here, in Schmitt's concept of war, the limitation of the use of force was restricted to *ius in bello*. A state's resort to war was clearly excluded from any normative limitation. Moreover, according to Schmitt and his followers, hedging the use of force *in* war was only possible because modern states had been freed from any normative judgement of their decision to *go* to war. 'That we have learned', Schmitt concluded along similar lines to Hobbes's philosophical justification of the absolute state,[37] 'from the feuds of the feudal age and from the creedal civil wars over theological truth and justice'.[38] Consequently, at the centre of Carl Schmitt's concept of *Ius Publicum Europaeum* stands the claim that with the emergence of modern sovereignty, states—and sovereign states alone—hold a 'free right to go to war'. With regard to the question of who could 'decide authoritatively on all the obvious, but impenetrable questions of fact and law pertinent to the question of *justa causa*', Schmitt therefore answered that '[t]here can be only a decisionist answer: each state-person decides autonomously concerning *justa causa*.'[39] According to Schmitt, the decision by a modern state to wage war against an enemy could never be governed by international law.[40]

---

[32] *Ibid.*
[33] *Ibid.*
[34] *Ibid.*, at 93 ff.
[35] Schmitt, 'Totaler Feind, totaler Krieg, totaler Staat', 4 *Völkerbund und Völkerrecht* (1937/38) 139.
[36] I.V. Hull, *Absolute Destruction: Military Culture and the Practices of War in Imperial Germany* (2005).
[37] On Hobbes, see R. Koselleck, *Kritik und Krise. Eine Studie zur Pathogenese der bürgerlichen Welt* (13th edn, 2017 [1954]), at 33.
[38] Schmitt (n. 20), at 156 ff.
[39] *Ibid.*
[40] Schmitt's praise for a 'modern' non-discriminatory concept of war does not mean that he accepted 'just war' as international law before this claimed transformation. To Schmitt, even before the 'transformation', the 'just war' doctrine had *moral* authority at best, as becomes clear in a passage on the Spanish *conquista* in his *Nomos* (*ibid.*, at 110). According to Schmitt, even 'a warrior like Cortes recognized questions of conscience. He also consulted theological moral counsellors. But certainly he would not have thought of allowing the right of his *conquista* to be challenged juridically for moral reasons, and even less of turning it over to the advocate of a political enemy.'

The 'transformation' of the early modern war discourse as claimed by Schmitt was supposedly completed in the 'long nineteenth century'. Accordingly, sixteenth and seventeenth-century efforts to replace justice with state sovereignty as the only valid vocabulary in war discourse are said to have been taken up and pursued further by authors such as Emer de Vattel at the threshold of the 'long nineteenth century'.[41] Vattel is often regarded as the scientific precursor of the nineteenth-century international order.[42] This already indicates that for the proponents of the *liberum ius ad bellum* proposition, the 'long nineteenth century' represents the main era of reference for the 'free right to wage war' in its alleged full bloom.

Much in this vein, German lawyer and diplomat Wilhelm G. Grewe has underlined the importance of the nineteenth century as the alleged golden era of *liberum ius ad bellum* in his *Epochs of International Law* (2000 [1984]). Alongside Schmitt's realist classic of 1950 and Stephen C. Neff's *War and the Law of Nations* of 2005, Grewe's *Epochs* is to be regarded as one of the most cited works in support of the assertion of the thesis of *liberum ius ad bellum*. In his magnum opus, the so-called 'doyen of the History of International Law in the German language',[43] has claimed that for

> the international legal positivism of the nineteenth century the 'justice' of wars was fundamentally, and more decidedly and radically than for many teachers of natural law in preceding centuries, a juridically irrelevant problem of political ethics .... Whenever the problem of war was seriously discussed from an international law perspective, the principle of the freedom to wage war ... emerged.[44]

This passage is of utmost importance here: to Grewe, it was nineteenth-century international legal positivism that deprived the doctrine of 'just war' of its last remaining authority.

The claimed turn to positivism is crucial to understanding why the nineteenth century appears as the main reference period in the academic discourse on the

---

I therefore agree with Martti Koskenniemi that Schmitt must be understood as a mediator between early modern and modern thinkers of political realism in international relations: the 'Schmittian perspectives became absolutely central for international relations "realism"'. See M. Koskenniemi, *The Gentle Civilizer of Nations. The Rise and Fall of International Law 1870–1960* (2002), at 494.

[41] Schmitt (n. 20), at 165; Nakhimovsky, 'Carl Schmitt's Vattel and the "Law of Nations" between Enlightenment and Revolution', 31 *Grotiana* (2010) 141; a critical account is offered by Zurbuchen, 'Emer de Vattel on the Society of Nations and the Political System of Europe', in S. Kadelbach, Th. Kleinlein, and D. Roth-Isigkeit (eds), *System, Order, and International Law. The Early History of International Legal Thought from Machiavelli to Hegel* (2017) 263.

[42] C. van Vollenhoven, *The Three Stages in the Evolution of the Law of Nations* (1919); E. Jouannet, *The Liberal-Welfarist Law of Nations* (2012); Neff (n. 6), at 195; Zurbuchen (n. 41), at 263.

[43] '*Senior der deutschsprachigen Völkerrechtsgeschichte*', see Hueck, 'Völkerrechtsgeschichte: Hauptrichtungen, Tendenzen, Perspektiven', in W. Loth and J. Osterhammel (eds), *Internationale Geschichte. Themen - Ergebnisse - Aussichten* (2000) 267.

[44] Grewe (n. 27), at 531.

alleged emergence of a 'free right to go to war'. As is generally known, the nineteenth century was not only the 'golden age of the state',[45] but it is also usually considered a 'positive century'[46] in the History of International Law. Indeed, a new generation of professional international legal scholars[47] has focused increasingly on what Mónica García-Salmones Rovira has both pointedly and critically described as 'the project of positivism in international law'.[48] This 'project' and its different sub-projects[49] aimed at the unification and standardization of international legal vocabulary in favour of 'positive' law derived from empirical historical sources such as state practice and international consent—even if the actual sources of these positivist projects remained much more vague and controversial among legal scholars than is often assumed.[50]

However, a common denominator of these nineteenth-century 'projects of positivism' was the conviction that natural law had to be 'dethroned' as the leading vocabulary for speaking the language of international law.[51] Yet, there was dissent about the speed of such a transition. The clash between reformist and more radical conceptions of positivism should be understood as a crucial point in the debate on the legitimacy of war. It was because of this clash that the question of the legitimacy of waging war (*ius ad bellum*) became closely intertwined with theoretical and methodological debates on valid—and invalid—sources of modern international law.[52]

Thus, to properly understand the proposition of *liberum ius ad bellum* and its methodological foundation, we must read it against the background of the widespread perception of the nineteenth century as a century of international legal positivism. For, according to proponents of the *liberum ius ad bellum* proposition, the 'just war' doctrine, built mainly on *natural law*, was now completely disputed and seen as 'a juridically irrelevant problem of political ethics'.[53] Furthermore, and quite paradoxically, since the nineteenth century allegedly knew no rules on when

---

[45] J. Osterhammel, *The Transformation of the World: A Global History of the Nineteenth Century* (2014), at 573.
[46] Neff (n. 6), at 215; see also K.H. Ziegler, *Völkerrechtsgeschichte* (1994), at 213; for a critical account, see Vec, 'Sources in the 19th Century European Tradition: The Myth of Positivism', in S. Besson and J. d'Aspremont (eds), *The Oxford Handbook of the Sources of International Law* (2017) 121.
[47] Koskenniemi (n. 40); L. Nuzzo and M. Vec (eds), *Constructing International Law. The Birth of a Discipline* (2012); M.M. Payk, *Frieden durch Recht? Der Aufstieg des modernen Völkerrechts und der Friedensschluss nach dem Ersten Weltkrieg* (2018).
[48] M. García-Salmones Rovira, *The Project of Positivism in International Law* (2013); see also Kammerhofer, 'International Legal Positivism', in A. Orford and F. Hoffmann (eds), *The Oxford Handbook of the Theory of International Law* (2016) 407; and Hall, 'The Persistent Spectre: Natural Law, International Order and the Limits of Legal Positivism', 12 *European Journal of International Law* (2001) 269.
[49] Neff identifies three versions (or projects) of positivism in the nineteenth century: an empirical, a voluntarist, and a common-will variant, see Neff (n. 6), at 226–43; see also Chapter 7 in this book.
[50] García-Salmones (n. 48); Vec (n. 46).
[51] Neff (n. 6), at 222; S. Zurbuchen (ed.), *The Law of Nations and Natural Law, 1625–1800* (2019).
[52] See Chapters 5, 6, and 8 in this book.
[53] Grewe (n. 27), at 531.

wars could be waged, proponents of the *liberum ius ad bellum* proposition also claim that this new project of positivism prevailed not only over natural law, but also over any legal positivist limitation of *ius ad bellum*.[54] In the words of one of the most important scholars working on war in the history of international law, Stephen C. Neff: 'The idea of law governing the resort to war—the *ius ad bellum* of lawyers—shrivelled into virtual nothingness in the face of the positivist challenge.'[55] According to the thesis of *liberum ius ad bellum*, war was thus 'permitted' because it was not expressly forbidden by positive international law: 'Might was right.'[56]

Although the thesis of *liberum ius ad bellum* is formulated based on the positivist legal projects that were seen as materializing in the nineteenth century, it should now become clear why this doctrine is ultimately not based on a positivist norm of international law at all. Instead, the Hobbesian 'state of nature' (*status naturalis*) is said to have been transferred to interstate relations:[57] thus, the alleged 'free right to wage war' is understood as an 'essential sovereignty right'[58] beyond international legal regulation, as a 'prerogative of policy, not of law'.[59] To be quite clear: *liberum ius ad bellum* is not about *ius* at all. It is all about realpolitik: instead of universal normativity, the sovereign's 'monopoly to decide'[60] is the key justificatory argument, as Schmitt claimed. In this sense, sovereign was he who decided on the state of war,[61] i.e. who made the state of war the norm and was thus able to equate fact and law, constituent violence and political order, *nómos* and *physis*, and, finally: politics and the decision about life and death.[62]

With normativity supposedly eliminated, for proponents of the *liberum ius ad bellum* proposition, sovereignty became the perfect determinant of international relations[63] as a realist substitute religion[64]—with the absolute *Machtstaat* as its substitute house of prayer. Accordingly, political sovereignty became the epitome of *liberum ius ad bellum*, as much as *liberum ius ad bellum* became 'the epitome of sovereignty'.[65] In other words, as should have become clear by now, the idea of

---

[54] *Ibid.*
[55] Neff (n. 10), at 161 ff.
[56] O.A. Hathaway and S.J. Shapiro, *The Internationalists: How a Radical Plan to Outlaw War Remade the World* (2017), at xv.
[57] Koselleck (n. 37), at 33.
[58] G. Dahm, R. Wolfrum, and J. Delbrück, *Völkerrecht/Die Formen des völkerrechtlichen Handelns* (2nd edn, 2002), at 818.
[59] Neff (n. 10), at 161 ff.
[60] C. Schmitt, *Politische Theologie: Vier Kapitel zur Lehre von der Souveränität* (2nd edn, 1934), at 19 ff.
[61] This is a modification of the first sentence from C. Schmitt's *Politische Theologie* (1934), at 11.
[62] This is a modification of a phrase by G. Agamben, *Homo sacer: Sovereign Power and Bare Life* (1998), at 27.
[63] Fassbender, 'Die souveräne Gleichheit der Staaten – ein angefochtenes Grundprinzip des Völkerrechts', 43 *Aus Politik und Zeitgeschichte* (2004) 7, at 8 ff.
[64] O. Chadwick, *The Secularization of the European Mind in the Nineteenth Century* (1975), at 132.
[65] Peters, 'Membership in the Global Constitutional Community', in J. Klabbers, A. Peters, and G. Ulfstein (eds), *The Constitutionalization of International Law* (2009) 153, at 183.

a 'free right to wage war' is ultimately based on a realist understanding of international relations. It is a synonym for political arbitrariness—and thus the opposite of international law.[66]

As I have shown in this section, the proposition of *liberum ius ad bellum* is to be assigned to the theoretical tradition of political realism.[67] This is to say that the thesis is built on realist premises regarding the relationship between war, power, and normativity in international relations. For realists, law is an expression of the factual power of the sovereign state; its authority does not originate from the authority of an international or supranational order, but from state sovereignty as a precondition of (international) law, or *Rechtsvoraussetzungsbegriff* (Carl Schmitt).[68] Accordingly, international relations are characterized by anarchy—international cooperation is unlikely, 'peace through law' seems impossible. Along this *narrative of anarchy*, Wilhelm Grewe described liberals' legal pacifism as a 'mistaken belief...of reality-blind, idealist friends of peace'.[69]

From a realist point of view, the 'free right to go to war' tells us basically everything we need to know about the interrelationship between law and politics when it comes to (the justification of) war. In an anarchical state of nature, sovereign states are not obliged to follow the rules of an international legal order, which is 'ineffective'[70] anyway: 'War is just, if it is necessary' (Machiavelli).[71]

Beyond Anarchy: The Discursive Construction of Legal Progress

Interestingly enough, however, the thesis of a nineteenth-century 'free right to go to war' is not only supported by realists. It is also advocated by a majority of scholars who have little in common with a *Machiavellian*, *Hobbesian*, or *Clausewitzian* agenda for dealing with war.[72] As indicated in the introductory chapter, Hans Wehberg referred to the nineteenth century as an era of anarchy.[73] Wehberg has

---

[66] For an analysis of the opposition of force and law, see O'Connell, 'Peace and War', in B. Fassbender and A. Peters (eds), *Oxford Handbook of the History of International Law* (2nd edn, 2014) 272, at 272.

[67] For an introduction to realism in international law, see Jütersonke, 'Realist Approaches to International Law', in A. Orford and F. Hoffmann (eds), *The Oxford Handbook of the Theory of International Law* (2016) 327; for a classic text, see Morgenthau, 'Positivism, Functionalism, and International Law', 34 *American Journal of International Law* (1940) 260.

[68] See also M. Koskenniemi, *From Apology to Utopia. The Structure of International Legal Argument. Reissue with a New Epilogue* (2005), at 227.

[69] W.G. Grewe, *Friede Durch Recht?* (1985), at 21.

[70] K.N. Waltz, *Theory of International Politics* (1979). Interestingly enough, this argument has been put forward more recently also by non-realist just war thinkers like Chris Brown: see Brown (n. 5).

[71] I. Brownlie, *International Law and the Use of Force by States* (1963), at 19; Q. Wright, *A Study of War* (2nd edn, 1965), at 5; see also G. Ritter, *Die Dämonie der Macht. Betrachtungen über Geschichte und Wesen des Machtproblems im politischen Denken der Neuzeit* (6th edn, 1948), at 29; H. Münkler, *Machiavelli. Die Begründung des politischen Denkens der Neuzeit aus der Krise der Republik Florenz* (1984), at 397.

[72] See Chapter 1, n. 2.

[73] Wehberg, 'Universales oder Europäisches Völkerrecht? Eine Auseinandersetzung mit Professor Carl Schmitt', 41 *Die Friedens-Warte* (1941) 157, at 162.

frequently been echoed in research discourses to this day in order to characterize the nineteenth century as a *'laissez-faire* era for war-makers',[74] in which state sovereignty found its limits 'only in the power of other states'.[75]

Jürgen Habermas—as a critical Frankfurt School thinker in the liberal tradition of Kant—for instance assumes that *liberum ius ad bellum* constituted the structural core of classic international law.[76] Even Michael Walzer—'on most people's reckoning, the single most influential just war thinker of the last hundred years'[77]— concludes that from early modernity up to the nineteenth century, arguments of justice were replaced by political prudence in the sense of Niccolò Machiavelli.[78] Other important scholars, such as Mary Kaldor, Ernst-Otto Czempiel, or Beatrice Heuser, share Walzer's opinion.[79] And Yale lawyers Oona A. Hathaway and Scott J. Shapiro claim, with reference to Clausewitz, that the 'old world order' before the prohibition of war in 1920/28/45 'relied on and rewarded' war as an instrument of politics (for instance, in the 'right of conquest').[80] Astonishingly, the thinking of Carl von Clausewitz can be found in numerous current references to the thesis of a nineteenth-century *liberum ius ad bellum* made by non-realist scholars.[81] 'Clausewitz is alive', as Michael Bothe has put it.[82]

What distinguishes legal pacifist and liberal internationalist approaches,[83] such as those of Wehberg, Habermas, or Hathaway and Shapiro, from those of realists, however, is the role which they attribute to *liberum ius ad bellum* in their histories of modern international law. By constructing ideal-type dichotomies between 'classical' and 'modern' international law (Habermas) or 'old' and 'new world orders' (Hathaway and Shapiro), they transform the alleged 'free right to go to war' of the nineteenth century into a negative, anarchic converse of the 'universal' legal order that rose from the ashes of the two world wars. The darker the

---

[74] Neff (n. 10), at 161, 168.

[75] Dahm, Delbrück, and Wolfrum (n. 58), at 818.

[76] J. Habermas, *The Divided West*, edited and translated by C. Cronin (2006), at 118.

[77] Brown, 'Michael Walzer', in D. Brunstetter and C. O'Driscoll (eds), *Just War Thinkers. From Cicero to the 21st Century* (2017) 205, at 205.

[78] Walzer, 'The Triumph of Just War Theory (and the Dangers of Success)', 69 *Social Research* (2002) 925, at 927.

[79] M. Kaldor, *New and Old Wars. Organized Violence in a Global Era* (3rd edn, 2012), at 19; E.-O. Czempiel, *Friedensstrategien. Eine systematische Darstellung außenpolitischer Theorien von Machiavelli bis Madariaga* (2nd edn, 1998), at 89; B. Heuser, *War: A Genealogy of Western Ideas and Practices* (2022), at 189 ff.

[80] Hathaway and Shapiro (n. 56), at 33.

[81] Reference to war as a 'political procedure among others' in the nineteenth century can be found in Koskenniemi, 'The Politics of International Law', 1 *European Journal of International Law* (1990) 4, at 6; see also Koskenniemi (n. 40), at 85 ff.; reference to the phrase 'a pursuit of policy by other means' is also made in Neff (n. 10), at 162; Hathaway and Shapiro (n. 56), xv; and C. Henderson, *The Use of Force and International Law* (2018), at 11.

[82] Bothe, 'An den Grenzen der Steuerungsfähigkeit des Rechts. Kann und soll es militärischer Gewalt Schranken setzen?', in P. Becker, R. Braun, and D. Deiseroth (eds), *Frieden durch Recht* (2010) 63, at 70. See also Conclusion.

[83] Joyce, 'Liberal Internationalism', in A. Orford and F. Hoffmann (eds), *The Oxford Handbook of the Theory of International Law* (2016) 471.

image of the nineteenth century portrayed, the brighter and more progressive the Kellogg-Briand Pact and the UN Charter's ban on violence appear. It is therefore not surprising that liberals argue that it was only once *liberum ius ad bellum* was prohibited that international law transformed from a law of war to a law of peace.[84]

This becomes particularly clear in Hathaway and Shapiro's widely received *The Internationalists*, first published in 2017. At the heart of their book is the thesis that the Kellogg-Briand Pact of 27 August 1928 outlawed war for the first time ever and was thus 'among the most transformative events of human history'—an event 'that has, ultimately, made our world far more peaceful'.[85] Hathaway and Shapiro come to this conclusion by constructing a dichotomy between a vaguely defined 'old world order', which the authors locate between 1600 and 1945, and a 'new world order' thereafter.

According to Hathaway and Shapiro:

- while in the 'old order', not only was war legal, but power and law were ultimately identical, the 'new order' emerged through the gradual prohibition of war (1920 and 1928) and, more generally, of the use of force (1945);
- while in the 'old order', conquests, threats of violence, and killings in war were always legitimate, in the 'new order', conquests and threats of violence are illegal and war crimes can be prosecuted;
- while in the 'old order', economic sanctions were illegitimate, in the 'new order', they are legitimate.[86]

In short, based on this comparison, the 'new world order' of 1920/28/45 not only overcame the normative shortcomings of the 'old order' but, by outlawing war, it became the latter's 'photo negative'.[87] Hathaway and Shapiro go so far as to claim that, whereas in the 'old world order', power and law were identical,[88] the Kellogg-Briand Pact of 1928 facilitated the emergence of a better, more peaceful order.[89] And Jürgen Habermas even makes the argument that with the abolition of *liberum ius ad bellum* after the Second World War, international law had taken a decisive step towards a cosmopolitan state of law.[90]

Black-and-white dichotomies like this one make for an effective narrative—even more so when the dichotomy is between 'old' and 'new'. For the contrast between 'old' and 'new' is at the centre of human experience, as Susan Sontag aptly

---

[84] Heintze, 'Frieden und Völkerrecht', in H.-J. Gießmann and B. Rinke (eds), *Handbuch Frieden* (2019) 753; Hathaway and Shapiro, 'International Law and Its Transformation Through the Outlawry of War', 95 *International Affairs* (2019) 45.
[85] Hathaway and Shapiro (n. 56), at xiii.
[86] Ibid., at xv.
[87] Ibid., at xvii, 304.
[88] Ibid., at xv.
[89] Ibid., at 422.
[90] Habermas (n. 76), at 34.

reminded us in her acceptance speech for the German Book Trade Peace Prize in 2003.[91] Only a distinction between 'old' and 'new' allows us to compare, order, and periodize socio-political phenomena historically. At the same time, however, the distinction between 'old' and 'new' is attractive in its simplicity. It may seduce us into simplifying historical ambiguity and exaggerating supposed progress. My argument is that this is precisely what happens in view of the way many liberals deal with the thesis of *liberum ius ad bellum*: the latter is not even questioned in order to uphold liberal histories of progress—decreasing violence, international legalization, rule of law, cosmopolitanism. I will return to this argument in more detail in Chapter 10.

Strictly speaking, then, there are two main historiographical narratives building on the thesis of the 'free right to go to war'. While realists may feel vindicated by the thesis of an anarchic *ius ad bellum* in their assumption of an eternal 'right of the strongest',[92] for the liberal teleology of 'peace through law'[93] and its *narrative of progress*, the (anti)thesis of nineteenth-century *liberum ius ad bellum* serves to emphasize the legal progress that the international order has achieved in comparison to the pre-1920/28/45 order.[94]

Like the realist narrative of anarchy, however, this liberal teleological narrative of progress is highly questionable. This is because it does not really reflect the nineteenth-century international order governing the use of force. In Hathaway and Shapiro's *The Internationalists*, the nineteenth century does not appear as an era in its own right at all—and as a result, the Congress of Vienna, the Concert of Europe, and nineteenth-century European lawyers and their 'radical ideas to outlaw war' are largely missing as well. The uncritical assumption of the Kantian Habermas that there was a *liberum ius ad bellum* before the twentieth-century prohibition of war is also surprising: Kant—as Habermas admittedly mentions—denied any legal status to the 'free right to wage war'.[95] Equally unconvincing is the argument by Michael Walzer, Mary Kaldor, Ernst-Otto Czempiel, and many others, that only after the First World War was a discriminatory concept of war introduced again. The fact that such discrimination did in fact also exist in the nineteenth century—as I will show in the two historical parts of this book—is generally omitted here.

---

[91] S. Sontag, *Literature Is Freedom* (28 October, 2003). I thank Lothar Brock for pointing out this analogy.
[92] R.N. Lebow, *The Tragic Vision of Politics* (2003), Chapters 2 and 3.
[93] On this narrative, see Brock, 'Frieden durch Recht?', in P. Becker, R. Braun, and D. Deiseroth (eds): *Frieden durch Recht* (2010) 15; Brock and Simon, 'Liberal European Peace Theories and their Critics', in K.E. Jørgensen (ed.), *The Liberal International Theory Tradition in Europe* (2020) 73.
[94] Hathaway and Shapiro (n. 56); see also Heintze (n. 84); for critical reviews, see Peevers, 'Liberal Internationalism, Radical Transformation and the Making of World Orders', 29 *European Journal of International Law* (2018) 303; and Simon, 'Das Alte in der neuen Ordnung', 27 *Rechtsgeschichte – Legal History* (2019) 448.
[95] Habermas (n. 76), at 117 ff.

This is not to say that liberal internationalism with its telos of international legalization has it all wrong: not at all. In critical, self-reflective forms of this theoretical tradition, which are sensitive to historical contingency, the legalization of international relations as famously spelled out by Kant[96] can be understood as a long, perhaps even 'perpetual', 'heuristic process'[97] marked by both progress and regression.[98] This legal progress is real but it is challenged by ever new violence, be it the now dominant intrastate warfare,[99] or aggressive war, such as that of Russia against Ukraine,[100] as a correlate of the 'civilizational turn' in Russian politics of international law.[101] Whether war—and more generally, political violence—decrease with legal progress is, of course, a rather different matter.[102] Progress is a highly ambivalent issue.[103] And sometimes, the dead live longer.

However, the long history of this legal prohibition and the dual role of international law as both enabling and hedging violence[104] is worth emphasizing more strongly. In teleological narratives of legalization, in contrast, positive legal progress appears more 'radical'[105] and unambiguous. Historical complexity and contingency are then replaced by notions of ahistorical inevitability. That which is ambiguous is made unambiguous—and thus easier to consume and reproduce in discourse.

---

[96] Kant, 'Toward Perpetual Peace. A Philosophical Sketch (1795)', in I. Kant, *Toward Perpetual Peace and Other Writings on Politics, Peace, and History*, edited by P. Kleingeld (2006) 67.

[97] Vec, 'Verrechtlichung internationaler Streitbeilegung im 19. und 20. Jahrhundert? Beobachtungen und Fragen zu den Strukturen völkerrechtlicher Konfliktaustragung', in S. Dauchy and M. Vec (eds): *Les conflits entre peuples. De la résolution libre à la résolution imposée* (2011) 11.

[98] In a similar vein, Lothar Brock and I introduced the term 'reflexive legalization' (*reflexive Verrechtlichung*) in a critical examination of Kant's project of 'peace through law', see Brock and Simon (n. 93).

[99] Kaldor (n. 79); Kalyvas, 'The Landscape of Political Violence', in E. Chenoweth, R. English, A. Gofas, and S.N. Kalyvas (eds), *The Oxford Handbook of Terrorism* (2019) 11; Daase et al., 'Transformations of Political Violence? A Research Program', *TraCe Working Paper No. 1* (2022).

[100] Hathaway, 'International Law Goes to War in Ukraine', *Foreign Affairs* (15 March 2022).

[101] Mälksoo and Simon, 'Aggression and the "Civilizational Turn" in Russian Politics of International Law: An Interview with Lauri Mälksoo', *Völkerrechtsblog* (25 February 2022), available at: https://voelkerrechtsblog.org/de/aggression-and-the-civilizational-turn-in-russian-politics-of-international-law/ (last visited 1 December 2022); Kotova and Tzouvala, 'In Defense of Comparisons: Russia and the Transmutations of Imperialism in International Law', 116 *American Journal of International Law* (2022) 710.

[102] Mann, 'Have Wars and Violence Declined?', 47 *Theory and Society* (2018), 37; S. Malešević, *The Rise of Organised Brutality. A Historical Sociology of Violence* (2017).

[103] Forst, 'The Justification of Progress and the Progress of Justification', in A. Allen and E. Mendieta (eds), *Justification and Emancipation: The Critical Theory of Rainer Forst* (2019) 17.

[104] Simon and Brock, 'The Justification of War and International Order: From Past to Present', in L. Brock and H. Simon (eds), *The Justification of War and International Order: From Past to Present* (2021) 3.

[105] Hathaway and Shapiro (n. 56).

Disenchantment: Ordering War as a Modern Discourse of Rationalization?

To summarize, the two central narratives structuring the modern historiography of war and international order *both* proceed from the proposition of *liberum ius ad bellum*—even though they pursue contrary projects in political and historical theory: the realist narrative of anarchy and the liberal/idealist narrative of legal teleological progress. Both narratives use the proposition of a nineteenth-century *liberum ius ad bellum* to develop an ontological, ultimately philosophical statement on the connection between war and normativity. For realists, *liberum ius ad bellum* points to the national 'telos' of absolute sovereignty in the modern *Machtstaat*. According to them, the latter must prevail at all costs under the conditions of international anarchy. In contrast, for liberal teleologists, *liberum ius ad bellum* is perceived as a pre-modern doctrine of the nineteenth century, which was abolished by an assumed radical transformation of the international order at the beginning of the twentieth century. Thus, a realist theorem of 'eternal anarchy' confronts an idealistic theorem in the tradition of the occidental belief in (legal) progress.[106]

What is more, regardless of whether they are written from a realist or an idealist perspective, modern historiographies of war and the international order usually start from their rejection of 'just war' theory as a supposedly pre-modern tradition. Both realist and liberal approaches of ordering war seek to go beyond 'just war' in favour of either absolute political sovereignty in international relations or international legal peace. According to these two mainstream narratives, the formation of the modern discourse of war and international order is currently remembered as a communicative process of rationalization: as a process of *Entzauberung der Welt* ('disenchantment of the world'), to refer to Max Weber's famous concept here.

As is well known, Weber used the term *Entzauberung* to describe what he understood as an 'increasing intellectualization and rationalization' in modern society having the consequence

> that principally there are no mysterious incalculable forces that come into play, but rather that one can, in principle, master all things by calculation. This means that the world is disenchanted. One need no longer have recourse to magical means in order to master or implore the spirits, as did the savage, for whom such mysterious powers existed.[107]

---

[106] For an optimistic account see D. Thürer, *International Law as Progress and Prospect* (2009); for a critical account see Altwicker and Diggelmann, 'How is Progress Constructed in International Legal Scholarship?', 25 *European Journal of International Law* 425.

[107] Weber, 'Science as a Vocation [1922]', in H.H. Gerth and C. Wright Mills (eds), *Max Weber: Essays in Sociology* (1946) 129.

My argument is that modern historiographies of war and international order share a close affinity to Weber's concept of 'disenchantment'. They seek to exclude all vocabularies of religion and natural law. They move away from the 'savage', 'vague', 'mysterious', and 'incalculable' vocabulary of 'just war', which was supposedly no longer regarded as 'true law',[108] but only as 'political ethics',[109] and towards rational and uniform modern 'languages' of either sovereign realpolitik or positivist legal assessments of violence.

The idea of a modern 'intellectualization and rationalization' on a national or global level against any non-positivist argument is inherent in both historiographies. Thus, the proposition of *liberum ius ad bellum* and the supposed overcoming of the concept of 'just war' are to be understood as part of Weber's grand narrative of the 'secularization' of the modern world.[110]

However, in recent years, this very grand narrative has been increasingly criticized and questioned. Inter alia, it has been countered with alternative narratives and concepts such as 'modern sacralization'[111] or 'post-secularism',[112] as well as by research on modern 'international law and religion'.[113] In these different academic contexts, the normative plurality and diversity of modern society has been highlighted. This book's argument that the 'free right to go to war' represents a myth in the history of international thought is consistent with this more recent critique of Weber's thesis of 'disenchantment': from a historical perspective, mainstream narratives of linear rationalization of the war discourse are just as unacceptable as the narrative of the essential continuity of power politics.

Taking a critical look at the assumed transformation from *bellum iustum* to *liberum ius ad bellum* in the nineteenth century involves a critique of both realist and liberal narratives of 'anarchy' and 'legalist'[114] 'progress'. Ultimately, both standard narratives are oversimplifying the nineteenth-century discourse on the justification of war and international order. Since the complexity of the nineteenth-century war discourse is still largely ignored today, advocates of these narratives fundamentally misunderstand the role of 'just war' in the formation of the modern normative order. Although 'just war' did not fit neatly with the emerging legal positivism, it continued to be accepted as a legal concept—both in nineteenth-century legal theory and political practice. Against Carl Schmitt's standard narrative of a 'transformation of the early modern war discourse', in Part I of this book, I will

---

[108] Neff (n. 10), at 167.
[109] Grewe (n. 27), at 531.
[110] Weber (n. 107).
[111] Joas, 'Sacralization and Desacralization: Political Domination and Religious Interpretation', 36 *Journal of the Society of Christian Ethics* (2016) 25.
[112] A. Abeysekara, *The Politics of Postsecular Religion. Mourning Secular Futures* (2008); Habermas, 'Secularism's Crisis of Faith: Notes on Post-Secular Society', 25 *New Perspectives Quarterly* (2008) 17.
[113] Koskenniemi, García-Salmones Rovira, and Amorosa (n. 18); Esther D. Reed, *Theology for International Law* (2013).
[114] Hoffmann, 'International Legalism and International Politics', in A. Orford and F. Hoffmann (eds), *The Oxford Handbook of the Theory of International Law* (2016) 954.

highlight the continuity of the vocabulary of 'just war' in the nineteenth century. The doctrine of 'just war' was not, as is widely claimed, 'reborn' after 1919.[115] It had never gone away.

2.3 The Discursive Power of Normativity: Towards a Genealogy of Modern War Justifications

The main thesis of this book is that, in contrast to the notion of a nineteenth-century 'free right to wage war', the modern international order governing the use of force in international relations is rooted in the 'long nineteenth century'. To support this argument, the study will examine the normative status of war in nineteenth-century Europe. The analysis first addresses the genealogy of justifying war both in European legal theory and political practice (Part I). It then turns to the emergence of the proposition of *liberum ius ad bellum* in late nineteenth-century Germany (Part II). This comparison of European rule and German exception will enable me to paint a more complex picture of nineteenth-century war discourses than those of the prevailing grand narratives of 'anarchy' and 'progress'.

With regard to the methodology for such a historical examination, an approach oriented towards purely formal law hardly seems sufficient. A mere analysis of (peace) treaties and codified norms governing the use of force is unlikely to be a constructive endeavour for the present research interest—not least since the interpretation of these treaty norms was contested among politicians and lawyers in concrete cases of conflict.[116] This impression is reinforced by the poorly formalized character of the nineteenth-century international order governing the legitimacy of waging war.

It seems more promising to understand peace treaties as part of a broader political and legal discourse on war and international order and to place this discourse at the analytical centre. Particularly in the highly political field of the use of force, international law has always been what legal historian Heinhard Steiger called a *Kulturleistung*.[117] This German term is interesting, due to its twofold meaning. On the one hand, *Kulturleistung* can be translated as 'cultural achievement'—here the term refers to the liberal hope of civilizational progress taming arbitrary violence through law. On the other hand, *Kulturleistung* can also be translated as 'cultural

---

[115] However, this argument is made, for example, by Walzer (n. 78), at 927; Johnson, 'Paul Ramsey and the Recovery of the Just War Idea', 1 *Journal of Military Ethics* (2002) 136; Neff (n. 10), at 277; and Elbe (n. 7).

[116] Tischer, 'Princes' Justifications of War in Early Modern Europe: the Constitution of an International Community by Communication', in L. Brock and H. Simon (eds), *The Justification of War and International Order: From Past to Present* (2021) 65.

[117] Steiger, 'Ius bändigt Mars. Das klassische Völkerrecht und seine Wissenschaft als frühneuzeitliche Kulturerscheinung', in R.G. Asch, W.E. Voß, and M. Wrede (eds), *Frieden und Krieg in der Frühen Neuzeit. Die europäische Staatenordnung und die außereuropäische Welt* (2001) 59.

practice',[118] which is closer to what Steiger meant here in line with constructivist thinking as well as critical legal theory: international law emerges, falls, and proves itself in cultural practices, through socio-political interaction, contestation, and application.

In perhaps no other policy field is this observation more pertinent than in the use of force. By combining the political and legal debates of justifying war in the historical analysis, it is possible to show that the decisive ideas, practices, and international norms for prohibiting war began to emerge in political and scientific discourses on the justification of war and international order in the 'long nineteenth century'. Against the background of this discourse (Part I), it can be shown that the German discourse on justification became an exception to the European rule (Part II). In the debates that arose, both meanings of the term *Kulturleistung* played a role: international law as cultural practice and as cultural achievement.

Discourses Remembered—Discourses Forgotten

A normative reinterpretation of the nineteenth-century war discourse as envisaged in the present study may provoke opposition. For it contradicts firm established convictions and narratives across disciplines. These narratives have generally not been challenged, given that the nineteenth century has long been neglected in research on international politics, war, and order.

This is particularly true for the discipline of International Relations (IR): 'The first way that IR approaches the nineteenth century is by ignoring it', Barry Buzan and George Lawson observed in their ground-breaking book on *The Global Transformation* in 2015.[119] Although, more recently, Historical International Relations have been gaining in importance again,[120] the nineteenth-century international order governing the use of force still plays only a marginal role here. For instance, in the very same book in which they rightly criticize IR's blindness to the nineteenth century, Buzan and Lawson claim that if states in the nineteenth century 'wanted to go to war, they could'.[121] However, like most other IR scholars, they provide no evidence or more detailed empirical justification for this claim. Rather, when it comes to the legitimacy of war in the nineteenth century, Buzan

---

[118] J. Rogge (ed.), *Making Sense as a Cultural Practice. Historical Perspectives* (2013).
[119] B. Buzan and G. Lawson, *The Global Transformation: History, Modernity and the Making of International Relations* (2015), at 48; but see J. Rosenberg, *The Empire of Civil Society. A Critique of the Realist Theory of International Relations* (1994).
[120] See, for example, A. Acharya and B. Buzan, *The Making of Global International Relations: Origins and Evolution of IR at its Centenary* (2019); B. de Carvalho, J. Costa Lopez, and H. Leira (eds), *Routledge Handbook of Historical International Relations* (2021); K. Schlichte and S. Stetter (eds), *The Historicity of International Politics. Imperialism and the Presence of the Past* (2022); M. Bukovansky, E. Keene, C. Reus-Smit, and M. Spanu (eds), *The Oxford Handbook of History and International Relations* (2023); M. Albert, H. Brunkhorst, I.B. Neumann, and S. Stetter, *The Social Evolution of World Politics* (2023).
[121] Buzan and Lawson (n. 119), at 50; referring to Neff (n. 10).

and Lawson refer to a standard book of the History of International Law—Stephen C. Neff's *War and the Law of Nations* (2005), which, as I pointed out in the previous section, affirms the thesis of *liberum ius ad bellum*. Similarly, Beatrice Heuser, in her new book *War: A Genealogy of Western Ideas and Practices* (2022), refers to Neff to claim that in the nineteenth century:

> any sovereign State was ... assumed to have the right to go to war. As legal historian Stephen Neff comments, 'issues related to ... the ius ad bellum ... were quietly dropped from legal consideration.' In general, until the First War ... there was what Stephen Neff has called an 'atomistic' view of the world as composed of sovereign, indivisible nation-States, all of which were relentlessly pursuing their selfish interests in a Hobbesian world which would necessarily lead them to clash and to wage war.[122]

This affirmative reference is surprising, particularly since Historical IR has debunked the 'Myth of Westphalia'[123]—the proposition that the Westphalian Peace settlements of 1648 gave rise to the modern state system—and correctly located the emergence of modern international order in the nineteenth century.[124] Strangely enough, however, IR then stopped halfway: despite important research on Great Power politics in the Concert of Europe,[125] the discipline was not critical of the thesis of *liberum ius ad bellum*, but rather continued to perpetuate it by not treating it as a problem.

In International History as a discipline, things are a little different. The nineteenth century is certainly not deliberately neglected here. But since international law and normative orders have long played only a subordinate role in this discipline, the result is still pretty much the same:[126] unsurprisingly, the thesis of the 'free right to go to war' is also extremely popular among historians (of international relations). Analyses of the nineteenth-century international order governing the use of force are largely lacking.

This also applies to the discipline of International Law as well as to the interdisciplinary field of the History of International Law. As Neff has correctly stated, the

---

[122] Heuser (n. 79), at 189 ff.; referring to Neff (n. 10).

[123] Osiander, 'Sovereignty, International Relations, and the Westphalian Myth', 55 *International Organization* (2001) 251; B. Teschke, *The Myth of 1648: Class, Geopolitics, and the Making of Modern International Relations* (2003).

[124] Buzan and Lawson (n. 119).

[125] J. Mitzen, *Power in Concert: The Nineteenth-century Origins of Global Governance* (2013); H. Müller and C. Rauch (eds), *Great Power Multilateralism and the Prevention of War—Debating a 21st Century Concert of Powers* (2018).

[126] Fisch, 'Völkerrecht', in J. Dülffer and W. Loth (eds), *Dimensionen internationaler Geschichte* (2014) 151, at 151; Payk (n. 47), at 9; see also Payk, 'Institutionalisierung und Verrechtlichung. Die Geschichte des Völkerrechts im späten 19. und frühen 20. Jahrhundert', 52 *Archiv für Sozialgeschichte* (2012) 861.

nineteenth century was for a long time, 'extraordinarily ... the least explored area of the history of international law'.[127]

In the wake of the 'historiographical turn in international law',[128] much has clearly changed and several studies have highlighted an unprecedented *Verrechtlichung* ('legalization' or 'juridification') in nineteenth-century international relations.[129] It has been shown that the nineteenth century was not only a century of political and social but also legal innovations. Not only did the nineteenth century see 'the birth of international relations as we know it today',[130] but also 'international law as we know it today took shape'.[131] European international law became an increasingly important language for ordering international and global political discourses. It was understood as a yardstick of cultural progressiveness, as 'the conscience of the civilized world'.[132] It created public normative expectations.

Politicians could refer to these expectations in order to justify their politics, but at the same time these very expectations were no longer easily evaded.[133] While politics and law—not least in war discourses—often came into conflict with each other,[134] they were also closely connected.[135] This was reflected not least in the fact that seemingly contradictory phenomena developed simultaneously and were sometimes interwoven: war and peace, nationalism and internationalism, or cosmopolitanism and imperialism. The 'normative paradoxes'[136] of international law's close entanglement with Great Power politics[137]—and with violence[138]— become particularly clear in the context of the claim of European civilizational

---

[127] Neff, 'A Short History of International Law', in M. Evans (ed.), *International Law* (2010) 3, at 10; see also Kennedy, 'International Law and the Nineteenth Century: History of an Illusion', 65 *Nordic Journal of International Law* (1996) 385.

[128] Galindo, 'Martti Koskenniemi and the Historiographical Turn in International Law', 16 *European Journal of International Law* (2005) 539.

[129] See e.g. M. Vec, *Recht und Normierung in der industriellen Revolution. Neue Strukturen der Normsetzung in Völkerrecht, staatlicher Gesetzgebung und gesellschaftlicher Selbstnormierung* (2006); Vec (n. 97); Keene, 'The Treaty-Making Revolution of the Nineteenth Century', 34 *The International History Review* (2012) 475; Payk (n. 126); Payk (n. 47), Chapter 1.

[130] Osterhammel (n. 45), at 393; see also Buzan and Lawson (n. 119).

[131] Neff (n. 6), at 219.

[132] Koskenniemi (n. 40); see also G.W. Gong, *The Standard of 'Civilization' in International Society* (1984); M. Pauka, *Kultur, Fortschritt und Reziprozität. Die Begriffsgeschichte des zivilisierten Staates im Völkerrecht* (2012); Obregón, 'Completing Civilization: Creole Consciousness and International Law in Nineteenth-Century Latin America', in A. Orford (ed.), *International Law and its Others* (2006) 247; N. Tzouvala, *Capitalism As Civilisation. A History of International Law* (2020).

[133] For the context of the First World War and its aftermath, see Payk (n. 47); for the theoretical argument underlying the present study, see Chapter 2.3.

[134] For a critical account, see Hoffmann (n. 114).

[135] Koskenniemi (n. 68); Simon, 'Theorising Order in the Shadow of War. The Politics of International Legal Knowledge and the Justification of Force in Modernity', 22 *Journal of the History of International Law* (2020) 218.

[136] Honneth and Sutterlüty, 'Normative Paradoxien der Gegenwart', in H.-G. Soeffner and K. Kursawe (eds), *Transnationale Vergesellschaftungen* (2013) 897; T. Hippler and M. Vec (eds), *Paradoxes of Peace in Nineteenth Century Europe* (2015).

[137] G.J. Simpson, *Great Powers and Outlaw States: Unequal Sovereigns in the International Legal Order* (2004).

[138] Brock and Simon (n. 8).

superiority over the non-European world: it served as a justification narrative for colonialism, war, and forceful 'civilizing missions'.[139] State sovereignty as a basic condition for participation in the legal community was systematically denied to non-European political entities, even though global 'inter-polity relations' were much more complex than often assumed.[140]

Back in Europe, the increasing importance of international law was demonstrated on the one hand by the emergence of the science of modern international law,[141] and on the other, by the culmination of a 'treaty-making revolution of the 19th century'.[142] As Miloš Vec has put it, certain types of treaties even 'functionally compensated for the lack of codification of international law, and they were therefore called "law-making treaties"'.[143] Both developments were particularly pronounced in the second half of the nineteenth century (a fact which should not, however, lead one to overlook the roots of legal transformation in Europe and the world in the early nineteenth century, as will be shown in Chapters 3 and 4).[144] Accordingly, the First World War and the subsequent peace agreements became a 'struggle for law' (*Kampf um das Recht*) to quote Rudolf von Jhering's famous words.[145] Much in this vein, Isabel V. Hull and Marcus M. Payk have pointed to processes of making and breaking *ius in bello* in the First World War (Hull)[146] and the role of normative expectations in the subsequent peace settlement (Payk).[147]

After all, even the use of force in international relations was increasingly regulated under international law in the nineteenth century, albeit to a much more limited extent than less politicized fields of international relations.[148] This applies in particular to the legal codifications of the laws of war in the second half of

[139] Anghie (n. 8); B. Barth and J. Osterhammel (eds), *Zivilisierungsmissionen. Imperiale Weltverbesserung seit dem 18. Jahrhundert* (2005); L.A. Benton and L. Ford, *Rage for Order. The British Empire and the Origins of International Law, 1800–1850* (2016); Tzouvala (n. 132); see also Chapters 4 and 6.

[140] Benton, 'Protection Emergencies: Justifying Measures Short of War in the British Empire', in L. Brock and H. Simon (eds), *The Justification of War and International Order: From Past to Present* (2021) 167; for an account of early modernity, see Becker Lorca (n. 8).

[141] Koskenniemi (n. 40); Nuzzo and Vec (n. 47); Payk (n. 47).

[142] Keene (n. 129).

[143] Vec, 'Challenging the Laws of War by Technology, Blazing Nationalism and Militarism: Debating Chemical Warfare before and after Ypres, 1899–1925', in B. Friedrich, D. Hoffmann, J. Renn, F. Schmaltz, and M. Wolf (eds), *One Hundred Years of Chemical Warfare: Research, Deployment, Consequences* (2017) 105, at 107, referring to Keene (n. 129).

[144] See also Benton and Ford (n. 139), and Benton (140).

[145] R. von Jhering, *The Struggle for Law*, translated by J. J. Lalor (1997 [1915]), at 1; see also Cotterrell, 'The Struggle for Law: Some Dilemmas of Cultural Legality', 4 *International Journal of Law in Context* (2009) 373.

[146] I.V. Hull, *A Scrap of Paper: Breaking and Making International Law during the Great War* (2014).

[147] Payk (n. 47); see also M.M. Payk and R. Pergher (eds), *Beyond Versailles. Sovereignty, Legitimacy, and the Formation of New Polities after the Great War* (2019).

[148] See also Vec, 'Intervention/Nichtintervention. Verrechtlichung der Politik und Politisierung des Völkerrechts im 19. Jahrhundert', in U. Lappenküper and R. Marcowitz (eds), *Macht und Recht. Völkerrecht in den internationalen Beziehungen* (2010) 135.

the nineteenth century.[149] According to Martti Koskenniemi, the norms of *ius in bello* were studied with enthusiasm in the period between 1870 and 1914.[150] And as Maartje Abbenhuis has shown, the institute of neutrality under international law became an important 'tool of diplomacy and statecraft'[151] in nineteenth-century Great Power politics. While the emergence of neutrality was long regarded as evidence for the parallel emergence of a *liberum ius ad bellum*—since it supposedly contradicted the classical doctrine of *bellum iustum* (see above)—, it can also be understood as calling for the keeping of peace instead of going to war (see Chapter 5).

However, this 'overall friendly-sounding panorama of legal internationalism'[152] should not detract attention from the fact that the normative regulation of war differed greatly from the regulation of other political and legal fields in the nineteenth century. Despite the unquestionably important—and often underestimated—*ius ad bellum* limitations in treaties such as the Final Act of the Congress of Vienna (1815), the Troppau Treaty (1820), the Treaty of Paris (1856), and especially the Hague Conventions (1899 and 1907), the highly political question of a state's decision to use military force remained only marginally regulated by nineteenth-century international treaty law. A clear regulation would have been contrary to the interest of the Great Powers to remain the sole judges of the international use of force: treaties should not silence the Great Powers' vocabulary for justifying force.

That said, my argument is that while the international legitimacy of a state's decision to wage war largely was not regulated by international treaty law, it *was* nonetheless regulated by international norms. In the lively discourse on the normativity of war, appropriate reasons for waging war were debated in political practice and legal theory throughout the course of the nineteenth century. Surprisingly, this discourse has so far largely been ignored and seems to have been forgotten in the academic debates on the *liberum ius ad bellum*.

It is only recently that the continuing importance of natural law in nineteenth-century discourses on the use of force has been problematized. Although Stephen C. Neff, in his seminal *War and Law of Nations* (2005), adheres to the thesis that there was a 'free right to wage war' in the nineteenth century, he puts this view in perspective by showing that 'measures short of war', such as reprisals or interventions, continued to be legitimized by referring to the doctrine of *bellum iustum*.[153] They were, writes Neff, 'the nineteenth-century version of just wars'.[154] However,

---

[149] Alexander, 'A Short History of International Humanitarian Law', 26 *European Journal of International Law* (2015) 109, at 112 ff.; K. von Lingens, *Crimes Against Humanity. Eine Ideengeschichte der Zivilisierung von Kriegsgewalt 1864–1945* (2018).
[150] Koskenniemi (n. 40), at 87.
[151] Abbenhuis, 'A Most Useful Tool for Diplomacy and Statecraft: Neutrality and Europe in the "Long" Nineteenth Century, 1815–1914', 35 *The International History Review* (2013) 1; M. Abbenhuis, *An Age of Neutrals. Great Power Politics, 1815–1914* (2014).
[152] Vec (n. 143), at 107.
[153] Neff (n. 10), at 226 ff.; see already Brownlie (n. 71), at 27.
[154] Neff (n. 10), at 216.

why would states have bothered justifying, say, reprisals if the use of force in the nineteenth century depended purely on the political will of the sovereign state? Neff answers this question by recourse to Clausewitz. According to Neff, in addition to 'perfect wars', in which states were in an existential struggle with each other for survival, there were also 'imperfect wars', waged 'when issues of only slight importance were at stake'.[155] However, as we will see below, such a distinction between 'perfect violence', which needed no justification, and 'imperfect violence', which needed justification, was unknown in nineteenth-century political practice and mainstream legal doctrine. It is part of the *Clausewitzian* myth this book seeks to deconstruct.

First direct (albeit brief) contestations of the thesis of the 'free right to go to war' in recent research can be found in the works of Anthony Carty[156] and Mary Ellen O'Connell.[157] Carty's article on German legal scholarship in the *Kaiserreich* published in the *German Yearbook of International Law* in 2007 is particularly interesting for my analysis. In this article, Carty aims to show that late nineteenth-century German international legal doctrine was not very different from that of other countries. In a way, my research on the nineteenth-century use of force[158] follows up on Carty's brilliant article—even if I come to the completely opposite conclusion that late nineteenth-century German international legal doctrine *did* differ markedly from other European legal scholarship. It was in the context of the German *Kaiserreich* that the thesis of *liberum ius ad bellum* was born. On this point I disagree with Agatha Verdebout, who, building on Emmanuelle Tourme-Jouannet's work,[159] has argued that it was only 'during the interwar years, that the narrative of indifference first surfaced in scholarship'.[160] As will be shown in Part II of this book, the thesis of indifference (which holds that nineteenth-century

---

[155] *Ibid.*, at 215 ff. A somewhat similar differentiation between 'ontological' and 'order-related' justifications was introduced by Bernstorff, 'The Use of Force in International Law before World War I: On Imperial Ordering and the Ontology of the Nation State', 29 *European Journal of International Law* (2018) 233.

[156] Carty, 'The Evolution of International Legal Scholarship in Germany during the Kaiserreich and the Weimarer Republik (1871–1933)', 50 *German Yearbook of International Law* (2007/2008) 29, at 45–55.

[157] O'Connell (n. 7), at 38–40; M.-E. O'Connell, *The Art of Law in the International Community* (2019), at 163.

[158] Simon, 'Über das "freie Recht zum Krieg" in Politik und Völkerrecht des 19. Jahrhunderts', *Research Paper/Max Planck Institute for European Legal History* (2012); Simon, 'The Myth of Liberum Ius ad Bellum. Justifying War in 19th-Century Legal Theory and Political Practice', 29 *European Journal of International Law* (2018) 113; Simon, 'Anarchy over Law? Towards a Genealogy of Modern War Justifications (1789–1918)', in L. Brock and H. Simon (eds), *The Justification of War and International Order: From Past to Present* (2021) 147.

[159] E. Jouannet, *The Liberal-Welfarist Law of Nations* (2012), at 130: 'Throughout the inter-war years there was an avalanche of studies on the law of peace.... In an over-hasty amalgam, commentators inferred that states legally had the right to trigger any war at any time. Nothing could have been more mistaken.'

[160] A. Verdebout, *Rewriting Histories of the Use of Force. The Narrative of 'Indifference'* (2021), at 231; see also Verdebout, 'The Contemporary Discourse on the Use of Force in the Nineteenth Century: A Diachronic and Critical Analysis', 1 *Journal on the Use of Force and International Law* (2014) 223.

international law was indifferent to war), like the more radical nineteenth-century thesis of *liberum ius ad bellum* (which holds that under international law, states had a right to go to war),[161] was an invention of legal doctrine not of the early twentieth century, but in fact of the late nineteenth century. Against the European tradition of justifying war (Part I), legal scholarship *and* political practice in the German Empire took a *Sonderweg*. Thus, Jochen von Bernstorff's claim that the German entry into the war in 1914 was not illegal according to *ius ad bellum*[162] is historically unconvincing. Aggressive war was *not* permitted in 1914—neither according to political practice nor the prevailing legal doctrine.[163]

While this is undoubtedly pioneering work, recent accounts on nineteenth-century use of force suffer, in my view, from three main, interrelated shortcomings. *First*, as already addressed, European legal theory is essentially treated as a monolith, with only marginal deviations. The fact that there was a realist tradition in German legal scholarship that systematically developed the *liberum ius ad bellum* against the liberal mainstream is completely overlooked. As a result, the historical roots of the myth of *liberum ius ad bellum* are ignored (see Part II).

Second, the monolithic treatment of legal theory is related to the fact that essentially only scholars of the nineteenth century's 'last five minutes'[164] are analysed. Normative innovations, continuities, and changes in legal discourse during the nineteenth century are barely addressed, and the same applies to the fact that concepts of *ius contra bellum* were already developed in the first half of the 'long nineteenth century'.[165]

Third, and perhaps most consequential, most research on historical war discourses still prioritizes international legal doctrine. The political practice of justifying force is essentially analysed from the perspective of contemporary international (legal) scholars. As a result of this methodological bias, which has long been criticized in the History of International Law and International Relations,[166] the central question of how the nineteenth-century international order was normatively constituted remains marginalized. As Lothar Brock and I have argued elsewhere,[167] this question can only be resolved by at last bridging the gap between theory and practice in the analysis of discourses of violence and normativity.

---

[161] For a differentiation between the narrative of 'indifference' and the narrative of *liberum ius ad bellum* in nineteenth-century international legal scholarship, see Chapter 7.5.
[162] Bernstorff (n. 155).
[163] See also Simon 'Anarchy over Law?' (n. 158); Lesaffer, 'Aggression before Versailles', 29 *European Journal of International Law* (2018) 773; and Hull, 'The Great War and International Law: German Justifications of "Preemptive Self-Defense"', in L. Brock and H. Simon (eds), *The Justification of War and International Order: From Past to Present* (2021) 183.
[164] Kennedy (n. 127), at 391.
[165] See Chapter 4.
[166] W. Preiser, *Die Völkerrechtsgeschichte, ihre Aufgaben und ihre Methode* (1964); W. Janssen, *Die Anfänge des modernen Völkerrechts und der neuzeitlichen Diplomatie. Ein Forschungsbericht* (1965); Tischer (n. 14); Tischer (n. 116); Benton and Ford (n. 139); Hull (n. 163); Simon and Brock (n. 104); see also Chapter 1.2.
[167] Simon and Brock (n. 104).

This is all the truer since previous research on war justifications in political practice largely omits the nineteenth century. For instance, even though Hathaway and Shapiro's *The Internationalists*[168] is based on the authors' particularly rich research on war manifestos,[169] the nineteenth century is not analysed as an independent era when it comes to justifications and norms of war. Rather, the general acceptance of the proposition that there was a 'free right to wage war' in the nineteenth century has for a long time made in-depth analyses of contemporary debates on war and international normativity seem superfluous. Thus, contemporary political and legal narratives which deviated from the thesis of *liberum ius ad bellum* by referring to normative spheres are still barely considered today. Largely forgotten, they are buried under a thick layer of one-sided memory and historiography.

This neglect has contributed to fostering the erroneous image of the nineteenth century as a century of anarchy in the field of the use of force. The analysis in this book of the norms, rules, and values stated, debated, and contested in this discourse provides an insight into what was understood as a legitimate reason for waging war in the poorly formalized international order of nineteenth-century Europe—and accordingly, it shows whether a 'free right to go to war' was claimed or not. Combining the perspectives of contemporary legal theory and political practice, it is this discourse and the norms emerging from it that is the focus of the present book.

War and Order: The Dialectics of a Normative Dichotomy

My argument starts from a simple, but often neglected observation with far-reaching historiographical consequences: when political actors resort to violence, they usually do so as 'justifying beings'.[170] This is to say that throughout history, the use of force has been accompanied by attempts to publicly (de)legitimize it.[171] This finding applies to various types of violence and violent actors, such as guerrilla soldiers, revolutionaries, partisans, terrorists, or militias—and it also applies to states. The question of when and under what circumstances military force can be considered '(un)just' or '(il)legal' in international relations has been discussed for thousands of years, not only by scholars and theorists,[172] but also by politicians and the general public.[173]

---

[168] Hathaway and Shapiro (n. 56).
[169] Hathaway et al. (n. 19).
[170] R. Forst, *Normativity and Power. Analyzing Social Orders of Justification* (2017), at 32.
[171] On the 'fateful' continuation of violence in an order, see Benjamin, 'Critique of Violence [1920/21]', reprinted in P. Demetz (ed.), *Walter Benjamin, Reflections: Essays, Aphorisms, Autobiographical Writings* (1978) 277; for an account of the field of (international) law, see McWilliams, 'On Violence and Legitimacy', 79 *Yale Law Journal* (1970) 623, at 628; Schachter, 'In Defense of International Rules on the Use of Force', 53 *University of Chicago Law Review* (1986) 113.
[172] R. Tuck, *The Rights of War and Peace: Political Thought and the International Order from Grotius to Kant* (1999); Neff (n. 10); Bartelson (n. 10).
[173] K. Repgen, *Kriegslegitimationen in Alteuropa. Entwurf einer historischen Typologie* (1985); Tischer (n. 14); Simon and Brock (n. 104).

The possibility of justifying war may be bewildering at first sight. In modern occidental political thinking, violence and language have often appeared as fundamental opposites.[174] Violence is regarded as what Hannah Arendt has called '*wortloses Handeln*' ('speechless action')[175] that silences, traumatizes, and claims 'victims'.[176] However, the widespread juxtaposition of barbaric violence and civilized culture is undoubtedly questionable insofar as it is not only war that has played a crucial role in the emergence of modern political orders,[177] but also the discourse on the justification and critique of violence.[178] In other words, the history of modernity is also a history of war—and the history of war is also a history of its justification and critique.

According to Jan Philipp Reemtsma, it is precisely the legitimacy requirements that any political actor must fulfil when using force that form the basis of trust in modernity.[179] My argument is that this assumption holds true not only for domestic, but also for international affairs, an argument that is supported by recent research on war and order in the early modern period. As Anuschka Tischer has shown in her pioneering study on war manifestos that were issued between 1492 and 1792,[180] belligerent princes in early modern Europe continuously felt the obligation to publicly justify war to their enemies and to the general public.

This brings us back to Carl Schmitt's thesis of an early modern transformation of the European war discourse. For Tischer's observations call into question Schmitt's claim of the emergence of a 'non-discriminating concept of war' (*nicht-diskriminierender Kriegsbegriff*)[181] in the early modern era: contrary to what Schmitt and others assumed, 'just war' retained its discursive authority in early modern political discourse. Much in this vein, Benno Teschke has argued that 'the praxis of *Ancien Régime* warfare contrasts sharply with Schmitt's non-discriminatory concept of war as a bracketed war in form'.[182] Schmitt's false concept of early modern war as a 'military relation between states'[183] thus points to

---

[174] A. Hirsch, *Recht auf Gewalt. Spuren philosophischer Gewaltrechtfertigung nach Hobbes* (2004), at 178; C. Thürmer-Rohr, *Fremdheiten und Freundschaften. Essays* (2019), at 85–96.
[175] H. Arendt, *Macht und Gewalt* (1970), at 64.
[176] S. Goltermann, *Victims: Perceptions of Suffering and Violence in Modern Europe* (2023).
[177] M. Foucault, *Society Must Be Defended: Lectures at the Collège de France, 1975–76* (2004); A. Linklater, *Violence and Civilization in the Western States-Systems* (2017); Bartelson (n. 10); D. Langewiesche, *Der gewaltsame Lehrer. Europas Kriege in der Moderne* (2019).
[178] Benjamin (n. 171); Simon and Brock (n. 104); Menke, 'Law and Violence', in C. Menke et al. (eds), *Law and Violence. Christoph Menke in Dialogue* (2018) 3.
[179] J.P. Reemtsma, *Trust and Violence: An Essay on a Modern Relationship* (2012); for a perspective of International Relations, see also Simon and Brock, 'Trust and International Violence. Revisiting "a Modern Relationship" in Times of Uncertainty', manuscript; and Brock and Simon, 'Vom Krieg zum Frieden. Vertrauen im Konflikt', 40–41 *Aus Politik und Zeitgeschichte* (2022) 14.
[180] Tischer (n. 14); Tischer (n. 116); see also Chapter 1.
[181] Schmitt (n. 20); Schmitt (n. 23).
[182] Teschke, 'Carl Schmitt's Concepts of War: A Categorical Failure', in J. Meierhenrich and O. Simons (eds), *The Oxford Handbook of Carl Schmitt* (2016) 367, at 388; on 'the myth of the cabinet war', see also Heuser (n. 122), at 41.
[183] Schmitt (n. 20), at 309.

a problematic concept of early modern international relations. Or, in Teschke's words: 'Schmitt's whole account of the Westphalian system is both empirically and theoretically deeply flawed.'[184]

These critical new perspectives on early modern political practice coincide with more recent reinterpretations of early modern legal theory. To construct his narrative of the 'non-discriminatory concept of war', Carl Schmitt deliberately 'simplified the political and philosophical complexities of the early modern discourse', as Peter Schröder has put it.[185] However, contrary to Schmitt's thesis, more recent research has argued that early modern legal theory by no means eradicated the doctrine of 'just war'. Not even seventeenth- or eighteenth-century ideas of *bellum legale* questioned the normative order of *bellum iustum* and the necessity of offering a *iusta causa*.[186]

These early modern justifications of violence in theory and practice are of utmost importance here since they point to the fundamental dialectic of violence and order in the history of international relations. For in justifying their violence, political actors at the same time recur to political order. The early modern princes' practice of justifying wars, Anuschka Tischer has explained,

> indicates that they accepted, at least in theory, a kind of control, contrary to the popular view that an early modern prince was a ruler who could do more or less what he wanted and did not care for others' opinions.[187]

In the name of order, in turn, violence is easier to justify. It is therefore no coincidence that the history of international order, in the absence of a monopoly on the use of force, is at the same time a history of international violence, and that the enforcement of the norms of the international order has always been accompanied by warlike violence.[188] War shaped the international order, and the international

---

[184] Teschke (n. 182), at 389.

[185] Schröder, 'Carl Schmitt's Appropriation of the Early Modern European Tradition of Political Thought on the State and Interstate Relations', 33 *History of Political Thought* (2012) 348, at 371. Claire Vergerio has recently argued that Schmitt referred to a distorted reading of Gentili's doctrine of the laws of war, which had been constructed by late nineteenth-century international legal scholars; see C. Vergerio, *War, States, and International Order. Alberico Gentili and the Foundational Myth of the Laws of War* (2022).

[186] Haggenmacher, 'Grotius and Gentili: A Reassessment of Thomas E. Holland's Inaugural Lecture', in H. Bull, B. Kingsbury, and A. Roberts (eds), *Hugo Grotius and International Relations* (1990) 133; A.H. Aure, *The Right to Wage War (jus ad bellum). The German Reception of Grotius 50 Years after De iure belli ac pacis* (2012); Lesaffer (n. 4), at 40; Simone Zurbuchen (n. 41) has shown that this was even true for Vattel, who is commonly regarded as 'a founding father of positivism'. In fact, a plurality of normative concepts emerged in early modernity. According to Randall Lesaffer, Europe went to a 'just war', but 'made a formal peace'; see Lesaffer, 'Peace Treaties and the Formation of International Law', in B. Fassbender and A. Peters (eds), *The Oxford Handbook of the History of International Law* (2nd edn, 2014) 71, at 88.

[187] Tischer (n. 116), at 76.

[188] See also H. Bull, *The Anarchical Society: A Study of Order in World Politics* (2nd edn, 1995), at 180–3.

order shaped war, is how one could sum up this seemingly paradoxical dialectic of war and international order, referring freely to Charles Tilly.[189]

But is there not then something 'desperate in the attempt to rise up against it', to modify Theodor W. Adorno's words here,[190] if war itself is inscribed within the civilizing process of international order? It is not possible to answer this normative question conclusively here.[191] But what must be noted from an analytical standpoint is that the formation of international order should not only be understood as eradicating or as a critique of violence, it must also be understood as its origin, as justification of violence. An international discourse of justifying war is a discourse on the formation of the international normative order. Order and violence refer dialectically to each other. The medium that communicatively connects them is the discursive practice of justifying violence.

A Constructivist Argument: The Discursive Co-constitution of the Justification of War and International Order

The dialectic of war and order also indicates that the norms of the international order are subject to discussion in a discourse of war. Drawing on insights from constructivist research on norms, I argue that the attempt at a normative justification of violence reflects the fact that the actors justifying violence have developed an awareness that by using violence they are potentially violating previously internalized, intersubjective obligations imposed by the international order.[192] The need for the legitimation of international violence expressed in these discursive practices thus refers to the internalization of normative expectations. If these expectations become stable, trust in the norms of the international order and their binding power can emerge.[193]

This constructivist approach to war justifications obviously contradicts realists' claims that there is not and cannot be any need for a justification of violence beyond the guiding vocabulary of power politics. For realists of all types, a legitimization of violence only comes into question when such a justification could serve

---

[189] Tilly, 'War Making and State Making as Organized Crime', in P.B. Evans and D. Rüschemeyer (eds), *Bringing the State Back In* (1985) 169.
[190] T.W. Adorno, *Education After Auschwitz* (1966).
[191] For an attempt, see Brock and Simon (n. 8).
[192] On norms in general, see Forst (n. 170); on norms in international relations, see F. Kratochwil, *Rules, Norms and Decisions, On the Conditions of Practical and Legal Reasoning in International Relations and Domestic Society* (1991); Finnemore and Sikkink, 'International Norm Dynamics and Political Change', 52 *International Organization* (1998) 887, at 891; Jepperson, Wendt, and Katzenstein, 'Norms, Identity, and Culture in National Security', in P.J. Katzenstein (ed.), *The Culture of National Security: Norms and Identity in World Politics* (1995), at 54; A. Wiener, *The Invisible Constitution of Politics. Contested Norms and International Encounters* (2008).
[193] For domestic affairs, see Reemtsma (n. 179); for international affairs, see Simon and Brock (n. 179).

their own political interests. For according to the founder of twentieth-century realism in International Relations, Hans J. Morgenthau,

> It is a characteristic aspect of all politics, domestic as well as international, that frequently its basic manifestations do not appear as what they actually are—that is, manifestations of a struggle for power. Rather, the element of power as the immediate goal of the policy pursued is explained and justified in ethical, legal, or biological terms. Statesmen generally refer to their policies not in terms of power but in terms of either ethical and legal principles or biological necessities. In other words, while all politics is necessarily pursuit of power, ideologies render involvement in that contest for power psychologically and morally acceptable to the actors and their audience.[194]

More recently, Eric A. Posner and Jack L. Goldsmith have argued similarly. They write that 'nations acting aggressively need some convenient rhetoric with which to influence speculation about their preferences. They do so by describing their motives in universalistic or semi-universalistic terms.'[195] It is hardly surprising that one of the most radical rejections of international normativity in international discourses on violence can be found in Carl Schmitt's work: 'Whoever invokes humanity wants to cheat.'[196]

This criticism certainly contains a kernel of truth: practices of justification are always based on political interests[197] as well as on structural power asymmetries.[198] This is especially true in the highly political field of the military use of force:[199] a legitimation of force that refers to norms of the international community can always be used with manipulative intent. It can be used as an apology for belligerents who are in fact pursuing political aims that may contradict the international norms they refer to.[200] No one would dispute that justifications of war are often built on lies.[201]

---

[194] H.J. Morgenthau, *Politics Among Nations: The Struggle for Power and Peace* (7th edn, 2006 [1948]), at 61.
[195] Goldsmith and Posner, 'Moral and Legal Rhetoric in International Relations: A Rational Choice Perspective', 108 *John M. Olin Program in Law and Economics Working Paper* (2000), at 21.
[196] C. Schmitt, *The Concept of the Political* (Expanded Edition 2008 [1932]), at 55; see also Chapter 10.
[197] Forst (n. 170).
[198] Teschke, 'Capitalism, British Grand Strategy, and the Peace Treaty of Utrecht: Towards a Historical Sociology of War- and Peace-making in the Construction of International Order', in L. Brock and H. Simon (eds), *The Justification of War and International Order: From Past to Present* (2021) 107.
[199] Kritsiotis, 'When States Use Armed Force', in C. Reus-Smit (ed.), *The Politics of International Law* (2004) 45.
[200] C. Peevers, *The Politics of Justifying Force. The Suez Crisis, the Iraq War, and International Law* (2013); I. Hurd, *How to Do Things with International Law* (2017); and T.M. Fazal, *Wars of Law: Unintended Consequences in the Regulation of Armed Conflict* (2018).
[201] Repgen (n. 173), at 19 ff.; Brock and Simon, 'Discourses of Power and Normativity. Ordering the International via War Justifications', *Völkerrechtsblog* (4 June 2021), available at: https://voelkerrechtsblog.org/de/discourses-of-power-and-normativity/ (last visited 1 December 2022).

At the same time, this is by no means the end of the story—but in fact its beginning. As Lothar Brock has convincingly argued, when political actors refer to norms, they are trying 'to make something available to themselves, the value of which for them is its unavailability'.[202] After all, reference to norms would be meaningless—and ultimately unwise even from a perspective of realpolitik—if they were regarded as *principally* irrelevant and non-binding. But even if a norm—as realists claim—is invoked as a justification for war waged for illegitimate political reasons, and is thus used to facilitate a lie, the normativity of this norm must be accepted in principle. Otherwise, it could never develop the desired discursive 'authority'[203] in a communication community. Thus, I agree with Konrad Repgen that for the scientific analysis of war justifications, it is irrelevant whether the justifications put forward by states really correspond to their political interests or motives. The issue here is the discursive authority of norms in different historical contexts.

It is, of course, true that norms which are constantly violated lose authority.[204] However, as IR norm research has convincingly explicated, looking at norm compliance is not enough. Even if a norm is openly contested and its validity disputed, the norm can still develop discursive authority precisely because of the recourse to it.[205] The decisive factor for the authority of a norm is not only actual compliance with it. A communicative recourse to a norm confirms its normative authority—*even* if that recourse is driven by instrumental motives or takes the form of a rejection. An (unfortunately not entirely) fictional example supports this argument. When a state violates the prohibition of the use of force as laid down in Article 2(4) UN Charter by invading another state, but knowingly uses the factually inaccurate justification of self-defence, it is doing two things: it is clearly violating the legal norm that prohibits war, but at the same time it is communicatively confirming the discursive authority of that norm. To be clear, normatively speaking, the deliberately false reference to norms is doubly reprehensible (first the breach of law itself, and second the lie about it). Analytically, however, it is particularly interesting as, even in violating it, the aggressor proves the rule. We will encounter several such cases in the historical analysis.

In view of these constructivist objections, it should have become clear that the realist understanding of war justifications as an instrument of power politics is not entirely wrong, but it is insufficiently complex. Realism can, based on an individualistic rationalist logic of action, establish and criticize which power-political interests may lie behind a moralizing legitimation of violence. However, realism cannot convincingly explain why states should resort to normative justifications

---

[202] Brock (n. 93), at 31.
[203] M. Zürn, *A Theory of Global Governance. Authority, Legitimacy, and Contestation* (2018).
[204] Vec (n. 143); see also Theresa Reinold's review of Lothar Brock's and my *The Justification of War and International Order: From Past to Present* (2021), in 63 *Politische Vierteljahresschrift* (2022) 145, at 147.
[205] Wiener (n. 192); Zürn (n. 203).

of violence in intersubjective practices, yet fail to grant any discursive validity to international norms. Realism lacks insight into the normative power of intersubjective discourses. But the justification of war is always more than just empty 'propaganda', in the sense of realists such as Wilhelm Grewe.[206]

A discourse on legitimate reasons to wage war, therefore, points to the fact that norms do matter in international relations. Again, this by no means excludes the importance of power. Rather, every justification of war that refers to international norms is, at the same time, always also an exercise of power—but not exclusively so: it is shaped by interests as well as norms, which, in turn, it shapes. According to Rainer Forst, power can be 'the art of binding others through reasons; it is at the core of normativity'.[207] In a discourse on the justification of war and international order, normativity and political power are dialectically intertwined. *Both* are real.

Accordingly, international order is understood here not only as ' "governing" arrangements among a group of states including its fundamental rules, principles, and institutions'.[208] The focus is also on its character as an 'order of justification', i.e. as an order of 'narratives of the justification and critique'[209] of violence. This is to say that war justifications and the international orders surrounding them co-constitute each other in discourse.[210] In narratives of justification, the norms of the international order are communicatively (re)produced, modified, or contested. The discourse on legitimate reasons to wage war shapes the international order. Conversely, the international normative order also has an important influence on justification narratives. It offers normative narratives to be used in discourse.[211] The decisive factor is how other members of the communication community react to concrete justifications and whether they recognize them as legitimate or illegitimate. This can result in discourse oppositions as well as discourse alliances between members of the same communication community.

Discourses of violence are, therefore, at the same time discourses of the formation, enforcement, and contestation of norms and normative orders in international relations. As such, they are highly interesting as complex objects of historical research, since they comprise what was accepted, aspired to, or disputed as an appropriate reason for waging war in each historical communication community. After all, in the assumed co-constitution of international order and narratives of justification lies the analytical key for the genealogy of the modern discourse of war and international order—and for testing the historical validity of the proposition of 'the free right to wage war'.

---

[206] Grewe (n. 27), at 531.
[207] Forst (n. 170), at 64; R. Forst and K. Günther (eds), *Die Herausbildung normativer Ordnungen. Interdisziplinäre Perspektiven* (2011).
[208] G.I. Ikenberry, *After Victory* (2001), at 23.
[209] Forst (n. 170); Forst and Günther (n. 207); A. Fahrmeir, *Rechtfertigungsnarrative. Zur Begründung normativer Ordnung durch Erzählungen* (2012).
[210] Simon and Brock (n. 104).
[211] M. Foucault, *L'Archéologie du savoir* (1972); Koskenniemi (n. 68), at 7.

With this, the analytical focus shifts away from an idealized or even timeless understanding of war discourses and 'normative orders'[212] towards an analysis of historical practices of legitimizing violence. Here, norms lose the static character of formally fixed rules, standards, and/or expectations. Instead, they become objects of social action, and can be historicized as communicative practices. Although norms—understood as the legitimation of expectations—reduce the complexity of reality, their validity as norms is ultimately based on their acceptance as valid and appropriate arguments in discourse. This discursive acceptance in turn is based on the reflexive examination and normative evaluation of the appropriateness of a narrative of justification, i.e. on the ability of norms to bind the members of a communication community. This reflection does not take place in timeless discourses; it is negotiated in specific historical contexts. Thus, its genealogy can be reconstructed by tracing narratives of justification and critique that have been performed on the stages of domestic, international, and transnational affairs.

Accordingly, I understand war discourses not only as the sum of disputes over 'justifying reasons',[213] but also as the sum of different narratives and traditions of justification and critique. This underlines, once again, that the legitimacy of norms is the result of socio-political negotiations and thus subject to historical changes. The identities of who or what is regarded as possessing normative authority in discourse change, as do the vocabulary and the normative sources of that vocabulary that are deemed valid. In the words of Martti Koskenniemi:

> Words are politics. When vocabularies change, things that previously could not be said, are now spoken by everyone; what yesterday seemed obvious, no longer finds a plausible articulation.[214]

Continuity, Contingency, and Change: The Nineteenth Century as the Era of Birth of Modern International Order

Bearing in mind the historical openness of war discourses, the question of continuities, continuity, and change arises. Even if the question of progress is difficult—at times precarious—given the fundamental dialectic of war and order, it seems to me, as already noted above, it is ultimately inescapable. After all, the question of whether the justificatory practices of the early modern period continued into the nineteenth century or whether they were modified, remains unanswered. As Anuschka Tischer has shown, in early modern Europe, war was considered 'just',

---

[212] Forst (n. 170); Forst and Günther (n. 207).
[213] Forst (n. 170); Forst and Günther (n. 207).
[214] Koskenniemi, 'Miserable Comforters: International Relations as New Natural Law', 15 *European Journal of International Relations* (2009) 395.

first, if it responded to a breach of law or, *second*, if it was an act of self-defence.[215] My argument to be developed in this book is that beyond early modernity, these two justifications were, in more or less modified form, to remain central in modern history of war justifications. A crude periodic distinction between the discourses of pre-modernity and those of modernity therefore seems questionable.

However, despite these clear continuities, there was also change in the nineteenth-century international discourse of war and international order. As I argue in Chapter 4, 'Vienna 1814/15' became such an important historical caesura because from here on, the European discourse of war and international order underwent an unprecedented institutionalization. A state's decision to wage war was not only to be justified publicly, it was also assessed by an international institution: the Concert of Europe,[216] whose members were England, Russia, France (after 1818), Austria, and Prussia (with the Ottoman Empire and Italy joining in the second half of the century). The Concert sought to establish a stable architecture of peace in Europe, which also included the use of legitimate force by its members: multilateral congresses and conferences became diplomatic forums for the perpetuation and institutionalization of this peace order and the war discourse accompanying it.[217] Against this background, the characterization of the European Concert as a 'nineteenth-century Security Council'[218] seems plausible.

To this day, how long the Concert lasted is a matter of debate. Particularly with regard to the nineteenth-century discourse on the legitimacy of war, I agree with those scholars who argue that the Concert and the Vienna Order principally, if in modified versions, remained intact throughout the entire century, only to perish in the First World War.[219] The Concert worked so well that the nineteenth century has even been described as the 'most peaceful century of modern times'.[220] The 'Hundred Years Peace'[221] between the Great Powers was interrupted but not ended[222] by the mid-century crises. Again, the Great Power community that

---

[215] Tischer (n. 14). This confirms Brian Rathbun's argument that even states that feel wronged always refer to norms, not to power politics; see B. Rathbun, *Right and Wronged in International Relations. Evolutionary Ethics, Moral Revolutions, and the Nature of Power Politics* (2023).

[216] P.W. Schroeder, *The Transformation of European Politics, 1763–1848* (1994); Mitzen (n. 125); M. Jarrett, *The Congress of Vienna and its Legacy: War and Great Power Diplomacy after Napoleon* (2013); Payk (n. 47).

[217] See e.g., Schroeder (n. 216); Vec (129), at 75.

[218] M. Schulz, *Normen und Praxis. Das europäische Konzert der Großmächte als Sicherheitsrat, 1815–1860* (2009), at 527.

[219] See e.g. J. Paulmann, *Globale Vorherrschaft und Fortschrittsglaube. Europa 1850–1914* (2019), at 356; Schulz (n. 218); R.J. Evans, *The Pursuit of Power: Europe, 1815–1914* (2017); and Langewiesche (n. 177).

[220] J. Levy, *War in the Modern Great Power System. 1494–1975* (1983), at 90 ff., 138.

[221] K. Polanyi, *The Great Transformation. The Political and Economic Origins of Our Times* (1944), at 16; see also H. Kissinger, *A World Restored. Metternich, Castlereagh and the Problems of Peace, 1812–22* (1957), at 5; for critical accounts, see A. Zamoyski, *Rites of Peace. The Fall of Napoleon & the Congress of Vienna* (2007); and recently Lybeck, 'The Myth of the Hundred Years Peace: War in the Nineteenth Century', in M. Forough (ed.), *At War for Peace* (2020) 33.

[222] See also J. Dülffer, M. Kröger, and R.-H. Wippich, *Vermiedene Kriege: Deeskalation von Konflikten der Großmächte zwischen Krimkrieg und Erstem Weltkrieg, 1865–1914* (1997); Evans (n. 219).

created nineteenth-century normativity was based on hierarchies, exclusion, unequal property relations,[223] and claims of civilizational superiority,[224] exploitation, and domination. It served to establish coercion, repression, and military force against medium-sized and smaller as well as non-European powers and their people.[225]

Thus, here the dialectic of war and order reveals itself once again: the limitation of force in the European order went hand in hand with the legitimation of that very same force. To quote Rudolf von Jhering once more: 'The end of the law is peace. The means to that end is war.'[226] This, again, points to the double function of an international normative order: it limits, but it also legitimates force;[227] it judges violence, and thus curtails it; and at the same time it justifies violence, and, as Walter Benjamin has described it,[228] 'fatefully' perpetuates it. It is in this complex and paradoxical discursive field between restraining and enabling war that the formation of the modern order governing the use of force, which began to emerge in the nineteenth century, must be located.

Despite its many 'dark side(s)',[229] however, the Vienna Order was more than an order based on power and interest. The Great Powers' normativity and their realpolitik were interwoven but did not merge. Thus, while the thesis of *liberum ius ad bellum* emphasizes the importance of state sovereignty in the supposedly anarchic war discourse of the nineteenth century, it overlooks important normative innovations of this era. By making concerted decisions about legitimate force, the Great Powers placed violence in Europe under the collective obligation of justification. Accordingly, the use of force was regarded as an exception to the norm of international peace. In order to be brought publicly into line with the norms of the Vienna Order, the use of force had to be justified to an international public. In their international justifications of war resulting from this pressure for legitimation, states therefore referred, whether critically or approvingly, to norms of the international order of Europe when depicting their own violence as legitimate, i.e. 'appropriate behaviour'.[230]

In the nineteenth century, the common internalization and institutionalization of norms fell on such fertile ground in this context because the Great Powers saw themselves as part of the same elitist and powerful communication community.

---

[223] Teschke (n. 198).
[224] M. Wight (ed.), *Systems of States* (1977); Linklater (n. 177).
[225] Fahrmeir, 'The Dark Side of the European Concert of Powers: Caveats to be Taken into Account for Successfully Managing Peace', in H. Müller and C. Rauch (eds), *Great Power Multilateralism and the Prevention of War: Debating a 21st Century Concert of Powers* (2018) 65; Simpson (n. 137); Zamoyski (n. 221); Hippler and Vec (n. 136).
[226] Jhering (n. 145), at 81.
[227] Simon, 'Das Recht des Krieges', 24 *Rechtsgeschichte – Legal History* (2016) 508, and Simon and Brock (n. 104).
[228] Benjamin (n. 171); see also Menke (n. 178).
[229] Fahrmeir (n. 225).
[230] Finnemore and Sikkink (n. 192); Jepperson, Wendt, and Katzenstein (n. 192), at 54.

However, the interests and identities of the Great (and those of the less 'Great') Powers were not static as (neo-)realist theories[231] claim. Rather, they were shaped in intersubjective communicative practices[232] and were therefore subject to historical change. Accordingly, the emergence of a nineteenth-century institutionalized Great Power discourse on the legitimacy of war is ultimately to be understood as a discursive process not only of the establishment and internalization, but also of the contestation of common principles, rules, norms, and procedures.

As the historical analysis will show, the long discourse of European war justification was continued in the nineteenth century. At the same time, however, I argue that the strong institutionalization of the discourse of war laid the foundation for the modern international order governing the use of force. Starting in 1814/15, the modern prohibition of war was constructed as an emerging norm.[233]

Legalization, Moralization, Politicization: A Discourse of Multinormativity

Another important phenomenon should be briefly introduced here, one which had shaped the European discourse on war in the early modern period and continued to do so in the nineteenth century: that of 'multinormativity'.[234] Beyond its broader institutionalization and legalization, in the nineteenth-century international order, too, it was unclear which normative language should be used for the justification of force. Contrary to the thesis of a consolidation of the vocabulary used in nineteenth-century war discourse in the form of realpolitik or legalism,[235] much was in flux in this century of general social and political transformation.[236] The debates on the justification of war were by no means only conducted in the area of conflict between power and normativity.[237] Instead, a complex and paradoxical plurality of different normative and political vocabularies and arguments from spheres such as law, morality, ethics, social custom, honour, or technological

---

[231] Waltz (n. 70).
[232] Foucault (n. 211); Ashley, 'The Poverty of Neorealism', 38 *International Organization* (1984) 225.
[233] On the concept of 'emerging norms', see Finnemore and Sikkink (n. 192); Deitelhoff, 'The Discursive Process of Legalization: Charting Islands of Persuasion in the ICC Case', 63 *International Organization* (2009) 33; Forst (n. 170); Forst and Günther (n. 207).
[234] Vec, 'Multinormativität in der Rechtsgeschichte', in Berlin-Brandenburgische Akademie der Wissenschaften (vormals Preußische Akademie der Wissenschaften) *Jahrbuch 2008* (2009) 155, at 162–5; M. Stolleis, *Geschichte des öffentlichen Rechts in Deutschland. Staats- und Verwaltungsrechtswissenschaft in West und Ost 1945–1990*, vol. 4. (2017), at 684, 696; Duve, 'Was ist "Multinormativität"? – Einführende Bemerkungen', 25 *Rechtsgeschichte—Legal History* (2017) 88; see also Vec's Preface to this book.
[235] See Chapter 2.2.
[236] Osterhammel (n. 45), at 393; see also Buzan and Lawson (n. 119).
[237] Forst (n. 170).

standards regulated the justification of war 'norms ... without binding rules of collision in the case of conflicts of norms'.[238]

As I argue, this empirical descriptive 'multinormativity' is a characteristic feature of the modern war discourse from the nineteenth century to the present day. Even the general prohibition of violence under positive law in Article 2(4) of the UN Charter has by no means brought an end to the legitimation of violence using non-legal means.[239] This is quite obvious in the current debate on 'humanitarian intervention'[240] (also a product of the nineteenth century in the strictest sense[241]).

For the purposes of the genealogical analysis, this once again raises the important question of the change in the war discourse of the nineteenth century beyond realist or liberal narratives of anarchy and linear progress. For, while the Vienna Congress set in motion the modern process of narrowing down the legitimate causes for waging war to self-defence and embedded this process in international institutions as well as in law, multiple normative spheres remained relevant throughout the century. In international law, a dualism of natural and positive spheres of law can be identified in nineteenth-century war discourse.[242]

As will be shown in the historical analysis, this plurality of norms had various effects which cannot easily be generalized: political, legal, or moral arguments could, in war discourse, contradict each other, simply coexist, or even support each other.[243] However, what can already be stated here as a thesis is that the manifold forms of normativity that can be found in the discourse of the justification of war in the nineteenth century clearly contradict the Schmittian concept of a non-discriminatory concept of war and thus the thesis of *liberum ius ad bellum*. The latter constitutes a myth in the History of International Relations and International Law.

2.4 Conclusion: On the Front Stages of Diplomacy

To summarize, in a historical perspective, the formation of the modern discourse of war and international order has taken place in the context of a multitude of not only political but also normative spheres of reference for justifying and criticizing military force. In the following historical discourse analysis, the thesis of *liberum ius ad bellum* and its underlying realist thesis of anarchy in nineteenth-century international relations will be countered by this assumed multinormativity of

---

[238] Vec (n. 234), at 162–5.
[239] Simon and Brock (n. 104).
[240] Brock (n. 93).
[241] See Chapter 4.3.
[242] For a general account of this dualism, see Vec (n. 46); D. Klippel, *Naturrecht und Staat. Politische Funktionen des europäischen Naturrechts (17.–19. Jahrhundert)* (2006).
[243] See also Vec (n. 234).

modern war discourse. The history of the international order is thus not told here as a history of linear progress of a single normative sphere (such as law), but as a history of the sometimes quite conflictive interaction of multiple political and normative claims.

For this very reason, (historical) norm research must focus more on those interactions in which arguments and claims from different normative spheres meet and struggle with each other for discursive authority. Looking solely at law or morality, for example, is not sufficient to grasp the complexity of normative communication. It is important not to reduce a discourse's multinormative complexity to simplistic, uniform ex post narratives of politicization, moralization, or linear teleological juridification. For it was precisely in cases of conflict that contested norms became particularly evident.[244]

This will be shown in the historical discourse analysis in the following chapters. The genesis of modern war discourse and the accepted causes for war can only be understood in a longer historical perspective, which juxtaposes the wider European discourse (Part I) with the birth context of the myth of *liberum ius ad bellum* (Part II).

As the empirical parts of the book will also show, the history of the justification of war can be told as an almost endless tragedy. For, as is well known, the notion of 'tragedy', according to Georg Friedrich Wilhelm Hegel, refers to a fateful collision of viewpoints, interests, or norms.[245] This is especially true in international relations. In no other sphere, as claimed by Toni Erskine and R. Ned Lebow, 'are clashes between competing ethical perspectives more prevalent than in the realm of international relations'.[246]

Frankfurt philosopher Christoph Menke believes that:

> The genre of tragedy and the institution of law are genetically and structurally interlinked: Tragedy is the genre of law; law is the justice of tragedy.... The suit of the individual, the antagonism and the dialogue between the parties, the responsibility that comes with action, the significance and consequences of the decision, the questions and mysteries of interpretation—these are structural elements of both tragedy and law.[247]

When political actors claim that their violence against other actors is legitimate according to shared norms and rules, they are inevitably confronted with a plurality of competing political and normative claims and justifications. In Thucydides'

---

[244] Schulz (n. 218), at 616; Vec (n. 234); see also Chapter 4.2.
[245] W. Kaufmann, *Tragödie und Philosophie* (1980), at 223; R.R. Williams, *Tragedy, Recognition, and the Death of God: Studies in Hegel and Nietzsche* (2012); see also W. Benjamin, *Ursprung des deutschen Trauerspiels* (2019 [1928]).
[246] T. Erskine and R.N. Lebow (eds), *Tragedy and International Relations* (2012).
[247] Menke (n. 178), at 6.

classic example of the tragedy of justifying war—*the Melian Dialogue*[248]—two narratives on the legitimacy of violence are irreconcilably opposed to each other. On the one hand, the Athenians' use of violence according to the politically 'wise' or 'necessary' based on a 'right of the strongest',[249] an ancient *liberum ius ad bellum*, so to speak; on the other, the counter-demand of the Melians that the Athenians should act according to the customs, values, and norms shared by the Greek *poleis* and should not exercise unjustified violence and rule. Power and normativity are thus an irreconcilable thesis and antithesis in the *Melian Dialogue*. A mutual understanding seemed completely impossible. Friedrich Nietzsche thus described the dialogue between Attic and Melian envoys as a *'furchtbares Gespräch'* ('terrible conversation').[250] As is well known, in Thucydides' story, the Athenians ignore the warnings of the Melians—and with them the Greek norms—, conquer Melos, but ultimately perish from their own hubris. With the Attic tragedy, Thucydides underlines the fact that international relations require not only power but also legitimacy.[251] Research in ancient history has proven the Melians right. For with the emergence of public war in the early Greek period, violence between Greeks had to be justified by a preceding violation of rights and within the framework of a formal declaration of war.[252]

However, the behaviour of the Athenians in Thucydides' *Melian Dialogue* is historically completely atypical. It is an ideal-typical fiction.[253] When political actors resort to war, I argue, they (can) *never* claim a 'right of the strongest', a 'non-discriminatory concept of war', or *liberum ius ad bellum*—this neither happened in classical Greece nor in (early) modernity. Rather, even states must always justify their international violence. To do this, political actors enter what Erving Goffman has called the 'front stage':[254] they slip into roles as diplomats and try to convince their audience with their communicative performance. On these diplomatic front stages, they basically do two things: *first*, they problematize the use of force in international relations; if war was not deemed a problem in international relations, there was no need to justify it. And *second*, they refer to norms, rules, and rituals

---

[248] Thucydides, *History of the Peloponnesian War*, translated by R. Crawley, vol. 5, Ch. 17 (1874 [~400 BC]).
[249] Lebow (n. 92).
[250] F. Nietzsche, *Menschliches, Allzumenschliches: Ein Buch für freie Geister* [1878] (1954), at 501.
[251] Lebow (n. 92).
[252] E. Baltrusch, *Symmachie und Spondai: Untersuchungen zum griechischen Völkerrecht der archaischen und klassischen Zeit (8.–5. Jahrhundert v. Chr.)* (1994), at 97, 193; Baltrusch, '"I Have Set Out First the Grievances and Disputes:" Greek International Law in Thucydides', in C.R. Thauer and C. Wendt (eds), *Thucydides and Political Order: Lessons of Governance and the History of the Peloponnesian War* (2016) 3.
[253] Thucydides may have wanted to highlight the Athenian hubris, and therefore presented their motives rather than their actual speech acts in the *Melian Dialogue*; for this interpretation, see *ibid*.
[254] On Goffman in International Relations, see e.g. Schimmelfennig, 'Goffman Meets IR: Dramaturgical Action in International Community', 12 *International Review of Sociology* (2002) 417.

to depict their violence as internationally appropriate behaviour, i.e. as a legitimate exception from the rule.

Clearly, the justifications expressed on these front stages often conceal true war motives and economic or power-political interests, which are only expressed on the 'back stages' and thus remain invisible. However, this is of little relevance for the analysis of what are considered to be 'sayable' norms on the diplomatic front stages. For it is precisely the lies that actors utter on the diplomatic front stages that enlighten us as to what norms and rituals they consider appropriate behaviour.[255] In Goffman's words:

> In their capacity as performers, individuals will be concerned with maintaining the impression that they are living up to the many standards by which they and their products are judged. Because these standards are so numerous and so pervasive, the individuals who are performers dwell more than we might think in a moral world. But, qua performers, individuals are concerned not with the moral issue of realizing these standards, but with the amoral issue of engineering a convincing impression that these standards are being realized. Our activity, then, is largely concerned with moral matters, but as performers we do not have a moral concern with them.[256]

Even if Goffman's conclusion might appear too pessimistic (in my opinion it is not necessary, but conceivable, that actors are seriously convinced of the morality of their violence), what is decisive is that there are other actors to judge the respective performances. Justifications are often met with resistance and criticism. It is precisely these normative oppositions, contestations, and negotiations that indicate whether an asserted norm is also accepted in the broader communication community. Thus, in the communicative dialectic of justification and critique lies the key for the following historical discourse analysis. Analysing these communicative performances and reactions thus tells us much about those norms of the international order that are considered valid. In the sense of a genealogical discourse analysis, this involves reconstructing historical continuities and changes over time. Having set the scene by plotting thesis and antithesis in this chapter, this very reconstruction of different scenes of the perpetual tragedy of war justifications will be conducted in the following chapters. *Curtain up!*

---

[255] Repgen (n. 173); Simon and Brock (n. 104).
[256] E. Goffman, *The Presentation of Self in Everyday Life* (1959), at 251.

PART I
JUSTIFYING WAR IN THE NINETEENTH CENTURY
A European Discourse

3
On the Threshold of Modernity
From Revolutionizing to Reordering War

3.1 Introduction: The Change of an Epoch

'In the beginning was Napoléon.' These are the famous opening words of Thomas Nipperdey's *Geschichte der Deutschen*.[1] Clearly, this personification of the French Revolution was a gross simplification. But the socio-political innovations that emanated from the Revolution were real—and they were already perceived as radical by contemporaries: 'Those living at the time were aware that this [was a] change of an epoch', Michael Stolleis has argued.[2]

Similarly, Reinhart Koselleck has described the Revolution as the peak in the transition from 'Old Europe' to 'Modernity'. In this 'saddle period' (*Sattelzeit*) between about 1750 and 1850 a transformation of contemporary political language and semantics took place.[3] The French Revolution became a culmination point for new ideals, values, and norms. It 'touched the fundamental, legitimizing thought of the time and abruptly opened new perspectives'.[4] Before the actual 'revolution of fact', claimed revolutionary leader Dominique Joseph Garat, a 'revolution of ideas' was necessary.[5] For the new socio-political order demanded new ideas and a new normative vocabulary with which these ideas could be publicly communicated. For political discourse, therefore, the year 1789 marks the threshold of modernity.[6]

Is this true also for the discourse justifying the use of force? The emergence of a new socio-political vocabulary in Revolutionary France might indeed suggest that something changed in the way war was legitimized. This seems even more plausible when one considers the constitutive role of military violence in this period: for twenty-three years, the French Revolution was closely linked to the experience of war. This applies in particular to the Coalition Wars: five million Europeans died in battle or from war-related diseases—more than 2.6 percent of the European

---

[1] T. Nipperdey, *Germany from Napoleon to Bismarck: 1800–1866* (2016), at 1.
[2] M. Stolleis, *Public Law in Germany, 1800–1914* (2001), at 3.
[3] Koselleck, 'Einleitung', in O. Brunner, W. Conze, and R. Koselleck (eds), *Geschichtliche Grundbegriffe. Historisches Lexikon zur politisch-sozialen Sprache in Deutschland* (1979) xiii.
[4] Stolleis (n. 2), at 3.
[5] J. Israel, *Revolutionary Ideas: An Intellectual History of the French Revolution from the Rights of Man to Robespierre* (2015), at 15.
[6] R. Koselleck, *Vergangene Zukunft. Zur Semantik geschichtlicher Zeiten* (1988); see also D. Andress, *The Threshold of the Modern Age* (2008).

population around 1800.[7] The Coalition Wars were the traumatic events that would serve as the driving force behind the multiple attempts to reorder Europe between 1792 and 1815.[8] Tim Blanning has rightly emphasized that it 'was not the French Revolution which created the modern world, it was the French Revolutionary Wars'.[9] In a sense, Blanning's finding echoed J.-W. Goethe's recollection of the Cannonade of Valmy (20 September 1792): 'Here and today, a new epoch in the history of the world has begun, and you can boast you were present at its birth.'[10]

Given the centrality of war in the era of the French Revolution, the question thus arises: did the revolutionaries and their enemies justify their use of violence—and if so, *how* did they do it? The main argument of this chapter is that the revolutionary/Napoleonic era should be understood as the period during which the modern discourse of war and international order was born. Both in political practice (Chapter 3.2) and political/legal theory (Chapter 3.3), the justification of war was, in one sense or another, revolutionized. In a dialectical way, this revolutionization of the European discourse of justifying war between 1792 and 1815 was to have ground-breaking effects on the international reordering of violence in 1814/15. Modernity took its course.

3.2 Justifying Revolutionary War—Revolutionizing War Justifications?

This argument may come as a surprise—at least when considering the current state of research. For the (de)legitimization of war in the revolutionary age has played only a minor role so far.[11] Usually ignored or subsumed under broader perspectives, the revolutionary/Napoleonic era in general appears as a peripheral side event in textbooks on (the history of) international law.[12]

So, why is this the case? Randall Lesaffer's take on this question is particularly convincing. Lesaffer argues that the French Revolution, with its 'new' ideas of popular sovereignty, self-determination of peoples, and cosmopolitanism, does not fit into the classical historiographical narrative of modern international law. According to this narrative, after its supposed peak in the nineteenth century,

---

[7] Hewitson, 'Princes' Wars, Wars of the People, or Total War? Mass Armies and the Question of a Military Revolution in Germany, 1792–1815', 20 *War in History* (2013) 452, at 453.

[8] P.W. Schroeder, *The Transformation of European Politics, 1763–1848* (1994), at vi; C.J. Esdaile, *The French Wars, 1792–1815* (2001); M. Bélissa, *Fraternité universelle et intérêt national (1713–1795): Les cosmopolitiques du droit des gens* (1998).

[9] T.C.W. Blanning, *The Origins of the French Revolutionary Wars* (1986), at 211.

[10] W. Doyle, *The Oxford History of the French Revolution* (2nd edn, 2002), at 193.

[11] Bélissa, 'War and Diplomacy (1792–95)', in D. Andress (ed.), *The Oxford Handbook of the French Revolution* (2015) 418, at 419; E.J. Kolla, *Sovereignty, International Law and the French Revolution* (2017) at 124, 298.

[12] Sometimes it appears in an excursus, as, for instance, in W.G. Grewe, *The Epochs of International Law*, translated and revised by M. Byers (2000), at 415.

state sovereignty was limited for the first time with the Treaty of Versailles and the founding of the League of Nations in 1919/1920.[13] In other words, the international thinking on war and order in the revolutionary era might challenge the narrative that depicted the nineteenth century as anarchic, as well as the narrative of the linear progress of modern international law. What is more, this observation indicates that the revolutionary era does not fit neatly into the thesis of an emerging *liberum ius ad bellum*. In fact, it creates historiographical confusion.

Interestingly, however, Wilhelm G. Grewe has tried to incorporate the revolutionary era into his narrative of the emergence of a 'free right to go to war'. Grewe has argued that ultimately almost all international legal postulates of the Revolution—'the right of national self-determination and other fundamental rights such as the equality of States, the principle of non-intervention and the idea of the natural boundary'—pursued the ideological aim of completing 'the process of rendering the doctrine of sovereignty absolute'.[14] In Grewe's *Epochs*, the Revolution thus strictly forms part of the history of a 'free right to go to war' in the 'long nineteenth century', becoming the decisive moment in the transformation of the modern vocabulary of the justification of war in the sense of a supposed *liberum ius ad bellum*. In the Napoleonic era, according to Grewe, international relations even entered a 'state of anarchy'.[15] For Grewe, Nipperdey's introductory sentence—'In the beginning was Napoléon'—was thus tantamount to the claim that 'in the beginning was anarchy'.

As should now be clear, it is worthwhile to take a closer look at the political practice of justifying war in the revolutionary era. In this subchapter, I will contradict Grewe's thesis of the emergence of a *liberum ius ad bellum* in the revolutionary/Napoleonic era. Undoubtedly, the Revolution and the emergence of popular sovereignty as a narrative of justifying war correlated with tendencies towards a complete removal of the limits of violence. However, this use of force was constantly justified with reference to a variety of 'old' and 'new' normative claims.

'*Au nom de la nation*': The Revolution as the Birth of Modern War Discourse

What made the French Revolution the birth era of the modern discourse of justifying war? An important difference with their US-american counterparts was that the French revolutionaries were less willing to adapt to the international (legal) order of the European monarchies. Instead, they sought a radical transformation

---

[13] Lesaffer, 'In the Embrace of France. An Introduction', in B. Jacobs, R. Kubben, and R. Lesaffer (eds), *In the Embrace of France: The Law of Nations and Constitutional Law in the French Satellite States of the Revolutionary and Napoleonic Age (1789–1815)* (2008), at 7.
[14] Grewe (n. 12), at 413.
[15] *Ibid.*

of this very order.[16] Accordingly, the central characteristic of the revolutionary war discourse was the close interweaving of domestic and foreign policy *au nom de la nation*. This 'imagined community'[17] as a political and legal subject was to become formative for the modern discourse of justifying war. It was shaped by a fundamentally new and particularly influential narrative of justification: popular sovereignty (*souveraineté populaire*).

Initially, however, it did not look as if a typical revolutionary narrative to justify war would emerge. The revolutionary elites only gradually became aware of the explosive international power of popular sovereignty, as Edward J. Kolla has recently shown.[18] Moreover, a pacifist critique of war—perceived as a political instrument of monarchies—was predominant in early revolutionary discourse. This is particularly clear from a decree of 22 May 1790, in which the National Assembly spoke out against the legality of wars of conquest: '*l'Assemblée nationale déclarant à cet effet que la nation française renonce à toute espèce de conquête, et qu'elle n'emploiera jamais ses forces contre la liberté d'aucun peuple.*' The decree was adopted verbatim in the Constitution of 3 September 1791 (Title VI, Sentence 1). Military violence should now only be justifiable in defence of the sovereignty, freedom, and property of a people, as Grégoire put it.[19] What is more, in France, waging an illegal war of aggression was to be punishable as high treason![20]

With these provisions, an important first contribution was made to the modern discourse on the prohibition of war in international and constitutional law—albeit only in rudimentary form, as neither a clear and precise definition of 'conquest' or 'aggression' was provided, nor had the definition of 'aggression' yet been narrowed 'to mean the first-use of armed force'.[21] It is nevertheless significant that Carl Schmitt saw in this prohibition of aggressive war a break in the alleged genesis of the 'free right to wage war'.[22] The prohibition clearly contradicts Schmitt's thesis of the validity of a non-discriminatory concept of war in the revolutionary era.[23] For Schmitt, this legal progress was undoubtedly a political regression.

What was also revolutionary was the public nature of the debates on the legitimacy of war in the National Assembly. These debates closely linked normative theory and political practice. Stephen C. Neff has noted that the French revolutionaries produced neither an important international legal theorist, nor a monumental

---

[16] Kolla (n. 11), at 176 ff.; see also R. Redslob, *Völkerrechtliche Ideen der französischen Revolution* (1916).
[17] B.R. Anderson, *Imagined Communities: Reflections on the Origin and Spread of Nationalism* (1988).
[18] Kolla (n. 11), at 178.
[19] Steiger, 'Das natürliche Recht der Souveränität der Völker – Die Debatten der Französischen Revolution 1789–1793', in J. Fisch (ed.), *Die Verteilung der Welt. Selbstbestimmung und das Selbstbestimmungsrecht der Völker* (2011) 51, at 55.
[20] Grewe (n. 12), at 423.
[21] Ibid.
[22] C. Schmitt, *The Nomos of the Earth in the International Law of the Jus Publicum Europaeum*, translated by G.L. Ulmen (2006 [1950]), at 150.
[23] For an account of Schmitt's thesis, see Chapter 2.2.

work on revolutionary international law.[24] This is true insofar as revolutionary international political and legal thought was primarily developed in political discourse and based on concrete cases of conflict.[25] Yet, many members of parliament were lawyers and philosophers. Practice and theory were thus often interwoven. Moreover, these debates were published, especially in the *Gazette Nationale ou Le Moniteur Universel*, edited by Charles-Joseph Panckoucke since 1789. The public word, according to Heinhard Steiger,[26] had become a decisive political weapon, both internally and externally.

For the increasing publicity and immediacy of political discourse could be used not only to criticize violence, but also to legitimize it. For example, in its declaration of war on Austria on 20 April 1792, France referred to the entire French nation, and justified the war '*au nom de la nation*'.[27] The pacifism of the Revolution was abandoned. War had been justified—and thus begun.

Paradoxes of Popular Sovereignty: From Limitation to Legitimation of Violence

The French declaration of war on Austria was preceded by a gradual radicalization of revolutionary foreign policy. Between 1789 and 1792, the dominant tack among revolutionary leaders changed: from limiting violence to legitimizing it. An important turning point was the French reaction to the counter-revolutionary Pillnitz Declaration (27 August 1791). This declaration was a direct result of the new alliance between Prussia and Austria, and was made under pressure from French *émigrés*.[28] In the declaration, Leopold II of Austria and Friedrich Wilhelm II of Prussia demanded, under threat of sanctions, the reinstatement of Louis XVI, following his attempted flight to Varennes in June 1791.[29] The declaration did not fail to have an effect—albeit not the one intended: despite the fact that a military intervention by Austria and Prussia was rather unlikely in the summer of 1791,[30] most of the French feared it.[31] This public anxiety was exploited by the French war hawks—even to the extent of justifying preventive war.

Notably, the war against Austria was not referred to as a war 'of nation against nation' in the French war declarations, but as a 'just defence of a free people against

---

[24] S.C. Neff, *War and the Law of Nations: A General History* (2005), at 93.
[25] See also Steiger, 'Das Völkerrecht und der Wandel der Internationalen Beziehungen um 1800', in A. Klinger, H.-W. Hahn, and G. Schmidt (eds), *Das Jahr 1806 im europäischen Kontext: Balance, Hegemonie und politische Kulturen* (2008) 23; Kolla (n. 11).
[26] Steiger (n. 19), at 53.
[27] *Déclaration de guerre de la France au roi de Bohême et de Hongrie* (20 April 1792).
[28] E. Schulin, *Die Französische Revolution* (4th edn, 2004), at 123.
[29] M. Erbe, *Revolutionäre Erschütterungen und erneutes Gleichgewicht: Internationale Beziehungen 1785–1830* (2004), at 293 ff.
[30] Schulin (n. 28), at 123.
[31] Bélissa (n. 11), at 423; Hewitson (n. 7), at 467.

the aggression of a king' (meaning Leopold's successor, Franz II).[32] This formulation is highly interesting as it clearly comprises recourse to the fundamental justification principles of the doctrine of 'just war'. The centuries-old European tradition of justifying war[33] was now to be secularized according to the ideas of freedom, national independence, and popular sovereignty. Tradition and innovation merged.

Clearly, the main French narratives of justifying had already begun to emerge before war was declared in April 1792. In 1791, Jacques Pierre Brissot, spokesman for the pro-war Girondists, argued that war against Austria was necessary to protect liberty against internal and external enemies, and to remove men who might 'poison' it.[34] According to Brissot, France would be dishonoured if, after the completion of its constitution, it tolerated insults which 'a despot would not have put up for a fortnight'.[35] Sovereignty, morality, liberty, 'purity',[36] and honour of the nation were the main narratives of justification here. They were to remain central throughout modernity.

These arguments had both a legitimizing and a delegitimizing impetus. While they would gradually justify the need for a new international order, they could at the same time be used to delegitimize what revolutionaries called 'old' or 'dynastic' international law. Accordingly, revolutionary international thought polemicized against fundamental rules, norms, and principles of the 'old' international order, such as that of the 'balance of power'.[37] 'Old' international law was broken where doing so served the goals of the Revolution.

In the case of the debates on French sovereignty in Alsace of 1790, the *princes possessionnés* under Article 87 of the Peace of Münster (30 January 1648) were clearly violated.[38] However, for Philippe Antoine Merlin de Douai, a *juriste en politique*,[39] experienced both in legal theory and practice, this violation of the law was easily justifiable. He argued that the *princes possessionnés d'Alsace* arose from an 'old language' of dynastic international law: according to the French lawyer, this

---

[32] *Decree of the French National Assembly* (21 April 1792), at 2. The decree addressed Franz II not as Holy Roman Emperor, but as King of Hungary and Bohemia. The idea behind this was to declare war not on the Empire, but on Austria alone.

[33] For a more in-depth account of 'just war', see Chapter 2.2.

[34] P.B. de Brissot, *Second Discours De J.P. Brissot, Député, Sur la nécessité de faire la guerre aux Princes allemands; Prononcé à la société, dans la séance du vendredi 30 décembre 1791* (1791), at 15.

[35] Translation of Brissot in J. Gilchrist and W.J. Murray (eds), *The Press in French Revolution. A Selection of Documents Taken from the Press of the Revolution for the Years 1789–1794* (1971) 215, at 215.

[36] B. Moore, *Moral Purity and Persecution in History* (2000), at 59.

[37] See the Decree of the National Convention … declaring that the French Republic is at war with Spain (1793), available at: https://documents.law.yale.edu/manifestos (last visited 1 December 2022).

[38] Kolla (n. 11), at 37–40; Pierre Muret noted in 1899 that this dispute between French and German jurists remained unresolved, see Muret, 'L'affaire des princes possessionnés d'Alsace et les origines du conflit entre la Révolution et l'Empire', 1 *Revue d'Histoire Moderne & Contemporaine Année* (1899) 433, at 434.

[39] H. Leuwers, *Un Juriste en Politique: Merlin de Douai, 1754–1838* (1996).

'old', 'dynastic' treaty law had simply been invalidated by the expression of the will of the Alsatian people to reunite with Revolutionary France.[40]

Merlin de Douai is a good example of a politicized jurist in the sense of Kelsen's 'real type', described above.[41] He did not hesitate to break international law in the name of the political goals of his client, Revolutionary France. To him (and many others), the 'old' was no longer valid in view of the promises of the 'new'.

Popular sovereignty was also used as an argument in the case of the annexation of Avignon in 1791. Here, legal rights competed with the alleged 'will of the people' (*volonté générale*) for discursive acceptance: conservative Catholics in Avignon opposed annexation by France. They invoked the historical rights of the Pope. In contrast, one of the leading Brissotins, Jérôme Pétion de Villeneuve, justified the invalidity of these rights in the spirit of Rousseau by arguing that the social contract was concluded between (free) individuals, not between rulers and the ruled. The rights of the sovereign were to be subordinated to the will of the sovereign people '*aux éternels principes de la justice*'.[42] Avignon could therefore be incorporated into the French kingdom even against the will of the Pope. In adopting this position, Pétion openly accepted a breach of international law.[43] Pétion admitted that this would not be possible without injustice or without injuring the laws of nations ('*je ne dis pas sans injustice, je ne dis pas sans blesser les droits des nations*').[44] But illegality by the standards of the 'old' order ultimately seemed irrelevant to him in the face of 'justice' by the standards of the Revolution.

The dichotomy of 'legitimate republic' and 'illegitimate monarchy' expressed in these French justifications of violence was quite consistent with the teachings of the Enlightenment: Montesquieu, Voltaire, and Rousseau had explicitly written against the elitist, anti-democratic, and bellicose politics of monarchies as favoured by Machiavelli or Hobbes.[45] But if monarchy was the cause of war, then it had to be defeated to defend the republic—by force if necessary. The juxtaposition of republic and monarchy was therefore also accompanied by further escalations of revolutionary violence against the old elites, both at home and abroad. The more the unity of the nation seemed to be in danger, the greater the revolutionaries' willingness to use excessive violence and justify it accordingly. Self-declared atheist Anacharsis Cloots claimed that a 'holy war' was being waged by the French in 1792: the fate of humanity lay in the hands of France. If the German princes were to destroy the Republic, they would first have to bathe in the blood of a nation defending itself to the utmost.[46] In this vein, Condorcet defended the offensive war against Austria on

[40] Kolla (n. 11), at 64–6.
[41] See Introduction.
[42] J. Pétion, *Discours sur la réunion d'Avignon à la France* (1790), at 28.
[43] Ibid.
[44] Ibid.
[45] T.L. Knutsen, *A History of International Relations Theory* (1997), at 124.
[46] Cloots, 'Discours prononcé à la barre de l'Assemblée nationale le 12 avril 1792, l'an IV de la liberté, par Anarcharsis Cloots, Orateur du genre humain', in M. Duval (ed.), *Écrits révolutionnaires 1790–1794* (1979) 338, at 338.

the grounds that the sovereignty of the people had to be protected by force against the threat of military interference by the European monarchies.[47]

The narrative of defending the Revolution, based on popular sovereignty, retained its fundamental meaning from the war justifications in 1792 to the Napoleonic Wars, but it was modified and reinterpreted several times during this period. Although the early, pacifist voices of the Revolution had forbidden wars of aggression and conquest, since 1792 offensive war was increasingly legitimized as a necessary evil. In this process of political radicalization, the principle of non-intervention was de facto reinterpreted as a responsibility to intervene for the liberation of 'oppressed peoples':[48] Anacharsis Cloots, much like ancient theologian Augustine, recognized peace as the purpose of war. To some extent anticipating H.G. Wells, General Charles-François Dumouriez spoke of the coming war as 'the last war'.[49]

With this, in addition to a 'just cause' (*iusta causa*), a 'right intention' (*intentio recta*) was given by revolutionary leaders. As in early modernity,[50] the argument of 'liberty'—now interpreted in a more cosmopolitan manner—gained important legitimizing power: France promised Europe freedom from monarchical foreign rule. Merlin de Thionville summed up this ideology in the oft-quoted formula: 'war to kings, peace to nations'.[51] And Robespierre, who had initially argued against the expansionism of the Girondists ('no one likes armed missionaries'), spoke on 2 January 1792 of a war of the European peoples against 'liberty's enemies'.[52]

However, liberation and domination were two sides of the same coin. Radical, bellicose interpretations of Jean-Jacques Rousseau's ideas on popular sovereignty and 'forced freedom'[53] served to justify French expansion in Europe.[54] Occupied territories were forced to republicanize. As a *pouvoir révolutionnaire*, or revolutionary power, the French army increasingly became a constitution-making force after 1792—even against the will of the population to be 'liberated'. In case of doubt the latter were incapacitated as the 'slaves of the tyrants'.[55] The Revolutionary Wars were thus clearly justified as civilizing violence. With increasing radicalization, all actions that served the survival and preservation of the 'indivisible' Republic,

---

[47] Steiger (n. 19), at 59.
[48] See also A. Cassese, *Self-Determination of Peoples. A Legal Reappraisal* (1995), at 12.
[49] J.R. Hayworth, *Revolutionary France's War of Conquest in the Rhineland: Conquering the Natural Frontier, 1792–1797* (2019), at 76 ff.
[50] See also A. Tischer, *Offizielle Kriegsbegründungen in der Frühen Neuzeit. Herrscherkommunikation in Europa zwischen Souveränität und korporativem Selbstverständnis* (2012), at 52; Tischer, 'Princes' Justifications of War in Early Modern Europe: the Constitution of an International Community by Communication', in L. Brock and H. Simon, *The Justification of War and International Order: From Past to Present* (2021) 65.
[51] Grewe (n. 12), at 423.
[52] Bélissa (n. 11), at 424.
[53] Rousseau, 'The Social Contract [1762]', in J.J. Rousseau, *The Basic Political Writings of Jean-Jacques Rousseau*, edited by D.A. Cress (2nd edn, 2012) 141, at 162.
[54] Kolla (n. 11), at 157 ff., 187.
[55] D.W. Bates, *States of War. Enlightenment Origins of the Political* (2012), at 215.

including plundering, occupation, and annexation, were seen as legitimate.[56] Danton famously spoke of war as the 'destroying angel of liberation'. The 'just' end seemed to justify the means.

Did this development in French discourse not, as Grewe claims, pave the way for the doctrine of a 'free right to go to war' as a pure and normatively unrestricted doctrine of (popular) sovereignty? The fact that war was seen as justified if it was understood as 'necessary' for the purposes of the Revolution might indeed support this assumption. The revolutionaries offensively challenged the norms of the international order—as well as those of their own constitution—and acted in the spirit of the alternative normative order they were striving for. Furthermore, some revolutionaries no longer merely perceived war as a 'necessary evil', as *ultima ratio*, but glorified it as the 'bloody regeneration' of the French nation.[57] Seen from the perspective of the then prevailing international legal order, they clearly acted arbitrarily.

However, the fundamental justification of French violence always remained the alleged self-defence of the Republic—even if 'self-defence' in fact now meant more and more 'conquest'. But the language glorifying violence continued to be located within the framework of the revolutionary ideology and its claimed 'just cause'. Here it was not only normative arguments of legitimacy or legality that came into play, but also references to the 'honour' and 'greatness' of the nation. Revolutionary war was stylized as an existential war against an unjust enemy (*iniustus hostis*) in the sense of *bellum iustum*. This enemy was also personified in British Prime Minister William Pitt, who was summarily declared an 'enemy of mankind' by the Jacobins in 1793 due to his financial support of the military campaigns against France.[58] The Revolution had found its 'unjust enemy'.

It was only this connection between the Revolution and the doctrine of 'just war' that legitimized the violence, both internally and externally. In this way the Revolution itself was sacralized as an ideology of justification. In other words, even massive violence did not primarily appear to be just because it was considered necessary in the sense of *liberum ius ad bellum*; quite to the contrary in fact, it only appeared to be necessary when it was also considered just in terms of the 'just cause' of the Revolution. There was no revolutionary violence without justification.

Moreover, while defending popular sovereignty was the main narrative of justifying war in the revolutionary era, the French justifications for war of that time were more complex, at times even self-contradictory. Where doing so promised argumentative advantages, references were made not only to 'new' principles, but

---

[56] Kolla (n. 11), at 187; D.A. Bell, *The First Total War. Napoleon's Europe and the Birth of Modern Warfare* (2007).
[57] Bell (n. 56), at 117.
[58] 'Decree of the French National Convention declaring William Pitt an "Enemy of Mankind" (7 August 1793)', in W.G. Grewe (ed.), *Fontes Historiae Iuris Gentium (FHIG), Sources Relating to the History of the Law of Nations*, vol. 2: 1493–1815 (1988) 661.

also to 'old' international law. When, for instance, Brissot described the Pillnitz Declaration as an 'unjust' and 'illegal' intervention in France's internal affairs,[59] he also referred to it as a serious violation of international treaty law, namely, of the defensive alliance between Austria and France established in the Treaty of Versailles (1756). In the case of the reunion with Alsace, the revolutionaries referred to the Peace of Nijmegen (1679), through which Alsace had allegedly become French.[60] Paradoxically, revolutionary lawyers wanted to use 'old', 'dynastic' international law as justifications for the violent establishment of a 'new' international order.

These debates were thus characterized by multinormativity. Revolutionary elites justified war with reference to a plurality of normative orders: morality, natural and cosmopolitan law, the liberation of peoples, positive law, or French constitutional law. In addition, there were justifications based on national security and geopolitical interests, such as the increasing rivalry with England or the idea of the *frontières naturelles de la France*. On 31 January 1793, Danton had called for the completion of the Republic, describing its natural borders as the banks of the Rhine, the ocean, the Pyrenees, and the Alps.[61] Economic motives also played a role, as in the context of Dutch republicanization in 1795.[62]

Justifications of violence such as those by Brissot, Merlin de Douai, or Villeneuve therefore not only point to the legitimizing authority of 'popular sovereignty'; they also offer strong indications that the revolutionary practice of legitimizing war was in a state of normative disorder. The, at times contradictory, justificatory narratives defied simple dichotomies of 'old' and 'new' because multiple claims of morality, 'old' and 'new' international law, and other normative and political spheres were mixed. Wilhelm Grewe spoke of a 'particular, transitory state'.[63] This description may seem accurate at first sight. But it is grossly simplistic, for it declares the simultaneity of multiple normative claims in the revolutionary period to be a pathological condition. This is only plausible if simplistic historiographical narratives of 'anarchy' or 'linear progress' are followed.[64] But neither the history of international order, nor that of the justification of war is unambiguous or linear.

Emperor of the Revolution: Rise, Decline, and Justification of Napoléon's Hegemony

Whereas the justification strategies in the early revolutionary years were characterized by a plurality of political and normative claims, a certain disorder of

---

[59] Steiger (n. 19), at 57.
[60] *Ibid.*, at 68.
[61] M. Biard and H. Leuwers, *Danton: Le mythe et l'histoire* (2016), at 84.
[62] Steiger (n. 25), at 34.
[63] Grewe (n. 12), at 413.
[64] For more on these narratives, see Chapter 2.

justification narratives can be identified in the Napoleonic era. Yet, if Napoléon's imperial justifications for violence were smoothly adapted to each respective case of conflict, and thus appeared arbitrary, even he could not do without justifying his violence. The revolutionary narrative of the defence of the French nation retained its central importance here, but became more mixed with other narratives than before.

A good example of this mixing of narratives is Napoléon's justification of his invasion of Ottoman Egypt in 1798, at that time still on behalf of the Directorate, which Napoléon would overthrow a year later. In Egypt, Napoléon had printed proclamations which he distributed to the population. In these, he referred—before even mentioning the French nation—to 'God Almighty', 'and also his prophet Mohamed and the glorious Koran', whom Napoléon claimed to worship more 'than the Mamluks do'.[65] This presumptuous claim was followed by a bizarre conflation of references to the French nation and Islam to justify French violence against the scourge of the Mamluks (who de facto ruled Egypt at the time).[66] Cairo cleric Abd al-Rahman al-Jaharti angrily rejected the proclamations—not only because of the poor quality of the Arabic translation, but also because of Napoléon's inconsistent argumentation.[67] However, al-Jaharti reported that parts of the Egyptian rural population in fact believed the justifications Bonaparte gave in the proclamations.[68]

When it came to his Russian campaign in 1812, Napoléon refrained from formally declaring war on Tsar Alexander I. This ran counter to the practice hitherto in Revolutionary France as well as in Europe. That said, albeit not in a formal declaration of war, Napoléon *did* justify his disastrous 1812 campaign, which would usher the beginning of his Empire's end. It was not long since Napoléon had been at the height of his power: after the victories against Prussia in the twin battles of Jena and Auerstedt (1806) and against Russia in the battle of Friedland (1807), the path from the European balance of power to French hegemony seemed clear.[69] The Franco-Russian alliance that had now been formed, however, was soon confronted with conflicts between Napoléon and Alexander I, especially with regard to Poland.[70] Both sides prepared for war. In June 1812, the Russian ambassador, Alexander Borisovich Kurakin, left Paris. Napoléon had warned Kurakin several times that his departure would be taken as a Russian declaration of war.[71] Napoléon

---

[65] B. Tibi, *Vom Gottesreich zum Nationalstaat. Islam und panarabischer Nationalismus* (1987), at 65 ff.
[66] J.R. Cole, *Napoléon's Egypt: Invading the Middle East* (2008), 30–4.
[67] *Ibid.*, at 32.
[68] *Ibid.*, at 34.
[69] A.D. Bernstein, *Von der Balance of Power zur Hegemonie: Ein Beitrag zur europäischen Diplomatiegeschichte zwischen Austerlitz und Jena/Auerstedt 1805–1806* (2006).
[70] C. Esdaile, *Napoleon's Wars: An International History, 1803–1815* (2008), Chapter 9; D. Lieven, *Russland gegen Napoleon: Die Schlacht um Europa* (2011), at 101 ff.
[71] A. Zamoyski, *1812. Napoleons Feldzug in Russland* (2012), at 129.

let it be known in the *Bulletins de la Grande Armée* that he had sought peace, while Russia had sought war.[72]

In further proclamations, Napoléon stated that the successful campaign against Prussia and Russia of 1806/07 had ultimately served to free Poland and protect Europe from the Russian yoke; the 'barbarians of the North' were to be 'thrust back into their snow and ice so that for a quarter of a century at least they will not be able to interfere with civilized Europe'.[73] Napoléon therefore linked his justification of war not only to the (false) promise of 'liberating' Poland and to the assertion of the 'civility', 'honour', and 'glory' of the French army. He also complained that Russia had broken the alliance with France established in the Peace of Tilsit (1807).[74] With this, he referred to positive law to clarify his 'just cause' for war. Napoléon envisaged the goal of war as being a more stable peace, thus attempting to underscore the 'just intention' of his Russian campaign. In short, Napoléon located his violence in the classical criteriology of *bellum iustum*. By no means did he claim to be allowed to wage war without justification.

Nevertheless, the members of the European communication community dealing with the ethics of war were certainly not inclined to believe his justifications. Even French soldiers, who read Napoléon's bulletins, considered them to be lies *(menteur)*.[75] Multiple normative claims of the old and new world order had been combined too arbitrarily and opportunistically.[76] Napoléon's justification strategy lacked any logical stringency.

In addition, Napoléon blatantly contradicted some of the principles of the Revolution he claimed to defend, as became particularly evident regarding the question of the emancipation of slaves in the French colonies. This issue is somewhat under-researched, although discussions have recently become livelier.[77] Not least due to military strategic considerations and in view of the situation on Saint-Domingue[78] (today's Haiti), the National Convention had decided in February 1794 to abolish slavery in the French colonies. In 1802 Napoléon reintroduced slavery. In doing so, he violated the Declaration of the Rights of Man and of the Citizen of 26 August 1789.[79] However, Napoléon was unable to prevent Haiti from gaining independence in 1804.[80]

---

[72] 'Napoleon's Proclamation of 1812', reprinted in *ibid.*, at 171 ff.
[73] Esdaile (n. 70), at 442 ff.
[74] 'Napoleon's Proclamation of 1812', reprinted in Zamoyski (n. 71), at 171 ff.
[75] C. Emsley, *Napoleon: Conquest, Reform and Reorganisation* (2nd edn, 2015) at 27.
[76] See also Steiger (n. 25), at 50.
[77] Claude Ribbe drew a comparison between Napoléon's colonial and Hitler's extermination policies; C. Ribbe, *Le crime de Napoléon* (2005). The book sparked fierce reactions in France, see Bickerton, 'France's History Wars', *Monde Diplomatique* (February 2006), available at: https://mondediplo.com/2006/02/14postcolonial (last visited 1 December 2022).
[78] Emsley (n. 75), at 27.
[79] Slaves and women were largely deprived of these rights in the patriarchal politics of the Revolution; for a contemporary criticism, see O. de Gouges, *Déclaration des droits de la femme* (1791).
[80] C. Fick, *Making Haiti: The Saint Domingue Revolution from Below* (1990); see also S. Buck-Morss, *Hegel, Haiti, and Universal History* (2009).

The extent to which Napoléon led the usurped Revolution *ad absurdum* was particularly evident in his self-coronation as Emperor of the French in Notre-Dame de Paris on 2 December 1804. Here, Napoléon referred to the Revolution as the original source of his imperial dignity. However, in the eyes of many contemporaries, the combination of imperial dignity, pre-revolutionary ceremonial, and revolutionary ideology was a self-contradictory farce.[81]

So, what does all this imply for the assessment of the legitimacy of law in the Napoleonic era? Under Napoléon, popular sovereignty was ultimately reduced to a justification for an imperial order. In its early phases (1789–91 and 1792–94), Revolutionary France had proclaimed—though not consistently adhered to—a restructuring of international law based on the principle of popular sovereignty.[82] In contrast, Napoleon made use of largely classical diplomatic and legal instruments of 'dynastic' international law. Europe's international relations thus once again played out within the framework of the dialectic of striving for hegemony and the balance of power, i.e. within the 'old' order that had developed in Europe since the Peace of Utrecht (1713).[83] Thus, paradoxically, Napoléon had helped the Revolution to spread as far as possible and at the same time swept its core principles aside. The Revolution was devoured by its strongest child.

To conclude the discussion on the need to justify violence in the revolutionary/Napoleonic era, what is decisive for this study's research interest is that all French actors in the revolutionary and Napoleonic era—despite the ideological polarization between France and the European monarchies—always sought to justify their violence internationally with reference to normative arguments. At no time did they assume that violence was to be used arbitrarily, but in fact acknowledged that it required (de)legitimization. Even particularly cruel violence remained the subject of controversial debates in France. Revolutionary violence was always committed—at least superficially—in the name of the nation, liberty, and popular sovereignty. But there were also other narratives: political interests, universal morality and natural law, the honour and glory of the nation, (anti-)religious arguments, as well as positive international law came together in an eclectic mix to (de)legitimize military force.

A proposition of *liberum ius ad bellum*, however, was *not* part of their vocabulary for justifying war. The revolutionaries did not use it. Nor were they familiar with it. And the reason for that? It simply did not exist.

---

[81] Jacques-Louis David vividly depicted the spectacle in his *Le Sacre de Napoléon*, completed in 1807. The painting can be viewed online at: https://histoire-image.org/etudes/sacre-napoleon (last visited 1 December 2022)

[82] Cassese (n. 48); Kolla (n. 11).

[83] Steiger (n. 25), at 50; Teschke, 'Capitalism, British Grand Strategy, and the Peace Treaty of Utrecht: Towards a Historical Sociology of War- and Peace-making in the Construction of International Order', in L. Brock and H. Simon (eds), *The Justification of War and International Order: From Past to Present* (2021) 107.

Between 'Old' and 'New': Europe's Reactions to Revolutionary Violence

So, how did the other European states react to the new narratives the Revolution tried to introduce into the European war discourse? The answer might initially seem rather obvious: since all other European Great Powers were at war with France at least once between 1792 and 1815, it seems logical that they would have resolutely opposed the Revolution. As always, the historical reality, however, was considerably more complex—even if research to date has largely overlooked this complexity. If, as stated above, there is a blind spot in the Histories of International Law and International Relations with regard to the French Revolution and its war discourse, this applies all the more to the complex diplomatic interactions between Revolutionary/Napoleonic France and the major European powers.[84]

This research gap cannot—and need not—be comprehensively closed here. However, it is worth noting that among the European Great Powers, there were three principal reactions to the French conceptions of justifying war and international order, although these were neither applied by all Great Powers at the same time nor in this chronological order. The reactions were:

first, coexistence and arrangement;
second, rejection and, closely related to this, political/normative opposition; as well as
third, (partial) adoption of the revolutionary vocabulary of justifying war.

As this ideal-typical distinction suggests, there was no single, unified reaction from Europe to the French justifications of violence. Not only were the competing political interests of the Great Powers too different, but so too were their normative ideas of war and international order. For despite the fact that France's war opponents were united by a common enemy, throughout the era between the French declaration of war in 1792 and the 'wars of liberation' against Napoléon, the Great Powers pursued unilateral, in part thoroughly contradictory interests—especially with regard to the Polish and Eastern Questions.[85]

This complexity of interests is illustrated especially clearly by reactions in the German lands, and Prussia in particular. The Holy Roman Empire was directly affected by revolutionary violence and would eventually meet its end at the hands of Napoléon in 1806 (which in turn favoured Prussian reforms). However, initially, the reactions of the German populations to the French Revolution were largely positive. This applied to the middle and upper classes as well as to so-called

---

[84] Bélissa (n. 11), at 433; but see Kolla (n. 11), and L. Frey and M. Frey, *The Culture of French Revolutionary Diplomacy* (2018).
[85] E. Fehrenbach, *Vom Ancien Régime zum Wiener Kongress* (5th edn, 2010), at 41 ff.

'common people'. Among Protestant theologians, the Revolution was even interpreted as a religious event, although it was disputed whether it was an anti-church apocalypse or an act of liberation of the 'divine creation', in other words: man.[86] The reason many reactions in the German lands were positive was not because the German population also longed for a comprehensive revolution; rather, the pre-revolutionary French monarchy was regarded by many 'Germans' as corrupt and despotic.[87]

Even arch-conservative Prussian King Friedrich Wilhelm II was not initially hostile to the French Revolution. Indeed, he expected political advantages from the fact that it would weaken not only France but also Austria, with whom Prussia competed for power until the alliance of 1791. After the outbreak of the Liège Revolution in 1789, Prussia thus only intervened under pressure from the Empire—de facto, however, in favour of the rebels, in order to prevent Austria from gaining influence in the north-west of the Empire.[88] Overall, the impact of the Revolution and the principle of popular sovereignty on the international order was initially underestimated—not only by the revolutionaries themselves, but also by Europe as a whole. Brissot certainly recognized the European powers' lack of zeal for war. Since he wanted to use the war to boost his own domestic reputation, he promoted a 'preventive defence' against Austria for this very reason.[89] If the European powers did not invade, France would have to make the first move to defend itself.

With the French declaration of war of 20 April 1792, the European perceptions of Revolutionary France changed abruptly. Moreover, the European public reacted with horror to the execution of Louis XVI on 21 January 1793. Those European monarchies that were not already fighting France now also declared war. These declarations of war are remarkable, for it was not only the revolutionaries who formally declared war on the 'old', 'dynastic' order. The European monarchies also continued to inform the European public about their 'just causes' of war. Clearly, they questioned the legitimacy of the revolutionary government and popular sovereignty as a valid basis for rule. Nevertheless, for them, the Revolution did *not* undermine the binding force of the international norm of justifying wars publicly. Even in the revolutionary era, a public discourse on the legitimate international use of force unfolded.

---

[86] Graf, 'Sakralisierung von Kriegen: Begriffs- und problemgeschichtliche Erwägungen', in K. Schreiner and E. Müller-Luckner (eds), *Heilige Kriege: Religiöse Begründungen militärischer Gewaltanwendung: Judentum, Christentum und Islam im Vergleich* (2008) 1, at 21.
[87] W.W. Hagen, *German History in Modern Times: Four Lives of the Nation* (2012), at 98.
[88] See the justification by C.C.W. Dohm, *Die Lütticher Revolution im Jahr 1789 und das Benehmen Sr. Königl. Majestät von Preussen bey derselben* (1790); Neugebauer, 'Brandenburg-Preußen in der Frühen Neuzeit. Politik und Staatsbildung im 17. und 18. Jahrhundert', in W. Neugebauer (ed.), *Handbuch der Preußischen Geschichte. Das 17. und 18. Jahrhundert und Große Themen der Geschichte Preußens* (2009) 113, at 375.
[89] Schulin (n. 28), at 125.

This is particularly clear in the Vienna counter-declaration of 1792, in which the Viennese Court refuted the individual accusations of the French declaration of war in detail. Franz II rejected the accusation 'that the sovereignty of the French nation had been violated by the establishment of an alliance [between Austria and Prussia, HS]' (*par l'etablissement d'un concert*); rather, according to Franz II, the primary aim of this alliance was to guarantee the legitimate sovereignty of France, since it was being attacked daily by the French revolutionaries.[90] Subsequently, Franz II referred, for his part, to the narrative of self-defence that the French had previously claimed. In the face of the 'unjust' French attack, Franz II argued, he was entitled to 'call for the indignation and support of all Europe in the name of a common cause for the honour and safety of governments'. The 'perpetrators of such unjust and odious aggression' ('*odieuse aggression*'), Franz II continued, were to be held 'responsible before the court of the universe and of posterity for all the evils' that were the inevitable consequences of the war.[91] Obviously, Franz II was not at all keen to recognize the revolutionaries as sovereigns of France. Nevertheless, he publicly justified his violence as self-defence.

This Austrian counter-declaration was followed in March 1793 by a second war manifesto in which Franz II, by now crowned Holy Roman Emperor of the German Nation (14 July 1792), declared an imperial war (*Reichskrieg*) on France. In the manifesto, addressed 'to the kings of Europe and, in particular, to France', Franz II declared that he was going to war against France not only in defence of Austria, but of all Germany.[92] To justify his action, Franz II first listed in detail the legal violations he accused the Revolutionary French of committing, including:

- violation of the rights and possessions of the German princes in Alsace and Lorraine;
- attacking the German lands with the aim of overthrowing the 'good order' there (*renversér le bon ordre*);
- deposition of the legitimate government in France;
- use of force against his family, especially his uncle, Louis XVI; and
- France's unjust war against England and Holland.[93]

Franz II also made certain to emphasize the right intention (*intentio recta*) of his campaign. He claimed to have no intention whatsoever of using the war to enrich himself through conquests.[94] According to Franz II, his aim was solely 'to put

---

[90] Franz II, *Contre-Declaration de la Cour de Vienne au Sujet de l'Agression de la France* (5 July 1792), at 5, 8.
[91] Ibid.
[92] Franz II, *Manifeste de François II, empereur très chrétien, roi de Bohème et de Hongrie; fait à Vienne et envoyé à tous les rois de l'Europe, sur l'attaque de la Turquie contre l'Empire, sur l'invasion prochaine des troupes françoise; sur la levée de 700 mille hommes de troupes dans ses états, et sur la déclaration de guerre de la France contre l'Angleterre et la Hollande* (30 January 1793), at ii ff.
[93] Ibid.
[94] Ibid., at ii ff.

an end to the anarchy in the interior of France' as well as 'to the French attacks'.[95] The Holy Roman Emperor claimed that there were no plans to interfere with the affairs of the government of France and that he only wanted to see his aunt Marie-Antoinette and her family freed from captivity.[96] However, this hardly fits with the fact that Franz II, 'convinced that the healthy part of the French nation abhors the excesses of the faction subjugating it', called on the French to 'return without delay to the voices of reason and justice, of order and peace' ('*retourner sans delais aux votes de la raison et de la justice, de l'ordre et de la paix*').[97] According to Franz II, the Revolution was to be reversed.

The Holy Roman Emperor's rejection of the 'anarchy of revolution' was thus at the same time linked to a normative opposition. The restoration of the monarchy as a legitimate order of rule had become his wartime goal within the first anti-French coalition. Like Franz II, British Prime Minister Pitt criticized the 'public anarchy' emanating from the Revolution. Pitt was primarily concerned with maintaining the balance of power in Europe, but also with British commercial interests, which were severely threatened by the French invasion of Holland.[98] Conservatives such as Edmund Burke feared the spillover of the Revolution to the Holy Roman Empire and early on advocated violent action against France: non-intervention, Burke argued, was 'a false principle in the law of nations'.[99] However, conservatives faced strong public opposition and pro-revolutionary sentiments such as those of Thomas Paine.

After the French declaration of war on Great Britain, however, it became easier to legitimize military 'counter-violence'. On 12 February 1793, King George III declared to the House of Commons that Britain was facing a 'wanton and unprovoked aggression' based on untenable claims by France.[100] The war against France was therefore 'just and necessary'[101] to oppose a system that attacked the security and peace of all free nations as well as the principles of restraint, good faith, humanity, and justice. Again, the aim, argued George III, was to prevent the spread of 'anarchy'.[102] George's III statement was followed by Prime Minister Pitt's appeal to parliamentarians. Although there had previously been different opinions on what was happening on the continent, according to Pitt, a decisive response to the French declaration of war must now follow. After all, the French declaration of war was aimed at 'the total ruin of the freedom and independence of this country'.[103]

[95] *Ibid.*
[96] *Ibid.*, at vi.
[97] *Ibid.*, at iii.
[98] Pitt, 'The French Declaration of War (February 12, 1793)', in R. Coupland (ed.), *The War Speeches of William Pitt the Younger* (1915) 52.
[99] B. Simms, *Europe. The Struggle for Supremacy, from 1453 to the Present* (2013), at 144.
[100] George III, 'Message from George III (12 February 1793)', in R. Coupland (ed), *The War Speeches of William Pitt the Younger* (1915) 52, at 52.
[101] *Ibid.*
[102] *Ibid.*, at 53.
[103] Pitt (n. 98) at 54.

It was not only the French revolutionaries who were aware of the superior legitimizing power of the narrative of 'self-defence' against unjust aggression. Franz II and William Pitt had also mastered the unwritten rules of effectively justifying war.

Disagreement about developments in France persisted in the USA, with pro-French US Secretary of State Thomas Jefferson and Anglophile Secretary of the Treasury Alexander Hamilton at odds with each other.[104] On 22 April 1793, President George Washington—like Hamilton, strongly influenced by Vattel's doctrine of international law—declared US neutrality in the Revolutionary Wars. Citizens of the United States were prohibited from interfering in the conflict between France and its enemies.[105] The tensions with Great Britain that had existed since the American War of Independence were to be resolved through commissions for conflict management, as regulated in the Jay Treaty of 19 November 1794.[106] Many Americans, but also America's former ally in the War of Independence, France, saw American neutrality and the Jay Treaty as a betrayal of one republic by the other. Tensions between France and the United States increased. Between 1794 and 1800, French privateers raided hundreds of defenceless US ships.[107]

The policy pursued by Prussia was decisive for the further course of war in Europe: after numerous defeats, it withdrew from the First Coalition and concluded the Peace of Basel with France (5 April 1795). This was accompanied by Prussian recognition of Revolutionary France as a full legal subject in the European legal community—the first monarchy to do so, and thus a novelty in international law. Friedrich Wilhelm III would explicitly remind the French of this fact in his declaration of war in 1806, with which Prussia joined the Fourth Coalition.[108] In 1795, an even larger part of the war burden rested on Austria's shoulders. Prussia's exit from the war was publicly criticized in several Austrian manifestos.[109] Furthermore, numerous German scholars reacted to the Peace of Basel and a lively debate on the problem of peace and war emerged around 1800. In 1795, Immanuel Kant published his famous peace memorandum, *Zum ewigen Frieden* ('Toward Perpetual Peace') as a direct response to the Peace of Basel. It was to become the most important legal pacifist stimulus for the emerging modern discourse of war and international order (see below).

Prussia's withdrawal from the war in 1795 was undoubtedly driven by primarily military and political considerations. Friedrich Wilhelm II welcomed peace with

---

[104] L. Müller, *Neutrality in World History* (2019), at 69.
[105] G. Washington, *The Proclamation of Neutrality 1793* (1897).
[106] Lingens, 'Der Jay-Vertrag (1794) als Geburtsstunde der modernen internationalen Schiedsgerichtsbarkeit? Zur Entstehung eines undifferenzierten Geschichtsbildes', in S. Dauchy and M. Vec (eds), *Les conflits entre peuples. De la résolution libre à la résolution imposée* (2011) 65.
[107] Müller (n. 104).
[108] Friedrich Wilhelm III, 'Manifest des Königs von Preußen Friedrich Wilhelm III. zur Begründung der Kriegserklärung an Frankreich vom 9. Oktober 1806', in P.A.G. Meyer (ed.), *Corpus Juris Confoederationis Germanicae oder Staatsacten für Geschichte und öffentliches Recht des Deutschen Bunds* (3rd edn, 1858) 150.
[109] K.O. Aretin, *Vom Deutschen Reich zum Deutschen Bund* (2nd edn, 1993), at 78 ff.

the French Republic, not least because Prussia could now focus on the last of the three Partitions of Poland (1772, 1793, and 1795) alongside Russia and Austria.[110] In a sense, Prussia made peace with one republic to dismantle the other. As the example of Prussia makes clear, not only rejection and normative opposition, but also coexistence and arrangement with the Republic were policy options open to the European monarchs in dealing with Revolutionary France. Despite the French gaining power, the European powers continued to pursue unilateral political interests along similar lines to the eighteenth century. The Revolution had not suspended the informal rules of politics.

The Battle of the 'Nations': The Birth of Modern Mass War and its Justification

Besides normative opposition and coexistence, as mentioned, there was a third reaction of European states and populations to the revolutionary war discourse, which was used in particular in the struggle against Napoléon: the partial adoption of the revolutionary vocabulary. The Spanish counter-government to Napoléon's occupation, the *Junta Suprema Central,* was the first to adopt this approach. After Napoléon had invaded the Iberian Peninsula in 1808, the *Junta* published the manifesto *El Tirano de la Europa Napoleon Primero.* In it, Napoléon was accused of waging an 'unjust war' against Spain ('[Napoléon, HS] *provora iniquamente la guerra*') with the aim of making the Spaniards 'vile slaves of his greed, his tyranny, his perfidy, and his false glory'. The Spanish claimed the sanctioning of the injustice suffered and the liberation of the Spanish nation ('*salvado la Nacion*') as the war's goal and their justification for the use of force. Napoléon was considered an unjust enemy. The Spanish War of Independence (1808–1813) that now began was a hybrid war in which various forms of political violence were interwoven: one of these was guerrilla warfare that the Spaniards waged against Napoléon.[111] Its brutality was vividly captured by the Spanish artist Francisco de Goya in the series of prints *Desastres de la Guerra* ('The Disasters of War'), created between 1810 and 1814, but not published until 1863.

The 'liberation of the nation' was also to become the central narrative for the ultimately victorious wars against Napoléon in the years 1813 to 1815. While the French had gone to war for 'nation and fatherland' in 1792—being forced to do so, with the introduction of compulsory military service in 1793—these legitimations of violence now came back to haunt Napoléon, the Emperor of the Revolution. After the disaster of the *Grande Armée* in the Russian campaign of 1812,[112] his enemies recognized their opportunity to bring Napoléon down.

[110] Fehrenbach (n. 85), at 42.
[111] Esdaile (n. 70).
[112] Zamoyski (n. 71); see also A. Mikaberidze, *The Napoleonic Wars: A Global History* (2020).

Nevertheless, Prussian King Friedrich Wilhelm III was reluctant to switch sides, for fear of Napoléon's power. However, this decision was soon taken out of his hands: General Yorck, commander of the Prussian auxiliary forces against Russia, allowed himself to be persuaded by a Prussian officer in the service of Russia, Carl von Clausewitz, to make a declaration of neutrality and then to go to war against Napoléon with a volunteer army. In a letter to Friedrich Wilhelm III, Yorck justified his action against the Franco-Prussian alliance by referring to the urgency of liberating the 'nation': 'Now or never', claimed Yorck, was the moment to 'regain freedom, independence, and greatness...'.[113] The war seemed necessary to Yorck—but only because it also seemed just to him. Thus, no 'free right to go to war' can be found in the justifications of the 'wars of liberation'. The use of force continued to be legitimized with reference to the defence of the nation.

Friedrich Wilhelm III was annoyed at Yorck's actions. At the same time, however, he bowed to immense pressure from his own generals out of a 'fear of revolution'.[114] On 17 March 1813, Friedrich Wilhelm III declared a 'people's war' against Napoléon. In his declaration, the Prussian king referred to the Peace of Tilsit of 1807, which had stripped him of half his subjects and thus inflicted 'deeper wounds than even war'. He countered this negative memory with positive images of the Prussian state under Friedrich II 'the Great', 'mindful of the goods that ... our ancestors fought for in blood: freedom of conscience, honour, independence, trade, artistic diligence, and science'.[115] Finally, Friedrich Wilhelm III summed up that 'the last, decisive battle ... for our existence, our independence, our prosperity' was at hand, which alone would distinguish between an 'honourable peace' and a 'glorious downfall'.[116] The war against Napoléon was thus stylized as a decisive war, 'for the sake of honour; because Prussians and Germans cannot live without honour'. At the same time, however, the Prussian king expressed confidence that 'God and our firm will ... will give victory to our just cause' and 'with it a secure, glorious peace and the return of a happy time'.[117] In his justification of violence, Friedrich Wilhelm III thus made use of a variety of normative spheres: the nation, justice, religion, honour, positive law, as well as Prussian history, culture, and prosperity. He also addressed the people of Prussia and Germany directly.

Thus, the Prussian justifications of war are strongly reminiscent of those of the French revolutionaries in 1792 (see above). Prussia, for its part, declared the war to be a war of fate. In its declaration of war to the French government on 18 March 1813, Prussia argued that after France's 'terrible' violations of their sovereignty

---

[113] Quoted from G.H. Pertz, *Das Leben Des Ministers Freiherrn Vom Stein* (1851), at 258.
[114] Aschmann, '"Das Zeitalter des Gefühls?" Zur Relevanz von Emotionen im 19. Jahrhundert', in B. Aschmann (ed.), *Durchbruch der Moderne? Neue Perspektiven auf das 19. Jahrhundert* (2019) 83, at 104.
[115] Friedrich Wilhelm III, 'An mein Volk. Se. Majestät der König haben mit Sr. Majestät dem Kaiser aller Reußen ein Off- und Defensiv-Bündniß abgeschlossen', *Schlesische privilegirte Zeitung* (20 March 1813) 593 ff.
[116] *Ibid.*, at 594.
[117] *Ibid.*

since 1807, the Prussian king would now give his monarchy back its independence.[118] Thus, in keeping with the European tradition of justifying war, a previous breach of law by the French was claimed as a 'just cause' for the 'defence' of Prussian sovereignty. The French Revolution thus had a catalytic effect—albeit one that undoubtedly evolved dialectically—on the development of modern war and its discourse, which is made particularly evident here. The wars against Napoléon's armies had, in a sense, been 'wars of state formation'.[119] For it was only with a reformed army—conscription was introduced in 1814—and the legitimizing involvement of volunteer units that it seemed possible to wage war against Napoléon. The Prussian royal physician Christoph Wilhelm Hufeland, for example, noted in his *Selbstbiographie* that the Prussian spirit had awoken with 'boundless enthusiasm and fearful courage, willing to sacrifice everything, even the dearest of things, to regain freedom'.[120] Prussia experienced its 'national saddle period'.[121]

The battle between the 'nations' went hand in hand with a further removal of the limits of the violence used in the war. The French foreign minister, Duke Bassano, warned Napoléon that in view of the deployment of irregular troops on the side of the coalition forces, the French people 'must make efforts in proportion to those of the enemy in order to achieve a lasting peace'.[122] Violence and counter-violence each removed the limits of the other.

The language of legitimizing violence increasingly took on features reminiscent of total war—in clear analogy to the discourse of Revolutionary France. The 'just war' was now also secularized on the German side and enriched with Prussian-German nationalism against the French '*Erbfeind*', a sinister term that was introduced into the war discourse by historian Franz Rühs.[123] Although its roots lay in the eighteenth century, German nationalism now became, as the nationalist poet Ernst Moritz Arndt put it, the 'highest religion' of the fatherland.[124] Ernest Gellner

[118] Hardenberg, 'Kriegserklärung an Frankreich, 16. März 1813', in P.A.G. Meyer (ed.), *Corpus Juris Confoederationis Germanicae oder Staatsacten für Geschichte und öffentliches Recht des Deutschen Bundes* (3rd edn., 1858) 163.
[119] Burkhardt, 'Die Friedlosigkeit der Frühen Neuzeit. Grundlegung einer Theorie der Bellizität Europas', 24 *Zeitschrift für historische Forschung: ZHF* (1997) 509; see also O. Asbach and P. Schröder (eds), *War, the State, and International Law in Seventeenth-Century Europe* (2010).
[120] Hufeland, 'Flucht nach Schlesien 1813-1814', in W. v. Brunn (ed.), *Selbstbiographie von Christoph Wilhelm Hufeland* (1937), at 111.
[121] Planert, 'Wann beginnt der "moderne" deutsche Nationalismus? Plädoyer für eine nationale Sattelzeit', in J. Echternkamp and S.O. Müller (eds), *Die Politik der Nation: Deutscher Nationalismus in Krieg und Krisen, 1760-1960* (2002) 25; U. Planert, *Der Mythos vom Befreiungskrieg: Frankreichs Kriege und der deutsche Süden; Alltag—Wahrnehmung—Deutung; 1792-1841* (2007).
[122] Bassano, 'Bericht des französischen Außenministers Herzog Bassano an den Kaiser von Frankreich und König von Italien Napoleon bezüglich der Kriegserklärung Österreichs an Frankreich (20 August 1813)', in P.A.G. Meyer (ed.), *Corpus Juris Confoederationis Germanicae oder Staatsacten für Geschichte und öffentliches Recht des Deutschen Bunds* (3rd edn., 1858) 191.
[123] Rühs, 'Über die Forderungen Hamburgs an Frankreich', in F. Rühs (ed.), *Zeitschrift für die neueste Geschichte, die Staaten und Völkerkunde* (1815) 314, at 316; see also Planert, 'Nationalismus und Befreiungskrieg?: Das Zeitalter Napoleons in Augenzeugenberichten', in S. Feucht (ed.), *1810, die vergessene Zäsur: Neue Grenzen in der Region Bodensee-Oberschwaben* (2013) 17, at 17.
[124] Quoted from H.-U. Winkler, *Germany: The Long Road West*, vol. 1: 1789-1933 (2006), 53; see also Planert (n. 121).

has aptly described the socio-cultural phenomenon of 'nationalism' as a nation's 'self-worship'.[125] This religion found its 'holy writings' in a bellicose 'liberation poetry'.[126] Prussian-German publicists such as Ludwig Uhland, Theodor Körner, Max von Schenkendorf, Friedrich Ludwig Jahn, Joseph Görres, and Arndt now called for a 'holy war' or a 'sacred sacrificial battle' against the 'usurper Napoléon.[127]

The rhetorical exaltation of the war against Napoléon was accompanied by an affirmation of modern mass warfare as distinct from early modern 'cabinet war' (which had also been a reaction to the unbounded violence of the Thirty Years' War). Johann Gottlieb Fichte wrote that it was 'finally time ... to keep the designs of a petty calculating cabinet policy away from this holy struggle'. Fichte even called for a war manifesto in which not only the defence of a state, but a 'war for the human race' would be declared.[128] Napoléon was now seen exactly as the revolutionaries had perceived the monarchies and statesmen such as Pitt: as the 'unjust enemy' of humankind.

According to Dieter Langewiesche, the discourses of the 'wars of liberation' thus revealed a dualism of 'participation' and 'aggression' that would become constitutive for modern nationalism.[129] For the 'self-worship of the nation' was accompanied by disdain for other nations. Freiherr vom Stein legitimized the campaign against France by referring to it as a 'crusade' against the 'impudent and lewd French race'.[130] But nationalists such as Arndt and Rühs were also looking for supposed enemies of the nation within the German lands. German Jews were dehumanized and described as 'horrors corrupting Germany' ('*Teutschland verderbende Gräuel*').[131] The particularly strong Prussian-German militarism and nationalism of the later nineteenth century[132] was thus anticipated here. As Reinhart Koselleck has summed up, the fundamental exclusion criteria in the modern socio-political discourse were 'laid out in the German semantics' of that era.[133]

However, it was not because of war propaganda that the armies were popular for volunteers. Rather, the German populations (and particularly those in

---

[125] E. Gellner, *Nationalismus und Moderne* (1991).
[126] E. Weber, *Lyrik der Befreiungskriege (1812–1815): Gesellschaftspolitische Meinungs- und Willensbildung durch Literatur* (1991); C. Jürgensen, *Federkrieger: Autorschaft im Zeichen der Befreiungskriege* (2018).
[127] Graf (n. 86), at 22 ff.
[128] Fichte, 'Anhang zu den Reden an die deutsche Nation, geschrieben im Jahre 1806', in J.H. Fichte (ed.), *Johann Gottlieb Fichte's sämmtliche Werke* (1846) 505, at 508.
[129] D. Langewiesche, *Nationalismus im 19. und 20. Jahrhundert. Zwischen Partizipation und Aggression; Vortrag vor dem Gesprächskreis Geschichte der Friedrich-Ebert-Stiftung in Bonn am 24. Januar 1994* (1994).
[130] H.-U. Wehler, *Nationalismus: Geschichte—Formen—Folgen* (2001), at 68.
[131] Hagemann, 'Aus Liebe zum Vaterland. Liebe und Hass im frühen deutschen Nationalismus', in B. Aschmann (ed.), *Gefühl und Kalkül: Der Einfluss von Emotionen auf die Politik des 19. und 20. Jahrhunderts* (2005) 101, at 118.
[132] See Part II in this study.
[133] Koselleck et al., 'Volk, Nation, Nationalismus, Masse', in O. Brunner, W. Conze, and R. Koselleck (eds), *Geschichtliche Grundbegriffe: Historisches Lexikon zur politisch-sozialen Sprache in Deutschland* (1997) 141, at 396 ff.

south-western Germany), battered by war for decades, longed for a stable peace. Since the monarchs had so far failed to secure permanent peace through agreements, the people were now prepared to enforce it themselves by military force.[134] But even where propaganda was actually effective among the masses, the narrative was not necessarily that of German nationalism. In order to address the rural population, in particular, it made more political sense to justify the war with 'classical', e.g. religious arguments. For the nationalist war was primarily an elitist project. Clearly, the Prussian king had no interest in German unity or a free national movement. But he understood the great propagandist value of 'national honour'[135] and used the latter not to defeat the authoritarian Prussian state—but rather to merge nationalism and the Prussian state.[136] This instrumental use of nationalism from above would become characteristic of Prussian politics. Accordingly, the German 'people's war lacked one thing above all: the people'.[137]

But even if the Prussians did use the concepts of the nation and freedom in an instrumental way, constantly linking them with the Prussian authoritarian state, there had undoubtedly been a *partial adoption* of the revolutionary vocabulary of justifying war. In one way or another, the Prussian elites had been eager students of the Revolution, its warfare, and not least its justification. That did not make the Prussian reformers French revolutionaries. But the victory in the so-called *Völkerschlacht bei Leipzig* (Leipzig Battle of the Nations) from 16 to 19 October 1813 made clear that the reformers were able to live up to the demands of revolutionary mass warfare. Napoléon had devoured the Revolution; now, its stepchildren devoured him.

3.3 Kant versus Clausewitz: Law, Politics, and the Formation of the Modern Discourse of Justifying War

The Revolution had sparked lively discussions on normative and socio-political conceptions of war and order, and not only in contemporary political practice. But it did not stop there: the Revolution also left its mark in political and legal theory. What is more, the Revolution was to become the starting point for the modern discourse on war and peace in political and normative theory. In this discourse, the fundamental methodological and theoretical questions about the legal character and legal sources of 'modern international law' were discussed anew.

The Revolution provoked three main reactions in contemporary theoretical discourse on war and international order, which determine the structure of this

---

[134] Planert 'Wann beginnt der "moderne" deutsche Nationalismus?' (n. 121).
[135] Aschmann (n. 114), at 105.
[136] Planert (n. 121).
[137] A. Bleyer, *Auf gegen Napoleon! Mythos Volkskriege* (2013), at 238.

subchapter. *First*, using Jeremy Bentham and Georg Friedrich Martens as examples, I show that early legal 'positivists' fundamentally rejected revolutionary justifications of war. At the same time, however, these 'positivists' were just as incapable as those of the early modern period of conceptualizing the problem of the legitimacy of war beyond the doctrine of 'just war', i.e. of 'modernizing' it in positive law terms. A transformation or 'disenchantment' of the normative discourse on war did *not* take place here.

Second, I argue that demands for a full legalization of war in the sense of *ius contra bellum* did not emerge only at the end of the nineteenth century—or even at the beginning of the twentieth century.[138] Rather, the beginning of modern normative thinking on the prohibition of war is to be found in the revolutionary era. But this project did not emanate entirely from the legal sciences in the narrower sense. More innovative here was a thinker who could be found outside the law faculties: Immanuel Kant.

Third, when Kant launched the modern project of *ius contra bellum*, the prohibition of war, he was opposed by another Prussian thinker. This theorist's military *and* political theory of war was to become the central, antagonistic reference point in modern thinking about the legality and legitimacy of war to Kant's. He was ultimately to become the founder of the modern thesis of *liberum ius ad bellum*. This theorist was Carl von Clausewitz.

Revolutionizing Reform? The 'Positivist Turn(s)' in International Legal Thought: British Edition (Bentham)

While the Bastille was stormed and the course for political modernity was set in Paris, international legal scholarship in Europe did not find itself in a revolution. It was in the midst of reform. Legal doctrine was permeated by ideas of the Enlightenment and new conceptions of scientific knowledge, expressed, for example, in the progressive tendencies towards a de-theologization of law.[139]

Nevertheless, a core problem of the debates on international law in the 'saddle period' remained: the tension between natural and positive law. Jurists were less willing to accept law as given by nature alone. They were certain that law was (also) made by people or by their sovereigns.[140] Correspondingly, legal scholarship was characterized by a strong turn to the scientific systems of legal positivism[141]—or

---

[138] O.A. Hathaway and S.J. Shapiro, *The Internationalists: How a Radical Plan to Outlaw War Remade the World* (2017).

[139] F.S. Ruddy, *International Law in the Enlightenment: The Background of Emmerich de Vattel's Le droit des gens* (1975).

[140] G.W. Gong, *The Standard of 'Civilization' in International Society* (1984); H. Kleinschmidt, *Diskriminierung durch Vertrag und Krieg: Zwischenstaatliche Verträge und der Begriff des Kolonialkriegs im 19. und frühen 20. Jahrhundert* (2013), at 286.

[141] Alexandrowicz, 'The Afro-Asian World and the Law of Nations (Historical Aspects)', *Recueil des cours/Académie de Droit International de La Haye* (1968) 121; Orakhelashvili, 'The Idea of European

rather to different positivisms.[142] This growing scholarly interest in positive law coincided with a 'treaty-making revolution'[143] that began in the 1790s and only reached its peak during the nineteenth century. Gradually, at least according to Grewe, the universalism of natural law was to be replaced by a new universalism of the law of the sovereign state.[144]

But is this narrative of a turn to a modernity based on legal positivism historically convincing? Indeed, the vocabulary of natural law used by many revolutionary leaders contradicted the *zeitgeist* of European lawyers. Jeremy Bentham's neologism of 'international law' expressed a stronger focus of scholars on law that was not given to all peoples or nations by nature but concluded by states with equal rights. Accordingly, the first motive of Bentham's 'radical reform' of international law, as it was called in Bluntschli and Brater's *Deutsches Staats-Wörterbuch*,[145] was an outright rejection of any natural law. Bentham not only called the French Declaration of the Rights of Man and of the Citizen for its natural law vocabulary 'nonsense upon stilts'.[146] Due to the continuing importance of natural law, he also criticized 'The Law [of Nations]' as consisting 'partly of a thing that isn't Law at all'.[147] Bentham was no denier of international law. But according to him, only through a positivist turn could international law become 'genuine law', analogous to state law.[148]

As far as questions of war and peace in international law are concerned, in his essays on the *Principles of International Law* (1786–89), Bentham anticipated some aspects of Kant's peace treatise and set out the central demands of modern international liberal thought.[149] Bentham called for comprehensive disarmament and institutionalization of international relations, an international court of justice, an end to secret diplomacy, free trade, and 'codification' of international law—another

---

International Law', 17 *European Journal of International Law* (2006) 315; Mälksoo, 'Sources of International Law in the Nineteenth-Century European Tradition: Insights from Practice and Theory', in S. Besson and J. d'Aspremont (eds), *The Oxford Handbook of the Sources of International Law* (2017) 146.

[142] Vec, 'Sources of International Law in the Nineteenth-Century European Tradition: The Myth of Positivism', in S. Besson and J. d'Aspremont (eds), *The Oxford Handbook of the Sources of International Law* (2017) 121.
[143] Keene, 'The Treaty-Making Revolution of the Nineteenth Century', 34 *The International History Review* (2012) 475.
[144] Grewe (n. 12), at 503.
[145] Gundermann, 'Bentham', in J.C. Bluntschli and C L.T. Brater (eds), *Deutsches Staats-Wörterbuch* (1857) 42, at 42.
[146] Bentham, 'Critical Examination of the Declaration of Rights', in J. Bowring (ed.), *The Works of Jeremy Bentham* (1843) 496, at 501.
[147] Quoted from Janis, 'Jeremy Bentham and the Fashioning of "International Law"', 78 *American Journal of International Law* (1984) 405, at 406.
[148] Quoted from *ibid.*, at 409.
[149] M. Howard, *War and the Liberal Conscience: The George Macaulay Trevelyan Lectures in the University of Cambridge, 1977* (1981); Baum, 'A Quest for Inspiration in the Liberal Peace Paradigm: Back to Bentham?', 14 *European Journal of International Relations* (2008) 431.

of his neologisms.[150] At the same time, however, Bentham differed from some of his 'liberal' successors in Britain. Unlike John Stuart Mill, who blatantly justified British imperialism,[151] Bentham recommended that several (though not all) nations should give up their colonies, as this would be conducive to peace.[152]

Bentham's thinking on war, law, and peace was undoubtedly utilitarian.[153] Bentham believed in a mutually positive correlation between peace and free trade.[154] War, in contrast, he considered to be a 'mischief upon the largest scale'.[155] According to Bentham, it was essentially heads of state who profited from conquests, while citizens had to bear the costs of war, not least through increasing tax burdens: 'Conquer little or much, you pay for it by taxes.'[156] Bentham's rejection of war was therefore not based on a categorical imperative of reason, but on citizens' political and economic interests. Yet the theorist was not always consistent in practice. During Britain's war against Napoléon, in 1811, Bentham attempted to fit out a privateer so that he could benefit financially from war with France.[157] Bentham's quest for peace was clear—his quest for profit obviously no less so.

Despite the ethically problematic inconsistency of his own actions, it was unclear on what normative order Bentham's interest-driven theory of peace and a radically positivist international law should be based. Bentham's ideas were hardly compatible with the dominant legal theory of his time.[158] His project of international juridification lacked an ultimate normative justification.

It is thus perhaps not unsurprising that Bentham was unable to present an innovative approach to dealing with the problem of justifying war. Rather, he treated the problem largely in accordance with the European tradition. Bentham argued that '[a]ggressive war is a matter of choice: defensive, of necessity'.[159] Bentham thus understood Britain's war against Napoléon as a legitimate defensive war,[160] confirming the central justification narrative of *bellum iustum*. For Bentham, too, war was ultimately 'a species of procedure by which one nation endeavours to enforce its rights at the expense of another nation'.[161] What these 'rights' could consist of in

---

[150] Janis (n. 147), at 414; Augusti, 'Peace by Code: Milestones and Crossroads in the Codification of International Law', in T. Hippler and M. Vec (eds), *Paradoxes of Peace in Nineteenth Century Europe* (2015) 37, at 41.
[151] Jahn, 'Kant, Mill, and Illiberal Legacies in International Affairs', 59 *International Organization* (2005) 177.
[152] Bentham, 'A Plan for an Universal and Perpetual Peace', in J. Bowring (ed.), *The Works of Jeremy Bentham* (1843) 546, at 546 ff.
[153] G.J. Postema, *Utility, Publicity, and Law: Essays on Bentham's Moral and Legal Philosophy* (2019).
[154] Bentham (n. 152), at 557.
[155] *Ibid.*, at 544.
[156] *Ibid.*, at 557.
[157] Conway, 'Bentham on Peace and War', 1 *Utilitas* (1989), at 85 ff.
[158] See also Augusti (n. 150).
[159] Bentham (n. 152), at 555.
[160] Conway (n. 157), at 85.
[161] Bentham, 'Objects of International Law', in J. Bowring (ed.), *The Works of Jeremy Bentham* (1843), 537, at 538.

more concrete terms, however, remained open. Although his writings were praised by nineteenth-century scholars,[162] Bentham's work would not become a decisive caesura in international legal thought on war and normativity. His project of international legalization was missing a normative core.

Revolutionizing Reform? The 'Positivist Turn(s)' in International Legal Thought: German Edition (Martens)

Georg Friedrich von Martens was more strongly oriented towards the political practice of his time than Bentham. The Göttingen lawyer is generally regarded as the legal founder, and sometimes even as the 'deserving champion'[163] of modern legal positivism. Much in this vein, Martti Koskenniemi has called Martens 'the most significant representative of the "internationalist" branch of German public law at the time'.[164]

This characterization is in keeping with the argument repeatedly presented by Koskenniemi that 'there is a specifically "German" heritage to international law', and, what is more, that 'in view of its history and its problems, international law is a "German discipline" in a way that it cannot be said to be "French", "British" or indeed an "American" discipline'.[165] What Koskenniemi meant here was 'that the way we theorise about international law has grown out of German public law'.[166] This argument refers in particular to the early modern German problem of forming an overarching binding law in the 'anarchic society'[167] of the Holy Roman Empire of the German Nation and in view of the 'Westphalian settlement'.[168] Furthermore, new forms of thinking about public law emerged at new universities such as Halle or Göttingen in the seventeenth and eighteenth centuries. Their legal protagonists increasingly based their arguments on European state practice. Martens was able to bring together these positivist influences. He engaged with the work of Pufendorf, Pütter, Achenwall, and Johann Jacob Moser[169]—and went further. In his studies,

---

[162] R. von Mohl, *Die Geschichte und Literatur der Staatswissenschaften: In Monographien dargestellt* (1858), at 384.
[163] Hubrich, 'Georg Friedrich von Martens und die moderne Völkerrechtswissenschaft', *Zeitschrift für Politik* (1914) 362, at 362; see also Grewe (n. 12), at 346 ff.
[164] Koskenniemi, 'Georg Friedrich von Martens (1756–1821) and the Origins of Modern International Law', 13 *IILJ Working Paper 2006/1* (2006), at 1 ff.
[165] Ibid.; Koskenniemi, 'Between Coordination and Constitution: International Law as a German Discipline', 15 *Redescriptions* (2011) 45; M. Koskenniemi, *To the Uttermost Parts of the Earth: Legal Imagination and International Power, 1300–1870* (2021), at 800.
[166] Koskenniemi (n. 164), at 1 ff.; see also Brock and Simon, 'Die deutsche Sprache des Rechts', in S. Jäger and W. S. Heinz (eds), *Frieden durch Recht: Rechtstraditionen und Verortungen* (2020) 33; and Kemmerer, 'Martti Koskenniemi's (German) Legal Imagination and the Politics of Panorama', *Völkerrechtsblog* (25 August 2021), available at: https://voelkerrechtsblog.org/de/martti-koskenniemis-german-legal-imagination-and-the-politics-of-panorama/ (last visited 1 December 2022).
[167] H. Bull, *The Anarchical Society: A Study of Order in World Politics* (2nd edn, 1995).
[168] Koskenniemi (n. 164), at 1 ff.
[169] On Moser, see M. Stolleis, *Geschichte des öffentlichen Rechts in Deutschland*, vol. 1 (1988), at 258 ff.

he brought out the tension between sovereignty and the superior legal order on the basis of political state practice.

Martens's textbook on international law was entitled *Droit des Gens Moderne de l'Europe* (1789). A German translation was published in 1796 under the title *Einleitung in das positive Europäische Völkerrecht auf Verträge und Herkommen gegründet*. This title may have seemed inconspicuous but was in fact quite telling. It referred to both the narrowing of international law to Europe and to the increasing importance of positivisms. Two theoretical premises introduced by Kant were central to Martens's understanding of international law: the distinction between morality and law, on the one hand, and a teleology of positive law as civilizational progress, on the other.[170]

Accordingly, Martens's history of international law as a civilizing history was geared towards a steadily increasing consolidation of positive law along the lines of political practice in Europe. The European states—regardless of their size or religious denomination—formed a whole through common values, practices, and legal transactions even without a constitution. The goal, according to Martens, should be cooperation between states to maintain peace through a balance of power.[171] Here, the 'German' legal tradition after Pufendorf once again clearly comes to the fore. International law should evolve from a law of coexistence into a law of cooperation between sovereign states.[172] Martens recognized a general, positive European international law in the unity of treaties, customs, and the behaviour of the European powers.[173] In a sense, he anticipated Heinhard Steiger's concept of international law as *Kulturleistung*.[174] Martens saw positive international law as a European cultural achievement—from which he excluded non-European powers.[175]

However, Martens was no radical positivist like Bentham. He was a conservative legal reformer who wanted to maintain the 'old' international order. From his perspective, neither a radical turn to natural law (Grégoire) nor to positive law (Bentham) seemed appropriate.[176] While Bentham advocated a radical rejection of *all* natural law, Martens drew on the European tradition and thus on the dualism of natural law and positive law. For Martens, positive law was by no means opposed to natural law in principle. Positive law was rather a historically empirically

---

[170] Koskenniemi (n. 164).
[171] Blom, 'A Very Uncertain Perspective... The Revolutionary and Napoleonic Age and International Relations in Europe, in the Views of Georg Friedrich von Martens (1756–1821)', in B. Jacobs, R. Kubben, and R. Lesaffer (eds), *In the Embrace of France: The Law of Nations and Constitutional Law in the French Satellite States of the Revolutionary and Napoleonic Age (1789–1815)* (2008) 127, at 130 ff.
[172] For a general account of this narrative, see W. Friedmann, *The Changing Structure of International Law* (1964).
[173] G.F. von Martens, *Einleitung in das positive Europäische Völkerrecht auf Verträge und Herkommen gegründet* (1796), at 6.
[174] See Chapter 2.3.
[175] Martens (n. 173), at 6 ff.
[176] On Grégoire, see Blom (n. 171).

observable and thus systematizable concretization of the law of reason through state practice.[177] Martens would be proven right: the dualism of natural law and positive law was to retain validity even in the supposedly 'positivist century'.[178]

While he accepted traditional natural law in European international law, Martens clearly rejected the new natural law claims of the Revolution. He dismissed Abbé Grégoire's *Déclaration du Droit des Gens* as utopian.[179] Furthermore, he warned that the revolutionaries' principles of natural law could be used to justify violent interference in any constitution that was not recognized as free. According to Martens, these principles went hand in hand with war and its justification.[180] Martens was therefore relieved at the failure of the Revolution in Europe. In the preface to the 1796 edition of *Droit des Gens*, he had expressed the fear that his book would soon be out of date.[181] In the new edition of 1821, on the other hand, Martens noted with satisfaction that Europe had returned to its old principles, having thrown off the 'yoke' of Napoléon, without having refused the advances of the Enlightenment.[182] Due to his close connection to political practice—especially to the Hanoverian Electorate—Martens was to personally witness the reorganization of Europe after Napoléon's defeat. In 1814, he took part in the Congress of Vienna as part of Hanover's diplomatic delegation.

In his rejection of revolutionary violence, Martens's scholarly engagement with the use of force becomes visible. It is not true that Martens accepted war as fact. To him, the debates on 'just war' were not at all 'unfruitful and unnecessary', as claimed by Koskenniemi.[183] Quite the opposite is true: Martens understood war as a highly relevant field of international law. To deal with it scientifically, he once again drew heavily on early modern debates. Martens referred[184] to the writings on war and law by, for example, Grotius, Bynkershoek, Moser, Leibnitz, Wolff, and Vattel, as well as to the chapter on resorting to war in Ompteda's bibliography of international law.[185]

A positivist turn towards a 'free right to go to war' cannot, however, be identified in Martens's work. Rather, Martens emphasized that public war manifestos were considered 'essential' in state practice, not only throughout early modernity, but 'even now' (that is, in 1796).[186] Martens also confirmed the two central justification

---

[177] This becomes evident from the title of H.G. Scheidemantel, *Das Staatsrecht nach der Vernunft und den Sitten der vornehmsten Völker betrachtet* (1771).
[178] For a critical account, see Vec (n. 142).
[179] Martens (n. 173), at ix.
[180] *Ibid.*, at xv.
[181] *Ibid.*, at xvi.
[182] G.F. von Martens, *Précis du droit des gens moderne de l'Europe fondé sur les traités et l'usage: Pour servir d'introduction à un cours politique et diplomatique* (3rd edn, 1821), at 17; see also Blom (n. 171), at 139.
[183] Koskenniemi (n. 164).
[184] Martens (n. 173), at 298.
[185] D.H.L. von Ompteda, *Litteratur des gesammten sowohl natürlichen als positiven Völkerrechts* (1785).
[186] Martens (n. 173), at 300.

narratives for the use of 'physical means' ('*thätlicher Mittel*') as being self-defence and the violation of one's own rights.[187] Moreover, Martens also believed that war could only be legitimate as *ultima ratio*. Before going to war, a state had to prove that its decision to do so was justified and that a (futile) retaliation or reprisal in an attempt to enforce its rights by force had preceded it. Martens thus fully endorsed the classic criteria for the legitimacy of war in the European tradition.

However, as in the early modern theory of international law, a more precise differentiation of legitimate violations of rights was lacking in Martens's work (although Martens could perhaps have provided such a distinction, given his greater interest in state practice). As Martens conceded, there was still a great deal of room for interpretation in the justification of war, especially about alleged violations of law, since no nation was the judge of another. In any case of doubt, therefore, the reasons for war given by both warring parties would have to be considered equally just.[188] According to Martens, in almost every war there was a dispute over which side was to be considered 'defensive'.[189] This even applied to 'wars of the Africans', whose true motive was so often mere rapacity, as Martens claimed in typical European superiority habitus.[190]

Martens is generally regarded as a pioneer of positivism in modern international law. In view of his positions on the justification of war, however, it must be emphasized that there are far more similarities than differences between the early modern legal literature on the justification of war and that of Martens. For Martens, too, war had to be justified publicly and with reference to legitimate reasons for war, which could originate from positive law, but also from natural law. Martens's work also lacked a 'free right to wage war'. And he, too, could not imagine a public legal order in which war would be generally forbidden—perhaps even less so than some of his early modern predecessors, due to his 'positivism'. After all, it was not Martens who was to provide the decisive impetus in the modern conception of a prohibition of the use of force, but Immanuel Kant.

Peace through Legalization: Towards a Modern Prohibition of War (Kant)

Kant's contribution to the modern discourse on war and normativity was nothing short of revolutionary. Whereas European legal doctrine from ancient times up to Martens had adhered to the doctrine of 'just war', Kant rejected any extra-legal justification of international violence as claimed by theorists of *bellum iustum* as

---

[187] *Ibid.*, at 289.
[188] *Ibid.*, at 297.
[189] *Ibid.*, at 299.
[190] *Ibid.*, at 297.

well as those of absolute statehood in the tradition of Machiavelli or Hobbes. The central telos of Kant's international theory was an 'order of justification'[191] in which positive law alone would be accepted as a valid argument for judging violence. To this end, law had to be distinguished both from morality and from politics—a radical step towards normative homogenization.

And yet Immanuel Kant did share some of the views of realists, such as Hobbes's negative view of man. Georg Geismann has convincingly argued that Kant completed the work of Hobbes and Rousseau.[192] But what exactly does that mean? For Kant, too, the state of nature (*status naturalis*) was an anarchic 'state of war'.[193] This was especially true for international relations: peoples organized as states 'bring harm to each other already through their proximity to one another'.[194] However, Kant drew completely different conclusions from the assumption of a warlike state of nature at the international level than Hobbes: he fully rejected states' 'lawless freedom, preferring to fight continually amongst one another'.[195] His aim was perpetual peace based on a prohibition of war by positive law. Kant thus sought to transform international law from a law of war into a law of peace.[196]

For although drafts on 'perpetual peace' had been presented long before,[197] Kant became *the* foremost modern thinker on *ius contra bellum* in the European tradition.[198] Accordingly, Kant's project of pacification through law was already widely received in politics and theory in his time. This would remain the case throughout the nineteenth and twentieth centuries and to this day.

While the Königsberg philosopher Kant addressed his legal pacifist project in various of his writings, *Toward Perpetual Peace* is certainly the most important of them on this issue. The 'philosophical sketch', as its subtitle reads, was published in 1795, during the turmoil of the Revolutionary Wars. The Peace of Basel had motivated Kant to make his ideas on international law public to a wider audience. Yet Kant was rather ambivalent about the peace agreement. On the one hand, he understood the treaty as an opportunity for the legal pacification of the international conflicts between the French Republic and the European monarchies; on the other hand, however, the peace was overshadowed by the Third Polish Partition.

---

[191] R. Forst, *Normativity and Power. Analyzing Social Orders of Justification* (2017), at 15.
[192] Geismann, 'Kant als Vollender von Hobbes und Rousseau', 21 *Der Staat* (1982) 161.
[193] Kant, 'Toward Perpetual Peace. A Philosophical Sketch [1795]', in I. Kant, *Toward Perpetual Peace and Other Writings on Politics, Peace, and History*, edited by P. Kleingeld (2006) 67, at 72.
[194] Ibid., at 78.
[195] Ibid.
[196] Brock, 'Frieden durch Recht?', in P. Becker, R. Braun, and D. Deiseroth (eds): *Frieden durch Recht* (2010) 15.
[197] Ghervas, 'Balance of Power vs. Perpetual Peace: Paradigms of European Order from Utrecht to Vienna, 1713–1815', 39 *The International History Review* (2017) 404; K. von Raumer, *Ewiger Friede: Friedensrufe und Friedenspläne seit d. Renaissance* (1953).
[198] On Kant and international law, see the Special Issue: The Kantian Project of International Law in 10 *German Journal of International Law* (2009); J. Habermas, *The Divided West* (2006); one of the best introductions to Kant's thinking on peace and law is Eberl and Niesen, 'Kommentar', in I. Kant, *Zum Ewigen Frieden* (2011 [1795]).

Unlike the conservative Martens, Kant, as a liberal cosmopolitan, had sympathies for the Revolution and the legal progress it brought about.[199] The intertwining of republicanism and legal pacifism was indeed the innovative force of Kant's writing on perpetual peace.[200] Echoing Heinrich Heine, Marx would later refer to Kant's philosophy as 'the German theory of the French revolution'.[201]

In his peace treatise, Kant drew on the 'typically German' public law tradition of the early modern period outlined above. Nevertheless, Kant set himself apart from this tradition. Thus, with the different emphasis of the status quo (Martens) and the incremental progress of a cosmopolitan legal pacifist teleology (Kant), the two central standpoints of modern legal positivist discussions are identified. They were to be weighed against each other repeatedly in the course of the nineteenth century but were ultimately based on the same fundamental legal premise: according to both Martens and Kant, a pacifying process in international relations required positive law.[202]

The importance of public law for Kant's idea of peace is already evident in the fact that he wrote *Toward Perpetual Peace* in the form of a treaty. The text was divided into six preliminary and three definitive articles. In his preliminary articles, Kant named conditions for a lasting legal peace. In the first preliminary article, he distinguished peace from a 'mere cease-fire'[203] (*'bloße Waffenstillstand'*), in the second he rejected annexations, and in the third he pleaded, not only for disarmament, but for a ban on standing armies[204] At the same time, citizens should be allowed to periodically practise using arms on a voluntary basis in order to be prepared for the event of an external attack. Kant, too, considered self-defence a legitimate exception to the prohibition of war. In the fifth, and probably most controversial, preliminary article, Kant put forward a prohibition of intervention in view of the interference of the European monarchies vis-à-vis France and Poland.[205] Kant justified this prohibition with the 'autonomy of all states' as moral persons, with 'the idea of an original contract, upon which all laws legislated by a people must be based'.[206]

---

[199] Pfordten, 'Kant on the Right of Resistance', in J.-C. Merle and A. Trivisonno (eds), *Kant's Theory of Law* (2015), 101; Eberl, 'Kant's Rejection of Just War: International Order between Democratic Constitutionalism and Revolutionary Violence', in L. Brock and H. Simon (eds), *The Justification of War and International Order: From Past to Present* (2021) 129.

[200] J. Bohman and M. Lutz-Bachmann (eds), *Perpetual Peace: Essays on Kant's Cosmopolitan Ideal* (1997); Hans-Christian Lucas has argued that a summary of Kant's entire philosophy of law, 'admittedly not as a systematic synthesis', can be found in his *Toward Perpetual Peace*, Lucas, 'Geschichte, Krieg und Frieden bei Kant und Hegel', in D. Hüning and B. Tuschling (eds), *Recht, Staat und Völkerrecht bei Immanuel Kant* (1998) 247, at 248.

[201] Marx, 'The Philosophical Manifesto of the Historical School of Law (1842)', in *Marx and Engels Collected Writings* (1975), vol. 2, 203; see also Ypi, 'On Revolution in Kant and Marx', 42 *Political Theory* (2014) 262.

[202] Koskenniemi (n. 164), 23 ff.

[203] Kant (n. 193), at 68.

[204] *Ibid.*, at 68.

[205] *Ibid.*; see also Eberl and Niesen (n. 198), at 196.

[206] Kant (n. 193), at 73, fn.

This points to the central postulate of Kant's peace project, 'that all people who can mutually exert influence on one another must be party to some civil constitution'.[207] In the three definitive articles of his peace treatise, Kant developed a tripartite public legal system consisting of the 'right of citizens of a state governing the individuals of a people (*ius civitatis*)' (First Definitive Article of Perpetual Peace), the 'international right governing the relations of states among one another (*ius gentium*)' (Second Definitive Article of Perpetual Peace), and the 'cosmopolitan right, to the extent that individuals and states, who are related externally by the mutual exertion of influence on each other, are to be regarded as citizens of a universal state of humankind (*ius cosmopoliticum*)' (Third Definitive Article of Perpetual Peace). But since 'peace can be neither brought about nor secured without a treaty among people', according to Kant, at the same time, legal peace had to be secured institutionally—be that in the form of a world state, be it in the form of a 'pacific federation (*foedus pacificum*)' as a 'negative surrogate' of the former.[208] This was the idea of a legally founded permanent institution.

Unlike Bentham, Kant's turn to positive law was not based on considerations of interest. Instead, Kant had confidence in reason and normativity. He saw it as a dictate of reason to outlaw war. Since 'from the throne of the highest moral legislative authority, reason looks down on and condemns war as a means of pursuing one's rights, and makes peace an immediate duty',[209] for Kant it followed that every state could demand of any other that it leave this state of nature and entrust itself to positive law as a regulative of behaviour, i.e. that it give up unilateral moral and political considerations on the use of force in favour of a multilateral institutionalized decision based on law.[210]

Against this background, it becomes clear why Kant defended not only the right to free philosophizing but also free publicity: they both favoured the development of natural reason. In this sense, as Kant had already sketched out in his *Idea for a Universal History from a Cosmopolitan Perspective* (1784), positive law was the best indicator of progress in history demanded by reason, i.e. a key human cultural achievement. Unlike Martens, Kant envisaged a world that was clearly beyond his time, pointing towards 'an ideal moral world, which the sensible world should approximate through historical progress'.[211] He outlined a cosmopolitan universal history with law as its main narrative of justification—or in other words: *a history of international law with a cosmopolitan purpose.*

---

[207] *Ibid.*, at 72.
[208] *Ibid.*, at 80.
[209] *Ibid.*
[210] Habermas, 'Kant's Idea of Perpetual Peace, with the Benefit of Two Hundred Years Hindsight', in J. Bohman and M. Lutz-Bachmann (eds), *Perpetual Peace: Essays on Kant's Cosmopolitan Ideal* (1997) 113.
[211] Kleingeld, "What do the Virtuous Hope for? Re-reading Kant's Doctrine of the Highest Good", in H. Robinson (ed.), *Proceedings of the Eighth International Kant Congress: Memphis* (1995) 91.

In view of the virtually sacral significance of positive law in Kant's international thought, it becomes clear why his teleology of legalization was accompanied by a complete rejection of any extra-legal argument in the discourse on war and peace. Against the backdrop of the historical experience of his time, Kant resolutely set himself apart from the two main theses in the political and international legal theory of the early modern period.

First, he opposed the continuing importance of the doctrine of 'just war'.[212] After all, the problem of vague and thus widely interpretable criteria for a 'just cause' had remained unresolved in legal theory throughout early modernity. It is true that Kant also saw a certain normative power in the obligation to justify in the legitimation discourses of 'just war'. Thus, in view of the 'maliciousness of human nature', which 'can be observed openly in the free relations between the peoples', Kant understood it as 'astonishing that the word *right* has not yet been able to be fully banished from war politics as pedantic, and that no state has yet dared to publicly endorse doing so'.[213]

However, Kant rejected any justification of war by natural law and, with it, the natural law of international law of the early modern period. To him, theorists of *bellum iustum* such as Grotius, Pufendorf, and Vattel were 'tiresome comforters'[214] ('*leidige Tröster*'), since their writings had not yet prevented a single war, 'but are still faithfully cited to justify an offensive war'.[215] Kant might have underestimated the potential of a critique of violence based on natural law. However, he recognized that the entire discourse of *bellum iustum* was not only aimed at limiting violence but made its very legitimation possible.

Second, Kant also resolutely opposed the idea of absolute sovereignty and Machiavelli's conviction that war was always just if it was politically necessary. Against political realists, Kant[216] stated:

> One cannot conceive of international right as a right *to* war (since this would be a presumptive right to determine what is right, not according to universally valid external laws that restrict the freedom of every individual, but rather by means of violence, according to one-sided maxims).

This was a clear rejection of war as an instrument of politics and of any notion of *liberum ius ad bellum*—a rejection that was to become constitutive for the modern legal pacifist discourse. It substantiates Kant's importance as *the* pioneer of *ius contra bellum*.

---

[212] See also H. Williams, *Kant and the End of War: A Critique of Just War Theory* (2012); Eberl (n. 199).
[213] Kant (n. 193), at 80.
[214] *Ibid.*, at 80.
[215] *Ibid.*, at 79.
[216] *Ibid.*, at 81.

With this dual denial of existing approaches to justifying war, Kant laid the foundation for the liberal telos of the full legalization of the modern discourse on war and peace at the beginning of the 'long nineteenth century'. Kant's innovation in addressing the justificatory spheres of politics, law, and morality can therefore be summarized as follows: for Kant, war as a political instrument had to be prohibited by positive law because the moral vocabulary was not sufficient to contain the evil nature of man. For modern international legal doctrine in the tradition of Kant, the distinction between law and morality—and derived from that: between is and ought (*Sein und Sollen*)—was therefore central. But twentieth-century positivism was still a long way off. The ideal-typical separation of law and other normative spheres was to be put to the test several more times in the nineteenth century.

And yet even the main protagonist of modern legal pacifist discourse shows ambivalences in his thinking about violence and law. Kant anticipated Hegel's dialectic to a certain extent, when he attributed war with progressive power.[217] According to Kant, what guaranteed perpetual peace was 'nothing less than the great artist nature (*natura daedala rerum*)': its 'mechanical course ... visibly reveals a purposive plan to create harmony through discord among people, even against their own will'.[218] In other words, human nature could lead man through the barbarity of war back to reason—and thus to working on legal peace. Paradoxically, Kant of all people also saw in the violent barbarity of war a kind of cultural catalyst if human reason should ever fail.[219] However, and this *does* make a distinct difference, for Kant, war did not serve the unilateral political purpose of creating a state or expanding its power—but the establishment of eternal global peace.

This points to a second ambivalence in Kant's thinking on violence and law, namely his assessment of revolutionary violence. Kant observed the unfolding of the revolution with mixed feelings. While he criticized violence and the forced spread of revolution, he accepted the legal progress brought about by revolutionary violence: recent studies even point out that Kant was not only indifferent to the execution of King Louis XVI,[220] but also accepted a right to resist tyrants and despots.[221]

A third ambivalence in Kant's writings supports Kelsen's differentiation between real and ideal types of 'objective' and 'politicized science', as summarized above.[222] For all the distinction between law, politics, and morality, Kant's plea for legal

---

[217] See also Schoch, 'Frieden als Progress? Ein Großbegriff zwischen politischem Projekt und Geschichtsphilosophie', in M. Albert, B. Moltmann, and B. Schoch (eds), *Die Entgrenzung der Politik: internationale Beziehungen und Friedensforschung: Festschrift für Lothar Brock* (2004), 13, at 18 ff.; and D. Langewiesche, *Der gewaltsame Lehrer. Europas Kriege in der Moderne* (2019).
[218] Kant (n. 193), at 85.
[219] *Ibid.*, at 81.
[220] Paula Olivieira, 'Compatibility of the Moral Foundation of Law in Kant with the Theory of Reflective Judgment and with the Kantian Theory of Revolution', in J.-C. Merle and A. Trivisonno (eds), *Kant's Theory of Law* (2015) 35.
[221] Pfordten, 'Kant on the Right of Resistance', in *ibid.* 101.
[222] See Introduction.

positivism was ultimately, as Walter Benjamin[223] would later emphasize, a thoroughly political—and also moral—project. After all, Kant's idea of an objective law initially stemmed from a non-legal sphere, since it was demanded by pure reason. The Scottish philosopher Walter B. Gallie has therefore, for good reason, described Kant's peace pamphlet as a 'political act' with which Kant publicly promoted his project of a legal prohibition of war.[224]

Nevertheless, these ambivalences do not fundamentally discredit the Kantian project. An ideally *reflexive legalization of international relations* is preferable to the anarchy of arbitrary violence and an arbitrary expansion of 'just causes' for war.[225] The fact that Kant resolutely opposed an expansion of 'just causes' for war is also illustrated by the discussion of a false ambivalence in Kant's international thought, with some researchers attempting to assign Kant to the tradition of 'just war'.[226] But this argument is not convincing. It is true that, following German legal scholar Gottfried Achenwall, Kant discussed 'just reasons for war' in his *Fundamental Principles of Jurisprudence as the Science of Right* (*Metaphysische Anfangsgründe der Rechtslehre*) published in 1797. It is also true that, in doing so, he described just causes that could be interpreted quite broadly. But Kant's intention here was to reveal what he saw as the self-contradictory nature of the natural law of nations in its attempt to regulate a warlike state of nature based on considerations of justice.[227] In other words, his argument referred to the state of nature between states that he wanted to do away with through legalization. Kant was not a theorist of 'just war'.

Therefore, the assumption that Kant advocated a particularly far-reaching and normatively unrestricted use of force by democracies against undemocratic, and thus 'unjust enemies',[228] is ultimately unconvincing.[229] It is true that Kant did discuss the concept of the 'unjust enemy' borrowed from the doctrine of *bellum iustum* (he again referred to Achenwall here). But Kant used this concept only at the *in bello*, not the *ad bellum* level. Unlike Vattel, Kant did not see it as legitimate to declare war on an 'unjust enemy' or even to wage a war of extermination against such an enemy. Rather, he only envisaged a collective defence against an enemy who used means of war that would make it impossible to achieve peace at a later date. A contemporary example is the destruction of Paris threatened by the

---

[223] Benjamin, 'Critique of Violence [1920/21]', reprinted in P. Demetz (ed.), *Walter Benjamin, Reflections: Essays, Aphorisms, Autobiographical Writings* (1978) 277.

[224] W.B. Gallie, *Philosophers of Peace and War: Kant, Clausewitz, Marx, Engels and Tolstoy* (1978), at 8; R. Maliks, *Kant's Politics in Context* (2014).

[225] For an account of both, see Brock and Simon, 'Die Selbstbehauptung und Selbstgefährdung des Friedens als Herrschaft des Rechts. Eine endlose Karussellfahrt?, 59 *Politische Vierteljahresschrift* (2018) 269.

[226] B. Orend, *War and International Justice: A Kantian Perspective* (2000).

[227] See also Eberl and Niesen (n. 198), at 343 ff.; and Eberl (n. 199).

[228] Müller, 'Kants Schurkenstaat: Der "ungerechte Feind" und die Selbstermächtigung zum Kriege', in A. Geis (ed.), *Den Krieg überdenken: Kriegsbegriffe und Kriegstheorien in der Kontroverse* (2006), 229.

[229] See also Eberl (n. 199).

Prussian commander-in-chief in 1792.[230] Unlike the French revolutionaries, Kant cannot serve as a pioneer in the justification for 'democratic wars'.[231]

Kant's writings on peace, normativity, and war were not free of antinomies and paradoxes.[232] These paradoxes, however, hardly diminish Kant's merit in exposing the inadequacies of the doctrine of 'just war' as well as those of the thesis of the 'free right to wage war', thus opening them to criticism. Kant was to become central to the political and theoretical debates of the nineteenth century. It therefore seems exceedingly surprising that the influence Kant had on nineteenth-century liberal legal theorists in their struggle against war as an instrument of politics (Chapters 4 and 6) has been neglected. Even in recent debates on the outlawing of war,[233] Kant, arguably the most important visionary of the modern legal prohibition of war, is hardly considered. This once again underlines the scope of the thesis of *liberum ius ad bellum* in current academic discourse.

Kant's vision of *ius contra bellum* was in fact to become the most important counter-thesis of *liberum ius ad bellum*—and vice versa. Although the latter was not advocated in international legal discourse for the first time until the late nineteenth century (see Part II), it was developed in modern political theory in the same context as Kant's legal pacifism (having found precursors such as Hobbes and Machiavelli in political discourses of the early modern period). Like Kant's project of *ius contra bellum*, it was also drafted by a Prussian, against the background of the French Revolution as well as influenced by new scientific concepts of the Enlightenment. And like Kant's peace treatise, the military—and political—theory of Carl von Clausewitz was to become a landmark in the formation of the modern discourse on war and peace.

War as an Instrument of Politics: On the Realist Discourse of Modern Warfare (Clausewitz)

Clausewitz and Kant shared the goal of going beyond moral justifications of war in the sense of *bellum iustum*. However, it is here that the similarities in their thinking on war and order end. For Kant and Clausewitz envisaged bringing an end to the doctrine of 'just war' by contrasting means. While Kant became the most important modern theorist of the legal prohibition of war, Clausewitz emerged as one of the

---

[230] See also Eberl and Niesen (n. 198), at 164–70, 332–4.

[231] For an analysis of this type of war, see A. Geis, L. Brock, and H. Müller (eds), *Democratic Wars: Looking at the Dark Side of Democratic Peace* (2006); A. Geis, H. Müller, and N. Schörnig (eds), *The Militant Face of Democracy: Liberal Forces for Good* (2013).

[232] P. Kleingeld, *Kant and Cosmopolitanism: The Philosophical Idea of World Citizenship* (2012), Chapter 4; Eberl, 'Kant on Race and Barbarism: Towards a More Complex View on Racism and Anti-Colonialism in Kant', 24 *Kantian Review* (2019) 385.

[233] Hathaway and Shapiro (n. 138); see also Chapter 2.

most important, if not the most important, modern theorists of war.[234] The central innovation in Clausewitz's theory of war is its primacy of politics. Unlike military theorists such as Heinrich Dietrich von Bülow or Antoine-Henri de Jomini, Clausewitz turned to the nexus of politics and war. Accordingly, in his *Vom Kriege* (1832–34), he developed his military theory as a *political* theory of war.[235]

Two definitions of 'war' can be found in the first volume of *Vom Kriege*. Clausewitz began the first chapter not with a political, but rather with an existential concept of war. He defined 'war' as a mere fact of violence, 'nothing but a duel on a larger scale'.[236] 'War is thus an act of force to compel our enemy to do our will', Clausewitz wrote.[237] For this purpose, the enemy must be rendered 'powerless', since this 'is the true aim of warfare'.[238] According to Clausewitz: 'Force—that is, physical force, for moral force has no existence save as expressed in the state and the law—is thus the means of war; to impose our will on the enemy is its object'.[239]

This factual description of war, however, was followed by a second definition at the end of the chapter that gets to the heart of Clausewitz's political theory: 'War is merely the continuation of policy by other means'.[240] (*'Der Krieg ist eine bloße Fortsetzung der Politik mit anderen Mitteln.'*) He continued: 'war is not merely an act of policy but a true political instrument, a continuation of political intercourse, carried on with other means'.[241] According to Clausewitz, the political object was therefore 'the goal, war is the means of reaching it, and means can never be considered in isolation from their purpose'.[242] War as mere violence is thus contrasted with Clausewitz's concept of war as an instrument of politics.

To explain this simultaneity of a factual and a political concept in Clausewitz's work, Weber's differentiation between ideal and real types is helpful: war as a duel represents an ideal type of physical combat, a *'Reagenzglaskrieg'* ('test-tube war')[243] in which variable factors such as time, space, and culture are largely ignored. With this ideal type, Clausewitz referred to what he saw as the essence of war: its violent nature.[244] This concept of war may be 'pure'—but is also 'empirically empty'.[245]

---

[234] B. Heuser, *Clausewitz lesen!: Eine Einführung* (2005); B. Heuser, *War: A Genealogy of Western Ideas and Practices* (2022), at 189.

[235] A. Herberg-Rothe, *Clausewitz's Puzzle: The Political Theory of War* (2007); see also Daase, 'Clausewitz and Small Wars', in H. Strachan and A. Herberg-Rothe (eds), *Clausewitz in the Twenty-First Century* (2007) 182; and Wille, 'Politik und ihre Grenzen in Clausewitz' Denken über den Krieg', 62 *Politische Vierteljahresschrift* (2021) 45.

[236] C. von Clausewitz, *On War*, edited and translated by M. Howard and P. Paret (1976 [1832]), at 75; for the German terms, see Clausewitz, 'Vom Kriege', in M. von Clausewitz (ed.), *Hinterlassene Werke über Krieg und Kriegsführung des Generals von Clausewitz* (1832).

[237] *Ibid.*
[238] *Ibid.*
[239] *Ibid.*
[240] *Ibid.*
[241] *Ibid.*, at 87.
[242] *Ibid.*

[243] R. Beckmann, *Clausewitz trifft Luhmann: Eine systemtheoretische Interpretation von Clausewitz' Handlungstheorie* (2011).

[244] Nitschke, 'Clausewitz ohne Ende – Oder die Existenzialität des Krieges', in H. Zapf and S. Salzborn (eds), *Krieg und Frieden: Kulturelle Deutungsmuster* (2015) 11.

[245] U. Kleemeier, *Grundfragen einer philosophischen Theorie des Krieges: Platon – Hobbes – Clausewitz* (2002), at 231.

Hence, in order to establish the primacy of politics in war, Clausewitz contrasted his ideal type of war with historicized real types of war. In his ideal-typical depiction of the duel the '*immediate* aim is to *throw* his opponent in order to make him incapable of further resistance'.[246] However, according to Clausewitz, everything changed when moving 'from the abstract to the real world'.[247] With this, Clausewitz now emphasized the political purpose of war. After all, war was never an act that suddenly appeared, in isolation from the former life of the state. For Clausewitz, it was permeated through and through by politics in its historical variability.

Against this background, it is also possible to explain why Clausewitz regarded war as a 'true chameleon'[248] ('*wahres Chamäleon*'). War can take on completely different forms in different historical contexts, as Clausewitz illustrated with his concept of the 'remarkable' or 'paradoxical trinity' ('*wunderliche Dreifaltigkeit*').[249] Clausewitz saw war as varied in its manifestation along the three elements of 'blind natural force' ('*blinder Naturtrieb*'), the 'freedom of the creative spirit' ('*freie Seelentätigkeit*'), and 'pure reason' ('*bloßer Verstand*'),[250] or in other words: between self-sufficient brutality, strategic creativity, and political rationality.[251]

It reflects Clausewitz's own political agenda that he equated the people with the category of 'blind natural force' and the government with 'political rationality'. Just as for Bentham, Martens, and Kant, the context of the Revolutionary and Napoleonic Wars was central here.[252] But unlike his legal and philosophical contemporaries, Clausewitz took part in the wars as a combatant: first from 1793—as a then thirteen-year-old—until the Peace of Basel, then in the disastrous Fourth Coalition War in 1806, and finally in 1812, now in the service of Russia.

Clausewitz thus experienced the end of eighteenth-century 'cabinet warfare' and the superior power of the warfare conducted by mobilized people, which he summarized as follows:

> Suddenly war again became the business of the people—a people of thirty millions, all of whom considered themselves to be citizens of the State.... The people became a participant in war; instead of governments and armies as heretofore, the

---

[246] Clausewitz (n. 236), at 78.
[247] *Ibid.*, at 75.
[248] *Ibid.*, at 89.
[249] Herberg-Rothe (n. 235).
[250] Clausewitz (n. 236), at 89.
[251] Münkler, 'Clausewitz über den Charakter des Krieges', in R. Hohls, I. Schröder, and H. Siegrist (eds), *Europa und die Europäer: Quellen und Essays zur modernen europäischen Geschichte* (2005) 385.
[252] Hahlweg, 'Clausewitz und die Französische Revolution: Die methodische Grundlage des Werkes "Vom Kriege"', 27 *ZRGG* (1975) 240; Moran, 'Clausewitz and the Revolution', 22 *Central European History* 183 (1989); Herberg-Rothe, 'Clausewitz und Napoleon – Jena, Moskau, Waterloo', in K.-H. Lutz and G. Bauer (eds), *Jena 1806: Vorgeschichte und Rezeption* (2009) 81.

full weight was thrown into the balance. The resources and efforts now available for use surpassed all conventional limits; nothing now impeded the vigor with which war could be waged, and consequently the opponents of France faced the utmost peril.[253]

As can be observed here, Clausewitz became, in the words of Christopher Daase, 'one of the first theorists of wars of national liberation'.[254] For Clausewitz, as a liberal nationalist, this analytical finding was linked to a political project. His aim was to understand this new type of people's war in order to make it useful, first of all, for the German nation (earlier Clausewitz) and then for the Prussian authoritarian state (later Clausewitz). For this, the revolutionary people's war had to be scientifically understood. Thus, at the beginning of Clausewitz's theory of war, too, 'there was Napoléon'.

At the same time, Clausewitz reversed the Kantian assumption that greater participation of the people in the discourse on war would serve peace.[255] Clausewitz understood the people not as a pacifist force but as the central agent of the modern 'national bellicism'.[256] His ideal of the well-organized, monarchical administrative state was incompatible with Kant's notion of a state and legal discourse based on the general will of free and responsible *citoyens*. For Clausewitz, on the contrary, a citizen was first and foremost *Untertan*. The emergence of Clausewitz's dual definition of war may thus be explained against the background of the revolutionary people's wars. The revolutionary war initially struck Clausewitz as an existential threat to Prussia. By joining the Russian army in 1812, Clausewitz even violated the primacy of the political sphere that he later declared in order to protect the Prussian nation. Clausewitz did *not* subordinate his sense of national and soldierly honour to the political calculations of King Friedrich Wilhelm III, who was at that time allied with Napoléon. On the contrary, in his 1812 *Bekenntnisdenkschrift* ('Notes of Confession') Clausewitz invoked these very emotions to justify his decision to join the Russian army.[257] The young, liberal Clausewitz was concerned with the survival or national rebirth of Prussia by any means necessary. Accordingly, Clausewitz pleaded for warfare in the sense of existential warfare. The latter was to be committed solely to the freedom and honour of the Prussian people, but not to international law:

---

[253] Clausewitz (n. 236), at 592.
[254] Daase (n. 235), at 182 ff.
[255] Münkler (n. 251).
[256] J. Leonhard, *Bellizismus und Nation: Kriegsdeutung und Nationsbestimmung in Europa und den Vereinigten Staaten 1750–1914* (2008).
[257] Münkler, 'Instrumentelle und existentielle Auffassung vom Krieg bei Carl von Clausewitz', 16 *Leviathan* (1988) 235.

I believe and confess, that there is nothing more worthy of a people's respect than the dignity and freedom of its existence; that these must be defended to the last drop of blood; that there is no duty more holy to fulfil and no higher law to obey.[258]

This passage is not only interesting as a legitimization of the anti-Napoleonic 'people's war', however. It also suggests that Clausewitz was prepared to suspend the rules of international law (*ius in bello*) for the sake of the Prussian nation's existential struggle. In this case, then, war for Clausewitz essentially leaned towards the 'blind natural force' element of the remarkable/paradoxical trinity notion he later formulated. Political reason, which after all might have recognized the legal regulation of violence in war as politically prudent—not least to spare the troops—hardly came into play here. In this conception of war, the people were not to be subsumed under the will of the political sovereign; rather, the Prussians expressed their political will in the form of excessive violence in the first place.[259] Thus, violence in war was to be conducted without limits, the end justifying the means.

After 1815, Clausewitz turned away from this existential conception of war. Interestingly, this turn anticipated the further political-historical developments of Prussia/Germany and its war discourse in the nineteenth century. Clausewitz's hopes for a unification of the German nation were bitterly disappointed after the allied victory over Napoléon. In the era of European reorganization ushered in by the Congress of Vienna,[260] the promise of a German people united in a nation-state failed to materialize. Disillusioned, Clausewitz now more and more adopted conservative political positions.[261] Instead of the Prussian nation, the Prussian state increasingly became the focus of Clausewitz's political analysis. Clausewitz's conception of war also changed. He no longer understood it as a revolutionary essentialist act capable of creating a new national order. Rather, in the spirit of political realism following Machiavelli and Hobbes, war became an instrument of the existing political order—the (Prussian) state. Clausewitz's realist telos thus turned into the transfer of the unbounded people's war into the firm hand of the Prussian state. At the same time, this implied a limitation of war. Not the people, but the sovereign state alone was to decide on war and peace according to purely political calculations. Extra-political narratives of law, morality, and emotion no longer had a place in this political demystification of war. For Clausewitz, war was now subsumed under the primacy of state policy.

Clausewitz simultaneously shifted the decision regarding the legitimacy of war to the primacy of politics. An international normative order for the regulation of war played no role in his theory. His theory was normatively empty. The natural

---

[258] C. von Clausewitz, *Clausewitz On Small Wars*, edited and translated by C. Daase and J. Davis (2015), at 176.
[259] Münkler (n. 257), at 240 ff.
[260] See Chapter 4.
[261] Münkler (n. 257), at 240.

law criteria of 'just war' had to be denied any authority. And the positive law utopia of Kant—with whose philosophy Clausewitz was fundamentally familiar through his teacher Kiesewetter[262]—was diametrically opposed to the intended primacy of the political interests of the state. On the threshold of modernity, Clausewitz had become the foremost modern theorist of the thesis of the 'free right to wage war'.

Only the objective law of war (*ius in bello*) could claim some relevance in *Clausewitzian* war theory. Nevertheless, Clausewitz noted that attached to force were 'certain self-imposed, imperceptible limitations hardly worth mentioning, known as international law and custom'.[263] Thus, Martin van Creveld has rightly remarked that '*Vom Kriege* dismisses the entire body of international law and custom in a single irreverent sentence'.[264]

However, there were contemporary military authors who addressed normative aspects of justifying war in greater detail than Clausewitz: for example, the Prussian military theorist August Rühle von Lilienstern, who is comparatively unknown today. From him, Clausewitz had not only taken the title of his book *Vom Kriege*, but also many other ideas on the nexus of war and politics, including the notorious characterization of war as a continuation of politics by other means.[265] Unlike Clausewitz, Rühle did discuss the normativity of war in its relation to the primacy of politics, arguing that law was unfortunately often ambiguous and it was never easy to tell which side it was on. For Rühle, too, war therefore did not serve the violent enforcement of law, but rather political ends.[266]

In other words, for military authors such as Clausewitz and Rühle, international law was ultimately incapable of settling conflicts between states. Thus, neither public discourse nor a positive prohibition of war, but only the political interests of the state were the true purposes of war. Clausewitz ignored the role of international normativity. After all, he was not concerned with a 'pedantic, literary definition of war', Clausewitz argued,[267] but solely with the factual violence of war and its subsumption under the interests of politics.[268] Thus, in *this* sense, Clausewitz can indeed be understood as anti-Kantian.

However, as already indicated above, Clausewitz must not be misunderstood as a warmonger here. Reading war glorification into Clausewitz's theory of war does not do it justice. While the young Clausewitz may have euphorically legitimized existential warfare, the Clausewitz of *Vom Kriege* was neither a bellicist nor an

---

[262] Münkler (n. 251).
[263] Clausewitz (n. 236), at 75.
[264] Creveld, 'The Clausewitzian Universe and the Law of War', 26 *Journal of Contemporary History* (1991) 403, at 404.
[265] Heuser, 'Rühle von Lilienstern', in T. Jäger and R. Beckmann (eds), *Handbuch Kriegstheorien* (2011) 206, at 208 ff.
[266] J.J.O.A. Rühle von Lilienstern, *Handbuch für den Offizier zur Belehrung im Frieden und zum Gebrauch im Felde* (1818), at 12 ff.; quoted from *ibid.*, at 209.
[267] Clausewitz (n. 236), at 75.
[268] See also Tashjean, 'Pious Arms: Clausewitz and the Right of War', 44 *Military Affairs* (1980) 79.

advocate of Prussian/German hegemony in Europe.[269] Later *Clausewitzians* would thus go beyond the Prussian thinker himself with their euphoria about war. We will find enough illustrative material to prove this argument in Part II of this book.

The importance Clausewitz attributed to political primacy, however, also contained the idea of this primacy's function to limit violence. The political sovereign was supposed to steer the actual and boundless violence—even during a war that had broken out—onto a common path. In this context, Clausewitz's juxtaposition of the existential and the political conceptions of war is reminiscent of the Hobbesian—and also Kantian—juxtaposition of the state of nature and political order. In Clausewitz's thinking, the *political control* of war thus became the 'telos' of his realist doctrine of war.[270] The ideal war for Clausewitz remained the duel, a war which was waged in the name of sovereigns' political interests. Accordingly, war was primarily considered to be the war of states. State sovereignty was thus a condition for the legitimate use of force. In the spirit of *realism*, Clausewitz recognized only the balance of powers at the international level as a structure of order that did not oppose Prussia's security but was complementary to it.[271] This balance had to be protected in Prussia's interest—as was shown not least in Clausewitz's plea for a preventive war against Revolutionary France in 1830.[272]

Clausewitz's political theory thus centres on the political will of the state, its *raison d'être* and power. Consequently, Clausewitz should not only be understood as a modernizer of the realist thesis of absolute statehood in the sense of Hobbes or Machiavelli—even though he did not literally speak of a 'free right to go to war'. He is also the founder of a theory of war that is genuinely oriented towards the Prussian authoritarian state, which realist thinkers in the nineteenth and twentieth centuries were to take further. However, Clausewitz's work is not free of inner contradictions. Rather, it stands—due also to the biographical breaks—exactly between the politically liberal and conservative positions that were to become central to Prussian-German history in the rest of the nineteenth century. According to Gian Enrico Rusconi, Clausewitz found himself,

> in terms of his habitus, at an apex of Prussianism of the classical period, with all its possibilities and dispositions, which could develop in both liberal-democratic and national-chauvinist directions.[273]

---

[269] See also K.J. Gantzel, *Der unerhörte Clausewitz. Zur Korrektur gefährlicher Irrtümer – eine notwendige Polemik* (2001); Rusconi, 'Wiederbegegnung mit Clausewitz', in H. Böhme and M. Formisano (eds), *War in Words. Transformations of War from Antiquity to Clausewitz* (2011) 61, at 68.
[270] See also P. Paret, *Clausewitz and the State. The Man, His Theories, and His Times* (1976).
[271] Rusconi (n. 269), at 64.
[272] *Ibid.*, at 66.
[273] *Ibid.*, at 65.

The late, conservative Clausewitz, in any case, favoured the Prussian authoritarian state, which relied on a 'combination of economic-administrative modernization, domestic rule of law, and *Machtstaat* in its foreign policy'.[274]

The multifaceted nature of Clausewitz's thinking about war has certainly not diminished its success in political and military theory. It explains why he was to become an authority for so many different, indeed downright contrary, recipients. However, Clausewitz arguably 'became effective less in his own time than in the realm of his afterlife'.[275] In late nineteenth-century international legal discourse, his political primacy was to become the definitive antithesis of the Kantian project of *ius contra bellum*—and thus the central justification of the thesis of the 'free right to war'.[276]

3.4 Conclusion: 'In the Beginning was Napoléon'

Due to the eventually successful political and military resistance of the European monarchs, a radical transformation of international law as envisaged by revolutionary international thought failed to materialize. This failure has long fuelled the opinion among researchers that the French Revolution had no lasting impact on political and legal discourse on the legitimacy of war.[277] However, this impression is deceptive. Rather, in the revolutionary era, the decisive concepts, ideas, and narratives of modern war discourse began to emerge. This applied first and foremost to the ideas of the nation and popular sovereignty, but also to notions to legitimize or limit popular war. The Revolution left deep traces in modern thinking about war, politics, and normativity, which were to remain influential throughout the whole nineteenth century.

As I have argued in the present chapter, the transition from pre-modern to modern war discourse can therefore be located in the revolutionary era—in the discourses both of political practice (Chapter 3.2) and political theory (Chapter 3.3). The revolutionary era should therefore not be marginalized as it tends to be in the Theory and History of International Law and International Relations. Instead, it is to be understood here as the historical starting point of the genealogy of modern war discourse.

It is important to emphasize that both Revolutionary/Napoleonic France and its monarchical enemies continued to declare war with recourse to the criteria of 'just war'. War was continuously seen as requiring justification by all conflict parties over the period from 1789 to 1815. France's most important justification narrative was

---

[274] *Ibid.*, at 84.
[275] W. Hahlweg, *Carl von Clausewitz. Soldat, Politiker, Denker* (1957), at 83.
[276] I will come back to this argument in Part II of this book.
[277] On this point, see S.C. Neff, *Justice among Nations. A History of International Law* (2014), at 210 ff.

defending—and later expanding—the Revolution and its achievements: popular sovereignty, human rights, and liberty. These justificatory strategies were not free of paradoxes. For instance, the revolutionaries postulated a principle of non-intervention in defence of the Republic. But they themselves repeatedly violated this principle to 'liberate' oppressed peoples by military means. 'Liberation', 'emancipation', and force went hand in hand—*liberté, égalité, brutalité*.

So, 'nation' and 'popular sovereignty' became central concepts of the revolutionary politics of international law. Not only was the entire nation to be mobilized for the first time in the name of the Revolution, but the wars were also intended to bring about a comprehensive reordering of Europe and the world. This new kind of nationalized war already pointed to the destructiveness of warfare in the (late) nineteenth and twentieth centuries. Accordingly, David Bell (2007) has even called the revolutionary era the birth epoch of the 'first total war'.[278]

However, it should not be overlooked that the revolutionary narratives of 'nation' and 'popular sovereignty' were always linked with the doctrine of 'just war'. And even the enemies of the Revolution did not claim to be allowed to use force against Revolutionary France without justification. Despite all ideological innovations, we can clearly identify continuities with the war discourse of the 'pre-modern era' in the 'modern' war discourse emerging between 1789 and 1815: neither the revolutionaries nor their monarchical enemies defeated *bellum iustum*. Indeed, both sides continued to use this tradition of justification to excuse their use of force: be it to declare themselves defender of Europe's liberal peoples or of the dynastic legal community. It is true that the French revolutionaries tried to secularize and modernize 'just war' in a novel combination of natural law and political radicalism in order to distance themselves from the 'old' international legal order.[279]

In their 'new' justifications of violence, however, the revolutionaries clearly also referred to the ideas, norms, and values of the 'old' order: they combined 'old', 'dynastic' international law with morality, national honour, and security—unmistakably revolutionary values. Under Napoléon's reign, French diplomats even referred to religion and legal claims of medieval imperial dignity. But even in their enemies' war justifications, monarchical and revolutionary conceptions of order were mixed since the European monarchs, for their part, started to recognize the legitimating power of the nation. They, too, instrumentalized this modern concept to legitimize their own 'counter-violence' against France. Thus, multinormativity can be observed both in revolutionary *and* dynastic war discourse, which obviously contradicts Grewe's thesis of a narrowing of the justificatory vocabulary in the sense of *liberum ius ad bellum*. 'Just war' had not been replaced by radical political or legal positivism. The revolutionary era thus cannot

---
[278] Bell (n. 56).
[279] Neff (n. 277), at 205.

be integrated into the narrative of a supposedly emerging 'free right to go to war', as Grewe claims. In fact, it strongly contradicts this narrative.

The second part of the chapter turned to normative and political theory in the 'saddle era' by examining four important authors of the time—Bentham, Martens, Kant, and Clausewitz. While Bentham, who is neglected in German research discourses to this day, argued for a radical positivism *de lege ferenda*, Martens, a representative of the German public law tradition, still adhered in principle to the early modern dualism of *bellum iustum* and *bellum legale*. Here too, then, historical continuities can be identified rather than radical transformations.

Two Prussian theorists outside the law faculty were clearly more innovative: Immanuel Kant and Carl von Clausewitz became the two leading thinkers of modern war discourse. Unlike Martens, Kant and Clausewitz embody an attempt at a radical cut with early modern war discourse: both theorists clearly rejected the assumption of a 'justice' of war—albeit with diametrically opposed arguments. The two Prussian theorists established the argumentative framework for modern war discourse in the dichotomy between a political and a legal primacy—which, it must be noted again, did not coincide with the war discourses of political practice in the revolutionary era. Here, modern efforts at homogenization and unification were opposed by the plurality of legal, moral, and political justifications of war.

The aim of this chapter was to highlight the constitutive importance of the French Revolution for the formation of the modern discourse on war. Not only was modern warfare born at this time,[280] but so too was the modern discourse of the (de)legitimation of war. When Napoléon was finally defeated by the Sixth Coalition (and then again by the Seventh Coalition, at the Battle of Waterloo), the major European powers sought to reorder Europe at the Congress of Vienna in 1814/15—which is the subject of the next chapter. But in the period of supposed 'restoration' that now began, the Revolution continued to exert a dialectical influence on international relations. Early nineteenth-century discourse of war and normativity was clearly shaped by the experience of the revolutionary people's wars. The Revolution had reordered the world. It was necessary to react. If a new revolutionary danger was to be averted, the European monarchs had to control and oppress the new narratives of justified violence and international order.

The revolutionary and Napoleonic epoch was not only 'the connection between the early modern feudal state system and the bourgeois social order since the 19th century'.[281] It was, at the same time, the link between pre-modern and modern conceptions of war, law(making), and international order. Consequently, when it comes to the genealogy of modern war discourse, what I asserted at the beginning of this chapter can now be confirmed: in the beginning, there was Napoléon.

---

[280] Bell (n. 56).
[281] Frevert, 'Auftakt zum 19. Jahrhundert: Die Neuordnung der Welt im Zeitalter Napoleons', in B. Aschmann (ed.), *Durchbruch der Moderne? Neue Perspektiven auf das 19. Jahrhundert* (2019) 29, at 34.

4
Birth of an International Order

4.1 Introduction: Peace and Coercion after an Epoch of War

After war came peace—after anarchy came law and order. This is, in crudely simplified terms, how the anti-Napoleonic coalition itself assessed the results of the Congress of Vienna in 1814/15. Not only had France revolutionized European warfare, but it had also transformed the European discourse on the legitimacy of war. The victorious monarchies, in turn, were now focused on securing a lasting peace in Europe. This goal was largely achieved—if 'peace' is defined as the absence of violence between the major European powers. Some scholars have therefore called the nineteenth century the 'most peaceful century in modern history'.[1] Some speak of a '100-year peace' between the major European powers[2]—even if, to be precise, this peace in fact consisted of two different phases interrupted by the Crimean War and the Italian and German Wars of Unification.

In search of reasons for this long European Great Power peace, important innovations in the international order founded in 1814/15 stand out. Undoubtedly, there were fundamental continuities from early modern times and even from Greek and Roman antiquity.[3] And yet, viewed from a perspective of *longue durée*, it becomes clear that the Vienna Order differed considerably from earlier 'international' orders. Its political as well as normative core was the institutionalization of a new type of Great Power diplomacy under the guiding principles of the Concert of Europe.[4] Multilateral crisis communication, consolidated at congresses and conferences, not only enabled the building of solidarity and interpersonal trust between princes and diplomats.

---

[1] J. Levy, *War in the Modern Great Power System. 1494–1975* (1983), at 90 ff., 138; K.J. Holsti, *Peace and War: Armed Conflicts and International Order, 1648–1989* (1991), at 142; M. Schulz, *Normen und Praxis. Das europäische Konzert der Großmächte als Sicherheitsrat, 1815–1860* (2009), at 5.

[2] K. Polanyi, *The Great Transformation. The Political and Economic Origins of Our Times* (1944), at 16; H. Kissinger, *A World Restored. Metternich, Castlereagh and the Problems of Peace, 1812–22* (1957), at 5; Holsti (n. 1), at 142; Schulz (n. 1), at 5; J. Osterhammel, *The Great Transformation. A Global History of the Nineteenth Century* (2014), Chapter 4; R.J. Evans, *The Pursuit of Power: Europe, 1815–1914* (2017).

[3] See Chapter 2.

[4] M. Holbraad, *The Concert of Europe: A Study in German and British International Theory, 1815–1914* (1970); P.W. Schroeder, *The Transformation of European Politics, 1763–1848* (1994); Schulz (n. 1); J. Mitzen, *Power in Concert: The Nineteenth-Century Origins of Global Governance* (2013); M. Jarrett, *The Congress of Vienna and its Legacy: War and Great Power Diplomacy after Napoleon* (2013); G. Sluga, *The Invention of International Order: Remaking Europe after Napoleon* (2021).

It also increased the role of international norms in an unprecedented way—but not only in the heyday of international law during the second half of the century. Rather, even at this stage, European international law was attributed a pacifying effect that it had not possessed to such an extent hitherto. From 1814/15 on, international law was understood as an integral part of European 'civilization', 'culture', and 'progressiveness'. The course for modern international law as a 'gentle civilizer of nations'[5] was already set in the first half of the century.

As I will argue in this chapter, the rising importance of international normativity was also significant in the field of the use of force: from now on, international conflicts were to be settled peacefully by the Great Powers. Hegemonic and imperial ambitions were to be constrained. Pan-European war was to be avoided at all costs.[6] The revolution of the people was followed by a revolution of Great Power diplomacy. If the French Revolution had given birth to the modern discourse of (nationalist) war justifications, 'Vienna 1814/15' gave birth to the modern order of international violence.

This had far-reaching consequences that research to date has barely acknowledged (Chapter 4.2). The early modern war justifications, which had been relatively vague,[7] were now gradually narrowed. The Concert's institutionalized peace became the new norm in European international relations. Consequently, the political *and* normative roots of the modern prohibition of wars of aggression under international law are not to be found in the early twentieth century,[8] but in the early nineteenth century—despite the lack of a codified prohibition of war or force.

Paradoxically, however, interstate violence was not unfamiliar to the Vienna order—neither factually nor normatively. The discourse on war remained susceptible to competing interests and norms among the Great Powers. Moreover, the Concert as the central institution of the Viennese order not only limited, but also legitimized violence (Chapter 4.3). Coordinated concert diplomacy served to pacify relations between Great Powers, but it also enabled the latter to govern medium and small powers more effectively. And it was only the Great Powers peace within Europe that made the 'successful bellicism of European states outside Europe' possible.[9] Peace, coercion, and imperialism went hand in hand. It is these 'normative paradoxes'[10] that will be analysed in this chapter.

---

[5] M. Koskenniemi, *The Gentle Civilizer of Nations. The Rise and Fall of International Law 1870–1960* (2002), at 494.

[6] J. Dülffer, M. Kröger, and R.-H. Wippich, *Vermiedene Kriege: Deeskalation von Konflikten der Großmächte zwischen Krimkrieg und Erstem Weltkrieg, 1865–1914* (1997); G.J. Ikenberry, *After Victory. Institutions, Strategic Restraint, and the Rebuilding of Order after Major Wars* (2001), Chapter 4; Jarrett (n. 4).

[7] Tischer, 'Princes' Justifications of War in Early Modern Europe: the Constitution of an International Community by Communication', in L. Brock and H. Simon (eds), *The Justification of War and International Order: From Past to Present* (2021) 365.

[8] Yet this is the prevailing research opinion to this day; see Introduction and Chapter 2.

[9] D. Langewiesche, *Der gewaltsame Lehrer. Europas Kriege in der Moderne* (2019), at 86.

[10] Honneth and Sutterlüty, 'Normative Paradoxien der Gegenwart', in H.-G. Soeffner and K. Kursawe (eds), *Transnationale Vergesellschaftungen* (2013) 897; T. Hippler and M. Vec (eds), *Paradoxes of Peace in Nineteenth Century Europe* (2015).

4.2 Towards a Modern Order of International Violence

For a long time, scholarly reflections on the nineteenth-century European peace rarely addressed the concept of the 'European Concert of Great Powers'. Realist approaches tended to regard the 'Vienna System' as a particularly successful result of the European politics of equilibrium. The Concert was mostly ignored, equated with the balance of power and/or the Holy Alliance. A comprehensive study of the European Concert combining theory and practice, however, has been lacking for a long time. This changed with the declining popularity of realism after the end of the Cold War. Paul W. Schroeder's study on the *Transformation of European Politics. 1763-1848*, published in 1994, was crucial in paving the way for constructivist-inspired interpretations of the Concert. Now, the Congress of Vienna was seen as a 'decisive turning point', leading to a fundamental transformation of diplomatic culture, procedures, and norms.[11] This was indeed also a transformation 'from eighteenth-century bellicism to the idea of the Concert', as Matthias Schulz has put it.[12]

But what exactly *was* the 'Concert'? Winfried Baumgart has aptly defined it as 'the mode of consultation and cooperation among the major European powers for the purpose of settling or overcoming international crises and of ending and preventing wars'.[13] More generally, the Concert involved 'a group of great powers working together in a permanent and institutionalized way with the aim of shaping and maintaining the international order as well as managing change within that order'.[14] As a 'network of institutions geared toward cooperation',[15] it represented a form of governance, of 'public international power', since states assumed international responsibility through shared intentionality and thus developed collective authority.[16] It is true that the nineteenth-century Concert of Europe was also based on a 'balance of power system with built-in checks'; however, this balance of power was 'reformed, multipolar, and intertwined'.[17] It was no longer a mechanical political principle, but rather a central factor of normative ordering.[18] Power and normativity were by no means mutually exclusive in the Concert.

---

[11] Schroeder (n. 4), at vii–ix.
[12] Schulz (n. 1), at 36.
[13] W. Baumgart, *Vom Europäischen Konzert zum Völkerbund. Friedensschlüsse und Friedenssicherung von Wien bis Vesailles* (1974), at 1.
[14] Müller and Rauch, 'Machtübergangsmanagement durch ein Mächtekonzert—Plädoyer für ein neues Instrument zur multilateralen Sicherheitskooperation', 4 *Zeitschrift für Friedens- und Konfliktforschung* (2015) 36, at 49.
[15] Evans (n. 2), 59.
[16] Mitzen (n. 4), at 11.
[17] Gruner, 'Was There a Reformed Balance of Power System or Cooperative Great Power Hegemony?', 97 *The American Historical Review* (1992) 725.
[18] Schulz (n. 1), at 591.

For the genealogy of the modern discourse of war justifications to be developed here, the more recent liberal institutionalist and constructivist studies on the Concert are highly relevant. However, a closer look reveals an astonishing lacuna even in the most innovative research on the Concert's 'culture of peace'.[19] So far, there has been barely any attempt to critically relate it to the thesis of *liberum ius ad bellum*. This may be due to researchers' focus on the dramatically increasing legalization of international relations, particularly in the second half of the nineteenth century.[20] This focus may have obscured the fact that the normative roots of the modern institutionalization of the discourse of international violence *(ius contra bellum)* can already be found in the first half of the century—in the early phase of the Concert. With regard to the discourse on war and order, David Kennedy's assumption once again proves true: histories of international law in the nineteenth century are often limited to the century's 'last five minutes'.[21] This narrow focus will be abandoned in the present chapter by tracing the formation of the modern order of international violence to 'Vienna 1814/15' and the political and legal discourses related to it.

The Emergence of the Concert between Revolution and Reform

It was the third anti-French coalition that would pave the way for the genesis of the Concert. In 1804/05, Tsar Alexander I and Prime Minister William Pitt envisaged a new international order for the post-Napoleonic period. It should not come as a surprise that for Pitt and Alexander, peace was to be based on Russian and British power. But both knew that power alone was not enough to preserve peace. They also relied on the power of normativity and, more precisely, on international treaty law: Alexander I understood the restoration of international law as a central wartime objective, '*qu'en même temps le droit des gens, qui règle les rapports de la fédération européenne, aura été rétabli sur ses véritables principes*'.[22]

In a very similar vein, Pitt set the aim

> to form a treaty to which all the principal Powers of Europe should be parties, by which their respective rights and possessions, as they shall then have been

---

[19] Ibid., at 4.
[20] Chapter 2.3.
[21] Kennedy, 'International Law and the Nineteenth Century: History of an Illusion', 65 *Nordic Journal of International Law* (1996) 385, at 391. Kennedy's argument has recently been reiterated by Lauren Benton and Lisa Ford with regard to the 'origins of international law' in the British Empire; see L.A. Benton and L. Ford, *Rage for Order. The British Empire and the Origins of International Law, 1800–1850* (2016).
[22] '... that at the same time the law of nations, which regulated the relations of the European federation, is restored to its true principles', quoted from J. ter Meulen, *Der Gedanke der Internationalen Organisation in seiner Entwicklung* (1968), at 122.

established, shall be fixed and recognized; and They should all bind Themselves mutually to protect and support each other, against any attempt to infringe them.[23]

This new peace treaty, Pitt argued,

> should re-establish a general and comprehensive System of Public Law in Europe, and provide, as far as possible, for repressing future attempts to disturb the general tranquillity, and above all, for restraining any projects of Aggrandizement and Ambition similar to those, which have produced all the calamities inflicted on Europe since the disastrous era of the French Revolution.[24]

Alexander I and Pitt's draft peace conceptions clearly pointed beyond both a mere peace treaty with France and a defensive alliance against it. After victory over Napoléon, the European order had to be guaranteed in a strong treaty framework, protected from aggressors by the 'principal powers of Europe'.[25] Ten years before the 1814/15 reorganization, its central elements were already anticipated:

first, the Final Act of Vienna;
second, the Concert of Europe.

The 'transformation of political thinking' described by Schroeder[26] can thus be clearly identified in emerging peace conceptions such as those of Alexander I and Pitt. Both material and ideational factors were important prerequisites for this: the trauma of the Revolutionary and Napoleonic Wars had significantly strengthened the monarchs' commitment to peace, mutual solidarity, political restraint, and a willingness to compromise as fundamental principles of Great Power diplomacy.[27] In a dialectical way, the war made it necessary for the monarchs to engage in co-operative relations with each other and to build mutual trust.

All the monarchs and ministers involved in the formation of the Concert were influenced not only by the events of the French Revolution, but also by the political philosophy of the Enlightenment.[28] This was especially true for Kant's peace project: it was not only Kant's personal disciples such as Friedrich von Gentz who were

---

[23] 'Extract from an Official Communication made to the Russian Ambassador at London, on the 19 January, 1805', in House of Commons [UK], *Miscellaneous Papers. Also, Treaties with Foreign Powers* (1814–1815), at 264.
[24] *Ibid.*
[25] *Ibid.*
[26] Schroeder, 'The Transformation of Political Thinking, 1787–1848', in J. Snyder and R. Jervis (eds), *Coping with Complexity in the International System* (1993) 47.
[27] Mitzen (n. 4); Ikenberry (n. 6).
[28] Jarrett (n. 4), at 72–84.

familiar with the idea of a 'federative system of European states'.[29] Other peacemakers of 1814/15 also explicitly referred to Kant's perpetual peace and his idea of a permanent congress of states, understood as multilateral diplomatic meetings.[30] To some extent, theory and practice interacted in the discourse on war and peace.

But there were also unilateral interests: Great Power ambitions and the Concert were no strange bedfellows at all. Great Britain was particularly concerned that a stable concerted Great Power peace should be achieved on the continent in order to focus on its global 'web of British connections'[31] and the resulting imperial 'inter-polity relations'.[32] London internalized the normative foundations of the European peace order more strongly than any other Great Power. It would go on to vehemently defend this political, normative, and economic order.[33] To this end, Britain even renounced territorial gains at the Congress of Vienna.

The narrower starting point for the Concert in terms of international law was the Treaty of Chaumont (1/9 March 1814), signed at the Congress of Châtillon (5 February/19 March 1814). Here, British Foreign Minister Viscount Castlereagh (who had also contributed to Pitt's peace draft of 1805) persuaded the Allies to take joint action against Napoléon: no separate peace was to be concluded, of the type being considered by Metternich and Alexander I: Napoléon was to be overthrown, Europe was to be jointly reorganized.[34] Even before the Congress of Châtillon, Castlereagh had stressed that the

> present Confederacy may be considered as the union of nearly the whole of Europe against the unbounded and faithless ambition of an individual .... As opposed to France, a peace concluded in concert, though less advantageous in its terms, would be preferable to the largest concessions received from the enemy as the price of disunion[35]

Much in this sense, the Treaty of Chaumont established the Quadruple Alliance (Preamble and Article 3). As the title suggests, this was an anti-French defensive alliance, concluded by the four anti-Napoleonic Great Powers for twenty years. But the Quadruple Alliance was clearly more than that: in Article 1 of the Treaty

---

[29] Gentz, 'Ueber de Pradt's Gemälde von Europa nach dem Kongreß von Aachen', in G. Schlesier (ed.), *Kleinere Schriften* (1839) 88; on Gentz, see also R. Cahen, *Friedrich Gentz (1764–1832): Penseur post-Lumières et acteur du nouvel ordre européen* (2017).

[30] Schulz (n. 1), at 42, 44 ff.; For Kant's project of international legalization, see Chapter 3.3.

[31] J. Darwin, *The Empire Project. The Rise and Fall of the British World-System, 1830–1970* (2009), at 1.

[32] Benton and Ford (n. 21); Benton, 'Protection Emergencies: Justifying Measures Short of War in the British Empire', in L. Brock and H. Simon (eds), *The Justification of War and International Order: From Past to Present* (2021) 167.

[33] Holbraad (n. 4) at 139; Schulz (n. 1), at 596.

[34] Holbraad (n. 4) at 136; Schulz (n. 1), at 56.

[35] 'Castlereagh to Cathcart (No. 65.) Foreign Office, September 1813', in C.K. Webster, *British Diplomacy, 1813–1815: Select Documents Dealing with the Reconstruction of Europe* (1921), at 19 ff.

of Chaumont, the Great Powers expressed their explicit will to establish a general European peace—'in perfect concert'.[36]

The catalyst for the foundation of the latter was undoubtedly the Congress of Vienna, originally planned as a brief meeting to confirm and supplement the provisions of the First Peace of Paris (Treaty of Paris)[37]—as a 'European peace enforcement congress'.[38] However, the Vienna negotiations would last nine months, from 18 September 1814 to 9 June 1815. Myths and legends have grown up around this marathon negotiation: rarely in history has there been so much intrigue, greed, espionage, sex, and splendour in one place, as Adam Zamoyski has observed.[39] The lavish balls and festivities earned the spectacle in Vienna great admiration, but also drew harsh criticism. Charles Joseph de Ligne's *bon mot* about the Congress has become famous: '*Le congrès danse beaucoup, mais il ne marche pas.*'[40]

But the Congress was by no means all parties and dancing. Rather, the monarchs and their ministers were focused on the comprehensive territorial—and normative—reorganization of Europe. The Napoleonic conquests were to be redistributed; 'legitimate' dynasties were to be reinstated—without, however, 'restoring' the *ancien régime*.[41] The Great Powers were not squeamish in their aim to reorder Europe. According to Dieter Langewiesche,

> the new legitimacy always emerged from a breach of legitimacy. In their willingness to do so, the princely breakers of legitimacy were no different from the revolutionary ones. Probably never before in Europe had so many states been wiped out in so few decades.[42]

This becomes particularly clear with regard to the German lands. While there had been no less than 314 sovereign dominions in the Old Empire, now only 35 states and 4 free cities remained in the German Confederation (*Deutscher Bund*). The formation of modern international order was accompanied by an increasing standardization of its legally equal subjects: sovereign states.

---

[36] For an account of the conceptual history of the 'Concert of Europe', see Schulz (n. 1), at 36–9.

[37] Art. 32 of the First Peace of Paris (1814) provided that within two months all belligerents would send delegates to Vienna 'to settle in a general congress the arrangements which shall complete the provisions of the present treaty': '*Dans le délai de deux mois, toutes les puissances qui ont été engagées de part et d'autre dans la présenté guerre, enverront des plénipotentiaires à Vienne, pour régler, dans un congrès général, les arrangemens qui doivent compléter les dipositions du présent traité*'; see *Traité de paix entre la France et les puissances alliées, conclu a Paris, le 30 Mai 1814, et traités et conventions signés dans la même ville le 20 Novembre 1815* (1815), at 27.

[38] E.R. Huber, *Deutsche Verfassungsgeschichte seit 1789*, vol. 1 (1990), at 543 ff.

[39] A. Zamoyski, *Rites of Peace: The Fall of Napoleon and the Congress of Vienna* (2007).

[40] '*Le congrès danse beaucoup, mais il ne marche pas*'—literally at first probably '*Le congrès ne marche pas, il danse*'; on the genesis of the quotation, see G. Büchmann, *Geflügelte Worte. Der Citatenschatz des Deutschen Volkes* (1882), at 357.

[41] Evans (n. 2), at 60 ff.

[42] Langewiesche (n. 9), at 80 ff.

A central motive for convening the Congress of Vienna was therefore to deal with territorial conflicts between the Great Powers. It was particularly the Polish-Saxon Question which divided the alliance. At its centre was Alexander's demand to rule as king over a united Poland. This Russian demand was linked to Prussia's claims to Saxon territory in order to restore its great power status, which it had lost in 1807. To the other Great Powers, these plans seemed disproportionate. Even more than Russia's territorial gains, Metternich feared a united Poland, which he associated with a breeding ground for nationalism and revolution—an existential threat to the multi-ethnic state of Austria.[43] In the winter of 1814/15, the Polish-Saxon Question brought the Great Powers to the brink of a new war. But a compromise was reached. Russia received large parts of Poland, but not Austrian Galicia or Prussian Posen; Prussia received two-fifths of Saxony, but the latter remained a kingdom; Austria gained territories in northern Italy and in the Adriatic; and Great Britain renounced territorial gains on the continent.[44]

In peacefully resolving the Polish-Saxon Question, the functioning of the Concert's diplomacy crystallized in a prototypical manner. The Great Powers met confidentially and clandestinely to settle conflicts between them and, by doing so, they prevented war in Europe.[45] However, this informal diplomatic practice had not been envisaged at first. In fact, Article 32 of the Treaty of Paris (30 May 1814) suggested that the whole international community of Europe (*société générale de l'Europe*)[46] should be involved in the continent's reorganization. French negotiator Talleyrand, however, succeeded in excluding smaller and medium-sized powers from the negotiations.[47] While the Committee of the Five Great Powers had initially been set up only to negotiate the Polish-Saxon Question, the Concert would no longer meet in public after its solution. Wilhelm von Humboldt concluded that the Committee was the true Congress of Vienna.[48]

So, were the spectacles of 'Vienna 1814/15' merely diplomatic facades, 'Potemkin villages' hiding the power-hungry grimaces of the Great Powers on their secret 'back stages'?[49] Some medium-sized powers and political commentators undoubtedly saw it this way. With the emergence of a two-class society of European powers, Spain refused to sign the Congress's Final Act until 1817. In 1883, Scottish international legal scholar James Lorimer wrote that 'the representatives of the smaller powers might, for the most part, just as well have stayed at home'.[50]

---

[43] Schroeder (n. 4), at 525 ff.
[44] W. Bleek, *Vormärz: Deutschlands Aufbruch in die Moderne* (2019), at 21 ff.
[45] Schroeder (n. 4), at 504; Jarrett (n. 4), at 358.
[46] W.G. Grewe, *The Epochs of International Law*, translated and revised by M. Byers (2000), at 430.
[47] See C.K. Webster, *The Congress of Vienna. 1814–1815: Publ. for Hist. Sect. of the Foreign Office* (1919), at 72; T. Lentz, *1815. Der Wiener Kongress und die Neugründung Europas* (2014).
[48] Webster (n. 47), at 75.
[49] For an account of Goffman in the context of diplomacy and the justification of war, see Chapter 2.4.
[50] J. Lorimer, *The Institutes of the Law of Nations. A Treatise of the Jural Relations of Separate Political Communities*, vol. 1 (1883), at 176.

Other commentators were more positive. One of them was the German constitutional lawyer Johann Ludwig Klüber, who was to become the 'great leading figure of pre-March liberalism'.[51] Klüber had attended the Congress of Vienna as part of the Prussian delegation and edited the Congress records in eight volumes. In 1816, Klüber wrote that the Congress of Vienna concluded:

> a quarter of a century, which equals a millennium, if one measures it by the amount and variation of its most important events, especially by the misfortunes for states and mankind. Great, immense was the task, the solution of which was incumbent upon that gathering. A world political hurricane had wreaked havoc in the European community, not only geographically and politically, but also in terms of morality and international law. It was expected that a moral order would be restored and ensured in the relations between states. Through it, states, as well as individuals, were to be compelled to return to the noble habit of not wanting anything unlawful.[52]

Despite—or because of—the diplomatic two-class society, Great Power meetings continued to be held following the Vienna model after 1815. According to Article 6 of the renewed Quadripartite Alliance Treaty (20 November 1815), the four victorious Great Powers should perpetuate their diplomatic meetings 'for the maintenance of general peace' in Europe.[53] The ambassadorial conferences now established monitored compliance with the Paris Peace Treaties. But they did more than this: they also served as broader discussions on the political implementation of key provisions of the Final Act of the Vienna Congress,[54] such as the formal outlawing of the slave trade,[55] one of the few non-European aspects of the multilateral negotiations.

This practice of multilateral, informal, and confidential diplomacy between the Great Powers was finally consolidated at the Congress of Aix-la-Chapelle in September 1818. Unlike in Vienna, Aix-la-Chapelle dispensed with pompous balls and lavish festivities.[56] Any public was excluded from the diplomatic meetings. For the European Concert, 'Aix-la-Chapelle 1818' was decisive. After its defeat in 1814/15, France accepted the invitation to be consulted under Article 6 of the Quadruple Alliance of November 1815.[57] With this, France became a member of the '*concert*

---

[51] G. Schuck, *Rheinbundpatriotismus und politische Öffentlichkeit zwischen Aufklärung und Frühliberalismus. Kontinuitätsdenken und Diskontinuitätserfahrung in den Staatsrechts- und Verfassungsdebatten der Rheinbundpublizistik* (1994), at 93.
[52] J.L. Klüber, *Uebersicht der diplomatischen Verhandlungen des Wiener Congresses* (1816).
[53] 'Protocol of the French Accession to the Quadripartite Alliance', in W.G. Grewe (ed.), *Fontes Historiae Iuris Gentium (FHIG), Sources Relating to the History of the Law of Nations*, vol. 3/1: 1815–1945 (1992) 104 ff.
[54] Schulz (n. 1), at 63.
[55] F. Klose, *In the Cause of Humanity. A History of Humanitarian Intervention in the Long Nineteenth Century* (2021), Chapter 5.
[56] H. Duchhardt, *Der Aachener Kongress 1818. Ein europäisches Gipfeltreffen im Vormärz* (2018).
[57] Holbraad (n. 4), at 24; Schulz (n. 1), at 70 ff.

diplomatique entre les cinq course, ayant pour but unique et explicite le maintien de la paix générale.[58] Once again, the Congress Protocol underlined that it was only the Concert that could guarantee a lasting European peace.[59]

Indeed, the hope of the peacemakers of 1814/15 to establish a peaceful order among the Great Powers through a new type of confidential diplomacy was successful until 1914—albeit interrupted by the mid-century military conflicts. As I argue in the following section, this was mainly due to a normative achievement which has so far been overlooked in research. For with the unprecedented institutionalization of a new type of multilateral diplomacy in the sense of Kant's *permanenten Staatencongress* ('permanent congress of states'), the central norm of the modern international order began to emerge not after the First World War, but in 'Vienna 1814/15': the legal prohibition of aggressive war.

Against War: Political and Normative Contours of a Modern Order of International Violence

The Vienna Peace Order was accompanied by a normative reordering of international violence in Europe: from now on, the legitimacy of any decision to go to war was measured by the European Concert in terms of whether it posed a threat to the peace order of 1814/15. The Peace of Vienna thus became an international norm.

This was a historical novelty. Admittedly, it is true that also in the early modern period, despite de facto 'bellicosity',[60] interstate peace was regarded as the desired norm in 'international' relations.[61] With the emergence of the European Concert, however, the safeguarding of peace became the responsibility of a largely stable international institution for the first time in modern history. If the 'communication community'[62] in the early modern discourse of war (de)legitimization extended across a multitude of hierarchically unequal sovereign actors, in the Concert it was centralized, narrowed, and thus unified among legal equals. This process of unification was by no means completed in the context of the Treaty of Westphalia

---

[58] 'Quadripartite Alliance of the Great Powers (20 November 1815)', in W.G. Grewe (ed.), *Fontes Historiae Iuris Gentium (FHIG), Sources Relating to the History of the Law of Nations*, vol. 3/1: 1815–1945 (1992) 100, at 103 ff.

[59] Art. 3 of the 'Protocol of the French Accession to the Quadripartite Alliance/Aix-la-Chapelle' (15 November 1818), in W.G. Grewe (ed.), *Fontes Historiae Iuris Gentium (FHIG), Sources Relating to the History of the Law of Nations*, vol. 3/1: 1815–1945 (1992) 104, at 105.

[60] Burkhardt, 'Die Friedlosigkeit der Frühen Neuzeit. Grundlegung einer Theorie der Bellizität Europas', 24 *Zeitschrift für historische Forschung: ZHF* (1997) 509.

[61] A. Tischer, *Offizielle Kriegsbegründungen in der Frühen Neuzeit. Herrscherkommunikation in Europa zwischen Souveränität und korporativem Selbstverständnis* (2012); Tischer (n. 7).

[62] *Ibid.*

of 1648, as is often erroneously claimed.[63] It can only be identified with historical accuracy since the French Revolution or, reacting dialectically to it, the Viennese Order.[64]

So, the clocks were not turned back to the *Ancien Régime* period in 1814/15— even if the term 'restoration', coined by the conservative Swiss constitutionalist Karl Ludwig von Haller, suggests just that. But this term is highly misleading, for at the Congress of Vienna, 'restoration' did not become a guiding principle at all.[65] Rather, the nascent modern nation-state now received its sovereignty in a territorial sense,[66] which at the same time was increasingly depersonalized, i.e. transferred from the monarch to the nation-state.[67] The anti-revolutionary, dynastic legitimacy argument of 1814/15 did nothing to change this.

In the Vienna Peace Order, the comprehensive contractual regulation of borders was explicitly directed against hegemonic violence of the type that Europe had experienced under Napoléon.[68] The territorial and normative basis for this reorganization of international law was the Congress's Final Act (9 June 1815). This 'Charter of Europe',[69] with its 122 articles in the main text, and 17 supplements with another 118 articles, regulated the new borders of Europe in detail. Since a state had to sign all components of the Final Act to enjoy the legal protection of its own interests, the treaties were signed by all European parties except the papal delegation. As a result, they were under the special protection of all of Europe.[70]

The aim of the territorial reorganization of Europe was to reduce the likelihood of violent territorial conflicts and thus of wars: to this end, buffer zones were established between Great Powers. The most important example of this is the *Deutsche Bund* (German Confederation), founded at the Vienna Congress on 8 June 1815. The *Bund* served as a Central European buffer. As a defensive system of collective security, it was supposed to protect the relatively weak thirty-nine individual German states against illegitimate territorial ambitions, both from

---

[63] For critical accounts, see Osiander, 'Sovereignty, International Relations, and the Westphalian Myth', 55 *International Organization* (2001) 251; B. Teschke, *The Myth of 1648: Class, Geopolitics, and the Making of Modern International Relations* (2003).

[64] B. Buzan and G. Lawson, *The Global Transformation: History, Modernity and the Making of International Relations* (2015).

[65] R. Stauber, *Der Wiener Kongress* (2014), at 11 ff.; for a critical account, see also A. Fahrmeir, *Europa zwischen Restauration, Reform und Revolution 1815–1850* (2012), at 143.

[66] For a nuanced account, see L.A. Benton, *A Search for Sovereignty. Law and Geography in European Empires, 1400–1900* (2010); Steiger, 'Das natürliche Recht der Souveränität der Völker – Die Debatten der Französischen Revolution 1789–1793', in J. Fisch (ed.), *Die Verteilung der Welt. Selbstbestimmung und das Selbstbestimmungsrecht der Völker* (2011) 51; J. Bartelson, *War in International Thought* (2017), at 88.

[67] Evans (n. 2), at 60.

[68] Jarrett (n. 4).

[69] Adapted from Webster (n. 47), at 6; see also Hull, 'The Great War and International Law: German Justifications of "Preemptive Self-Defense"', in L. Brock and H. Simon (eds), *The Justification of War and International Order: From Past to Present* (2021) 183.

[70] Webster (n. 47), at 82.

within and without.[71] However, the Confederation was no sovereign actor in its own right. It was therefore unpopular among German *Vormärzler* (pre-March activists)[72]—not least because Austria held the presiding power in the Federal Convention (*Bundesversammlung*) in Frankfurt. Metternich knew how to use imperial interventions (*Reichsexekution*) to repress national and liberal aspirations in the German states.[73] The *Bund* was thus merely a 'passive ordering factor in the European state system':[74] preservation of the Vienna Order against wars of aggression was its central task.

Another innovative 'tool of diplomacy and statecraft'[75] was the legal institution of neutrality. On 20 November 1815, Switzerland's 'perpetual neutrality' (*la neutralité perpétuelle*) was declared at the Congress of Vienna. The Great Powers saw the neutrality of a state in the centre of Europe which was shaped by German, French, and Italian nationalities as being 'in the political interests of the whole of Europe'.[76] For the member states of the Holy Alliance—Russia, Prussia, and Austria—this was all the more true, given that the decision concerned a republic.[77] Neutralizing politically disputed territories and regions underscored the Great Powers' desire to maintain European peace.[78]

This contradicts the widespread view, according to which the (alleged) 'free right to wage war' and the institution of neutrality under international law were two sides of the same coin, as Wilhelm Grewe put it.[79] Liberal legal scholar Hersch Lauterpacht would also refer to 'the unrestricted right of war' as 'the historical foundation of absolute neutrality'.[80] While I will discuss the historical narratives of twentieth-century realist and liberal scholars in more detail later,[81] it is important to note here that the view that neutrality in some way supported the emergence of a *liberum ius ad bellum* in the nineteenth century is not at all convincing. On the contrary, neutrality became a central institution of peacekeeping,[82] intended to

---

[71] Art. II of the 'Constitution of the Germanic Confederation (8 June 1815)', in W.G. Grewe (ed.), *Fontes Historiae Iuris Gentium (FHIG), Sources Relating to the History of the Law of Nations*, vol. 3/1: 1815–1945 (1992) 174, at 175.

[72] Bleek (n. 44).

[73] Schroeder (n. 4), at 593–606; D. Willoweit, *Reich und Staat. Eine kleine deutsche Verfassungsgeschichte* (2013), at 81 ff.

[74] A. Doering-Manteuffel, *Die deutsche Frage und das europäische Staatensystem 1815–1871* (2010), at 6 ff.

[75] Abbenhuis, 'A Most Useful Tool for Diplomacy and Statecraft: Neutrality and Europe in the "Long" Nineteenth Century, 1815–1914', 35 *The International History Review* (2013) 1; M. Abbenhuis, *An Age of Neutrals. Great Power Politics, 1815–1914* (2014), at 1.

[76] '... in den politischen Interessen von ganz Europa'; see J.C. Bluntschli, *Das moderne Völkerrecht der civilisierten Staaten als Rechtsbuch dargestellt* (2nd edn, 1872), at 404.

[77] Ibid.

[78] Abbenhuis (n. 75).

[79] Grewe (n. 46), at 535.

[80] Lauterpacht, 'Neutrality and Collective Security [1936]', in E. Lauterpacht (ed.), *International Law. Being the Collected Papers of Hersch Lauterpacht* (2005) 611, at 623.

[81] See Chapter 10.

[82] Webster (n. 47).

prevent the escalation of violence between Great Powers.[83] As Prussian diplomat Chevalier Bunsen aptly summed it up in 1847: 'Aggressive warfare and neutrality are absolutely contradictory terms.'[84]

Defining state borders, buffer zones, and neutralized territories guaranteed by treaty law was the condition for the second structural element of the Vienna Order: the subordination of international force to the authority of the Concert. This was accompanied by a narrowing of the range of legitimate reasons for war, with numerous types of war and justifications of the early modern period, especially wars of succession and dynastic disputes, being normatively abolished.[85] Conquests and annexations had to be prevented at all costs in the name of the European peace.[86] Renunciation not only of annexations but also of wars of aggression now became the norm. It is true that aggressive war had already been considered problematic or illegitimate before.[87] However, it was not until the European Concert that an institutional framework was created for the gradual normative ordering of war at congresses and conferences. This was a thoroughly revolutionary development in the history of international relations and international law. The decision to go to war was now judged by the Concert against the backdrop of the new territorial order and its normative framework.

In this context, two basic patterns of justification for the use of force in the nineteenth century thus emerged, starting with the Congress of Vienna,[88] which have been preserved in principle in contemporary positive international law (see Chapter VII of the UN Charter).

War was now only legitimate:

first, to secure European peace, as legally and institutionally established by the Final Act of Vienna and the European Concert; and
second, for the self-defence—and thus the self-preservation—of a state in the face of aggression against its sovereign territory.

With this narrowing of the range of legitimate justifififications of war, the Vienna Order laid the foundation for the modern order of the international use of force. Violence that could not be justified in terms of either the Vienna Order or of self-defence was seen as aggression against European peace. The modern prohibition of war had begun to emerge.

---

[83] For the example of Belgium in World War I, see Chapter 9.3.
[84] Bunsen, 'The Chevalier Bunsen to Viscount Palmerston, 28. November 1847', in Foreign Office (ed.), *British and Foreign State Papers*, vol. 57: 1866–1867 (1871) 949.
[85] Schulz (n. 1), at 71.
[86] See also Hull (n. 69).
[87] Tischer 'Offizielle Kriegsbegründungen in der Frühen Neuzeit' (n. 61); Lesaffer, 'Aggression before Versailles', 29 *European Journal of International Law* (2018) 773.
[88] For an analysis of their continuing importance in the nineteenth century, see the following chapters, and especially Chapters 5 and 6.

Hybrid Normativity: Two Paths to the Prohibition of War Beyond International Treaty Law

It remained unclear, however, in which normative vocabulary this first modern norm—defined on the basis of state territory—for the prohibition of aggressive war in 1814/15 was to be formulated. For the Great Powers had *not* enacted a general prohibition of war under treaty law. Such a prohibition can be inferred neither from the Congress's Final Act of 1815 nor from the founding treaties of the Concert. Lord John Russell put it accurately in 1841 when he said that there was no 'undeviating rule applicable to all ... cases', but that decisions had to be made based on the circumstances of each case—'and upon these circumstances you must judge what course is best for the preservation of the peace of Europe, and the honour and dignity of the Crown'.[89]

From its creation, the Vienna Order was situated in the nexus between normativity and power.[90] One must not make the mistake of weighing one with the other. This order was not *either* normative *or* political, but always both: a highly political catalyst for the emergence of modern international norms. According to Lassa Oppenheim, the Final Act of Vienna had 'asserted for the first time the quasi-legislative authority of the international agreement'. International law was 'from now on often produced by legislative agreement'.[91] However, sensitive policy areas were shaped less by treaty law than by political and normative principles such as legitimacy, solidarity, trust, political restraint, and mediation among Great Powers.[92] As a result, whether certain norms were positive law, natural law, moral law, or political norms remained open at all times.[93] An important example is the principle of 'balance of power', which could be interpreted from a political but also a legal point of view.[94] Klüber aptly called it 'legally and politically considered, an indefinite idea'.[95] For this reason, he wished 'that the ambiguous word "political balance," might be banished from the language both of politics and of international law'.[96]

Hence, a closer look at the political and theoretical discourses of war (de)legitimization is likely to prove more revealing than an analysis focused solely on the

---

[89] Quoted from Schulz (n. 1), at 617; see also Simon, 'The Myth of *Liberum Ius ad Bellum*. Justifying War in 19th-Century Legal Theory and Political Practice', 29 *European Journal of International Law* (2018) 113.

[90] Simon (n. 89).

[91] Oppenheim, Die Zukunft des Völkerrechts", in *Festschrift für Karl Binding 1911* (1911) 141, at 146.

[92] A. Osiander, *The States System of Europe, 1640–1990. Peacemaking and the Conditions of International Stability* (1994); Vec, 'Grundrechte der Staaten. Die Tradierung des Natur- und Völkerrechts der Aufklärung', in 18 *Rechtsgeschichte* (2011) 66; Ikenberry (n. 6).

[93] See also Schulz (n. 1).

[94] Vec, 'De-Juridifying "Balance of Power" – A Principle in 19th Century International Legal Doctrine', *ESIL Conference Paper* (2011).

[95] J.L. Klüber, *Europäisches Völkerrecht* (1821), at 81.

[96] '... dass das zweideutige Wort "politisches Gleichgewicht", aus der Sprache sowohl der Politik als auch des Völkerrechtes, möge verbannt werden.', see ibid., at 83.

treaty law of 1814/15. As will be systematically analyzed below, a complex, multinormative discourse of war legitimization emerged. This discourse was marked by historical continuities, being based in part on early modern narratives of justifying wars. However, it also produced change. To sum up the following historical discourse analysis in a single argument: in this discourse of war justifications, the authority of the European Concert and its norms would remain abundantly clear. The political and normative ostracism of unilateral military force remained intact throughout the century.

Moreover, I argue, the discourse on the justification of war was permeated by two ways of norming war under international law: *first*, in 1814/15, a legal prohibition of war gradually began to emerge. Any use of force that potentially endangered the Vienna Order and its territorial boundaries violated the treaties guaranteed by almost all European powers. Even though this was still only a *desired* norm of positive law, i.e. not yet universally applicable (*de lege ferenda*), and its details only gradually became more defined, this emerging norm[97] already had its regulative effects. As the century progressed, the international community moved closer to this legal prohibition of aggression through treaties and state practice.[98] However, a general prohibition of law governed by positive law of war cannot be derived from this process. Violence which the Great Powers understood as not directly endangering the Vienna Order, such as regional wars or wars on the European 'periphery', remained largely unaffected by this emerging norm.[99]

Second, in the absence of a treaty-based prohibition of war, political practice as well as legal theory continued to refer to 'just war'. Legal doctrine in the first half of the century followed on relatively seamlessly from the justificatory tradition. In his 'often translated and reprinted'[100] *Droit des gens moderne de l'Europe* (1819), Johann Ludwig Klüber referred to Ompteda's bibliography as well as to ancient and early modern authors such as Cicero, Grotius, Bynkershoek, Burlamaqui, Kahle, Vattel, Moser, Kamptz, and Martens.[101] Klüber thus directly reaffirmed the long European tradition of justifying war in the vocabulary of *bellum iustum*. However, while Klüber also briefly mentioned Kant, he did *not* discuss the latter's rejection of the doctrine of 'just war' and the project of *ius contra bellum* related to it. This, too, is a clear sign that Klüber remained wedded to the traditional discourse.

In line with his early modern predecessors, Klüber began his chapter on the laws of war by stating that hostile relations between states arise 'through violations of

---

[97] On 'emerging norms', see Finnemore and Sikkink, 'International Norm Dynamics and Political Change', 52 *International Organization* (1998) 887, at 891; Deitelhoff, 'The Discursive Process of Legalization: Charting Islands of Persuasion in the ICC Case', 63 *International Organization* (2009) 33; see also Chapter 2.3.
[98] See Chapters 5 and 6.
[99] See also Schulz (n. 1), at 633; Hull (n. 69), at 185.
[100] R. von Mohl, *Die Geschichte und Literatur der Staatswissenschaften in Monographien dargestellt*, vol. 2 (1856), at 473.
[101] Klüber (n. 95), at 377–93.

rights,[102] real or threatened'. War was therefore 'just' for the state that was 'compelled to wage it for the protection of its rights', but 'unjust' for the state to which violations of rights were to be attributed.[103] Klüber therefore considered the purpose of a 'just war' to be 'satisfaction, or defence, or security, insofar as these cannot be obtained in any other way'.[104] On the other hand, war was 'unjust' for the state 'which is charged with violations of the law of the kind indicated' or which waged war only out of self-interest or wrong motives. Among the latter, Klüber counted lust for conquest, rapacity, 'prevention of the just increase of the power of another state', 'leaving the so-called political equilibrium', 'moral or religious crudeness of the other people', and 'true or supposed immorality of the same'.[105]

Another central legal treatise of the first half of the century was August Wilhelm Heffter's *Das europäische Völkerrecht der Gegenwart* (1844), published 25 years after Klüber's first edition of *Droit des gens moderne de l'Europe*. Heffter's work was soon to become a standard book in international legal scholarship, in Robert von Mohl's opinion even the 'best by far that exists in any language'.[106] Others praised it 'for its genuinely legal character'.[107] This was not by chance: Heffter was regarded as *the* international legal positivist par excellence in the first half of the century, 'one of the most recent and distinguished public international lawyers of Germany', as Henry Wheaton, the predominant Anglo-American public international lawyer of his time,[108] put it.[109] Heffter's turn to positivism was a continuation of the work of Martens and Klüber. In the study of international law, 'nothing significant' had 'been accomplished in Germany since Klüber', Heffter himself claimed.[110] Indeed, as a result of the political censorship during the *Vormärz* period, there had been a

---

[102] *Ibid.*, at 377.
[103] *Ibid.*, at 386.
[104] '*Genugthuung, oder in Verteidigung, oder in Sicherheit, so fern diese auf andere Art nicht zu erlangen ist.*', see *ibid.*, at 386.
[105] *Ibid.*
[106] Alphonse Rivier also agreed with Mohl; see A. Rivier, *Lehrbuch des Völkerrechts* (1889) at 61. As did F.F. Martens, *Völkerrecht. Das internationale Recht der civilisirten Nationen*, vol. 1 (1883), at vii, and P. Resch, *Das Völkerrecht der heutigen Staatenwelt Europäischer Gesittung. Für Studierende und Gebildete aller Stände* (2nd edn, 1890), at 24. Surprisingly, there is no in-depth study or annotated biography on Heffter. There is no brief biographical sketch of Heffter in *The Oxford Handbook of the History of International Law* either. But see Hueck, 'Pragmatism, Positivism and Hegelianism in the Nineteenth Century. August Wilhelm Heffter's Notion of Public International Law', in M. Stolleis and M. Yanagihara (eds), *East Asian and European Perspectives on International Law* (2004) 41.
[107] H. Rettich, *Zur Theorie und Geschichte des Rechts zum Kriege. Völkerrechtliche Untersuchungen* (1888), at 31.
[108] M.W. Janis, *The American Tradition of International Law. Great Expectations 1789–1914* (2004); H. Kleinschmidt, *Diskriminierung durch Vertrag und Krieg: Zwischenstaatliche Verträge und der Begriff des Kolonialkriegs im 19. und frühen 20. Jahrhundert* (2013), at 127; Liu, 'Henry Wheaton (1785–1848)', in B. Fassbender and A. Peters (eds), *The Oxford Handbook of the History of International Law* (2014) 1132.
[109] H. Wheaton, *Elements of International Law* [1836]. Edited, with Notes, by Richard Henry Dana (1866), at 16.
[110] A.W. Heffter, *Das europäische Völkerrecht der Gegenwart* (1844), at iv ff.

weakening of public law at German universities.[111] In this respect, Heffter's textbook pointed to a resurgent interest in the discipline in the 1840s.

So, what did one the most important representatives of international legal positivism think about the legitimacy of international force? Surprisingly or not, no major innovations can be found since Klüber's book. Like Klüber, Heffter held the view that a war was only justified if it was waged 'for the realization of legal purposes' ('*zur Realisirung rechtlicher Zwecke*').[112] But what did Heffter see as the basis for the legal character of war? The answer is surprising indeed, for even the 'pragmatist, Hegelian, and positivist'[113] Heffter continued to refer to the hardly pragmatic, hardly Hegelian, and hardly positivist theory of 'just war'. Heffter tried to integrate the latter into his positivist theory of international law.

It is true that Heffter equated the effects of an 'unjust war' with those of a 'just war'—and, analogously to Hegel, justified the indistinguishability between 'just' and 'unjust wars' by the absence of an earthly judge.[114] Nevertheless, Heffter *did* normatively distinguish between wars to defend against an 'unjust' attack and illegitimate wars of aggression.[115] On the one hand, the German scholar referred to the historical dialectic of war and international order when he argued that war replaced order with chaos, 'from which it must first arise anew'. On the other, however, Heffter normatively emphasized that

> the moral consequences of the unjust war [will be] different from those of the just, and never will mere reasons of political utility or morally good ends, without the existence of an imminent or already inflicted violation of rights, be able to remove the injustice of a war.[116]

War was, in other words, a state's ultimate self-help,[117] while its ultimate justification of war was the restoration of law and peace. In discussing (il)legitimate reasons for war, Heffter referred also—and of all things—to a passage in Friedrich II's *Anti-Machiavel*, according to which all wars were in accordance with justice, if their sole purpose was the defence against usurpers, the maintenance of legitimate

---

[111] R. von Mohl, *Staatsrecht, Völkerrecht und Politik*, vol. 1: Staatsrecht und Völkerrecht (1860), at 580; M. Stolleis, *Geschichte des öffentlichen Rechts in Deutschland*, vol. 2: Staatsrechtslehre und Verwaltungswissenschaft 1800–1914 (1992), at 81; M. Koskenniemi, *To the Uttermost Parts of the Earth. Legal Imagination and International Power, 1300–1870* (2021), at 959.
[112] Heffter (n. 110), at 195; see also Simon, 'Anarchy over Law? Towards a Genealogy of Modern War Justifications (1789–1918)', in L. Brock and H. Simon (eds), *The Justification of War and International Order: From Past to Present* (2021) 147.
[113] The formulation is based on the title of Hueck (n. 106).
[114] Heffter (n. 110), at 195; see also Wheaton (n. 109), at 368.
[115] Heffter (n. 110), at 195.
[116] *Ibid.*, at 195 ff.
[117] Heffter (n. 110), at 195; see also Wheaton (n. 109), at 368.

rights, the safeguarding of general liberty, and the prevention of violence and oppression by rising powers.[118]

In the international legal doctrine of the first half of the century, too, war was a state's *ultima ratio regum* for the defence of its rights.[119] Robert von Mohl argued that in 'such a case, the state is in the position of an individual who is in a state of self-defence and who is forced to use the utmost means to defend himself, and who is therefore also entitled to do so'.[120] Private-public analogies like this one were typical in contemporary scholarship on international law. While arguing in favour of a state's right to defend itself, Mohl was fully aware of the risks of the 'legal remedy of war'. According to Mohl, it was 'an uncertain one, because victory on the side of the right is by no means inevitable', a 'daring one ... , because in case of defeat not only the intended defence against injustice is not achieved, but easily a further and perhaps greater injury to right and interests is inflicted', and a painful one, 'which even in the best case is bought with the most painful sacrifices' and 'inevitably leads to innumerable human misery in its wake'. And yet, war waged in defence of a state's rights was unavoidable, Mohl argued, if 'not every right was to be finally exposed to the act of violence'. It was unilateral force sanctioned by law.[121]

But war was also ascribed the character of a *collectively legitimized* force in the legal doctrine of the first half of the nineteenth century. It was not only a legal instrument of the state, but also a legal instrument of the international order. Kaltenborn-Stachau referred to the international community as the actual authority for the (de)legitimization of the use of force in international law. To this end, he also drew analogies to state law: he argued that just as in private law physical execution was usually imposed on property, and in criminal law it was imposed on the person, in international law war was the 'peculiar execution of international legal decisions' ('*eigenthümliche Vollziehung internationaler Rechtssprüche*').[122] For according to Kaltenborn-Stachau, all 'individual rights of the peoples', those 'members of the organism of international law as a whole', were simultaneously also 'a matter for the international community'.[123]

War consequently derived its legitimacy not from the defence of the law of an individual state alone, but from the defence of the entire international peace order. According to Kaltenborn-Stachau, law was enforced by war as the 'final execution of legal claims' and by the totality of 'the international community'—

---

[118] '"*toutes les guerres qui n'auront pour but que de repousser des usurpateurs, de maintenir des droits légitimes, de garantir la liberté de l'univers et d'éviter les violences et les oppressions des ambitieux*", als "*conformes à la justice*"', Heffter (n. 110), at 194.

[119] The same is still true today for self-defence in the sense of Art. 51 of the UN Charter.

[120] R. von Mohl, *Encyklopädie der Staatswissenschaften* (1859), at 454.

[121] *Ibid.*

[122] K. von Kaltenborn-Stachau, *Kritik des Völkerrechts nach dem jetzigen Standpunkte der Wissenschaft* (1847), at 312.

[123] *Ibid.*

admittedly not as supreme state power, for this would turn international law into state law, but as international common power, which differs from state power in that it recognizes its members, the states, as sovereign.[124]

The aim was not to destroy the lawbreaker, Kaltenborn-Stachau emphasized, but 'only to maintain the rights that had not been recognized or had been violated, and in general to maintain the international order'.[125] War was to be separated from political arbitrariness. It was solely to serve the cause of European legal peace.

As can be seen here, Neff's distinction between 'perfect' and 'imperfect' wars[126] was unknown in contemporary legal doctrine. War, and not only 'measures short of war', such as reprisals[127] or interventions, continued to be referred to in recourse to just war theory. They were all part of the same legal escalation strategy, provided—and this was, as shown, the mandatory condition for both—that there had been a violation of rights. Before war was waged to sanction the violation of rights, according to Heffter, 'such measures of force' could be used 'whereby persons or things are subjected to a temporary injunction by the other party to pursue or defend its right, in order thereby to make the former yield or to pay a debt of satisfaction'.[128] War and 'measures short of war' were parts of the same order of justification.

As can be seen in the works of Klüber, Heffter, Wheaton, Zachariä, H.B. Oppenheim, Kaltenborn-Stachau, and somewhat later Mohl, legal doctrine in the first half of the nineteenth century by no means accepted war as an instrument of politics in the sense of a supposed *liberum ius ad bellum*. On the contrary, war was seen as a means of enforcing law, securing peace, and sanctioning violations of rights. The above-mentioned central narratives of justification in state practice were confirmed. The legal discourse of the early and mid-nineteenth century continued to rely on a modification of *bellum iustum*, although an increasingly strong commitment to positivist modification can be observed. But there was no break with the tradition of 'just war' in favour of a strictly positivist *ius contra bellum*, as demanded by Kant in his critique of early modern lawyers as 'tiresome comforters'.[129]

---

[124] *'freilich nicht als oberste Staatsgewalt, denn dadurch würde sich das Völkerrecht in Staatsrecht verwandeln, sondern als internationale Gemeinmacht, die sich dadurch von der Staatsgewalt unterscheidet, dass sie ihre Glieder, die Staaten als souveraine anerkennt'*, ibid.
[125] Ibid.; see also Z. von Lingenthal and K. Salomo, *Vierzig Bücher vom Staate. Regierungslehre* (1826), at 200 ff.
[126] See Chapter 2.3; S.C. Neff, *War and the Law of Nations: A General History* (2005), at 62; see I. Brownlie, *International Law and the Use of Force by States* (1963), at 27.
[127] Stephen C. Neff has aptly defined a 'reprisal' as 'an action which is inherently unlawful but which is permitted, exceptionally, as a means of counteracting a prior violation of law'; see Neff, 'Reprisals', in *The Encyclopedia of War* (2011).
[128] Heffter (n. 110), at 191.
[129] See Chapter 3.3.

For the normatively hybrid treatment of war in international legal doctrine reflected a central challenge: to find a legal framework for judging war in the context of an international order that constituted a normative proscription of war, but that had not yet prohibited the latter under treaty law.

'Positivists' without Positivism: A Methodological Tragedy

This lack of a contractual prohibition sometimes led to (self-)contradictory arguments in the treatises of the self-professed 'positivists'. Politics, law, and other normative spheres were not always sharply distinguished from one another. Klüber for instance listed 'exiting from the so-called political balance'—clearly a *political* act—, '*moral* or *religious* crudeness', and the 'true or supposed *immorality*' of a state as legal reasons for waging war on the opposing side.[130] This mixing of normative spheres is surprising, since, according to Klüber, law demanded 'only legality, not morality, not propriety, not prudence, not mere customs without moral necessity'.[131] Klüber clearly saw law as separable from morality and '*Staatsklugheit*' ('state wisdom').[132] In fact, Klüber himself referred to non-legal criteria. Religion, politics, and morality thus continued to play a relevant role in Klüber's discussion of legal reasons for war. Similar ambivalences can be identified in Heffter's discussion of (il)legitimate reasons for war. While the Berlin law professor emphasized that international law was not a 'mere morality of states or an aggregate of political maxims'[133] he, however, warned against the 'moral after-effects of unjust war'.[134]

These normative contradictions are related to the fact that legal scholarship in the early nineteenth century found itself in the unfortunate situation of, on the one hand, striving for the separation of law and morality introduced by Kant, yet, on the other, not finding a prohibition of war under international treaty law.

The fact that the legal scholars were to some extent bound to fail in their 'project of positivism'[135] can be seen in the numerous and pointed, sometimes polemical commentaries of their respective predecessors. Heffter, for example, complained that Martens, Günther, Schmalz, Klüber, Schmelzing, Pölitz, and Zachariä wanted to write the history of law based on treaties and conventions without being able to sufficiently justify this positivist character of law. According to Heffter, however, these authors were unable 'to consistently present the doctrines presented as positive'.[136] The positivist Heffter, however, was criticized as well. Kaltenborn-Stachau

---

[130] Klüber (n. 95), at 18.
[131] *Ibid.*
[132] *Ibid.*
[133] '*bloße Staatenmoral oder ein Aggregat politischer Maximen*': Heffter (n. 110), at vi.
[134] *Ibid.*, at 195 ff.
[135] M. García-Salmones Rovira, *The Project of Positivism in International Law* (2013).
[136] Heffter (n. 110), at 21.

claimed that Heffter did not always strictly distinguish between philosophy and positive law.[137] And even Kaltenborn-Stachau himself could be accused of having understood war as a legal remedy, while at the same time trusting not only in the 'deeply spiritual power of law' (*'intensive Geistesmacht des Rechts'*) but also 'in the just providence of God', so that 'even through war, in the course of the development of world history, every nation will come to its rights'.[138] Others went even further: in his *Systematischer Grundriss des praktischen europäischen Völkerrechts*, Julius von Schmelzing continued to refer to 'holy war'.[139] Tragically, the so-called 'positivist turn' in nineteenth-century international law lacked positivism.

After all, the doctrine of international law in the nineteenth century was still characterized by a hybridization of philosophical, natural, historical, and positive law traditions.[140] The distinction between 'rationalists' and 'empiricists'[141] thus only made limited sense. In many treaties, the boundaries between different legal traditions continued to be fluid. Parallel to positive law, the 'philosophical law of nations'[142] retained its importance—at least as an 'influential motive of ... positive [law]' (*'influenzirendes Motiv des Positiven'*),[143] a 'guiding principle of reason'[144] in the case where 'there is a lack of a positive norm'. In no other field was the latter truer than in the highly political field of the use of force.

Thus, the question of the legitimacy of war was closely linked to theoretical and methodological debates on valid sources of international law. In these debates, the indeterminacy of the sources of international law was recognized as a fundamental problem. In particular, Kant's separation between *Sein und Sollen* became the standard of criticism. Kant's writings had an enormous influence on legal theory in the first half of the century.[145] Kaltenborn-Stachau, for example, referred to Kant's numerous followers among legal scholars on the threshold of modernity, including Hufeland, Schaumann, Hoffbauer, Heydenreich, Schmid, Jakob, Abicht, Mellin, Pölitz, and Zachariä.[146] However, Kaltenborn-Stachau also claimed that

---

[137] Kaltenborn-Stachau (n. 122), at 210.
[138] *Ibid.*, at 315 ff.
[139] J. von Schmelzing, *Systematischer Grundriss des praktischen europäischen Völkerrecht, Dritter Theil* (1820), at 113.
[140] See also Vec, 'Sources of International Law in the Nineteenth-Century European Tradition: The Myth of Positivism', in S. Besson and J. d'Aspremont (eds), *The Oxford Handbook of the Sources of International Law* (2017) 121.
[141] Warnkönig, 'Die gegenwärtige Aufgabe der Rechtsphilosophie nach den Bedürfnissen des Lebens und der Wissenschaft', 7 *Zeitschrift für die gesamte Staatswissenschaft/Journal of Institutional and Theoretical Economics* (1851) 662, at 637.
[142] See e.g. Fallati, 'Die Genesis der Völkergesellschaft. Ein Beitrag zur Revision der Völkerrechtswissenschaft', 1 *Zeitschrift für die gesamte Staatswissenschaft* (1844) 160, at 160; Mohl (n. 120), at 404; Resch (n. 106), at 21.
[143] Heffter (n. 110), at 21.
[144] Mohl (n. 120), at 404.
[145] Rückert, 'Kant-Rezeption in juristischer und politischer Theorie (Naturrecht, Rechtsphilosophie, Staatslehre, Politik) des 19. Jahrhunderts', in M.P. Thompson (ed.), *John Locke und/and Immanuel Kant. Historische Rezeption und gegenwärtige Relevanz* (1991) 144.
[146] Kaltenborn-Stachau (n. 122), at 136 ff.

'the present standpoint of science' had transcended the merely 'aphoristic sketch' of Kant's theorem on international law.[147] Yet this assertion is not entirely convincing. Martti Koskenniemi has recently pointed out that the contemporary reception of Kant's work is difficult to measure.[148] Kant was 'not only complicated, but also ambivalent', as Joachim Rückert put it.[149]

This was also the view of many nineteenth-century legal scholars. Kant's work on international law and war drew not only substantive support, but also methodological criticism and contradiction. Tübingen scholar Leopold August Warnkönig saw a self-contradiction in Kant basing 'all real international law on treaties between nations' and allowing 'no natural, but only a positive law', although Kant's imperative for states to turn to positive law was, in the lawless state of nature, merely a 'moral obligation'.[150] The legal scholars of the early and mid-nineteenth century thus also criticized what has been explained in more detail above: Kant wanted to establish a strictly positive *ius contra bellum*, but could only justify this prohibition of war based on positive law in a non-legal, moral ought of reason.[151]

International legal scholars in the first half of the nineteenth century did not get beyond Kant's contradiction 'of himself'[152] on peremptory and provisional state law.[153] They had to accept it. In this respect, Kaltenborn-Stachau's demarcation from the 'indeterminacy of Kant's philosophy' is to be understood primarily as another attempt by a (would-be) positivist to demarcate himself from 'philosophical international law'.[154] However, not only legal philosophers, but also 'positivist' legal scholars continued to refer to Kant. In his textbook of 1847, Kaltenborn-Stachaus, for instance, agreed with Kant's rejection of war as a political means.[155] For all the criticism of its philosophical rationale, jurists held to the project of international legalization and also engaged in discussions on Kant's 'political project'[156] of *ius contra bellum*.

From the Trauma of War to the Institutionalization of Peace

The reason for this was partly the trauma of the Revolutionary Wars, which persisted for the first half of the century. For it was not only the monarchs and their ministers (see above), but also legal scholars who were clearly impressed by the

---

[147] *Ibid.*
[148] Koskenniemi (n. 111), at 876 n. 17.
[149] J. Rückert, *August Ludwig Reyschers Leben und Rechtstheorie. 1802–1880* (1974), at 306.
[150] Warnkönig (n. 141), at 640.
[151] Chapter 3.3.
[152] Warnkönig (n. 141), at 640.
[153] Kaltenborn-Stachau (n. 122), at 138.
[154] *Ibid.*, at 142.
[155] *Ibid.*, at 134.
[156] W.B. Gallie, *Philosophers of Peace and War: Kant, Clausewitz, Marx, Engels and Tolstoy* (1978), at 8.

'world hurricane' ('*Weltorkan*') of the Revolutionary Wars, as Klüber put it.[157] Heidelberg professor Karl Salomo Zachariä likewise emphasized that the 'war of the French Revolution' had shaken and reshaped the 'constitution of the European state of nations'. The trauma of the Revolutionary Wars was also reflected in the fear of new mass wars. Long before Moltke's oft-quoted—and oft-misunderstood[158]— speech in the *Reichstag* on 14 May 1890, the liberal Heidelberg legal scholar Heinrich Bernhard Oppenheim prognosticated in 1845 that the war of the future would no longer be a single war between two sovereigns in the sense of a duel. Rather, according to Oppenheim, it would be a general European mass war, a 'historical philosophical crisis' ('*allgemeiner Krieg, eine geschichtsphilosophische Krisis*').[159]

However, there was also hope. Oppenheim was optimistic that 'the present and the future are too mature and too wise' for specific wars of the past, and 'especially religious wars'.[160] He argued that wars of extermination or mere conquest should not and could no longer be waged in the 'civilized world' ('*civilisirten Welt*'). Oppenheim thus reaffirmed the Kantian connection between law, peace, and civilizational progress.[161]

But if previous types of war could be eliminated, why should new ones not be preventable? Like the political practice of their time, legal scholars put their faith in the progress of international law. From this perspective, the Napoleonic Wars appeared to liberal jurists from the pre-March period, such as Lorenz von Stein, to be a radical, violent caesura between an old and a new international order. In light of the differentiation of law since 1815, Stein argued around the middle of the century that this was a 'point of transition to a new era'.[162]

Lawyers of the first half of the century working on international law also saw the importance of the European Concert of Great Powers as a catalyst for the further emergence of the international normative order. Thus, they recognized the role of the European Concert as a guarantor of the new international order. Klüber saw in the 'system of Europe' created at the Congress of Vienna one of 'the greatest advances of human reason on the level trajectory of civilization'.[163] As a reaction to the Napoleonic Wars, Klüber argued, this system had preserved peace

---

[157] Klüber (n. 52), at 3.
[158] See also Peters, Schäfer, and Simon, '(Writing) International Legal Histories – Continuation of Politics by Other Means?: An Interview with Anne Peters and Raphael Schäfer', *Völkerrechtsblog* (17 September 2021), available at: https://voelkerrechtsblog.org/de/writing-international-legal-histories-continuation-of-politics-by-other-means/ (last visited 1 December 2022).
[159] H.B. Oppenheim, *System des Völkerrechts* (1845), at 272.
[160] *Ibid.*
[161] *Ibid.*, at 272.
[162] Koskenniemi (n. 111), at 961.
[163] '... größten Fortschritte der menschlichen Vernunft auf der ebenen Bahn der Civilization', J.L. Klüber, *Pragmatische Geschichte der nationalen und politischen Wiedergeburt Griechenlands, bis zu dem Regierungsantritt des Königs Otto* (1835), at xi ff.

by joint mediation, by congresses of monarchs and ministers, by exchanges of notes and protocols of diplomatic conferences, by means of protective and reconciliatory alliances, by peaceful, if necessary armed, interposition, even by precautionary military occupation, on the part of neutral powers.[164]

Zachariä praised the innovations of the Concert. The Kantian scholar wrote that, partly according to the wording, partly according to the spirit of the law, there existed in Europe 'an association embracing all peoples and powers of this part of the world, which, one may call it a state of nations or a league of nations, approaches the idea of a state association'.[165] According to Zachariä, the Congress of Vienna had given the latter 'state' a 'new constitution appropriate to the circumstances of the time':[166] with the Final Act of Vienna as its 'fundamental law' or 'constitutional document', the Protocol of the Congress of Aachen (Aix-la-Chapelle) as an 'organic law', and the pentarchy of the Great Powers as the autocratic supreme leadership of European affairs, the 'Directorium Europae'.[167] The European Concert was thus seen as a catalyst for progress and pacification.

The liberal H.B. Oppenheim basically agreed with this view when he contrasted the Concert with the 'old balance system' of the eighteenth century. According to Oppenheim, the latter had 'caused as many wars as it was intended to eliminate'.[168] Oppenheim also referred to the Concert's guarantee of territorial order and highlighted that after the Congress of Vienna, no state was allowed to make territorial changes without the approval of the Concert: 'Any unilateral possession, without the determination of the upper house of European diplomacy [the Concert, HS], would therefore, as an exit from the balance system, be to be considered a casus belli'.[169]

Liberal jurists of the mid-century, such as Zachariä, H.B. Oppenheim, and Kaltenborn-Stachau, thus assigned to the Concert of Great Powers the authority, as an institution of the international legal community, to watch over the preservation of peace and, if necessary, to enforce it. This was the argument put forward by Carl von Kaltenborn-Stachau.[170] According to him the pentarchy had 'taken over the execution, and in general the regulation of the legal relations of international life in recent times in the name of the entirety'. Thus, Kaltenborn-Stachau saw the pentarchy—at least 'for the time being' ('*für's Erste*')—as the representative of the international legal community, which had the right, but also the power, to 'bring

---

[164] Ibid.
[165] '... *ein alle Völker und Mächte dieses Weltteiles umfassender Verein, welcher sich, man mag ihn nun einen Völkerstaat oder einen Völkerbund nennen, der Idee eines Staatsvereines nähert*', K.S. Zachariä von Lingenthal, *Vierzig Bücher vom Staate. Regierungslehre* (1841), at 218.
[166] Ibid.
[167] Ibid., at 218–20.
[168] '... *so viele Kriege hervorgerufen, als es beseitigen sollte.*', Oppenheim (n. 159), at 272.
[169] Ibid., at 273.
[170] Kaltenborn-Stachau (n. 122), at 313.

disputed or violated rights of the peoples to recognition through martial execution.[171] In the shadow of the Revolutionary Wars, the Concert was seen as an institution that allowed for progress in the pacification of international relations and the expansion of international law.

At the same time, however, liberal lawyers of the first half of the century described the Concert only as a provisional institution. Due to its highly political character, many international lawyers had mixed feelings about the Concert: some called it a 'political balance',[172] while for other authors it was the foundation of international law or even a 'constitution existing in the state of nations'.[173] But liberal scholars of the first half of the century were also critical of the arbitrary rule of the Concert, which resulted from its highly political character. H.B. Oppenheim clearly addressed the ambivalences, which will be examined in more detail in the following section. In his view, the 'newer system of balance' of the eighteenth century had given way to 'an allied supremacy of the great powers, which, however, sits in judgment over war and peace, but decides according to its very own rules'.[174]

4.3 Peace through Coercion: Limitation as Legitimization of Violence

The fundamental paradox of the Vienna Order was its dual character as a frame of reference that both limited and legitimized violence. This was particularly evident in the central institution of this order. The European Concert of Great Powers was supposed to prevent a new hegemony in Europe and to preserve peace; with this aspiration, however, the Concert itself became the collective hegemon of the new international order.[175] The arbitrariness of individual states was thus transferred to the multilateral arbitrariness of the Concert. The Concert, with its far-reaching competences, established a *'tradition directoriale'*,[176] which to some extent continues today in the United Nations Security Council and its undemocratic constitution.[177]

---

[171] '*streitige oder verletzte Rechte der Völker durch kriegerische Execution zur Anerkennung zu bringen.*', ibid.
[172] Klüber (n. 95), at 83.
[173] '*in dem Völkerstaate bestehende Verfassung*', see K.S. Zachariä von Lingenthal, *Vierzig Bücher vom Staate. Regierungslehre* (1826), at 200.
[174] Oppenheim (n. 159), at 272.
[175] G.J. Simpson, *Great Powers and Outlaw States: Unequal Sovereigns in the International Legal Order* (2004).
[176] Arcidiacono, 'For a Genealogy of the United Nations Charter: The Directorial Tradition', 127 *Relations internationales* (2006) 5.
[177] Afoaku and Ukaga, 'United Nations Security Council Reform: A Critical Analysis of Englargement Options', 18 *Journal of Third World Studies* (2001) 149; Binder and Heupel, 'Rising Powers, UN Security Council Reform, and the Failure of Rhetorical Coercion', 11 *Global Policy* (2020) 93.

In the following section, the paradoxical simultaneity of violent coercion and peace in the Vienna Order will be examined with a focus on the discourse on the legitimization of violence in the first half of the century. Only from these practices of justification can the normative structure of Europe's international order in the nineteenth century (and beyond) be understood. For to maintain hegemonic peace, the Great Powers used not only political repression but also military force. This included war in the name of peace.

An Order Built on Normativity and Power

The central normative paradoxes of the Vienna Order can be identified during the Congress of Vienna. In the negotiations on the Polish-Saxon Question in the winter of 1814/15, Castlereagh had made it clear to Hardenberg that he would not accept a Prussian annexation of Saxony without a collective decision by the Concert or a contractual basis. Castlereagh even threatened to break off the Vienna negotiations.[178] The British foreign minister wanted to put a stop to Prussia's unilateral arbitrariness—especially after Prussia's decision to support Russia in its ambitions in Poland. This statement by Castlereagh has recently been interpreted as an example of an emerging prohibition of conquest.[179]

Is this interpretation correct? The British foreign secretary certainly took a different tack on 20 March 1815 when he gave a speech in the House of Commons. According to Castlereagh, his threat to Hardenberg had been deliberately exaggerated. In contrast, Castlereagh wanted to make clear that he had *not* argued in favour of a ban on conquest:

> But let me not be misunderstood. I never was one of those who contested the point upon the principle assumed by the honourable gentleman, that it must, in any case, be inconsistent with the duties of the Powers of Europe assembled at Vienna, with the express leave of the nation itself, to annex even the whole of Saxony to Prussia. I never opposed it on the ground of mere abstract right; and I broadly and avowedly deny any assertions that may have been made regarding my conduct in that respect.[180]

---

[178] Castlereagh, 'Castlereagh to Liverpool. (No. 44.)', in C.K. Webster (ed.), *British Diplomacy 1813-1815. Select Documents Dealing With the Reconstruction of Europe* (1921), at 278 ff.

[179] Hull (n. 69), at 185.

[180] Castlereagh, 'Extracts from a Speech of Castlereagh in the House of Commons, March 20th, 1815', in C.K. Webster (ed.), *British Diplomacy 1813-1815. Select Documents Dealing With the Reconstruction of Europe* (1921) 396, at 402.

What is more, Castlereagh also did not dispute

> the right of conquest [sic!], under the qualifications which I shall presently state, was a right which gave the conqueror a perfect warrant to annex the whole of a subjugated country to another State. I deny that I had argued this matter on any other principle, and cannot suffer the honourable member to give me credit for a line of conduct which he may perhaps applaud, but which I did not think fit to follow in this particular transaction.[181]

Finally, Castlereagh even argued 'with perfect confidence, that never was the principle of conquest more legitimately applicable, or more justifiably exercisable than in the case of Saxony'.[182]

Was this not a fundamental contradiction to Castlereagh's rejection of a Prussian conquest of Saxony vis-à-vis Hardenberg? At first glance it would certainly seem so. A closer inspection, however, reveals that Castlereagh's chain of arguments was self-contradictory, yet consistent. For in Vienna, Castlereagh had objected solely to a *unilateral* annexation of Saxony not legitimized by the Concert. Furthermore, he held that a *full* annexation was too great a sacrifice 'in the eyes of Europe'.[183] To a *partial* annexation justified by the Concert, on the other hand, Castlereagh agreed. In addition, he referred to the Saxon king's enduring support of Napoléon, from which a Prussian title of conquest could have been derived according to the doctrine of 'just war'.[184] Castlereagh also referred to the restoration of Prussia's status as a Great Power as being 'necessary to the general repose and safety of Europe'.[185]

Castlereagh's argument was also consistent in the sense that it was entirely in favour of the Concert. It underlined the Concert's unrestricted international authority in questions concerning the violent restructuring of European borders. Only if a justification of force—in this case, the conquest of parts of Saxony by Prussia—was deemed appropriate by a majority of the Great Powers, was it considered legitimate. Moreover, Castlereagh's chain of arguments once again underlines the space of tension between the political and normative claims in which the Concert operated. Castlereagh argued normatively *and* politically. A uniform language of justification and critique was lacking. It remained to a certain extent up to the Great Powers which narratives they wanted to use in the Concert's often tough negotiation processes. For the Concert made its decisions over the decades by no means unanimously,[186] but by changing voting alliances, or, as I call them, *discourse alliances*. The legitimacy of war always had to be negotiated. As a result, whether or not an argument was accepted

---

[181] *Ibid.*
[182] *Ibid.*
[183] *Ibid.*, at 403.
[184] Klüber (n. 95), at 412 ff.
[185] Castlereagh (n. 180), at 402.
[186] Schulz (n. 1), at 554–8.

continued to be subject to historical fluctuations. The international community thus remained first and foremost a community of communication—albeit under increasingly institutionalized conditions after 1815.

The most important cause for disagreement between the Great Powers was at once the greatest challenge for the European peace order: dealing with nationalism.[187] Although the Great Powers had themselves invoked the 'nation' in the anti-Napoleonic 'wars of liberation',[188] they then tried to ban this narrative from the political discourse. The Final Act of Vienna of 9 June 1815 was therefore no longer to apply '*au nom de la Nation*', but '*au nom de la très-Sainte et indivisible Trinité*'.[189] Nevertheless, the 'nation' remained an influential political concept in contemporary political and legal debates on war and peace. It would also—and especially—become constitutive for the justification of modern wars between Great Powers.

Of central importance for the European war discourse was also the *Eastern Question*. The latter can be defined, albeit in a slightly pointed manner, as 'the problems connected to the withdrawal of the Turks from Europe',[190] also magnified due to the increasing national movements on Ottoman territory and especially in the Balkans. The Eastern Question was of the utmost importance for the discourse on the legitimacy of war in the nineteenth century (see below). Here, too, the question of nationality played a huge role. However, it would be a mistake to assume that there was a dichotomy between empire and nation in the nineteenth century. The international order proved to be more flexible. The Great Powers succeeded not only in largely limiting the regional violence that accompanied the emergence of the modern nation-state, but also in reconciling monarchy and nation-state, at least in principle, in the form of nation-state monarchies.[191] Nevertheless, the radicalization of nationalisms caused the most serious dissonance in the European Concert—and ultimately led to it being silenced.

Inventing Intervention: War in the Name of Peace

But even in its early phase, the Concert's diplomacy was by no means free of political conflicts and different preferences. No political issue made this clearer than the dispute over the legitimacy of military interventions. Although there had been inventions before the nineteenth century,[192] the question of intervention was of enormous importance for the Concert. It brought together fundamentally different

---

[187] See also Langewiesche (n. 9), at 83.
[188] Chapter 3.2.
[189] 'Final Act of the Congress of Vienna (9 June 1815)', in W.G. Grewe (ed.), *Fontes Historiae Iuris Gentium (FHIG), Sources Relating to the History of the Law of Nations*, vol. 3/1: 1815–1945 (1992) 3.
[190] Baumgart (n. 13), at 23.
[191] Evans (n. 2), at 64; Langewiesche (n. 9), at 82 ff.
[192] Kampmann, 'Vom Schutz fremder Untertanen zur Humanitären Intervention. Einleitende Bemerkungen zur diachronen Analyse einer aktuellen Problematik', 131 *Historisches Jahrbuch* (2011) 3.

views on central principles of the emerging modern international order such as (popular) sovereignty. Stanley Hoffmann's thesis, according to which all central themes of international relations to this day converge in the question of 'intervention', also seems plausible for the nineteenth century.[193]

The crux of intervention was—and still is[194]—that it could also be used to justify a de facto unilateral war as violence in the name of the international order and thus provide it with higher authority. As a result, the distinction between foreign and domestic policy guaranteed under international law in the Peace of Vienna[195] could, if necessary, be eliminated by force. Advocates of intervention thus always legitimized military intervention as a means of securing international order and maintaining peace. At the same time, military intervention—at least in the first half of the century[196]—was below the threshold of a major war, and thus, a 'measure short of war'. In the words of Jürgen Osterhammel: 'The small war was to become a substitute for the large one that had been avoided.'[197]

However, the Concert was divided on the question of intervention during its early phase, in the so-called Congress System (1815–23). On the one hand, the sovereigns of the Holy Alliance, founded in September 1815 and led by Russia, Austria, and Prussia, advocated a principle of intervention based on dynastic legitimacy and 'religion, justice, and peace' in Europe against revolution and national uprisings.[198] By contrast, Castlereagh and his successor George Canning vehemently denied interfering in a state's constitution.[199] The question of intervention, which had not been regulated in detail in the Vienna Treaties,[200] thus became the ideal-typical conflict of norms in the international discourse on the use of force in the early nineteenth century. The principles of intervention and non-intervention were mutually exclusive.

The first reason for the debates on military intervention was the revolutionary uprisings in Spain and Italy.[201] In March 1820, a military coup had taken place in Spain. For most of the Great Powers, the developments in Spain appeared to

---

[193] Hoffmann, 'The Problem of Intervention', in H. Bull (ed.), *Intervention in World Politics* (1984) 7.
[194] N.J. Wheeler, *Saving Strangers: Humanitarian Intervention in International Society* (2003); A. Orford, *Reading Humanitarian Intervention. Human Rights and the Use of Force in International Law* (2011); Jahn, 'Humanitarian Intervention: Justifying War for a New International Order', in L. Brock and H. Simon (eds), *The Justification of War and International Order: From Past to Present* (2021) 355.
[195] Vec, 'Inside/Outside(s): Conceptualizations, Criteria, and Functions of a Dichotomy in Nineteenth-Century International Legal Doctrine', in A. Fahrmeir, G. Hellmann, and M. Vec (eds), *The Transformation of Foreign Policy. Drawing and Managing Boundaries from Antiquity to the Present* (2016) 51.
[196] Unlike, for example, in 1877/78, see Chapter 9.2.
[197] Osterhammel, 'Krieg im Frieden: Zu Form und Typologie imperialer Interventionen', in J. Osterhammel (ed.), *Geschichtswissenschaft jenseits des Nationalstaats. Studien zu Beziehungsgeschichte und Zivilisationsvergleich* (2003) 283, at 298.
[198] 'The "Holy Alliance" (14/26 September 1815)', in W.G. Grewe (ed.), *Fontes Historiae Iuris Gentium (FHIG), Sources Relating to the History of the Law of Nations*, vol. 3/1: 1815–1945 (1992) 107.
[199] Schulz (n. 1), at 85 ff.
[200] Osterhammel (n. 197), at 298.
[201] This paragraph is based on Schroeder (n. 4), at 606–14.

present no threat to European peace—only the Tsar wanted to convene a congress. The situation came to a head, however, in July 1820, when revolutionaries followed the Spanish example, first in Naples, and later in Piedmont in March 1821. In 1821, Austria successfully intervened militarily in Naples and Piedmont. The Austrian army defeated the rebels (who fled, for example, to neutral Switzerland) within a few days, but without changing the territorial order of Europe.

How was Austria's intervention in Naples legitimized? Metternich did *not* refer to a 'free right to go to war', but to an internationally valid justification, in other words one based on a treaty: the Alliance Treaty of 1815, by which the Kingdom of the Two Sicilies had become Austria's satellite state in Italy. In accordance with the treaty, any change to the constitution in Naples was dependent on Austria's consent.[202] The planned Austrian use of force became a subject of negotiation in multilateral Great Power diplomacy at the initiative of both Russia and France. Not only the Italian princes,[203] but also France and Russia feared a growing influence of the Habsburg monarchy in Italy.[204] Britain, on the other hand, was keen to prevent the Concert from negotiating intervention in Naples according to anti-revolutionary principles. Metternich was now in a diplomatic quandary. He had to side against either Castlereagh, alongside whom he had successfully contained Alexander's expansionism in Poland, or the Tsar, who espoused the same anti-revolutionary principle of intervention as Metternich.[205] Metternich opted for common cause with the Tsar.

Now, nothing stood in the way of the Congress of Troppau, chaired by Metternich in November 1820. Great Britain attended the meeting only as an observer, determined to avoid the impression that the Concert was officially concerned with revolutions.[206] Surprisingly, although it had co-initiated the Congress, France followed the British example. Consequently, in Troppau, only the Eastern powers Austria, Russia, and Prussia established an anti-revolutionary principle of intervention. In the Troppau Protocol of 19 November 1820, they jointly stated that they would refuse to recognize domestic 'changes brought about by illegal methods' (Article 2) and, in extreme cases, would use force to do so (Article 3). Article 4 covered Austria's violent interference in the Kingdom of the Two Sicilies under the newly asserted principle of intervention. Considering the principle of intertemporality (*lex retro non agit*), this was a problematic argument: the Eastern powers were attempting to legitimize their intervention *ex post facto* with a principle that had not previously existed under treaty law.[207]

---

[202] H. von Rotteck, *Das Recht der Einmischung in die inneren Angelegenheiten eines fremden Staates* (1845), at 26.
[203] Schulz (n. 1), at 79.
[204] Schroeder (n. 4), at 609.
[205] Jarrett (n. 4).
[206] Schulz (n. 1), at 79.
[207] 'The Congress of Troppau (19 November 1820)', in W.G. Grewe (ed.), *Fontes Historiae Iuris Gentium (FHIG), Sources Relating to the History of the Law of Nations*, vol. 3/1: 1815–1945 (1992) 110.

Yet they did not assume that they could act solely on the basis of their own political discretion. In the face of vehement British criticism,[208] they endeavoured to present the intervention as appropriate action in line with the Vienna peace order. In their joint circular despatch of 8 December 1820, Austria, Prussia, and Russia recalled the collective trauma of the Great Powers inflicted on Europe by the 'military tyranny of the Representative of Revolution',[209] without, however, mentioning Napoleon by name. The Eastern powers claimed that they were acting altruistically, that they were not aiming for conquest, and that they only wanted to protect Europe from the scourge of new revolutions.[210] They thus tried to locate their violence in the European tradition of legitimizing war.

Reconciling the desired principle of intervention with British policy was, however, impossible. At the monarchs' meetings in Laibach (1821) and Verona (1822), the Eastern powers further extended the anti-revolutionary principle of intervention. Whereas Metternich had been able to refer to the Treaty of 1815 in the case of Naples, in 1822 the Eastern powers supported France in its military intervention in Spain in favour of the Bourbon Ferdinand VII solely on the basis of their new principle of intervention.[211] The Holy Alliance now claimed to authorize military force in the name of international order and general peace.

However, this claim by no means remained unchallenged. As early as 5 May 1820, Castlereagh had written a state paper with regard to the uprisings in Spain. Mid-twentieth-century British historians described this as the state paper with the most far-reaching consequences in British history.[212] In the paper, Castlereagh formulated a non-intervention principle that became seminal for British European policy through the century. Castlereagh argued with regard to Spain that for the Concert, there was 'no Order of Things upon which to deliberate',[213] for the Spanish Revolution posed no threat to European peace. Accordingly, there was no reason for European intervention.[214] For Castlereagh, the aim of the principle of non-intervention was, in particular, to prevent intervention to avert purely potential dangers: 'We shall be found in our place when actual Danger menaces the System of Europe', wrote Castlereagh, 'but this Country cannot and will not act upon abstract and speculative Principles of Precaution'.[215]

With regard to the anti-revolutionary principle of intervention, Castlereagh also stated: 'The [Quadruple] Alliance which exists had no such purpose in view in

---

[208] Schulz (n. 1), at 80.
[209] 'Austro-Prusso-Russian Circular Dispatch (8. December 1820)', in W.G. Grewe (ed.), *Fontes Historiae Iuris Gentium (FHIG), Sources Relating to the History of the Law of Nations*, vol. 3/1: 1815–1945 (1992) 113, at 114.
[210] *Ibid.*
[211] Schulz (n. 1), at 85.
[212] H. Temperley and L.M. Penson, *Foundations of British Foreign Policy* (1938), at 47.
[213] Castlereagh, 'Lord Castlereagh's Confidential State Paper of May 5th, 1820', in A.W. Ward and G.P. Gooch (eds), *The Cambridge History of British Foreign Policy, 1783–1919*, vol. 2 (1923) 621, at 624.
[214] *Ibid.*, at 624.
[215] *Ibid.*, at 632.

its original formation.'[216] The principle of intervention proclaimed by the Eastern powers, Castlereagh stated unequivocally, contradicted the political and normative foundations of the Concert, which had anchored the inviolability of sovereign borders in the Final Act of Vienna.[217] Nevertheless, for Castlereagh, it was acceptable to deviate from the principle of non-intervention in two exceptional circumstances: multilaterally to secure peace 'when actual Danger menaces the System of Europe',[218] and unilaterally when a state's rights had been violated. Castlereagh thus confirmed the narrowing of the justification narrative of military force outlined above, which the Concert had introduced in Vienna in 1814/15.

Austria's intervention in Naples was indeed an example of a legitimate unilateral intervention in the sense intended by Castlereagh, especially since this interference was considered by Great Britain not to be a threat to European peace and British interests.[219] Metternich's justification, the breach of the 1815 Treaty of Alliance by the new government in Naples, was convincing even to Castlereagh. Since Castlereagh, however, could not express his support for unilateral intervention for diplomatic reasons (approval could easily have been misinterpreted as approval of the anti-revolutionary principle of intervention as well), Metternich argued that the British foreign minister was behaving like a music lover in church—he wanted to clap but was not allowed to.[220]

Castlereagh's strict non-intervention principle was continued by his successor Canning. Great Britain, as a persistent objector, took a firm stand against the legal opinion of the Holy Alliance. In doing so, it prevented the emergence of a customary law anti-revolutionary principle of intervention.[221] What is more, the British principle of non-intervention would even prevail after the end of the Congress System. After 1823, the Great Powers would no longer collectively intervene against revolutions, not even in the face of the revolutions of 1830 and 1848.[222] The British principle of non-intervention also received important transatlantic reinforcement through the cooperation between Canning and US President James Monroe.[223] Monroe's Declaration of 2 December 1823 prohibited interference by the major European powers in the Americas. This did not, however, prevent the USA from carrying out military interventions in the late nineteenth century, even on humanitarian grounds, as part of its imperial policy in South America.[224]

---

[216] Ibid.
[217] Ibid., at 631 ff.
[218] Ibid., at 624.
[219] Jarrett (n. 4) at 241.
[220] Schroeder (n. 4), at 609.
[221] Schulz (n. 1), at 82.
[222] See also Langewiesche (n. 9), at 82.
[223] Schroeder (n. 4), at 632.
[224] A particularly important example is the Spanish-American War of 1898, see also Klose (n. 55), Chapter 9. On the consequences in the twentieth century, see L. Brock, *Entwicklungsnationalismus und Kompradorenpolitik. Die Gründung der OAS und die Entwicklung der Abhängigkeit Lateinamerikas von den USA* (1975).

After 1823, intervention in state practice and international law doctrine remained a 'highly political field'.[225] However, the central justification was no longer anti-revolutionary. Rather, according to Baden historian and jurist Hermann von Rotteck, the July Revolution of 1830 marked the beginning of 'a new period for international law, since the absolute powers have been forced by the general constellation of European affairs to deviate from their previous system': with the recognition of the 'facts of Paris', the Great Powers—and 'even Metternich'—had proclaimed the principle of non-intervention, hitherto championed by England alone, as 'the only true one that secures peace and justice'.[226] The principle of non-intervention had prevailed.

In fact, the July Revolution of 1830 was not perceived as a threat to European peace. In the cases of the revolutions in Greece (1821–32, see below) and Belgium (1830), the Concert even intervened in a pro-revolutionary way: Belgium became an independent state in 1839 under guarantee of the Concert and on condition of its neutrality.[227] For the first time since 1815, a territorial change in the European peace order had been made by the Concert.[228] In line with Castlereagh, from now on the significance of a domestic conflict for European peace alone was the only decisive reason for the authorization of military intervention. This also means that military interventions always required justification by the Concert. No reference was made to a 'free right to go to war' or 'to intervene'.

Debating Intervention beyond Positive Law

But it was not only in political practice that intervention was considered one of the most controversial international issues of the nineteenth century. The same view dominated among international lawyers, theologians, and political scholars.[229] Assessing the legitimacy of an intervention was a delicate undertaking. In what was probably the first detailed nineteenth-century analysis of 'intervention', Hermann von Rotteck wrote that an 'incorrect assessment' had 'already brought innumerable misfortunes upon mankind'.[230] Here, the liberal Rotteck referred to military interference against national and revolutionary movements.

---

[225] See also Vec, 'Intervention/Nichtintervention. Verrechtlichung der Politik und Politisierung des Völkerrechts im 19. Jahrhundert', in U. Lappenküper und R. Marcowitz (eds), *Macht und Recht. Völkerrecht in den internationalen Beziehungen* (2010) 135.
[226] Rotteck (n. 202), at 85.
[227] Schroeder (n. 4), at 681 ff.; Schulz (n. 1), at 112 ff.; Abbenhuis (n. 75).
[228] Simms, '"A False Principle in the Law of Nations": Burke, State Sovereignty, [German] Liberty, and Intervention in the Age of Westphalia', in B. Simms and D.J.B. Trim (eds), *Humanitarian Intervention: A History* (2011) 89, at 92.
[229] Heffter (n. 110), at 85 ff.; Strisower, 'Intervention', in K. Strupp (ed.), *Wörterbuch des Völkerrechts und der Diplomatie*, vol. 1 (1924) 581; Vec (n. 225); see below.
[230] Rotteck (n. 202), at xxviii.

According to Rotteck's statement, the principle of non-intervention was broadly accepted in international legal doctrine.[231] Important nineteenth-century international legal scholars such as Klüber, Heffter, Bluntschli, Westlake, Oppenheim, and Fiore denied the legality of interventions against liberal revolutions.[232] There was 'generally no justification' for intervention, according to Heffter, but the principle of non-intervention was the rule.[233] In this context, referring to the Holy Alliance's intervention in Spain (1820), the Berlin constitutional lawyer Albert Friedrich Berner asked: 'Has the principle of intervention thereby become a principle of European international law?' His answer: 'This cannot possibly be affirmed.'[234] After all, as Berner observed, Castlereagh had protested directly against an anti-revolutionary principle of intervention (see above).

Although the majority of European international legal scholars advocated the principle of non-intervention in favour of state sovereignty,[235] intervention remained only vaguely regulated. According to Berner, 'as far as intervention is concerned', no fixed political practice had emerged until 1860. Nor had Europe reached an agreement on certain principles, nor could a single state claim to have a consistent stance on its part.[236] During the Belgian Revolution of 1830, for example, according to Berner, the principle of non-intervention found favour mainly for the reason that—

> it was desired to avoid the armed clash of Western Europe with Eastern Europe here as well as there; for the sympathies of the governments of England and France were this time as decidedly in favour of the independence of Belgium as the sympathies of the governments of Prussia, Austria and Russia were in favour of the restoration of the House of Orange.[237]

But legal scholars agreed with political practice that there were exceptions to the principle of non-intervention—particularly if they were in favour of European peace.[238] No 'non-intervention machine' was without an 'emergency valve', wrote Berner.[239] According to Strisower, the nineteenth-century international legal doctrine was quite inclined to allow intervention, 'when it concerns certain violations of law of general interest, violations of generally recognised principles of law... or in

---

[231] See e.g. Heffter (n. 110), at 85; Berner, 'Intervention', in J.C. Bluntschli and C.L.T. Brater (eds), *Deutsches Staats-Wörterbuch*, vol. 5 (1860) 341, at 345; Bluntschli (n. 76), at 89; Martens (n. 106), at 300; L.M. Drago, *Cobro Coercitivo de Deudas Públicas* (1906); F. von Liszt, *Das Völkerrecht. Systematisch dargestellt* (11th edn, 1920), at 50–65, 270 ff.; see also Strisower (n. 229); Vec (n. 229), at 158.
[232] See also Strisower (n. 229).
[233] Heffter (n. 110), at 85.
[234] Berner (n. 231), at 345.
[235] Heffter (n. 110), at 85.
[236] Berner (n. 231), at 350.
[237] *Ibid.*, at 349.
[238] Osterhammel (n. 197), at 298.
[239] Berner (n. 231), at 354.

certain cases of generally punishable violations of international law'.[240] According to Heffter, such exceptions to the principle of non-intervention were consent by the state affected by an intervention and violated rights of the intervening power, such as 'feudal claims' or an 'aimless state of war pending in the interior of a country'.[241] Thus, while an intervention continued to be deemed an international use of force, it was considered an exception—and accordingly had to be legitimized in terms of the international order of justification.

In this context, legitimizations in the language of natural law once again represented a solution given the lack of positive legal regulations.[242] In the highly political field of 'intervention', a plurality of legal concepts can therefore be found in nineteenth-century international legal theory. In 1845, Hermann von Rotteck, for example, initially argued in favour of the principle of non-intervention on the basis of rational law.[243] However, Rotteck argued, this principle had not yet become a principle of positive international law due to a lack of *opinio iuris* on the part of the Great Powers.[244] Similar to Heffter, Rotteck therefore concluded entirely in line with a normative hybridization of international law, that:

> the positive law of nations does not contain a definite provision, to another conclusion, namely that we say: in the silence of positive law, natural law, which never renounces its claim to power, enters into legislative activity. As long, therefore, as a certain principle of intervention is not permanently established, generally recognized and thus incorporated into the body of international law, the dictum of the natural law of nations ... applies.[245]

The supposedly positivist legal scholars thus admitted to themselves that where positive international law was lacking, they continued to rely on morality and natural law. In no other political field was this truer than in the field of the use of international force.

Ungentle Civilizers: Violence in the Name of Humanity?

Violence in favour of or against revolutions was not the only problem in the debates on intervention. In the first half of the nineteenth century, another justification narrative emerged that 'increasingly absorbed all other grounds for intervention' and 'tended in practice to be executed collectively':[246] the nineteenth century

---

[240] Strisower (n. 229), at 587.
[241] Heffter (n. 110), at 106.
[242] Vec (n. 140).
[243] Rotteck (n. 202), at 36.
[244] *Ibid.*, at 92.
[245] *Ibid.*, at 93.
[246] Grewe (n. 46), at 493.

was to become the 'true "century of humanitarian intervention"'.[247] According to Fabian Klose, this was the period—

> in which the idea of protecting and enforcing humanitarian norms by military force emerged across a variety of theatres in Africa, Asia, Europe and America, took on a definite shape in colonial and imperial contexts, and ultimately was enshrined in core texts in international law.[248]

Under the impact of the transatlantic revolutions, the discourse on the violent protection of religious minorities became increasingly secularized at the threshold of modernity. As Fabian Klose has shown, this new civil humanitarianism culminated in abolitionism: the latter was pushed politically and militarily by Great Britain, from 1807 onwards on the West African coast, and later also throughout the Atlantic region.[249] The genesis of 'humanitarian intervention' as a novel way of justifying force was therefore closely intertwined with the British Empire. While London was a staunch opponent of the anti-revolutionary principle of intervention, at the same time it was a key actor in the formation of humanitarian intervention.[250]

'Humanitarian intervention' was thus not something that appeared out of nowhere in the context of the Eastern Question.[251] Nonetheless, the European Concert primarily used it in the context of the Eastern Question, and exclusively on Ottoman territory. Eliana Augusti has thus aptly argued that European intervention in the Orient was not 'an intervention legitimized by exception, but rather a geographical exception that legitimized any form of intervention'.[252] In his important treatise *La théorie de l'intervention d'humanité*,[253] French international legal scholar Antoine Rougier emphasized that Europe's theory of intervention had developed explicitly within the framework of the Eastern Question.[254] For the

---

[247] Klose (n. 55), at 4; see also Trachtenberg, 'Intervention in Historical Perspective', in L.W. Reed and C. Kaysen (eds), *Emerging Norms of Justified Intervention* (1993); M. Swatek-Evenstein, *A History of Humanitarian Intervention* (2020); D. Rodogno, *Against Massacre. Humanitarian Interventions in the Ottoman Empire, 1815–1914* (2011); Simms und Trim (n. 228).

[248] Klose (n. 55), at 4.

[249] *Ibid.*, at 69; Benton (n. 32), at 180; Benton and Ford (n. 21).

[250] The idea of violent protection of rights could also be applied within Europe, for example to enforce the protection of own citizens in foreign states. The so-called Don Pacifico affair, in which Great Britain used military threats against Greece, is the most prominent example here; see Grewe (n. 46), at 526 ff.; Benton (n. 32) at 180.

[251] Rodogno (n. 247); Klose (n. 55); Benton (n. 32).

[252] 'Un intervento legittimato dall'eccezione, ma un'eccezione geografica che legittimava qualsiasi forma d'intervento.' Augusti, 'L'intervento europeo in Oriente nel XIX secolo: storia contesa di un istituto controverso', in L. Nuzzo and M. Vec (eds), *Constructing International Law. The Birth of a Discipline* (2012) 277, at 322.

[253] According to Umut Özsu, Rougier's essay is the most important academic treatise on 'humanitarian intervention' before 1914 ; see Özsu, 'Ottoman Empire', in B. Fassbender and A. Peters (eds), *The Oxford Handbook of the History of International Law* (2nd edn, 2014) 429, at 440 n. 54.

[254] Rougier, 'La Théorie de l'intervention d'humanité', 17 *Revue Génerale de Droit International Public* (1910) 468, at 472.

Ottoman Empire was regarded by the European Great Powers as 'the sick man of Europe',[255] a 'semi-civilized' and only 'semi-sovereign' state on the 'semi-periphery' of Europe.[256] This political and normative discrimination of the Ottoman Empire made it much easier for the Great Powers to limit the former's sovereignty with reference to universal morality and humanity. At the same time, their own violence could be presented as a 'civilizing mission'.[257]

It was in the context of the Greek War of Independence (1821–32) that the first 'humanitarian intervention' of the European Great Powers along these lines took place. Insurgents of the Greek national movement had declared a 'holy war' in the name of the nation against the 'cruel yoke' of the 'frightful tyranny, iniquitous in its very essence,—an unexampled despotism to which no other rule can be compared'.[258] This Greek war included massacres of Turkish and Jewish inhabitants.[259] In 1822, the Ottoman central administration reacted to the violence of the Greek independence movement by issuing marching orders to the regional pashas. The latter armies now, in turn, committed their own massacres. Particularly the massacre at Chios and the enslavement of Greek prisoners that followed caused an outcry among the European public. Due to biased reporting, many Europeans branded only the Ottoman, but not the equally brutal Greek use of violence a scandal.[260]

The Greek uprising now became an international political issue, for the question of the protection of humanity and Christianity, as well as the defence of abolitionism, arose in the context of the Eastern Question. However, intervention did not necessarily follow in such cases.[261] Rather, the Great Powers always found themselves in the space of tension between international norms and unilateral political interests. It was therefore necessary to debate intervention on a case-by-case basis.[262]

Russia was the first Great Power to plead for European intervention in favour of the Greeks, as early as 1821, a plea which, however, was denied by the other

---

[255] This phrase was coined by Tsar Nicholas I on the eve of the Crimean War.
[256] On 'semi-sovereignty', see Genell, 'The Well-defended Domains: Eurocentric International Law and the Making of the Ottoman Office of Legal Counsel', 3 *Journal of Ottoman and Turkish Studies* (2016) 255; see also Nuzzo, 'The Birth of an Imperial Location. Comparative Perspectives on Western Colonialism in China', 31 *Leiden Journal of International Law* (2018) 569; Hulle, 'British Humanitarianism, International Law and Human Sacrifice in West Africa', in I. van Hulle and R.C.H. Lesaffer (eds), *International Law in the Long Nineteenth Century (1776–1914)* (2019) 105; Genell and Aksakal, '"Salvation through War?" The Ottoman Search for Sovereignty in 1914', in L. Brock and H. Simon (eds), *The Justification of War and International Order: From Past to Present* (2021) 207.
[257] Rodogno (n. 247), at 48; Kleinschmidt (n. 108).
[258] 'Greek Declaration of Independence (1822)', in Hathaway et al. (2017), *War Manifesto Database* available at: https://documents.law.yale.edu/manifestos (last visited 1 December 2022).
[259] Rodogno (n. 247), at 65 ff.
[260] Castlereagh, however, had pointed out the atrocities committed by both sides; see Klose (n. 55), at 167.
[261] Klose (n. 55), at 168.
[262] This continues to apply to this day. See ICISS, *The Responsibility to Protect. Report of the International Commission on Intervention and State Sovereignty* (2001).

Great Powers. This pro-revolutionary line is remarkable, since Russia had only just proclaimed an *anti*-revolutionary principle of intervention in Troppau (see above). Historically, however, Russian sympathy with the Greek Revolution is relatively easy to explain: for centuries, Russia had waged wars against the Ottomans on religious grounds. In addition, Russia derived from Article 7 of the 1774 Treaty of Küçük Kaynarca the highly questionable claim to be the sole protector of the Christian Orthodox minority, not only in the 'Holy Land' but in the entire Ottoman Empire. The Russian intervention policy was thus decidedly selective,[263] insisting on the sovereignty of the European monarchs, yet denying it to the Ottoman rulers.

Great Britain and France, on the other hand, were concerned with preserving the Ottoman Empire and its sovereignty—not least to prevent a Russian rise to power in south-eastern Europe, and Russian access to the Mediterranean.[264] Great Britain saw the Ottoman Empire as a buffer against Russian influence in India.[265] Austria and Prussia, in turn, adhered to the anti-revolutionary policy they had established at the Congress of Troppau. They thus largely became passive observers in the Greek Question. Russia, Great Britain, and France, however, were able to claim the authority of the Congress even without the direct participation of Austria and Prussia.[266]

Yet direct intervention by the Great Powers in the Greek War of Independence did not occur until 1825. Influenced by the unverifiable rumour that the Ottoman Empire was seeking to deport all Greek Christians into slavery,[267] Great Britain agreed to a British-Russian pacification plan, which France joined. In the Treaty of London of 6 July 1827,[268] Great Britain, Russia, and France declared their intention to put 'an end to the sanguinary struggle' and to restore peace 'by a formal treaty... between the contending parties, by means of an arrangement called for, no less by sentiments of humanity, than by interests for the tranquillity of Europe'.[269] In order to achieve a Greek-Ottoman peace, the Great Powers offered to provide diplomatic mediation (Article 1). However, they reserved wider options in a secret additional article. The mandate of the Concert's majority did not exclude the collective use of force against the Ottoman Empire.

Violence was not long in coming. As the Greek-Turkish fighting continued, British, French, and Russian warships entered the port of Navarino in October 1827 to enforce a naval blockade against the Egyptian-Ottoman fleet. When a shot

---

[263] It has remained so, in a modified form, to this day, see Robinson and Antonov, 'In the Name of State Sovereignty? The Justification of War in Russian History and the Present', in L. Brock and H. Simon (eds), *The Justification of War and International Order: From Past to Present* (2021).
[264] Klose (n. 55), at 163.
[265] O. Figes, *Crimea: The Last Crusade* (2011), at 48 ff.
[266] Schulz (n. 1), at 102.
[267] Klose (n. 55), at 175.
[268] 'Franco-Anglo-Russian Treaty for the Pacification of Greece (6 July 1827)', in W.G. Grewe (ed.), *Fontes Historiae Iuris Gentium (FHIG), Sources Relating to the History of the Law of Nations*, vol. 3/1: 1815–1945 (1992) 150.
[269] *Ibid.*

was fired from an Ottoman ship, the far superior British-French-Russian warships sank the entire Egyptian-Ottoman fleet.[270] A French expeditionary force was then deployed to pacify the conflict between the Greeks and the Turks.[271] In 1830, an independent Greek state was created by the Concert—not least to limit the Russian expansion of power in southern Europe after the Russo-Turkish War of 1828/29.

The Ottoman Empire and the major European powers blamed each other for the naval battle of Navarino.[272] From the Ottoman point of view (1828), Russia, in particular, was responsible as the 'principal enemy of the Sublime Porte'.[273] The European Great Powers, in turn, tried to justify their collective intervention vis-à-vis the Ottoman Empire—even though the latter was not a member of the European legal community at the time.[274] This behaviour underlines that even between the European Great Powers and the Ottoman Empire, aggression was, fundamentally, considered illegitimate. In the process, however, the Ottoman Empire was portrayed as 'savage' and 'uncivilized'.[275] Such 'othering' speech acts went hand in hand with a self-portrayal of Europe as a civilized legal community. However, a 'free right to go to war' was by no means claimed, even in the dealings of the Great Powers with a supposedly 'semi-civilized' empire on the European 'semi-periphery'.

Violence as a Herald of Legal Progress?

The fact that 'humanitarian intervention' was understood as part of the Concert's politics of ordering the international is also reflected in the lively debates in international legal scholarship[276]—even if the term 'humanity' was not yet defined in international law. What was the relationship between humanitarian intervention and the non-intervention principle, which was accepted by the majority of international legal scholars? As an important representative of the latter, Heffter wrote that 'even the most flagrant injustice committed in one state' could not justify intervention, since no state was 'in the position to judge another'.[277]

Other authors argued in favour of humanitarian intervention. Antoine Rougier, for example, wrote that a third party's right to intervene—be it an individual state

---

[270] O. Schulz, *Ein Sieg der zivilisierten Welt? Die Intervention der europäischen Großmächte im griechischen Unabhängigkeitskrieg (1826–1832)* (2011), at 298.
[271] Schulz (n. 1).
[272] *Ibid.*, at 95.
[273] 'Manifesto of the Ottoman Porte – Issued in the beginning of January, after the Departure of the Ambassadors (within the Annual Register) (1828)', in Hathaway et al. (2017), *War Manifesto Database* available at: https://documents.law.yale.edu/manifestos (last visited 1 December 2022) 397, at 397.
[274] Özsu (n. 253); Genell (n. 256).
[275] *Ibid.*
[276] Vec (n. 225); Simon (n. 112); A. Heraclides and A. Dialla, *Humanitarian Intervention in the Long Nineteenth Century* (2016), at 60.
[277] Heffter (n. 110), at 89.

or a group of states—was justified if a state massively violated the (natural) laws of humanity ('*les droits de l'humanité*').[278] To stop the violence within, the latter state's sovereignty was to be removed in the name of the '*société internationale*', Rougier argued.[279] Other international lawyers argued in a very similar way. For Gustave Rolin-Jacquemyns and Aegidius Rudolph Nicolaus Arntz, excessive cruelty was an attack on 'the mores of civilization'.[280]

Although nineteenth-century debates on 'humanitarian intervention' are usually dated to the second half of the century,[281] Henry Wheaton dealt with the issue as early as 1836. Wheaton explicitly welcomed the intervention of the 'Christian powers of Europe' in favour of the Greeks, who 'after enduring ages of cruel oppression ... had shaken off the Ottoman yoke'. Intervention, Wheaton argued, was authorized by the principles of international law—

> not only where the interests and safety of other powers are immediately affected by the internal transactions of a particular state, but where the general interests of humanity are infringed by the excesses of a barbarous and despotic government.[282]

In Wheaton's view, the Christian powers had a particular right to intervene militarily in the name of humanity against a 'barbaric and despotic government'. This violence was nevertheless not legitimized based on inner-European international (treaty) law, but precisely on the distinction between 'civilized' and 'uncivilized' communities.[283]

In other words, Wheaton and the legal scholars who followed him did not argue in the language of positive law, but with direct recourse to asserted natural law as well as religion, progress, and culture—explicitly and exclusively against the Ottoman Empire, which was described as the backward and barbaric 'other'. This was bluntly expressed by the Russian legal scholar Fedor Fedorovich Martens when he claimed that intervention was lawful 'in regard to Turkey, China, Japan, and other Asiatic states' when the Christian population was subjected to persecution or 'slaughter'.[284] Such intervention, Martens argued, could be justified by the 'commonality of religious interests and the dictates of humanity, i.e. the principles of natural law'.[285]

---

[278] Rougier (n. 254), at 468.
[279] *Ibid.*, at 472.
[280] Rolin-Jacquemyns, 'Note sur la théorie du droit d'intervention', 8 *Revue de Droit Internationale et de Législation Comparée* (1876) 673, at 675.
[281] Heraclides and Dialla (n. 276), at 59.
[282] Wheaton (n. 109), at 113.
[283] Klose (n. 55), at 182; Swatek-Evenstein (n. 247), at 66.
[284] Martens (n. 106), at 302.
[285] *Ibid.*

The European discourse on 'humanitarian intervention' in the nineteenth century was therefore dominated by arguments of natural law, morality, religion, and the claimed cultural superiority of Europe. These spheres of argumentation were mixed together and could be put forward as a characteristically European justification narrative against the non-European 'Other'. However, there was no positive legal norm of 'intervention' or 'humanitarian intervention' in the nineteenth century. Rather, as Rougier admitted, 'humanitarian intervention' was incompatible with certain traditions of international law, especially with the independence ('*l'indépendance*') and equality ('*l'égalité*') of states.[286]

In this respect, then, it is perhaps not surprising that throughout the century there was also scepticism towards this new pattern of justification.[287] By the end of the century, Franz von Liszt argued that general interests of humanity or culture as a basis for intervention opened the door to arbitrariness.[288] Yet the potential norm conflicts between legitimacy under natural law and legality under positive law were also identified by international lawyers in the first half of the century. Hermann von Rotteck, for example, argued in one of the first detailed analyses on 'humanitarian intervention' in favour of a clear separation of morality and law.[289] Even if morality approved of 'humanitarian intervention' in individual cases, it contradicted 'formal law' and the 'principle of non-intervention', Rotteck argued.[290]

And yet, Rotteck found the Concert's intervention in the Greek War of Independence to be justified. He came to this conclusion, however, not 'out of the title of intervention', but because Greece, after its declaration of independence in 1822, had, according to Rotteck, no longer been part of Turkey, 'but an independent state in its own right'. The liberal Rotteck thus addressed a delicate and particularly controversial justification for war that was to become decisive for the discourse on the legitimacy of war in the second half of the century: the asserted right to national unification (even) through military force.[291]

From today's perspective, however, the most interesting argument in the nineteenth-century intervention debate probably came from Antoine Rougier. The French scholar interpreted the intervention discourse in the context of the broader debates on the institutionalization and legalization of international relations. Rougier presupposed the authorization of the international community as a central condition for legitimate intervention.[292] Thus, according to Rougier, the European Concert, despite its varying membership, had acquired the character of a consistent international legislature in Europe.[293] In this context, according

---

[286] Rougier (n. 254), 468.
[287] See also the critical account by Heraclides and Dialla (n. 276), at 60.
[288] Liszt (n. 231), at 63.
[289] Rotteck (n. 202), at 56.
[290] *Ibid.*
[291] *Ibid.*, at 42.
[292] Rougier (n. 254), at 502 ff.
[293] *Ibid.*, at 510.

to Rougier, the 'theory of humanitarian intervention' could perhaps be seen as a sign of a new conception of the 'international community':[294] in it, nations were to be organized in close solidarity and interdependence under one authority. This authority should then be charged with guaranteeing respect for justice and with taking collective coercive measures in the name of civilization against states that violated human rights[295]—if necessary, even against Great Powers.[296]

With this plea, Rougier anticipated the debate on the tension between sovereignty and human rights, which has continued to the present day. Particularly noteworthy is the similarity of Rougier's arguments to a famous thesis put forward by Jürgen Habermas in the context of the discussion regarding the NATO intervention in Kosovo (1999): Habermas saw the intervention as a 'humanitarian intervention' and as an anticipation of a transition from state law to cosmopolitan law.[297] Much like Rougier, Habermas concluded that, in favour of a more sophisticated institutionalized international order, a 'humanitarian intervention' could exceptionally also be legitimized against international law.[298] However, Rougier's anticipation of Habermas's anticipation has not yet been realized. A legal institution of 'humanitarian intervention' still does not exist to this day. Nevertheless, the power of this justification of military force as an *ungentle civilizer of nations* is unbroken.

4.4 Conclusion: The Janus Face of the Vienna Order

In 1865, on the occasion of its fiftieth anniversary, the Austrian historian Joseph Alexander Freiherr von Helfert—the only one of his profession to do so[299]—wrote a tribute to the Congress of Vienna: 'In the midst of the incessant alternation of war declarations and military campaigns', it was, according to Helfert, comforting 'to encounter, for once, periods of time where peace among nations allows its mild scepter to prevail'.[300]

Indeed, the monarchs and ministers at the Congress of Vienna had ushered in an era of peace after the traumatic experiences of the Napoleonic Wars. This peace, defined as the absence of wars between the Great Powers, was constituted

---

[294] *Ibid.*, at 468.
[295] *Ibid.*
[296] *Ibid.*, at 508 ff.; see also Chapter 5.
[297] Habermas, 'Bestiality and Humanity: A War on the Border between Legality and Morality', 6 *Constellations* (1999) 263.
[298] For a critical account on Habermas's narrative, see Brock, 'Normative Integration und kollektive Handlungskompetenz auf internationaler Ebene', 6 *Zeitschrift für Internationale Beziehungen* (1999) 323.
[299] Werner, 'Ein Mahnmal des Friedens – Der Wiener Kongress in den europäischen Erinnerungskulturen', 22–24 *Aus Politik und Zeitgeschichte* (2015) 3, at 3.
[300] J.A. Freiherr von Helfert, *Fünfzig Jahre nach dem Wiener Congresse von 1814-15. Mit besonderem Hinblick auf die neuesten österreichischen Zustände* (1865), at 1.

in the Vienna Order. From now on, the legitimacy of violence was judged by the European Concert. Violence was only considered legitimate if it was either a threat to European peace or an act of self-defence. The Peace of Vienna thus became an international norm, its breach an illegitimate aggression. Since 'Vienna 1814/15', war was thus considered to be in particular need of justification. The normative architecture of the 'order of justification'[301] created in Vienna diametrically opposes the thesis of a nineteenth-century *liberum ius ad bellum*.

The first half of the nineteenth century was thus of utmost importance for the emergence of the modern international order governing the use of force. Overlooked by research on the history of international law with its focus on the century's 'last five minutes',[302] the roots of this order lie in the political and international legal debates on the legitimacy of war in the first half of the century. After Vienna in 1814/15, a legal prohibition of war began to evolve as an *emerging norm*—even though, in the absence of the development of treaty-based norms on the question of violence, political practice and international legal theory continued to refer to the justificatory tradition of 'just war'. This was still a long way from the treaty-based prohibition of war in the Kellogg-Briand Pact of 1928. The discourse on the legitimization of violence in the early nineteenth century was shaped by political interests as well as multiple normative spheres. Nevertheless, a first step towards the prohibition of aggressive war had been taken.

This assessment is also reflected in the legal debates in the first half of the nineteenth century. As has been demonstrated in this chapter, there were lively discussions about law, peace, and war well before the legal debates of the late nineteenth century, that is the debates of the 'men of 1873'.[303] The discourse on the (de)legitimization of violence under international law in the first half of the century is still largely neglected by researchers today.

The authority of the Concert as an institution of the normative order of international violence was clearly accepted in early nineteenth-century political and academic debates. By the middle of the century, however, (national) liberal international lawyers had become increasingly critical of the darker side of the Concert. According to this criticism, the Concert primarily represented the interests of the monarchs and not those of the peoples. Now, liberals not only perceived a gap between a (sometimes) desired 'perpetual peace', on the one hand, and the actual Concert's diplomacy on the other. The problem of legal sources with which a desired prohibition of aggression could be justified was also clearly revealed. For in the highly political field of the international use of force, the Great Powers' discussions were primarily based on vague normative principles, not formal codified,

---

[301] R. Forst, *Normativity and Power. Analyzing Social Orders of Justification* (2017).
[302] Kennedy, 'International Law and the Nineteenth Century: History of an Illusion', 65 *Nordic Journal of International Law* (1996) 385, at 391.
[303] Koskenniemi (n. 5).

positive legal norms. Since the teachers of international law wanted to separate law and morality in the Kantian sense, they had to find a remedy by hybridizing the sources of law: they sought a positive law regulation of *ius ad bellum*. In the absence of a prohibition of war under treaty law, however, they continued to argue with reference to the doctrine of 'just war' and thus to natural law—even though they tried to 'modernize' *bellum iustum* by using positive law vocabulary.

Normatively hybrid legitimizations also retained their significance in the discourse of political practice. While there was no war between major European powers between 1815 and 1853, military intervention developed into the Concert's violent means of suspending the state sovereignty guaranteed in the Final Act of Vienna, if necessary. Military intervention became firmly tied to the mandate of the Concert. What all justifications of intervention therefore had in common was that they always referred to the European peace and the norms of the international order—even if these norms were disputed between the anti-revolutionary principle of intervention and the principle of non-intervention. Recourse to natural law, religion, and humanity remained common in political practice and legal doctrine for lack of positive legal norms.

The Vienna Order was thus characterized by a fundamental Janus face: it was a normative frame of reference for the pacification of international relations through trust, solidarity, and normativity among the Great Powers; at the same time, however, it was also a 'legalised hegemony'[304] with the aim of enforcing the Great Powers' norms and interests. Thus, it was an institution of critique *and* justification of violence.

These practices of justification and critique at the same time confirm that military force was considered in need of justification in the first half of the nineteenth century. An alleged 'free right to go to war' was not claimed anywhere. Even vis-à-vis the Ottoman Empire, which European powers considered 'barbaric', i.e. 'uncivilized' or 'semi-civilized', violence would always have to be justified. The binding force of international norms can thus also be seen in Europe's chauvinistic behaviour towards the Ottoman Empire.

The further development of the discourse on *ius contra bellum* did not proceed in a linear fashion. Rather, it reconfirmed what has already been asserted above about the historical dialectic of war and international order. In the further course of the nineteenth century, war became the central catalyst for normative advances in international relations towards a prohibition of war under treaty law. As long as there were no wars between Great Powers, there was no reason to develop *ius contra bellum* further. This changed with the Great Power wars in Europe that were waged in the middle of the century. The following chapter deals with these wars and their justification.

---

[304] Simpson (n. 175).

5
Between Might and Right
Justified Wars and Multiple Normativities

5.1 Introduction: Normativity in Times of War

The robustness of orders is revealed in their crises.[1] For by criticizing specific norms, rules, and institutions, the legitimacy of an entire order can become contested. Windows of opportunity for transformation open. At the same time, what we understand as a crisis is often only vaguely defined and may change in retrospect: the definition of a specific crisis—like the iridescent concept of 'crisis' itself—is historically contingent.[2]

This indistinct definition of a 'crisis' also applies to the military conflicts of the mid-nineteenth century. The years 1848/49 saw not only a renewed wave of revolutions in Europe but also, for the first time since 1815, wars between European Great Powers: the Crimean War (1853–56), the Italian Wars of Unification (1848/49, 1859, and 1866) in the context of the *Risorgimento*; and the three German Wars of Unification in 1864, 1866, and 1870/71. There is no doubt that these wars were serious social, political, and humanitarian crises: more than a million people were killed or wounded. But were they also normative crises of the Vienna Order? Did they call into question the normative core of this order—the international norm of peace founded in 'Vienna 1814/15'? And was the increasing importance of the principle of nationality in international relations connected with a shift toward a 'free right to go to war', as is still claimed today?[3]

The current research literature offers no clear answers to these questions. For Paul W. Schroeder, the mid-century wars resulted in a 'revival of bellicist values'—and the end of the European Concert.[4] It is said that the 'age of realpolitik' now dawned, and idealism was displaced by realism, international Great

---

[1] R. Koselleck, *Kritik und Krise. Eine Studie zur Pathogenese der bürgerlichen Welt* (13th edn, 2017 [1954]), at 33; Luhmann, 'Kommunikation über Recht in Interaktionssystemen', in E. Blankenburg, E. Klausa, and H. Rottleuthner (eds), *Alternative Rechtsformen und Alternativen zum Recht* (1980), at 101; M.M. Mbengue and J. d'Aspremont (eds), *Crisis Narratives in International Law* (2022).
[2] Koselleck, 'Krise', in O. Brunner, W. Conze, and R. Koselleck (eds), *Geschichtliche Grundbegriffe*: H–Me (1982) 617; F. Bösch, N. Deitelhoff, and S. Kroll (eds), *Handbuch Krisenforschung* (2020).
[3] See Introduction, note 2.
[4] Schroeder, 'The Vienna System and Its Stability: The Problem of Stabilizing a State System Transformation', in P. Krüger (ed.), *Das europäische Staatensystem im Wandel: Strukturelle Bedingungen und bewegende Kräfte seit der Frühen Neuzeit* (1996) 107, at 121.

Power solidarity by egotistic state politics.[5] Much in this vein, in 1860, Austrian foreign minister Bernhard von Rechberg complained that 'the European equilibrium ... has become a dead letter': 'only the law of the strongest still applies; international anarchy reigns in Europe'.[6]

In the following chapter, I will examine whether this is true, i.e. whether realpolitik gained the upper hand over the Viennese peace norm in the mid-century discourse of justifying war. For in line with the basic theoretical assumption of this study, a declining discursive authority of the international normative frame of reference would, at the same time, have to manifest itself in a change in the practice of justifying war.[7] The absence of a practice of legitimizing war would fulfil the premise of the thesis of *liberum ius ad bellum*. In contrast, a continuing reference to the international order in justifications of war must be understood as a discursive strengthening of the Vienna norm of peace.

The first pan-European war after 1815 developed in the context of the Oriental Question. While Russia had acted as the guardian of the European monarchies in the revolutionary years of 1848/49,[8] it now confronted the Sublime Porte as the presumptive protective power of the Orthodox Christians. After failed diplomatic negotiations, the Ottoman Empire declared war on Russia in 1853. Britain, France, and Sardinia-Piedmont joined on the Ottoman side in 1854 (Chapter 5.2). This war thereby became, I assert, a struggle for law. This is also true for the Italian and German Wars of Unification (Chapters 5.3 and 5.4). The chapter's main argument is that there was a continuing need for justification of international violence—even for *Realpolitiker* such as Cavour, Napoléon III, and Bismarck.

5.2 Europeanizing the Eastern Question: The Struggle for Law at its 'Semi-periphery'

The Crimean War (1853–56) seems to have been forgotten by the wider public, as well as by parts of the research community.[9] This oblivion of the only pan-European war of the nineteenth century is surprising, as the Crimean War and the

---

[5] A. Doering-Manteuffel, *Die deutsche Frage und das europäische Staatensystem* (2010), at 38; see also T. Nipperdey, *Deutsche Geschichte: 1800–1866. Bürgerwelt und starker Staat* (1983), at 718; for a nuanced perspective on the concept of 'realpolitik', see J. Bew, *Realpolitik. A History* (2016); and N. Doll, *Recht, Politik und 'Realpolitik' bei August Ludwig von Rochau (1810–1873)* (2005).

[6] Quoted from W. Baumgart, *Europäisches Konzert und nationale Bewegung. Internationale Beziehungen 1830–1878* (2nd edn, 2007), at 158.

[7] See Chapter 2.

[8] M. Schulz, *Normen und Praxis. Das europäische Konzert der Großmächte als Sicherheitsrat, 1815–1860* (2009), at 149.

[9] O. Figes, *Crimea: The Last Crusade* (2011), at xviii.

Treaty of Paris (1856) were the 'clearest turning points'[10] in European international politics between 1815 and 1914/18.

With the Crimean War, 'modernity... found its way into warfare'.[11] The 'technological modernity' of the Crimean War correlated with 800,000 soldiers being killed.[12] The boundary between the military and society shifted, with countless—and uncounted—civilians losing their lives in the bombardments, sieges, and 'ethnic cleansings' of the war. Orlando Figes has called the Crimean War 'the first "total war", a nineteenth-century version of the wars of our own age'.[13] According to Winfried Baumgart, the Crimean War, with its secondary theatres in northern Europe, the Danube region, the Caucasus, the White Sea, and the north-west Pacific, even contained features of a 'world war'.[14] Furthermore, the Crimean War developed into the first modern media war.[15] As Ulrich Keller has illustrated, images of the war were conveyed through new visual media such as photography, lithography, and press illustration to broad sections of the population that until then had hardly participated in visual culture.[16] The Crimean War became the 'ultimate spectacle' with veritable 'image battles'.[17] It was a seminal moment for war propaganda.

As will be argued here, the Crimean War was also significant in normative terms: the Oriental Question was finally Europeanized. This became particularly evident in the contemporary discourse of justification and critique of the war, where the international norms of the legitimate use of force came to be disputed. My thesis is therefore that the war that was waged on Europe's 'semi-periphery' was at the same time a struggle for the European normative order.

The 'Last Crusade'? From the 'Monks' Quarrel' to the Ottoman Declaration of War

But what was the origin of the first pan-European war since 1815? Its narrower cause was religious disputes between Roman Catholic and Greek Orthodox clergy and pilgrims over access to the 'Holy Places' in Jerusalem and Bethlehem.[18] These conflicts among worshippers were unfortunately not resolved in the spirit of

---

[10] W. Baumgart, *The Crimean War, 1853–1856* (2nd edn, 2020) at 224; Craig, 'The System of Alliances', in J.P.T. Bury (ed.), *The New Cambridge Modern History* (1960) 246, at 267.
[11] Maag, Pyta, and Windisch, 'Einleitung', in G. Maag, W. Pyta, and M. Windisch (eds), *Der Krimkrieg als erster europäischer Medienkrieg* (2010) 7, at 7.
[12] Figes (n. 9), at xix.
[13] *Ibid*. It should be noted that the coalition wars have also been described as such recently, see Chapter 3.2.
[14] Baumgart (n. 10), at 12, 53–6.
[15] Maag, Pyta, and Windisch (n. 11).
[16] U. Keller, *The Ultimate Spectacle. A Visual History of the Crimean War* (2012).
[17] *Ibid*.
[18] Baumgart (n. 10), at 12.

Christian charity, but were violently fought out with fists, candlesticks, crucifixes, knives, and pistols.[19] While these local religious conflicts were in no way serious enough to cause the outbreak of a pan-European war, they lent themselves perfectly to politicization by the Great Powers.

Karl Marx argued in the *New York Daily Tribune* of 15 April 1854 that there was 'no sanctuary, no chapel, no stone of the Church of the Holy Sepulcher, that had been left unturned for the purpose of constituting a quarrel between the different Christian communities'.[20] In historical research, the impression has prevailed that for Tsar Nicholas I, the religious question was 'mere camouflage' for his actual power interests, i.e. propaganda.[21] In contrast, Orlando Figes, in his fundamental reinterpretation of the Crimean War as the 'last crusade', has argued that politics and faith were closely intertwined, 'and every nation, none more so than Russia, went to war in the belief that God was on its side.'[22]

This intertwining of religion and politics was also evident in the Great Powers' war justifications. Russia claimed to represent the Orthodox Christians and therefore to be allowed to expand its influence in the 'Holy Land' and in Southern Europe at the expense of the Ottoman Empire.[23] France, which after Louis Napoléon's coup d'état (2 December 1851) wanted to finally restore its status as a Great Power, also used religious sentiments against Russia.[24] While French leftists saw the Tsarist Empire as the counter-revolutionary gendarme of 1848/49, rightists saw it as a backward representative of Orthodox heresy.[25]

With this antagonism between France and Russia, the religious conflict over the 'Holy Places' was internationalized. Particularly after 1851, the conflict continued to escalate. In the process, religious claims were once again combined with political and legal ones, with both sides invoking capitulations that the Ottomans had bestowed upon them. But this was the problem: capitulations were not only awarded to one major European power. Rather, according to Marx's precise definition, they were

> imperial diplomas, letters of privilege, octroyed by the Porte to different European nations, and authorizing their subjects to freely enter Mohammedan countries, and there to pursue in tranquillity their affairs, and to practice their worship. They differ from treaties in this essential point, that they are not reciprocal acts contradictorily debated between the contracting parties.... On the contrary, the capitulations are one-sided concessions on the part of the Government granting them,

[19] Figes (n. 9), at 2.
[20] Marx, 'Declaration of War. – On the History of the Eastern Question', *New York Daily Tribune* (15 April 1854).
[21] Baumgart (n. 10), at 29.
[22] Figes (n. 9), at xxiii.
[23] Baumgart (n. 10), at 28 ff.
[24] Figes (n. 9), at 168 ff.
[25] *Ibid.*

in consequence of which they may be revoked at its pleasure…. This precarious character of the capitulations made them an eternal source of disputes, of complaints on the part of Embassadors, and of a prodigious exchange of contradictory notes and firmans revived at the commencement of every new reign.[26]

Although both Russia in 1774 and Napoléon in 1802 had translated Ottoman capitulations into international treaty law, neither side could claim an exclusive right to represent the Christian population in the Ottoman Empire. Nevertheless, Russia wanted to derive such an exclusive right from the vaguely defined Article 7 of the Treaty of Küçük Kaynarca (1774). However, this claim was hardly justifiable in terms of treaty law.[27]

While the Ottoman authorities tried to signal concessions to both sides using their 'troublesome *système de basculea*',[28] Russia and France exerted increasing pressure. In 1852, France sent a warship and forced renewed concessions from the Sultan, and Russia even demanded a protectorate of Orthodox Christians throughout the Ottoman Empire and mobilized 140,000 soldiers on the border with the Danubian principalities.[29] As Matthias Schulz has correctly argued, if Russia's demand had been met, the Ottoman Empire would have been de facto degraded to a Russian protectorate, with Russia having a permanent right to intervene.[30] The Russian demand was unacceptable.

It is therefore reasonable to assume that Russia had anticipated a negative response from the Sublime Porte. This was to provide a favourable justification for further escalation of the conflict: Russia rejected a compromise reached under British mediation in Constantinople. Instead, it repeated its demand for a protectorate of the Orthodox Christians. After a five-day ultimatum had expired, the Russian army occupied Moldavia and Wallachia as a 'bargaining chip', but without declaring war on the Turks.[31] The European Concert reacted to this 'illegitimate reprisal' with renewed mediation efforts in Vienna.[32] The Porte, however, was not consulted here. The result was a technically flawed note, which gave the false impression that Russia had been granted its privileges in the Ottoman Empire through international treaty law, and not through the voluntary action of the Sublime Porte. For the latter, this meant a difference for the sake of the whole. Thus, it had to reject the note and insist on a contractual guarantee of its sovereignty.

When the Tsar, for his part, refused to change the Vienna Note, it became perfectly clear that Russia was seeking escalation. The Western powers now turned

---

[26] Marx (n. 20).
[27] Figes (n. 9), at 7.
[28] Marx (n. 20).
[29] Figes (n. 9), at 108.
[30] Schulz (n. 8), at 303.
[31] On this paragraph, see *ibid.*, at 308–12.
[32] *Ibid.*, at 308.

against St Petersburg. For its part, the Porte issued an ultimatum to Russia to vacate the occupied Danubian principalities. This move was encouraged by Russia's diplomatic (self-)isolation—but also by nationalist and religious protests in Constantinople, where Islamists called for a 'holy war' against Russia.[33] When the Russians refused to vacate the Danubian principalities—Ottoman territory at the time—even after the deadline was extended, the Ottoman Empire declared war on Russia.

Law vs Religion? War Justifications in 1853/54

The Turkish declaration of war on 4 October 1853 emphasized the impossibility of accepting the Vienna Note.[34] Moreover, the Sublime Porte underscored Russia's violation of the international principle of moderation. Even if Russia had been able to raise legitimate criticisms with regard to the Holy Places, it would have had to stay with that issue in the negotiations, 'and not put forth pretensions which the object of its claims could not bear out.'[35] Russia's attempts at intimidation through the early mobilization of its troops were also criticized.

The actual *casus belli* for the Porte, however, was the Russian occupation of Moldova and Wallachia, which was described as a clear breach of international law: 'Who, then, can doubt that Russia is the aggressor?'[36] The Porte therefore described it as its firm and laudable intention to defend 'the sacred Rights of Sovereignty and the Independence of its Government'.[37] Consequently, the declaration of war against Russia was referred to as 'just Reprisals against a violation of Treaties which it looks upon as a casus belli.'[38] The core narrative of the Ottoman declaration of war was thus the Russian breach of international law, which was described as aggression.

How did Russia respond to these accusations? The Russian counter-declaration of 1 November, for its part, accused the Ottoman Empire of aggression. According to this document, the Ottoman Empire had responded to Europe's peaceful efforts with a declaration of war and false accusations against Russia.[39] Like the Sublime Porte, the Tsarist Empire was eager to justify its violence as self-defence.

In a comparison of the Ottoman and Russian declarations of war, however, the differences in the importance attached to international law is striking. The Ottoman

---

[33] Figes (n. 9), at 126–9.
[34] 'Turkish Declaration of War against Russia, 4 October 1853', in E. Hertslet (ed.), *The Map of Europe by Treaty*, vol. 2 (1875) 1171.
[35] *Ibid.*, at 1172.
[36] *Ibid.*
[37] *Ibid.* at 1176.
[38] *Ibid.*
[39] 'Russian Declaration of War against Turkey, 20 October/1 November 1853', in E. Hertslet (ed.), *The Map of Europe by Treaty*, vol. 2 (1875) 1177, at 1177.

declaration of war focused on the Russian breach of international law and positive treaty law (Treaty of Küçük Kaynarca of 1774)—and proved it in detail. Religious, nationalist, or moral arguments, on the other hand, were completely absent. The brief Russian declaration of war, in contrast, contained a mixture of various normative spheres. Particular reference was made to religious arguments in order to construct the image of an uncivilized, peace-threatening enemy, with Russia arguing that the war was a matter of 'defending the Orthodox faith in the East'.[40] Moreover, the Ottoman army was accused of tolerating revolutionaries of all countries in its ranks.[41] This anti-revolutionary argument was self-contradictory, as Russia itself supported pan-Slav nationalists in the Balkans in their revolts against the Ottoman Empire.[42] Russia's international legal argument was decidedly weak. It consisted primarily of a barely convincing interpretation of the 1774 treaty. The fact that this argument was later presented only very briefly by Russian diplomats suggests that Russian diplomacy became aware of its own misinterpretation.[43] Instead of international law, however, the Russian justification strategy mainly relied on narratives of religion, security, and counter-revolution.

The Sublime Porte, on the other hand, based its declaration of war almost exclusively on sound arguments of international law. This is particularly remarkable since the Ottoman Empire was defamed by Europeans for being excessively religious. German historian and lawyer Friedrich Heinrich Geffcken, for example, wrote in his *Geschichte des Orientalischen Krieges* that nowhere were religion, politics, laws, and customs so closely interwoven.[44] A declaration of war in Islam was 'no less a religious question than faith in paradise', according to Geffcken.[45] It is true that scholars of Islamic law had considerable influence on the Sultan.[46] Precisely for this reason, however, it is striking that the Turkish declaration of war in 1853 meticulously used arguments derived from international law, and what is more: positive international law. The Sublime Porte understood that referring to international law was a particularly effective means of branding the Russian aggression a scandal. Paradoxically, then, it was Ottoman reasoning that supported the norms of the Vienna Order—even though the Ottoman Empire was not a formal member of the Concert at that time. Russia, in contrast, as a member of the European Concert, was willing to undermine this order.

So, did Russian aggression and its attempted justification trigger a normative crisis of the Vienna Order? The key to answering this question is knowing which

---

[40] *Ibid.* at 1178.
[41] *Ibid.* at 1177.
[42] J. Milojković-Djurić, *Panslavism and National Identity in Russia and in the Balkans, 1830–1880: Images of the Self and Others* (1994).
[43] Schulz (n. 8), at 306.
[44] F.H. Geffcken, *Zur Geschichte des Orientalischen Krieges* (1881), at 312.
[45] *Ibid.*
[46] On the complex role of Islamic scholars as a means of legitimizing the Sultan's rule, see L. Benton, *Law and Colonial Cultures. Legal Regimes in World History, 1400–1900* (2001), at 109 ff.

arguments were accepted in the communication community of the European Great Powers; and the fact that the other Great Powers endorsed the Ottoman position. France justified its entry into the war in March 1854 by accusing Russia of being solely responsible for the war.[47] In the treaty of 12 March 1854, Great Britain, France, and the Ottoman Empire explicitly described the Russian occupation as 'aggression' against the integrity of the Ottoman Empire and the independence of the Sultan.[48] In addition, the existence of the Ottoman Empire 'in its present limits' was described as essential for the European 'balance of powers' and thus for the Vienna Order.[49] This was the decisive argument for the establishment of the wartime alliance. For European societies were divided in their assessment of the conflict.[50] Entering the war on behalf of a Muslim power represented a hurdle to legitimization for the racist and chauvinist European empires. Even Stratford Cannings, British ambassador to Constantinople and an expert on the Ottoman Empire, described Islam in 1850 as the 'master mischief' associated with 'tyrannical domination'.[51] Thus, Paris had to urge London to gradually support its anti-Russian position.[52]

This step was facilitated by the so-called 'Massacre of Sinope' of 30 November 1853, which involved the Russian destruction of an Ottoman squadron in the port of Sinope.[53] Lord Palmerston, who unlike Prime Minister Aberdeen, advocated war against Russia, recognized its high potential for public politicization.[54] *The Times* wrote on 14 December that the English people demanded Russia receive 'punishment' for its 'hypocrisy'. Russia should not be allowed to turn the Black Sea into 'a Russian lake'.[55] In some British dailies, the Tsar was also portrayed as a religious fanatic, referred to as 'the mad Tsar'.[56] The dismantling of one enemy image—the 'barbaric' Ottoman Empire—was thus accompanied by the construction of another.

In the British declaration of war of 27 March 1854, the different narratives of the British discourse can be clearly identified. The declaration first emphasizing the joint diplomatic efforts of the Ottoman Empire and the Great Powers 'to meet any just demands of the Emperor of Russia without affecting the dignity and

---

[47] 'Message of the French to the Senate and Legislative Assembly, relative to the War with Russia, 27 March 1854', in E. Hertslet (ed.), *The Map of Europe by Treaty*, vol. 2 (1875) 1186, at 1186.

[48] 'Treaty between Great Britain, France, and Turkey. Military Aid to Turkey, 12 March 1854', in E. Hertslet (ed.), *The Map of Europe by Treaty*, vol. 2 (1875) 1181, at 1181.

[49] *Ibid.*

[50] Geffcken (n. 44), at 73.

[51] Figes (n. 9), at 59 ff.

[52] Baumgart (n. 10), at 13 ff.; 106 ff.

[53] *Ibid.*

[54] Figes (n. 9), at 123.

[55] Geffcken (n. 44), at 47.

[56] Stenzel, '"The Mad Czar" und "King Clicquot": Russland und Preußen als Feindbilder in den Karikaturen des "Punch"', in G. Maag, W. Pyta, and M. Windisch (eds), *Der Krimkrieg als erster europäischer Medienkrieg* (2010) 139.

independence of the Sultan'.[57] Then Russian misconduct was blamed. If Russia had really been concerned with the protection of the Christian subjects in the Ottoman Empire, the declaration read, it could have a guarantee of this in the offers made by the Sublime Porte. But the object the Russian Government sought to achieve, the manifesto continued, was a 'right for Russia to interfere in the ordinary relations of Turkish subjects to their Sovereign, and not the happiness of Christian communities'.[58] The Sultan could not agree to such a demand. Therefore, 'His Highness, in self-defence, declared war upon Russia.'[59]

This approval of the Ottoman right to self-defence against an 'unprovoked aggression'[60] was followed by a more extensive justification of the British entry into the war. Having made efforts, together with other European Great Powers, to pacify the conflict, the time had now come to accept that these efforts had been in vain. Russia was held responsible for this. Hence, the declaration continued,

> Her Majesty feels called upon by regard for an Ally, the integrity and independence of whose empire have been recognized as essential to the peace of Europe, by the sympathies of Her people with right against wrong, by a desire to avert from Her dominions most injurious consequences, and to save Europe from the preponderance of a Power which has violated the faith of Treaties, and defies the opinion of the civilized world, to take up arms in conjunction with the Emperor of the French, for the defence of the Sultan.[61]

The British declaration, closely aligned with the French position, thus confirmed the two basic exceptions of legitimate reasons for war in the Vienna Order: self-defence and the preservation of the European peace. But it also included references to unilateral British interests—the protection of its own dominions (the trade routes to India come to mind). Russia, on the other hand, was portrayed as a lawbreaker who had not only violated international treaties, but also used the Christian religion as a pretext 'to cover an aggression undertaken in disregard of its holy precepts'.[62] Russia's actions were not only contrary to the sense of justice of the British population, the declaration read, but even more so to the convictions of the 'civilized world'. In addition, recourse was made to the 'legitimate authority' of the Allied declarers of war as well as to the 'right intention' for entering the war: 'Her Majesty humbly trusts that Her efforts may be successful, and that, by the blessing of Providences, peace may be re-established on safe and solid foundations.'[63]

---

[57] Westminster, 'War Declaration', *The London Gazette* (28 March 1854), at 1008.
[58] Ibid.
[59] Ibid.
[60] Treaty between Great Britain, France, and Turkey (n. 48), at 1184.
[61] Westminster (n. 57), at 1008.
[62] Ibid.
[63] Ibid.

The British declaration of war in 1854 therefore represents a prime example of a justification of war in the long European tradition. It smoothly combined classical elements of the European discourse on the legitimacy of war (at the latest) since Thomas Aquinas with 'modern' arguments of the nineteenth century. Accordingly, the declaration was characterized by a multitude of normative spheres: politics, positive international law, morality, religion and—in keeping with the international zeitgeist—historical civilizational arguments. Continuity and change in the European discourse on the legitimacy of war can thus be vividly depicted here.

What was new in the war declarations of France and Great Britain was that the Eastern Question was fully integrated into the European discourse of war: the independence of the Ottoman Empire was considered essential for the European peace. The Eastern Question was thus framed as a European Question. This framing was important in order to justify force against a Christian Great Power in favour of a Muslim empire. France and Great Britain joined the Crimean War not primarily in the name of Turkey, but rather in the name of Europe.[64] The Russian violence was condemned as aggression, to which it was necessary to react together in concert, after failed attempts at negotiation. Given the decisive military reaction of the Western powers, it was evident that the Russian action had challenged the norms of the Vienna Order—but it had not undermined them. On the contrary, the declarations of war by the Western powers and the Ottoman Empire confirmed and reaffirmed the norms of the Vienna Order.

Norm Emergence in Conflict: The Treaty of Paris as an International Suborder

Austria's reaction to the Russian violence against the Ottoman Empire further confirmed those norms. The multi-ethnic state, shaken by the wave of revolutions in the middle of the century, perceived a general European war as a threat to its existence.[65] Austria remained neutral in the Crimean War, but increasingly distanced itself from Russia. In the end, Austria even threatened to enter the war on the side of the Western powers. In fact, after the fall of Sevastopol on 8 September 1855, Austria succeeded in persuading the Tsar to give in,[66] for which it paid a high price: in the face of the British-French-Austrian offensive and defensive alliance of 2 December 1854, the Holy Alliance finally broke down.

Prussia also remained neutral in the Crimean War, but did not distance itself from Russia as clearly as Austria. In fact the reason for Prussia's neutrality was paralysis. Public opinion was divided during the Crimean War. Russophile and Russophobic

---

[64] Geffcken (n. 44), at 73; A.J.P. Taylor, *The Struggle for Mastery in Europe 1848–1918* (1986), at 61.
[65] Schulz (n. 8), at 315, 626.
[66] Figes (n. 9), at 408.

voices competed with each other, with the one side calling for the defence of the Christian faith alongside Russia and against the 'fanaticism of the Muslims', and the other demanding that action be taken against the aggression of the Russian 'barbarians'.[67] While his brother, who went on to become Emperor Wilhelm I, campaigned for entry into the war on the side of the Concert, King Friedrich Wilhelm IV hesitated[68]—for which certain British newspapers mockingly referred to him as 'King Clicqout' (because of his alleged fondness for Clicquot champagne)[69]. In fact, Prussia did not live up to its responsibilities as a member of the European Concert. It deserted in the face of the challenges of its time, as Matthias Schulz aptly puts it.[70] Politically, this was not entirely unwise: Prussia would benefit most from the estrangement between Russia and Austria.

But even without direct military support from Prussia or Austria, the anti-Russian alliance of the Ottoman Empire, France, Great Britain, and Sardinia-Piedmont was successful. After a two-year war with heavy losses, the Tsarist Empire finally gave in. This was triggered above all by the storming of Sevastopol by the Allies and, not least, the threat of Austria's entry into the war.[71] Alexander II, Russian Tsar since 1855, was persuaded by his advisors to enter into peace negotiations.[72]

The Treaty of Paris, signed on 30 March 1856 after 24 negotiating sessions, ended the first pan-European war since 1815 to establish 'Peace and Friendship... in perpetuity' between the Allies and Russia.[73] For the further development of international order, this oft-neglected peace treaty was, as Franz von Liszt correctly argued, 'of the greatest importance'.[74] According to Winfried Baumgart, the treaty was 'undoubtedly the most important document of the Ius publicum Europaeum' since the Congress of Vienna.[75] It was to be understood, Baumgart argued, as part of the series 'of great peace congresses from Westphalia 1648 to Berlin 1878'.[76]

The enormous significance of the peace treaty is indicated by the fact that, in addition to the Ottoman Empire and Sardinia-Piedmont, all five major European powers became contracting parties—i.e. also Austria and Prussia, which had not

---

[67] M. Hewitson, *Absolute War. Violence and Mass Warfare in the German Lands, 1792–1820* (2017), at 224.
[68] Kraus, 'Wahrnehmung und Deutung des Krimkrieges in Preußen: Zur innenpolitischen Rückwirkung eines internationalen Großkonflikts', in G. Maag, W. Pyta, and M. Windisch (eds), *Der Krimkrieg als erster europäischer Medienkrieg* (2010) 235.
[69] Stenzel (n. 56), at 152.
[70] Schulz (n. 8), at 320.
[71] Baumgart (n. 10), at 21.
[72] Figes (n. 9), at 408.
[73] Art. 1, 'Peace Treaty Concerning the Termination of the Crimean War/Paris (30 March 1856)', in W.G. Grewe (ed.), *Fontes Historiae Iuris Gentium (FHIG), Sources Relating to the History of the Law of Nations*, vol. 3/1: 1815–1945 (1992) 19, at 20.
[74] F. von Liszt, *Das Völkerrecht. Systematisch dargestellt* (11th edn, 1920), at 18.
[75] W. Baumgart, *Der Friede von Paris 1856. Studien zum Verhältnis von Kriegführung, Politik und Friedensbewahrung* (1972), at 279.
[76] Ibid., at 12 ff.

participated in the Crimean War. By providing European answers to the Oriental Question, the Treaty of Paris can even be seen as forming a normative (sub)order of the Vienna Order.[77] The connection between the Oriental Question and the Vienna Peace Order became particularly clear in Article 7 of the Treaty, in which the Great Powers and Sardinia-Piedmont declared the formal admission of the Sublime Porte 'to participate in the advantages of the Public Law and System (*Concert*) of Europe'.[78] However, this formulation requires two explanations: *first*, it has been rightly argued that Turkey had concluded international treaties with European powers even before 1856. Informally at least, the Sublime Porte was already part of the European legal community.[79] That said, it is true that the formal admission of the Ottoman Empire into the Concert and the European legal community only took place with the Treaty of Paris in 1856. As Bluntschli put it:

> Admittedly, for centuries it had been impossible to avoid concluding treaties under international law with the High Porte. But it was not until the Paris Peace Congress of 1856 that Turkey was accepted as a legitimate member of the European community of states, thereby proving the universal human character of international law. Since then, it has been recognized also in practice that the borders of Christendom are not at the same time the borders of international law.[80]

The rising importance of international law is also clearly illustrated by the increasing number of publications of Ottoman legal doctrine on European international law after 1856.[81]

Second—and this point is missing in Bluntschli's argument—the Ottoman Empire continued to be politically and legally discriminated against after 1856.[82] It remained the object of European intervention. This should be borne in mind when reading Bluntschli's praise for the fact that international law had further spread—

> over other Muhammadan states and likewise over China and Japan, and demands respect for its principles of law from all peoples, whether they worship God in

---

[77] Similarly, Werner Eugen Mosse has argued that the Treaty of Paris established an international (sub)system, see W.E. Mosse, *The Rise and Fall of the Crimean System, 1855–71: the Story of a Peace Settlement* (1964).

[78] 'Peace Treaty Concerning the Termination of the Crimean War/Paris (30 March 1856)' (n. 73), at 22.

[79] Palabiyik, 'The Emergence of the Idea of "International Law" in the Ottoman Empire before the Treaty of Paris (1856)', 50 *Middle Eastern Studies* (2014) 233.

[80] J.C. Bluntschli, *Das moderne Völkerrecht der civilisierten Staaten als Rechtsbuch dargestellt* (2nd edn, 1872), at 19.

[81] Palabiyik, 'International Law for Survival: Teaching International Law in the Late Ottoman Empire (1859–1922), 78 *Bulletin of the School of Oriental and African Studies* (2014) 271; for a general account, see A. Becker Lorca, *Mestizo International Law. A Global Intellectual History 1842–1933* (2014).

[82] Genell and Aksakal, '"Salvation through War?" The Ottoman Search for Sovereignty in 1914', in L. Brock and H. Simon (eds), *The Justification of War and International Order: From Past to Present* (2021) 207.

the manner of Christians or Buddhists, in the manner of Muhammadans or the disciples of Confucius. Finally, the truth has penetrated: Religious belief does not establish or impede legal duty.[83]

On closer inspection, the 1856 treaty already points to this legal discrimination: in Article 7, the Ottoman Empire was invited to participate in the benefits of the European legal community—and to submit to its legal vocabulary.

Submission: Law as an Imperial Project

It was only the acceptance of international norms that allowed the Ottoman Empire's integration into the European international order. The Ottoman Empire was tied to a 'voluntary' assurance by the Sultan in the form of a new firman to improve the situation of the Christian population in his territory and to 'modernize'[84] its legal system. With this, the sovereignty and territorial integrity of the Ottoman Empire (Article 7) was obliged to guarantee the 'human rights'[85] of its Christian subjects (Article 9).

The treaty was clearly part of an imperialist and racist project of forced pacification, secularization, and capitalization under the Eurocentric justification narrative of 'civilization'.[86] What constituted civilization, however, was kept deliberately vague, in order to be able to formulate the conditions to be imposed on 'uncivilized' or 'semi-civilized' powers as flexibly as possible.[87] While 'semi-civilized' states such as the Ottoman Empire were usually only admitted to the European community of international law under certain conditions, the affiliation of the USA was taken for granted.[88]

The references to positive international law in the Ottoman war declaration of 1853 thus also appear to be an act of Ottoman 'submission'[89] and 'Westernization'.[90]

---

[83] *Ibid.*, at 19.
[84] 'Peace Treaty Concerning the Termination of the Crimean War/Paris (30 March 1856)' (n. 73), at 19 ff.
[85] On the role of the legally not yet fully defined 'human rights' in the historical context of the nineteenth century, see also Chapter 4.3.
[86] G.W. Gong, *The Standard of 'Civilization' in International Society* (1984); Genell, 'The Well-defended Domains: Eurocentric International Law and the Making of the Ottoman Office of Legal Counsel', 3 *Journal of Ottoman and Turkish Studies* (2016) 255.
[87] N. Tzouvala, *Capitalism As Civilisation. A History of International Law* (2020); S. Spitra, *Die Verwaltung von Kultur im Völkerrecht. Eine postkoloniale Geschichte* (2021); see also Tzouvala and Simon, 'Relapse Into "Civilisation?!" A Narrative's Continuity and Change. An Interview with Ntina Tzouvala', *Völkerrechtsblog* (01 February 2023), available at: https://voelkerrechtsblog.org/de/racial-capitalism-and-international-law-ii/ (last visited 1 March 2023).
[88] M.M. Payk, *Frieden durch Recht? Der Aufstieg des modernen Völkerrechts und der Friedensschluss nach dem Ersten Weltkrieg* (2018), at 41; Becker Lorca (n. 81), at 17 ff.
[89] Baumgart (n. 10), at 207 ff.
[90] Schulz (n. 8), at 343.

under the European 'imperialism of statehood'.[91] The Ottoman submission was an expression of a 'politics in a coercive community', which, in Lothar Brock's words, went hand in hand with the 'increasing futility of all efforts to escape the cohesion instituted from Europe'.[92] But while assimilation was expected from the Sublime Porte, the European Great Powers did not limit themselves to secular war justifications. They flexibly and eclectically combined law, religion, morality, and politics. In this sense, the Treaty of Paris was an unequal treaty between European and non-European powers. While the Ottoman Empire accepted the primacy of European international law as an indicator of civilizational progress, the major European powers clung to their normative hybrid vocabulary of regulating war as it had emerged since 1815/18. Formally, the invocation of God (*invocatio dei*) at the beginning of the treaty already points to this asymmetry.[93] Christian European civilization was at its centre.

But what did the Ottoman Empire receive in return for its submission to international law? The answer is relatively simple: it hoped for legally guaranteed protection against Russia. And this was certainly granted with the Treaty of Paris. Along with the latter came, as I argue, an expansion of international norms against unilateral violence. The treaty of 1856 went beyond the treaties of 1815/17, with the highly political question of intervention, in particular, being more strongly standardized under treaty law in the context of the Oriental Question. Articles 9, 22, 27, and 29, for example, established a prohibition of intervention in the territory of the Ottoman Empire under treaty law.

According to Article 9, it was—

> clearly understoood, that it [the Sultan's guarantee to protect his Christian subjects, HS] cannot, in any case, give to the said Powers the right to interfere, either collectively or separately, in the relations of his Majesty the Sultan with his subjects, or in the Internal Administration of his Empire.[94]

To this end, Article 22 placed the principalities of Wallachia and Moldavia under the sovereignty of the Porte and under the guarantee of the contracting parties. Article 22 clearly states that '[n]o exclusive Protection shall be exercised over by them by any of the guaranteeing powers' and thus that '[t]here shall be no separate right of interference in their Internal Affairs'.[95] Articles 27 and 29 further specified

---

[91] O. Eberl, *Naturzustand und Barbarei. Begründung und Kritik staatlicher Ordnung im Zeichen des Kolonialismus* (2021); see also Becker Lorca (n. 81); L.A. Benton and L. Ford, *Rage for Order. The British Empire and the Origins of International Law, 1800–1850* (2016).
[92] Brock, 'Normative Integration und kollektive Handlungskompetenz auf internationaler Ebene', 6 *Zeitschrift für Internationale Beziehungen* (1999) 323, at 325.
[93] 'Peace Treaty Concerning the Termination of the Crimean War/Paris (30 March 1856)' (n. 73), at 19. Moreover, the *invocatio dei* has remained relevant in the history of constitutional law to this day.
[94] *Ibid.*, at 24.
[95] *Ibid.*, at 30.

that no armed intervention in the principalities (Article 27) or in Serbia (Article 29) could take place without the consent of the Great Powers.[96] With this, the authority of the Concert as the decisive institution for assessing legitimate reasons for the use of force in international relations was confirmed.

This prohibition of intervention, which was particularly robust under treaty law but limited to the Ottoman Empire, was clearly directed against the Russian war justifications of 1853.[97] The Russian (mis)interpretation of the Treaty of Küçük Kaynarca (1774) and the resulting claim of an exclusive right of Russia to represent the Christians in the Ottoman Empire was rejected by Articles 9, 22, 27, and 29. Russia was clearly regarded as an aggressor against the European legal order. The neutralization of the Black Sea (Article 11) and the closure of the straits of the Bosphorus and the Dardanelles (Article 10) underscore this statement.

The anti-Russian thrust of the Treaty of Paris was further underlined by the British-French-Austrian Convention (15 April 1856). In this treaty, the supposed Russian responsibility to protect Christians in the Ottoman Empire was once again explicitly denied. A renewed violation of Turkish integrity, as had been regulated in Article 7 of the Treaty of Paris, was established as a sufficient reason for war.[98] It is noteworthy that this convention was initiated by the Austrian foreign minister Karl Ferdinand von Buol. The diplomatic rift between the long-standing allies Austria and Russia was now evident.[99]

The Abolition of Privateering: Towards Universal International Law

The great importance of the Crimean War for the history of the international legal order governing the use of force is also evident in two other fields of regulation: 'Of particular importance', according to Franz von Liszt, was the Paris Declaration Respecting Maritime Law of 16 April 1856.[100] The Declaration was of crucial importance for the universalization of international law, since it was open to states that had not negotiated it. The Declaration was also particularly significant in the field of warfare; its description as the 'grandfather of all modern international law agreements on the conduct of war' is not without reason.[101] It regulated the abolition of privateering, the freedom of private property in naval warfare, 'insofar as it

---

[96] *Ibid.*, at 31 ff.
[97] Baumgart (n. 75), at 252.
[98] *Ibid.*
[99] Mosse, 'The Triple Treaty of 15 April 1856', 67 *English Historical Review* (1952) 203.
[100] F. von Liszt, *Das Völkerrecht. Systematisch dargestellt* (11th edn, 1920), at 19; see also Anderson, 'Some Further Light on the Inner History of the Declaration of Paris', 76 *The Law Quarterly Review* (1960) 379.
[101] J.M. Lemnitzer, *Power, Law and the End of Privateering* (2014), at 203; on the emergence of privateering, see J.F. Ford, *The Emergence of Privateering* (2023).

is not either war contraband or enemy property under an enemy flag', as well as the binding of the legality of a blockade to its effectiveness.[102] While this was not the first codification of the laws of war in modernity, it was certainly—

> the first general agreement on naval warfare that was also valid beyond the European circle of international law ... to which only the USA, Spain and a few South American states remained outside of the maritime states in the period that followed.[103]

For some contemporary diplomats, the Paris Declaration was a testimony to the 'spirit of the century' and the 'progress of culture': the French foreign minister Alexandre Colonna-Walewski even described the Declaration as the special historical achievement of the Congress of Paris, comparable with the Congress of Westphalia and the Vienna Congress.[104]

'A Vague Promise' as 'a First Step in the Right Direction'? The Mediation of Mediation

Here, however, another aspect of the peace agreement after the Crimean War seems even more interesting. In addition to the area of naval warfare, the Congress of Paris also included a rarely remembered norm in the still very vaguely regulated field of *ius contra bellum*. Article 8 of the Treaty of Paris had introduced mediation as an international norm:

> If there should arise between the Sublime Porte and one or more of the other Signing Powers any misunderstanding which might endanger the maintenance of their relations, the Sublime Porte, and each of such Powers, before having recourse to the use of force, shall afford the other Contracting Parties the opportunity of preventing such an extremity by means of the Mediation.[105]

With this regulation, the dispute settlement mechanism and the subsequent three-month cooling-off period of the League of Nations were anticipated in the treaty law of 1856—even if this regulatory anticipation was regionally limited to the Eastern Question.

But that was not all—at least not entirely: towards the end of the Congress of Paris, the British foreign secretary Lord Clarendon proposed that the mediation

---

[102] Liszt (n. 100), at 19.
[103] Baumgart (n. 75), at 219.
[104] Liszt (n. 100), at 220.
[105] 'Peace Treaty Concerning the Termination of the Crimean War/Paris (30 March 1856)' (n. 73), at 23.

requirement of Article 8 be extended to conflicts of all Congress participants and thus for it to be universalized. However, Lord Clarendon's proposal soon failed due to resistance from the other participants in the Congress, who invoked their sovereign independence.[106]

This recourse to one's own sovereignty, however, in no way implied a claim to a 'free right to war', since it did not call into question the existing norms and institutions of the Vienna Order and the necessity of legitimizing war. It did, however, make clear the desire of the European powers not to transform the Concert's *political* principle of mediation into a *legal* requirement. Here, too, the normative asymmetry of the European legal project became apparent. While Article 8 of the Treaty of Paris obligated the Ottoman Empire to mediate in the event of conflicts, the European powers wanted flexibility of choosing their own conflict resolution mechanisms. Law's limitation of political arbitrariness was to be limited to the European semi-periphery.

Nevertheless, 'the first attempt ... undertaken jointly by the decisive political power centres of Europe ... to preserve peace by establishing the principle of peaceful settlement of disputes'[107] should not be underestimated. This at least is how the European powers' aim was recorded in the Congress minutes: '*que les États etc. avant d'en appeler aux armes, eussent recours, en tant que les circumstances l'admettraient, aux bons offices d'uns Puissance amie*'.[108] After the Congress, more than 30 powers joined in this attempt.[109]

This was a success of the peace societies, pacifist organisations founded after the Napoleonic Wars, which had put the mediation clause on the British foreign policy agenda.[110] The subsequent wars of the nineteenth century were usually preceded by attempts at mediation[111]—even if German jurist Friedrich Heinrich Geffcken erroneously denied this: Geffcken claimed that the subsequent wars after 1856 had shown 'how ineffective this vague promise was'.[112] In fact, this 'vague promise' was indeed promising, for the demand for peaceful settlement of disputes corresponded to the mid-century zeitgeist and, closely related to this, to the increasing importance of the peace movements in Great Britain, the USA, and continental Europe.[113]

The Brussels Peace Congress of 1848 had called for the introduction of international arbitration, an increasing codification of international law, and comprehensive disarmament. In 1849, Liberal politician Richard Cobden introduced a motion in the British Parliament for the conclusion of arbitration treaties between

---

[106] Geffcken (n. 44), at 279.
[107] Baumgart (n. 75), at 224.
[108] J. von Jasmund, *Aktenstücke zur orientalischen Frage*, vol. 2. (1855), at 466.
[109] Schulz (n. 8), at 347; Baumgart (n. 75), at 224.
[110] Geffcken (n. 44), at 279.
[111] Baumgart (n. 75), at 231.
[112] Geffcken (n. 44), at 347.
[113] J. ter Meulen, *Der Gedanke der Internationalen Organisation in seiner Entwicklung* (1968).

Great Britain and other states.[114] Clarendon's proposal in Paris directly reflected this increasing importance of the peace movements. This is not altered by the fact that, contrary to the hopes of the 'friends of peace', there was no longer any talk of legalizing 'arbitration', but only of 'mediation'.[115]

The Congress of Paris was thus already influenced, at least on the margins, by voices and ideas that are usually not believed to have been influential until the end of the century—and especially in the context of the Hague Peace Conferences of 1899/1907.[116] According to Gladstone, the 'civilized powers' had even officially outlawed war for the first time in Paris.[117] And Clarendon assumed that 'reasonable people' would be pleased with the resolution as 'a first step in the right direction'.[118]

However, the Treaty of Paris did *not* establish a prohibition of war under positive international law. Nor did it prevent the outbreak of further wars in the second half of the nineteenth century. However, it is wrong to regard it as completely 'ineffective',[119] as contemporary defeatists claimed. This can clearly be refuted, not least in view of its discursive impact.

New Conflicts—New Principles: The Rise of the Nationality Principle

The Crimean War thus acted as a norming catalyst in international politics. At the same time, however, it also fuelled political tensions in Europe, with the Holy Alliance breaking down over the antagonism between Austria and Russia in the Crimean War. Both Vienna and St Petersburg now sought closer diplomatic relations with the main war victor, Paris. Nevertheless, the 'would-be revisionist' Napoléon III did not succeed in transforming the international order established in Vienna in 1814/15, which had followed the defeat of his uncle.[120] Napoléon's commitment to the principle of nationality prevented a stable alliance with any of the Eastern powers. At the Congress of Paris, however, Napoléon III was able to establish popular sovereignty as a desired principle in the debates on the independence of the Balkan principalities—even if these were placed under Ottoman sovereignty and European guarantee.[121]

However, the increasing importance of the nationality principle as a normative concept in international relations also contributed to the emergence of new

---

[114] Baumgart (n. 75), at 229.
[115] *Ibid.*
[116] *Ibid.*, at 231.
[117] *Ibid.*, at 229.
[118] Geffcken (n. 44), at 279.
[119] *Ibid.*
[120] Senner, 'Mainz Wien 1855 – Paris 1856. Zwei Friedenskonferenzen im Spiegel einer neuen Aktenedition', *Francia* 26 (1999) 109.
[121] *Ibid.*, at 124; Schulz (n. 8), at 346.

conflicts, as well as the intensification of old ones.[122] Since the revolutionary wave of 1848/49—and despite its 'failure'—international relations had already been much more strongly characterized by nationalistically motivated antagonisms.[123] The national independence and unity movements benefited from the end of the Holy Alliance. The right to self-determination of peoples under natural law, which had emerged in 1789, and the international territorial order guaranteed by positive law in 1814/15 now clearly collided. 'The monarchical and the popular principle', Heffter argued with regard to the revolution of 1830, 'have watched over each other in European politics ever since. Neither principle denies the law of nations, but certainly the conception of the latter is not the same.'[124] Arguments from natural law and positive law collided. And there was no rule to resolve this collision of norms.

However, this did not necessarily mean war. A pan-European war had already been prevented in 1848/49—not least because France, unlike in 1789, did not attempt to change the international order by force.[125] But even after 1856, in the context of the Neuchâtel crisis and the Romanian Question, the conflict over norms could be resolved peacefully through the Concert.[126]

But conflict resolution was more of a challenge when major powers took clear sides in this conflict of norms and rejected the mediation of the Concert. There were three contexts in which the Concert could not prevent war: in the Balkans,[127] in the Italian, and in the German lands. In the following sections, the Italian and German Wars of Unification will be used to examine which patterns of justification were used in these conflicts: did the norms of the Vienna Order maintain their discursive authority? Or did *Realpolitiker* à la Bismarck, Cavour, Gorchakov, Napoléon III, and Schwarzenberg, in their instrumentalization of the national, supersede the necessity of justifying war in terms of a 'free right to wage war'?

5.3 '*Viva l'Italia*'—*e Viva l'Ordine Internazionale?* The Justification of War in the *Risorgimento*

A particularly important example of the conflict of norms between the Viennese territorial order under positive international law and popular sovereignty based on natural law can be found in Italy between 1848 and 1861—in the *Risorgimento* ('Resurgence'), with the Italian independence movements primarily being directed

---

[122] A.W. Heffter, *Das europäische Völkerrecht der Gegenwart* (1844), at 10.
[123] Hahn, 'Die Revolutionen von 1848 als Strukturkrise des europäischen Staatensystems', in P. Krüger (ed.), *Das europäische Staatensystem im Wandel. Strukturelle Bedingungen und bewegende Kräfte seit der Frühen Neuzeit* (1996) 131, at 151.
[124] Heffter (n. 122), at 10.
[125] Hahn (n. 123), at 137; D. Langewiesche, *Der gewaltsame Lehrer. Europas Kriege in der Moderne* (2019), at 203.
[126] Schulz (n. 8), at 360–442.
[127] The Russo-Turkish War of 1877/78 is discussed in Chapter 6.4.

against Austrian rule in Italy. The Habsburg monarchy in turn was able to justify its influence in Italy under international law with the Final Act of Vienna. Positive law and natural law were thus opposed to each other as they had been in the era of the French Revolution (Chapter 3).

Revolution from Above: The Justification of the First War of Independence

In 1848/49, there were numerous revolutionary uprisings in the Italian principalities, including Milan, Padua, Naples, Sicily, and Rome. These uprisings led to the first Italian War of Independence, with King Carlo Alberto I of Sardinia-Piedmont intervening militarily in the conflict in favour of the independence movements. Why did he do this? Contrary to the cosmopolitan republican ideas and principles of Guiseppe Mazzini, who envisaged Italian unification happening 'from below', Sardinia-Piedmont pursued realpolitik, and indeed anti-republican motives 'from above'. Carlo Alberto I was keen to place himself at the head of the independence movement—and steer it in a monarchical reformist direction.[128]

In his declaration of war on Austria of 23 March 1848, Carlo Alberto I appealed to the populations of Lombardo-Venetia in order to instrumentalize the national sense of unity in Italy for his cause. Sardinia-Piedmont, the declaration read, joined the insurgents out of love for their common ancestry and commonality of vows.[129] But the war was not only waged in the name of freedom, as a defence of the 'violated rights' of the Italian people (*difensori di conculcati diritti*), Carlo Alberto I claimed. Rather, war was also being waged in the name of God, *di quel Dio che con sì meravigliosi impulsi pose l'Italia in grado di fare da sè*.[130]

Thus, in his legitimization of violence, Carlo Alberto I combined new, nationalistic, with old, religious justification narratives. As becomes clear here, too, Sardinia-Piedmont followed a moderate reform course: nationalism and monarchy were to be reconciled. Influenced by the March Revolution, Sardinia-Piedmont introduced a constitution. However, the first Italian War of Independence of 1848/49 was not successful. Carlo Alberto I abdicated after Italy's decisive defeat in the battle of Novara (23 March 1849). His son Vittorio Emanuele II succeeded him.

---

[128] R.J. Evans, *The Pursuit of Power: Europe, 1815–1914* (2017), at 337.
[129] '*Per amore di stirpe, per intelligenza di tempi, per comunanza di voti, noi ci associamo primi a quell'unanime ammirazione che vi tributa l'Italia.*' C. Casati, *Nuove rivelazioni su i fatti di Milano nel 1847–1848* (1885), at 203.
[130] 'of that God who by such wonderful impulses put Italy in a position to do for itself', Manifesto of 23 March 1848 to Venice, in Venice governo provvisorio, in *Raccolta per ordine cronologico di tutti gli atti, decreti, nomine ecc. del governo prov. della Repubblica veneta (di Venezia)* (1848), at 148.

David against Goliath: Cavour's Strategy of Justifying War against Austria

Sardinia-Piedmont now found itself in a dilemma: national self-determination was discussed in Paris in 1856 as an internationally accepted principle (see above). Moreover, in Paris, Turin had been able to put the Italian Question before the Concert.[131] After 1856, Sardinian and Austrian newspapers engaged in an increasingly heated dispute over the Italian Question.[132] It had also become apparent that the Western European public were sympathetic to the Italian cause. Austrian superiority, however, stood in the way of Italian unification.

For Camillo Benso, conte di Cavour, prime minister of Sardinia-Piedmont since 1861, it was therefore clear that Italian unification could only be achieved by force. Like Schwarzenberg in Austria, Napoléon III in France, Gorchakov in Russia, and Bismarck in Prussia, Cavour stood for the supposed mid-century 'realist turn'[133] in European political culture. Cavour was primarily concerned with Sardinia-Piedmont gaining power in Italy and Europe. This required a unification of Italy under the leadership of Turin.

In Cavour's view, to unify Italy, the constitutional monarchy had to secure the military support not only of the national movement but also of at least one of the European Great Powers, in its struggle against Austria. This was achieved in 1858: following in the tradition of his uncle, Napoléon III wanted to 'liberate' the Italians from what he understood as an illegitimate Austrian expansion of power—undoubtedly not without following his own territorial interests in Italy.[134] At the same time, a failed bomb attack by the Italian revolutionary Felice Orsini in January 1858 had made it clear to Napoléon III that the Italian national movement needed to be suppressed.[135] In a secret meeting in Plombières-les-Bains, Napoléon III promised Cavour that France would support Sardinia-Piedmont with 200,000 soldiers in the event of Austrian aggression. In the event of war, an Italian confederation was to be created, the kingdom of Piedmont in northern Italy was to be enlarged, and Nice and Savoy were to be ceded to France.[136] A unification of all of Italy under the Sardinian crown, however, was not in Napoléon III's interest.

A justification strategy was now needed that could persuade the Concert to tolerate an unauthorized violent unification of Italy. For a legal title to unilaterally

---

[131] L. Gall, *Europa auf dem Weg in die Moderne. 1850–1890* (1997), at 46.
[132] F.W. Ghillany, *Diplomatisches Handbuch Sammlungen der wichtigsten europäischen Friedensschlüsse, Congreßacten und sonstigen Staatsurkunden vom Westphälischen Frieden bis auf die neueste Zeit; mit kurzen geschichtlichen Einleitungen*, vol. 7: Friede zu Zürich zwischen Österreich und Frankreich, 10. November 1859 (Der französisch-sardinisch-österreichische Krieg vom Jahr 1859) (1868), at 63.
[133] Nipperdey (n. 5), at 718.
[134] Schulz (n. 8), at 447.
[135] A. Blumberg, *A Carefully Planned Accident. The Italian War of 1859* (1990), at 21; Evans (n. 128), at 337.
[136] Evans (n. 128), at 340.

change the territorial order was by no means endorsed in international relations, despite the increasing acceptance of the nationality principle. After 1856, however, the prospects for such a justification of violence were not bad. Austria was isolated in the context of the Italian Question: in Western Europe, Austrian rule in Italy was perceived as increasingly outmoded.[137] In principle, the changeability of borders, in the spirit of popular sovereignty, was supported by the Western powers—as long as it did not touch upon the Vienna Order and was decided by the Concert. This was a clear rejection of Metternich's idea of Italy as a mere geographical concept. Vienna, moreover, could not hope for Russian support after the diplomatic rift in the Crimean War. Prussia and the German Confederation did not feel responsible. Since no federal territory was affected by the conflict in Italy, no collective case of defence in accordance with Article XI of the Federal Act was justified.[138]

Napoléon III and Cavour were now both waiting for the opportunity to present a good reason for war. Whether Napoléon III, like Cavour, wanted to provoke Austrian aggression through a 'carefully planned accident'[139] by any means, or whether he was also willing to find a diplomatic solution for the Italian Question, is disputed in the research.[140] But there is another decisive factor here: both statesmen were clearly aware that even a nationalistically charged use of force still required international justification. Napoléon III repeatedly emphasized that the French army could only intervene militarily in favour of Sardinia if the reason for the war held up before the diplomacy and public opinion of both France and Europe.[141] Clear evidence of the enduring normative power of the international order!

A suitable justification for violence could be put forward in 1859. After Austria had begun conscripting Italians into its army, Sardinia-Piedmont mobilized its troops—which in turn prompted Austria to demand unilateral disarmament by Sardinia-Piedmont.[142] Vienna evaded all attempts at mediation by the Concert, since it thought that war would be more effective.[143] In doing so, however, Austria violated the Concert norms of restraint and mediation and ultimately manoeuvred itself into further diplomatic isolation.

Vienna, however, made every effort to justify its violence nationally and internationally: on 29 April 1859, Franz Joseph I declared war on Sardinia-Piedmont after an ultimatum had expired. One day earlier, Franz Joseph I had explained the reasons for his declaration of war in detail in a manifesto entitled '*An meine Völker!*' ('To my peoples!'). The Austrian Emperor argued that the years of hostilities by

---

[137] Ghillany (n. 132), at 63; E.J. Kolla, *Sovereignty, International Law and the French Revolution* (2017), at 285.
[138] Ghillany (n. 132), at 63.
[139] Blumberg (n. 135).
[140] Schulz (n. 8), at 450.
[141] Cavour to Vittorio Emanuele II, 24 July 1858, in C.B. conte di Cavour, *Il carteggio Cavour-Nigra dal 1858 al 1861: Plombières*, vol. 1 (1926) 112 ff.
[142] Evans (n. 128), at 341.
[143] Schulz (n. 8), at 479–96.

Sardinia violating the indisputable rights of his crown and the integrity of the Empire entrusted to him by God were now to be ended.[144] Franz Joseph I started by referring to the first Italian War of Independence of 1848/49, claiming that 'the same enemy' had already broken international law and breached the customs of war more than ten years earlier when it invaded Lombardy and Veneto without due cause.[145] The recourse to international law here served the dichotomous construction of friend and foe. While Franz Joseph I described Sardinia-Piedmont as a law-breaking, unjust war party, he stylized Austria as a just, righteous, and benevolent victor. Although his 'brave army' had already defeated Sardinia twice, Franz Joseph I argued, he had behaved generously, stretched out his hand in reconciliation, and thus 'sacrificed the blood of my army for peace'.[146] The victorious Austria had not violated any of Sardinia's rights as a member of the European 'family of nations' and had not taken possession of any Sardinian territory.[147] The response to this unprecedented leniency, however, according to the Austrian Emperor, was Sardinia's increasingly treacherous agitation against its Lombard-Venetian kingdom.[148] But again, Franz Joseph I argued, he had reacted with patience to the new hostilities and accepted the mediation efforts of the other Great Powers—on the condition that Sardinia-Piedmont disarmed. Sardinia had not fulfilled this condition, which, the Emperor argued, was why he had ordered his army to enter Sardinian territory.[149] This justification strategy was coherent. However, it was not convincing: after all, it was Austria, not Sardinia, that had boycotted the Concert's many attempts at mediation.

The Austrian Emperor, however, clearly declared peace to be the norm of the international order: war was an evil of mankind and his Empire was dependent on peace.[150] But the monarch's heart must be silent in the face of duty and honour, he argued. Franz Joseph I thus used the narrative of a preventive defence, for the enemy was standing at the border to seize Austrian possessions in Italy, and France was interfering with legal relations in Italy on flimsy pretexts. Accordingly, the Austrian offensive was intended to prevent a Sardinian, possibly also a French attack.

In addition, Franz Joseph I also referred to Austria's 'glorious history'. It had often been Austria's sword, he argued, that had driven away the shadows of the revolution threatening the highest goods of mankind.[151] Here, Franz Joseph I alluded to the battle against Napoléon I. So, if he took up the sword, Franz Joseph

---

[144] 'Austrian Declaration of War against Sardinia, 28 April 1859', in E. Hertslet (ed.), *The Map of Europe by Treaty*, vol. 2 (1875) 1362, at 1362.
[145] *Ibid.*
[146] *Ibid.*
[147] *Ibid.*
[148] *Ibid.*, at 1363.
[149] *Ibid.*
[150] *Ibid.*
[151] *Ibid.*, at 1364.

I proclaimed, he did so in defence of the honour and law not only of Austria, but of all peoples, states, and mankind.[152] The Austrian Emperor thus not only appealed to the two central narratives for justifying war in the Vienna Order: self-defence and the restoration of peace. He also depicted the struggle as a renewed battle of destiny against revolution on behalf of Austria, Europe, and, indeed, all of humanity.

A reason for this argument was Franz Joseph's I hope that Austria would not stand alone in the battle. Thus, he argued that the ground on which the battle was now to be fought had been 'made fertile by the blood of the German brothers'. It had long been the place where the 'cunning enemies of Germany' usually began their game to break Germany's inner power.[153] Franz Joseph I was once again alluding to Napoléon Bonaparte, since the feeling prevailed in all parts of Germany, the Austrian Emperor asserted, that such a danger was once again imminent. This was a clear message to the German Confederation and to Prussia.

Austria's justifications for war can thus be interpreted as an attempt to extricate itself from its self-inflicted diplomatic isolation in the Italian Question. The Emperor wanted to win over the Confederation and Prussia as allies for a war against Sardinia-Piedmont and France by referring not only to violated legal titles, the 'justice' of their own violence, God, and honour, but also to common European values and the 'German' struggle against Napoléon I. Austria was thus to be presented as the defender of the international order in general and of Germany in particular.

Although the multiple justificatory arguments were skilfully combined, Franz Joseph I's efforts were in vain. Not one of the other Great Powers saw the Austrian preventive war as legitimate. Instead, they all perceived it as an aggression against Sardinia-Piedmont.[154] The Concert did not intervene violently in the Austro-Sardinian War of 1859, but it did deprive Austria of any Great Power solidarity in the conflict. Austria was left to its own devices.

For Sardinia-Piedmont and France, this offered a decidedly favourable opportunity to implement their plans. Now that Austria was seen as the aggressor, could the two Allied powers confine themselves to a purely nationalistic legitimation strategy of realpolitik to mobilize their own population and refrain from any recourse to international norms?

Not at all! In his counter-declaration, which he addressed to his people on 29 April 1859, King Vittorio Emanuele II also referred to the typical narratives of the international order. By portraying Austria as the aggressor, Vittorio Emanuele II recalled the Vienna Order's prohibition of aggressive war.[155] This impression was

[152] *Ibid.*
[153] *Ibid.*
[154] Schulz (n. 8), at 489.
[155] 'Sardinian Declaration of War against Austria, 29 April 1859', in E. Hertslet (ed.), *The Map of Europe by Treaty*, vol. 2 (1875) 1365, at 1365.

further strengthened by emphasizing that Austria was attacking 'with a mighty army'. Thus, the Sardinian David faced the Austrian Goliath.

As Austria had warned against the 'revolutionary' Sardinia, the former was now portrayed as a backward power, 'unable' to modernize its political order as well as 'unwilling' to diplomatically negotiate the Italian Question in the Concert.[156] This was a brilliant rhetorical move. By referring to the Concert, Vittorio Emanuele II clearly located himself within the international order of Europe. In doing so, he made himself immune to Franz Joseph I's accusation of bringing a renewed revolutionary danger upon Europe. At the same time, Vittorio Emanuele II portrayed the Austrian Emperor as an outsider to the socio-political and legal order of Europe. According to Vittorio Emanuele II, Austria was neither capable of domestic reforms nor diplomatic cooperation. Sardinia thus presented itself as the progressive power of a 'new Europe', Austria on the other hand as the backward remnant of an 'old Europe'. As already outlined above, a useful discursive sounding board for this narrative had emerged in Western European politics at the latest from 1856.[157]

Vittorio Emanuele II then skilfully combined legitimizing narratives of the international order with those of his Italian nationalist agenda, claiming that Sardinia was fighting together with 'the brave soldiers' of Napoléon III for 'freedom' and 'justice', since Austria had dared to demand the limitation of the Sardinian troops. This, Vittorio Emanuele II argued, was tantamount to handing over the 'brave youth' who had joined the national independence movement from all parts of Italy to Austrian rule.[158] In the Sardinian justifications of war, nationalism and internationalism were not opposites. Rather, they were linked together.

This is also reflected in the second paragraph of the Sardinian counter-declaration. Now addressing the entire 'Italian people', Vittorio Emanuele II stressed that Austria was attacking Sardinia-Piedmont because the latter had represented the cause of Italy in the councils of Europe. Austria had violated treaties by force, which meant that all law was now on the side of the Italian nation. Accordingly, Vittorio Emanuele II argued, he was defending not only his throne, but also the freedom of his people, the honour of Italy, and the rights of the entire nation with arms. In doing so, the king relied on God, Italian concord, the bravery of Italian soldiers, the alliance with France, and the sense of justice in public opinion.[159] Finally, Vittorio Emanuele II also asserted his *intentio recta*. He only wanted to be 'the first soldier of Italian independence', the king wrote, before concluding the justification of the war with a '*Viva l'Italia*'.[160]

This combination of national and international justifications for war was echoed in Napoléon III's public war declaration of 3 May 1859, in which Austria was

---

[156] *Ibid.*
[157] Ghillany (n. 132), at 63.
[158] 'Sardinian Declaration of War against Austria, 29 April 1856' (n. 155), at 1365.
[159] *Ibid.*
[160] *Ibid.*, at 1366.

once again assigned the role of aggressor.[161] By entering the territory of France's Sardinian ally, Napoléon III claimed, Austria had at the same time declared war on France: Austria had violated international treaty law and threatened French borders. The reference to a violation of the law was followed by a recourse to diplomacy. All the Great Powers had protested Austrian aggression, Napoléon III argued. However, since Austria, unlike Sardinia, had not agreed to mediation, the only reason for the Danube monarchy's aggression could be the desire to further expand its rule.

At the same time, Napoléon III also emphasized that he was not seeking any conquests with his support of the Italian people and that he wanted to comply with treaties under international law. The French war aim, according to Napoléon III, was to promote Italian independence. What Napoléon III concealed was the fact that he himself hoped for territorial gains from the war against Austria (Savoy and Nice) as well as for more French influence in Italy. Instead, according to Napoléon III, France's entry into war was based on justice, humanity, love for the fatherland, bravery, and independence. The French Emperor also referred to religion: in the eyes of God, he argued, this was a holy war.[162]

In Napoléon III's multinormative war justification, France's progressive reformist politics of international law are clearly revealed: the French Emperor rejected Franz Joseph I's assertion of a revolutionary danger to the international order. However, he also argued that France's natural allies were always those who strove for the betterment of 'the human race'. Accordingly, the French sword was not carried to rule, but to liberate.[163] As Napoléon III claimed, the war against backward Austria served the further development of international law—a narrative that was to become increasingly important in the second half of the century.[164]

Sardinia-Piedmont and France thus succeeded in integrating Italian independence into a defensive justification strategy after the Austrian offensive. Now liberation from the Austrian yoke seemed a logical next step following Sardinia's self-defence. Clear evidence, then, of the need for justification of war in the middle of the century! In the Sardinian and French justifications of war, old and new legitimations were carefully weighed against each other. Even though the Austrian justification of war also combined old and new legitimation narratives, the excellently planned and successfully implemented Sardinian-French justification strategy prevailed here. The Austrian narrative of prevention failed, and Vienna appeared as the aggressor. With this, its domination in Italy was seen as illegitimate.

---

[161] 'French Declaration of War against Austria, 3 May 1859', in E. Hertslet (ed.), *The Map of Europe by Treaty*, vol. 2 (1875) 1368.
[162] *Ibid.*, at 1369.
[163] *Ibid.*, at 1368.
[164] Chapter 6.

Liberation of Italy—Sardinian Rule: A Contradiction of the International Order?

The war between Austria and the Sardinian-French alliance was decided in the Battle of Magenta on 6 June 1859 and that of Solferino on 24 June 1859. The latter was in fact the largest battle since Waterloo in June 1815, with around 300,000 soldiers fighting.[165] For the codification of *ius in bello*, the battle is famed to have had the greatest significance[166]—in a dialectical way. Shocked by the brutality of the battle, the Geneva merchant Henry Dunant founded the Red Cross Society, from which the Geneva tradition of international humanitarian law emerged.[167]

The Battle of Solferino ended with the defeat of the Austrian army. France now withdrew from the war: Napoléon III wanted Austria to be weakened in Italy, but he did not want an Italian nation-state.[168] Furthermore, public opinion in Germany was turning in favour of Austria: Prussian Prince Regent Wilhelm considered— albeit reluctantly—entering the war.[169] The war ended with the preliminary peace of Villafranca on 11 July 1859 and the Peace of Zurich on 10 November 1859.

Contrary to Napoléon III's expectations, the French withdrawal from war did not mean the end of Italian unification. First in northern Italy, but soon also in southern Italy after Garibaldi's 'Train of a Thousand' (*'Spedizione dei Mille'*), plebiscites were held, and annexations followed, the likes of which had not been seen since the Napoleonic Wars.[170] The plebiscites promised democratic participation, but were organized in a non-transparent manner. Many Sicilians, for example, did not realize that they were not confirming their 'liberator' Garibaldi as Sicilian ruler, but voting on the annexation of Sicily to Sardinia-Piedmont.[171]

After the republican Garibaldi had subordinated himself to the liberal-conservative reformer Cavour, the unification of Italy under the supremacy of Sardinia-Piedmont could be completed. This was achieved with the incorporation of Veneto (1866) and Rome (1870) during the German Wars of Unification. Sardinia's constitution was extended to the entire Italian state—Cavour's plan had succeeded. Nevertheless, the organization of (albeit non-transparent) plebiscites made it clear that even Cavour needed legitimacy within the Italian populations. Realpolitik thus by no means excluded recourse to principles. The German cultural

---

[165] Evans (n. 128), at 341.
[166] H. McCoubrey, *International Humanitarian Law. Modern Developments in the Limitation of Warfare* (1998), at 16.
[167] Greenwood, 'Historical Development and Legal Basis', in D. Fleck (ed.), *The Oxford Handbook of International Humanitarian Law* (2008) 101; Alexander, 'A Short History of International Humanitarian Law', 26 *European Journal of International Law* (2015) 109.
[168] Evans (n. 128), at 345.
[169] Schulz (n. 8), at 406 ff.
[170] Kolla (n. 137), at 285.
[171] M.I. Finley, D. Mack Smith, and C. Duggan, *Geschichte Siziliens und der Sizilianer* (4th edn, 2010), at 292 ff.

historian Johannes Scherr argued in 1888 that it was not only Cavour, but rather three men who created the '*Regno d'Italia*':

> Mazzini, Garibaldi, Cavour. Mazzini was the heart, Cavour the head, Garibaldi the arm of the Italian unity movement .... Without the two idealist politicians Mazzini and Garibaldi, where would Cavour have been with all his realpolitik? In his little Piedmontese ministerial chair.[172]

To be able to establish the Kingdom of Italy at all, Sardinia-Piedmont had modified the territorial order decided in Vienna. In the process, Italian states had been annexed. In conclusion, the question must be asked here: did the Italian unification and Cavour's realpolitik trigger a normative crisis of the international order?

There can be no doubt, Italian unification had been achieved by force without a mandate by the Concert, and Austria's legal rights in Italy had thus clearly been violated. Nevertheless, the European Concert tolerated the unilateral annexations. What is more, in 1867 Italy was accepted as a member of the European Concert of Great Powers. Since Austria was seen as aggressor, Sardinia-Piedmont could justify its war of unification—and ultimately even its (nevertheless illegal) annexations—as (a consequence of) self-defence. Furthermore, the violent unification of Italy 'from above' hardly affected the Concert's 'dynastic family cartel'.[173] It simply posed no threat to the general European peace. Indeed, Great Britain even saw an Italian kingdom as a guarantor of international peace, because it freed Italy from Austrian and French hegemonial claims.[174]

The fact that Sardinia-Piedmont succeeded in unifying Italy militarily was due not least to its mastery of the unwritten rules of contemporary discourse on the justification of war. A national unification without recourse to international norms and justifications for war would not have been in the spirit of Cavour or Napoléon III. Both wanted to reform the international legal order in favour of popular sovereignty, but without calling into question this order's fundamental norm of the legitimate use of force as a result. Rather, all warring parties confirmed the two central justification narratives of the international order: they each claimed to defend themselves against an (imminent or actual) attack and to take up arms in the name of European peace. In this respect, the discourse of justified war differed only slightly from that of the first half of the century. The Italian Wars of Unification did *not* cause a crisis of the international normative order.

---

[172] J. Scherr, *Menschliche Tragikkomädien* (1884), at 70.
[173] Langewiesche (n. 125), at 214 ff.
[174] Schulz (n. 8), at 519.

5.4 Blood, Iron—and Law?! Justifying German Unification

The 'failed'[175] revolution of 1848/49 had left 'the political organization of Germany an unresolved political problem'.[176] Following the successful Italian Wars of Unification, the continent was gripped by a new wave of national euphoria, for example in Hungary, Poland—and the German lands. National liberals recognized that a unification of Germany in the sense of a *Kleindeutsche Lösung* (little German solution) was only possible by abolishing the German Confederation, which had been reinstated in 1850 under its hegemon Austria.[177] This meant that German unification had to be enforced by unilateral military violence.

'Blood and Iron': Laying the Foundations of Bismarck's Realpolitik

This required the military support of another major German power.[178] All the hopes of the national liberals were therefore pinned on the Prussian monarchy. Not only had the political and economic power rivalry between Prussia and Austria reached its peak in the 1860s,[179] Prussia also potentially had the necessary military clout. This was due not least to the importance of the Rhineland and Westphalia as industrial centres and 'Prussia's armouries'.[180] In 1862, the publicist Rudolf Löwenstein argued—anticipating John Maynard Keynes—that German unity would be achieved less by 'blood and iron' than by 'coal and iron'.[181]

While to liberals, Prussia appeared militarily powerful, there was a significant problem: under Friedrich Wilhelm IV, the Prussian state was anything but liberal.[182] This changed only briefly under his successor, Wilhelm I. The 'New Era' ended as early as 1862 in a power struggle between king and parliament, which escalated in the debate on army reform. In the ensuing constitutional conflict, in September 1862 Wilhelm I appointed one of Prussia's most conservative politicians and diplomats as prime minister: Otto von Bismarck.

Although he himself is unlikely to have ever used the term,[183] realpolitik is probably more strongly associated with Bismarck than with any other statesman

---

[175] Wolfram Siemann has rightly pointed out that the concept of the 'failure' of the revolutions needs to be reconsidered, due to their lasting effects; W. Siemann, *Die deutsche Revolution von 1848/49* (1985), at 223.
[176] Siemann (n. 175), at 218.
[177] Evans (n. 128), at 351.
[178] Evans (n. 128), at 350 ff.; Langewiesche (n. 125), at 214.
[179] Doering-Manteuffel (n. 5), at 38 ff.
[180] C. Jahr, *Blut und Eisen. Wie Preußen Deutschland erzwang: 1864–1871* (2020), at 94.
[181] Ibid.
[182] Evans (n. 128), at 350 ff.
[183] Bew (n. 5), 47.

of the nineteenth century.[184] Bismarck was aware of the growing public influence of the liberals.[185] He tried to convince the latter that Prussia's political importance in Germany and Europe depended on its power, not its freedom. In his famous speech to the Prussian House of Representatives on 30 September 1862, Bismarck argued that '[n]ot through speeches and majority decisions will the great questions of the day be decided—that was the great mistake of 1848 and 1849—but by iron and blood.'[186]

Bismarck's goal in foreign policy was Prussian hegemony in Germany. This goal included the unilateral use of military force. Austria had to be pushed out of Germany. Given that Austria was diplomatically isolated in Europe after the Crimean War and its aggression against Sardinia-Piedmont, the 1860s offered the ideal opportunity: in 1866, Bismarck was able to replace the German Confederation by the North German Confederation after the Prussian victory over Austria. In 1870/71, the victory over Napoléon III was followed by the founding of the German Empire under Prussian domination. In both wars, Prussia annexed German states. Bismarck's realpolitik, it could be argued, had prevailed against the norms of the Vienna Order. Was this the end of the Concert and the international norm of peace? Did Bismarck's blood-and-iron also refer to an unlimited 'right to go to war'?

What is certain is that Bismarck's belligerent unification policy undoubtedly meant a serious violation of the norms of the Viennese order—much more serious than that committed by Sardinia-Piedmont in the Italian Wars of Unification. In the case of Prussia, a Great Power violated the Vienna norms, the German Confederation as a central element of the international security order was eliminated, and Bismarck's wars of 1864, 1866, and 1870/71 brought about a fundamental restructuring of the European power constellation.

However, my argument is that Bismarck had indeed internalized the international norm of peace. For an excessively linear retrospective on the victorious Prussian wars overlooks the fact that Bismarck's foreign policy was initially by no means 'one track, fixated on conflict, even on war'.[187] In his memoirs, Bismarck stated that historical developments could not be anticipated.[188] Lothar Gall is correct with his claim that the insinuation of a continuous consistency and unambiguity of Bismarck's policy is 'neither subjectively nor objectively' accurate.[189]

---

[184] Faber, 'Realpolitik als Ideologie. Die Bedeutung des Jahres 1866 für das politische Denken in Deutschland', 203 *Historische Zeitschrift* (1966) 1; D. Haffer, *Europa in den Augen Bismarcks. Bismarcks Vorstellungen von der Politik der europäischen Mächte und vom europäischen Staatensystem* (2010), at 47.
[185] Bew (n. 5), 37.
[186] Bismarck, 'Reden 1847–1869', in W. Schüßler (ed.), *Bismarck: Die gesammelten Werke*, vol. 10 (1928), at 139 ff.
[187] K. Canis, *Bismarcks Aussenpolitik 1870 bis 1890. Aufstieg und Gefährdung* (2 end., 2008), at 28.
[188] S.A. Silverstone, *From Hitler's Germany to Saddam's Iraq. The Enduring False Promise of Preventive War* (2018), at 103.
[189] Gall (n. 131), at 304.

So, even if Bismarck rather carefully and deliberately took one step after another 'as if on marshy ground'[190]—was his foreign policy not nevertheless characterized by a dominance of might over right? This question is generally answered in the affirmative in the research. However, to this question too, a more nuanced response will be provided in the following. The norms of the international order were unquestionably opposed to Bismarck's political objective. Yet the Prussian could not ignore them. Bismarck's realpolitik was by no means accompanied by the assertion of a 'free right to wage war'.

1864: Bismarck Turns Law against Law

The first opportunity for Prussia's violent expansion of power, was, quite unexpectedly, the conflict over Schleswig and Holstein, which flared up again in 1863. In this conflict, questions of nationality, power, and law were so intricately intertwined that Lord Palmerston is said to have once claimed that only three people ever understood it: 'the Prince Consort, who is dead—a German professor, who has gone mad—and I, who have forgotten all about it'.[191]

To summarize the causes of the conflict very briefly, despite Palmerston's scepticism: as early as the 1830s, the German-speaking population of Schleswig and Holstein had been demanding that Schleswig become a separate state so that it could join the German Confederation. At that time, Schleswig was a Danish fiefdom, but it was also connected to Holstein; Holstein, like Lauenburg, was, on the one hand, connected to Denmark in a personal union, but on the other, was also a member state of the German Confederation. The German-speaking side in Schleswig now invoked the real union between the two duchies, which had (supposedly) been guaranteed by treaty since 1460. The Danish side under King Frederik 7., on the other hand, sought an incorporation of Schleswig into the Danish state.[192] When the revolutions in the spring of 1848 led to the formation of a provisional Schleswig-Holstein government in Kiel by the German-speaking side, Denmark saw its sovereign rights as having been violated and marched into Schleswig. Both sides thus put forward competing historical legal arguments for their violence, which were now charged with the respective nationalist emotions in both Copenhagen and in Schleswig and Holstein.

The conflict was internationalized when the Frankfurt Federal Assembly recognized the government in the duchies and decided to defend the real union between Holstein and Schleswig by force. Prussia entered the war against Denmark in order, according to King Friedrich Wilhelm IV's justification, to restore the international

---

[190] M. Epkenhans, *Die Reichsgründung 1870/71* (2020), at 38.
[191] See also Marriott, 'Modern England', in *The Fortnightly Review* (1. April 1907) at 606.
[192] G. Koeppen and G.A. Zimmermann, *Bismarck: Seine Zeit und sein Wirken* (1899), at 200.

legal status quo 'before the Danish invasion'.[193] The European Concert, however, now intervened to end the war between Prussia and Denmark.[194] Denmark was subsequently victorious over the German-speaking rebels and thus decided the First Schleswig War, or *Treårskrigen* (Three Years' War) in its favour.

The London Protocols of 2 August 1850 and 8 May 1852 regulated the Danish right of succession to Schleswig and Holstein. Denmark had thus won an important legal victory and in turn inflicted a decisive defeat on the German national movement. What did Bismarck do now? Did he use national sentiment to challenge the London Protocol and immediately declare war on Denmark in the name of the nation? Quite the opposite. Adherence to the London Protocols in fact became, according to Michael Epkenhans, 'the guiding principle of Bismarck's policy' on the Schleswig-Holstein Question[195]—much to the annoyance of the German national movement.

However, Bismarck's strategy of respecting international law in 1850/52 and dissuading the German middle powers from hastily declaring war against Denmark was to pay off politically. For under strong public pressure from the national liberal parliament, Danish King Christian 9., who had ruled since 1863, signed the November Constitution drafted by Orla Lehmann in the same year. The constitution provided for the separation of Schleswig and Holstein and the incorporation of Schleswig into Denmark. With this, German historian Wilhelm Müller argued in 1889, Denmark 'threw down the gauntlet to the German Confederation'.[196] The German Confederation now initiated a federal execution (*Bundesexekution*) granting it the right to act militarily against Holstein and Lauenburg. After all, the November Constitution massively violated the London agreements—and in particular the Danish circular notes of 1852.[197] Christian 9's predecessor, Frederik 7., had assured Austria and Prussia that he did not want to incorporate Schleswig into the Danish state.

Bismarck had found an excellent justification for a war against Denmark, which, unlike in the First Schleswig War, would prevent an intervention by the Concert.[198] Bismarck also benefited from the fact that Russia was still favourably disposed towards Prussia after its support for the counter-insurgency in Poland (1863).[199] French intervention would have contradicted Napoléon III's commitment to the principle of nationality, and Great Britain did not see Prussia's regional war politics as representing any kind of danger to European peace.[200] The timing was perfect for a violent expansion of power.

[193] Schulz (n. 8), at 208.
[194] On the negotiations, see Schulz (n. 8), at 208.
[195] Epkenhans (n. 190), at 38.
[196] W. Müller, *Deutschlands Einigungskriege 1864–1871* (1889), at 9.
[197] W. Oncken, *Das Zeitalter des Kaisers Wilhelm*, vol. 1 (1890), at 480 ff.
[198] *Ibid.*, at 498.
[199] Canis (n. 187), at 29 ff.
[200] *Ibid.*

The Danish breach of law was followed by an Austro-Prussian ultimatum to Copenhagen on 16 January 1864, initiated by Bismarck. Austria and Prussia were pursuing very different agendas. While Prussia wanted to expand its influence in the north through annexation or the establishment of a dependent middle state, Austria was keen to steer the national movement in the north in the right direction.[201] The ultimatum to Denmark stated that if the latter did not rescind its November Constitution, the two German powers would 'see themselves compelled to use the means at their disposal to establish the status quo and to secure the treaty rights of the Duchy of Schleswig'[202] and Prussia and Austria declared that the 'conditions under which we agreed in the spring of 1852' were 'violated by the present action of the Royal Danish Government'.[203]

Denmark thus provided Bismarck with an opportunity to legitimize Prussian force by presenting it as a defence of international law. After Denmark's negative response, the Austrian and Prussian armies marched into Schleswig on 1 February. In particular, the Battle of Dybbøl on 16 April 1864 decided the war in favour of the two German Great Powers. It was therefore stated in the Treaty of Vienna (30 October 1864) that:

> His Majesty the King of Denmark renounces all His rights to the Duchies of Schleswig, Holstein, and Lauenburg in favor of Their Majesties the Emperor of Austria and the King of Prussia, agreeing to recognize the agreements which Their said Majesties shall make in connection with these Duchies.[204]

After creating a condominium over Schleswig and Holstein, the two German Great Powers initially agreed in the treaty of 14 August 1865 that Schleswig should be placed under Prussian and Holstein under Austrian administration—despite protests from the German Confederation as well as the other European Great Powers. Bismarck's justification strategy had succeeded. In terms of realpolitik, it may have been a 'tactical masterstroke'.[205] Normatively, however, Bismarck's politics of international law were highly cynical.[206] In his justifications of war, the Prussian prime minister referred to the London Protocols of 1850/52—only to bury them afterwards. Bismarck turned international law against itself.

---

[201] Epkenhans (n. 190), at 39.
[202] L.K. Aegidi and A. Klauhold (ed.), *Das Staatsarchiv. Sammlung der officiellen Actenstücke*, vol. 6 (1864), at 613.
[203] Quoted from L. Hahn, *Fürst Bismarck, sein politisches Leben und Wirken urkundlich in Tathsachen und des Fürsten eigenen Kundgebungen dargestellt*, vol. 1 (1878), at 125.
[204] Art. 3, 'Prusso-Austrian Peace Treaty with Denmark (30 October 1864)', in W.G. Grewe (ed.), *Fontes Historiae Iuris Gentium (FHIG), Sources Relating to the History of the Law of Nations*, vol. 3/1: 1815–1945 (1992) 63, at 64.
[205] Doering-Manteuffel (n. 5), at 41.
[206] Ibid.

1866: An Austro-Prussian Duel?

After the victorious Second Schleswig War, Bismarck's next war was already in the offing. A dispute over the occupied duchies flared up between the newly allied German Great Powers. While Austria—like many German middle powers—was prepared to install Friedrich VIII, Duke of Schleswig-Holstein as legitimate ruler, Bismarck intended to annex the duchies once and for all. In early 1866 Prussia and Austria were heading for war.[207]

Bismarck now had to come up with as legitimate a reason for war as possible. Therefore, he escalated the conflict. To provoke Austria, Bismarck demanded general elections of the Federal Convention in Frankfurt on 9 April 1866—a demand which the multi-ethnic Habsburg Empire could not possibly agree to.[208] Austria reacted to the Prussian provocation by beginning to prepare the installation of Friedrich VIII in Schleswig-Holstein. Austria had thus fallen into Bismarck's trap. For Bismarck could now present Austrian action as a scandalous breach of law. Prussia argued that Austria had broken the Gastein Convention and the unity of Schleswig formulated therein.[209]

The war that now broke out, which lasted from 14 June to 23 August 1866, is often described as a 'political duel'[210] or a 'cabinet war'[211]. It thus seems to correspond to Clausewitz's ideal of a 'classical', interstate war. The Prussian Chief of General Staff and Clausewitz's student Helmuth Graf von Moltke also saw the war against Austria as representing the ideal of a 'cabinet war', defined by limited, short, and decisive battles, and by the absence of ideological public debates.[212] For Stephen C. Neff, the war of 1866 was thus the nineteenth-century war in which the primacy of politics over law—and thus the 'free right to go to war'—was most evident.[213]

So, did the war of 1866 bring about a turn towards *liberum ius ad bellum*? Its characterization as a 'cabinet war' may at first seem reasonable. There was a precise political goal (a decision on the political order of Germany) and, moreover, this military decision was quickly brought about, predominantly in the Battle of Königgrätz and Sadowa on 3 July 1866. The lack of formal war declarations further substantiates the impression that a primacy of might over a right—and thus a 'free right to go to war'—dominated in the military conflict of 1866.

Yet this impression is deceptive. It is based on the—factually questionable—perspective of Prussia in the conflict. For legally speaking, the conflict was not an

---

[207] Epkenhans (n. 190), at 40–3.
[208] Jahr (n. 180), at 102 ff.
[209] Lesaffer, 'The War of 1866 and the Undoing of Vienna', *Oxford Public International Law* (2016), available at: https://opil.ouplaw.com/page/549 (last visited 1 December 2022).
[210] S.C. Neff, *War and the Law of Nations. A General History* (2005), at 164.
[211] J. Leonhard, *Die Büchse der Pandora. Geschichte des Ersten Weltkriegs* (2014), at 30.
[212] *Ibid.*
[213] Neff (n. 210), at 164.

international war, but a federal execution of the German Confederation against Prussia, which Austria obtained in the Frankfurt *Bundestag* on 14 June 1866. The military conflict was preceded by a legal dispute in which both sides presented their arguments for discussion in Frankfurt. Prussia, Austria argued, had violated the prohibition of self-help under Article 19 of the Final Act of Vienna with its invasion of Holstein.[214] This also removed the need for a formal declaration of war. The Austrian legal position was convincing, and the initiation of a federal execution was accordingly legal and legitimate.

This argument was firmly rejected by Bismarck, who argued that the German Confederation had no authority in the case of the duchies under Prussian-Austrian rule, and the federal execution was thus illegal.[215] Bismarck used this alleged Austrian breach of the constitution to unilaterally declare the German Confederation dissolved. This was a mistake,[216] for in doing so, Bismarck violated Article 5 of the Final Act of Vienna, according to which '[t]he Confederation is established as an indissoluble Union, and therefore none of its Members can be at liberty to secede from it.'[217]

The Prussian army won the war, which was largely fought by the northern German states on Prussia's side and the southern German states on Austria's side— not least because of its superiority in terms of weaponry. In the preliminary Peace of Nikolsburg, Austria had to accept the dissolution of the German Confederation violating monarchical rights, Prussia annexing Hanover, Electoral Hesse, Nassau, and the Free City of Frankfurt, and concluding protective alliances with the southern German states.[218] The German Confederation, dominated by Austria, was replaced by the North German Confederation, with Prussia as hegemon. Bismarck had reached his goal: Austria was ousted from Germany.

However, in doing so, Bismarck did *not* refer to a 'free right to wage war'. In his legitimization of violence, he referred to international law. Bismarck tried to portray his violence as a legitimate exception to the international norm of peace— albeit using questionable arguments. Nevertheless, Bismarck's justification strategy was politically successful. This is shown not least by the fact that the failed federal execution against Prussia is still erroneously remembered today as an interstate war and not as a federal execution.

But if, as I argue, the Vienna Order and its norm of international peace was still intact in 1866, why did the other major European powers not intervene in the escalating conflict? A meaningful answer to this question can only be provided by

---

[214] M. Kotulla, *Deutsches Verfassungsrecht 1806–1918* (2006), at 109.
[215] E.R. Huber, *Deutsche Verfassungsgeschichte seit 1789*, vol. 1 (1990), at 540.
[216] See also Kotulla (n. 214), at 109; Jahr (n. 180), at 104.
[217] Art. 5, 'Final Act of the Minsterial Conference Concerning the Organization of the German Confederation (15 May 1820)', in W.G. Grewe (ed.), *Fontes Historiae Iuris Gentium (FHIG), Sources Relating to the History of the Law of Nations*, vol. 3/1: 1815–1945 (1992) 178, at 178.
[218] Lesaffer (n. 209).

historically contextualizing the arguments presented to legitimize force. Although Austria was undoubtedly able to present more cogent legal arguments, it must be emphasized that both sides argued in the language of constitutional and international law. Prussia's legal strategy was admittedly weak. Unlike Russia in the context of the Crimean War,[219] Bismarck nevertheless continued to argue in terms of positive law, thus having no need to resort to vague patterns of natural law. In 1864, Bismarck had turned international law against itself. Now he tried to play constitutional law and international law off against each other.

More importantly, Austria had not learned from its diplomatic mistakes in the Second Italian War of Independence. When Great Britain, France, and Russia proposed a congress to discuss the German and Italian issues in May 1866, neither Austria nor Prussia were inclined to participate.[220] Both states saw the achievement of their political goals as being more feasible in a war. However, by pre-empting Prussia with its cancellation of the congress, it was once again Austria that isolated itself diplomatically within the Concert.[221]

But the decisive factor for the non-intervention of the other Great Powers, apart from the shortness of the war, was probably that the Concert did not see any immediate threat to the general peace of Europe. The war remained largely confined to federal territory, although it was intertwined with the Third Italian War of Independence through the Prussian-Italian alliance. Bismarck was also aware that an overly bold expansion of Prussian power would make intervention by the Concert more likely. When Wilhelm I advocated a continuation of the campaign to Vienna, Bismarck ended the war on his own authority and against Wilhelm I's 'flush of victory'.[222]

All this proves that as in 1864, the possibility of interference by the authority of the Concert was clearly right before Bismarck's eyes in 1866. Violence was bound to appear legitimate on the international stage. Politically arbitrary action was not accepted as appropriate behaviour by any of the politicians involved. This proves that even the supposed 'duel' between Austria and Prussia did not result in a 'free right to go to war'.

1870/71: An 'Unprovoked Attack'?

The war of 1866 had considerably strengthened Prussia's power in Germany. For many contemporaries, the Battle of Königgrätz had become an almost 'revolutionary' turning point in German history.[223] 'If, until then, it had been completely

---

[219] Chapter 5.3.
[220] Doering-Manteuffel (n. 5), at 44 ff.
[221] Ibid.
[222] Epkenhans (n. 190), at 45.
[223] Faber (n. 184), at 4; G. Wawro, *The Franco-Prussian War. The German Conquest of France in 1870–1871* (2003), at 16.

open as to how, to what extent, and by whom the highest political goal of the German bourgeoisie would be realized', according to Karl-Georg Faber, 'the year 1866 provided an answer which, although not clearly determining the final outcome of 1871, decisively narrowed the scope for resolving the German question.'[224]

Nevertheless, the war of 1866 had not answered the 'German question'. The founding of the North German Confederation by no means automatically meant that German unification would follow. In the elections to the Customs Parliament in February 1868, for example, a number of 'anti-Prussian particularists' were elected in the southern German states.[225] The decisive catalyst for unification would be another Prussian war, this time with the fading hegemonic power of continental Europe: France.

A military conflict between Prussia and France had become increasingly likely since 1866.[226] A violent scenario in the sense of the International Relations 'transition of power theory'[227] had occurred in an almost ideal typical form: the increasingly weakened hegemon France saw itself threatened by the growing power of Prussia. Prussia, on the other hand, strengthened by its victories in 1864 and 1866, was dissatisfied with its position in the international order. Its leadership hoped that a victory over France would not only enable it to push for German unification but also assert its own claim to hegemony in Europe.[228]

The conflict between Prussia and France had already become more volatile in 1866 when Bismarck ignored France's desire for territorial compensation on the Rhine, in Luxembourg, and/or Belgium for its non-intervention in the Austro-Prussian War of 1866.[229] Bismarck instead wooed the French Emperor and his ambassadors, publishing the French draft treaties, and thus the French annexation plans, in French and English journals. Not only German but also European public opinion now turned against France.[230] Bismarck also proceeded in a very similar way in 1867. He made public the French attempt to acquire Luxembourg, which had been fully sovereign since the dissolution of the German Confederation, at the same time as the Prussian protective and defensive alliances were concluded with the southern German states. In this way, Bismarck dealt Napoléon III's honour two major blows.[231]

In a sense, the constellation of justificatory arguments used in the German campaign against Napoléon in 1813 was now repeated.[232] Like his uncle, Napoléon

---

[224] Faber (n. 184), at 2.
[225] Jahr (n. 180), at 168.
[226] Siemann (n. 175), at 218, at 299; B. Aschmann (ed.), *Durchbruch der Moderne? Neue Perspektiven auf das 19. Jahrhundert* (2013), at 342; D. Wetzel, *Duell der Giganten. Bismarck, Napoleon III. und die Ursachen des Deutsch-Französischen Krieges 1870/71* (2005).
[227] A.F.K. Organski, *World Politics* (1958); R.L. Tammen, *Power Transitions: Strategies for the 21st Century* (2000).
[228] Evans (n. 128), at 364–4; Wetzel (n. 226).
[229] Aschmann (n. 226), at 341–66.
[230] *Ibid.*, at 345.
[231] *Ibid.*, at 349.
[232] See also Chapter 3.2.

III faced a Prussian state that invoked the nation and its honour as a pretext[233]—precisely the ideas that Napoléon III had made his foreign policy dogma. The Revolution was now also to devour its grandchildren.

Yet war between France and Prussia was by no means inevitable at the end of the 1860s. Communication and cooperation between the two powers remained possible.[234] The Luxembourg Crisis of 1867 was settled peacefully through mediation at a conference of the Great Powers—especially because neither side wanted war at that time.[235] The treaty of 11 May 1867 that concluded the conference left Luxembourg in a personal union with the Kingdom of the Netherlands (Article 1), but at the same time insisted on its neutrality analogously to Belgium under 'the Guarantee of the Courts of Great Britain, Austria, France, Prussia, and Russia'.[236]

Contrary to what is sometimes maintained in retrospective accounts of German unification, war did not seem at all inevitable even for the leaders of the two countries. As late as spring of 1870, Bismarck had assumed that 'at least for the foreseeable future' neither the French Emperor nor the French people would seek war.[237] The fact that war did break out in 1870 was therefore not structurally determined. Rather, war was brought about by the actors involved.

This, however, raises the delicate and still controversial question of 'war guilt' in/for the Franco-Prussian War of 1870. In narratives that see Prussia as primarily responsible, the notorious 'Ems Dispatch'—or more precisely, its shortening by Bismarck—is central to the line of argument used in the context of the Spanish Succession Crisis. After Spanish officers had chased Queen Isabel II from the throne in 1868, the Spanish government offered the crown to Leopold von Hohenzollern in February 1870.[238] From the French point of view, this offer was highly problematic: Leopold was a prince of the Catholic line of the Hohenzollerns and a distant relative of the Prussian king. Consequently, France feared a Prussian embrace. The (alleged) escalation of the conflict took place in Ems.[239] Wilhelm I stayed as a guest at the restorative spa there in July 1870. On 7 July, the French foreign minister, Antoine Duke of Gramont, sent ambassador Count Benedetti to Ems. The Prussian king was to be persuaded to ask the Hohenzollerns to renounce the throne. Gramont had already indirectly threatened war. Benedetti was successful: after several talks, Wilhelm I agreed to the French demand. He wanted to keep the peace.

---

[233] Aschmann (n. 226), at 488.
[234] Jahr (n. 180), at 174.
[235] Aschmann (n. 226), at 362 ff.
[236] Art. 2, 'Treaty on the Neutralization of Luxemburg and its Sovereignty/London (11 May 1867)', in W.G. Grewe (ed.), *Fontes Historiae Iuris Gentium (FHIG), Sources Relating to the History of the Law of Nations*, vol. 3/1: 1815–1945 (1992) 169.
[237] Quoted from Epkenhans (n. 190), at 55.
[238] *Ibid.*, at 54.
[239] On the following paragraph, see Jahr (n. 180), at 183–5; see also V. Benedetti, *Le Comte: Ma Mission en Prusse* (1871).

Gramont, however, was not satisfied. After the humiliation inflicted on France, it was now Prussia's turn.[240] Wilhelm I was to apologize personally to Napoléon III and declare that he would *never* agree to the nomination of a Hohenzollern candidate for the Spanish throne.[241] But the Prussian king refused. He wanted to decide on a case-by-case basis. Things got rolling when a summary of Wilhelm I's conversation with Benedetti was telegraphed to Bismarck. Bismarck had the telegram published the same day in a heavily abridged version. Bismarck's version, however, suggested that Benedetti had acted in an extremely improper manner towards Wilhelm I.[242] Accordingly, the events in Ems came across as a massive affront to Benedetti and thus also to France[243]—or to Wilhelm I and thus to Prussia. In falsifying the Ems Dispatch, Bismarck instrumentalized the honour of both France and Prussia.[244] In doing so, he successfully achieved his aim: the outrage provoked by Bismarck in Prussia and France was enormous.

The widespread narrative is that the forged Ems Despatch was an expression of Bismarck's long-cherished plan to provoke France into declaring war. Along similar lines, Wilhelm Liebknecht claimed twenty years later that 'the so-called "Ems Dispatch"' was a forgery, and that the man who perpetrated this forgery wanted war with France and also made it inevitable.[245] This narrative has two sides: on the one hand, the main responsibility for the war is attributed to Bismarck. On the other, however, Bismarck also comes across as a strategic genius. His abuse of international norms for unilateral goals seems to be excused or at least tolerated by his admirers.

Against this narrative, it has been argued that France had already decided to declare war on Prussia after Wilhelm I had refused to grant a perpetual guarantee regarding the Spanish throne.[246] The Ems Dispatch was then only a pretext.[247] Another argument against the narrative of Bismarck's strategic genius is put forward by Birgit Aschmann: she has argued that Bismarck simply underestimated how much France would perceive the Hohenzollern candidacy as a question of rank and status.[248] Accordingly, Bismarck did not follow a sophisticated escalation strategy, but wrongly expected France to grudgingly accept the Hohenzollern candidacy. Aschmann concludes: 'Bismarck, celebrated as the greatest diplomat of the 19th century, had miscalculated.'[249] In 1870, the genius of realpolitik thus made a serious diplomatic mistake.

---

[240] Quoted from Epkenhans (n. 190), at 56 ff.
[241] Jahr (n. 180), at 183.
[242] H.-U. Winkler, *Germany: The Long Road West*, vol. 1: 1789–1933 (2006) 53, at 182 ff.
[243] Jahr (n. 180), at 184.
[244] Aschmann (n. 226), at 487.
[245] W. Liebknecht, *Die Emser Depesche oder wie Kriege gemacht werden* (1891), at 4.
[246] Epkenhans (n. 190), at 57; see also M. Stürmer, *Das ruhelose Reich. Deutschland 1866–1918* (1994), at 164.
[247] R. Wilhelm, *Das Verhältnis der süddeutschen Staaten zum Norddeutschen Bund (1867–1870)* (1978), at 163 ff; Wetzel (n. 226); Canis (n. 187), at 29 ff.
[248] Aschmann (n. 226), at 402.
[249] *Ibid.*

This unresolved historical dispute about German or French 'war guilt' of 1870 does not need to be decided here. However, *both* research positions underline the extraordinary importance that nationality and national honour had attained in Europe since the middle of the nineteenth century. Accordingly, the French declaration of war of 19 July 1870 was justified as a defence of national honour, which had been violated by Prussia. In the process, the 'plan to raise a Prussian prince to the throne of Spain' was described as 'an enterprise directed against the territorial security of France'.[250] The Prussian king, the declaration read, had refused to provide the requested assurance that he would not support such a candidacy—an assertion which is only true with regard to a permanent assurance independent of the case in hand. Moreover, the declaration wrongly stated that Wilhelm I refused to meet with Benedetti. Here, interestingly enough, according to the declaration, Bismarck's abridged Ems Dispatch was received—although Benedetti *had* indeed met Wilhelm I and even reported to Paris about the meeting. The declaration stated, however, the French government had come to the conclusion that it had a duty to immediately enter into a state of war with Prussia '*à la défense de son honneur et de ses intérêts compromis*'.[251]

According to France's justifications for war, Prussia's behaviour was directed not only against the French government, but also against the French people. In his speech of 21 July 1870, Napoléon III claimed that the entire nation had demanded the decision to go to war.[252] In the *Journal Officiel*, the French government emphasized on 4 August that France was not at war with Germany, but only with Prussia, and in particular with Bismarck's policies. Neither Napoléon III nor his government had held 'anything but the friendliest attitude' towards the 'great German people'.[253] The Peace of Villafranca of 1859, the French argued, had been concluded in the war against Austria because Napoléon III had not wanted to fight the German princes, with whom he maintained friendly relations.

At the centre of the French argumentation was thus a nationally charged friend/foe construction. Napoléon III was portrayed as a friend of the German nation; Bismarck, on the other hand, as an enemy not only of the French but also of the German nation. Bismarck had even become a 'traitor to the common country' by pushing Austria out of Germany, the French government argued.[254] The countries annexed by Prussia in 1866, according to the French government, 'deeply regretted' the loss of their own princes: peaceful, rich, honoured, and lightly taxed, they had previously been a model of moral and material prosperity[255] Now, however, they

---

[250] '*une entreprise dirigée contre la sécurité territoriale de la France le projet d'élever un prince prussien au trône d'Espagne*', French Declaration of War (19 July 1870), in M. Schilling, *Quellenbuch zur Geschichte der Neuzeit. Für d. oberen Klassen höherer Lehranst* (1884), at 464 ff.
[251] H. Kohl (ed.), *Die politischen Reden des Fuersten Bismarck*, vol. 4 (1893), at 429.
[252] C. Abel (ed.), *Letters on International Relations Before and During the War of 1870*, vol. 2 (1871).
[253] *Ibid.*, at 223.
[254] *Ibid.*, at 224.
[255] *Ibid.*

were forced to waste 'their gold and blood' on Prussian politics—even though they were worthy of fighting for a 'better cause'. This, of course, meant a unified fight against Prussia, as France hoped to win Prussia's former enemies, especially Austria and Denmark, over to its side.[256] Thus, in the *Journal Officiel*, the French government also addressed the southern German states: the Germans were prepared to participate in a 'truly national war', yet they had to take part in a 'purely Prussian war'.[257]

Rhetorically, this was a very clever move. France linked the reference to the illegal Prussian annexations of 1866 with the right of self-determination of the German peoples in order to justify its own war of aggression as a war to liberate Germany 'from Prussian oppression'. Accordingly, France defined its war aims as:

- reconciling the 'rights of sovereigns' with the 'legitimate aspirations of the peoples';
- ending the 'incessant encroachments' of Prussia, which posed a 'constant threat to Europe';
- saving the Danish nation from 'utter ruin'; and
- enforcing a 'just and lasting peace' based on 'moderation, justice, and law'.

The justification of the war in the *Journal Officiel* concluded by emphasizing France's 'right intention'. Addressing European public opinion, it referred to France as 'the arbiter of peoples and kings' and the justification as being a defence of 'the weak against the strong', the redress of 'great injustices', the sanction of 'unjust acts'.[258]

Despite the increasing importance of national honour and self-determination as justificatory claims, the French legitimation strategy thus also continued to be in keeping with the proven European practice of war legitimation. Even a thoroughly nationalistic legitimation of war could not forgo recourse to international norms. This is made clear by the recourse to the claimed 'just cause' in the French war justifications.[259] The French justifications of war also clearly rejected the arbitrary use of force, which is the basis of the thesis of the 'free right to go to war'. The rights of each nation, 'like the rights of each individual', the French government claimed, are limited by the rights of others. It was therefore not permissible for a nation to threaten the existence or security of a neighbouring nation under the pretext of exercising its own sovereignty.[260] The idea that states were allowed to make policy at the expense of others was thus clearly and unequivocally rejected. A state's sovereignty thereby ended at its own territorial borders.

---

[256] *Ibid.*
[257] *Ibid.*, at 225.
[258] *Ibid.*
[259] *Ibid.*, at 190.
[260] *Ibid.*, at 175.

France's arguments justifying a preventive war against Prussia were technically and rhetorically well 'composed'. According to these justifications, the war was to be understood not only as a preventive defence of France's honour, but also of the international order. To this end, the French government mixed classic and new justificatory arguments, combining territorial security, national honour, and self-determination with European peace, international law, and Prussian breaches of law. In this respect, the French justifications for war corresponded almost completely to the spirit of the times and the state of the art of European discourse.

But not even the rhetorically brilliant French formulations and attempts to position the German nation against Prussia could hide a fundamental flaw: ultimately, the French offensive was a unilateral preventive war, and thus a form of war that was generally considered particularly illegitimate against the background of the Vienna Order. The fact that he ignored this taboo of preventive war contributed to Napoléon III's downfall. It is actually quite astonishing that Napoléon III let himself be allured into declaring a preventive war, since he himself, together with Cavour, had provoked Franz Joseph I into declaring an illegitimate preventive war in 1859 (see above).

For regardless of whether the provocation was long planned or not, it was now easy for Bismarck to portray Napoléon III as the aggressor before the German and European communication communities. In his circular to the diplomats of the North German Confederation of 19 July 1870, 'concerning the French declaration of war', Bismarck for his part portrayed the French Emperor as a lawbreaker, stating that the French declaration of war was 'the first and only official communication' which 'we have received from the Imperial French Government in the whole affair which has occupied the world for 14 days'. Bismarck thus claimed the French deliberately escalated the crisis leading to a war, 'which it imposes on us'.[261]

Bismarck then criticized the French government's justifications for the war. He argued that Wilhelm I had never thought of raising the hereditary prince of the Hohenzollerns to the Spanish throne. The demands made by France on the Prussian king 'of promises for the future' were therefore 'unjustified and presumptuous' (*'ungerechtfertigt und anmaßend'*).[262] With this argument, ironically, Bismarck now repudiated the impression he himself had previously deliberately created by shortening the Ems Dispatch. For in contrast to what Bismarck's abridgement of the dispatch wrongly suggested, he now argued that Benedetti had indeed met Wilhelm I in Ems. In short, according to Bismarck, the French reasons for war were fictitious.

Following on from this argument, the chancellor of the North German Confederation constructed the image of a French aggressor, mirroring the French accusations. The German nation, Bismarck claimed, had recognized that 'the

---

[261] Bismarck's Declaration of War, in *ibid.*, at 430.
[262] *Ibid.*, at 175.

demands of the French government were directed towards a humiliation which the nation cannot bear'.[263] The war, 'which could never have been Prussia's intention', had been forced on Prussia by France.[264] For his part, Bismarck now appealed to the southern German states. According to Bismarck, both the North German Confederation and the governments of southern Germany allied with it protested 'against the unprovoked invasion' ('*gegen den nicht provocierten Überfall*') by France and were prepared to 'repel it with all the means which God has given them'.[265] But Bismarck addressed not only the German states, but also Europe: the 'entire civilized world' would realize, Bismarck predicted, that 'the reasons given by France do not exist but are invented pretexts'.[266]

Since France had declared war first, Bismarck was in an exceptionally favourable position to present a convincing legitimization of war. He could credibly point to the Vienna Order's most effective reason for unilateral force: self-defence against aggression. Bismarck could thus present his own violence as legitimate counter-violence in keeping with the norms of the international order. However, Bismarck mixed the classical reference to self-defence with stronger recourse to national honour. Bismarck's justification strategy was thus entirely in tune with the increasingly nationalized discourse on the legitimacy of war of that time.

The nationalist-oriented war legitimation strategy was also supported by Wilhelm I, who in his proclamation 'to the German People' ('*An das deutsche Volk!*') of 25 July 1870, emphasized that the war against France was a fight 'for the honour and independence of Germany'. According to Christoph Jahr, from the outset, the war 'was also perceived as a war of ideologies, in which both sides saw themselves as the executors of a "higher truth" '.[267] Both sides presented themselves as embodying honour, law, and civilization, and demonized the other as an enemy of their own nation as well as of the international community.

But there were also critical voices on both sides that argued against war. The future President of the Third Republic, Adolphe Thiers, for example, warned of the impending war, and the author Gustave Flaubert cautioned that there was insufficient pretext for the 'terrible slaughter'.[268] Anti-Prussian voices were also heard in German discourse, each of which appealed to or questioned law, honour, custom, and the 'national necessity' of the war.[269] Even in 1870, the nations were not quite as united in their war euphoria as the statesmen portrayed them.

Although both sides justified their violence, the Prussian justification for the war prevailed in the European communication community as the more convincing

---

[263] *Ibid.*
[264] *Ibid.*
[265] *Ibid.*, at 431.
[266] *Ibid.*
[267] Jahr (n. 180), at 197.
[268] *Ibid.*, at 186.
[269] *Ibid.*, at 189.

one. Benedetti's demand that Wilhelm I guarantee that no Hohenzollern would ever accept the throne of Spain was understood as improper. In the liberal *National-Zeitung*, for example, France's demands were described as an 'insolence exceeding all moderation' (*'jedes Maass überschreitende Frechheit'*).[270] Some German legal scholars, too, placed the blame for the war on France: Bluntschli, for instance, argued in September 1870 that—

> public opinion in the entire civilized world ... was not in doubt that the responsibility for the war, which had been started wantonly, lay exclusively on the imperial government and, since the representatives of the French nation applauded this policy of aggression, also on the latter.[271]

By declaring a preventive war, France moved outside the framework of legitimately accepted justifications for violence. This was never going to be a convincing reason.

Prussia, on the other hand, succeeded in generating solidarity—or at least neutrality—in the European communication community: the southern German states of Baden, Württemberg, Bavaria, and Hesse-Darmstadt joined the war against France, following the 1866 treaties with Prussia. Other European (Great) Powers did not intervene in the war. Great Britain and Russia remained neutral, and Denmark could not satisfy its desire for revenge for 1864 without British backing. Austria was militarily unprepared, and Italy used the war to occupy Rome after the withdrawal of the French Guard in 1870.[272] The way was clear for German unification.

The war that now broke out between the German states and France can be described as a hybrid war:[273] the character of the war changed with the decisive French defeat at the Battle of Sedan on 1 and 2 September 1870. The French army surrendered, Napoléon III was captured, the French government was overthrown, and the Third French Republic was proclaimed. But even with the proclamation of the German Empire in the Hall of Mirrors at the Palace of Versailles on 18 January 1871, the war did not end. Rather, it turned into an industrialized people's war, characterized by partisan attacks on the Prussian invaders as well as Prussian violence against the French civilian population.[274] Moltke denied the *Francs-tireurs* the status of combatants, and ordered summary executions.[275]

---

[270] Quoted from *ibid.*, at 188.
[271] J.C. Bluntschli, *Das moderne Völkerrecht in dem Kriege 1870. Rede zum Geburtsfeste des höchstseligen Grossherzogs Karl Friedrich von Baden und zur akademischen Preisvertheilung am 22. November 1870* (1870), at 8 ff.; the opinions of international legal scholars on the wars of the mid-century will be discussed in more detail in Chapter 6.2.
[272] Jahr (n. 180), at 192 ff.
[273] This paragraph is based on Simon, 'The Myth of *Liberum Ius ad Bellum*. Justifying War in 19th-Century Legal Theory and Political Practice', 29 *European Journal of International Law* (2018) 113.
[274] Leonhard (n. 211), at 30.
[275] *Ibid.*, at 30 ff.; M. Howard, *The Franco-Prussian War. The German Invasion of France, 1870–1871* (2nd edn., 2001), at 257 ff.

Like the Crimean War before it, the Franco-Prussian War, with more than 180,000 deaths, pointed to the later rise of total wars.[276] The legitimacy of German 'counter-violence' declined over the course of the war, losing acceptance precisely when it could no longer be justified as self-defence. When Prussia decided to annex parts of Alsace and Lorraine, international approval for the Prussian campaign fell rapidly.[277] After the decisive Battle of Sedan, the French pacifist Frédéric Passy reminded Wilhelm I on behalf of the *Ligue internationale et permanente de la paix* that Prussia had justified war in 1870 as self-defence against the French government, not as a war against the French people.[278] This was very much in line with the observation by Vienna law professor Leopold Neumann in his *Grundriss des heutigen europäischen Völkerrechtes*. Neumann wrote that a 'just war' became an 'unjust war' if the purpose of the war is exceeded.[279] With the founding of the German Empire under Prussian leadership, Bismarck had reached his main political goal.

So even in proclaiming the German Empire, Bismarck and Wilhelm I used the legitimizing force that came from the narrative of self-defence against foreign aggression. This underlines once again that international force was seen as requiring legitimization even in the *Eisen-und-Blut* policy of the man who was supposedly the most important nineteenth-century *Realpolitiker*. At *no* time did Bismarck claim a 'free right to go to war'. Rather, I have demonstrated in the preceding analyses that Bismarck's foreign policy between 1864 and 1871 could only be successful because the Prussian politician had mastered the normative language of justifying war. If Bismarck had not been able to portray his violence as an internationally accepted exception, he would never have succeeded in unifying Germany.

In his memoirs, Bismarck stated that 'even victorious wars can only be justified if they are imposed'.[280] This was a clear rejection of the idea of preventive war, which had been Napoléon III's undoing. But even Bismarck was not entirely immune to the hubris of waging a preventive war after the German Empire had been created, contrary to what is stated in his memoirs. Indeed, in the period between 1872 and 1874, as well as during the 'war in sight' crisis in 1875, Bismarck repeatedly threatened France with preventive war. Yet he evoked the illegitimacy of this justificatory argument in the face of clearly negative reactions from the international communication community.[281] Bismarck was able to learn that he had to subject his realpolitik, at least on the surface, to the normative force of international order.

---

[276] M. Epkenhans, *Der Deutsch-Französische Krieg 1870/1871* (2020).
[277] Baumgart (n. 6), at 399; Bring, 'The Westphalian Peace Tradition in International Law: From Jus ad Bellum to Jus contra Bellum', 75 *International Law Studies. US Naval War College* (2000) 57, at 72.
[278] S.E. Cooper, *Patriotic Pacifism. Waging War on War in Europe, 1815–1914* (1991), at 43.
[279] L. Neumann, *Grundriss des heutigen europäischen Völkerrechtes* (1877), at 93.
[280] '... auch siegreiche Kriege [können] nur dann, wenn sie aufgezwungen sind, verantwortet werden', O.E.L. von Bismarck, *Gedanken und Erinnerungen* (1959 [1890]), at 348.
[281] Hull, 'The Great War and International Law: German Justifications of "Preemptive Self-Defense"', in L. Brock and H. Simon (eds), *The Justification of War and International Order: From Past to Present*

Bismarck's recipe for success thus consisted not least in the fact that he sought to reconcile his violence with its international legitimacy. Even the fact that Bismarck subsequently praised himself in his memoirs for having circumvented the European Concert in his unification policy proves one thing above all: his awareness of the normative constraint of the Concert's powers in the event of an illegitimate use of force.

5.5 Conclusion: Law and Realpolitik—a Mid-century Crisis of the International Norm of Peace?

For the first time since the 1814/15 Congress of Vienna, in the years between 1853 and 1871 wars were again waged between European Great Powers. This renewed Great Power violence had profound consequences for the further development of international relations. The Ottoman Empire was admitted to the circle of Great Powers. Austria was forced out of Italy and Germany. Russia lost its latent hegemonic position to France in the Crimean War, which in turn had to surrender it to the German Empire in 1870/71. Then there were individual losers: more than a million soldiers and countless civilians lost their lives or were wounded in the wars between 1853 and 1878. The Crimean War and the Franco-Prussian War, in particular, were brutal harbingers of the industrialized mass wars of the twentieth century.

Were the Great Power wars simultaneously crises of the international peace norm, as is so often claimed?[282] To answer this question, in this chapter, I have examined the European discourse on the legitimation of war between 1853 and 1871 with a focus on its political and normative foundation. For if the normative frame of reference for the international use of force had indeed become meaningless with the supposed beginning of an 'age of realpolitik',[283] then the traditional European practice of legitimizing war would also have become superfluous by now. And the claims of the proposition of *liberum ius ad bellum* would thus be met.

However, as I have shown in this chapter, *all* European wars of the mid-century were comprehensively justified by *all* states involved in them. This applies to the only pan-European war of the time, the Crimean War, as well as to the German and Italian Wars of Unification. Even the failed federal execution of 1866 against Prussia, often described as an ideal typical example of a classic 'cabinet war',[284] was preceded by legitimations of force in the Frankfurt *Bundestag*. In short, not a

---

(2021) 183, at 189; in-depth K.-E. Jeismann, *Das Problem des Präventivkrieges im europäischen Staatensystem. Mit besonderem Blick auf die Bismarckzeit* (1975); and Silverstone (n. 188).

[282] Schroeder (n. 4); see above.
[283] Doering-Manteuffel (n. 5), at 38.
[284] Neff (n. 210), at 164.

single Great Power between 1853 and 1871 resorted to military force without engaging in the international discourse of its justification and critique. War remained a problem of international relations.

But not everything remained the same in the language of justifying the use of force. National self-determination became increasingly accepted as an international principle. To politicize the masses, *Realpolitiker* such as Napoléon III, Cavour, and Bismarck now referred to national honour, self-determination, self-preservation, and national enemy images in their legitimizations of violence. Michel Foucault was right to argue that wars were no longer waged only 'in the name of a sovereign who must be defended', but 'on behalf of the existence of everyone; entire populations are mobilized for the purpose of wholesale slaughter in the name of life necessity'.[285]

Jochen von Bernstorff is therefore principally correct that since the middle of the century, ontological justifications of war, oriented towards the survival of the nation, gained in importance—particularly, but not exclusively, in Italy and Germany.[286] However, Bernstorff's helpful, ideal typical comparison of ontological and order-related types of justification does not do justice to the historical complexity of justification practices. A sole reference to national honour and self-determination as a legitimate justification of war was by no means sufficient in the middle of the century. Quincy Wright's argument, according to which only 'reasons of state' were considered suitable justifications for war in the nineteenth century, can be clearly empirically refuted.[287] Without exception, all states recurred to the established norms of the international 'order of justification' in their war justifications.[288] Accordingly, war was justified as self-defence and/or as a violent means of securing European peace. By referring to these arguments in their justifications of violence, the warring parties reinforced the discursive robustness of the international norm of peace. Thus, when the Austrian foreign minister Bernhard von Rechberg argued in 1860 that 'the law of the strongest' or 'international anarchy' prevailed in Europe,[289] this was by no means an adequate analysis of the international normative order—but rather an expression of the helplessness of a multi-ethnic state that found itself diplomatically isolated.

But there were also innovations with regard to the norms of the international order: the Treaty of Paris created an international suborder and re-regulated the question of intervention in the Ottoman Empire. The still tentative calls for peaceful dispute resolution through mediation at the Congress of Paris (1856)

---

[285] M. Foucault, *The Will to Knowledge: The History of Sexuality*, vol. 1 (1998), at 137.

[286] Bernstorff, 'The Use of Force in International Law before World War I: On Imperial Ordering and the Ontology of the Nation State', 29 *European Journal of International Law* (2018) 233, at 236.

[287] Wright, 'Völkerrecht und internationale Organisation', *Zeitschrift für ausländisches öffentliches Recht und Völkerrecht* (1950) 266, at 266.

[288] R. Forst, *Normativity and Power. Analyzing Social Orders of Justification* (2017).

[289] Quoted from Baumgart (n. 6), at 158.

were also to have a lasting discursive effect. According to Hanns Göhler, this forced contemporary international legal doctrine to 'deal in detail with the question of the limitation of *ius ad bellum*'.[290] Nevertheless, the Great Powers did *not* expand the *ius contra bellum* in terms of treaty law. Robert von Mohl wrote in 1859 that there was no binding legal institution under international law to prevent war.[291] Hopes for legalization were undermined by the interest of the Great Powers in continuing to justify their violence with arguments from various normative areas.

The war legitimations of the mid-century confirm the ambivalent nexus between power and normativity in war discourses in an almost ideal typical way: for politicians like Cavour, Napoléon III, or Bismarck, norms were unquestionably a political tool. They could be used skilfully as arguments to confer international legitimacy on one's own political interests. Moreover, Cavour in 1859 and Bismarck in 1864, 1866, and 1870 invoked the law to justify campaigns which included annexations and thus also came into conflict with the territorial order constituted in Vienna. But even this in no way changed the fundamental logic of justification in European war discourse. Rather, this practice of legitimizing war proves that even *Realpolitiker* such as Bismarck, Napoléon III, and Cavour had internalized the international norms of the international order. They weighed the international acceptability of a justification for war against the likelihood of intervention by the Concert. For the authority of the latter remained intact throughout the period between 1853 and 1871, as can be seen from the many offers of mediation and diplomatic congresses. The most accepted justification was self-defence against aggression. Preventive war, on the other hand, was not accepted by the international communication community, as Franz Joseph I and Napoléon III painfully learned.

The norm of peace thus remained the guiding principle of the middle of the century. For recourse to international norms could only have any effect because all politicians assumed that these norms could claim discursive authority. The *Realpolitiker* of the mid-century were thus, to quote Lothar Brock's apt formulation again here, 'to make something available to themselves, the value of which for them is its unavailability'.[292] Thus, the Great Power wars at mid-century were not normative crises of the international order. The normative order with all its ambivalences and paradoxes was left intact.

---

[290] H. Göhler, *Freies Kriegsführungsrecht und Kriegsschuld* (1931), at 8.
[291] R. von Mohl, *Encyklopädie der Staatswissenschaften* (1859), at 454.
[292] Brock, 'Frieden durch Recht?', in P. Becker, R. Braun, and D. Deiseroth (eds): *Frieden durch Recht* (2010) 15, at 31; see also Chapter 2.3.

6
The Promise of 'Peace through Law' in the Shadow of War

6.1 Introduction: Plans to Outlaw War and Their Antinomies

The mid-century wars had not destroyed the international order established in Vienna in 1814/15; yet they marked a caesura. Besides the Crimean War (the only pan-European war), this was especially true of the Franco-Prussian War, which was perhaps even 'one of the great turning points in world history', as Bluntschli claimed from a purely Eurocentric perspective.[1] This industrialized mass war transferred France's latent hegemony to the German Empire. British lawyer and legal historian Henry Sumner Maine called the war of 1870/71 'one of the greatest of modern wars, which probably never had a rival in the violence and the passion which it excited'.[2]

This violence had to be ordered. The war of 1870/71 therefore became a catalyst for an unprecedented legalization of international relations—and thus a further example of the modern dialectic of war and international order (see Introduction): after 1871, treaties and codifications were literally the order of the day. International law, as Miloš Vec aptly sums it up, 'never had it as good as it did in the final years before the First World War'.[3] It is therefore perhaps not surprising that a considerable amount of recent research on the history of international law has focused on the late nineteenth century.[4] In his *The Gentle Civilizer of Nations* (2002), Martti Koskenniemi famously characterized the period between 1870 and 1960 as a period of the 'rise and fall of international law'.[5] Many studies have since followed Koskenniemi in this periodization.[6]

---

[1] J.C. Bluntschli, *Das moderne Völkerrecht in dem Kriege 1870. Rede zum Geburtsfeste des höchstseligen Grossherzogs Karl Friedrich von Baden und zur akademischen Preisvertheilung am 22. November 1870* (1870), at 23.
[2] H.S. Maine, *International Law: The Whewell Lectures* (1887), at 128 ff.
[3] Vec, 'Challenging the Laws of War by Technology, Blazing Nationalism and Militarism: Debating Chemical Warfare before and after Ypres, 1899–1925', in B. Friedrich, D. Hoffmann, J. Renn, F. Schmaltz, and M. Wolf (eds), *One Hundred Years of Chemical Warfare: Research, Deployment, Consequences* (2017) 105, at 107.
[4] For a critical account, see Kennedy, 'International Law and the Nineteenth Century: History of an Illusion', 65 *Nordic Journal of International Law* (1996) 385, at 391; L.A. Benton and L. Ford, *Rage for Order. The British Empire and the Origins of International Law, 1800–1850* (2016).
[5] M. Koskenniemi, *The Gentle Civilizer of Nations. The Rise and Fall of International Law 1870–1960* (2002).
[6] Galindo, 'Martti Koskenniemi and the Historiographical Turn in International Law', 16 *European Journal of International Law* (2005) 539; see also M. Koskenniemi, *To the Uttermost Parts of the Earth. Legal Imagination and International Power, 1300–1870* (2021), at 1, 966 ff.

The dramatic rise in the importance of international law towards the end of the century was particularly true for the legal regulation of war. Perhaps never before and never since, according to Koskenniemi,[7] was *ius in bello* studied with such enthusiasm as in the period between 1870 and 1914. The Paris Declaration (1856), the First Geneva Convention for the Amelioration of the Condition of the Wounded in Armies in the Field (1864), and the St Petersburg Declaration Renouncing the Use, in Time of War, of Explosive Projectiles Under 400 Grammes Weight (1868) had laid the foundation for the modern codification of the laws of war. The Brussels Declaration of 1874, the *Oxford Manual* of 1880, and the Hague Conferences of 1899 and 1907 followed and demonstrated the still growing interest of the Great Powers in a treaty-based regulation of war.[8]

But this growing interest actually raises the question of what had become of the politically even more fundamental problem of *ius ad/contra bellum*. How, then, was the legitimacy of war considered in the *fin de siècle* (1871–1914), a period in which European societies were shaped not only by internationalism and (legal) pacifism,[9] but also by militarism, nationalism, and imperialism?[10]

It is here that we find a remarkable blind spot in research on international legalization in the late nineteenth century. An important example of this is that in Martti Koskenniemi's *Gentle Civilizer*, the central question of the *ius ad/contra bellum* law does not play a major role. Rather, the thesis of the 'free right to go to war', which Koskenniemi had already advocated before,[11] is confirmed, but mentioned only briefly.[12] The (counter-)theories of 'just war', on the other hand, are at best a marginal note in the *Gentle Civilizer*;[13] according to Koskenniemi, these theories did not re-emerge until after the First World War.[14]

---

[7] Koskenniemi (n. 5), at 1, 966 ff.

[8] K. Nabulsi, *Traditions of War: Occupation, Resistance, and the Law* (1999), Chapter 1; Alexander, 'A Short History of International Humanitarian Law', 26 *European Journal of International Law* (2015) 109, at 112 ff.; K. von Lingens, *Crimes Against Humanity. Eine Ideengeschichte der Zivilisierung von Kriegsgewalt 1864–1945* (2018).

[9] F.S.L. Lyons, *Internationalism in Europe. 1815–1914* (1963); S.E. Cooper, *Patriotic Pacifism. Waging War on War in Europe, 1815–1914* (1991), at 43; M.H. Geyer and J. Paulmann (eds), *The Mechanics of Internationalism* (2001); C. Sylvest, *British Liberal Internationalism, 1880–1930: Making Progress?* (2013); F. Klose, *In the Cause of Humanity. A History of Humanitarian Intervention in the Long Nineteenth Century* (2021), Chapter 1.

[10] E. Hobsbawm, *The Age of Empire: 1875–1914* (1987); A. Anghie, *Imperialism, Sovereignty and the Making of International Law* (2004), Chapter 2; Jahn, 'Kant, Mill, and Illiberal Legacies in International Affairs', 59 *International Organization* (2005) 177; N. Tzouvala, *Capitalism As Civilisation. A History of International Law* (2020).

[11] Koskenniemi, 'The Politics of International Law', 1 *European Journal of International Law* (1990) 4.

[12] Koskenniemi (n. 5), at 85 ff.

[13] I have counted a total of eleven references in Koskenniemi (n. 5), at 230, 307, 320, 323, 334, 425 ff., 462 (in some cases, there are several references on one page).

[14] Other renowned scholars such as Gerry Simpson and Stephen C. Neff have also strengthened this narrative, see G.J. Simpson, *Great Powers and Outlaw States: Unequal Sovereigns in the International Legal Order* (2004), at 350, and S.C. Neff, *War and the Law of Nations: A General History* (2005), at 277. This is astonishing in Neff's case, because he identified references to natural law in the supposedly positivist legal discourse of the nineteenth century, see Chapter 2.2.

This impression is confirmed in Koskenniemi's new opus magnum, *To the Uttermost Parts* (2021), in which the chapters on the period between 1815 and 1870 address neither the doctrine of 'just war' nor the Concert's practice of ordering violence.[15]

However, as I have shown in Chapters 4 and 5, this impression is deceptive. Legal scholarship of the early and mid-nineteenth century did not abandon the theories of 'just war'. Nor did war become 'one political procedure among others', as Koskenniemi[16] has argued in line with prevailing opinion across disciplinary boundaries.[17] In the following chapter, I will argue that this was also—and especially—true for the debates in the second half of the nineteenth century. The Kantian idea of 'peace through law' established itself in the discourse on international law against realist opposition. However, it was also accompanied by inner-liberal ambivalences and antinomies. The prohibition of war, in Europe, became one of the main promises of liberal jurists in the shadow of war and imperialism.

6.2 Pacification Through Professionalization? Liberal International Legal Doctrine as the '*Conscience Juridique du Monde Civilisé*'

On 22 November 1870, Heidelberg constitutional lawyer Johann Caspar Bluntschli gave a speech on the occasion of the birthday of the Grand Duke Karl Friedrich von Baden. At that time, the Battle of Sedan had already been fought, Napoléon III had been captured, and the Third French Republic had been proclaimed. Hesse, Baden, Württemberg, and Bavaria now belonged to 'Bismarck's eternal union'.[18] But the fighting in France had not stopped.

Rather, the 'terrible war' entered a new phase.[19] The guerrilla warfare brought new battles—and new violations of rights. Both warring parties had repeatedly disregarded the Geneva Convention of 1864 and abused the emblem of the Red Cross.[20] In addition, the German occupiers had bombed French cities and cultural

---

[15] Koskenniemi juxtaposes his narrative of the genesis of modern international law in the late nineteenth century with the theories of 'just war', as if the latter had played no role in the nineteenth century: 'Although many readers reacted with sympathy to that account [of *The Gentle Civilizer*, HS], they also remained puzzled about how to think about the ealier times—"But what about Vitoria, Grotius and Vattel, theories of the just war and the Peace of Westphalia?"' The theories of 'just war' thus wrongly appear as a relic of the early modern period that was left behind in the nineteenth century; see also Koskenniemi (n. 6), at 1.

[16] Koskenniemi (n. 11), at 6.

[17] See Intro n. 2.

[18] O.F.R. Haardt, *Bismarcks ewiger Bund. Deutschland zwischen Fürstenbund und Reichsmonarchie 1871–1918* (2020).

[19] Bluntschli (n. 1), at 4.

[20] Koskenniemi (n. 5), at 39.

assets and appropriated the property of French citizens.[21] Now, summary executions were ordered:[22] the German warring parties refused to recognize the *Francs-tireurs* as legitimate combatants. The French government, for its part, would deny the status of legal combatants to irregular fighters of the Paris Commune and carry out summary executions.[23]

Struck by these violations of law, Bluntschli set out in his speech to analyse the war of 1870 from a legal perspective to 'focus on the experiences of this difficult time of war from the standpoint of modern international law'.[24] The Heidelberg professor began his speech 'with the shameful confession ... that the deficiencies and weakness of modern international law came to light in a frightening manner during this war'.[25] While 'for the first time ... the Geneva Convention of 1864 had proved its healing power', Bluntschli emphasized the excesses of violence, which he linked to hybrid warfare.[26]

How could these massive violations of law have occurred despite the codifications of the laws of war since 1864? For liberal jurists such as Bluntschli, the answer was relatively clear: one of the principal reasons was simply that 'the dissemination of the knowledge of the law, especially the law of nations, was still far too limited'.[27] Thus, Bluntschli argued, 'too little had been done before the war and during it to inform the soldiers and the citizens of the law'. Much like Bluntschli, Geneva lawyer Gustave Moynier, co-founder of the International Committee of the Red Cross (1863), saw one of the main reasons for the 'savagery unworthy of civilized nations' of 1870/71 as being the ignorance of the warring parties about the legal regulations.[28]

Bluntschli even speculated that 'the basic principles of international law' were as

> effective in practice as they are scientifically clear, and ... in particular, if they had been present at all times in public opinion and the conscience of state leaders ..., then this war would not have been dared, or the attempt to wage it would have been immediately suppressed.[29]

In other words, a stronger public awareness of international law, according to Bluntschli's self-confident credo, could have prevented war.

---

[21] Benvenisti and Lustig, 'Monopolizing War: Codifying the Laws of War to Reassert Governmental Authority, 1856–1874', 31 *European Journal of International Law* (2020) 127.
[22] M. Howard, *The Franco-Prussian War. The German Invasion of France, 1870–1871* (2nd edn., 2001), at 251 ff.
[23] Benvenisti and Lustig (n. 21).
[24] Bluntschli (n. 1), at 7.
[25] *Ibid.*
[26] *Ibid.*, at 21.
[27] *Ibid.*, at 13.
[28] Koskenniemi (n. 5), at 39.
[29] Bluntschli (n. 1), at 7.

It was therefore necessary, Bluntschli wrote in a letter to his friend Francis Lieber, for 'the law of nations and especially the law of war and the law of neutrals [to] be taught more carefully than hitherto in the war schools'.[30] Europe should hesitate no longer, Bluntschi argued, 'to follow the American example, and to give the most important legal regulations to officers and soldiers in a sharp version as printed service instruction'. This was an allusion to the addressee of Bluntschli's letter. Not long before this letter was written, in 1863, the 'Lieber Code' had become binding on Northern troops in the American Civil War through Abraham Lincoln's 'General Orders No. 100'.[31] In his letter, Bluntschli pleaded for more public presence of international law.

The prospects for such a public reappraisal of international law were not bad in the early 1870s. Calls for a pacification of international relations were clearly on the rise.[32] Again, the idea of 'peace through law'[33] was demanded by 'friends of peace'. This was not a foregone conclusion, as after five peace congresses between 1843 and 1851, the mid-century wars in Europe and the Civil War in the USA had brought the peace movements largely to a standstill.[34] The war of 1870/71 weakened the European peace movements further. But at the same time, it made the importance of their mission abundantly clear and thus also became a catalyst for their reform.

But there was a second reason for this new trust in international law: two years later, a long-standing dispute between the USA and Great Britain was settled peacefully by international arbitration.[35] The issue was whether Great Britain had violated neutrality in the US Civil War by tolerating Confederate privateers being equipped and armed in the port of Liverpool. The two conflict parties entrusted their dispute to an international arbitration tribunal in Geneva, which on 15 September 1872 ruled in favour of the USA. Great Britain was ordered to pay monetary compensation. The arbitration, which became famous as the *Alabama case* (named after one of the privateer ships, the CSS *Alabama*), greatly increased hopes for the peaceful resolution of international disputes.

Furthermore, fifty-six years before the Kellogg-Briand Pact, pacifist demands to prohibit aggression as a crime of international law now grew.[36] This finding fundamentally contradicts the thesis of a 'free right to wage war'. Peace was to be guaranteed by law, which suggested a strengthening of the codification of international

---

[30] J.C. Bluntschli, *Das moderne Völkerrecht der civilisierten Staaten als Rechtsbuch dargestellt* (2nd edn, 1872), at ix.
[31] P. Kalmanovitz, *The Laws of War in International Thought* (2020), at 14; for a critical perspective, see below.
[32] M.M. Payk, *Frieden durch Recht? Der Aufstieg des modernen Völkerrechts und der Friedensschluss nach dem Ersten Weltkrieg* (2018), Chapter 1.
[33] Chapter 3.3.
[34] Cooper (n. 9).
[35] Bingham, 'The Alabama Claims Arbitration', 54 *The International and Comparative Law Quarterly* (2005) 1.
[36] Bring, 'The Westphalian Peace Tradition in International Law: From Jus ad Bellum to Jus contra Bellum', 75 *International Law Studies. US Naval War College* (2000) 57, at 72 ff.

law, mediation, and arbitration courts as core demands of the moderate peace movement. But even before this, international law had been a subject of debate within the peace movements.[37] There had already been cooperation between liberal lawyers and (moderate) peace movements before 1870—although the latter sometimes relied less on state institutions than on the (similarly Kantian) idea of conflict resolution through public argumentation at its peace congresses.[38]

An important link between law scholarship and the peace movement in the middle of the century was Auguste Visschers. This Belgian lawyer was involved in the moderate peace movement and suggested a reform of international law long before the 'men of 1873'.[39] At around the same time, the young Belgian jurist Louis Bara was awarded the 1848 Essay Prize at the Third International Peace Congress in 1849 for his paper *La Science de la Paix* (1872), which dealt with the question of how international peace could best be established.[40] This is remarkable not only because Bara argued in favour of international law as the basis of peace, but also because he clearly affirmed the legitimacy of defensive war, which was controversial among pacifists. He made an analogy with the law of the state: just as the right to self-defence was a chapter in the code of private individuals, Bara argued, the right to self-defence of a state was a chapter in the code of peoples.[41]

After having been rediscovered by the liberal Belgian writer Charles Potvin, Bara's essay was reprinted in 1872. Moderate pacifists such as Potvin sought to present the plea for a lasting peace as scientifically as possible. They wanted to avoid being labelled 'utopians' at all costs.[42] To moderate pacifists, law was the most realistic option for a lasting pacification of international relations. They therefore turned to a negative concept of peace, which could be defined as the 'absence of direct violence'.[43] This legalistic orientation also provoked opposition in the peace movement—hardly surprising, given the movement's potpourri of anarchists, conservatives, socialists, nationalists, liberals, and feminists.[44] But the legalistic orientation of significant parts of the peace movement correlated with

---

[37] Cooper (n. 9); Hippler, 'From Nationalist Peace to Democratic War: The Peace Congresses in Paris (1849) and Geneva (1867)', in T. Hippler and M. Vec (eds), *Paradoxes of Peace in Nineteenth Century Europe* (2015) 170.

[38] Hippler (n. 37), at 181.

[39] Rycke, 'In Search of a Legal Conscience: Juridical Reformism in the Mid-19th Century Peace Movement', 80 *Studia Iuridica* (2019) 355, at 365–8.

[40] Cooper (n. 9), at 24, 29; Rycke, 'Legislating Utopia. Louis Bara (1821–1857) and the Liberal-Scientific Restatement of International Law in the Nineteenth Century Peace Movement', in 23 *Journal of the History of International Law/Revue d'histoire du droit international* (2020) 590.

[41] 'le jus belli est purement et simplement un chapitre du code d'instruction criminelle des peuples, comme le droit de légitime défense fait partie de celui des particuliers...': L. Bara, *La science de la paix: programme: mémoire couronné, à Paris, en 1849, par le congrès des sociétés anglo-américains des Amis de la paix* (1872), at 219.

[42] Cooper (n. 9), at 46.

[43] On the differentiation between 'positive' and 'negative peace', see Galtung, 'Violence, Peace, and Peace Research', 6 *Journal of Peace Research* (1969) 167; Senghaas, 'Peace Theory and the Restructuring of Europe', 16 *Alternatives: Global, Local, Political* (1991) 353.

[44] Cooper (n. 9), at 36.

the professionalization of international legal scholarship. As early as the 1860s, Gustave Rolin-Jaecquemyns, Tobias Asser, and John Westlake were increasingly thinking about the institutionalization of International Law as a secular, positivist, and liberal academic discipline.[45]

This project immediately found great support among liberal lawyers throughout Europe and in the USA. In September 1873, the first meeting of the *Institut de Droit International*, founded in Ghent, took place. In addition to Asser and Rolin-Jaecquemyns, founding members were Pascal Mancini (Rome), Émile de Laveleye (Liège), Tobie Michel Charles (Amsterdam), James Lorimer (Edinburgh), Vladimir Besobrassof (St Petersburg), Augusto Pierantoni (Naples), Carlos Calvo (Buenos Aires), David Dudley Field (New York), and the aforementioned Moynier and Bluntschli. In 1873, Rolin-Jaecquemyns prominently articulated the Institute's central idea of the progress of law through the professionalization of its science in an essay for the *Revue de Droit Internationale et de Législation Comparée*. According to Article 1 of its Statute,[46] the Institute's self-declared mission was to promote the progress of international law as the organ '*de la conscience juridique du monde civilisé*'. For the 'men of 1873', liberal legal scholarship was supposed to systematize, promote—and thus represent—both legal conscience and consciousness of the 'civilized world'.[47] Hence, for the members of the *Institut de Droit International*, international law was a process of civilization,[48] which should ideally lead to a pacification of international relations.

But this ideal was confronted with the reality that the international order still lacked a prohibition of war under international treaty law. Even—and especially— in the late nineteenth century, international relations were thus characterized by an asymmetrical codification of *ius in bello* and *ius ad bellum*, which I call '*semi-legalization of war*'. How did liberal legal scholars react to this uneven development of international law?

6.3 Mere Continuity? Liberal Legal Theory between Limiting and Outlawing War

Analysing the treatment of war in international legal literature after 1870, one is initially left with an impression of mere continuity. Like their predecessors in the first half of the century, most legal scholars after 1870 continued to refer to

---

[45] On its genesis, see Rolin-Jacquemyns, 'De la nécessité d'organiser une institution scientifique permanente pour favoriser l'étude et le progrès du droit international', 5 *Revue de Droit Internationale et de Législation Comparée* (1873) 463; and Koskenniemi (n. 5).
[46] *Statuts votés par la Conférence Juridique internationale de Gand, le 10 Septembre 1873* (1877), at 1.
[47] Koskenniemi (n. 5), at 47–51.
[48] Bluntschli (n. 30), at 19; H. Bonfils, *Lehrbuch des Völkerrechts für Studium und Praxis, durchgesehen und ergänzt von Paul Fauchille* (3rd edn, 1904), at 4.

the doctrine of 'just war'. Like Henry Bonfils, a professor in Toulouse, they distinguished between 'just and unjust wars'.[49]

As in the first half of the century, lawyers wanted the 'justice' of war to be replaced more and more by 'positive law'. War was therefore 'just' if it was 'legal'. The Argentinean jurist Carlos Calvo, who lived in Paris, succinctly summed up this principle in his treatise on '*légitimation de la guerre*': war could only be considered 'just' if international law permitted the taking up of arms; it would be considered 'unjust', on the other hand, if it ran counter to the principles of law.[50] The legal discourse of the former was echoed almost word for word in the formulations of the second half of the century.

In his 1868 textbook (second edition 1872), Bluntschli stated accordingly that war was 'just' if and insofar as armed legal assistance was justified by international law—and 'unjust' if it contradicted the provisions of international law.[51] However, Bluntschli claimed, this was not only a moral but also a legal principle ('*wirklicher Rechtssatz*').[52] Bluntschli emphasized that while war did not appear 'in the form of a legal remedy, but in the terrible shape of a physical struggle between conflicting powers',[53] it had 'a multitude of legal effects',[54] regardless of its legal basis. War was usually to be understood as a legal dispute between states, 'as parties warring over public law'. And against any political arbitrariness in international relations, Bluntschli argued that the 'mere interest of state does not justify war'.[55] Similarly, in his *Manuel de Droit International Public Droit Des Gens*, which was translated into German in 1904, Bonfils wrote with reference to the British jurist James Lorimer that war should not be an end in itself, but only a state of emergency of limited duration.[56] Lorimer had stated in his textbook of 1883 that accepting the factuality of war in no way meant accepting its legality:

> In accepting war and neutrality as inevitable, we accept them, not as indifferent, but as right—as jural, notwithstanding their abnormality. In consequence of their abnormality, however, they are right relatively only, not absolutely— temporarily only, not permanently. They are right only in relation to conditions that are wrong, because not wholly independent of human volition.[57]

---

[49] Bonfils (n. 48), at 538.
[50] '*Légitimation de la guerre*: ... En résumé, une guerre peut être considérée comme juste, lorsque le droit international autorise le recours aux armes; comme injuste lorsqu'elle est contraire aux principes de ce droit.' C. Calvo, *Dictionnaire de Droit International Public et Privé* (1885), at 366 ff.
[51] Bluntschli (n. 30), at 289.
[52] *Ibid.*
[53] *Ibid.*, at 286.
[54] *Ibid.*, at 287.
[55] '*Das blosse Statsinteresse rechtfertigt den Krieg nicht.*', *ibid.*, at 51.
[56] Bonfils (n. 48), at 538.
[57] J. Lorimer, *The Institutes of the Law of Nations. A Treatise of the Jural Relations of Separate Political Communities*, vol. 1 (1883), at 7.

These were clear rejections of a legal indifference to war as well as of narratives of realpolitik. The legal discourse of the 'men of 1873' was characterized by a primacy of law, which was positioned against a primacy of power in the sense of Carl von Clausewitz.[58]

The fact that the jurists still deemed as necessary this definitional demarcation from, for example, moral or political concepts and narratives of war, becomes clear when one recalls Fedor Fedorovich Martens's statement that 'everyone knows what war is; but to define it scientifically correctly does not seem so easy. The definitions so far show the greatest diversity.'[59] Martens did indeed refer to a large number of authors, relevant in late nineteenth-century war discourse, who used different definitions of war.[60] He mentioned military writers (Clausewitz, Rüstow, Ratzenhofer, Hartmann), philosophers (Spinoza, Kant, de Maistre, Mill, Proudhon [interestingly, Martens did not refer to Hegel here]), scholars (Cobden, Treitschke), a journalist (de Girardin), and international lawyers (Phillimore, and Martens himself).

Nevertheless, most of the literature on international law—the so-called 'prevailing opinion'—agreed with Bluntschli, Bonfils, Calvo, and Lorimer: a clear commitment to the need to justify war can also be found in the work of important European legal scholars such as William Edward Hall,[61] the Frenchman Pradier-Fodéré, the Baltic Germans Karl Bergbohm and August von Bulmerincq,[62] the Russian crown jurist Fedor Fedorovich Martens,[63] the Swiss jurist Alphonse Rivier,[64] the Germans Franz von Holtzendorff[65] and Fritz Stier-Somlo,[66] the Italian Pasquale Fiore,[67] and the Austrians Leopold Neumann[68] and Heinrich Lammasch (see below). They all confirmed the necessity of a legal reason for war. Furthermore, the two pivotal legitimate justifications of war remained the same: war was considered legitimate by lawyers if it was waged to sanction a violation of rights—and in particular for self-defence—or to secure general peace.

Thus, at the end of the nineteenth century, the mainstream of jurisprudence was situated in this consolidated European tradition of justifying war. Bluntschli, for example, explicitly referred to this tradition, thus confirming my perception of continuity in legal thinking on the legitimacy of war in the nineteenth century. In his speech in November 1870, Bluntschli affirmed that legal science 'has long proved the principle that every lawful war presupposes a legal ground and that a

---

[58] Chapter 3.3.
[59] F.F. Martens, *Völkerrecht. Das internationale Recht der civilisirten Nationen*, vol. 2 (1886), at 476.
[60] Ibid., at 476 ff.
[61] W.E. Hall, *A Treatise on International Law* (1890), at 63.
[62] A. von Bulmerincq, *Das Völkerrecht oder das internationale Recht. Systematisch dargestellt* (2nd edn, 1889), at 357.
[63] Martens (n. 59).
[64] A. Rivier, *Lehrbuch des Völkerrechts* (1889), at 367.
[65] F. von Holtzendorff (ed.), *Handbuch des Völkerrechts* (1889).
[66] F. Stier-Somlo (ed.), *Handbuch des Völkerrechts* (1912).
[67] P. Fiore, *Trattato di diritto internazionale pubblico* (2nd edn, 1879), at 86 ff.
[68] L. Neumann, *Grundriss des heutigen europäischen Völkerrechtes* (1877), at 93.

war of the nations can never be justified by mere interests or passions, only by violations or threats to law'.[69] Lawyers, however, no longer referred only to the early modern classics, such as Vitoria, Grotius, or Vattel, but just as clearly to the direct predecessors of the latter in the first half of the century.

In addition, international legal discourse continued to refer to non-lawyers—and in particular to philosophers of the Enlightenment. Bonfils, for example, agreed with Montesquieu that states as well as individuals were entitled, in the case of self-defence, to wage war 'for the purpose of self-preservation'.[70] This formulation is interesting for several reasons. Bonfils argued for a defence of the rights of the individual state, as becomes clear in the next paragraph of his treatise. Much like Montesquieu, Bonfils too contended:

> the publicists of the 19th century, notably Calvo, [Charles] Giraud, Heffter, Lorimer, Phillimore, Travers Twiss, hold in principle the legitimacy of war per se, as a means of providing the state with satisfaction for an injustice or a slight.[71]

Bonfils's recourse to 'self-preservation', however, also points to the definitional indeterminacy with which self-defence was treated in some law treaties. Although it was regularly stated that only defensive wars were justified under international law,[72] what exactly 'defence' meant nevertheless remained open in the absence of a clear definition of 'aggression' in international legal theory. August von Bulmerincq, Bluntschli's successor in Heidelberg after 1882, referred to the 'fundamental rights of international law', namely the 'existence, independence, equality, and honour of a state', as needing to be defended by force.[73] These, too, were decidedly vague concepts.[74] It is true that the self-preservation of a state was, in principle, covered by its right to self-defence, as Ian Brownlie has argued.[75] However, in parts of legal treaties—and in parts of state practice—attempts to expand self-defence under a broadly interpreted claim of preventive self-preservation of a state or people can be observed since the middle of the century.[76] However, these broad interpretations were difficult to reconcile with state practice. Any form of unilateral preventive use of force was considered strictly illegitimate, as I have already discussed in Chapter 5 regarding the mid-century wars.[77]

---

[69] '... schon lange den Grundsatz erwiesen [hat], dass jeder rechtmässige Krieg einen Rechtsgrund voraussetzt und dass niemals blosse Interessen oder Leidenschaften, sondern nur Verletzungen oder Bedrohungen des Rechts einen Völkerkrieg zu rechtfertigen vermögen', Bluntschli (n. 1), at 7.
[70] Bonfils (n. 48), at 538 ff.
[71] Ibid.
[72] Bulmerincq (n. 62), at 357.
[73] Vec, 'Grundrechte der Staaten. Die Tradierung des Natur- und Völkerrechts der Aufklärung', 18 Rechtsgeschichte (2011) 66.
[74] Bulmerincq (n. 62), at 357.
[75] I. Brownlie, *International Law and the Use of Force by States* (1963), at 42 ff.
[76] See below, Chapter 7; see also Lesaffer, 'Aggression before Versailles', 29 *European Journal of International Law* (2018) 773, at 795.
[77] For the debates in the context of the Great War, see Chapter 9.3.

Unsurprisingly, a 'free right to go to war' was not advocated by any of the luminaries of liberal international law doctrine. Rather, the liberal consensus that war was to be understood as an *'ultima ratio* for the settlement of disputes under international law'[78] persisted until after the First World War. One example is the 'standard book'[79] of Berlin legal scholar Franz von Liszt, which was published in twelve editions between 1898 and 1925 and became the most successful international law textbook of the Wilhelmine era.[80] However, Liszt doubted the rationality of this *'ultima ratio',* faced with the horrors of the First World War.[81] This—quite subtle—criticism also referred to the fact that a prohibition of war based on positive law was still lacking.

The impression of continuity since the first half of the century is therefore not deceptive. A distinction continued to be made between 'just(ified)' and 'unjust(ified)' wars. Since war was not yet outlawed in terms of positive law, this also meant that multiple non-legal, e.g. moral, arguments were still used to assert the (il)legality of war. Especially in the political field of ordering international violence, legal doctrine was shaped by normative plurality. The 'project of positivism in international law'[82] was often in fact the exact opposite: non-positivist.

Liberal Legal Theory between Grotius and Kant

For liberal scholars, this was an extremely unsatisfactory situation. It *had* to provoke more complex and multifaceted responses. My argument is that, despite all the continuities, the phase between 1870 and 1914 did indeed see important innovations in liberal thought about war and law. These theoretical innovations were to become groundbreaking for the further development of modern international law from a 'law of war to a law of peace'.[83] Thus, a complete legalization of war was now sought in the sense of *ius contra bellum*. At first, these ideas were formulated rather sporadically and tentatively, sometimes even contradictorily. However, by the outbreak of the First World War—and beyond—they gained argumentative traction.

The Kantian problem of *Sein und Sollen* (is and ought) thus also played a decisive role in the discourse on the legitimacy of war in the second half of the century. International lawyers did not stop at characterizing war as a legal means that

---

[78] F. von Liszt, *Das Völkerrecht. Systematisch dargestellt* (11th edn, 1920), at 275.
[79] F. Hermann, *Das Standardwerk. Franz von Liszt und das Völkerrecht* (2001).
[80] Liszt (n. 78), at 275.
[81] *Ibid.*
[82] M. García-Salmones Rovira, *The Project of Positivism in International Law* (2013); see also Vec, 'The Project of Anti-Positivism in International Law', 24 *Rechtsgeschichte* (2016) 505.
[83] On this narrative, see Brock, 'Frieden durch Recht?', in P. Becker, R. Braun, and D. Deiseroth (eds): *Frieden durch Recht* (2010) 15; Payk (n. 32); Brock and Simon, 'Liberal European Peace Theories and their Critics', in K.E. Jørgensen (ed.), *The Liberal International Theory Tradition in Europe* (2020) 73.

had to be limited and 'humanized'. Rather, after 1870 they began to formulate a general critique of war, first as a political, but later also as a legal means. Bonfils, for example, argued that war was an evil regardless of the reasons for it.[84] Even justified wars were morally reprehensible. Based on these moral scruples, liberal lawyers, such as Bluntschli,[85] Bonfils,[86] Yale's Theodore Dwight Woolsey,[87] or Hans Kelsen's teacher in legal philosophy, Leo Strisower, concluded that peace, not war, was the normal state of international relations.[88] In times of peace, law ruled, not force, argued Bluntschli.[89]

The liberal doctrine of international law was thus caught between a systematization of the legal limitation of violence in war and the anticipation of a positive legal prohibition of war. Referring to the three worldviews of the English School of International Relations theory—Hobbes, Grotius, and Kant—,[90] one could say that liberal legal theory at the end of the nineteenth century oscillated somewhere between Grotius and Kant.

But how could those liberals who sought a more ambitious regulation not only of *ius in bello* but also of *ius ad/contra bellum*, substantiate their arguments in the absence of a positive legal prohibition of war? It is striking that corresponding pleas in law books were also reinforced with extra-legal arguments of morality, humanity, civilization, economy, or the '(survival of) peoples'. Thus, although late nineteenth-century scholarship aspired to positive international law, it continued to be shaped by non-positivist influences.[91] Matthias Schmoeckel has correctly observed that 'positivism' is a vague and unreliable term applied to very different approaches.[92]

Bluntschli, for example, justified his appeal for war to be understood as a phenomenon of law with the existence of 'great human interest'.[93] The turn to law to limit legitimate reasons to justify war was thus based on considerations of morality and humanity.[94] Likewise, when Bluntschli argued—

---

[84] Bonfils (n. 48), at 538.
[85] Bluntschli (n. 30), at 9.
[86] Bonfils (n. 48), at 538.
[87] T.D. Woolsey, *Introduction to the Study of International Law: Designed as an Aid in Teaching, and in Historical Studies* (1897), at 183.
[88] L. Strisower, *Krieg und Völkerrechtsordnung* (1919), at 4.
[89] Bluntschli (n. 30), at 9.
[90] H. Bull, *The Anarchical Society. A Study of Order in World Politics* (1977).
[91] S.C. Neff, *Justice among Nations. A History of International Law* (2014), at 226–43; García-Salmones (n. 82); Vec, 'Sources of International Law in the Nineteenth-Century European Tradition: The Myth of Positivism', in S. Besson and J. d'Aspremont (eds), *The Oxford Handbook of the Sources of International Law* (2017) 121.
[92] Schmoeckel, 'The Internationalist as a Scientist and Herald: Lassa Oppenheim', 11 *European Journal of International Law* (2000) 699, at 701.
[93] Bluntschli (n. 30), at 289.
[94] On humanity and morality in nineteenth-century war discourse, see also K. Lovric-Pernak, *Morale internationale und humanité im Völkerrecht des späten 19. Jahrhunderts. Bedeutung und Funktion in Staatenpraxis und Wissenschaft* (2013); Klose (n. 9).

that it is not lawful for man to use force and coercion against man merely for the sake of advantage, or out of hatred and revenge or other excitation of passion, but only insofar as the necessity of law ennobles force and requires coercion for its protection,[95]

he also referred to the 'entire civilized world order' ('*gesammte civilisirte Weltordnung*') as the source of this unwritten rule.[96] This was accompanied by a condemnation of war as immoral. According to Bluntschli,[97] no violence was more terrible than that of war, 'which constantly threatens the lives, health, and property of many thousands and endangers the existence and welfare of entire peoples'. Bluntschli concluded that to 'start a war without a compelling legal reason is therefore the gravest crime against humanity'.[98] This was not yet a rejection of war as a legal *ultima ratio*. However, the criticism of an illegal war as 'inhumane' was disseminated by liberal lawyers in the second half of the nineteenth century.

But even this portrayal of war as a moral scandal and the linking of civilization and progress in the perception of law as an antipode to war as a political means was not fundamentally new. As has already been shown,[99] critical authors such as Kaltenborn-Stachau, H.B. Oppenheim, or the Kantian Zachariä had already developed the argumentative triad of law, civilization, and peaceful progress in the first half of the nineteenth century. In view of this continuity, the innovations of the 'men of 1873' are thus somewhat less significant.

However, there *were* innovations in legal theory in the second half of the century. With the rapidly increasing importance of international law after 1870, the ideas of pacification through civilization acquired more argumentative depth, were more widely disseminated, and thus gained significantly in political and normative weight. And more importantly, some international legal scholars after 1870 sought to completely eliminate war not only as a political tool, but also as a legal remedy. This was a decisive step in legal doctrine towards the outlawing of war.

A particularly prominent demand was to link the legalization and institutionalization of international relations. The idea of international courts of arbitration gained particular importance. The French jurist Charles Lucas, for example, emphasized in 1873 that he had long cherished the wish that mankind might achieve the abolition of war through the establishment of international courts of arbitration. Lucas, a member of the *Institut de Droit International* as well as

---

[95] '… dass es dem Menschen nicht verstattet ist, wider den Menschen Gewalt und Zwang zu üben, bloss um des Vortheils willen, oder aus Hass und Rache oder andern Reizungen der Leidenschaft, sondern nur soweit die Rechtsnothwendigkeit die Gewalt adelt und den Zwang zu ihrem Schutze erfordert': Bluntschli (n. 1), at 7.
[96] *Ibid.*
[97] *Ibid.*
[98] 'Einen Krieg ohne zwingenden Rechtsgrund zu beginnen ist daher das schwerste Verbrechen an der Menschheit.', ibid.
[99] Chapter 4.2.

the renowned French *Académie des Sciences Morales et Politiques*, hoped that the progress of public reason would make it possible to put an end to war in this way. Civilizing war, Lucas argued, meant publicly proclaiming that the only principle that could justify it was legitimate defence and, apart from that, war should be understood as criminal.[100] Thus, from the narrowing of legitimate reasons for war to self-defence, in particular, Lucas deduced a plea for overcoming war not only as a political means, but also in general. For if war of aggression were to be legally prohibited, Lucas logically concluded, defensive war would also have lost its basis for existence.[101]

Lucas was not a 'naïve idealist': he explicitly praised the codification of the laws of war since the First Geneva Convention of 1864. At the same time, however, he assumed, in light of the Franco-Prussian War and Bismarck's realpolitik, that Europe would continue to be helplessly at the mercy of outbreaks of violence without an international code of law prohibiting war. In Lucas's work, the liberal hope of outlawing war is thus clearly visible. Moreover, Lucas shared the liberal idea that a professionalization of international legal scholarship was crucial for the pacification of international relations. The two were interrelated: an international code of law would have to be drafted at diplomatic and scientific congresses.[102] This was also an (indirect) recourse to the Kantian idea of the development of reason in the communicative space of congress diplomacy.

Lucas thus presented a precise summary of liberal demands for gradual progress towards a legal peace through the narrowing of legitimate reasons for war, the establishment of international arbitration courts, and increasing solidarity between states.[103] For instance, Turin professor Pasquale Fiore quoted Lucas's vision of abolishing war and added optimistically that one could already observe—

> how the principle of isolation is being replaced by that of a solidarity of interests, how peoples economically obey the law of the division of labour, how each state, seeing itself as an autonomous and independent organism, feels the need to live in society with others.[104]

---

[100] 'Civiliser la guerre, c'est, selon moi, proclamer bien haut le seul principe qui puisse la justifier, celui de la légitime défense, et en dehors de ce principe la flétrir comme criminelle, en un mot c'est montrer ce qui est le droit, la guerre défensive, at ce qui est le crise, la guerre offensive de l'ambition et de la conquête.' C. Lucas, *Civilisation de la guerre: Observations sur les lois de la guerre et l'arbitrage international, à l'occasion de la lettre de m. le comte de Moltke à m. le professeur Bluntschli* (1873), at 2.

[101] 'Ce qu'il faut s'attacher à abolir, c'est la seconde, puisqu'alors la première n'aurait plus sa raison d'être.' Ibid.

[102] Ibid.

[103] Quoted from J. ter Meulen, *Der Gedanke der Internationalen Organisation in seiner Entwicklung* (1968), at 62 ff.

[104] '... come al principio dell'isolamento si va sostituendo quello della solidarietà degl'interessi, come i popoli obbediscono alla legge della divisione del lavoro, come ciascuno Stato sentendo di essere un organismo autonomo e indipendente sente il bisogno di vivere in società cogli altri', Fiore (n. 67), at 83.

Against this background, according to Fiore, it could clearly be seen—

how, beyond the particular interests of each State, the international interest, the interest of humanity, comes to the fore, binding the various members of the human family with ever closer ties.[105]

According to Fiore, the individual human entities—man, family, nation, confederation of states or world state, and, finally, humanity—were naturally interconnected, following one another, as it were. This was a conception of law that was strongly reminiscent of Kant's cosmopolitan teleology.[106] Reason as the standard of nations played a prominent role in Fiore's conception of international law. But Fiore was not 'naïve' either: rather, he combined the teleological cosmopolitan project of pacification with an organic understanding of law.[107] Here the influence of the Italian School,[108] and especially Pasquale Stanislao Mancini, on Fiori becomes clear. Like Bluntschli and Lieber, Mancini had been influenced by Savigny's concept of law.[109]

Johann Caspar Bluntschli also followed a teleological organic conception of law. The Heidelberg lawyer reflected on a future 'organization of mankind' ('*Organisation der Menschheit*') and a 'legislator for the world' ('*Gesetzgeber für die Welt*'). The latter should one day regulate the relations between states and 'mankind' through a 'world law' ('*Weltgesetz*') just as clearly, uniformly, and effectively 'as present state law does with regard to the relations of private individuals among themselves and to the state'.[110] Bluntschli took objections to such a utopia seriously. Sometimes he even shared them: one might have complete confidence in the 'lofty final goal' of a world legislator, 'whose pronouncement would be obeyed by all states and all nations', he wrote—adding, however: 'present-day international law ... does not correspond to this ideal'.[111] A world legislator was not in sight: 'the organization of the world ... does not exist', Bluntschli argued.[112] He knew that the process of progressing from the 'raw barbarism of violence and arbitrariness to civilized states of law' would be a slow and gradual one.[113] At best, the law of his time could facilitate a transition from the 'uncertain legal community of peoples to the finite, fully conscious legal unity of humanity'.[114] These were serious empirical objections.

---

[105] Ibid.
[106] See also A. Weinke, *Gewalt, Geschichte, Gerechtigkeit. Transnationale Debatten über deutsche Staatsverbrechen im 20. Jahrhundert* (2016), at 33.
[107] Bartolini, 'Italian Legal Scholarship of International Law in the Early Decades of the Twentieth Century', in G. Bartolini (ed.), *A History of International Law in Italy* (2020) 128, at 129.
[108] Focarelli, 'The Concept of International Law: The Italian Perspective', in P. Hilpold (ed.), *European International Law Traditions* (2021) 97.
[109] J. Summers, *Peoples and International Law* (2007), at 112.
[110] Bluntschli (n. 30), at 4.
[111] Ibid.
[112] Ibid.
[113] '*rohen Barbarei der Gewalt und Willkür zu civilisirten Rechtszuständen*', ibid.
[114] Ibid.

However, Bluntschli did not stop at pessimism. Rather, he contradicted the formalist argument that there was 'no law without written regulations' ('*Ohne Gesetz kein Recht*').[115] Admittedly, Bluntschli saw written laws as the 'clearest and most effective expression' of law; but they were not its 'only source'.[116] This is where the concept of 'legal consciousness of the civilized world' came back in. It had in fact been Bluntschli who introduced this concept into the discourse of the *Institut de Droit International*. For, according to Bluntschli, even in the 'youth of civilized peoples', written laws were lacking. This was also the case in international relations.[117] Instead of looking only at the treaties, Bluntschli focused on the 'intercourse of the peoples';[118] in other words: he turned to their practice.

In Bluntschli's dynamic understanding of law as an evolved cultural practice, the influence of Friedrich Carl von Savigny's *Historical School of Law* and its 'supranational historicism' becomes clear.[119] In contrast to Austin with his command theory, liberals such as Bluntschli or Fiore did not see the validity of law as being based on its enforceability, but rather, as Koskenniemi has summarized, on 'historical jurisprudence, linked with liberal-humanitarian ideals and theories of natural evolution of European societies'.[120] Accordingly, Bluntschli spoke of law as 'emerging' ('*werdendes Recht*') or 'living' ('*lebendiges Recht*').[121]

The task of legal scholarship was therefore not only to document valid legal regulations, but also *opinio iuris* or state practice amounting to legal obligations in European societies and states. According to Bluntschli, the 'right of the natural growth' of peoples, states, and humanity as a 'right of progressive life' must be

> more unequivocally and resolutely recognized and advocated by science than hitherto, if it is to fulfil its high moral and spiritual mission of carrying its shining torch forward on the paths of humanity.[122]

And for Bluntschli, this was even accompanied by legal scholars having the authority to declare what law is.[123] Given the lack of legislative bodies in international relations, 'which provide for the further development of international law', legal science should be allowed to assume this task.[124]

---

[115] *Ibid.*, at 3.
[116] *Ibid.*
[117] *Ibid.*
[118] *Ibid.*
[119] Koskenniemi (n. 5), at 45; see also Nuzzo, 'The Birth of an Imperial Location. Comparative Perspectives on Western Colonialism in China', 31 *Leiden Journal of International Law* (2018) 569; J. Rückert, *Friedrich Carl von Savigny. Leben und Wirken (1779–1861)* (2021).
[120] Koskenniemi (n. 5), at 51.
[121] Bluntschli (n. 30), at viii ff.
[122] *Ibid.*
[123] *Ibid.*, at 7.
[124] *Ibid.*, at viii.

From such a practice-oriented perspective, Bluntschli came to a much more optimistic conclusion about the present and future of international law than his objections analysed above suggest. According to Bluntschli, 'contemporary international law does not completely lack a common, authoritative articulation of its legal principles, which therefore has a quasi-legislative character' (*'gesetzähnlichen Character'*).[125] For by convening in large congresses and declaring their common *opinio iuris*, 'the civilized states', according to Bluntschli, 'have basically done the same thing as the legislator does'.[126] Moreover, it was their intention not only to create bilateral treaties, but rather general legal norms.[127]

Liberal lawyers thus perceived recent developments in international law in a twofold way: on the one hand, the shortcomings of international law were unmistakably extensive, albeit 'not so extensive as to impede its existence'.[128] For liberals, the century was

> marked by the struggle between politics and law, between the transitory and conditional interests of governments and the stable principles of individual and international law

as Pasquale Fiore aptly put it.[129] A multitude of obstacles emerged again and again, he added, 'which, in ever new forms, prevent the rules that arise from scientific deduction and emerge in the conscience of peoples from finally being accepted as the canon of law'.[130]

On the other hand, liberals felt that national law in European states had made considerable progress in the nineteenth century. Fiore wondered, in a typical analogy to national law, why this progress should not 'also happen in international society'? Even Kant's 'main demand' of world citizenship 'to some extent, already contains real truth today', as Bluntschli noted with reference to laws governing the position of aliens.[131]

Organizing Peace

It was a clear expression of the back and forth of liberal legal theory between recognizing the shortcomings of international law and hoping for its progress, 'between apology and utopia',[132] when Bluntschli relativized the reference to Kant's

---

[125] *Ibid.*, at 5.
[126] *Ibid.*
[127] *Ibid.*
[128] *Ibid.*, at 11.
[129] Fiore (n. 67), at 75.
[130] *Ibid.*
[131] Bluntschli (n. 30), at 27.
[132] M. Koskenniemi, *From Apology to Utopia. The Structure of International Legal Argument. Reissue with a New Epilogue* (2005).

Weltbürgerrecht (cosmopolitan law) in the same textbook. While 'the disposition for cosmopolitan law (Kant)' was already visible, he argued, its formation would only be possible 'when there is a political organization of the world' ('*Organisation der Welt*').[133]

This brings us back to the beginning of Bluntschli's textbook quoted above: for the '*Organisation der Welt*' did not yet exist.[134] With this, however, Bluntschli referred to what was probably the most significant innovation of liberal legal thinking on war and order at the end of the nineteenth century: to abolish war as a legal remedy, to establish binding international courts of arbitration; in short, to secure lasting peace through *ius contra bellum*, the establishment of an international or supranational organization was needed.

In the lively liberal debates on this issue, the term 'organization' even became the 'antithesis of anarchy', understood as an unregulated, disorderly state of international relations.[135] International organizations were now conceived as peace and identity-building institutions, sometimes even as precursors of a world state.[136] English scholar John Robert Seeley, for example, argued in a lecture in 1871 that an international court of justice in Europe would only be possible if the European nations simultaneously created an international state modelled on the USA.[137] Seeley argued that an international institution was needed to enforce arbitral awards.

According to a research overview published by Hans Wehberg in *Die Frieden-Warte* in 1941, James Lorimer and Johann Caspar Bluntschli were the first legal scholars to become seriously interested in 'the problem of a United States of Europe'.[138] Indeed, in a series of essays in the 1870s, as well as in the second edition of his *Institutes of the Law of Nations* (1884), translated into French and Spanish, Lorimer designed an international government based in Geneva, which should deal with all international *political* questions. In addition, all international *legal* questions were to be decided by a permanent court that was also to be established.[139]

While, according to Lorimer, the European organization to be founded had to be sovereign, Bluntschli's conception of *Die Organisation des europäischen Staatenvereines* (the Organization of the European Association of States, 1881 [1878]) did not go as far. Bluntschli proposed a confederation of states in which all

---

[133] Bluntschli (n. 30), at 68.

[134] *Ibid.*, at 4.

[135] M. Koch, *Internationale Organisationen in der Weltgesellschaft* (2017), at 37; see also B. Reinalda, *History of International Organizations. From 1815 to the Present Day* (2009); M. Herren, *Networking the International System. Global Histories of International Organizations* (2014).

[136] Koch (n. 135), at 37; see also M. Vec, *Recht und Normierung in der industriellen Revolution. Neue Strukturen der Normsetzung in Völkerrecht, staatlicher Gesetzgebung und gesellschaftlicher Selbstnormierung* (2006).

[137] Wehberg, 'Ideen und Projekte betr. die Vereinigten Staaten von Europa in den letzten 100 Jahren', 41 *Die Friedens-Warte* (1941) 49.

[138] *Ibid.*, at 77.

[139] Lorimer, 'Proposition d'un congrès international basé sur le principe de facto', 3 *Revue de Droit Internationale et de Législation Comparée* (1871) 1.

individual states should remain sovereign. To Bluntschli, Lorimer's proposal still seemed too unrealistic. An international senate or parliament constituted under international law, Bluntschli argued, would remain a 'pious wish' for a long time.[140]

In his conception, Bluntschli also referred to the European Concert and Kant's idea of the permanent congress of states (*'permanenter Staatencongress'*).[141] In doing so, his argument was very much in line with the (self-)contradiction typical of contemporary liberalism. On the one hand, Bluntschli criticized the Concert as an exclusive club of primarily monarchically constituted Great Powers.[142] This is reminiscent of H.B. Oppenheim's remark that the Concert judged the legitimacy of violence according to 'its very own rules'.[143] On the other hand, Bluntschli saw the pentarchy as the 'beginning of an organization of Europe, but ... not as its completion'. The institution of a 'general congress under international law' was still lacking and in its 'uncertain stumbling' beginnings.[144] As a liberal, Bluntschli dreamed of the parliamentary representation of nations in an international congress system— which, however, he still considered wishful thinking.[145]

Bluntschli's peace draft ultimately also reflected the oscillation of many liberals (like Kant before them) between the political realities of their time and legal ideals. He conceived of a dualistic organization of Europe in which states were to retain their sovereignty, but in which state sovereignty was at the same time to be restricted by inalienable human rights.[146] Here, too, Kant's influence can be glimpsed. For Kant's ideas also had a significant impact on the discourse on international law theory of the late nineteenth century.[147] This applies, for example, to Kant's ideas of the 'eternal' congress diplomacy, the public exercise of reason, and especially the telos of pacification through legalization and institutionalization.

Kant's peace treatise, in particular, was important for liberal debates on international law—but was by no means only referred to positively. Rather, opinions were very mixed, especially with regard to its feasibility. In *Die Idee des ewigen Völkerfriedens* (1882), for example, Franz von Holtzendorff wrote that, according to Kant, the problem of perpetual peace could only be understood as a slow process, at the same time emphasizing, in the spirit of Kant, that peace as a process must be worked on continuously. The conditions producing aggression through lust for power, desire for conquest, and national hatred or hostility to faith had to 'either give way to a morally perfect state or are gradually rendered ineffective by improved institutions of international law'.[148]

---

[140] Bluntschli (n. 30), at 108.
[141] *Ibid.*, at 198.
[142] *Ibid.*
[143] H.B. Oppenheim, *System des Völkerrechts* (1845), at 272; see also Chapter 4.2.
[144] Bluntschli (n. 30), at 108.
[145] *Ibid.*, at 111.
[146] Hobe, 'Das Europakonzept Johann Kaspar Bluntschlis vor dem Hintergrund seiner Völkerrechtslehre', 31 *Archiv des Völkerrechts: AVR* (1993) 367, at 378 ff.
[147] Wehberg (n. 137), at 52.
[148] F. von Holtzendorff, *Die Idee des ewigen Völkerfriedens* (1882), at 47.

But when Holtzendorff referred to Kant in order to call for 'the moral rebirth of humanity', 'which can only happen in peace and will have no other consequence than peace', this sounded like cynicism and mockery.[149] Kant's conception of peace then appeared as a kind of squaring of the circle. But it was Holtzendorff himself who objected a little later in his text that the idea of perpetual peace in Kant's sense was by no means deserving of derision and contempt.[150] Rather, times might come 'in which, through an enlightenment of human consciousness as yet undreamed of, the distances separating the spiritual and moral life of the world of states from one another will be reduced'.[151]

There is evidence of an ambivalent relationship between the liberal doctrine of international law at the end of the nineteenth century and Kant's peace draft. Liberals sympathized with Kant's philosophical sketch in principle, but at the same time they were sceptical about its feasibility. For example, Italian jurist Antonio Del Bon wrote in his *Istituzioni del diritto pubblico internazionale* that one must bow before the magnificent dreams of peace from St Pierre to Kant, but at the same time 'always compare them with the reality of things, of men and of peoples'.[152] This—indeed very Kantian[153]—comparison of ideals and realities explains why many liberals held to the doctrine of 'just war' and sought to modify it. German historian Veit Valentin even argued in 1920 that Holtzendorff had defended 'just war' 'against the attacks of the peace societies'.[154] In this paradoxical defence of 'just war' against a radical pacifism, the determination of liberal jurists to avoid being labelled utopian once again comes to the fore. For many liberal scholars, perpetual peace was desirable, yet unattainable. In a perhaps more optimistic vein, Austrian international lawyer and politician Heinrich Lammasch expressed this particularly succinctly when he wrote that he 'did not believe in perpetual peace' but that 'everything must be done to bring it about'.[155]

6.4 Antinomies of the 'Gentle Civilizers': Liberal Justifications of War

The present chapter could have ended with the last paragraph addressing the liberal efforts to order violence. However, this would repeat a mistake of liberal histories of progress that is still being made today—and that was also central to the

---

[149] *Ibid.*
[150] *Ibid.*
[151] *Ibid.*, at 47 ff.
[152] A. del Bon, *Istituzioni del diritto pubblico internazionale* (1868), at 399.
[153] Chapter 3.3.
[154] V. Veit, *Geschichte des Völkerbundgedankens in Deutschland: ein geistesgeschichtlicher Versuch* (1920), at 109.
[155] S. Verosta, *Theorie und Realität von Bündnissen. Heinrich Lammasch, Karl Renner und der Zweibund (1897–1914)* (1971), at 3.

formation of the myth of *liberum ius ad bellum*, as I will argue in Chapter 10. As critical and postcolonial approaches have emphasized,[156] the liberal project of legalization in the nineteenth century is not only characterized by its progress towards *ius contra bellum*, but also by its dark sides: violence and law were closely intertwined in liberal legal discourse. They converged in the concept of 'coerced civilization'.[157]

The latter development was not only due to *normative* but also *political* reasons. While liberal lawyers strove to narrow the range of legitimate reasons for war and ultimately for a legal prohibition of war *within Europe*, they simultaneously expanded these reasons for war in certain political constellations. This was the case, for example, when international lawyers used legal arguments to justify unilateral violence on behalf of third parties in order to lend them the consecration of scientific neutrality[158]—as Grotius had done for the East India Company in 1609.[159] The 'gentle civilizers of nations'[160] then became 'gentle' justifiers of violence.

Important, genuinely liberal narratives justifying violence were 'property', 'nation', 'progress', and 'civilization'. In principle, these narratives referred to liberal philosophers such as Adam Smith and, in particular, Immanuel Kant.[161] In their case-specific application, however, they could be seriously at odds with the Kantian ideal of a pacification of international relations. A central philosophical argument of liberal justifications of violence was Kant's idea of a dialectic of violence and (international) order:[162] Kant assumed that through the horrors of war, man could be reminded of their 'unsocial sociability..., i.e., their propensity to enter into society', and, thus, the necessity of legal peace.[163] For Kant, this dialectical role of war also included the 'destruction or at least dismemberment' of old political bodies to create new ones.[164]

In liberal international legal theory, this Kantian dialectic was frequently invoked, for example by Bluntschli.[165] The latter argued that in view of the 'appalling and often quite unnecessary suffering that man inflicts on man', he could not agree with the glowing praise of war, 'about which talented writers in Germany now also feel enthusiastic, as they did earlier in France'—here, Bluntschli was critically

---

[156] Anghie (n. 10), Chapter 3; Tzouvala (n. 10); Jahn (n. 10); Sylvest (n. 9).
[157] On the following paragraphs, see also Simon, 'Theorising Order in the Shadow of War. The Politics of International Legal Knowledge and the Justification of Force in Modernity', 22 *Journal of the History of International Law* (2020) 218.
[158] *Ibid.*
[159] Ittersum, 'The Long Goodbye: Hugo Grotius' Justification of Dutch Expansion Overseas, 1615–1645', 36 *History of European Ideas* (2010) 386.
[160] Koskenniemi (n. 5).
[161] Jahn (n. 10).
[162] Chapter 3.3.
[163] Kant, 'Idea for a Universal History from a Cosmopolitan Point of View' (1784), in I. Kant, *On History*, edited and translated by L.W. Beck (1963) 11, Fourth Thesis.
[164] *Ibid.*, Seventh Thesis.
[165] Bluntschli (n. 30), at 11.

referring to Heinrich Treitschke and Adolf Lasson. But the liberal lawyer also expressed his approval of what liberals understood as the civilizing power of war. It was still true, Bluntschli argued, that war retained a 'law-forming authority' ('*Rechtbildende Autorität*'). While it was not 'the ideal of humanity', he continued, 'it is still an indispensable means for the necessary progress of humanity'.[166] Here, Bluntschli also quoted from Friedrich Schiller's poem *Resignation* (1786): 'World history is the world's court.' Unlike his pen pal Francis Lieber, supposed war humanizer but actual war enthusiast, who had described the blood spilled on the battlefield as the 'vital juice' of civilization, Bluntschli *morally* condemned war.[167] However, at the same time, he saw war as a suitable instrument of *legal* progress.

According to the conviction of many liberals, war had been an engine of legal progress in European history. Franz von Holtzendorff made direct references to Kant's idea of war as a catalyst for legal progress.[168] No important historian 'has ever overlooked the fact', he argued, that war, 'in its imperfect state, has been an enormous mediator of culture for mankind'.[169] '[E]ven Kant', he continued, had 'stated this fact most emphatically'.[170] However, for late nineteenth-century liberals, this dialectical connection between war and order was by no means just a matter of history. Rather, they could still take recourse to the narrative of 'legal progress' to justify force—in the name of the international community. In doing so, liberal international lawyers could even come into contradiction with existing treaty law (*lege lata*). This is evident in political fields where competing principles, norms, and state interests collided. In the second half of the century, this was particularly true for two debates: the first, on the conflicting norms of national self-determination and the inviolability of territorial borders,[171] and, the second, dealing with non-European political entities.

As for the former issue, in fact, many liberals understood nationalism and internationalism not as opposing but as successive principles. In 1910, British legal scholar John Westlake warned that nationalities, 'though often important in politics, must be kept outside of international law'.[172] However, nationalism was seen by liberals as a mission of anti-imperial emancipation and liberation. Italian legal scholar Pasquale Stanislao Mancini, for example, invoked the French Revolution to argue in favour of the moral and legal right of peoples to unite in a common state. However, the jurists' 'reflexive relationship' to the spirit of the people, as Savigny had described it, also increasingly tied liberal lawyers to national—and

---

[166] *Ibid.*, at 11.
[167] S. Moyn, *Humane. How the United States Abandoned Peace and Reinvented War* (2021), Chapter 1.
[168] F. von Holtzendorff, *Die Idee des ewigen Völkerfriedens* (1882).
[169] *Ibid.*
[170] *Ibid.*
[171] Chapter 5.
[172] Quoted from Summers (n. 109), at 112.

thus political—projects.[173] From now on, it could make a big difference whether an international lawyer was German, French, or Russian.

A particularly revealing example is the justification of the German Wars of Unification by an important protagonist of the liberal project that wanted to tame war through law: Johann Caspar Bluntschli. While Bluntschli rejected any war waged in the 'mere interest of the state' as illegitimate,[174] at the same time, the Heidelberg professor sympathized with Bismarck's violent unification politics— and agreed with his approach not only as a member of the First Baden Chamber, but also as an academic.[175] In his treatise on international law, Bluntschli wrote that the validity of a law that has evolved historically also depended on whether it was contemporary and viable.[176] Here, Bluntschli's dynamic understanding of law (see above) once again becomes clear. However, this also meant that Bluntschli did not see treaty law as irrevocable. Rather, it could be broken in favour of the 'living nature of law' ('*lebendigen Natur des Rechts*') and the further development of law as a means of 'self-realization of peoples' ('*Selbstverwirklichung der Völker*')—even by using military force.[177] In an interesting analogy to the justifications of force by French revolutionary lawyer Merlin de Douai,[178] Bluntschli argued that the people had the right to adopt 'the form of government necessary for the development of its natural faculties, for the fulfilment of its destiny, for the guarantee of its security, and for the preservation of its honour'.[179] Therefore, it also had 'the right to take up arms if necessary'. For this was, Bluntschli argued, 'a much more sacred, natural, and important right than any dynastic law'.[180]

Advocating the forcible achievement of legal progress, the liberal Bluntschli justified the wars of the *Realpolitiker* Bismarck. Bluntschli claimed these were legitimate defensive wars, emancipatory and 'necessary' acts of the German nation to 'preserve its honour, and therefore its right'. In doing so, Bluntschli paradoxically also referred to Treitschke to justify a 'necessary' 'little German solution' under Prussian leadership, even against the resistance of smaller German states.[181] With this aim in mind, Bluntschli went as far as to endorse Bismarck's—factually incorrect[182]—assertion that the war against Austria in 1866 had been an international war and not a federal execution against Prussia.[183] And Bluntschli also

---

[173] Koskenniemi (n. 5), at 43.
[174] Bluntschli (n. 30), at 290.
[175] On Bluntschli's professional biography straddling politics and international law, see B. Röben, *Johann Caspar Bluntschli, Francis Lieber und das moderne Völkerrecht 1861–1881* (2003); Senn, 'Rassistische und antisemitische Elemente im Rechtsdenken von Johann Caspar Bluntschli', 110 *Zeitschrift der Savigny-Stiftung für Rechtsgeschichte: Germanistische Abteilung* (1993) 372.
[176] Bluntschli (n. 30), at 290.
[177] *Ibid.*, at 290.
[178] Chapter 3.2.
[179] Bluntschli (n. 30), at 290.
[180] *Ibid.*
[181] *Ibid.*, at 174 ff.
[182] Chapter 5.4.
[183] Bluntschli (n. 30), at 289.

agreed with Bismarck's justification strategy of 1870/71.[184] While the former argued that 'such a terrible struggle between two civilized peoples' had never 'been started with such shameless recklessness', he made Napoléon III responsible for this 'recklessness', arguing that there was not even a 'semblance' of a German violation of rights.[185] The French demand that Wilhelm I reject any future Hohenzollern candidacy for the Spanish throne, he claimed, was not a legal demand, 'but a deliberate insult to the triple honour of the head of the [Hohenzollern, HS] family, the German king, and the German people'. The public had understood that France alone was to blame for the 'policy of aggression' and the 'criminal war' that followed.[186]

Unsurprisingly, French international legal scholar Henry Bonfils disagreed with Bluntschli's opinion.[187] According to Bonfils, Prussia's desire to expand had already caused the war against Denmark in 1864.[188] The war of 1870, in turn, had been caused by Prussia's insult to France. According to Bonfils, Bismarck had 'deliberately misrepresented' the incident with the Ems Dispatch in order 'to incite popular passion in Germany and France'. The 'real reason' for the war had therefore been Prussia's aim 'to unify Germany under Prussian domination through brotherhood in arms'.[189] As has already been shown above,[190] Bonfils's assessment may have been closer to the historical truth. But something else is more decisive here: liberal international lawyers allowed themselves to be overcome by national sentimentality, ultimately speaking in favour of the realpolitik of the Great Powers in their legal treatises. Both Bonfils and Bluntschli had been politicized. Bluntschli even called Bismarck one of the 'two most brilliant statesmen' in German history alongside Friedrich II 'der Große'.[191] How strange that an important liberal scholar should have such admiration for Prussian realpolitik!

Similarly, liberal lawyer Rudolf von Jhering also expressed sympathy for Bismarck's wars. Particularly noteworthy here is Jhering's inner conflict, which he conveyed to his Austrian colleague Julius Glaser in a private correspondence. Jhering wrote on 1 May 1866 that perhaps never before had a war been started with such 'shamelessness' ('*Schamlosigkeit*') and 'horrible frivolity' ('*grauenhaften Frivolität*') as Bismarck's war against Austria.[192] Jhering was outraged by such a 'violation of all principles of law and morality'. This, at least, was Jhering's legal

---

[184] Bluntschli (n. 1), at 8 ff.
[185] *Ibid.*
[186] *Ibid.*, at 9.
[187] Bonfils (n. 48), at 539.
[188] *Ibid.*
[189] *Ibid.*, at 540.
[190] Chapter 5.4.
[191] J.C. Bluntschli, *Allgemeine Staatslehre* (6th edn, 1886), at 84.
[192] R. von Jhering, *Briefe an seine Freunde* (1866/1913), at 196–8; quoted from Faber, 'Realpolitik als Ideologie', 203 *Historische Zeitschrift* (1966) 1, at 15 (my translation).

assessment (in which he mixed law and morality, demonstrating nineteenth-century multinormativity once again).

At the same time, however, Jhering reported to Glaser that his sense of law and his political convictions had come into 'an almost tragic conflict' with each other.[193] From a *legal* point of view, it was his duty to wish Austria luck in the war. For *political* reasons, on the other hand, he felt the need to hope for victory for the 'unjust cause' (*'ungerechten Sache'*): in other words, a Prussian victory. Obviously, two hearts were beating in Jhering's chest, one political and one legal. In the end, Jhering's political heart was the one that beat louder. After the Prussian victory over Austria, Jhering wrote in a letter to Leipzig legal scholar Bernhard Windscheid on 15 June 1866 that he bowed before the genius of Bismarck.[194] Mocking the 'powerless honesty' (*'machtlose Ehrlichkeit'*) of the liberals, Jhering stated that Bismarck had achieved 'a political masterpiece'. Thus, Jhering asserted, full of national pride, that he would give a hundred liberals 'for a political genius like Bismarck'.[195]

Bluntschli and Jhering thus ultimately became defenders of Prussian war politics. This ingratiation of the liberal middle classes with the Prussian state was not atypical after Bismarck's victory over Austria.[196] Liberals were torn between euphoria over Prussian victories and rejection of Bismarck's blood-and-iron policy. Jhering's letters are clear evidence of this. In fact, liberal legal scholars now sometimes became de facto *Realpolitiker* themselves. While the founder of realpolitik, August Ludwig von Rochau, was *not* concerned with abandoning liberal values in favour of political power,[197] the 'conservative liberal' Bluntschli linked Great Power politics with national/international legal progress.[198] Law was the goal—realpolitik sometimes the means.

But were the liberal justifications of the wars of national unification not ultimately claims to a nation's 'free right to go to war'? Not at all. Liberal scholars claimed a clear separation between political and legal arguments in their academic treatises—even if both actually merged in their justifications of wars of national unification. Yet Bluntschli justified violence with the aim of national unification not as a political, but as a genuinely *legal* means. For, according to Bluntschli, it was

> more of a childish than a legal opinion that a people is entitled to wage war in defence of the dynastic patrimonial right of a prince, but is not entitled to take up arms for its national unification, because that patrimonial right has been reserved in a medieval document, while national unification has hitherto been prevented

---

[193] Jhering (n. 192), at 197 ff.; Faber (n. 192), at 15.
[194] Jhering (n. 192), at 199; Faber (n. 192), at 16.
[195] Jhering (n. 192), at 197 ff.; Faber (n. 192), at 15.
[196] Faber (n. 192).
[197] J. Bew, *Realpolitik. A History* (2016); N. Doll, *Recht, Politik und 'Realpolitik' bei August Ludwig von Rochau (1810–1873)* (2005).
[198] M. Stolleis, *Geschichte des öffentlichen Rechts in Deutschland*, vol. 2: Staatsrechtslehre und Verwaltungswissenschaft 1800–1914 (1992), at 432.

and inhibited by a mournful history. Nevertheless, this whimsical opinion found many representatives in Germany in 1866.[199]

The justification of violence in the name of a nation's right of self-determination was—at least in theory—not supposed to affect Europe's peace.[200]

Nevertheless, this theoretically valid demarcation of law from politics sometimes became vague and permeable in the admiration of *Realpolitiker*. Once again, it becomes apparent that the liberal project of legalization in its ultimate justification is always also a political project.[201] In the words of Gerry Simpson: 'All books about international law are a politics of international law, no?'[202] This is undoubtedly true. Nevertheless, an approval of liberals for a 'free right to go to war' can by no means be derived from this antinomy. Rather, Bluntschli's nationalist justification of violence was clearly based on an understanding of the nation as a catalyst for civilizational and, thus, legal progress. Violence was acceptable in this process—but *only* if it served *legal* progress.

Their enthusiasm for the national self-determination of 'civilized peoples' should not, however, lead to the false assumption that liberal legal scholars aimed at a radical upheaval of European societies. The liberal project was clearly too exclusive and discriminatory for that in several respects. The supposedly boundless cosmopolitanism of the bourgeois 'men of 1873' found its, in fact rather narrow, limits with regard to non-Europeans, workers, and women.[203] The Fourth Estate of the industrial proletariat, which Rochau, for example, had called the 'big bunch' ('*großen Haufen*'),[204] was to remain largely excluded from political participation. Leading liberal scholars of the *Institut de Droit International*, such as Rolin, Rivier, Bluntschli, Lorimer, Martens, and Westlake, warned publicly against 'communism', 'anarchy', and 'nihilism', which they associated with the radical democratic peace and workers' movements. The language of the 'men of 1873', as Martti Koskenniemi has particularly aptly put it, sometimes took on a tone of agitation 'that appears symptomatic of the repressive impulses their otherwise balanced centrism must have entailed'.[205]

---

[199] Bluntschli (n. 30), at 290.
[200] Chapter 5.
[201] Chapter 3.3; Simon (n. 157); see also Peters, Schäfer, and Simon, '(Writing) International Legal Histories – Continuation of Politics by Other Means?: An Interview with Anne Peters and Raphael Schäfer', *Völkerrechtsblog* (17 September 2021), available at: https://voelkerrechtsblog.org/de/writing-international-legal-histories-continuation-of-politics-by-other-means/ (last visited 1 December 2022).
[202] Simpson and Simon, 'Sentiment without Sentimentality: An Interview with Gerry Simpson', *Völkerrechtsblog* (08 April 2022), available at: https://voelkerrechtsblog.org/de/sentiment-without-sentimentality/ (last visited 1 December 2022).
[203] See below; Anghie (n. 10); see also Koskenniemi, 'Race, Hierarchy and International Law: Lorimer's Legal Science', 27 *European Journal of International Law* (2016) 415; Khan and Kirchmair, '"All's Well That Ends Well?" Zum Verbot der Rassendiskriminierung im Völkerrecht', in I.U. Schraut and S. Schraut (eds), *Rassismus in Geschichte und und Gegenwart. Eine interdisziplinäre Analyse. Festschrift für Walter Demel* (2018) 337.
[204] Doll (n. 197), at 58, 93.
[205] Koskenniemi (n. 5), at 68.

The discourse on international law of the '1873s' was characterized not only by nationalist, but also racist and antisemitic tones. For Bluntschli, a state did not have to be ethnically homogeneous, but it should have a certain 'civilized' status. According to Bluntschli, the 'Aryan spirit' (*'arische Geist'*) could serve as a model for other states. It was, according to Bluntschli, 'most richly endowed by creation' and was therefore destined to 'enlighten mankind with its ideas of law and state and to take over and carry out the rule of the world ... by educating the rest of mankind to civilization'.[206]

Bluntschli distinguished not only non-European peoples from the state system of the 'Aryan Volksgeist', but also 'Semitic Jews' in Europe.[207] He argued that the latter could only be granted equal rights by 'European Aryan peoples' after successful assimilation. Racism and antisemitism were, of course, widespread throughout society in the nineteenth century. They were not unique to liberal legal discourse.[208] Conservative lawyers such as Lorimer also held racist, anti-Islamic, and antisemitic views. Nevertheless, racism, antisemitism, anti-feminism, and classism were constitutive elements of liberal legal thinking.[209] This also became clear in the liberal discourse on the justification of violence.

Liberal Justifications of Illiberal Violence

The exclusionary power of the European legal project became most evident in the second half of the century in Europe's dealings with political entities that were denied civilized status in their entirety or in part. The European 'standard of civilization' was used to deny states in the European (semi-)periphery their own sovereignty and thus the status of legitimate warring parties. Violent interventions, protectorates, and colonial usurpation could be legitimized with recourse to this flawed sovereignty. Liberal legal scholars actively participated in these justificatory practices.[210]

As already shown in detail above,[211] the debate on civilization was especially prevalent in confrontations with the Ottoman Empire. Interventions in Ottoman territory could be justified as 'humanitarian interventions' by accusing the Ottoman authorities of 'barbaric' and 'inhumane' treatment of their Christian population. In 1856, the Ottoman Empire had been admitted to the European

---

[206] Bluntschli, 'Arische Völker und arische Rechte', in J.C. Bluntschli and C.L.T. Brater (eds), *Deutsches Staats-Wörterbuch*, vol. 2 (1857), at 331.
[207] *Ibid.*, at 319, 331; Khan and Kirchmair (n. 203), at 331.
[208] Koskenniemi (n. 203); Tzouvala (n. 10).
[209] Anghie (n. 10); Koskenniemi (n. 5); Tzouvala (n. 10).
[210] G.W. Gong, *The Standard of 'Civilization' in International Society* (1984); Benton and Ford (n. 4); Genell, 'The Well-defended Domains: Eurocentric International Law and the Making of the Ottoman Office of Legal Counsel', 3 *Journal of Ottoman and Turkish Studies* (2016) 255; Tzouvala (n. 10).
[211] Chapter 4.3; Chapter 5.2.

Concert not least because it was willing to submit to the European legal project and guarantee the protection of its Christian subjects.[212] This was therefore a process of legal assimilation, such as that which Bluntschli demanded of European Jews (see above). However, the legal discrimination against the Ottoman Empire did not end there.[213] Indeed, Turkey's status as a member of the European legal community was fragile and always subject to the scepticism of the European powers.

Liberal legal scholars agreed with the discrimination against the Ottoman Empire. When it came to the Eastern Question, this was especially true of Russian international legal scholar Fedor Fedorovich Martens. The Tsar's crown lawyer found himself in the paradoxical situation of being a liberal in the diplomatic service of the most illiberal Great Power in Europe. Indeed, the Tsar wanted to style Russia as a 'defender of international law' in foreign policy—not least to position the latter against its new geopolitical challenger, the German Empire.[214] Legalization and politicization went hand in hand. This was particularly the case in relations with powers outside Europe. After its defeat in the Crimean War of 1856, Russia declared war on the Ottoman Empire again in 1877.[215] This declaration of war was made in the context of what was referred to as the 'Great Eastern Crisis' (1875–78). In the summer of 1875, there had been uprisings among parts of the Christian populations in Herzegovina and Bosnia and, soon after that, also in Bulgaria.[216] With the help of irregular troops known as the *Bashibosuks*, the Ottoman authorities succeeded in brutally suppressing the uprisings. Between 12,000 and 15,000 of the Bulgarian population died, including many civilians.[217]

One-sided reports about the mass killings caused public outrage in the European public. English dailies ran the headline 'The Bulgarian Horrors'. The liberal statesman William Gladstone demanded the complete liberation of Bulgaria from the Turks in the name of 'civilisation which has been affronted and shamed; to the laws of God or, if you like, of Allah, to the moral sense of mankind at large'.[218] Conservative Prime Minister Benjamin Disraeli did not comply with the demand of his predecessor (and successor) Gladstone. Nevertheless, anti-Turkish

---

[212] Chapter 5.2.
[213] Genell and Aksakal, '"Salvation through War?" The Ottoman Search for Sovereignty in 1914', in L. Brock and H. Simon (eds), *The Justification of War and International Order: From Past to Present* (2021) 207.
[214] Mälksoo, 'F.F. Martens and His Time: When Russia Was an Integral Part of the European Tradition of International Law', 25 *European Journal of International Law* (2014) 811, at 823; P. Holquist, *The Russian Empire as a 'Civilized State'. International Law as Principle and Practice in Imperial Russia, 1874–1878* (2004).
[215] H. Simon, *Zwischen Legalität und Legitimität. Rechtfertigung 'humanitärer Interventionen' im historischen Vergleich* (2013).
[216] A.A. Lobanov-Rostovsky, *Russia and Europe 1825–1878* (1954), at 263 ff.
[217] Anderson, 'Some Further Light on the Inner History of the Declaration of Paris', 76 *The Law Quarterly Review* (1960) 379; A. Pottinger Saab, *Reluctant Icon: Gladstone, Bulgaria, and the Working Classes, 1856–1878* (1991).
[218] Gladstone, 'The Bulgarian Horrors and the Question of the East (1876)', in W.D. Handcock and G.M. Young (eds), *English Historical Documents 1874–1914* (2nd end, 1996), at 351.

sentiment among the British public prevented London from taking decisive action against Russia's renewed offensive policy towards the Orient, which the Treaty of Paris of 1856 and the Anglo-French-Austrian Convention of 15 April 1856 should have countered. Britain did nothing but 'idly watch Russia's triumphal march in the Balkans'.[219]

Nevertheless, as usual, Russia justified its use of force against the Ottoman Empire. Moreover, the declaration of war on 24 April 1877 followed the European tradition of legitimizing war. It contained clear references to the 'justice' of its cause. Tsar Alexander II and foreign minister Alexander Gorchakov referred in their legitimations to 'humanity', 'European civilization', 'peace', 'popular sovereignty', 'economy (right to property)', 'honour', and 'religion'.[220] International law, on the other hand, was barely addressed in these legitimations with their normative symbiosis. Rather, Gorchakov criticized the prohibition of intervention in Article 9 of the Treaty of Paris—the thorn in the side of Russia's Oriental policy since 1856.[221] '[T]he European action in Turkey', Gorchakov argued, 'has been reduced to impotency by the stipulations of 1856'.[222] Already in 1870, Gorchakov had confidentially told Heinrich VII Reuß zu Köstritz, German ambassador in St Petersburg, that the Treaty of Paris should be declared null and void 'because of its defectiveness' and that the neutrality of the Black Sea should be revoked.[223]

However, to re-establish a stable peace for the benefit of the Christian population in Turkey, the independence of Turkey guaranteed by the Treaty of 1856 was to be subordinated to 'the interests of humanity, the Christian community and general peace', Gorchakov stated on 19 November 1877.[224] Since Russia had already unilaterally revoked the neutrality of the Black Sea in 1870 during the Franco-Prussian War, revision of the Treaty of Paris was now the main aim of Russian politics of international law. Calling into question the Ottoman Empire's status as a civilized power, ultimately *the* prerequisite for admission into the European legal community, also meant delegitimizing it as a sovereign state. The question of a state's level of 'civilization' thus became a struggle for its international legal subjectivity.

It was Fedor Fedorovich Martens's task to bestow scientific consecration on this core argument of the Russian politics of international law. In 1877, Martens presented a 46-page 'historical study', in which he claimed, according to the title, to analyse the 'Russian politics in the Oriental Question'. According to the editors of

[219] E. Hösch, *Geschichte der Balkanländer. Von der Frühzeit bis zur Gegenwart* (2002), at 176.
[220] 'Alexanders II's Declaration of War, 24 April 1877', in E. Hertslet (ed.), *The Map of Europe by Treaty*, vol. 4: 1875–1891 (1891) 2599; and 'Alexander Gortschakow, 9 April 1878', in E. Hertslet (ed.), *The Map of Europe by Treaty*, vol. 4: 1875–1891 (1891) 2712; for a more in-depth analysis, see Simon (n. 215).
[221] Chapter 5.2.
[222] 'Alexander Gortschakow, 19 November 1876', in E. Hertslet (ed.), *The Map of Europe by Treaty*, vol. 4: 1875–1891 (1891) 2523.
[223] Report by Reuß to Bismarck, 12 September 1870, in H.G. Linke (ed.), *Quellen zu den deutsch-russischen Beziehungen. 1801–1917* (2001), at 146 ff.
[224] Gortschakow (n. 222), at 2524.

the German translation, which was printed in the *Russische Revue*, the aim of the publication 'by one of our most important teachers and experts on constitutional and international law' was to eliminate the 'still widespread misconceptions about Russia's Oriental politics and its aims in the Orient' before a Western and Central European audience.[225] Martens's self-formulated claim not to want to influence 'the judgement of our readers' is thus hardly credible.[226] Rather, the liberal was to provide a justification for the violence of illiberal Russia.

But how—and above all, with what arguments—could a famous liberal lawyer legitimize an obvious breach of law? Like Alexander II and Gorchakov, Martens referred to the need to improve the situation of the Christian population, which, he claimed, was threatened by 'Muslim fanaticism'.[227] According to Martens, Russia had therefore declared war on Turkey—

> in the name of the interests of humanity and in order to put an end to a state of affairs which offended the most sacred feelings of the Russian people and which constituted a constant threat against its own tranquillity.[228]

Martens's justification of war was thus based on a natural law argument, constructing a dichotomy between Christian, 'European civilization' and 'Ottoman backwardness'. Martens even wrote in his treatise that throughout history, relations between Christian and 'uncivilized states' were pervaded by 'eternal hostility'. 'They have almost nothing in common at all.'[229]

Martens also denied that Turkey had reached the level of European civilization with the conclusion of the Treaty of Paris, arguing that Turkey had been admitted to the 'Concert of European powers', but not to the 'family of civilized states'.[230] The admission was therefore premature. Moreover, Martens repeated almost like a prayer mill, the Treaty of Paris did not abrogate the (supposed) Russian right of Küçük Kaynarca of 1774 to interfere in Turkey's internal affairs for the protection of the Christian citizens.[231] Therefore, Martens concluded, Russia was free to act on its own if Europe did not make use of its collective right to intervene.[232] Article 9 of the Peace of Paris did not abolish the Russian right of intervention, but instead confirmed it. The article, Martens argued, could be interpreted no differently.[233]

Martens's obvious misinterpretation of the Treaty of Paris, which clearly prohibited unilateral intervention, is surprising. This is due not least to the fact that

---

[225] F.F. Martens, *Die russische Politik in der Orientalischen Frage. Eine historische Studie* (1877), at 1.
[226] *Ibid.*, at 2.
[227] *Ibid.*, at 45.
[228] *Ibid.*, at 2.
[229] Martens (n. 59), at 118.
[230] *Ibid.*, at 128.
[231] Martens (n. 225), at 4, 12, 15–17, 19–21.
[232] *Ibid.*, at 19.
[233] *Ibid.*, at 15.

Martens contradicted himself in the second volume of his textbook, where he criticized the Treaty of 1856 for the fact that Article 9 had abolished both the right of collective and solidarity intervention.[234] With this criticism, however, Martens *did* recognize the regional ban on intervention. Martens's manuscript of 1877 can thus be understood as Russian propaganda in line with Alexander II's anti-Ottoman politics of international law. With recourse to natural law, Pan-Slavism, and especially 'European civilization', the 1856 ban on intervention was to be reinterpreted, circumvented, and finally undermined.

This justification strategy succeeded. After its victory, Russia was able to overturn a collective right of intervention in the Ottoman Empire at the Berlin Congress of 1878.[235] The treaty law of 1856 had thus been successfully broken. It had been abolished through recourse to natural law and the constructed dichotomy between 'civilization' and 'barbarism'.

Justifying Liberal Empires

The narrative of 'civilization' also played an important role in justifying imperialism and colonialism. Particularly in the second half of the nineteenth century, the Great Powers were interested in colonial acquisitions in Africa, Asia, and the South Pacific. In the so-called 'Scramble for Africa', they competed for new colonies and protectorates—and thus also new sales markets.[236] International law(yers) were instrumental in (de)legitimizing this process. With cession and protectorate treaties, the European Great Powers and the USA sought to expand their territories overseas.[237] In doing so, however, they were faced with the problem that even unequal treaties ultimately recognized the other party as sovereign, while it was precisely this sovereignty that European powers subsequently denied to overseas treaty partners.[238] Africa was declared a sovereignty-free space (*terra nullius*) at the Berlin Conference on the Congo in 1885.[239]

---

[234] Martens (n. 59), at 127.
[235] 'Peace Treaty Concerning the Settlement of the Oriental Question (Act of the Congress of Berlin) (13 July 1878)', in W.G. Grewe (ed.), *Fontes Historiae Iuris Gentium (FHIG), Sources Relating to the History of the Law of Nations*, vol. 3/1: 1815–1945 (1992) 38, at 46, 50.
[236] M.E. Chamberlain, *The Scramble for Africa* (1990); W.M. Egner, *Protektion und Souveränität. Die Entwicklung imperialer Herrschaftsformen im 19. Jahrhundert* (2018).
[237] Tzouvala (n. 10).
[238] D. Wang, *China's Unequal Treaties: Narrating National History* (2005); M.R. Auslin, *Negotiating with Imperialism. The Unequal Treaties and the Culture of Japanese Diplomacy* (2006); H. Kleinschmidt, *Diskriminierung durch Vertrag und Krieg: Zwischenstaatliche Verträge und der Begriff des Kolonialkriegs im 19. und frühen 20. Jahrhundert* (2013), at 286; S. Kroll *Normgenese durch Re-Interpretation. China und das europäische Völkerrecht im 19. und 20. Jahrhundert* (2012), Chapter 2.
[239] Craven, 'Between Law and History: the Berlin Conference of 1884–1885 and the Logic of Free Trade', 3 *London Review of International Law* (2015) 31.

But even this discrimination was justified by its perpetrators. Since treaty law could limit the arbitrariness of the European Great Powers, other justifications were needed.[240] While navy captains developed local figures of justification, in the imperial epicentres of Europe, it was up to lawyers to develop narratives of justification for the deprivation of statehood.[241] This is reminiscent of the early modern debates on *La Conquista*—with the difference that in the late nineteenth century the aim was to circumvent treaty law, not natural law, by recourse to 'civilization'.

A decisive justification strategy for the withdrawal of sovereign statehood was to limit the possibility of legitimate use of force to 'civilized peoples'. A mastermind of this narrowing of definitions was British officer Charles Edward Callwell, the 'Clausewitz of colonial warfare' (Douglas Porch). According to Callwell, 'savage tribes' were neither sovereign actors in the sense of European states, nor were they capable of following the rules of regular war. Accordingly, they were not permitted to wage anti-imperial war against European Great Powers.[242] On the other hand, the violence of European empires against 'half-civilized races or wholly savage tribes' was, according to Callwell, not war in the sense of the European law of war, but constituted a form of 'small wars' for purposes of counterinsurgency. What was special about this figure of justification was that it denied 'half-civilized' or 'uncivilized states' any right to violent resistance—while justifying normatively unbounded violence of European empires beyond the application of *ius in bello*.

Liberal international lawyers participated in this narrowing of the concept of war, much in the spirit of Callwell. This was quite paradoxical and demonstrates the double standards in European liberalism: while liberals in Europe were antipodes of imperialism, which they saw as an anti-national and anti-liberal project, outside Europe, they supported imperialism. Thus, even for liberal international lawyers such as Travers Twiss, King Leopold's 'ghost writer',[243] August von Bulmerincq, or John Westlake, only 'civilized states' could be legitimate participants in war.[244] Lassa Oppenheim even argued that the concept of a protectorate in treaties between European and non-European powers was ultimately only a temporary placeholder for future occupations and annexations.[245] As shown in this chapter, liberal legal scholars sought increasing containment—and ultimately an abolition—of war in Europe. In the imperial context, however, they justified

---

[240] Kleinschmidt (n. 238), at 151.
[241] Benton, 'Protection Emergencies: Justifying Measures Short of War in the British Empire', in L. Brock and H. Simon (eds), *The Justification of War and International Order: From Past to Present* (2021) 167; see also Szabla, 'Civilising Violence: International Law and Colonial War in the British Empire, 1850–1900', 24 *Journal of the History of International Law* (2023) 1; L. Benton, *They Called It Peace: Worlds of Imperial Violence* (2024).
[242] On this paragraph, see Kleinschmidt (n. 238).
[243] A. Fitzmaurice, *King Leopold's Ghostwriter. The Creation of Persons and States in the Nineteenth Century* (2021).
[244] Sylvest, '"Our Passion for Legality": International Law and Imperialism in Late Nineteenth-century Britain', 34 *Review of International Studies* (2008) 403; Kleinschmidt (n. 238).
[245] L.F.L. Oppenheim, *International Law. A Treatise* (3rd edn, 1920); Kleinschmidt (n. 238), at 133 ff.

increasing containment of legitimate subjects of war with a simultaneous removal of the limits of imperial violence.

6.5 'The Right Path': Toward Reflexive Legal Peace (Schücking)

But not *all* liberal legal scholars allowed themselves to be subjected to such political instrumentalization. There were also (self-)critical voices and approaches that took a self-reflexive perspective on the relationship between violence, law, and peace.[246] For example, a year before the outbreak of the First World War, the left-liberal German legal scholar Walther Schücking explicitly warned against liberals ingratiating themselves with the realpolitik of the Great Powers and a 'Prussification' ('*Verpreußung*') as an 'official uniformization of intellectual life'.[247] Instead of collaborating with conservative political elites, Schücking heavily criticized German policy for its anti-international law course at the Hague Peace Conferences.[248]

Although Schücking did not formulate a robust critique of the colonialism of his time, he *did* support the First Universal Races Congress in London in July 1911, whose self-declared goal was—

> to discuss, in the light of science and modern conscience, the general relations subsisting between the peoples of the West and those of the East, between the so-called 'white' and the so-called 'colored' peoples, with a view to encouraging between them a fuller understanding, the most friendly feelings, and the heartier co-operation.[249]

Much in this vein, Schücking criticized Bluntschli's idea of a world organization for being too strongly focused on Europe. In other words, Schücking criticized Bluntschli for being Eurocentric.[250]

Schücking thus clearly addressed antinomies and ambivalences of liberal legal doctrine in order to self-critically extract the liberal legal project from its entanglement with violence. The neo-Kantian was thus more coherent in his legal theory than conservative liberals such as Bluntschli. He was not only concerned with finally abolishing war as a means of politics. Following on from the Hague Peace Conferences, legal pacifist Schücking also demanded that war should cease to be

---

[246] For an account of *reflexive legalization*, see Brock and Simon, 'Die Selbstbehauptung und Selbstgefährdung des Friedens als Herrschaft des Rechts. Eine endlose Karussellfahrt?', 59 *Politische Vierteljahresschrift* (2018) 269.
[247] W. Schücking, *Neue Ziele der staatlichen Entwicklung. Eine politische Studie* (1913), at 17.
[248] On the Hague Conferences, see Chapter 9.2.
[249] 'Call for the Congress', in G. Spiller (ed.). *Papers on Inter-racial Problems Communicated to the First Universal Races Congress* (1911), at 477.
[250] W. Schücking, *Die Organisation der Welt* (1909), at 63–6; see also Wehberg (n. 137), at 82.

'a legal institution'.[251] In Schücking's (and Hans Wehberg's) view, this required a strong international organization that was not only capable of pronouncing law but also enforcing it.[252]

Schücking resolutely dismissed the doubts of many liberals of the 1870s and 1880s about the realizability of perpetual legal peace in Kant's sense. For Schücking, the century after 1815 was an 'epoch of an emerging international organization'.[253] Following in the footsteps of his academic teacher Ludwig von Bar, the Marburg legal scholar envisioned a republican '*Weltstaatenbund*'. In this 'World Confederation', interstate conflicts should be dealt with peacefully in accordance with the law. War, in turn, should be completely outlawed.[254] Schücking introduced his 1909 treatise *Die Organisation der Welt* with a quote from Victor Hugo:

> A day will come when a cannon will be exhibited in museums just as an instrument of torture is now, and people will be astonished how such a thing could have been.[255]

Schücking saw the peace conferences of 1899 and 1907 as a breakthrough on this path to perpetual legal peace, though less in terms of the actual material results of the conferences. To him, it was their procedural institutionalization that was more important. Schücking argued that the federal parliament ('*Bundestag*') of a future 'World Confederation' should be composed in the same way as the Hague Conferences.[256] As outlined above, Schücking was by no means the first to put forward a blueprint for international pacification through the establishment of an international organization. Nevertheless, his analysis of the Hague Peace Conferences as an emerging 'World Confederation' was pioneering.[257] The problem of the politically and normatively precarious peace between the Great Powers was to be resolved by a stable world organization. This was a high point of nineteenth-century liberal legal theory dealing with the problem of war.

For Schücking positioned himself more clearly than many of his predecessors, who vacillated between 'is and ought', in the tradition of the legal pacifist Immanuel Kant and his 'critical idealism'.[258] But Schücking was no naïve utopian either: like Kant, he argued that the question of whether 'a development from a confederation

---

[251] Schücking (n. 250), at 83.
[252] Daase and Deitelhoff, 'The Justification and Critique of Coercion as World Order Politics', in L. Brock and H. Simon (eds), *The Justification of War and International Order: From Past to Present* (2021) 489.
[253] Schücking (n. 250), at 74.
[254] *Ibid.*, at 80.
[255] *Ibid.*, cover.
[256] *Ibid.*, at 80.
[257] F. Bodendiek, *Walther Schückings Konzeption der internationalen Ordnung. Dogmatische Strukturen und ideengeschichtliche Bedeutung* (2001); Bodendiek, 'Walther Schucking and the Idea of "International Organization"', 22 *European Journal of International Law* (2011) 741.
[258] *Ibid.*

of states to a federal state will eventually take place' could ultimately 'only be decided in the distant future'.[259] In any case, Schücking argued, 'when the states get used to working together within the World Confederation, they will increasingly abandon the idea of shooting at each other'.[260] For according to Schücking, the decisive thing was 'that we get on the right path, the path of law instead of force'. The journey was the reward.[261]

Behind Schücking's scholarly commitment to a universal legal peace was, once again, an evolutionary, dynamic—or one could also say, political—approach to law. In striking analogy to Bluntschli's idea of a 'legal conscience of the civilized world', Schücking, too, saw it as a lawyer's moral political responsibility to go beyond positivist law. Law was to be conceptualized as being against war, and was projected into the future based on the normative trends of the present.[262] Schücking could not entirely avoid the ambivalence between the legalization of politics and the politicization of law—but unlike many liberals before him, the left-liberal neo-Kantian did not merely accept this fact. Rather, he critically emphasized it, as Schücking also understood that an escape from politics into law was not possible. To abolish war legally, this law first had to be fought for politically.

For Schücking, cooperation between international legal doctrine and the peace movement was of central importance. Pacifists such as Bertha von Suttner, author of the widely acclaimed novella *Die Waffen nieder!* ('Down With Weapons!'), and Alfred H. Fried had vigorously campaigned for European statesmen to take up their demands. Schücking recognized the value of the peace movement for his work on international law. According to him, it was not war but organized pacifism that was the decisive catalyst for progress in international law. Thus, for Schücking, international law and pacifism should go hand in hand.[263] While there had already been precedents for such cooperation in other European countries, Schücking's turn towards 'organizational pacifism', as Fried and Schücking called it,[264] was quite revolutionary. One can 'rightly say', Klaus Schlichtmann has argued, that with this conception, Schücking 'juridically founded pacifism as a science'.[265]

Politically, his commitment to (legal) pacifism made Schücking an outsider in the conservative and positivist international legal scholarship in the German Empire, with conservatives even considering him politically dangerous.[266] In Europe, on the other hand, he was soon regarded as a luminary of international

---

[259] Schücking (n. 250), at 81.
[260] Ibid.
[261] Ibid., at 64.
[262] Bodendiek (n. 257).
[263] Ibid.
[264] Bodendiek, 'Walther Schücking und Hans Wehberg. Pazifistische Völkerrechtslehre in der ersten Hälfte des 20. Jahrhunderts', 74 *Die Friedens-Warte* (1999) 79, at 84.
[265] Schlichtmann, 'Walther Schücking (1875–1935) – Völkerrechtler, Pazifist und Parlamentarier', 15 *Historische Mitteilungen* (2002) 129, at 130.
[266] Bodendiek (n. 264), at 83 ff.

law, as is evident not least from his work as a judge at the Permanent Court of International Justice in The Hague from 1931 to 1935. The fact that Schücking took part in the negotiations for the Treaty of Versailles in 1919 as part of the German delegation does not change this finding.[267]

As Anthony Carty has also argued, Schücking was an exceptional lawyer who, unlike most of his German colleagues, behaved in an intellectually and politically exemplary manner.[268] Although liberals before Schücking had also called for a pacification of international relations through law, these calls had at the same time been strongly interwoven with the nationalism, racism, chauvinism, antisemitism, classism, and imperialism of the time.[269] Schücking, on the other hand, understood legal pacifism as a reflexive, i.e. self-critical process. To him, it was clear that war had to be outlawed. Peace was only conceivable through law. Liberal lawyers therefore had the political task of not only systematizing this historical process, but also actively promoting it. According to Schücking, an ingratiation with realpolitik ran counter to this goal. He thus clearly positioned himself against war as a political tool and 'showed the way'.[270]

In short, according to Schücking, not a 'free right to go to war', but the law prohibiting war (*ius contra bellum*) was the main item on the agenda of international law at the end of the nineteenth century. The goal was thus a legal primacy in international relations. With Schücking at the latest, the liberal doctrine of international law took the final step against war—and thus from Grotius to Kant.

6.6 Conclusion: Politicized Depoliticizers between Utopias of Peace and Apologies of Violence

Influenced by the new Great Power wars in the middle of the nineteenth century, European liberal lawyers argued for a stronger legal norming of war. To this end, they were able to build on the debates their predecessors conducted during the first half of the century. This is particularly evident in the continuing importance of the doctrine of 'just war'. According to liberals, a war could only be waged for a 'just cause'—even if 'just' now increasingly (also) meant 'legal'. The legal discourse on the legitimacy of war in the nineteenth century was thus essentially characterized by continuity. However, the professionalizing discipline of International Law went beyond the international lawyers of the first half of the century in its plea for a stronger codification of the laws of war.

---

[267] Chapter 10.
[268] Carty, 'The Evolution of International Legal Scholarship in Germany during the Kaiserreich and the Weimarer Republik (1871–1933)', 50 *German Yearbook of International Law* (2007/2008) 29, at 63.
[269] Wehberg (n. 137), at 82.
[270] Schücking (n. 250), at 64.

Immanuel Kant was an important point of reference and the feasibility of his legal pacifist project was controversially discussed in international legal theory. For many liberal scholars, long before the Kellogg-Briand Pact of 1928 it was clear that war as a political means, in the sense of Carl von Clausewitz, should be abolished. The debates on legitimate reasons for war were to be resolved by a clearly positivist *ius contra bellum*. International legal doctrine thus aspired to positivism—or more precisely, to various positivisms.[271] However, scholars had to continue to stop short of the claim of a purely positive conception of law, in the absence of a general prohibition of war under treaty law. Like Kant, they had to refer to reason, morality, and the law yet to be formed (*de lege ferenda*) in the ultimate justification of a legal prohibition of war. Moreover, liberals based their arguments on evolutionary, dynamic understandings of law, which always contained legal political components. The preachers of positivism therefore always had other normative fixed points besides positive law. Nationalism, natural law, and 'civilizational superiority' were their three most important references.

Thus, international law scholarship found itself in an ambivalent nexus between politicization and depoliticization. For the core goal of liberal legal scholarship remained the depoliticization of international relations through their legalization. At the same time, however, the European project of legalization was always a political project *sui generis*. This becomes particularly clear in liberal legal scholars' aim to 'civilize' international relations.[272] However, this politicization of the depoliticizers not only had effects that were conducive to a further legal restriction of war. It also had its darker sides which legitimized violence. Liberal legal scholars not only justified war as a catalyst of international legal progress in the sense of Kant's philosophy of history. They also got involved in the justification of war and imperial expansion—be it from a distance in terms of legal theory, be it in close proximity in terms of legal practice.

As damaging as this pandering to realpolitik by some liberals may have been from a critical liberal perspective, it nevertheless does *not* prove a 'free right to go to war' in the late nineteenth century. On the contrary, it once again underlines the need of the Great Powers to hide their political violence behind a façade of legitimacy. Liberals thus became the legitimizing mouthpiece of the powerful. But paradoxically, in their acceptance of political arbitrariness, they themselves affirmed the political 'unavailability' of law.[273] For why would there have been a need for justification by lawyers if the powerful had not—and moreover, increasingly—assumed the necessity of a legal justification of violence?

While numerous liberals hesitated to make a radical turn to *ius contra bellum* and even began to identify with national realpolitik, there were also genuine

---

[271] S.C. Neff, *Justice among Nations. A History of International Law* (2014), at 226–43.
[272] Koskenniemi (n. 5); Tzouvala (n. 10).
[273] Brock (n. 83).

pioneers of *ius contra bellum* in the late nineteenth century. One of these pioneers was Walther Schücking, who clearly and consistently strove for *ius contra bellum*. In doing so, he reflected self-critically on the liberal legal project and advocated a reflexive analysis of legalization beyond conservative power elites, racism, imperialism, classism, and anti-feminism. Although Schücking's reflexive approach in the tradition of Kant could not prevent the World War, it refers to a tradition of justifying and criticizing war in the nineteenth century, which it simultaneously went beyond.

This tradition—full of ambivalences and paradoxes—did not grant a 'free right to go to war', as liberal voices made very clear at the end of the century. War in the nineteenth century was never 'simply the continuation of policy with the addition of other means'. It always needed justification—and thus always referred to the international normative order.

Since Part I of this book has now made clear that the nineteenth-century *liberum ius ad bellum* is a myth, two questions remain to be clarified. *First*, how has this thesis been able to endure until today? And *second*, when did it emerge in the first place?

Part II will answer these questions by showing that after the wars of the mid-century, it was not only liberal efforts of *ius contra bellum* that were advanced. Rather, a second, now largely forgotten language in the politics of international law emerged, one that was to enjoy particular popularity in the German Empire that was formed in 1870/71. This language was explicitly directed against the increasing efforts of liberal international lawyers to abolish war as a political—or even legal—tool. In this context, a thesis was developed which so far this study has searched for in vain in the genealogy of war justifications: the thesis of the 'free right to go to war'.

PART II
EMERGENCE OF A MYTH
A German Sonderweg?

7
Recht zum Krieg
A Clausewitzian Tradition

7.1 Introduction: German Realism and the 'Right to War'

In 1913, on the occasion of the twenty-fifth anniversary of the reign of Kaiser Wilhelm II, a commemorative publication of the *Rundschau für den deutschen Juristenstand* (Review for the German Legal Profession) was produced. In it, the Freiburg professor of criminal law and legal philosophy, Woldemar von Rohland, reported that he had the impression that the period between 1888 and 1913 represented the most significant stage in the development of international law to date: an almost incalculable number of state treaties had created a wealth of material. More and more new matters were legalized in connection with technological progress, including the telephone, wireless telegraphy, and the invention of the automobile. According to Rohland, this progressive legalization applied not only to peaceful international relations.[1] The Hague Peace Conferences of 1899 and 1907 as well as the London Declaration Concerning the Laws of Naval War of 1909 were also landmarks of the rule of law in matters of war.

Woldemar von Rohland's argument was partly true: the period between 1871 and 1918 did become formative for German international legal discourse. After the Empire had been founded by force in 1871—'overnight, so to speak'[2]—as a new federal state[3] in the centre of Europe, German jurists faced the challenge of reconciling the Empire's enormous increase in power with the normative expectations of the international legal community.[4] An unprecedented number of international legal textbooks and handbooks were published. Anthony Carty speaks of the production of international law writings on an almost 'industrial scale'. According to Carty, it was impossible for a single person to read all the international law texts produced during the Empire.[5]

---

[1] Rohland, 'Völkerrecht während der Regierungszeit Kaiser Wilhelms II', *Festschrift der Rundschau für den deutschen Juristenstand* (1913) 257.

[2] I. Geiss, *Zukunft als Geschichte: historisch-politische Analysen und Prognosen zum Untergang des Sowjetkommunismus, 1980–1991* (1998), at 202.

[3] O.F.R. Haardt, *Bismarcks ewiger Bund. Deutschland zwischen Fürstenbund und Reichsmonarchie 1871–1918* (2020).

[4] M. Koskenniemi, *The Gentle Civilizer of Nations. The Rise and Fall of International Law 1870–1960* (2002), at 204 ff.

[5] Carty, 'The Evolution of International Legal Scholarship in Germany during the Kaiserreich and the Weimarer Republik (1871–1933)', 50 *German Yearbook of International Law* (2007/2008) 29, at 29.

However, this was only half the truth. In his praise of international law in the Wilhelmine era (1890–1918), Woldemar von Rohland concealed the dark sides of the German politics of international law. Germany had certainly not exactly helped strengthen the law against war. On the contrary, diplomatic initiatives to prevent war by establishing compulsory international arbitration failed at the Hague Peace Conference of 1899 due to German resistance.[6] The transfer of power from Bismarck, who had almost unlimited freedom of action under Wilhelm I, to Wilhelm II (after the ninety-nine days of Friedrich III's government) was accompanied by a change in the diplomatic culture of the Empire. After founding the Empire by force, Bismarck had turned to a policy of balancing German and other Great Powers' interests within the international order[7]—not least to consolidate Germany's status in Europe. Under Wilhelm II, things were different: the Empire now strove more and more for hegemony in Europe and for a 'place in the sun' in the world political context. Germany thus increasingly turned away from the European Concert's consensus on the norms of restraint, mediation, and diplomatic compromise.

What consequences did this diplomatic turning point have for the legal approach to what is probably the most political field of international relations, the legitimation of force? To what extent, then, did the German Empire pursue a *Sonderweg* ('special path') in the discourse on the justification of war in international law?

So far, the research reveals very few answers to this question. Surprisingly—or significantly?—international law in the German Empire has long received relatively little scholarly attention.[8] As late as 2003, the doyen of German legal history, Michael Stolleis, rightly stated that 'the history of international law scholarship between the Kaiserreich and National Socialism has not yet been written.'[9] Particularly when it comes to the justification and criticism of war in international law, little has changed in this regard to this day.[10]

My argument is that with the limited research on the discourse of international law in the Empire, the origin of the thesis of the 'free right to go to war' has also been overlooked so far. For, as will be argued below, under Wilhelm II, the new 'central power'[11] of continental Europe became a challenger to the international legal order. The German Empire now turned out to be an extraordinarily favourable context, both socio-politically and from the perspective of its militaristic culture, for a power-based reorientation of parts of international legal doctrine. This took the form of a

---

[6] Chapter 9.
[7] L. Gall, *Bismarck: The White Revolutionary* (2019), vol. 2, Chapter 10.
[8] See also Stolleis, 'Schmidt, Julia, Konservative Staatsrechtslehre und Friedenspolitik. Leben und Werk Philipp Zorns', 120 *Zeitschrift der Savigny-Stiftung für Rechtsgeschichte: Germanistische Abteilung* (2003) 779; S. Wiederhold, *Die Lehren vom Monismus mit Primat staatlichen Rechts* (2018), at 38.
[9] Stolleis (n. 8), at 780.
[10] But see I.V. Hull, *Absolute Destruction: Military Culture and the Practices of War in Imperial Germany* (2005); Vec, 'Challenging the Laws of War by Technology, Blazing Nationalism and Militarism: Debating Chemical Warfare before and after Ypres, 1899–1925', in B. Friedrich, D. Hoffmann, J. Renn, F. Schmaltz, and M. Wolf (eds), *One Hundred Years of Chemical Warfare: Research, Deployment, Consequences* (2017) 105; and Simon, 'The Myth of *Liberum Ius ad Bellum*. Justifying War in 19-Century Legal Theory and Political Practice', 29 *European Journal of International Law* (2018) 113.
[11] Geiss (n. 2), at 202.

turn towards the idea of the sovereign state as a central actor, bound at most to its 'inner morality'. These developments were clearly helped by increasing tendencies towards a radical positivism in parts of German international legal doctrine.[12] At the centre of this positivist trend was the thesis that states had a 'free right to war'.

7.2 A Positivist Polemic

Figure 7.1 Frontispiece to Rettich's *Zur Theorie und Geschichte des Rechts zum Kriege* (1888)

---

[12] On positivism in the nineteenth century, see M. García-Salmones Rovira, *The Project of Positivism in International Law* (2013).

How much ... the opinions of Fichte and Hegel, of Bluntschli and Gneist, and no doubt of so many others, diverge about war and its function in the life process of mankind![13]

German lawyer Heinrich Rettich recorded this observation in his 300-page treatise *Zur Theorie und Geschichte des Rechts zum Kriege*, in 1888. Although Rettich wrote what I consider to be the most comprehensive (and a particularly problematic) legal treatise on *ius ad bellum* in the nineteenth century,[14] it has rarely been studied in detail so far. This may be due to the fact that Rettich, if considered at all, has been characterized as a relatively unimportant scholar.[15] As a result, Rettich's significance for the contemporary discourse on the legitimacy of war under international law has been underestimated. On closer examination, however, this ignorance is difficult to justify. Rettich's study was pioneering in its content and scope. Largely forgotten today, it was widely received and reviewed in German academic discourse (see below).

The trail that this reception of Rettich's treatise has laid, leading to the German discourse of war justification on the *ad bellum* level,[16] however, has not yet been picked up. This is surprising, as in view of his particularly detailed historical, theoretical, and methodological reflections, no other scholarly text of the late nineteenth century seems a more suitable starting point to analyse changes in the German legal discourse concerning the (de)legitimization of war. I therefore propose that Rettich be understood as an important pioneer of the realist doctrine of a 'free right to go to war'.

Rettich's intention may in fact have been to disrupt legal discourse on *ius ad bellum* by publishing his book. For he criticized the nineteenth-century doctrine of international law for not having developed an understanding of war and its role in history formulated in the vocabulary of legal positivism. According to Rettich,[17] however, what was even more unsatisfactory, and sometimes 'highly unclear and illogical', was the contemporary 'scientific treatment of the law of nations on war, or, in the words that are commonly used with the theory, the doctrine of the justifying causes of war' ('*die Lehre von den rechtfertigenden Kriegsursachen*').

In his analysis, Rettich did not mince his words: he harshly criticized famous 'positivist' authorities in his field, such as J.J. Moser, Georg Friedrich von Martens,

---

[13] '*Wie sehr ... gehen nicht über den Krieg und seine Funktion im Lebensprozesse der Menschheit die Meinungen eines Fichte und Hegel, eines Bluntschli und Gneist und zweifelsohne noch so vieler auseinander!*', H. Rettich, *Zur Theorie und Geschichte des Rechts zum Kriege. Völkerrechtliche Untersuchungen* (1888), at 34.

[14] Ibid., at viii; Rettich correctly noted the research desideratum: '*Irgend eine vorgängige gleichen Zweck verfolgende Arbeit ist mir dabei nicht zu statten gekommen ...*'

[15] Carty (n. 5), at 45.

[16] On the *in bello* level, see the important work by Hull (n. 10).

[17] Rettich (n. 13), at 37.

Klüber, Heffter, and Bluntschli, whom he held responsible for the failure of a positivist legal definition of the right to war.[18] Rettich went on to address these 'most striking example[s]': J.J. Moser, 'the father of proud positivism', had declared his 'complete impotence ... to bring war into the framework of norms of international law'.[19] Georg Friedrich von Martens's argumentation was 'shallow' and 'blurred'. It consisted, Rettich claimed, of 'analogies from theological morality, the principle of which is in no way transferable into a legal principle'.[20] '[H]is nebulous constructions and agonizing twists' pointed to the 'complete inability even of the positivist Martens to establish any doctrine at all on the right to war', Rettich followed.[21]

Rettich even claimed that Heffter, praised as a positivist,[22] was in fact *non-positivist*. In Heffter's treatment of the justification of war, Rettich wrote, it is 'impossible to see any proof of his legal conception and clear treatment of international law that is generally so vaunted'. Heffter's thinking about the 'justice of war', Rettich claimed, was 'moralizing, politicizing, at times mere phraseology'—but involved no legal analysis.[23] Rettich had a valid point when he berated Heffter for referring to the 'justice of war' and at the same time criticizing the lack of a praetor in interstate relations in the Hegelian tradition.[24] In Rettich's view—

> the positivist Heffter senses this gap in international law, or rather in its scientific treatment, just as much as he is disinclined to enter into its investigation whose juridical difficulty is only surpassed by the degree of its positive legal precariousness.[25]

And, finally, Rettich also attacked Bluntschli, claiming that his analysis of the 'serious violation of rights' as the 'legitimate cause' of war was 'naturally devoid of any legal usefulness'.[26]

Rettich was clearly dissatisfied with the (alleged) lack of positivist argumentation in legal scholars' analyses of *ius ad bellum* up to 1888. He wrote that—

> both with regard to the science of international law in itself, and especially with regard to humanity and the strengthening of peace, which it has the most beautiful and useful vocation to promote, it is a saddening and discouraging

---

[18] Ibid., at 38–42.
[19] 'völlige Impotenz erklärt, ... den Krieg in den Rahmen völkerrechtlicher Normen zu bringen', ibid., at 40.
[20] 'Analogien aus der theologischen Moral, deren Prinzip absolut nicht in ein Rechtsprinzip übertragbar sind', ibid., at 41.
[21] Ibid.
[22] But see Chapter 4.2.
[23] Rettich (n. 13), at 43.
[24] Chapter 4.2.
[25] Rettich (n. 13), at 43.
[26] Ibid., at 45.

circumstance, although excused by many things, that most modern theorists believe they can dispense with treating this central point of the whole law of nations [*ius ad bellum*, HS].[27]

And Rettich added that—

it must seem like a bitter irony if, on the other hand, relatively minor questions of the law of war, such as the right of search, the right of prise, etc., are discussed and volumes upon volumes are edited.[28]

Rettich's critique had some merit. Indeed, more academic studies were systematically published on *ius in bello* than on *ius ad bellum*. Rettich thus addressed the 'semi-legalization of war' in the nineteenth century. To Rettich, this unequal scholarly interest in *ius in bello* and *ius ad bellum* was—

as if in their systems the criminal lawyers did not get involved at all in the legal question of whether and why a person may be sentenced to death, but, on the other hand, would use all their acumen to find out whether it is right and permissible to cut off the poor sinner's hair before execution.[29]

However, Rettich did not stop at criticizing the majority of legal scholars who continued to invoke the doctrine of *bellum iustum*. Rather, he wanted an answer to the question of the extent to which 'a positive right to war' could be constructed.[30]

To this end, the German lawyer juxtaposed aggressive anarchy and peaceful rule of law. At first glance, Rettich's description of the telos of international law could also have come from a Kantian scholar. If international law had found its 'ultimate aim' in initiating the intercourse of sovereign states not through arbitrary but ordered and peaceful channels, Rettich argued, then law needed to be sharply demarcated from everything—to the extent 'that no transgression ever dares to excuse itself with "ignorantia"'.[31] 'Whoever wants to enact law must be able to distinguish it from lawlessness'.[32] Unlike private and state law, international law as 'law between sovereign states'[33] was still a long way from this ideal. Nevertheless, according to Rettich, the state of law, even between nations, was peace. The conceptual negation of peace, war, Rettich argued, therefore required justification in order not to be qualified as a crime.

---

[27] *Ibid.*, at 44.
[28] *Ibid.*
[29] *Ibid.*
[30] *Ibid.*
[31] *Ibid.*, at vii.
[32] 'Wer Recht setzen will, muss es von Unrecht unterscheiden können.', *ibid.*, at vii f.
[33] *Ibid.*, at viii.

Rettich now asked whether such a justification could be recognized in the *opinio iuris* of nations.[34] This question and the problems behind it were not new. Some of the jurists criticized by Rettich had already expressed their disquiet about the lack of a codification of *ius ad/contra bellum*. They had emphasized the continuing importance of war justifications, and some had begun to construct an emerging prohibition of war *de lege ferenda*.[35] Rettich, on the other hand, came to a completely different conclusion than liberals. He was not interested in states' normatively vague convictions and justifications of violence. For as long as legal scholarship was unable—

> to sufficiently fix the substantive law that is to be realized, its attempt to present war as a formal legal means of the same will also have to be declared as fanciful a beginning as if one wanted to endeavour to build steps into mountains of clouds in order to climb them.[36]

Thus, according to Rettich, the legal opinion that war was a legal remedy clearly fiction. However, as I have reconstructed in Part I of this book, it was precisely this opinion that prevailed in nineteenth-century legal theory. Rettich knew that too. His argumentation strategy therefore included the clear delegitimization of the legal mainstream of his time. In the absence of a positive legal norm, Rettich argued, legal scholarship was forced to further investigate what constituted a legal violation—and 'here it failed completely'.[37] It had, Rettich contended, 'made little progress for centuries'.[38] As far as the justifying causes of war were concerned, legal scholarship was 'completely in the dark' ('*völlig im Dunkeln*'). After all, Rettich reasoned, science could not judge the legitimacy or illegitimacy of a war if it was unable to name these causes concretely. The view of the prevailing doctrine was therefore, according to Rettich, 'theoretical fiction, which is in no way suitable to provide a norm for the judgement of concrete cases'.[39] It lacked 'any positive basis' and had 'not been able to prove even the most basic prerequisites and conceptual characteristics of the legal remedy in war'.[40]

This says a lot about Rettich's methodological basis. He claimed to be representing a strict 'scientific positivism' ('*wissenschaftlichen Positivismus*'),[41] in line with which he asserted—entirely in the sense of Wilhelm Grewe[42]—that states had 'a positive right to war'. Rettich defined this '*positive Recht zum Kriege*' as

---

[34] *Ibid.*
[35] Chapters 4.2 and 6.2.
[36] '*in Wolkenberge Stufen einzuhauen, um sie zu besteigen*', Rettich (n. 13), at 67.
[37] *Ibid.*, at 140.
[38] *Ibid.*
[39] *Ibid.*, at 52.
[40] *Ibid.*
[41] *Ibid.*, at 34.
[42] Chapter 2.2.

follows: 'The conviction of a state that it can only achieve an end necessary for its well-being by warlike means is the perpetually valid legal title for the declaration of war.'[43] For the first time in international legal discourse, the thesis that sovereign states had a free right to wage war was systematically developed!

But how did Rettich justify this alleged 'positive right to war' when there was no treaty granting such a 'right'? Rettich chose a legal historical approach in his analysis, which demonstrates the dominance of empirical historical approaches in the legal discourse of the German Empire (see below). Rettich's rejection of any definition of war based on natural law and the legitimation of war, which he disqualified as 'unscientific' (*'unwissenschaftlich'*),[44] is striking. While 'the positivists' before him had 'not provided any kind of scientific definition of war', Rettich considered the definitions offered by the 'philosophers' of international law, the natural lawyers, to be useless for the positivist definition he aspired to.[45] Accordingly, he blamed natural law for having metamorphosed 'war into a process'.

In his treatise, Rettich had therefore 'sought to establish the historical concept of war alone' since only 'history' with its 'real laws' could testify against this idea of an 'artificially abstract' concept of war.[46] Here, Rettich referred to warlike conflicts in the High and Late Middle Ages, as well as in the early modern period, to 'private wars' (feuds) in 'that bloody period in the process of the development of large state structures, where all legal life finds its beginning and end in the right of self-help'.[47] Political practice had tried to humanize 'private wars' by means of the 'gentle cover of litigation' (*'sanfte Maske des Rechtsstreits'*), and science had willingly provided it with the praxeology and the technical vocabulary.[48] However, according to Rettich, 'society, which does not educate itself according to the opinions of artificial abstractions', had tirelessly denied the idea of war as a 'legal dispute'. Thus Rettich asserted that 'after centuries' there was 'no longer anyone serious' referring to the 'emperorless, i.e. the lawless, terrible time', to a warlike legal process. Rather, Rettich claimed, it was referred to as the 'time of ... violence.'[49]

Starting from war as the mainspring of state-building in the early modern period, Rettich contrasted violence (*violentia*) and (legal) order (*potestas*) in the spirit of Hobbes, arguing that there was no longer any room for the right of the strongest within the modern constitutional state. Rather, violence was 'placed entirely and solely in the service of the state'. The latter alone was entitled and empowered to exercise violence—all violence in the state came from the state.[50] For Rettich, the

---

[43] '*Die Überzeugung eines Staates, einen für sein Wohl nötigen Zweck nur auf kriegerischem Wege erreichen zu können, ist der stetsfort gültige Rechtstitel zur Erklärung des Krieges*', Rettich (n. 13), at 142 ff.
[44] *Ibid.*, at xii.
[45] *Ibid.*, at ix.
[46] *Ibid.*
[47] *Ibid.*, at xii.
[48] *Ibid.*
[49] *Ibid.*
[50] *Ibid.*

experience of war was linked to the emergence of peace, as he illustrated with the (early) modern 'pacification of Germany under international law', which he identified in the Perpetual Peace (1495), the Peace of Westphalia (1648), the German Federal Act (1815), the constitution of the North German Confederation (1867), and finally, as the keystone, in the constitution of the German Empire (1871).

Rettich contended that the anarchic 'law of the fist' in private wars was finally defeated with an 'eternal pacification' (*'ewige Befriedung'*) in the modern state's monopoly of force. This, Rettich argued, excluded the right of private individuals to use force against one another—both within the national and the international legal communities. The state, on the other hand, could renounce the means it had forbidden its citizens to use. Free and defenceless though it once was, Rettich wrote, the state was still dependent on its own power. With this, Rettich argued entirely in the spirit of modern realist theory. A state must use force—and here lies the quintessence of Rettich's definition of *liberum ius ad bellum*—'as soon as it deems it necessary for its interest. The conviction of such necessity is its right to war!'[51]

In principle, this historiographical turn in international law was by no means limited to realists. Rettich praised Bluntschli for his insight that the 'eternally living, eternally fluid law-forming element of history' was 'entitled to have a necessary influence' in international law.[52] But Rettich did not conclude that a right against war (*ius contra bellum*) was to be developed. Instead, he concluded that the (supposed) facticity of *liberum ius ad bellum* had to be accepted. For the constantly new forms and necessities that resulted from historical development opposed a 'theoretical attachment' of war to 'a magnificent veto', Rettich claimed.[53] In other words, the never-ending necessity of war in the historical development of peoples and states made the normative limitation of its justifications largely impossible. Following his historical positivist approach, Rettich also derived the 'morality' of the 'positive right to go to war' from its asserted factuality: 'Precisely because its historical positivity is beyond all doubt, this is also its moral positivity.'[54] Rettich asserted that all states, in deciding whether or not to go to war, were guided only 'by consideration of their own interests', since it was 'the noblest obligation of every state system to always strive for only the most useful and expedient for its citizens'.[55] As a consequence, political arbitrariness in international relations was morally justified in the name of the nation. According to Rettich, war in the nineteenth century was thus, as it is still referred to in research to this day, a 'political procedure among others'.[56]

---

[51] *Ibid.*, at xii ff.
[52] *Ibid.*, at 45.
[53] *Ibid.*
[54] *Ibid.*, at 143.
[55] *Ibid.*
[56] Koskenniemi, 'The Politics of International Law', 1 *European Journal of International Law* (1990) 4, at 6; S.C. Neff, *War and the Law of Nations: A General History* (2005), at 161, 197; and O.A. Hathaway and S.J. Shapiro, *The Internationalists: How a Radical Plan to Outlaw War Remade the World* (2017), at xv.

Based on the analysis presented in this book so far, a critique of Rettich's thesis is not too difficult. *First*, in theoretical terms: as already discussed above,[57] the 'free right to go to war' was not a positive international legal norm, but an absolute right of state sovereignty. Rettich thus believed in a norm without normativity: if there was no treaty prohibiting war, in his view, war was legal. This understanding of the law is already highly problematic. But *second*, especially from a historical point of view, Rettich's thesis was unacceptable. He ignored the discourse on legitimacy in the nineteenth century, which clearly pointed in the direction of a normative prohibition of war.

Rettich's positivism can thus also be criticized in terms of craftsmanship, because it simply did not do historical justice to the multinormative grounding of the legitimation discourse. A sole focus on positive law, which Rettich demanded, fundamentally overlooked the reality of the international discourse on the legitimization of violence. Rettich's flight into a pure positivism of power ultimately amounted to a capitulation to war. Conceptions of a 'perpetual peace' were now countered by the assumption of a continuation, ad infinitum, of human history as the history of war. Paradoxically, Rettich thus strived for absolute objectivity in positive law—but in so doing legitimized absolute political arbitrariness. His plea against liberal moralizing and politicizing was thus just that: a politicization of legal discourse.

Rettich's oversimplified legal historical analysis did not start with the nineteenth century. His analysis of the early modern period already draws various erroneous conclusions. Remarkably, Rettich anticipated Carl Schmitt in that he implicitly conceived of a non-discriminatory concept of war, which he derived from the concept of *bellum iustum ex utraque parte* in order to assert a transformation of the European discourse on the legitimacy of war in the course of the early modern period.[58] In Rettich's view, German lawyer Karl Theodor Pütter had already ultimately arrived at the proposition of a 'positive right to go to war' when he wrote that in violent disputes between sovereign peoples it could never be questioned—

> whether one is in the wrong and which of the two that is, but both have the right to legally carry out their state will, which is to be considered just at all times and which has been legally and constitutionally established, with all power and force.[59]

According to Pütter, Rettich summarized, war was a divine judgement. Science could give its 'Amen' to this 'sermon' of Pütter's without hesitation—although Rettich[60] rebuked the 'pious Pütter' for continuing to refer to war as a 'legal remedy'

---

[57] Chapter 2.
[58] Chapters 2 and 10.
[59] K.T. Pütter, *Beiträge zur Völkerrechts-Geschichte und Wissenschaft* (1843), at 18 ff., in Rettich (n. 13), at 143 n. 1.
[60] *Ibid.*

and thus 'misusing clearly delimited legal terms in such a way'.[61] Once again, jurisprudence was to be cleansed of non-legislative terms.

However, Rettich misunderstood the early modern concept of *bellum iustum ex utraque parte* or *bellum legale*, just as others, such as Carl Schmitt, Wilhelm Grewe, and the prevailing doctrine to this day, did after him. For the concept of lawful war (*bellum legale*) had *not* replaced the doctrine of *bellum iustum* at the level of the legitimation of war *(ius ad bellum)*.[62] The Pütter quote cited by Rettich also points to this. Pütter still saw war as God's judgement on the side of the 'just' warring party, and second, both parties to the conflict were only allowed to carry out their violence within the framework of the law. If one looks up the brief excerpt that Rettich cites from Pütter's textbook, it becomes clear that Pütter was writing with *ius in bello* in mind, and in doing so was entirely in keeping with the prevailing doctrine of the early modern period that states should value themselves as moral beings even when violence breaks out, and should understand war as a legal remedy.[63] And what is more, explicitly distancing himself from Machiavelli, Pütter spoke out against a state policy oriented towards arbitrary increase in power. '[G]eneral laws of reason and law', Pütter argued, had to prevail in 'the mutual relations of sovereign peoples'.[64] A 'free right to war' could by no means be derived from this—despite Rettich's abbreviated exegesis of Pütter. Rettich's historical argument was thus just as one-sided as that of Carl Schmitt et al. later.[65]

Although Heinrich Rettich's radical positivism ultimately confused politics and law,[66] Rettich was not a bellicist. In his *Theorie und Geschichte des Rechts zum Krieg*, he did assert a historical necessity for war. He did not, however, go into raptures about war as a catalyst of the *Machtstaat*, nor did he make affirmative references to realist theorists such as Machiavelli, Clausewitz, (in his conservative interpretation) Hegel, or to realist politicians such as Friedrich II or Bismarck. When Rettich then listed the 'landmarks'[67] of the pacification of Germany in terms of international law, he did so in a soberly descriptive manner and without national pathos.

Finally, Rettich's absence of bellicism also becomes clear in his assertion that fundamental legal restrictions of the 'positive right to go to war' existed through treaty law, for positive international law had indeed 'imposed substantial and extensive restrictions on the "right to war" over the centuries'.[68] Among the formal conditions for the realization of the 'positive right to war', Rettich counted 'preceding peaceful negotiations' and 'in the most extreme case, the dispatch of an

---

[61] Pütter (n. 59), at 19.
[62] Chapter 2.3.
[63] Pütter (n. 59), at 18 ff.
[64] *Ibid.*, at 8 ff.
[65] Chapter 2.2.
[66] Chapter 3.2.
[67] See above, Rettich (n. 13), at 132.
[68] *Ibid.*, at 145.

ultimatum before the opening of hostilities'.[69] Even Rettich's advocacy of a 'positive right to go to war' was not entirely unaffected by the experience of nineteenth-century diplomacy aimed at peace. There were restrictions to this 'right', which Rettich demonstrated, especially in his discussion of Bulmerincq's fundamental rights of the state under international law.[70] According to Rettich, there was 'no right to war' at all with regard to neutral states.[71] The emphasis on neutrality is not unusual for proponents of the thesis of *liberum ius ad bellum* to this day, since according to them, neutrality did not affect the right of the politically and militarily dominant Great Powers to wage war, but rather strengthened the character of war as a political duel.[72]

Nevertheless, Rettich also praised the 'merit, which cannot be appreciated enough' of the diplomats and statesmen gathered in Vienna in 1815 for realizing the idea of Switzerland's perpetual neutrality 'with a view to the pacification of Europe'.[73] Rettich recognized a certain authority of the Concert—even if, in his view, it had not developed a *ius contra bellum*. Within the international legal community, he argued, there was a lack of a monopoly on the use of force comparable with that of the state or the federal state. Here, in Rettich's view, war was 'permissible to a limited extent' ('*bedingt zulässig*'), and only as an interstate act. A war against 'the life, property, personal freedom, and religion of the vanquished', however, was not permissible, according to Rettich.[74]

All these reflections on the limits of *liberum ius ad bellum* ultimately led Rettich to the following conclusion, which he placed on the last page of his study and which is worth quoting in full:[75]

From these sentences the following 'right to war' can be inferred within the present international legal community: a state of the international legal community is entitled under community law to the use of warlike force against another state:

1. if the decision to use force is based on the realization that the use of force is unavoidable in order to achieve the desired end,
2. if the end sought is compatible
    a) with the continued legal existence of the neutralized States above the permanently pacified objects, as well as

---

[69] Ibid., at 144.
[70] Ibid., at 50–61.
[71] Ibid., at 145 ff.
[72] For a critical discussion, see Chapter 4.3.
[73] Rettich (n. 13), at 151.
[74] Ibid., at 290.
[75] Ibid., at 291.

b) with the continued existence of the four categories of human goods of life, property, personal liberty, and religion in the possession of those subjugated by war.

Rettich was not only *not* a bellicist (as far as we can judge from his book), he also rejected 'total war'. Although he did not mention it once in his 300-page paper, Rettich's concept of war clearly overlaps with that of Carl von Clausewitz.[76] War was supposed to be a political means of striking down the enemy and thus imposing one's own will. At the same time, war as a political means should only be permitted between states, i.e. in the sense of 'cabinet warfare'. It should not be waged by irregular troops. The defeated were to be spared, so the war was to cease as soon as its political goal had been achieved.

Heinrich Rettich's study can be considered the first comprehensive attempt at a positivist justification of a 'free right to war'. His study points to the increasing importance of historical and empirical positivist scientific standards towards the end of the nineteenth century. On closer inspection, however, it becomes clear that Rettich's work failed as a legal analysis. He presented—possibly unwittingly—a political manifesto that amounted to an absolutization of political sovereignty. Instead of treating the consequences under international law that resulted from the lack of a treaty-based prohibition of war as a serious problem, the lawyer Rettich ultimately capitulated to its lack of codification.

While Rettich cannot be accused of having a bellicose intention, other lawyers in the German Empire can. The increasing importance of realist narratives of war and state in the intellectual discourse of the Empire was also relevant here, as will be shown in the next section.

7.3 War in the Name of the *Machtstaat*: The Formation of the 'Right of the Strongest' in German Historicism

Today, German historians are once again discussing 'special paths'. Surrounding the publication of Hedwig Richter's *Demokratie. Eine deutsche Affäre* in 2020, in particular, there has been a recent debate on whether a German tradition of structural hostility to democracy developed in the face of a lack of parliamentarization. The following remarks are not intended as a direct contribution to these new attempts at reviving the '*Sonderweg*' debate(s). Nevertheless, the argument to be developed overlaps with these more recent discussions in some (contentious) points. My claim is that the rise of the myth of *liberum ius ad bellum* in the History of International Law and International Relations was favoured in the German

[76] Chapter 3.3.

Empire. For it fell on fertile ground, especially where realist and state-oriented political and legal discourses were dominant.

This was arguably not the case to the same extent in any other Great Power as in the German Empire. Martti Koskenniemi has spoken of a 'special path' with regard to the particular weight of the national versus the international perspective in German international legal discourse.[77] And Isabel V. Hull[78] has presented a 'fulminant revival of the *Sonderweg* thesis'[79] with her analysis of 'military culture' in the German Empire. There are thus indications that the German discourse on the legitimacy of war also differed from that of other European states at the end of the nineteenth century. This is something that warrants discussion.

From Freedom to Power (Ranke)

A turn towards realist positions had already taken place in German discourses on state and legal theory since the failed revolution of 1848 and especially with the Prussian victory over Austria in 1866.[80] Some liberal legal scholars were infected by the enthusiasm for realpolitik[81]—even if they sometimes vacillated between euphoria over and rejection of Bismarck's blood-and-iron policy. National conservatives, however, were particularly strongly gripped by the idea of the German power state (*Machtstaat*). In 1867, for example, the *völkisch* author and politician Wolfgang Menzel wrote that 'if the great hopes of the German nation came true', they owed it 'solely to the warlike spirit of the people in arms, to blood and iron, not to the chatter of liberal chambers, not to the toasts of the *Classen-Kappelmänner*, not to the Jewish press'[82]. The reference to the power state was accompanied by a demarcation against actual and imagined enemies of this state. This was particularly strongly influenced by racism, antisemitism, chauvinism, anti-feminism, and classism.

Of particular interest in this context is Birgit Aschmann's observation that in German discourse after 1848, the conceptual pair of 'honour and freedom' was replaced primarily by that of 'honour and power'.[83] The 'will of the state' or 'will of the

---

[77] Koskenniemi (n. 4), at 210; for a critical account, however, see Carty (n. 5); for a nuanced account, see Vec (n. 10).

[78] Hull (n. 10).

[79] Kühne, 'Review of Hull, Isabel V.: Absolute Destruction. Military Culture and the Practices of War in Imperial Germany. Ithaca 2005', *H-Soz-Kult* (30 June 2005).

[80] A.L. von Rochau, *Grundsätze der Realpolitik, angewendet auf die staatlichen Zustände Deutschlands* (1859); Faber, 'Realpolitik als Ideologie. Die Bedeutung des Jahres 1866 für das politische Denken in Deutschland', 203 *Historische Zeitschrift* (1966) 1; N. Doll, *Recht, Politik und 'Realpolitik' bei August Ludwig von Rochau (1810–1873)* (2005); and J. Bew, *Realpolitik. A History* (2016).

[81] Chapter 6.3.

[82] By '*Classen-Kappelmänner*', Menzel was referring to the liberal politician and industrialist Johann Classen-Kappelmann, leading member of the *Deutsche Fortschrittspartei*, W. Menzel, *Der Deutsche Krieg im Jahr 1866*, vol. 1 (1867), at viii.

[83] B. Aschmann (ed.), *Durchbruch der Moderne? Neue Perspektiven auf das 19. Jahrhundert* (2013), at 297.

ruler' also became an especially important narrative in academic writings.[84] For the conservative Carl Friedrich von Gerber, Leipzig law professor and long-time Saxon Minister of Culture, state power was the 'willpower of a personified moral organism'.[85] Accordingly, the state's will was not guided by the norms of the international community, but by domestic morality and necessity.[86] The state became its own standard.

The most important thinker, when it comes to the idea of the state as the highest 'whole', as the 'self-realization of absolute spirit' ('*Verwirklichung des objektiven Geistes*'), was Georg Wilhelm Friedrich Hegel.[87] His idea of the *Machtstaat* was partly distorted in its reception, or at least detached from its dialectical complexity. Characterizations of Hegel as the mastermind of German realpolitik and militarism in the German Empire—or even of German totalitarianism up to Hitler— have remained controversial to this day.[88] What is undisputable, however, is that Hegel's philosophy of state and law was of outstanding importance for those legal scholars who strove for a unification or even expansion of the German state.[89] In their conceptions of the power state, they went beyond Hegel. The idea of morality directed towards the end of the state was in marked contrast to every cosmopolitan ethic in the tradition of Kant, as Hermann Heller would later aptly observe.[90] It was an important theoretical starting point for the absolutization of the power state that was now strongly taking hold, as well as for bellicist tendencies in Germany. For example, Helmuth von Moltke argued in a speech to the *Reichstag* on 16 February 1876 that the existence of a state was only protected by power.[91] According to Moltke, a great state existed only through itself and by its own strength.[92]

This 'new idealization of the real'[93] was supported by the growing importance of the empirical, i.e. natural and historical sciences.[94] Especially in German diplomatic discourse, historiography gained significance as a leading empirical

---

[84] Koskenniemi (n. 4), at 204 ff.
[85] C.F.W. von Gerber, *Grundzüge des deutschen Staatsrechts* (3rd edn, 1880), at 19; Koskenniemi (n. 4), at 183.
[86] A. Gat, *A History of Military Thought. From the Enlightenment to the Cold War* (2001), at 240 ff.; Koskenniemi (n. 4), at 184.
[87] Hegel, 'Die Verfassung Deutschlands (1802)', in E. Moldenhauer and K.M. Michel (eds), *Hegel. Werke*, vol. 1 (1986), at 452.
[88] See also Goldstein, 'The Meaning of "State" in Hegel's Philosophy of History', 12 *The Philosophical Quarterly* (1962) 60; Pfordten, 'Zum Begriff des Staates bei Kant und Hegel', *Internationales Jahrbuch des Deutschen Idealismus/International Yearbook of German Idealism* (2004) 103; Spitra, 'Normativität aus Vernunft: Hegels Völkerrechtsdenken und seine Rezeption', 56 *Der Staat* (2017) 593.
[89] N. Meier, *Warum Krieg? Die Sinndeutung des Krieges in der deutschen Militärelite, 1871–1945* (2012), at 75.
[90] *Ibid.*, at 76.
[91] *Ibid.*
[92] *Ibid.*
[93] B. Aschmann, *Preußens Ruhm und Deutschlands Ehre. Zum nationalen Ehrdiskurs im Vorfeld der preußisch-französischen Kriege des 19. Jahrhunderts* (2013), at 290.
[94] J. Liebrecht, *Brunners Wissenschaft. Heinrich Brunner (1840–1915) im Spiegel seiner Rechtsgeschichte* (2014).

discipline. This historical primacy is pivotal for the further development of the German discourse on war and law. Unlike in Great Britain or France, in Germany, the relationship between the state and the European order was primarily discussed by historians.[95] As in political practice, there was also a 'realist turn' in the German historical sciences. The Enlightenment scholars were now replaced entirely by historicism in the Ranke tradition.[96] This remained dominant in Germany until 1945 and, via Friedrich Meinecke, Ludwig Dehio, Gerhard Ritter, and Theodor Schieder, even continued to play an important role in the great historical debates in the Federal Republic until the mid-1980s.[97]

At the centre of this tradition was the 'spiritualization of power' following Hegel.[98] Leopold von Ranke's doctrine of the Great Powers was characterized by the idea that states were 'thoughts of God', whose independence through the preservation of power was accordingly willed by God. This 'mystification of the idea of the state'[99] in the first generation of German historians of the nineteenth century was supplemented in Ranke's work by a second point of reference in international history, that of the Vienna Order. The latter, however, was only a moral balance of power in Ranke's international thought.[100] Ranke was clearly convinced of the primacy of power over international law. This becomes clear in the way Ranke justified the conquest of Silesia by Friedrich II '*der Große*'. Ranke adopted the figure of preventive war, which was highly problematic not only in the nineteenth century, but also in 1740.[101] Furthermore, he characterized Friedrich's annexation of Silesia in terms of a Machiavellian 'right of the strongest'. According to this 'right', Ranke argued, Friedrich II had been allowed to wage war because he saw the conquest of Silesia both as necessary and possible in terms of Prussian political interests.

Ranke's affirmative view of Friedrich's violence had consequences. According to Mollin, by the fact that Ranke approved—

> the breach of law of 1740 ... without any distance ... the root of the intellectual dominance of the allegedly morally indifferent reason of state can be seen, as well as the disdain, bordering on contempt, for international law, which determined German politics for much of the 19th and 20th centuries.[102]

---

[95] See also M. Schulz, *Normen und Praxis. Das europäische Konzert der Großmächte als Sicherheitsrat, 1815–1860* (2009), at 598 ff.

[96] On this and other German traditions, see, e.g. F.C. Beiser, *The German Historicist Tradition* (2011).

[97] Mollin, 'Internationale Beziehungen als Gegenstand der deutschen Neuzeit seit dem 18. Jahrhundert', in W. Loth and J. Osterhammel (eds), *Internationale Geschichte. Themen – Ergebnisse – Aussichten* (2000) 3, at 3–5.

[98] T. Nipperdey, *Deutsche Geschichte: 1800–1866. Bürgerwelt und starker Staat* (1983), at 62, 518; *ibid.*, at 6.

[99] Daniel, '"Staaten sind Gedanken Gottes". Zur Mystifizierung des Staatsgedankens bei deutschen Historikern des 19. Jh', 29 *Sozialwissenschaftliche Informationen* (2000) 292.

[100] Mollin (n. 97), at 6.

[101] *Ibid.*, at 8 ff.

[102] *Ibid.*, at 9.

Ranke had created the basis for the primacy of power politics for the first generation of German historians of the 1870s. He had thus laid the theoretical foundations for the thesis that a 'free right to go to war' existed.

'Positive law is the only law that has real existence'—Immoral Realism (Treitschke)

This glorification of war in German historiography was most evident in the work of Ranke's successor in Berlin, Heinrich Treitschke.[103] Initially a national liberal, Treitschke became a national conservative during his time as member of the *Reichstag* in the 1870s. The reactionary historian was one of the most important representatives of the idea of the *Machtstaat*. Whereas Ranke's idea of the state as a divine creature was still loosely tied to Protestant morality, Treitschke in a sense secularized the historiographical image of war. He rejected Ranke's idea of a 'divine action in history' ('*göttliches Wirken in der Geschichte*') and thus, according to Karl Ferdinand Werner, unleashed—

> the idea of power and the 'power state' in the sense not merely of the de facto exercise of violence, but of the 'law of the strongest', i.e. the extinction of the idea of law, at least in intercourse between states, which in the totalitarian systems ... was very soon followed by its de facto denial.[104]

Chris Brown, Terry Nardin, and Nick Rengger therefore aptly describe Treitschke as 'representing the dark side of the realist approach to international relations',[105] as a prime example of an immoral realist—a label that is often wrongly ascribed to 'moral' realists such as Hans J. Morgenthau or George Kennan. For while war was morally reprehensible in the eyes of Morgenthau and Kennan, Treitschke, in contrast, understood it as a central political instrument of the state to increase its power. As Johann Baptist Müller has rightly summarized, Treitschke saw war as almost being 'surrounded by a metaphysical dignity'.[106] As Treitschke said in his Berlin lectures, to him it was clear that the 'appeal to arms will be valid until the end of history, and therein lies the sacredness of war'.[107]

For Treitschke, a legal limitation of legitimate reasons for war was out of the question. Rather, he polemicized explicitly against liberal legal scholars and their

---

[103] Schulz (n. 95), at 598 ff.
[104] Werner, 'Historisches Seminar–Ecole des Annales. Zu den Grundlagen einer europäischen Geschichtsforschung', in M. Jürgen (ed.), *Geschichte in Heidelberg* (1992) 1, at 26.
[105] C. Brown, T. Nardin, and N. Rengger (eds), *International Relations in Political Thought. Texts From the Ancient Greeks to the First World War* (2002), at 466.
[106] J.B. Müller, *Konservatismus und Aussenpolitik* (1988), at 12.
[107] H. von Treitschke, *Politics*, vol. 1 (1916), at 230.

conception of the legal consciousness of nations. 'The doctrinaire exponent of international law', Treitschke wrote contemptuously, 'fondly imagines that he need only emit a few aphorisms and that the nations of the world will forthwith, as reasonable men, accept them.'[108] But to accept them actually meant, Treitschke argued, to 'forget that stupidity and passion matter, and have always mattered in history'.[109] The state, according to Treitschke, did not recognize any authority above itself—and certainly not that of liberal teachers of international law: 'And whence do individuals—Rotteck, Bluntschli, Heffter, and others—say to States peremptorily, "Thou shalt"? No single man stands high enough to impose the doctrines on all States. He must be ready to see his theories crossed or crushed by actual life.'[110]

Treitschke contended that this was also due to methodological mistakes made by liberal lawyers: 'The delusion that there can be such a thing as hypothetical law is at the root of these errors.'[111] Due to German liberalism, the 'moral' conception, argued Treitschke, wrongly regarded the state 'as a good little boy, to be washed, brushed, and sent to school; he must have his ears pulled, to keep him good, and in return he is to be thankful, just-minded, and Heaven knows what else'.[112] 'This German doctrinaire theory', Treitschke continued, 'has done as much harm to our political thinking as to other forms of German life.'[113] Treitschke wanted to free law from any moralizing: 'Positive law is the only law that has real existence.'[114] The state, however, was in its sovereignty a profoundly political being. Treitsche therefore polemicized against international law and turned to history. He felt that it was necessary 'to work historically and consider the state as it actually is'.[115]

For Treitschke, international law was limited to a *lex imperfecta* based purely on reciprocity, which at most allowed states to enter a balance of power with one another: international agreements 'which limit the power of a State are not absolute, but voluntary self-restrictions', Treitschke contended.[116] Hence, he rejected the idea of a permanent international arbitration court as 'incompatible with the nature of the State, which could at all events only accept the decision of such a tribunal in cases of second- or third-rate importance'.[117] Treitschke justified this realist perspective by referring to distrust among states: 'When a nation's existence is at stake there is no outside Power whose impartiality can be trusted.'[118] Where there was fear and mistrust, international anarchy prevailed.

---

[108] H. von Treitschke, *Treitschke. His Doctrine of German Destiny and of International Relations* (1914), at 159.
[109] *Ibid.*
[110] *Ibid.*, at 160.
[111] *Ibid.*
[112] *Ibid.*, at 159.
[113] *Ibid.*
[114] *Ibid.*, at 160.
[115] *Ibid.*, at 161.
[116] Treitschke (n. 107), at 29.
[117] *Ibid.*
[118] *Ibid.*

From his distrust in international law, Treitschke concluded that 'every sovereign State has the undoubted right to declare war at its discretion, and is consequently entitled to repudiate its treaties'.[119] Treitschke supported the thesis of *liberum ius a bellum* from the perspective of a realist historian. Not surprisingly, he claimed that war was not waged in the name of internationally shared religious, legal, or moral norms, but only in the name of the power state. War's main motive was therefore the 'moral ideal of national honour [as] a factor handed down from one generation to another, enshrining something positively sacred, and compelling the individual to sacrifice himself to it'.[120]

In highlighting national honour as the ultimate justification of war, Treitschke tried to walk in Clausewitz's shoes. As discussed in Chapter 3.3, Clausewitz had justified joining the Russian army in the war against Napoléon in his *Bekenntnisschrift* ('Notes of Confession') of 1812, first published in 1869.[121] Clausewitz had argued that a nation must defend its honour to the last drop of blood. Referring to Clausewitz's confessions, Treitschke wrote in 1879 that even 'today' every 'German heart' must tremble with pride because of this text.[122] For Treitschke, as for the young Clausewitz, the power of a state was expressed 'in the currency of "honour" and its preservation'.[123]

Treitschke was thus particularly devoted to the young Clausewitz's idea of 'existential war'. As explained in more detail in Chapter 3.3, two concepts of war can be found in Clausewitz's work. According to his instrumental concept of war, politics provides the directives for war as a continuation of the political by other means. According to Clausewitz's existential concept of war, on the other hand, war is a fact that is not subject to external directives. It is thus beyond normative and, to a certain extent, also political limits: 'not an "act of violence to force the opponent to fulfil our will"', according to Herfried Münkler, 'but an act to prove to oneself one's will, to assure oneself of one's ability to have a will. War here is not an instrument of politics, but politics in its highest form.'[124]

The two concepts of war are not necessarily mutually exclusive, but they do stand in a certain tension with each other. While Clausewitz tended more towards an existential concept of war in his early writings, the primacy of politics over war clearly prevailed in his later works.[125] Thus, if Treitschke decisively took up the existential conception of war, this can also be seen as a potential conflict

---

[119] *Ibid.*, at 28.
[120] *Ibid.*, at 15.
[121] R. Parkinson, *Clausewitz: A Biography* (2002), at 134.
[122] H. von Treitschke, *Deutsche Geschichte im neunzehnten Jahrhundert*, vol. 1: Bis zum zweiten Pariser Frieden (2nd edn, 1879), at 391.
[123] Frevert, 'Die Gefühle der Staaten. Völkerrecht und politische Praxis', in H. Miard-Delacroix and A. Wirsching (eds), *Emotionen und internationale Beziehungen im Kalten Krieg* (2020) 25, at 27.
[124] Münkler, 'Instrumentelle und existentielle Auffassung vom Krieg bei Carl von Clausewitz', 16 *Leviathan* (1988) 235, at 247.
[125] Chapter 3.3.

of competence between the primacy of the political and the military. Treitschke, however, also went beyond Clausewitz's existential concept of war. The young Clausewitz had in mind the defence of Prussia and its honour against the Napoleonic Empire, but not the glorification of war as an instrument of power expansion. It was not Clausewitz the soldier, but Treitschke the historian who was the militarist.[126]

As one of the most widely read publicists, Treitschke had enormous discursive influence in the Empire. Moltke's thinking on war, politics, and history was significantly influenced by Treitschke. Chancellor Bernhard von Bülow claimed that Treitschke's *Deutsche Geschichte*[127] was the basis of his 'political thinking and feeling'.[128] The increasingly bellicose and realist discourse in Germany was also noticed abroad. British professor of international law Coleman Phillipson,[129] for example, became aware of a school of thought influenced by Clausewitz among German authors, in which Treitschke played a special role. In his *German Problems and Personalities*, published in 1917, the Belgian publicist Charles Sarolea wrote of the 'enormous influence of Treitschke on his countrymen'. Sarolea even described the German historian as the apostle and prophet of the political creed that plunged Europe into the World War:

> Those readers who will follow Treitschke's close reasoning to the end will probably agree with me ... that, more than any one thinker, much more certainly than Nietzsche, Treitschke must be held responsible for the catastrophe [of the Great War, HS]'.[130]

Sarolea's characterization of Treitschke was in keeping with the British strategy of delegitimizing Germany.[131] Indeed, Treitschke became *persona non grata* in international discourse after the First World War in view of his nationalist, reactionary, antisemitic, and sexist writings, as Chris Brown, Terry Nardin, and Nick Rengger point out.[132] Nevertheless, the increasing turn towards an expansive bellicose variant of realism in German discourse was by no means the conceit of British propaganda. It was exceedingly real.

---

[126] K.D. Rose, *The Great War and Americans in Europe, 1914–1917* (2017), at 117.
[127] Treitschke (n. 122).
[128] K. Canis, *Von Bismarck zur Weltpolitik: Deutsche Außenpolitik 1890 bis 1902* (2009), at 225.
[129] C. Phillipson, *International Law and the Great War* (1915), at 148.
[130] C. Sarolea, *German Problems and Personalities* (1917), at 104.
[131] Chapter 9.
[132] Brown, Nardin, and Rengger (n. 105), at 466.

'A people that cannot hate the foreign is a wretched people' (Lasson)

This was also noticed in Germany, where it met with divided and sometimes (self-) contradictory reactions. In the 'antisemitism controversy' initiated by Treitschke in 1879, for example, one of the most important philosophers of his time, Adolf Lasson, warned of a growing antisemitism in the student body.[133] The Hegelian Lasson opposed Treitschke in this debate. However, the same did not apply to another debate, that of war and political violence. Here, Lasson created a link between the Hegelian theory of the power state and the *Clausewitzian* theory of war even before Treitschke. It is therefore not surprising that Lasson's theory of war would have considerable influence on Treitschke.[134]

Like Treitschke, Lasson, in his *Princip und Zukunft des Völkerrechts* (Principle and Future of International Law), published in the year of the founding of the German Empire, saw international relations as dominated by enmity 'from time immemorial to the present day'.[135] The will of the state ('*Wille des Staates*') had 'its inner limit only in the certainty of its purpose', Lasson argued.[136] Lasson, too, was therefore of the opinion that statecraft was based solely on what was politically useful and necessary. For only in its state, Lasson argued, did a people develop its national culture, 'its supreme sanctuary, its true self' ('*sein höchstes Heiligthum, sein wahres Selbst*').[137] According to Lasson, it was true that the commonality of interests between states increased with culture. At the same time, however, he pointed out, that—

> unfortunately ... the progress of a people in the material and spiritual spheres [is accompanied by, HS] the physical strength of the state, the power and the temptation to harm the other, the claims to validity and supremacy; consequently, the competition between the various states in their progressive cultural work cannot be a permanently peaceful one, no matter how high common interests are raised. Conflict will therefore break out again and again.[138]

Just as for Treitschke, for Lasson, too, international relations were thus characterized by international anarchy. States were in a 'state of nature' ('*Naturzustand*') among themselves, Lasson claimed.[139] Lasson *did* see the need for states to live in

---

[133] U. Jensen, *Gebildete Doppelgänger. Bürgerliche Juden und Protestanten im 19. Jahrhundert* (2005), at 292 ff.
[134] U. Langer, *Heinrich von Treitschke. Politische Biographie eines deutschen Nationalisten* (1998), at 138.
[135] A. Lasson, *Princip und Zukunft des Völkerrechts* (1871), at 8.
[136] *Ibid.*, at 13.
[137] *Ibid.*, at 10.
[138] *Ibid.*, at 36.
[139] *Ibid.*, at 35.

peace with each other. Religious wars, wars for 'mere rapacity and vanity' or to impose 'one's own constitutional form', he argued, became increasingly improbable with growing culture.[140] Nevertheless, for the German philosopher, states could only effectively protect themselves from each other by establishing a balance of power. Peace, or in Lasson's words: 'tranquillity between states' ('*Ruhe zwischen Staaten*'), resulted from mutual recognition 'that one considers the other powerful enough to have to fear them, and therefore avoids conflict'.[141] This is clearly reminiscent of Hobbes's description of fear as a central motive in international relations. As a result, trust in international norms was impossible.

For ultimately—and here Hegel was speaking through Lasson—war was the 'only praetor who pronounces judgement on the states not according to a book of law, but according to justice'. But what did Lasson mean by 'justice'? Justice in Lasson's sense was the power of the state and his praetor was war as 'the only one that is just, because its decision is based on power'.[142] The more powerful state was thus at the same time the 'better state', its people the 'better people', its culture the 'more valuable culture'. Lasson's conception of war was based on an evolutionary, almost deterministic understanding of the supposedly natural rise and fall of powers. The weak perished, while the strong endured. For Lasson, however, this was no longer regrettable. He considered political weakness to be 'worthless'.[143] And what is more, according to Lasson, the health of a people also depended on their ability to hate the foreign: 'a people that cannot hate the foreign is a wretched people, unworthy of independence and destined only to be plundered and robbed'.[144] Hatred, fear, and power struggle were the central concepts of this German realist doctrine of war in history.

Based on these reflections on the meaning of war, it is not surprising that Lasson, even before Rettich, came to the conclusion that 'the sentence: war is a legal process between states' was a mere metaphor.[145] Lasson did not understand the state as bound by law and morality, but as a 'thoroughly heartless being' ('*durchaus herzloses Wesen*').[146] Accordingly, Lasson praised Machiavelli, whose sober, unemotional theory of the state he described as representing 'tremendous progress'.[147] For if the state waged war, it could only do so 'for its own interest; for there is no other motive for it'. However, Lasson was not entirely honest here. As shown above, he had considered hatred as an emotion between peoples quite desirable.

---

[140] *Ibid.*, at 38.
[141] *Ibid.*, at 37.
[142] *Ibid.*, at 75.
[143] *Ibid.*
[144] '*Ein Volk, welches das Fremde nicht hassen kann, ist ein erbärmliches Volk, unwerth der Selbstständigkeit und nur bestimmt, geplündert und beraubt zu werden.*' *Ibid.*, at 34.
[145] *Ibid.*, at 68.
[146] *Ibid.*, at 34.
[147] *Ibid.*, at 15.

So, it depended on the nature of the emotion: Lasson saw trust and love between peoples as taboo. Hate and fear, in contrast, were his guiding ideals in international relations.

Lasson was also critical of liberal lawyers (Bluntschli and Phillimore), whom he described as representatives of the '*Völker-Rechtsprocess-These*' of war. Similar to Rettich, Lasson criticized the legal mainstream for adhering to this thesis of war as an international legal process:

> Countless people repeat this. In recent times, people have got it into their heads to regard war as a kind of legal remedy; that is 'progress'. Yes, but progress in misunderstanding one of the basic phenomena of life.[148]

Thus, Lasson used a clear primacy of politics to oppose liberal lawyers with the primacy of law they aspired to. In his argumentation, Lasson affirmatively referred to Proudhon's conception of the 'right of strength'[149] in order to make clear that this was not a juridical but a political 'right' of violence.[150] This understanding became clear when he referred to Carl von Clausewitz's concept of war. Lasson praised Clausewitz's understanding of war as a 'mere continuation of politics by other means' ('*blosse Fortsetzung der Politik mit anderen Mitteln*') which he thought was 'excellent'.[151]

Lasson, whom Bluntschli criticized alongside Treitschke as a eulogist of war,[152] had thus presented a philosophical justification of a 'free right to go to war' in the founding year of the German Empire. In Lasson's work, the increasing importance of a political primacy in the German discourse on war is clearly visible. Lasson had created a theoretical foundation that historians like Treitschke and jurists like Rettich could now build on. However, there are differences between Lasson's 'law of strength' ('*Recht der Stärke*') and Rettich's 'positive law of war' ('*positives Recht zum Krieg*'). Unlike Rettich, the philosopher Lasson was not concerned with the theory of sources of international law. Lasson quoted multiple sources. Rettich, on the other hand, endeavoured to spell out the 'positive right to war' in legal vocabulary—even if he ultimately failed to do so. As a positive right, his 'right to go to war' remained a mere fiction. But while Rettich wanted to conceal the political character of his 'legal' conception, Lasson—and following him Treitschke—openly embraced the political primacy in his writing. Lasson even considered it an argumentative trump card in the analysis of war.

---

[148] *Ibid.*, at 171.
[149] P.-J. Proudhon, *La guerre et la paix. Recherches sur le principe et la constitution du droit des gens* (1863), at 203 ff.
[150] Lasson (n. 135), at 176.
[151] *Ibid.*, at 171.
[152] Chapter 6.4.

All three—the (right-)Hegelian philosopher Lasson, the historian Treitschke, and the lawyer Rettich—were interested in an empirical historical positivism, in the development of which power politics ultimately triumphed over law. Rettich, who was the last of the three to write—but one of the first lawyers to assert a 'free right to war'—was apparently the only one who had reservations about openly acknowledging the primacy of politics. This may also have been due to the fact that it would otherwise have become all too clear what the 'free right to go to war' was from the perspective of positive law: pure fiction.

7.4 A Clausewitzian 'Legal' Tradition

However, such reservations were not to endure among German lawyers. Instead, a new tradition began to emerge in parts of the legal theoretical discourse on the legitimization of war in the Wilhelmine era, which I call '*Clausewitzian*'. Lawyers now increasingly combined Rettich's thesis of the 'positive right to go to war' with a bellicist interpretation of Clausewitz and Hegel in the sense of Treitschke and Lasson. Whereas Rettich had tried to shroud his argument in the language of law, these jurists now blatantly expressed their argument in the language of politics. Realist authors such as Lasson, Treitschke, and Rettich had paved the way for (interpretations of) Clausewitz in German international law. From now on, parts of the German discourse on international law argued that war was a fact of physical violence, a continuation of politics by other means.

War—Always Factual and Very Often Political Violence (Lueder)

One prototypical example of a *Clausewitzian* in the legal discourse of the Empire was the Erlangen law professor Carl Lueder. Although Lueder has often been overlooked in research on the history of international law, he was arguably one of the most important legal authorities in the *Kaiserreich*'s discourse on war in international law. In 1874, Queen Augusta awarded him a prize for his history of the laws of war.[153] And the renowned US jurist John Bassett Moore, professor at Columbia University since 1891, member of the *Institut de Droit* and later judge at the Permanent Court of International Justice, called Lueder—along with Bluntschli!—one of the two most important German authors in the field of the laws of war.[154]

---

[153] Treuenpreuss, 'Queen Augusta and the Red Cross', *The International Review* (1876) 492, at 492.
[154] J.B. Moore, *A Digest of International Law, as Embodied in Diplomatic Discussions, Treaties*, vol. 7 (1906), at 338.

Lueder's importance is also evident in the fact that in the fourth volume of Franz von Holtzendorff's *Handbuch des Völkerrechts* (1889), he wrote the pivotal 175-page chapter on *Krieg und Kriegsrecht im Allgemeinen* ('War and the Law of War in General'). The chapter was to become an important reference text in the German international legal discourse. At the same time, it was to become groundbreaking for the justification argument which claimed a *liberum ius ad bellum* in recourse to Clausewitz's theory of war. Hardly any other legal text was so obviously influenced by military authors. Lueder introduced his treatise with a definition of terms. Since the given definitions of 'war' tended not to be blessed with great sharpness, brevity, and precision, according to Lueder, he wanted to present just such a short, sharp, and concise definition of war.[155] For this, however, he did not refer to the international lawyers who had written before him, but to a Prussian war theorist: Carl von Clausewitz.

On closer examination, Lueder's definition of war is not as sharp and concise as the German legal scholar himself claimed. It contained both Clausewitz's existential and instrumental conceptions of war. They were not only mixed with each other. What is more, they were in a certain tension with each other, since the instrumental conception of war pointed to a subordination of the military to politics, whereas the existential conception also made a primacy of the military conceivable.[156] Just as for Treitschke, for Lueder, too, Clausewitz's existential idea of war was particularly significant. Referring to Clausewitz, the lawyer Lueder saw war primarily as a 'fact of warlike violence' ('*Thatsache der kriegerischen Gewalt*'): war was

> the struggle waged between states or state-like sections of the population by force of arms. Its concept therefore consists in physical violence applied between states (or state-like subjects).[157]

Central to this idea was therefore the de facto violence of war between sovereign states in the sense of a duel.

Lueder argued, in the spirit of Clausewitz, that this interstate competition could only begin with defence, which meant that the attacked party accepted the challenge to a duel.[158] War presupposed reciprocity.[159] For only in the dialectic of attack and defence could war be understood as a two-sided struggle for military victory. This was a clear denial of war as a one-sided legal process in the sense of *bellum iustum*. The introduction of Carl von Clausewitz's theory of war was a fundamental

---

[155] Lueder, 'Krieg und Kriegsrecht im Allgemeinen', in F. von Holtzendorff (ed.), *Handbuch des Völkerrechts. Auf Grundlage europ. Staatspraxis*, vol. 4 (1889) 169, at 177.
[156] Chapter 3.3; see below.
[157] Lueder (n. 155), at 175 ff.
[158] *Ibid.*, at 172.
[159] *Ibid.*, at 177 n. 3.

prerequisite for the decisive turn away from war as a sanction. Instead, his theory favoured a theoretical de-normativization of war in the sense of a 'free right to go to war'. Accordingly, Lueder understood war as independent of its reasons or causes. It existed 'merely in the actual relationship of force between states'.[160]

Lueder thus saw war as a fact, a view which was particularly widespread among the military. As will discussed below, it contained the potential for removing the limits of violence. But Lueder also introduced Clausewitz's second, instrumental conception of war into his 'legal' discussion of this subject. If one wanted to bring the purpose and cause of war into its definition, Lueder claimed in reference to Clausewitz, then 'war would define itself as the use of force by one state to use coercion against another'. For only one purpose of war was unchangeable, Lueder argued: 'forcing the opponent and subjugating them to one's own will'.[161] Again, this was a clear reference to Clausewitz who had defined war as an 'act of force to compel our enemy to do our will'.[162] Combining Clausewitz's existential and instrumental conceptions of war, Lueder arrived at the definition of war as a natural force that was 'very often' expressed as a political instrument: a 'continuation of politics in another form' ('*Fortsetzung der Politik in anderer Form*').[163]

Lueder's definition of war was shared among other jurists in the *Kaiserreich*.[164] It became characteristic of *Clausewitzians* and was diametrically opposed to the position of liberal legal scholars such as Bluntschli, Bonfils, or later Schücking. Lueder categorically rejected a definition of war as a legal concept, even if this, as he critically noted, was often the preferred definition among scholars of international law.[165] However, according to Lueder, the legal dispute did not pertain to the essence and concept of war, but was, as the history and nature of 'the human race' showed, at best an 'accidental moment'.[166] To him, war was frequently 'the violent enforcement of a claim, but not the enforcement of a legal claim'.[167] Law was thus only one of many possible causes for war besides state politics and the 'natural historical development of the life of peoples and culture'.[168]

---

[160] *Ibid.*, at 176.
[161] *Ibid.*
[162] C. von Clausewitz, *On War*, edited and translated by M. Howard and P. Paret (1976 [1832]), at 75; for the German terms, see Clausewitz, 'Vom Kriege', in M. von Clausewitz (ed.), *Hinterlassene Werke über Krieg und Kriegsführung des Generals von Clausewitz* (1832); see Chapter 3.3.
[163] Lueder (n. 155), at 169, 180.
[164] Ullmann, 'Völkerrecht', in E. von Ullmann (ed.), *Handbuch des Öffentlichen Rechts* (2nd edn, 1898), at 313; R.R. Foulke, *A Treatise on International Law. With an Introductory Essay on the Definition and Nature of the Laws of Human Conduct* (1920), at 130 ff. Lueder also referred to W. Rüstow, *Die Feldherrnkunst des neunzehnten Jahrhunderts. Zum Selbststudium und für den Unterricht an höheren Militärschulen* (1857), at 1, see below.
[165] Lueder (n. 155), at 178.
[166] *Ibid.*, at 180.
[167] *Ibid.*, at 181.
[168] '*natürlichen geschichtlichen Weiterentwicklung des Völkerlebens und der Cultur*', *ibid.*, at 176.

However, on closer inspection, Lueder also implicitly relativized Clausewitz's instrumental conception of war and thus its political primacy, just as Treitschke did. When Lueder pointed out that war was 'very often' a political means, this left room for exceptions. Although Lueder located the 'military or political' standpoints close to each other and contrasted them with the understanding of war as a legal means, he repeatedly described war simply as physical violence, for example, in his examination of Bluntschli's analysis on war.[169] This position was also held by Geffcken, who argued that war was a 'physical struggle and only such a struggle'.[170]

The great importance of the facticity of violence in Lueder's work is also evident in the fact that he not only enthusiastically cited Clausewitz and Rühle Lilienstern, but also contemporary German military writers such as Moltke, Wilhelm Rüstow,[171] Julius von Hartmann,[172] Gustav Ratzenhofer,[173] and Bernhard Kiessling.[174] In addition, there are references to bellicose German philosophers and historians such as Adolf Lasson, Felix Dahn, and Heinrich Treitschke. This ingratiation with the militarists distinguished Lueder from Heinrich Rettich. The latter solely discussed the work of legal scholars. He emphasized the instrumental expediency of war in his definition of a 'positive right to war': to Rettich, war was only legal if it served a political (not a purely military) purpose.[175]

Lueder extended this primacy of politics. He supplemented it with a primacy of the military. In a sense, Lueder thus turned the military primacy of the early Clausewitz against the political primacy of the late Clausewitz.[176] This intra-*Clausewitzian* dispute over a primacy of politics and a primacy of the military was to become highly significant for the debates within Germany between 1914 and 1918.[177] What both *Clausewitzian* conceptions of war had in common, however, was the rejection of any legal character of war against the mainstream of the liberal, Kantian theory of international law.

Military Necessity: A German Cult

The basis for those realist lawyers, whom I call *Clausewitzians*, was thus a conception of war that understood physical violence as its natural essence, or, in

---

[169] Ibid., at 181.
[170] Geffcken, Comments in A.W. Heffter, *Das Europäische Völkerrecht der Gegenwart auf den bisherigen Grundlagen* (8th edn, 1888), at 246.
[171] W. Rüstow, *Die Feldherrnkunst des neunzehnten Jahrhunderts. Zum Selbststudium und für den Unterricht an höheren Militärschulen* (1857).
[172] J. von Hartmann, *Militärische Notwendigkeit und Humanität* (1878).
[173] G. Ratzenhofer, *Die Staatswehr* (1881).
[174] B. Kiessling, *Ewiger Krieg* (1885).
[175] Lueder (n. 155), at 291.
[176] Chapter 3.3, see above on Treitschke.
[177] Chapter 8.

Lueder's words, a law of nature (*lex lata naturae*) that was not to be judged normatively: morality, humanity, and law were not vocabularies to be spoken in the spheres of war.[178] There was no normative restriction of war—not least since this limitation of violence would have delayed the end of war, Lueder argued.[179] Rather, for realist lawyers, the only legitimate restriction of war resulted from its own necessity. The necessity of war constituted the third key criterion of *Clausewitzian* doctrine, alongside, *first*, war's facticity and, *second*, state sovereignty as a compelling prerequisite for waging war. For subjugation and assertion of will was accepted as legitimate because it was also considered necessary.[180]

In the *Kaiserreich*'s discourse on international law, the 'necessity of war' knew no limits. Whatever was expedient and thus necessary for coercion and victory was also permitted.[181] This resulted, according to Carl Lueder, in 'the rule of the sword and of military necessity'.[182] Here, Lueder directly anticipated the conception of war and sovereignty as the disposition of the state of exception that Carl Schmitt would later develop. General Julius von Hartmann, from whom Lueder had adopted the broad concept of the necessity of war, literally referred to war as a 'state of exception' ('*Ausnahmezustand*').[183] Direct continuities from the realism of the German Empire to the Weimar Republic and the Third Reich can be identified here.[184] Sovereign was he who decided on the state of exception.

Lueder's triad of facticity, sovereignty, and necessity of war in *ius in bello* was accompanied by the potential for a dissolution of the limits of violence. After all, according to Lueder, the state used its highest goods—'the blood and life of the citizens, the welfare, even the existence of the state, national honour'[185]—to defeat the opponent, to secure 'victory' and 'not to be defeated itself'. Nothing less than the loss of these goods, Lueder said, 'is decided by the outcome of the war'. Thus, according to Lueder, a belligerent state and its organs were 'in the position of an individual involved in a struggle for life and death'.[186] War was an existential struggle for survival. And in the struggle for survival, no one could feel bound by law, as the realist constitutional lawyer Max Seydel had argued in 1873: 'Between states, therefore, there can be no law, between them only force applies.'[187] In Lueder's view, this unconditional struggle for survival was not only natural, but 'also legal'.[188] Accordingly, Lueder drew analogies to self-defence and the state of necessity of the

---

[178] Lueder (n. 155), at 176.
[179] *Ibid.*, at 187.
[180] *Ibid.*, at 185.
[181] *Ibid.*, at 186.
[182] '*die Herrschaft des Schwertes und der militärischen Nothwendigkeit*', ibid.
[183] Hull (n. 10), at 123.
[184] Chapter 10.3.
[185] '*Blut und Leben der Bürger, Wohl, ja Bestand des Staates, nationale Ehre*', Lueder (n. 155), at 185.
[186] *Ibid.*, at 189.
[187] M. von Seydel, *Grundzüge einer allgemeinen Staatslehre* (1873), at 31.
[188] Lueder (n. 155), at 189.

individual to assert the state's unconditional and unlimited right to wage war.[189] Only the sovereign state could decide when to use physical force to put down its opponent.

Much in this vein, Erich Kaufmann wrote in 1911 that the state revealed its true essence in war, since war was 'its highest achievement, in which its distinctiveness reaches its fullest development'.[190] In war, a state had to prove itself. After all, according to Kaufmann, the 'victorious war' turned out to be 'the ultimate norm' that decided which of the states was right. Power and law were not contradictory. In Kaufmann's words: 'Only he who can, may.'[191]

The conservative jurist Philipp Zorn, law professor in Bonn, Crown Counsel, and legal delegate at the Hague Peace Conferences, did not completely oppose the possibility of international arbitration courts. Yet he emphasized that war 'as the utmost means in the state life of nations' could not be dispensed with as a means of coercion. For—

> in the life of nations there are always moments when only a decision by weapons is possible. Neither the creation of today's Kingdom of Italy nor the establishment of today's German Empire (or even the creation of the Kingdom of Belgium)—to offer but a few examples—would have been possible peacefully by means of 'law'; 'law' had become for these peoples an 'eternal disease' ['*ewigen Krankheit*', HS] which condemned them to impotence on the council and in the economic competition of nations.[192]

In reference to the German and Italian Wars of Unification, Zorn then also argued that—

> a decision by arms for the defeat of a 'right' which had become untenable and the establishment of a new right corresponding to the truth of things [had] to take place; for the Italian and German people have exactly the same claim to great state and economic power ['*staatliche und wirtschaftliche Grossmachtstellung*', HS] as the English and French, who have already enjoyed this position for centuries.[193]

---

[189] *Ibid.*, at 221.
[190] *Ibid.*, at 153; E. Kaufmann, *Das Wesen des Völkerrechts und die clausula rebus sic stantibus. Rechtsphilosophische Studie zum Rechts-, Staats- und Vertragsbegriffe* (1911), at 146.
[191] Nevertheless, it has been argued that Kaufmann's first monograph, despite passages like this one, should not be misunderstood as a mere plea for power political positivism, see F. Degenhardt, *Zwischen Machtstaat und Völkerbund. Erich Kaufmann (1880–1972)* (2008); see also Friedrich, 'Erich Kaufmann', 27 *Der Staat* (1987) 231.

[192] Zorn, 'Politik als Staatskunst. Ihr Begriff und Wesen', in W. Rothschild (ed.), *Handbuch der Politik*, vol. 1 (1914), at 6.
[193] *Ibid.*

Here the common narrative appears that Germany, as a belated great and colonial power, should not be prevented from fully developing its power through status quo considerations of international law.[194] For Zorn it was clear that the decision on the great 'imponderables' of 'the life of nations ... as far as human history records, are not factors of law, but factors of the power of nations'.[195] And according to his son, Albert Zorn, war proved that facts are the basis of law: law and power were therefore ultimately the same thing.[196] An astonishing thesis for a lawyer!

According to Lueder, the 'necessity' of war could even suspend the laws of war.[197] Lueder recognized *ius in bello* as a law binding on states.[198] It governed all relations relating to war, i.e. also those between the belligerents and the third states. In the true sense and in particular, it standardized the relations between the belligerents. It thus permitted violence, but at the same time prevented 'the unnecessary excess that goes beyond it'.[199] This sentence is telling: according to Lueder, law did indeed draw a barrier of humanity against the use of militarily unnecessary force. But humanity and law ultimately depended on the necessity of war—and thus on the primacy of the military!

This becomes particularly clear in Lueder's distinction between '*Kriegsmanier*' ('manners of war') and '*Kriegsraison*' ('reason for war'). '*Kriegsmanier (loi de guerre)*' was, according to Lueder, the law of war insofar as it established barriers with regard to the means of actual warfare. '*Kriegsraison (raison de guerre)*', on the other hand, meant the 'justification for deviating from the manners of war, which is necessary and permissible under certain circumstances due to the nature of war'.[200] Some form of 'necessity of war' was known in the early modern period and during the revolutionary era.[201] *Kriegsraison*, however, seemed to allow an almost unlimited deviation from *ius in bello*.[202] According to Lueder, this was possible in two cases:

> in the case of extreme necessity, when the purpose of the war can only be achieved by non-observance and would be thwarted by observance; then by way of retorsion, i.e. as a reply to unjustified non-observance of the manners of war by the other side.[203]

---

[194] Messerschmidt, 'Völkerrecht und "Kriegsnotwendigkeit" in der deutschen militärischen Tradition seit den Einigungskriegen', 6 *German Studies Review* (1983) 237, at 242.
[195] Zorn (n. 192), at 7.
[196] S. Wiederhold, *Die Lehren vom Monismus mit Primat staatlichen Rechts* (2018), at 10.
[197] See also Hull, '"Military Necessity" and the Laws of War in Imperial Germany', in S.N. Kalyvas, I. Shapiro, and T. Masoud (eds), *Order, Conflict, and Violence* (2008) 352.
[198] Lueder (n. 155), at 253.
[199] '*das darüber hinaus gehende unnöthige Mehr*', ibid., at 254.
[200] Ibid., at 254.
[201] Chapter 3.2.
[202] See also S.R. Johansen, *The Military Commander's Necessity. The Law of Armed Conflict and its Limits* (2019), at 113.
[203] Lueder (n. 155), at 254.

This was a very vague definition. What was considered a state of emergency in a specific case was not normed. It could be freely constructed by a state. Lueder was well aware of this vagueness. This becomes clear in a footnote in Lueder's text, the importance of which Isabel Hull has rightly emphasized.[204] In it, Lueder referred to General Julius von Hartmann[205] and argued in terms of his concept of 'military realism' (*'militärischer Realismus'*) that 'in case of doubt' military necessity took precedence over the manners of war. For 'in case of doubt', a decision could not be made in favour of the rule of law, but only in favour of military necessity.[206]

Ultimately, it remains completely unclear to Lueder how a law of war should be conceivable at all. For the vagueness of a formulation according to which mere 'doubt' made it possible to set aside the law opened the door to arbitrariness. Lueder's description of the law of war as a *'Kriegsmanier'* is already interesting, as it is reminiscent of the term 'custom of war' (*'Kriegsbrauch'*) used by the German Great General Staff (*Großer Generalstab*) instead of 'law of war'.[207] By *'Kriegsbrauch'*, military leaders such as Hartmann and Moltke meant customs of limiting violence that were common between states, but which had no binding *legal* power.[208] Lueder certainly spoke of law. Yet he also participated in the construction of a typically German narrative, which he accompanied with a strong glorification of war: necessity knows no law—'*Not kennt kein Gebot!*'[209]

War, 'a true necessary bearer of culture' (Lueder; Meurer)

Lueder's bellicism also resulted from a philosophical engagement with war. In addition to recourse to military writers, Lueder referred to De Maistre, Proudhon, and Lasson. Following De Maistre, Lueder argued that war was part of the divine world order and as such 'wholesome and good': war was thus 'a true necessary bearer of culture' (*'ein wahrer nothwendiger Culturträger'*).[210] Without it, humanity could scarcely achieve full development.

This idea is reminiscent of Kant's dialectic of war and order, which was shared by liberal legal scholars.[211] However, while war in the Kantian tradition could function as a violent corrective of reason on the path towards an international legal order, for Lueder it served only unilateral political and military purposes—namely, the full absorption of the individual into the army and the power state. According

---

[204] I.V. Hull, *A Scrap of Paper: Breaking and Making International Law during the Great War* (2014), at 71 ff.
[205] Hartmann (n. 172), at 74.
[206] Lueder (n. 155), at 254.
[207] See also Chapter 9.
[208] Messerschmidt (n. 194), at 240.
[209] See also Chapter 9.
[210] Lueder (n. 155), at 203 ff.
[211] Chapter 6.3.

to Lueder, war promoted 'first and foremost courage, sacrifice, obedience, a sense of honour, in short, everything that is manliness'.[212] War was also completely indispensable for the spread of civilization and the necessity of colonization.[213] Lueder saw war as a civilizational good. The telos of this civilization, however, was not legal peace, but the absolutized nation-state.

Würzburg's Christian Meurer argued along the same lines. Like Lueder, Meurer was an important legal scholar in the German Empire. Andreas Toppe has called Meurer the 'grandfather of German international laws of war'.[214] Meurer published the most important German-language commentary on the First Hague Conference.[215] In what he described as a 'popular scientific lecture' on international arbitral tribunals, which Meurer delivered on 27 February 1890 in the Schrannensaal in Würzburg, he argued that armies in war 'often replaced the recognition and always replaced the protection' of a superior community. This meant no less than the military taking the place of the legal order in the event of war. For law was 'recognized power protected by the community'.[216] Ultimately, however, international law abandoned the military. In Meurer's view, on the other hand, the army was the guarantor of the protection of the—admittedly national, not international—community. Like Lueder, Meurer represented a concept of the self-asserting state that was charged with images of masculinity: '*Selbst ist der Mann.*'[217]

Meurer therefore answered the question of whether war was politics or law by referring to the creative power of war as the physical, existential force, not of law but of the military: the army was the organized power of the people. What the nation possessed in terms of physical, moral, and spiritual power 'is developed in our army into a unified total power'.[218] Only the strength of a people in war was an expression of its moral and intellectual prowess, Meurer wrote, referring to Adolf Lasson. Thus, Meurer justified war as a purifying force, a political storm. The weak perished in the process: 'That is the eternal justice of world history'.[219]

Meurer can also be said to have permeated Clausewitz's existential conception of war with a bellicism based on Hegel and Lasson.[220] Like Lueder, Meurer advocated the 'popular educational importance of war' ('*volkserziehende Bedeutung des Krieges*') for nationalistic reasons: 'patriotism and discipline, garb and a sense of order, cleanliness and punctuality, public spirit and renunciation, openness and

---

[212] Lueder (n. 155), at 204.
[213] Ibid.
[214] A. Toppe, *Militär und Kriegsvölkerrecht. Rechtsnorm, Fachdiskurs und Kriegspraxis in Deutschland 1899-1940* (2008), at 12.
[215] Hull (n. 204), at 77.
[216] C. Meurer, *Völkerrechtliche Schiedsgerichte: ein populärwissenschaftlicher Vortrag* (1890), at 34.
[217] Ibid. To the best of my knowledge, there is no exactly accurate English translation. 'If you want something done well, do it yourself' fits best, but it lacks the clear reference to masculinity of the German original.
[218] Ibid., at 35.
[219] '*Das ist die ewige Gerechtigkeit der Weltgeschichte.*', ibid., at 33.
[220] Ibid., at 35.

straightness, in short physical and mental health'.[221] School and the military, according to Christian Meurer, were both 'excellent institutions of public education in Germany'. He, Meurer, would not want to forgo either of them 'for the development of our people'.[222] For the Würzburg lawyer, however, it was clear that the army was the real school of the nation.

Accordingly, Meurer even spoke out against disarmament and in favour of standing armies. This was in complete contrast to Kant and pacifist legal scholars such as Schücking. After all, in Meurer's view, disarmament would 'disrupt the organization of the people's power in a harmful way':

> Disarmament, even total disarmament, will no more eliminate war than ringing the bells will dispel a thunderstorm. Strife and feud, war and destruction existed long before the standing lords. They will remain as long as human nature does not change.[223]

Meurer wrote that he had greater hopes of wars being reduced through arbitration courts and congresses—only to immediately relativize this statement, by expressing his doubts that an arbitration award could have achieved anything in the war between Austria and Prussia in 1866. When 'freedom and honour, happiness, and the existence of a people' were at stake, 'the biological law of the organism ['*biologische Gesetz des Organismus*', HS] pushes to the extreme and thus to war', Meurer argued.[224] Supposedly empirical findings from historicism and biologism displaced normative arguments.

Meurer also referred to the plea for mediation at the Congress of Paris of 1856, reflecting on whether it might be a good idea to establish a binding mediation requirement under international law.[225] But he soon put this idea into perspective again. Instead, he reaffirmed that those who want war 'do not care about such pious recommendations' ('*fromme Empfehlungen*').[226]

Towards Perpetual War (Stengel)

It is not surprising that realist bellicist authors categorically rejected Kant's idea of perpetual peace. A world state and a permanent tribunal of nations were, according to Meurer, a 'blissful dream' ('*beseligender Traum*').[227] 'Real life' had nothing to do with it, for those who believed in a general world peace would do

---

[221] *Ibid.*, at 37.
[222] *Ibid.*
[223] *Ibid.*, at 36.
[224] *Ibid.*, at 32.
[225] *Ibid.*, at 38.
[226] *Ibid.*
[227] *Ibid.*, at 37.

well, Meuer argued, to 'first consider only what is attainable .... The spirit of the people [*Volksgeist*, HS] hit the nail on the head with the words: the better is the enemy of the good'.[228]

What is more, German realist lawyers polemicized against Kant's peace project. German lawyer Karl Michael Joseph Leopold Freiherr von Stengel, member of the German delegation to the First Hague Peace Conference, published a treatise entitled *Der ewige Friede* ('The Perpetual Peace') in 1899 and another treatise on *Weltstaat und Friedensproblem* ('World State and the Problem of Peace') in 1909. In both texts, Stengel—much like Lasson, Lueder, Zorn, and Meurer—presented an understanding of law that was clearly fixed on state sovereignty: if all states were united into a world federal state, Stengel argued,

> there would no longer be international law in the present sense, the relations of the member states of the world federal state would be governed by the world federal state law, which would, of course, restrict their independence and autonomy in a completely different way than the current international law.[229]

For, according to Stengel, the sovereignty of states was the basis of international law—and must remain so: 'international law presupposes states, i.e. autonomous and independent communities not subject to a higher power'.[230] In this point, too, Stengel was highly anti-Kantian. Against Kant's idea of a heuristic process of legalization, he tried to focus on the limitations of international law and use them to support his argument that cosmopolitan law was utopian. Stengel saw world peace as inconceivable, since it undermined the state and its 'struggle' ('*Kampf*') as a civilizing force:

> Without struggle and hardship, no individual can lead a life worth living, an extraordinary life. Struggle and hardship are needed by the collective being just as much, indeed far more, because its elements are much more loosely chained together than those of the individual.[231]

Finally, Stengel clearly expressed the political positions that were behind his understanding of international order. The best protection for 'the good right of a state' always remained 'its strong sword'.[232] For Stengel—again, the German representative at the First Hague Conference!—this applied in particular to the *Kaiserreich*: 'It is really said of Germany: "Enemies all around"' ('*Feinde ringsum*').[233] And indeed, they were, according to Stengel—both on the

---

[228] *Ibid.*, at 40.
[229] K. von Stengel, *Weltstaat und Friedensproblem* (1909), at 93 ff.
[230] *Ibid.*, at 93 ff.
[231] *Ibid.*, at 120.
[232] *Ibid.*, at 137.
[233] *Ibid.*, at 136.

international and on the national level.[234] Stengel polemicized against German social democrats as well as against pacifists. The enemy lurked everywhere—German angst at the end of the nineteenth century.

Carl Lueder was again a particularly vocal protagonist in the realist rejection of world peace, also referring to the well-known correspondence between Moltke and Bluntschli in November and December 1881.[235] Lueder's remarks suggest that he ultimately preformulated Moltke's argument in his reply to Bluntschli. In a lecture in Berlin in March 1880, Lueder stated that 'perpetual peace is a dream' ('*der ewige Frieden ist ein Taum*').[236] Moreover, the bellicist Lueder claimed that

> [w]ar is necessary for the attainment of the greatest common task, humanity cannot do without its discipline, it is the first to develop many brilliant sides and virtues of human history, it alone protects against pleasure-seeking laziness, against the curse of inaction, and a disgusting plunge into materialism.[237]

Lueder claimed that he had sent this lecture to Moltke before the latter's correspondence with Bluntschli. He also received Moltke's 'hitherto unpublished reply' to this letter on 21 June 1880—'and thus half a year earlier than [Moltke's] letter to Bluntschli' was written.[238] In his reply, Lueder made it clear that Moltke had agreed with him:

> Misery, sickness, suffering, and war are given elements in God's world order. After all, the so-called 'peaceful nature' is nothing but struggle and extermination. Where would the development of mankind have got to without those powerful means of coercion?[239]

Had Moltke adopted Lueder's formulation? In any case, what *is* certain is that the general and the lawyer were in agreement: perpetual peace was only a dream—'and not even a beautiful dream'.[240] Rather, war had to be used to sustain one's own people and the *Machtstaat*.

In the bellicose orientation of many *Clausewitzians*,[241] the assertion of a 'free right to go to war' was accompanied by a glorification of violence beyond legal

---

[234] Ibid., at 132.
[235] Chapter 9.
[236] Lueder (n. 155), at 210.
[237] Ibid.
[238] Ibid.
[239] Ibid.
[240] 'Moltke to Bluntschli (11 December 1880)', in T.E. Holland (ed.), *Letters to 'The Times' Upon War and Neutrality (1881-1909): With Some Commentary* (1909) 24; the German original can be found in H. von Moltke (ed.), *Gesammelte Schriften und Denkwürdigkeiten*, vol. 5 (1892), at 194 ff.
[241] As I already indicated above, the bellicist lawyers went beyond Clausewitz, who, especially in his late writings *On War*, showed no sign of bellicism. I thus put the *Clausewitzians* in italics since they referred to Clausewitz, while the bellicists among them at times even contradicted Clausewitz's political theory of war. On the latter, see Chapter 3.3.

limitations: perpetual peace was replaced by a plea for eternal war as a continuum of human history. Every law against war was rejected. War was not to be forbidden. It was to be perpetuated.

7.5 Varieties of Realism: Between Positivism and Bellicism

Arguments in favour of war in legal discourse noticeably increased in the *Kaiserreich*. In his book of 1888, Rettich had wanted to establish a purely 'positive right to go to war', which was not conceived as a bellicose but supposedly legal argument. Lueder, Meurer, Stengel et al. were different. They clearly called the 'right to war' for what it was: a political—or even military—justification of unrestricted warfare in the name of national honour.

Two Variations of a Thesis

What should become clear in the comparison between Rettich and Lueder et al. is that two varieties of the thesis of *liberum ius ad bellum* emerged in the *Kaiserreich*: a purely positivist and a bellicose variant.

The two varieties were related to each other and ultimately supported the same primacy of politics against the liberal primacy of law. However, the bellicist reading according to Lueder, Meurer et al. supplemented the 'positivist' thesis, which was based on a political primacy and the instrumental conception of war, with a military primacy and an existential conception of war. Yet, the purely positivist variety of *liberum ius ad bellum* continued to be advocated in parallel. For example, Emanuel Ullmann, Holtzendorff's successor in Munich from 1889 and author of the most important textbook on international law in the German Empire alongside that of Liszt,[242] argued that every war was legal because a sovereign state understood only its own policy as legally relevant.[243] And Berlin lawyer Paul Heilborn, whom Wilhelm Grewe cites in his *Epochen* to justify the thesis of the 'free right to wage war',[244] agreed with Ullmann: 'Today's international law', Heilborn wrote, knew no causes of war—

> no rules about when wars may be waged. If a state wants to use its own self, it may start war at any time. Violence is therefore absolutely permitted in the intercourse of states.[245]

---

[242] Koskenniemi (n. 4), at 224.
[243] Ullmann (n. 164), at 313.
[244] See Chapter 3.2.
[245] P. Heilborn, *Grundbegriffe des Völkerrechts* (1912), at 23.

Where there was no prohibition of war under treaty law, war was permitted. Like Rettich, Ullmann and Heilborn argued primarily in a legal positivist manner—although in Ullmann's case this formalism was expressed in a more sociologically oriented legal language.[246]

However, the two variants of the thesis of *liberum ius ad bellum* were neither explicitly contrasted nor clearly distinguished. Heilborn, for example, referred positively to *both* the positivist Rettich and the bellicist Lueder: the errors of the theory of war as a legal remedy, according to Heilborn, had been noticed by many.[247] Yet Lueder and Rettich, Heilborn observed, had 'so convincingly demonstrated' these errors that their remarks could be referred to without further ado.[248] Although Heilborn praised Lueder and Rettich for their rejection of the doctrine of 'just war' in nineteenth-century international legal theory, he also criticized both of them for the methodology they used. According to Heilborn, Lueder failed to answer the question of which part of international law war belonged to.[249] From this critique, an implicit criticism of Lueder's existential concept of war can be derived, for legal scholars should not be satisfied with statements such as war is a 'fact of life'.[250]

Here, Heilborn's position was closer to Rettich's,[251] who had also complained about the lack of legal norms in the field of *ius ad/contra bellum*. After all, this positivist criticism also reflected the actual pursuit of a stronger regulation of the prohibition of war. However, Heilborn also criticized Rettich's methodological approach.[252] By claiming that a state was always competent to declare war if its necessary purpose could only be achieved 'by warlike means' and not through prior peaceful negotiation, according to Heilborn, the self-declared 'positivist' Rettich had himself 'confused morality and law'. The 'formal requirement of peaceful negotiation' established by Rettich was neither proven nor 'transformed into a legally relevant fact'.[253] For Heilborn, the limitations to the 'positive right to war' introduced by Rettich were mere moralizing. Ironically, Heilborn now considered Rettich too 'non-positivist'. In the legal discourse at the end of the nineteenth century, positivism became a quality seal that no one deserved to receive.

According to Heilborn, a lawyer was not allowed to work with ethical, military, and psychological principles and Rettich violated the former principle, while Lueder violated the second and third.[254]

---

[246] Koskenniemi (n. 4), at 224 ff.
[247] *Ibid.*, at 330.
[248] *Ibid.*
[249] *Ibid.*, at 327.
[250] *Ibid.*
[251] Rettich (n. 13).
[252] Heilborn (n. 245), at 332.
[253] *Ibid.*
[254] *Ibid.*, at 330–2.

Radical Positivism beyond Germany: A Glimpse at Europe

But what was the situation outside Germany? Did both versions of the thesis of the 'free right to wage war' exist there as well? Perhaps needless to say, a German 'special path' in late nineteenth-century international legal discourse, the existence of which I expressly assert here, can logically only be established if the thesis of *liberum ius ad bellum* cannot also be found in other countries at that time. So, was this the case?

The impression from my comparative analysis of international legal scholarship of the nineteenth century is actually mixed. What is striking, however, is that the realist triad of facticity, absolute sovereignty, and necessity of war in the sense of Lueder et al. was in fact a German peculiarity. This school of thought, which glorified war and despised peace and law, can indeed only be found in in its full-fledged form in the *Kaiserreich*. This 'special path', which has so far been completely overlooked in research on nineteenth-century *ius ad bellum*, therefore undoubtedly existed.

However, it turns out that the radical positivist, non-bellicist version of *liberum ius ad bellum* à la Rettich or Heilborn was also occasionally advocated in textbooks by renowned lawyers outside Germany.[255] For example, British international legal scholar Thomas Joseph Lawrence, professor at the universities of Cambridge and Chicago, wrote that war, whether just or unjust, right or wrong, was a fact.[256] Lassa Oppenheim saw it similarly.[257] And the American lawyer Roland Roberts Foulke from Philadelphia asked: 'War is fighting, and there is nothing abnormal about a fighting man, so why should men fighting in a body be abnormal?'[258]

John Westlake, at that time professor of international law at Cambridge and member of the *Institut de Droit International*, formulated it in a particularly succinct way. He argued that international law, with regard to the legitimacy of war, 'says its last word ... when it pronounces the demand or the complaint to be legitimate or illegitimate, and if possible, offers arbitration'.[259] Nevertheless, according to Westlake, international law had to stand aside if a peaceful solution was not possible:

> [T]he want of organisation in the world of states compels the law which was concerned with their dispute to stand aside while they fight the quarrel out, in obedience not to the natural law of philosophers, which is a rule prescribing conduct,

---

[255] For the following paragraphs, see also Simon (n. 10).
[256] T.J. Lawrence, *The Principles of International Law* (2nd edn, 1895), at 292.
[257] L.F.L. Oppenheim, *International Law. A Treatise* (3rd edn, 1920), at 79 ff.
[258] Foulke (n. 164), at 130 ff.
[259] J. Westlake, *International Law* (2nd edn, 1910), at 56.

but to that of the natural historian, which is a record of the habits of the species, good or bad.[260]

This passage is quite telling here: for radical positivists like Westlake, Rettich, Heilborn, or L. Oppenheim, war was not a desirable fact. It was simply that: a fact. Since no treaty law had yet been developed to prohibit or limit war on the *ad bellum* level, under their postulate of radical positivism, this prohibition could not be derived *de lege ferenda*. Thus, positive international law could only offer mediation or, according to Westlake, 'stand aside while they [the states, HS] fight the quarrel out'.[261] The leading Italian international legal scholar of his time, Dionisio Anzilotti, professor in Rome and later judge at the Permanent Court of International Justice, argued along the same lines: 'International law cannot determine the cases in which the states are permitted to resort to war, but it can discipline the way they must wage it'.[262] *Ius in bello* was possible; *ius contra bellum* was not, these 'positivists' claimed.

This research view is described today as the thesis of 'indifference'.[263] As shown, however, even among radical positivists, law was by no means understood as indifferent to war, but rather powerless against it. This, however, made all the difference: radical positivists did not glorify war, they sometimes even portrayed it as a scandal. At the same time, they criticized the lack of a positivist norms on war. Randall Lesaffer is right when he asserts that radical positivists at the end of the nineteenth century were ultimately no longer prepared to allow rights and duties to apply that had not (yet) been formulated in international treaties.[264] As Lesaffer has correctly argued: they threw in the towel.[265] This distinguished them from liberal lawyers such as Bluntschli or Schücking—and led them to advocate a thesis that, at least when it came to the basic features, they shared with bellicists and that ultimately contradicted all principles of cooperative law in the nineteenth century. This assumption amounted to absolute political arbitrariness.

---

[260] *Ibid.*
[261] *Ibid.*, at 56.
[262] D. Anzilotti, *Corso di diritto internazionale* (1915), at 185.
[263] Bothe, 'Friedenssicherung und Kriegsrecht', in W. Graf Vitzthum (ed.), *Völkerrecht* (4th edn, 2014) 642, at 643; see also Bilfinger, 'Vollendete Tatsache und Völkerrecht', 15 *Zeitschrift für ausländisches öffentliches Recht und Völkerrecht: ZaöRV* (1953/54) 453.
[264] Lesaffer, 'Peace through Law. The Hague Peace Conferences and the Rise of the Ius Contra Bellum', in M. Abbenhuis, C.E. Barber, and A.R. Higgins (eds), *War, Peace and International Order? The Legacies of the Hague Conferences of 1899 and 1907* (2017) 31.
[265] *Ibid.*, at 37.

7.6 Conclusion: A Counter-Movement Against Liberalism

Whereas liberal lawyers throughout the nineteenth century were concerned with the possibility of limiting or even abolishing war,[266] after the Franco-Prussian War, a scholarly countermovement emerged. The latter rejected the mainstream description of war as a legal means.[267] In this process, two related but non-congruent varieties of a thesis were formulated. *First*, the thesis of indifference, or in other words: the thesis of the 'positive right to war',[268] which was advocated by radical positivists. Their main argument was that since positive law did not prohibit war, the latter was permitted. These radical positivist lawyers did *not* glorify war—some of them certainly regretted that international law did not prohibit war.

Second, in the German *Kaiserreich* of the Wilhelmine era, German legal scholars formulated a version of the thesis of *liberum ius ad bellum* which openly glorified war. To military theorists from Clausewitz to Hartmann and Moltke (the elder) as well as to right-Hegelian authors such as Treitschke and Lasson, the primacy of politics in the sense of the late Clausewitz and the primacy of the military in the sense of the young Clausewitz could coincide in the justification of the power state, but they could also come into tension with each other. However, what both variants of the thesis of *liberum ius ad bellum* had in common was the assumption that the use of force in international relations was principally legal.

This bellicose variant of *liberum ius ad bellum* has been completely overlooked in recent research—even by those researchers who have identified the radical positivists à la Rettich, Lawrence, and Anzilotti as such. In his important article on *The Evolution of International Legal Scholarship in Germany*, Anthony Carty has been one of the very few recent researchers to examine Heinrich Rettich's text on the 'positive right to war'.[269] However, Carty concluded that Rettich was a rather insignificant lawyer in Germany, and that the thesis of the 'free right to go to war' was a minor opinion in the *Kaiserreich*.

This conclusion was unjust. *First*, Rettich was widely read and cited.[270] *Second*, even Carty, whose 2008 article was pioneering when it came to research into the German discourse on the legitimacy of war in imperial Germany on the *ad bellum* level, has overlooked the bellicose tradition à la Lueder, Meurer, Zorn et al., who strongly advocated the thesis of *liberum ius ad bellum*. These proponents of a 'free right to go war' in the German Empire were by no means intellectually marginal individual cases.[271] Lueder and Meurer were two of the most important German

---

[266] Chapters 4 and 6.
[267] But see Heilborn (n. 245) and Westlake (n. 259), at 128.
[268] Rettich (n. 13).
[269] Carty (n. 5).
[270] See also Chapters 10.3.
[271] As e.g. Carty (n. 5) claims.

lawyers in the field of the laws of war. This was a robust German tradition of international legal thought.

This tradition, which, as I argue, was decisive for the formation of the thesis of the 'free right to wage war' and still resonates in scholarship today, is paradoxically hardly visible in today's research discourse—despite its enormous historical impact. However, if one wants to deconstruct the myth of *liberum ius ad bellum*, it is also necessary to uncover this buried realist discourse of war justification. This is what I have sought to do in the present chapter. The *Clausewitzian* tradition of justifying war emerged not only in its radical positivist, but especially in its bellicist variant in the German Empire of the Wilhelmine era. But did it also become dominant beyond Germany, e.g. in international relations? This is to be examined in the following chapter by juxtaposing the realist with liberal legal traditions in Germany and Europe.

8
A Hegemonic Discourse? On Mainstream(s) and Myth(s)

8.1 Introduction: The Exception to the Rule(s)

In the previous two chapters, I argued that the international legal discourse on the legitimacy of war at the end of the nineteenth century was bifurcated. While liberal international legal scholars strove for international pacification through law, realist lawyers understood the use of force in international relations as being characterized by anarchy. But which of these two legal theoretical traditions was dominant in Europe? And which one corresponded to actual political practice in the *fin de siècle*: the liberals in Kant's tradition or the realists in the (bellicose) Clausewitzian tradition?

These questions will be addressed in the following two chapters based on the levels of analysis that are central to this thesis. A comparison of realist and liberal perspectives within the theoretical discourse of international law (Chapter 8) is followed by a comparison with the discourse on political practice (Chapter 9)—deemed especially relevant since legal scholars and political practice continued to interact, as will be shown. The dichotomy of theory and practice was thus repeatedly blurred in the discourse on war and international order.

Two arguments are at the heart of what follows. *First*, I show that the liberal and realist positions in the literature on international law did not coexist. Rather, they critically—and directly—engaged with each other. They entered into a public academic dispute about the extent to which perpetual peace was possible and international violence needed to be justified. The ideal typical dichotomies that were formed here between 'ideals'/'realities', 'might'/'right', 'the power of law'/'the law of power', or 'pacifism'/'militarism' prototypically anticipated central elements of the 'First Great Debate' in International Relations theory, which is usually dated to the mid-twentieth century.[1]

Second, the comparative analysis of the theoretical and political discourses will show that among lawyers, military officers, and political elites, a political culture of justifying war emerged in the German Empire that was particularly hostile to

---

[1] Wilson, 'The Myth of the "First Great Debate"', 24 *Review of International Studies* (1998) 1; Ashworth, 'Did the Realist-Idealist Great Debate Really Happen? A Revisionist History of International Relations', 16 *International Relations* (2002) 33.

international law. This German tradition of justifying war was criticized not only by other European states but also by 'oppositional' liberal lawyers from within the Empire. The German Empire thus became an outsider in the international discourse on war and international order. It was an exception—which, however, in a dialectical sense confirmed the rule(s) of the international order.

8.2 A 'First Great Debate' between Realism and Liberalism

If we once again compare the core positions of those lawyers adopting realist and those adopting liberal arguments at the end of the nineteenth century with regard to the problem of the legitimacy of war, it is striking that they were almost antithetical to each other. Taken together, they form a photonegative (Figure 8.1).

First, while liberals wanted to limit or even abolish war, for realists, international relations were eternally characterized by war. Thus, while liberal jurists assumed the primacy of law, realists contrasted this with the primacy of politics and/or the military.

Second, while for liberals, war as legal means could be justified as self-defence or as a sanction for violated rights, realists, on the other hand, developed the thesis of *liberum ius ad bellum*, according to which only the sovereign will of the state (or even the will of the military) was decisive. While, from a liberal perspective, the justification of war was still needed, for realists, war was always permitted in international relations in the absence of a supranational praetor.

Third, whereas liberal lawyers referred to Kant's perpetual peace—arguing about whether it was feasible, but approving it in principle—realists rejected Kant's concept as a not only unattainable but also false ideal. While, on the other hand, realists referred to the young and/or old Clausewitz to legitimize and sometimes even glorify war as a means of politics, liberals rejected war as a 'continuation of politics by other means', as reprehensible, entirely in the spirit of Kant.

And finally, *fourth*, the two theoretical approaches can also be contrasted antithetically regarding the chosen methodological approaches. While liberals strove for a legal prohibition of war, they appealed to a dynamic historical understanding of law, which made a derivation of law *de lege ferenda* possible. Furthermore, they also referred to morality, civilization, and humanity. Their legal theoretical justifications were multinormative. Realist proponents of the thesis of *liberum ius ad bellum*, on the other hand, adhered to a radical positivist understanding of law, which was based on a strong historical empiricism and/or a bellicist glorification of war as a cultural catalyst.

When contrasting these theses put forward by liberal and realist legal scholars between 1871 and 1918, one is struck by the fact that they seem to be almost aligned with each other. This dichotomization of realist and liberal ideas and claims may seem like an ex-post construction. However, this is not the case. Rather, this

Liberal Legal Scholars	Realist Legal Scholars
1. Primacy of law	1. Primacy of the political / the military
2. War only justifiable by law/ to be **fully outlawed**	2. Thesis of liberum ius ad bellum
3. Positive reference to Kant: the aim of perpetual peace / Negative reference to Clausewitz: war as a political means is reprehensible	3. Positive reference to Clausewitz's theory of war / Negative reference to Kant: perpetual peace as a false ideal
4. Normative foundation: historical; de lege ferenda; multi-normative	4. Normative foundation: radical-positivist, historical; bellicist philosophy

Figure 8.1 A First Debate between Liberalism and Realism

dichotomization refers to a dispute between liberals and realists in late nineteenth-century discourse on the legitimization of war that has been largely forgotten in today's collective memory.

This finding contradicts the 'First Great Debate' in International Relations theory between realists and idealists in the 1930s and 1940s, a standard narrative of the political science subdiscipline of International Relations. The idealist/liberal tradition of thought that dominated at that time was dismissed as naïve after two world wars. It was replaced by realism in the sense of a Kuhnian paradigm shift. E.H. Carr's *The Twenty Years' Crisis. 1919–1939* (1939) was of especial importance in the genesis of the 'First Great Debate'. In this work, Carr presented realism and liberalism as the two most important poles of International Relations—and thus created the impression that the representatives of these directions were in a theoretical dispute with each other.[2] Especially since the end of the 1990s, however, it has been argued that this 'First Great Debate' was a myth[3] that distorted the history of the discipline in the twentieth century in favour of realism: for there was no actual debate at all.[4]

My argument is that this debate did indeed exist—but not in the 1920s. Rather, it began fifty years earlier! Between 1871 and 1918, liberal and realist legal scholars entered into a dispute with each other in lectures, publications, and letters about the legitimacy of war and the possibility of peace. The similarity of this debate, which *did* take place, to Carr's narrative of the supposed 'First Great Debate' of the 1930s and 1940s is striking. For, as I have shown above on the basis of Heinrich Rettich's polemic of 1888, realism also entered the fray as a reaction to the supposedly naïve idealism of liberal thinkers.

One possible objection might be that the protagonists of what was possibly the first theoretical dispute on war and peace in modern international thought were

---

[2] Devetak, 'An Introduction to International Relations: The Origins and Changing Agendas of a Discipline', in R. Devetak, A. Burke, and J. George (eds), *An Introduction to International Relations* (2017) 1, at 13.
[3] Wilson (n. 1); Ashworth (n. 1).
[4] Devetak (n. 2), at 11.

not political scientists, but lawyers. This argument, which focuses on disciplinary boundaries, is implausible for two main reasons. *First*, legal scholars were to become extremely important for the formation of modern International Relations. One notable example is the Frankfurt lawyer Hans Joachim Morgenthau, who became the founder of American realism in twentieth-century International Relations theory.[5] *Second*, however, disciplinary boundaries were not impermeable in the theoretical dispute over the normativity of war in the (late) nineteenth century. Liberal lawyers justified their arguments by recourse to philosophy (especially Kant), political analysts, and, last but not least, the peace movement.[6] Bellicose realists, on the other hand, referred to military authors (first and foremost Clausewitz, but also contemporaries such as Hartmann, Moltke, and Gläser), to philosophers such as Hegel and Lasson, to historians such as Treitschke, and sometimes also to Darwin's 'theory of evolution by natural selection'.[7]

And, possibly in contrast to the so-called 'First Great Debate' in International Relations, liberals and realists at the end of the nineteenth century also referred to the arguments of the opposing side in order to discredit them and to distinguish their own discursive position. This debate, which has been buried to this day, will be outlined in the following.

Un Dialogue de Sourds? From the Excavation Sketches of a Buried Debate (Bluntschli vs Moltke)

Today, much of the debate between liberals and realists in the late nineteenth-century discourse on the legitimacy of war justifications is buried under a thick layer of one-sided memory (which alone makes the popularity of the thesis of the 'free right to wage war' possible to this day). It is therefore necessary to uncover this debate between the two contrary positions. To do this, I start with a discourse fragment that even today stands out clearly from the more deeply buried parts of the contemporary debate—and at the same time underlines the transdisciplinary character of the nineteenth-century debate. This discourse fragment is the well-known exchange of letters between the liberal Johann Caspar Bluntschli and Field Marshal Helmuth von Moltke as a representative of the realist *Clausewitzian* tradition.

The exchange of letters began in November 1880, when the *Institut de Droit International*, in collaboration with Bluntschli, had just published the *Manuel: Les Lois de la Guerre sur terre*, which was to become known as the *Oxford Manual*. The lawyers had sent their Manual to numerous governments in the hope that it would be considered by political practice and implemented accordingly. Bluntschli had

---

[5] See Chapter 10.3.
[6] See Chapter 6.
[7] See Chapter 7.

already stressed the necessity of this during the Franco-Prussian War, in his speech on the occasion of the birthday of the Grand Duke Karl Friedrich on 22 November 1870.[8] In a short letter to Moltke, Bluntschli referred to the Manual, highlighting that it had been drafted in an 'honest endeavour' to bring the interests of the armies into harmony with the necessary principles of law and the needs of the 'civilized world'.[9] According to the liberal professor, a language was chosen for this purpose that was also comprehensible to what he called 'the simple mind of the common man and the common soldier'.[10]

Bluntschli and his co-editors hoped that Moltke would take good note of the *Oxford Manual* and put it to practical use in the Imperial German Army. Addressing Moltke was quite logical. He was chief of the German Great General Staff (*Großer Generalstab*), which de facto had a particularly strong position within the German political system, although it was not even mentioned in the Constitution of the German Empire.[11] In his role, Field Marshal Moltke could have worked towards compliance with the laws of war. Moltke certainly replied to Bluntschli—in other words, he corresponded not only with realists like Lueder, who were close to his own position. In his reply on 11 December 1880, Moltke acknowledged that the *Oxford Manual* sought a balance between humanity and the necessity of war.[12] However, he was not keen to limit the necessity of war at all. Instead, Moltke openly revealed himself as a bellicist. According to him,

> Perpetual peace is a dream, and is not even a beautiful dream. War is an element in the order of the world ordained by God. In it the noblest virtues of mankind are developed; courage and the abnegation of self, faithfulness to duty, and the spirit of sacrifice: the soldier gives his life. Without war the world would stagnate, and lose itself in materialism.[13]

Moltke's notorious dictum of perpetual peace being a dream—'and not even a beautiful dream'—was in the realist tradition already outlined above.[14] This position

---

[8] See Chapter 6.2.
[9] Quoted from H. von Moltke (ed.), *Gesammelte Schriften und Denkwürdigkeiten*, vol. 5 (1892), at 193 f.
[10] Ibid.; on the antinomies of large parts of liberal legal doctrine in the late nineteenth century, see Chapter 6.4.
[11] Khan, 'Der ewige Friede ist ein Traum, und nicht einmal ein schöner. Anmerkungen zu einem Briefwechsel zwischen Johann Caspar Bluntschli und Helmuth Graf von Moltke', in T. Groh, F. Knur, C. Köster, S. Maus, and T. Roeder (eds), *Verfassungsrecht, Völkerrecht, Menschenrechte – vom Recht im Zentrum der internationalen Beziehungen. Festschrift für Ulrich Fastenrath zum 70. Geburtstag* (2019) 159, at 166 f.
[12] Ibid.; N. Meier, *Warum Krieg? Die Sinndeutung des Krieges in der deutschen Militärelite, 1871–1945* (2012), at 124.
[13] 'Moltke to Bluntschli (11 December 1880)', in T.E. Holland (ed.), *Letters to 'The Times' Upon War and Neutrality (1881–1909): With Some Commentary* (1909) 24; for the German original, see H. von Moltke (ed.), *Gesammelte Schriften und Denkwürdigkeiten*, vol. 5 (1892), at 194 f.
[14] See Chapter 7.

may not have been unusual for a member of the military. Yet the vehemence with which Moltke questioned the validity of international law was astonishing even for contemporaries. In his letter to Bluntschli, Moltke wrote that in view of the St. Petersburg Declaration of 11 December 1868 (banning explosive munitions under 400 grams), he could

> by no means profess agreement that 'the weakening of the military forces of the enemy' is the only lawful procedure in war. No, you must attack all the resources of the enemy's Government, its finances, its railways, its stores, and even its prestige.[15]

In complete contrast to Bluntschli, who had taken the Franco-Prussian War as the occasion for his demand of the codification of the laws of war, Moltke argued that '[t]hus energetically, and yet with a moderation previously unknown, was the late war against France conducted'.[16] As Daniel-Erasmus Khan has recently rightly pointed out, Moltke, as the highest-ranking member of military staff in the German Empire, openly questioned a central norm of international law with this 'hitherto as far as can be seen little heeded statement'.[17] In this argumentation against the St. Petersburg Declaration, Manfred Messerschmidt has argued that Moltke had already 'envisaged the concept of a total war to be waged with the means of the time'.[18]

Not surprisingly, given Moltke's anti-legalistic stance, the Chief of the Great General Staff advocated a 'free right to go to war'. This becomes particularly clear in a letter Moltke wrote to the pacifist Goubareff in February 1881.[19] Goubareff, a Russian exile in France, had discovered Moltke's reply letter to Bluntschli in a newspaper. He wrote a letter to Moltke, in which he called war a crime. In his response, Moltke flatly contradicted Goubareff. 'You unconditionally declare war a crime', Moltke wrote, only to go on to define it in exactly the opposite way, as 'a last but perfectly justified means of asserting the existence, independence, and honour of a state'.[20]

For Moltke, war was thus also the last resort in international relations—but one that the state was allowed to use arbitrarily, beyond international norms, to assert itself in the struggle against other states. To justify this right of the state to fight, Moltke referred not only to the 'national honour' that had to be asserted, but also drawing on social Darwinian notions to 'nature' as the 'struggle of what is evolving

---

[15] Moltke to Bluntschli (n. 13), at 25.
[16] *Ibid.*
[17] Khan (n. 11), at 171 f.
[18] Messerschmidt, 'Völkerrecht und "Kriegsnotwendigkeit" in der deutschen militärischen Tradition seit den Einigungskriegen', 6 *German Studies Review* (1983) 237, at 241.
[19] Meier (n. 12), at 125.
[20] '... *vollkommen gerechtfertigtes Mittel, das Bestehen, die Unabhängigkeit und die Ehre eines Staates zu behaupten*', quoted after *ibid.*, at 125 f.

against what exists' ('*Kampf des Werdenden gegen das Bestehende*'). Nationalism and naturalism went hand in hand. But the Field Marshal was also deeply religious. In his view, war was a 'providence of God' ('*Fügung Gottes*').[21] Moltke's advocacy of *liberum ius ad bellum* was, in a sense, multinormative.

Bluntschli replied to Moltke's letter in a decidedly polite manner. Once again, he underlined the different perspectives of the military and the legal profession. He emphasized that for the military, the security and victory of the army always took precedence over the interests of the uninvolved population. The lawyer, on the other hand, could not free himself from the duty to ensure the indispensable legal guarantees for private individuals in the territories occupied by the enemy, Bluntschli claimed.[22] Bluntschli softened his position towards Moltke. However, this could also be read as the liberal ingratiating himself with the realist. It was true, Bluntschli wrote to Moltke, that some members of the *Institut* would not give up hope that mankind would one day succeed in replacing war between sovereign states with international jurisdiction ('*justice internationale organisée*'). 'But the body of the Institut, as a whole, well knows that that hope has no chance of being realised in our time', Bluntschli assured Moltke.[23] The *Institut*, Bluntschli continued, therefore limited itself to facilitating the legal process for 'trifling disputes' and to strengthening the legal order *in* war.[24] With this, Bluntschli emphasized once again that with the *Oxford Manual*, the *Institut* was not pursuing more ambitious peace designs but instead a project that it fundamentally shared with many military leaders: the 'humanization of war'.

The central concern of many liberal jurists to abolish war in the long term[25] took a back seat in Bluntschli's response to Moltke. It was precisely this focus of international legal doctrine on *ius in bello* that was to give rise to positivist critics such as Rettich.[26] Since Bluntschli was keen not to appear to Moltke as a utopian, in his letter, he became an apologist. Bluntschli even wrote that military leaders deserved most of the credit for the improvement of customs of war: 'Brutal and barbarous pillage was prohibited by generals before jurists were convinced of its illegality', he wrote.[27]

Bluntschli's ingratiation was not at all rhetorically clumsy, for in tipping his hat to the military leader, the jurist was at the same time reminding Moltke that other military leaders had fewer reservations about 'humanizing' war. He confronted Moltke with his deviation from the claimed norms of his own profession. Bluntschli ended his letter with a strong plea for international law, which

---

[21] *Ibid.*, at 125.
[22] 'Bluntschli's Reply to Count von Moltke (Christmas 1880)', in T.E. Holland (ed.), *Letters to 'The Times' Upon War and Neutrality (1881–1909): With Some Commentary* (1909) 26, at 27.
[23] *Ibid.*
[24] *Ibid.*
[25] See Chapter 6.
[26] See Chapter 7.2.
[27] Bluntschli's Reply (n. 22), at 27.

ran counter to his earlier ingratiation with Moltke. He explicitly distanced himself from Cicero's dictum of the silence of law in war (*inter arma enim silent leges*): at any rate, Bluntschli was convinced 'that this abominable error can but increase the unavoidable sufferings and evils of war without necessity...'.[28]

Against 'Prussian Ethics' (Pfau)

The correspondence between Bluntschli and Moltke was not the end of the debate between liberals and realists on the nature and legitimacy of war and peace, but rather its beginning. In particular, Moltke's dictum of perpetual peace being a dream—'and not even a beautiful' one—provoked indignation. It was taken up by numerous German scholars and daily newspapers. The emerging debate continued to be transdisciplinary: lawyers, military officers, and pacifists were all part of the discussion.

The political writer Ludwig Pfau, for example, countered Moltke in an essay written in 1895 entitled *Prussian Ethics* (*Preußische Ethik*). Pfau argued that states, for as long as they existed, had always suffered from injustice: 'and the highest expression of injustice is war. It is nothing other than predatory murder organized by the state.' The pacifist rejected the idea of the army as the school of the nation, which was widespread among members of the Prussian military and realist lawyers such as Meurer.[29] For Pfau, the army was not a school of the nation, but a 'school of sacrifice' ('*Schule der Opferung*') for those 'poor devils who have to pull others' chestnuts out of the fire'.[30] Pfau clearly rejected the realist understanding of the role of war in history. In his view, war had never been a catalyst for culture. It did not serve civilization or (inter)national progress, but only ruin, death, and destruction.

While Pfau clearly rejected the 'Prussian virtues' ('*Preußischen Tugenden*') propagated by the military and realist lawyers as unethical, the pacifist also recognized legitimate violence. Pfau acknowledged that there were also defensive wars that the attacked did not wage of their own free choice.[31] Self-defence remained legitimate. Nevertheless, 'on the whole', Pfau wrote, war was 'nothing but the crudest materialism', its real object 'the preservation and increase of power and property in the hands of the dynasties and ruling classes'. War was a political instrument of the ruling classes. As such, it could never be acceptable.

Ludwig Pfau ended his essay optimistically. Entirely in the spirit of Kant's teleology of history, he wrote that one 'fine day' and 'led by victorious reason', the nations would put a decisive end to the 'bloody mischief' of war. Once again, Pfau

---

[28] *Ibid.*, at 29.
[29] See Chapter 7.4.
[30] Pfau, 'Preußische Ethik', in L. Pfau (ed.), *Politisches und Polemisches aus den nachgelassenen Schriften, mit einem Vorwort von Dr. Ernst Ziel* (1895) 275, at 275.
[31] *Ibid.*

personally turned against Moltke. For even if an abolition of the war made 'battle theorists' ('*Schlachtendenker*') like Moltke fear that 'in the absence of a godly brawl, the mould might get into their brains, we other people, however, who still have enough to think about, even if there are no more battles, ... would bless the day when Field Marshals are no longer needed'.[32] Ludwig Pfau wanted to eradicate war and, with it, Moltke's profession.

Plea for a Public Science Beyond Realism (Lucas)

Moltke's letter to Bluntschli was not only taken up in the daily press and by pacifists, but also in academic journals. The French lawyer Charles Lucas provided the first contribution to the jurisprudential debate in two journal commentaries: one in the journal *Le Nord* on 17 February 1881 on the occasion of Moltke's letter to Bluntschli, and another in the *Revue Critique de Législation* in March 1881 on the occasion of Moltke's letter to Goubareff.

In his first letter in February, Lucas wrote that there were only two forces in the world: 'that of law and that of force'.[33] The French lawyer claimed that Prussia had produced two famous philosophers—Kant and Hegel. Each of them, he wrote, was an outstanding philosophical representative of one of these two poles: Kant had proclaimed the primacy of law in a rational order, for the observance of which force had to serve as a material guarantee, Lucas claimed; Hegel, on the other hand, reversed the roles of law and violence and, proclaiming the right of the strongest, made violence the incarnation of law.[34] According to Lucas, while Kant proclaimed peace through law, Hegel deified victorious war. In view of his letter to Bluntschli, Lucas felt that Moltke was clearly on Hegel's side[35]—and thus, according to Lucas's interpretation of Hegel, on the side of violence. For Moltke deviated strongly from Kant's teaching. The St. Petersburg Declaration of 1868, which Moltke disapproved of, Lucas wrote, was at the same time a declaration in the spirit of 'the Königsberg philosopher himself'.[36] According to Lucas, it was endorsed by all who were of the opinion 'that in waging war one must remember to make possible the work of

---

[32] *Ibid.*
[33] '*Il n'y a que deux puissances en ce monde: celle du droit et celle de la force.*' C. Lucas, *Civilisation de la guerre: Observations sur les lois de la guerre et l'arbitrage international, à l'occasion de la lettre de M. le comte de Moltke à M. le professeur Bluntschli* (1873).
[34] '*La Prusse a produit deux philosophes célèbres, l'un, Kant, proclame, dans l'ordre rationnel et providentiel, la primauté du droit au respect duquel la force doit servir de garantie matérielle; l'autre, Hegel, intervertit les rôles du droit et de la force, ou plutôt il fait de la force l'incarnation du droit en proclamant celui du plus fort, et dans son idolâtrie de la guerre, il va jusqu'à la déification du succès.*' *Ibid.*, at 5.
[35] '*On voit que la doctrine de M. le comte de Moltke s'éloigne singulièrement de celle de Kant pour se rapprocher beaucoup de celle d'Hegel*', *ibid.*
[36] '*... est celle même du philosophe de Königsberg...*', *ibid.*, at 7.

reconciliation in peace, so as not to be a source of national hatred'.[37] Moltke, on the other hand, mocked those who sought the rule of peace, Lucas argued.[38]

In the eyes of the French legal scholar, Moltke in 'his glorification of war' was clearly a militarist. Yet for Lucas, military leaders did *not* have to be militarists: he even contrasted Moltke's 'militarism' with the idea of the 'military spirit'. Lucas counted the loyalty and sacrifice of the soldier as being part of the latter—virtues that, according to Lucas, no one admired more than himself. These virtues, however, were not nourished by the glorification of war, but 'by the feeling of love for the fatherland, by the principle of law, and the duty of self-defence for the integrity of its territory and respect for its independence'.[39] Accordingly, fighting was honourable *only* in accordance with the law and in defence of the fatherland. This was a clear recourse to the core norms of legitimate use of force in the nineteenth century which I have reconstructed in Part I of this book.

In his response to the correspondence between Bluntschli and Moltke, Lucas positioned himself *expressis verbis* on the side of liberal, Kantian legal doctrine and thus in support of Bluntschli. Lucas congratulated the co-author of the *Oxford Manual* for his competent commitment to 'the progressive development of a general legal conviction … aimed at uniting all civilized peoples'.[40]

Nevertheless, Lucas also criticized Bluntschli's remarks in his correspondence with Moltke. It was 'undoubtedly good and useful to think about ways and means to alleviate the evils of war', Lucas wrote. However, he continued, wisdom advised above all to 'seek those [ways and means, HS] which prevent them as far as possible'. Lucas was obviously disturbed by Bluntschli's strategic ingratiation with Moltke. Limiting scholarship to *ius in bello* was not sufficient: according to Lucas, liberal international legal scholarship should rather devote itself to eradicating war as a means of politics, *ius contra bellum*. In his article in the *Revue Critique de Législation* of March 1881, Lucas made clear that he was ultimately not very encouraged by the 'precedent' set by the correspondence between Moltke and Bluntschli.[41] From Lucas's point of view, Bluntschli's approach of offering advice to governments on *ius in bello* as a liberal scholar was ultimately the wrong way to go. To Lucas (quite in the spirit of Kant), it seemed more sensible for liberal legal scholars to endorse public opinion on international law:

---

[37] '… *elle sera approuvée par tous ceux qui pensent avec Kant, que dans la conduite de la guerre il faut songer à rendre possible à la paix l'œuvre de réconciliation, afin de ne pas éterniser les haines nationales*', ibid.

[38] Ibid.

[39] Ibid.

[40] '*développement progressif d'une conviction juridique générale qui tend à unir tous les peuples civilisés*', ibid., at 9.

[41] '*Je ne trouve par fort encourageant le précédent de l'accueil fait par le comté de Moltke à l'hommage empressé du Manuel dû à l'initiative personnelle de M. le conseiller privé Bluntschli*', ibid., at 13.

In every respect, then, I repeat, public opinion must be addressed. This is the most correct, the most effective, and the most dignified process for science, because any ties to officials can only more or less hinder the independence of its situation, the freedom of its language, and the affirmation of its principles.[42]

But Lucas did not want to be a utopian, either. In his article of March 1881, he not only opposed Moltke's bellicism but also relativized the position of the radical pacifist Goubareff: although war was a crime to 'M. Goubareff', to Lucas[43] it was 'only a crime when ambition and conquest are at stake'. War in self-defence, on the other hand, was something Lucas wanted to maintain as legitimate, as did Pfau. After all, Lucas claimed, war was a right of legitimate defence 'when it protects the independence of the country and the integrity of its territory'. In his discussion of Moltke, Lucas not only distanced himself from realists, but also referred to debates between liberals about whether war should be contained or abolished in a discipline that was located somewhere between Grotius and Kant at the end of the nineteenth century.[44]

Peace through Law—or through 'Holy War' (Saripolos)

The correspondence between Bluntschli and Moltke was well noticed and actively received abroad. The Greek lawyer Nikolaos J. Saripolos, a member of the *Institut de Droit International*, mentioned the correspondence and Lucas's reaction in an article in the *Revue de Droit International* on the Greek-Turkish Question after the Russo-Turkish War of 1877/78. In his article, Saripolos agreed with Bluntschli and Lucas in their plea for the legalization of war.

At the same time, however, Saripolos's text once again illustrates what I have referred to above as the 'antinomies of the "gentle civilizers"'.[45] For Saripolos had no intention of denying 'that civilization can advance through war'.[46] In order to argue in favour of what he understood as the civilizing force of war, Saripolos used nationalist and anti-Turkish images and narratives. Europe had to be 'eternally grateful to the sacrifices of the Greeks' as well as to the Eastern Roman Emperor Herakleios because of their struggles 'against the victorious hordes of

---

[42] 'A tous les points de vue donc c'est à l'opinion publique, je le répète, qu'il faut selon moi, s'adresser. C'est le procédé le plus correct, le plus efficace et le plus digne pour la science, car toute attache officielle ne peut que gêner plus ou moins l'indé pendance de sa situation, la liberté de son langage, et l'affirmation de ses principes.' Lucas, Nécessité d'un Congrès Scientifique International relatif à la Civilisation de la Guerre et à la Codification du Droit des Gens (1873), at 13.
[43] *Ibid.*
[44] See Chapter 6.
[45] See Chapter 6.4.
[46] Saripolos, 'Nous partageons l'avis de ces derniers, sans toutefois méconnaître que la civilisation peut avancer par le moyen de la guerre', 13 Revue de droit international et de législation comparée (1881) 231, at 243.

Muhammad's successors'. Again and again, anything non-European was considered 'barbaric': 'Islamism', Saripolos claimed, only knew 'the power of arms and bows its head only to this'.[47]

Moreover, Saripolos referred to another classic liberal narrative justifying war. He expanded Lucas's formula of the evil of aggression and the right of defensive war as follows: 'If war is a right in the case of self-defence, it becomes sacred when it aims to restore liberty with all the rights and guarantees that are due to it.' According to Saripolos, a war of national unification was not only a just, but also a 'holy war'. Proof, in his view, was the Greek Revolution of 1821.[48] Even at the end of the nineteenth century, 'positivist' international law still spoke of 'holy wars'.

'A Prism without Colours and Shapes' (Beauharnais and Martens)

Even more strident criticism of Moltke's letter to Bluntschli than that of Saripolos was voiced in the same issue of the *Revue de Droit International* by two Russian authors: liberal lawyer Fedor Fedorovich Martens and Prince Nikolaus de Beauharnais, a member of the Russian military. In their correspondence, they clearly distanced themselves from Moltke's reply to Bluntschli.

Nikolaus de Beauharnais wrote in his letter to Martens on 19 February 1881 that Moltke's mistrust of the practical significance of the *Oxford Manual*, with 'all due respect for the authority of such an outstanding man as the Field Marshal ... seems somewhat exaggerated'.[49] Behind this courtesy hid a fundamental criticism of the German army leadership. For according to Beauharnais, Moltke's disrespect for the *Oxford Manual* was characterized by a desire to harm the enemy in war as arbitrarily as possible. According to Beauharnais, this was a specifically German perspective, 'a view fortunately not shared by other armies'. In contrast, Beauharnais himself, he claimed, was of the 'firm conviction that the level of modern civilization corresponds perfectly' to the humane principles that the *Oxford Manual* seeks to put into practice. The application of these principles depended entirely on the leaders, their moral development, their knowledge of the law, and, above all, on the requirements of the respective high command. Exceptional cases justifying a deviation were, 'if they existed at all', very rare.[50]

Nikolaus de Beauharnais skilfully combined his critique of Moltke with an emphasis on Russia's (alleged) loyalty to international law. To do so, the prince referred to his deployment in the Balkans as a Lt. General during the Russo-Turkish War of 1877/78.[51] Unfortunately, as Beauharnais pointed out, the *Oxford Manual*

[47] 'L'Islamismene connaît que la force des armes et ne courbe son front que devant elle.' Ibid.
[48] Ibid., at 244.
[49] de Leuchtènberg, 'Lettre de S. Â: î. le Nicolas de Leuchtènberg à M. de Martens', 13 *Revue de droit international et de législation comparée* (1881) 307, at 307 f.
[50] Ibid.
[51] Ibid.

did not exist at that time. In the absence of the Manual, precise rules, and therefore thorough knowledge of international law, had to be guided solely 'by logic and common sense'. Beauharnais reported anarchy in the region: 'Theft, robbery, arson, and murder were perpetrated on all sides.'[52] Moreover, he wrote, regular Turkish troops had committed cruel mutilations of the Russian wounded. In contrast, he claimed, the Russian army had retained a high level of moral discipline: 'Because they themselves refrained from excesses of violence and thus showed respect for the lives and property of the inhabitants, it was possible to master the situation.'[53]

According to Beauharnais, however, the allegedly exemplary behaviour of the Russian army in the Balkans was the international exception. Beauharnais contended that if this practice was not widespread, it was because 'most commanders do not know these laws and their application is not prescribed'.[54] This was once again a clear criticism of Moltke, who had just deliberately spoken out against the implementation of the *Oxford Manual* in Germany. The military leader Moltke was to be embarrassed and unmasked by the military leader Beauharnais.

Martens was even more explicit. In his reply to Beauharnais on 23 February 1881, he wrote that it was known that objects changed their shape and colour depending on the prism through which they were viewed.[55] Martens criticized that, by declaring that war was 'a given element in God's world order' and the source of 'the noblest virtues of man', Moltke had obviously viewed 'these serious objects' through a prism that robbed them of their natural colours and shapes. According to Martens, through this prism, it was inevitable that Moltke would see peace as a great misfortune for humanity and would declare any attempt to codify the law of war as impractical.[56] Martens underlined that the prism of realism was unrealistic.

While Moltke wanted to guarantee unlimited military freedom of action, Martens emphasized that lawyers were obliged to regulate relations between the warring nations.[57] But Martens did not leave it at that. According to him, it was the task not only of lawyers, but also of the military leadership, to enforce compliance with the laws of war in the army.[58] A clear critique of Moltke! Moltke, Martens argued, understood military discipline to be based on the principle of arbitrariness. But this was impossible, the Russian lawyer asserted, as concrete rules of conduct were absolutely necessary for military discipline. An army's awareness that the authority of the law imposed absolute obedience on everyone, 'from the commander down to the soldier', also increased its discipline, claimed Martens.[59]

---

[52] *Ibid.*, at 308.
[53] *Ibid.*
[54] *Ibid.*, at 308 f.
[55] Martens, 'Lettre de M. de Martens à S. Â: î. le Duc Nicolas de Leuchtènberg', 13 *Revue de droit international et de législation comparée* (1881) 309, at 310.
[56] *Ibid.*
[57] *Ibid.*, at 311.
[58] *Ibid.*
[59] *Ibid.*

Like Beauharnais, Martens was keen to highlight the exemplary Russian politics of international law. Having convened the Brussels Conference of 1874, the Russian government, Martens argued, had taken the decisive step in bringing about the *Oxford Manual* of 1888—a Manual that Moltke, on the other hand, now rejected. Russia, according to Beauharnais and Martens's message, was more favourably disposed to international law than Germany—and thus ultimately, more civilized.

8.3 Defending Law against War—Defending War against Law

As I outlined in the last section, Moltke's reply to Bluntschli was clearly branded as a scandal internationally by liberal lawyers such as Bluntschli, Lucas, Martens, and Saripolos, pacifists such as Pfau and Goubareff, as well as the Russian military leader Beauharnais. But Moltke's position was also defended in the debate.

Defending War against Law (Lueder vs the Liberal Mainstream)

Unsurprisingly, Carl Lueder took Moltke's side in the academic dispute over the correspondence between Moltke and Bluntschli.[60] Lueder's arguments were again reminiscent of the realist critique in the alleged 'First Great Debate' of International Relations. Lueder accused liberals of being idealistic and unworldly. They overlooked, he argued, 'with their intrinsically noble zeal the real conditions of life, especially of war, and therefore demand what is impracticable, and desire what is not desirable'.[61] The criticism voiced by Carl Gareis was in a similar vein. Gareis complained that Bluntschli had not spoken about prevailing, but about desired law (*de lege ferenda*) in his treatises on war and peace.[62]

Lueder's criticism was particularly harsh, however, when the military profession so revered by the realist was insulted by a liberal. While Ludwig Pfau had called Moltke a useless 'battle theorist' (see above), Lueder vehemently rejected 'Pfau's crudeness' ('*Pfau'sche Rohheit*'),[63] protesting that it was 'sad and shameful that unworthiness was printed in German against the statements of "the great German army leader"'.[64] The lawyer took the military's side against a pacifist.

Interestingly, Lueder countered liberals with the same accusation that Martens had made against Molke: both sides accused each other of being out of touch

---

[60] For more on Lueder, see Chapter 7.
[61] Lueder, 'Krieg und Kriegsrecht im Allgemeinen', in F. von Holtzendorff (ed.), *Handbuch des Völkerrechts. Auf Grundlage europ. Staatspraxis*, vol. 4 (1889) 169, at 210.
[62] C. von Gareis, *Institutionen des Völkerrechts* (1888), at 37.
[63] Lueder (n. 61), at 195.
[64] *Ibid.*, at 210.

with reality. Against this backdrop, a constructive dialogue between the realist and liberal perspectives was impossible. For while realists, basing their views on *Clausewitzian* primacy, saw war as an existential and/or instrumental factor in international relations, liberals completely disagreed. They wanted to limit war in the short term and, come what may, establish a lasting legal peace in the Kantian sense in the long term. This was a dialogue of the deaf (*'un dialogue de Sourds'*).

Nevertheless, a discursive terrain for mediating positions between the military and liberal legal scholars existed. This terrain, however, was exclusively *ius in bello*. The latter limited war, but at the same time legitimized it.[65] This was thus a field where a compromise between realists and liberals could be achieved—albeit not a far-reaching one. Bluntschli was criticized by some liberals and pacifists for not making more radical demands regarding *ius contra bellum* in his correspondence with Moltke.[66] The latter's rebuff of international law was so clear, however, that it appeared unusual. It may therefore come as no surprise that few lawyers took his side. One of those realist lawyers who nevertheless did so was Carl Lueder.

Defending Law against War (the Liberal Mainstream vs Lueder)

But this was not without consequences: Lueder soon had a reputation as a militarist among international lawyers in Europe. John Westlake noted that the German notion of 'military necessity being paramount to law'[67] ('*Kriegsraison geht vor Kriegsrecht*') was particularly evident in Lueder's chapter of Holtzendorff's *Handbook*.[68] Indeed, the latter contained perhaps 'the classical passage on the doctrine', described by Westlake as 'highly pernicious'.[69] According to Westlake, scholars should not instigate a breach of law, 'Otherwise, the most elementary restraints on war, which have been handed down from antiquity, are not safe'.[70]

Walther Schücking expressed a similar opinion when he noted 'the unbelievably reactionary and uncomprehending way in which the relevant problems of international organization' were treated in Holtzendorff's *Handbook*.[71] According to Schücking, in Holtzendorff's compilation,

---

[65] Simon, 'Das Recht des Krieges', 24 *Rechtsgeschichte – Legal History* (2016) 508; see Benvenisti and Lustig, 'Monopolizing War: Codifying the Laws of War to Reassert Governmental Authority, 1856–1874', 31 *European Journal of International Law* (2020) 127; S. Moyn, *Humane. How the United States Abandoned Peace and Reinvented War* (2021), Chapter 1.

[66] Lucas (n. 33).

[67] On this notion, see Woolsey, 'Retaliation and Punishment', in J.B. Scott, *International Law, Public Law and Jurisprudence* (1917) 167, at 168.

[68] Lueder (n. 61).

[69] J. Westlake, *International Law* (2nd edn, 1910), at 126 f.

[70] *Ibid.*, at 128.

[71] W. Schücking, *Die Organisation der Welt* (1909), at 65.

a certain Professor Lueder from Erlangen offers the ingenious view that the cessation of wars is not the right cultural ideal because it contradicts the divine world order. Unfortunately, however, Lueder does not give us the sources which have so precisely informed him about the plans of the divine world order concerning our cultural development.[72]

In his polemic against Lueder, Schücking also emphasized the bellicist 'special path' in German legal scholarship. Fortunately, Schücking continued, 'the academia of foreign countries had not adopted the same reactionary attitude'.[73] In other countries, Schücking wrote, legal scholars worked 'hand in hand' with pacifism. Here, Schücking referred to authors such as Rouard de Card, Mérignhac, Revon, Dreyfus, Kamarowski, and Descamps, who had recognized the duty of states to mediate and resolve conflicts peacefully.[74] In Germany, on the other hand, as a legal pacifist, Schücking must have felt like an outsider.

Sigrid Redse Johansen is right to highlight that the critique of Lueder and his concept of *Kriegsraison* must be contextualized, since Lueder's text in Holtzendorff's *Handbook* predated the Hague Conferences and thus the codification of major parts of the law of war.[75] It is also true that there were German authors such as Max Huber who, in 1913, and thus after both Hague Conferences, presented a more nuanced position on military necessity and international law than Lueder.[76] Particularly interesting is Johansen's reference to Swedish lawyer and diplomat Fredrik Herman Rikard Kleen, who, as Johansen argues, was strongly influenced by Lueder's thoughts.[77] Johansen thus rightly calls for the complexity of contemporary discourse on war and law to be emphasized. There were indeed also lawyers in Germany who thought about the law of war in a more nuanced way than Lueder. At the same time, Lueder's doctrine also influenced lawyers and diplomats outside Germany.

But does this change anything about Germany's 'special path' in its politics of international law and the justification of war? Hardly. Not only was Lueder's doctrine of German origin, without doubt, it remained particularly significant in German legal theory—and political practice, as we shall see below. Among the Great Powers, the doctrine of *Kriegsraison* remained a typically German one. Even Russian military and legal scholars criticized the German hostility towards international law (also for strategic reasons, no doubt). Within Germany, politically influential legal scholars who opposed Lueder's perspective were rare. Realist

---

[72] *Ibid.*, at 65 f.
[73] *Ibid.*
[74] See for example A. Mérignhac, *Traité de droit public international* (1912), at 3.
[75] S.R. Johansen, *The Military Commander's Necessity. The Law of Armed Conflict and its Limits* (2019), at 113.
[76] *Ibid.*
[77] *Ibid.*

lawyers dominated the discourse on the legitimization of war, especially within the German Foreign Office (*Auswärtige Amt*). Hans Wehberg noted in 1910 that the view that the necessity of war was above the law of war was generally accepted in the German literature, while it was rejected by practically all foreign writers.[78] Still in 1917, American legal scholar Theodore S. Woolsey described the doctrine '*Krieg's raison geht vor Krieg's recht*' [sic!] as 'the German theory'.[79]

As late as 1943, referring to Lueder's more than 100-page chapter of 1889, Arthur Nussbaum wrote that the Erlangen jurist had indeed attempted 'perhaps the most comprehensive refutation of the just war conception as a legal doctrine', adding that 'Lueder's discussion suffers, however, from the infusion of arguments which smack of enthusiasm of war'. In short: Lueder's militarism was acceptable among realist lawyers in the Kaiserreich, but by no means among the dominant liberal international legal scholars in Europe.

'Objections that are Easy to Refute': Peace through Polemics (Novicow vs Stengel)

Yet Lueder was not the only German scholar to be criticized by liberal scholars in Europe and beyond. Karl von Stengel met with a similar reception. As already hinted, this debate was both transnational and transdisciplinary. Russian sociologist Jacques Novicow, who lived in exile in France and was for a time vice president of the *Institut International de Sociologie* founded in Paris in 1893, presented a response to Stengel's *Der Ewige Friede* in 1899 titled *Der Ewige Krieg* ('Perpetual War'). Alfred Hermann Fried had translated the French manuscript into German, the language in which the book of Novicow's opponent had been published.

Novicow introduced his response with the remark that reading Stengel's pamphlet had been a real pleasure—not least because Stengel's 'objections raised in favour of war are easily refuted'.[80] Novicow drew an analogy to a traveller: if he had to climb a mountain for which his strength was not sufficient, he would be seized with apprehension; if, on the other hand, the terrain to be traversed was pleasant, the traveller would be overcome with a feeling of comfortable satisfaction. In other words, refuting Stengel was a walk in the park, Novicow argued.

But why then did Novicow even bother to reject Stengel's arguments? According to the Russian sociologist, the answer was to be found in Stengel's social background, 'a godsend for peace advocates'.[81] Novicow referred to Stengel's aristocratic

---

[78] I.V. Hull, *A Scrap of Paper: Breaking and Making International Law during the Great War* (2014), at 77.
[79] Woolsey (n. 67), at 168.
[80] J. Novicow, *Der ewige Krieg. Antwort auf die Schrift 'Der Ewige Friede' des Herrn Professor Karl Feiherr von Stengel. Aus dem französischen Manuskript übersetzt von Alfred Hermann Fried* (1899), at 1.
[81] Ibid.

status, his title of law professor, and the fact that he had been the representative of Germany, 'one of the most civilized countries on earth', at the Hague Conference in 1899.[82] In short, for Novicow, Stengel was an influential person. Thus, 'the arguments he makes in favour of the war' gained considerable weight, the Russian exile contended.[83]

In his *Perpetual War*, Novicow now went on to deconstruct Stengel's defence of war. The sociologist was able to rebut the German lawyer's argument that the German people were not unduly financially burdened by the possession of armaments,[84] for, Novicow argued, the Germans were still far from an adequate level of prosperity, if one looked at their average annual income.[85] Stengel had to admit, Novicow wrote, that 'the situation is rather sad'.[86] Although Stengel was his 'opponent' in this dispute, Novicow did not wish him to have to depend on the daily 27 pfennigs that was 'the average income of his countrymen'.[87] The average annual income would have to increase tenfold for a 'decent existence' to be possible in Germany. Novicow therefore asked why Germany should not use its budget more sensibly, instead of 'foolishly squandering it on expenditure for military purposes'.[88] It was not acceptable, Novicow argued, for Stengel to consider social and military questions from the standpoint of the 432,000 economically privileged, rather than the broad masses of his 53,948,000 countrymen.[89] This was the socio-economic dimension of Novicow's critique of Stengel's bellicism, strongly reminiscent of Norman Angell, who, in his book *The Great Illusion* (1909) would also criticize Stengel and Moltke for being militarists.

But the sociologist commented on not only the economic and social dimensions, but also the normative dimension. Novicow contradicted Stengel's argument that war would even be needed to enforce judgments if the entire 'human race' was organized into a federation and all international disputes were brought before a court of arbitration.[90] Novicow referred to the *Alabama* case[91] and the compensation payments made by Great Britain to the USA, arguing that in the spirit of reciprocity, it was in the self-interest of states to submit to arbitration.[92] But even if 'in some rare cases this sanctioning [of a judgment through war, HS] might become necessary', according to Novicow, such a judgment would nevertheless correspond to justice and be carried out in the sense of a federal execution on behalf of all parties against the lawbreaker, and not an unjust and arbitrary unilateral offensive.[93]

[82] *Ibid.*
[83] *Ibid.*
[84] *Ibid.*, at 13.
[85] *Ibid.*, at 9.
[86] *Ibid.*
[87] *Ibid.*
[88] *Ibid.*, at 10.
[89] *Ibid.*
[90] *Ibid.*, at 20.
[91] Chapter 6.2.
[92] Novicow (n. 80), at 16 f.
[93] *Ibid.*, at 17.

This was in effect a pre-emptive rejection of Carl Schmitt's criticism of the League of Nations and the doctrine of 'just war'.[94]

In Novicow's view, under a European federation, extensive disarmament was possible.[95] This would, he argued, allow Germany to save 500 million marks annually in military expenditure. Again, Novicow appealed to the principle of reciprocity.[96] According to him, 'the very conservative Herr von Stengel' could not 'emancipate himself from the old adage *"Si vis pacem, para bellum"*'. Novicow wanted to reassure Stengel, however, that no 'peace advocate' had ever suggested to Germany that it 'play the role of an imbecile and disarm while its neighbours remain in full armour from head to toe'.[97] The Russian Tsar Nicholas II, Novicow reminded his readers, had proposed a mutual disarmament agreement to Germany.[98] Novicow therefore wondered why Stengel saw this proposal as a trap and felt justified in discrediting those of his compatriots who were open to it.[99]

Novicow gave the following answer: Stengel was a pessimist, who had forgotten that not only was hatred 'a natural feeling of the human soul', but so too was sympathy for other people.[100] With this negative view of human beings, Novicow argued, one could not pursue politics.[101] Realism, and its assumption that 'the world will remain as it is now until the end of time', seemed unrealistic to liberals.[102] Stengel had overlooked the progress of international relations and was 'at least 60 years behind world history'.[103] According to Novicow, Stengel's negative view of humanity was also reflected in his anti-legalistic stance at the First Hague Peace Conference of 1899.[104]

Novicow also lamented the naïvety of German realism à la Stengel, in a manner which reminds me of the warnings of the Melians in Thucydides' fictional Melian dialogue.[105] Stengel was German, Novicow observed, 'and today Germany is the greatest military power on the continent'.[106] Stengel could therefore easily pronounce violence the basis of security. However, Novicow warned, this was shortsighted, because no one could guarantee that Germany would always remain the strongest: Prussia had been victorious against France at Roßbach in 1757, but was defeated at Jena in 1806. While Russia was weak 'today', if well lead, it could push Germany into second place, regardless of all the country's efforts.[107] Much in the

---

[94] See Chapter 10.3.
[95] Novicow (n. 80), at 12.
[96] *Ibid.*, at 21.
[97] *Ibid.*, at 25.
[98] See Chapter 9.2.
[99] Novicow (n. 80), at 25.
[100] *Ibid.*, at 19.
[101] *Ibid.*
[102] *Ibid.*
[103] *Ibid.*, at 30.
[104] *Ibid.*, at 19.
[105] See Chapter 2.4
[106] Novicow (n. 80), at 23.
[107] *Ibid.*, at 23 f.

sense of Thucydides, Novicow reminded his readers of what R. Ned Lebow has called the 'tragic vision of politics',[108] declaring that the 'right of the strongest' does not pay off in the long run.

Anarchy vs Pacifism

Stengel was also criticized by the pacifist opposition in Germany. Alfred H. Fried, for example, expressed surprise in *Die Friedens-Warte* of 4 September 1899 that Stengel had attended the Hague Conference as Germany's representative only to torpedo its decisions afterwards: 'it is a strange master builder who wishes that the house he has been working on for months might collapse!'[109] Stengel's bellicism was 'horrifying' to Fried. The latter countered that with increasing international legalization, however, no nation would be confronted with the kind of existential threat it faced 'in the times of international anarchy'.[110]

But, according to the Kantian Leonard Nelson, Stengel remained attached to the principle of international anarchy.[111] For Nelson, the fragility of law in the face of the dominance of sovereignty ultimately led to a radical polemic. He pointed to the fundamental paradox of modern international law described by Vattel, which was based on state sovereignty, but whose validity was repeatedly called fundamentally into question by the latter. In Nelson's view, international legal scholarship was thus ultimately 'jurisprudence without law'.[112] With this polemical formulation, Nelson criticized the entire doctrine of international law. However, in my opinion, it describes the German realists of the late nineteenth century particularly well.

Stengel's critique of perpetual peace was also noticed by US journals. His second book, *Weltstaat und Friedensproblem* ('World State and the Problem of Peace'), published in 1909, was reviewed in the *American Journal of International Law* by Frederick C. Hicks. It is quite remarkable that Hicks, a professor of legal bibliography at Yale University and once referred to as 'the dean of law librarians',[113] was interested in reviewing Karl von Stengel's anti-legalistic book. In his review, Hicks first referred to Stengel's bellicism and the narrative of Germany's encirclement to which Stengel adhered: 'With enemies all about, fully armed, of course von Stengel cannot see virtue in the paths of peace.'[114] What is also interesting about Hicks's review is the following: Hicks argued that Stengel had at least earned the merit of

---

[108] R.N. Lebow, *The Tragic Vision of Politics* (2003).
[109] Fried, 'Herr von Stengel und die Friedenskonferenz', 1 *Die Friedens-Warte* (1899) 53, at 53.
[110] *Ibid.*, at 53 f.
[111] L. Nelson, *Die Rechtswissenschaft ohne Recht. Kritische Betrachtungen über die Grundlagen des Staats- und Völkerrechts, insbesondere über die Lehre von der Souveränität* (1917), at 123.
[112] *Ibid.*
[113] Etheredge, 'Frederick C. Hicks: The Dean of Law Librarians', 98 *Law Libr. J.* (2006) 349.
[114] Hicks, 'Weltstaat und Friedensproblem. By Karl von Stengel. Berlin: Reichl & Co. 1909. pp. xiii, 145', 5 *American Journal of International Law* (1911) 1128, at 1129.

swimming against the tide of modern progress and having the courage to express his convictions—even if they should prove to be wrong.[115] The image of Stengel swimming against the tide proves once again that Stengel's bellicism and anti-legalism was perceived as an exception to the rule in international legal discourse.

Unsurprisingly, Stengel was defended by German bellicists. In the *Zeitschrift für Politik*, Richard Hamann, professor of art history at the Royal Academy of Posen, criticized the peace as well as the socialist movements for their cosmopolitan and 'anti-national' tendencies, whose roots he located in 'individualistic, unhistorical, and apolitical ideas of the 18th century'.[116] This was another reproach by a realist of liberals for pursuing supposedly 'unhistorical' ideals. But Hamann did not leave it at that: he called for the peace movement to be fought against for 'the sake of national and state interests'.[117] Here, Hamann also referred to Stengel, who, according to him, had rightly portrayed the social democrats and the peace movement as Germany's 'internal enemies'. This was, in Hamann's view, 'the valuable core of Stengel's remarks'.[118]

Moritz Adler sounded a much more progressive and pacific note in the journal *Waffen nieder!*, in which he criticized Zorn and Stengel for having failed to cut off the claw of the 'monster' called 'war' at the Hague Conferences; Adler countered with a 'triumphant march of new, loving powers', referring to Beecher Stowe's *Uncle Tom's Cabin* and Bertha von Suttner's *Die Waffen Nieder*:

> Love is victorious after all! These are books, these are successes, which give the thinking observer a justified and pleasant prophecy of a future development, of times that will come because they must come; in which the loving woman will have redeemed man from his own torpor and bondage, from his useless subtleties and blinkers.[119]

War the promoter of 'masculinity'[120] and peace the redeeming 'femininity': both stereotypes were *en vogue* in the *Kaiserreich*—with bellicose chauvinist and pacifist emancipatory intentions, respectively.

---

[115] *Ibid.*
[116] Hamann, 'Zur Literatur über die Friedensfrage. Rezension zu Die Grundlagen des revolutionären Pazifismus by Alfred H. Fried; Der kranke Krieg by Fried; Weltstaat und Friedensproblem by Karl von Stengel', 4 *Zeitschrift für Politik* (1911) 391, at 395.
[117] *Ibid.*
[118] *Ibid.*
[119] Adler, 'Kriegsritualmordschablone, Flottenrüstungen – Interventionspolitik, relativ gerechter casus belli – Emancipation des Mannes', 8 *Die Waffen nieder!* (1899) 414, at 423.
[120] Lueder (n. 61), at 204.

8.4 Conclusion: Bifurcation—The Ruling Doctrine vs the Doctrine of the Rulers

While it has been overlooked by recent research, at the end of the nineteenth century a public debate on the legitimacy and necessity of war gained prominence, conducted by politicians, military officers, and scholars of international law. In this debate, a dichotomy of two lines of thought soon crystallized. On the one hand, there was the thesis of self-declared realists, formulated with reference to Clausewitz and Hegel, that war was not only natural but also always legitimate in the name of the *Machtstaat*; on the other hand, and diametrically opposed to this, there was the liberal plea for a comprehensive prohibition of war under treaty law.

As Heinrich Rettich had argued, in accordance with the findings in Part I of this study, until 1890 the mainstream of international law clearly held the position that war required international justification.[121] Did that change afterwards? Not at all! Rather, the reactions to the correspondence between Bluntschli and Moltke show that Moltke's position was a minority opinion in European legal discourse. Only radical bellicose lawyers such as Carl Lueder took sides with Moltke in claiming a *liberum ius ad bellum*—Lueder himself recognized that he was arguing against the majority of liberal jurisprudence in Europe that was clearly on Bluntschli's side.[122]

According to a dictum by Holtzendorff, that was to be taken up even more frequently by liberals such as Otfried Nippold, Moltke's supporters were 'barrack ghosts trained in academic freedom'.[123] Among these 'barrack ghosts' were men whom Carl Lueder claimed to be 'of outstanding importance in all fields, the greatest philosophers, historians, publicists, statesmen, and military men'.[124] What is striking, however, is that Lueder named no lawyers. Nor could he have named them: the majority of bellicist legal authors published only after Lueder, and in Wilhelmine Germany. Accordingly, Lueder referred instead to (quite different) German military officers and military writers from Clausewitz to Moltke. Lueder wanted to replace the prevailing legal doctrine in Europe, according to which war was a problem of international law in need of legitimization, with the anti-legalistic opinions of German military leaders. Lueder became an advocate of German militarism.

But does this emerging militarist legal scholarship also mean that the German Empire trod a 'special path' in international law? Again, a typically German answer can be given to this question: it depends.

---

[121] H. Rettich, *Zur Theorie und Geschichte des Rechts zum Kriege. Völkerrechtliche Untersuchungen* (1888), at 34; see Chapter 7.2.
[122] Lueder (n. 61), at 209.
[123] It is interesting to note here that Holtzendorff was hostile to Lueder's realist and bellicist theory of war, but Lueder nevertheless ended up writing the important chapter on the law of war in Holtzendorff's *Handbuch des Völkerrechts*.
[124] Lueder (n. 61), at 210.

Three arguments seem particularly important here. *First*, legal discourse in the Empire also eluded simple black-and-white dichotomies. Moreover, after the emergence of the *Clausewitzian* school, there were critical lawyers who resolutely rejected *liberum ius ad bellum*. The legal pacifist Walther Schücking stood out among them.[125] But also the author of the most widely published textbook on international law, Franz von Liszt, was more critical of the realists than is sometimes assumed. Anthony Carty is right to point out that the chapter on the legitimacy of war in Liszt's textbook is surprisingly brief and thus somewhat sparse in content.[126] Carty's criticism of Liszt's 'mediocrity',[127] however, is too harsh: after having experienced 'Professors Stengel, Zorn, Kahle, Triebel, etc.', Alfred H. Fried praised Liszt's position as 'liberating, as redemptive, and as highly progressive'.[128] Perhaps, one could argue, that was not a high bar. But Liszt also did take a stand— for example, when he criticized Lasson, Philipp Zorn, and Albert Zorn for their 'dogma of absolute sovereignty' and as 'deniers of international law'.[129]

Second, there were undoubtedly militarists in other countries as well. In his *Great Illusion*, Norman Angell listed bellicists among military officers, philosophers, politicians, and even clergymen of various countries.[130] Novicow also referred to the Russian journalist Stieglitz, who distrusted joint disarmament and adopted very similar arguments to Stengel.[131] Nevertheless, the only bellicist lawyer named by Angell and Novicow was a German: Stengel. And it is precisely the international commentaries on realists such as Lueder and Stengel that underline that the bellicism that had become entrenched in parts of German legal scholarship was alien to other national cultures of international law.

Third, not all, not even the most important German international lawyers were militarists. But, nearly all bellicist lawyers of the late nineteenth century identified in my analysis were German. Lawyers such as Lueder, Meurer, or Stengel were the exception in Europe. Nevertheless, and this is the crucial point here, among lawyers in the diplomatic service of the *Kaiserreich*, there was a conspicuously large number of conservative realists such as Philipp Zorn, but also bellicists such as Stengel. Johannes Kriege, an anti-liberal monarchist, became head of the legal department of the *Auswärtige Amt* in 1911—after he had made himself unpopular during the Second Hague Conference of 1907 for his uncompromising assertion

---

[125] Chapter 6.5.
[126] Carty, 'The Evolution of International Legal Scholarship in Germany during the Kaiserreich and the Weimarer Republik (1871–1933)', 50 *German Yearbook of International Law* (2007/2008) 29, at 44.
[127] *Ibid.*, at 45.
[128] Fried, 'Prof. Dr. von Liszt über die Friedensidee', 3 *Die Friedens-Warte* (1901) 17, at 17; see also Porsch, 'Die Friedens-Warte zwischen Friedensbewegung und Wissenschaft', 74 *Die Friedens-Warte* (1999) 39.
[129] F. von Liszt, *Das Völkerrecht. Systematisch dargestellt* (11th edn, 1920), at 9; see also S. Wiederhold, *Die Lehren vom Monismus mit Primat staatlichen Rechts* (2018), at 98.
[130] N. Angell, *The Great Illusion. A Study of the Relation of Military Power in Nations to Their Economic and Social Advantage* (3rd edn, 1911), at 166–74.
[131] Novicow (n. 80), at 24.

of German interests.[132] Liberals did not form part of the German delegations of 1899 and 1907. They saw themselves as outsiders in the German legal discourse on war and peace. Only after the First World War had been lost did Schücking became a legal advisor to the German delegation—for strategic reasons. For the new German government, legal compliance now seemed opportune in the face of an impending 'dictatorial peace'.[133]

In the analysis of this 'First Great Debate' between liberals and realists at the end of the nineteenth century, it thus becomes clear that the *Clausewitzian* primacy of the political/military emerged predominantly in the German legal discourse of the Wilhelmine era. Conservative lawyers close to the military, but also to the German Foreign Office, such as Christian Meurer, Karl von Stengel, Philipp Zorn, and Albert Zorn now became diplomatically influential. Alongside these realist lawyers, right-Hegelian historians and philosophers such as Ranke, Treitschke, and Lasson were particularly important. They too were actively referred to in realist legal discourse when arguments in favour of military necessity were needed. It is therefore unsurprising that the thesis of the 'free right to go to war' was able to emerge in the military and legal discourse of the German Empire.[134]

Furthermore, realists who placed the necessity of war above the possibility of a law against war were the norm in diplomatic delegations. This distinguished them from delegations of other Great Powers.[135] As a rule, other Great Powers included lawyers in their delegations, who, in accordance with the prevailing doctrine of the nineteenth century, considered war to require justification and wanted to further legalize it. Thus, German realists were opposed to the opinions of legal scholars throughout Europe. In the German Empire, they did not follow the ruling doctrine—but they embodied the doctrine of their rulers.

---

[132] J. Dülffer, *Regeln gegen den Krieg? Die Haager Friedenskonferenzen von 1899 und 1907 in der internationalen Politik* (1981), at 312; M.M. Payk, *Frieden durch Recht? Der Aufstieg des modernen Völkerrechts und der Friedensschluss nach dem Ersten Weltkrieg* (2018), at 56; Schmoeckel, 'Haager Friedenskonferenz', *Staatslexikon online*, available at: https://www.staatslexikon-online.de/Lexikon/Haager_Friedenskonferenz (last visited 1 December 2022).
[133] Chapter 10.
[134] Chapter 7.
[135] Payk (n. 132), Chapter 1.

9
Antinomianism

The *Kaiserreich's* Politics of Justifying War

9.1 Introduction: Breaking and Confirming the Law

In the previous chapter, I have pointed out the bifurcation of the discourse on the legitimacy of violence in the late nineteenth century, which has largely remained buried in current research. I have shown that the liberal legal doctrine, which problematized war and considered it in need of justification, was predominant in Europe, while the realist thesis of the 'free right to go to war' was only advocated by a minority of scholars, mainly Germans. It is still an open question, however, which of the competing doctrines was more likely to reflect political practice in late nineteenth century. So how did Europe's political elites relate to the need to legitimize military force at the end of the nineteenth century? Did Germany occupy an outsider position in the discourse of political practice, as it did in the discourse of international legal theory?

In order to answer these questions, this chapter will take a final look at the political practice of legitimizing war in Germany and Europe in the late nineteenth century (1890–1918). To this end, a comparison of the German and European discourses on the legitimacy of war between 1890 and 1918 will be sketched out. I will focus on two moments of discourse: the German position at the Hague Peace Conferences of 1899 and 1907 (Chapter 9.2), and the German strategy of justification in the First World War (Chapter 9.3).

In analysing these two discourse moments, it will become apparent that not only the military and bellicose legal, but also the political discourse in the *Kaiserreich* was characterized by an extremely broad interpretation of the 'necessity of war'. However, the latter was not limited to the *ius in bello* level.[1] Rather, it also diffused into the political military discourse of justification on the *ad bellum* level.

---

[1] For an account of *ius in bello* in the German Empire, see Messerschmidt, 'Völkerrecht und "Kriegsnotwendigkeit" in der deutschen militärischen Tradition seit den Einigungskriegen', 6 *German Studies Review* (1983) 237; I.V. Hull, *Absolute Destruction: Military Culture and the Practices of War in Imperial Germany* (2005); and Vec, 'All's Fair in Love and War or The Limits of the Limitations. Juridification of Warfare and its Revocation by Military Necessity', in M. Killingsworth (ed.), *Who do the Laws of War Protect? Civility, Barbarity and IHL* (forthcoming).

The boundaries between politics and the military tended to blur in the Empire's war discourse. In the process, the primacy of the military increasingly dominated. While there was some resistance from the civilian leadership, ultimately, the political elite in Germany was prepared to abandon international law in favour of 'military realism'.[2] As a result, Germany violated fundamental norms of the Vienna Order at the end of the nineteenth century: the exception broke the rules—and at the same time confirmed them with this breach.

9.2 International Legalization and Its Circumvention

In the late nineteenth century, the European Great Powers were confronted with a fundamental dilemma. On the one hand, the political tensions among them increased. The Dual Alliance (1879) between the German Empire and Austria-Hungary, which Italy joined in 1882, was confronted with the Franco-Russian Alliance of 1894, from which the Triple Entente emerged by 1907 as an informal alliance between France, Great Britain, and Russia.[3]

However, the goal of a stronger legalization of war was not only supported by the transatlantic peace movements and liberal scholars. It was shared in principle by the European Great Powers, as became clear with the Brussels Declaration of 1874 and especially at the Hague Conferences of 1899 and 1907. For the Crimean War, the Franco-Prussian War, and the civil war of the Paris Commune that followed had not only revealed the destructive potential of new or renewed people's wars; they had also shown how difficult it was to control nationalist violence 'from above'.

Accordingly, Eyal Benvenisti and Doreen Lustig have recently argued that while the codification of the laws of war was initially inspired by 'humanist visionaries' such as Dunant, Moynier, and Lieber, in the shadow of the mass war of 1870/71, this codification project had increasingly become an 'aristocratic project bent on upholding the European order'.[4] In other words, the legalization of war did not contradict the political interests of the European Great Powers at the end of the nineteenth century. In fact, it served them. The Great Powers were concerned with preserving sovereignty in the 'new wars' of their time. International law seemed to be a suitable means for this.

---

[2] Messerschmidt (n. 1).
[3] On the 'polarization of Europe', see C. Clark, *The Sleepwalkers: How Europe Went to War in 1914* (2012), Chapters 3 and 4; on the alliances, see also K. Frehland-Wildeboer, *Treue Freunde? Das Bündnis in Europa 1714–1914* (2010), at 359–66.
[4] Benvenisti and Lustig, 'Monopolizing War: Codifying the Laws of War to Reassert Governmental Authority, 1856–1874', 31 *European Journal of International Law* (2020) 127, at 169.

However, not only a codification of *ius in bello*, but also bilateral treaties on arms limitation and disarmament, collective security, and the settlement of disputes through arbitration were on the Great Powers' political agenda.[5] Moreover, in 1886, during the Bulgarian Crisis, the Great Powers had underlined in collective démarches to Athens, Sofia, and Belgrade that aggressive war was illegitimate.[6] Here, too, the Concert's efforts to standardize *ius contra bellum* became clear. This objective, and the problem of achieving it without granting political privileges, would become apparent at the Hague Peace Conferences.

Peace at the Hague? An Unconventional Conference

The most important culmination points for the legalization of war were the Hague Peace Conferences of 1899 and 1907. Jost Dülffer has underlined in his groundbreaking study of the conferences that they were unconventional conferences: after all, there was no immediate reason for them.[7] It was unusual to convene peace congresses and conferences without an (imminent) violent conflict: the Congress of Vienna in 1814/15, the Congress of Paris in 1856, and the Congress of Berlin in 1878 all came about *after* wars. The location of the congresses also indicates the changing importance of the respective capitals over the century (Vienna—Paris—Berlin).

Since 1870/71, however, there had been no war between Great Powers in Europe. The Hague Conferences were thus rather an expression of the 'expanding international conference system ... which since the middle of the 19th century formulated the claim to modernize international relations', as Verena Steller has argued.[8] Establishing peace through law thus seemed to some, at least in principle, to be just as regulable under international law 'as the postal system, units of measurement, or means of payment'.[9] However, according to Dülffer, the unusual starting point of the conferences of 1899 and 1907 meant in equal measure 'a facilitation as well as a complication of the prospects for success'.[10] On the one hand, the opportunity existed,

---

[5] Lesaffer, 'Peace through Law. The Hague Peace Conferences and the Rise of the Ius Contra Bellum', in M. Abbenhuis, C.E. Barber, and A.R. Higgins (eds), *War, Peace and International Order? The Legacies of the Hague Conferences of 1899 and 1907* (2017) 31.

[6] W. Müller, *Politische Geschichte der Gegenwart* (1886), at 236; S. Verosta, *Theorie und Realität von Bündnissen. Heinrich Lammasch, Karl Renner und der Zweibund (1897-1914)* (1971), at 27; M. Schulz, *Normen und Praxis. Das europäische Konzert der Großmächte als Sicherheitsrat, 1815-1860* (2009), at 568.

[7] J. Dülffer, *Regeln gegen den Krieg? Die Haager Friedenskonferenzen von 1899 und 1907 in der internationalen Politik* (1981), at 12.

[8] V. Steller, *Diplomatie von Angesicht zu Angesicht. Diplomatische Handlungsformen in den deutsch-französischen Beziehungen 1870-1919* (2011), at 232.

[9] Ibid.

[10] Dülffer (n. 7), at 13.

unburdened by concrete and pressing clashes of interests, to discuss the possibilities and limits of an improved, more peaceful international order, and to create agreements that had not to be limited to day-to-day political balancing.[11]

On the other hand, without a concrete reason, there was no urgency for an agreement between the negotiating parties. However, because the successes of the conference had to be represented and justified 'rhetorically and with publicity' under the pressure of national and international public opinion, according to Dülffer—

> the real core of trust-building international cooperation [was] formulated more impressively in terms of future intentions, possibilities, and desires than it corresponded to the more modest binding commitments.[12]

Consequently, the results of the Hague negotiations were assessed differently, with some deeming them visionary, and others disenchanting (see below).

Russia's motives for convening the conference were also ambivalent and have traditionally been interpreted in terms of power politics. Nicholas II had initiated the 1899 conference because the Tsarist Empire was logistically and economically unable to keep up with the other powers in the arms race.[13] At the same time, however, Nicholas II also had idealistic motives for initiating the 1899 conference, not least due to his involvement with Jan Bloch's study on the future of war.[14] Political and normative objectives were by no means mutually exclusive.

Accordingly, Russian foreign minister Count Muravyev had, on the Tsar's orders, submitted to the diplomatic corps accredited in St Petersburg at the weekly meeting of 24 August 1898 the proposal for a disarmament conference, which would be 'with God's help, a favourable omen of the coming century':

> It would gather in one mighty bundle the efforts of all states sincerely striving to make the idea of perpetual peace triumph over the elements of disunity and discord.[15]

The reaction of the other Great Powers to this Tsarist manifesto was ostensibly positive. They replied that the Tsar's advance was to be seen as proof of his 'pure intentions'. In fact, however, the other Great Powers were thoroughly irritated, especially because of the Tsar's vague and unclearly defined objectives. 'Rarely', Dülffer argues, 'were governments' responses likely to have deviated so far from their true

---

[11] *Ibid.*, at 13.
[12] *Ibid.*
[13] *Ibid.*, at 19–53.
[14] M. Aust, *Globalisierung imperial und sozialistisch. Russland und die Sowjetunion in der Globalgeschichte 1851–1991* (2013), at 178.
[15] Quoted from Dülffer (n. 7), at 20.

assessment'.[16] This was another sign of how unconventional a peace conference that was not preceded by war in fact was.

It was the German Empire in particular that firmly rejected disarmament or arms limitation.[17] Berlin tried to convince London that the meeting proposed by St Petersburg might end in strife and thus be more conducive to war. This was an argument reminiscent of Stengel's reservations about diplomatic conferences and congresses. But just as Stengel had been unable to convince Novicow,[18] German diplomacy was unable to convince Britain to reject the Russian invitation.

International legal scholars such as the Briton Cecil Hurst, the Frenchman Louis Renault, or the American James Brown Scott were important in the process of organizing the diplomatic conferences of 1899 and 1907.[19] Since Russia had initiated the 1899 conference, Fedor Fedorovich Martens also played a crucial role. Martens chaired the Second Commission dealing with the systematization of *ius in bello*, which Moltke had so vehemently opposed in his correspondence with Bluntschli. The product of the negotiations was the Hague Convention (II) with Respect to the Laws and Customs of War on Land, which drew on the Brussels Declaration drawn up by Martens in 1874 and the *Oxford Manual* of 1880. In addition, the Geneva Convention of 1865 was confirmed and the firing of balloons, the use of deformation projectiles, and, for the first time, poisonous gases were prohibited.[20]

Once again, however, Martens found himself caught between his liberal cosmopolitan convictions and Russian political interests. In the preamble to the Hague Convention (II), according to which—

> in cases not included in the Regulations adopted by them, the inhabitants and the belligerents remain under the protection and the rule of the principles of the law of nations, as they result from the usages established among civilized peoples, from the laws of humanity, and the dictates of the public conscience,

liberal legalist expectations of the civilization of war through international law become visible. But this was not all, for the *Martens Clause* emphasized the continued validity of natural law and religion in the nineteenth-century discourse on war, and thus turned against an all too strict confinement of war by positive law.[21] So, the

---

[16] *Ibid.*, at 39.
[17] *Ibid.*, at 39 ff.
[18] Chapter 8.3.
[19] On this paragraph, see M.M. Payk, *Frieden durch Recht? Der Aufstieg des modernen Völkerrechts und der Friedensschluss nach dem Ersten Weltkrieg* (2018), at 45–56.
[20] Schmoeckel, 'Haager Friedenskonferenz', *Staatslexikon online*, available at: https://www.staatslexikon-online.de/Lexikon/Haager_Friedenskonferenz (last visited 1 December 2022); Vec, 'Juridification, Politicization, and Circumvention of Law: (De-)Legitimizing Chemical Warfare before and after Ypres, 1899–1925', in L. Brock and H. Simon (eds), *The Justification of War and International Order: From Past to Present* (2021) 221, at 223 ff.
[21] Giladi, 'The Enactment of Irony: Reflections on the Origins of the Martens Clause', 25 *European Journal of International Law* (2014) 847; Payk (n. 19), at 60 ff.

Martens Clause represents another myth in the history of international law. The intention of its author was the exact opposite of the objective usually attributed to it.[22] It was not (only) about humanization, but (at least initially) primarily about political interests.

Does this mean that Martens was not an 'architect of peace'[23] after all? Further doubts arise when one analyses Martens's reaction to the legal pacifist Tsarist Manifesto of 1898. The latter caused some confusion within Russia. Bertha von Suttner reported in her memoirs that at the 1899 conference some Russian military officers demanded the capture of Jan Bloch after his lecture on the war of the future from an economic perspective.[24] But not only Russian military officers, also numerous Russian diplomats rejected as utopian Nicholas II's call for a disarmament conference. They assumed that the conference would fail and feared that would damage Russia's reputation.[25] One of these diplomats was Martens. His diary makes it clear that Martens considered the Tsar's initiative for a peace conference an 'extravagant project' that was bound to end in a 'fiasco' for Russia. To Martens, in 1898/99 international disarmament simply seemed unrealistic.[26]

To avert a failure of the conference and thus embarrassment of the Tsar, Martens intervened in the conference programme. On his initiative, the focus of the conference was shifted away from the highly political question of disarmament and more towards questions of *ius in bello*. 'Regulating war was more than a placefiller on the conference agenda', argues Rotem Giladi: 'Its inclusion was designed to steer away from peace through disarmament, the thrust of the first Circular. It was a diversion.'[27] This diversion was successful. According to Giladi, the First Hague Peace Conference, 'in regulating war, has turned war into a legal regularity, averting the aversion of war'.[28] Seen thus, *ius in bello* was used against an expansion of arms control and disarmament. It therefore served as a kind of legalistic avoidance of law.

This finding underlines two things: *first*, the need to link the genealogies of *ius ad bellum* and *ius in bello* obligations, which are often treated separately in the history of the law of war, more closely; and *second*, that the First Hague Conference featured multiple legal and normative claims where not only references to humanity and morality circumvented legal constraints, but also the invocation of law itself. The limitation of law constituted a legitimization of war.

---

[22] Giladi (n. 21).
[23] V.V. Pustogarov, *Our Martens* (2000).
[24] B. von Suttner, *Memoiren* (1909), at 468 ff.
[25] Dülffer (n. 7), at 39–52.
[26] Giladi (n. 21), at 863; Pustogarov (n. 23), at 158–63.
[27] Giladi (n. 21), at 864.
[28] *Ibid.*, at 866.

'And shit on all the resolutions': German Anti-Legalism at the Hague Conference

However, the fact that the First Commission, which dealt with questions of disarmament, failed to reach a convention in The Hague in 1899 was not due to Martens's pessimism. It primarily failed due to the German delegation and its insistence on its national sovereignty.[29] After all, disarmament was diametrically opposed to the interests of Wilhelm II and his military advisors. Accordingly, the German delegates at the Hague Conference were instructed not to agree to any legal curtailment of German armaments.[30]

In Count Georg Herbert zu Münster, Karl von Stengel, and Phillip Zorn, the German Foreign Office (*Auswärtiges Amt*) had sent diplomats to The Hague who were themselves deeply opposed to strengthening the law against war. Hardly surprisingly, the German delegation was decidedly unpopular among the diplomats of other nations.[31] Bertha von Suttner described the encounters with Zorn and Stengel in her memoirs as cold during the conference. She remarked to Zorn that the industrially waged 'war of the future' needed to be confronted with peace.[32] According to Suttner, Zorn replied tersely: 'There is peace only in heaven.'[33] It should also be noted that Zorn was generally considered to be more accessible than Stengel.[34]

There is no doubt that the German Foreign Office had very deliberately selected legal experts who were enemies of peace. This becomes abundantly clear in the numerous exchanges of letters between the delegations and Berlin.[35] Furthermore, an entry in Suttner's memoirs is telling here.[36] Before the start of the First Hague Conference, British journalist and peace activist William Thomas Stead addressed Bülow, at that time state secretary for foreign affairs, about Stengel's 'anti-peace pamphlet', *Der ewige Friede*.[37] Bülow initially denied the existence of the pamphlet to Stead. He called it a fabrication. Bülow accused Stead of lying—and ironically lied himself, for when Stead pointed out that Stengel's book was already in its third edition, Bülow admitted its existence, but tried to play down its importance. According to Bülow, it had been a 'mere lecture among friends, printed by the publisher behind the author's back'.[38] So Bülow in fact *did* know of Stengel's bellicist book. Nevertheless, he had sent the very same Stengel to the Hague Conference.

---

[29] Schmoeckel (n. 20).
[30] Payk (n. 19), at 56–8.
[31] *Ibid.*
[32] Suttner (n. 24), at 469 ff.
[33] *Ibid.*
[34] Payk (n. 19), at 57.
[35] *Ibid.*, at 62.
[36] Suttner (n. 24), at 440 ff.
[37] Chapter 7.4.
[38] Suttner (n. 24), at 440 ff.

Perhaps the most honest answer that Bülow could have given to Stead would have been that he had no real choice: Stengel had been personally nominated by Wilhelm II. With this affront, the Kaiser aimed to express his disapproval of the Hague agenda.[39]

Because it became apparent early on that the original focus of the conference, disarmament, would fail, the question of arbitration became the real political issue of the event.[40] In the discussion, the positions of the French and German delegations were at odds with each other. Both in 1899 and 1907, the negotiations on the arbitration question were led by the former French prime minister and legal pacifist Léon Bourgeois, whose commitment to the legalization and institutionalization of the world of states threatened to fail due to a German veto.[41] For Germany, state sovereignty trumped international law. This is perhaps most evident in a circular in which Bülow stated after the conference that every independent state was an end in itself and that in the field of politics it recognized no higher aims than those of safeguarding its own interests: 'Under no circumstances', Bülow concluded, 'can any tangible barriers be imposed on our freedom of political action'.[42]

However, the Third Commission dealing with international arbitration was nevertheless able to present a result at the end of the 1899 Hague Conference. This was due to two reasons: *first*, breaking off the negotiations would have been tantamount to a massive violation of Tsar Nicholas's honour, and would have seriously damaged German-Russian relations.[43] Only after Bülow had urgently called attention to this dilemma did Wilhelm II agree to the decisions of the Third Commission. However, he made his position on international law unmistakably clear in an internal commentary:

> In Wiesbaden I promised to grant the Tsar my help to find a satisfactory solution! So that *he* does not make a fool of himself before Europe, *I* agree to this nonsense! But in practice and in future I shall look to none but God and my sharp sword! And shit on all the resolutions![44]

Second, the German delegation at the Hague had already demanded numerous concessions from the negotiating partners. The court of arbitration to be set up was only to be a voluntary procedural form of peaceful dispute settlement, not a binding legal authority for the prevention of war.[45]

---

[39] Dülffer (n. 7), at 127.
[40] *Ibid.*, at 80; Payk (n. 19), at 63.
[41] Payk (n. 19), at 65.
[42] Quoted from Dülffer (n. 7), at 137.
[43] *Ibid.*, at 39.
[44] Quoted from J.C.G. Röhl, *Wilhelm II: Into the Abyss of War and Exile, 1900–1941* (2017), at 60.
[45] Dülffer (n. 7), at 93 ff.

Contemporary reactions to the conference were mixed. Bertha von Suttner clearly expressed her disappointment—also with international lawyers—that progress had mainly been made in the field of *ius in bello*:

> The question of humanizing war cannot be of interest—especially in a peace conference.... It is, after all, about the codification of peace. Saint George rode out to slay the dragon, not to cut off its claws. Or, as Frédéric Passy says: '*On n'humanise pas le carnage, on le condamne, parce qu'on s'humanise.*' ['We don't humanize the carnage, we condemn it, because we humanize ourselves'].[46]

The 'most notable success of the conference', according to Mathias Schmoeckel, was the convention on the peaceful settlement of international disputes.[47] As in the Treaty of Paris (1856) at the regional level,[48] a general three-month cooling-off period was now agreed upon—thus foreshadowing the latter provision in the League of Nations Covenant. Baron Egor Staal also emphasized in his final speech of 29 July 1899 that the convention established 'a new era ... in the domain of international law'.[49] Similarly, French delegate Paul Henri Benjamin Balluet d'Estournelles noted optimistically that the conference may 'be a beginning, not an end' to further 'serve the cause of culture and peace!'[50]

This appeal was answered as early as 1907. The second conference in The Hague revealed the universalization of the international legal community: the number of participants had increased from twenty-six to forty-four states.[51] However, even in 1907, the negotiating parties failed to establish a permanent and compulsory court of arbitration. The US draft ultimately foundered due to a dispute over whether it was compatible with the sovereign equality of all nations if only the Great Powers were to provide permanent judgeships.[52] In particular, Brazilian international legal scholar Ruy Barbosa opposed the Great Powers' plans, much to the displeasure of the US delegates.[53]

With regard to obligatory international arbitration, it was once again the *Kaiserreich* that opposed Léon Bourgeois's efforts. German lawyer Johannes Kriege nipped all negotiation attempts in the bud with undiplomatic, formal legal interventions.[54] In doing so, Kriege lost any sympathy of other delegations.

---

[46] Suttner (n. 24), at 458 ff. Janne E. Nijman has identified an interesting analogy between Kant and Suttner's disenchantment with the legal doctrine of their times, see Nijman, 'Bertha von Suttner: Locating International Law in Novel and Salon', in I. Tallgren (ed.), *Portraits of Women in International Law: New Names and Forgotten Faces?* (2023) 87.
[47] Schmoeckel (n. 20).
[48] Chapter 5.2.
[49] On this paragraph, see Lesaffer (n. 5).
[50] Suttner (n. 24), at 458 ff.
[51] Schmoeckel (n. 20).
[52] Payk (n. 19), at 70.
[53] A. Becker Lorca, *Mestizo International Law. A Global Intellectual History 1842–1933* (2014), at 158.
[54] Dülffer (n. 7), at 312; Payk (n. 19), at 57.

Yet, his uncompromising approach was demonstrably desired by Bülow, by now *Reichskanzler* (Imperial Chancellor)![55]

Nevertheless, the Hague Conference of 1907 also achieved significant successes. For example, although the 'truly titanic debate'[56] on the compulsory nature of the court of arbitration did not produce a result at the conference, it was possible to pick up on this idea later. The dedicated campaign of many delegates for a compulsory court of arbitration underlined the growing importance of legal pacifist arguments. American lawyer Elihu Root was probably right that 'the most valuable services rendered to civilization by this Second Conference will be found in the progress made in matters upon which the delegates reach no definite agreement'.[57]

Moreover, not only was the cooling-off period of the First Hague Conference confirmed. The Hague Convention (II) of 1907 Respecting the Limitation of the Employment of Force for the Recovery of Contract Debts, also called the Drago-Porter Convention, provided for a further limitation of the *ius ad bellum*. Initiated by the Argentine foreign minister, Luis María Drago (1906), and presented at the Hague by the US diplomat Horace Porter, the convention prohibited the military collection of debts.[58] Finally, in 1907, the need to justify war was standardized in treaty law for the first time. In view of the delayed Japanese declaration of war on Russia in 1904, Article 1 of the Hague Convention (III) on the Opening of Hostilities provided that hostilities between states could not begin 'without prior unequivocal notification, which must take the form either of a reasoned declaration of war or of an ultimatum with a conditional declaration of war'.

What did the conferences of 1899/1907 mean for the analysis of the modern discourse on the legitimacy of war? Despite some setbacks, Martens's diversionary tactics, and German anti-legalism, important successes can ultimately be identified from the Hague Conferences. The Drago-Porter Convention introduced a limited prohibition of war under international treaty law, which can accurately be described as an important step towards the UN Charter's prohibition of the use of force.[59] However, this prohibition was not new. In fact, important progress towards a treaty-based standardization of the prohibition of war had already been made over the century since the Congress of Vienna.[60] Moreover, the new norms supported the prevailing doctrine of international law, that, in 1907, any decision to go to war would not be made in a legal vacuum.

---

[55] Dülffer (n. 7), at 312.
[56] Eyffinger, 'A Highly Critical Moment: Role and Record of the Second Hague Peace Conference', 54 *Netherlands International Law Review* (2007) 197, at 219; Tams, 'Die Zweite Haager Konferenz und das Recht der friedlichen Streitbeilegung', 82 *Die Friedens-Warte* (2007) 119, at 136.
[57] Quoted from Tams (n. 56), at 136.
[58] L. Heimbeck, *Die Abwicklung von Staatsbankrotten im Völkerrecht. Verrechtlichung und Rechtsvermeidung zwischen 1824 und 1907* (2013).
[59] Tams (n. 56).
[60] See Chapters 4–6.

The German Empire stood out at the conferences as an 'outsider no longer understood by the other sides'.[61] The *Kaiserreich* used a vocabulary of realpolitik that was scarcely compatible with the European—and global—communication community dealing with war and law. As delegates, it had sent authoritarian conservative, sometimes openly militaristic diplomats, who wanted to limit the scope of what could be said with the vocabulary of international law. Their understanding of war and international order was based on the realist theories that had become dominant among the political and military elites of the post-Bismarck Empire.[62] The contradiction between the legal pacifist efforts of the Western powers and the German Empire's anti-international law dogmas of sovereignty at the Hague Conferences thus ultimately pointed to a German *Sonderweg* in dealing with the international norms of the Vienna Order.

This dispute between German and internationally accepted concepts of international order came to a head when peace itself came to an end. In 1914, the Great War, which the European Concert had successfully prevented since 1814/15, broke out, ultimately becoming the 'primordial catastrophe of the 20th century' (George F. Kennan). The war erupted in contradictory times: on the one hand, increasing power-political tensions prevailed and, on the other, the Hague Conferences had strengthened the normative frame of reference of international politics. So how was entry into this war justified?

9.3 The End of an Era: Justifying the Great War

Although the First World War is better researched than almost any other military conflict in world history, its outbreak is still one of the greatest puzzles in the history and theory of international relations[63]—indeed the volume of historical sources has hardly changed over the years! Since the deeper causes of the war are manifold and disputed, this is not the place to discuss them. Instead, I will simply outline some of the political lines of conflict between the Great Powers.[64]

After the dissolution of Bismarck's alliance policy, Europe's international relations became increasingly polarized: on the one side stood the Dual or Triple Alliance; on the other, the Franco-Russian Alliance or Triple Entente of 1907.

---

[61] Dülffer (n. 7).
[62] Chapter 7.
[63] A. Mombauer, *The Origins of the First World War: Controversies and Consensus* (2002); J.S. Levy and J.A. Vasquez, *The Outbreak of the First World War: Structure, Politics, and Decision-Making* (2014); Hull, 'The Great War and International Law: German Justifications of "Preemptive Self-Defense"', in L, Brock and H. Simon (eds), *The Justification of War and International Order: From Past to Present* (2021) 183, at 192; F. Fischer, *Griff nach der Weltmacht. Die Kriegszielpolitik des kaiserlichen Deutschland 1914/1918* (1961); Clark (n. 3).
[64] For a nuanced overview, see Mombauer (n. 63), and G. Krumeich, *Juli 1914. Eine Bilanz* (2014), at 15–59.

This was accompanied by nationalist constructions of the enemy, including the German narrative of an 'encirclement' (*'Einkreisung'*), which can be found not only in the Great General Staff's *Schlieffen Plan* (see below), but even among some liberal German international lawyers.[65] The imperial conflicts between the Empire and France (Morocco Crises 1905/1911) and between the Empire and Great Britain (naval arms race) came to a head as a result of Wilhelm II's 'world politics' (*'Weltpolitik'*) initiated in 1897 and the related naval policy (*Tirpitz Plan*), as did the conflict between Austria-Hungary and Russia after the Austrian annexation of Bosnia and Herzegovina in 1908. This points to the smouldering ethno-nationalist conflicts in the Balkans, which erupted in two Balkan Wars.

At the same time, the Balkan Wars illuminate the narrower causes of the World War. Although the European Concert achieved peace agreements in 1912 and 1913, these were fragile and could not bring lasting peace to the Balkans. The bullets fired by Gavrilo Princip in Sarajevo on 28 June 1914 struck, as the Viennese press put it, not only the Crown Prince and Crown Princess, but also the 'Habsburg idea of the state'.[66] This was followed by the July crisis of 1914, which is still very central to the controversial scholarly debates on the question of war guilt today, a crisis that, according to Christopher Clark, was 'the most complex of modern times, perhaps of any time so far'.[67] For our purposes, what is of primary interest about this complexity is: how was the entry into the war at the end of this crisis justified?

Caught in Lies: Justifying the Unjustifiable

First of all, it can be noted that all European Great Powers sought to legitimize their entry into the war by means of declarations of war. In his declaration of war to Belgrade on 28 July 1914, Emperor Franz Joseph I referred to the classical justification pattern of the nineteenth century. He argued that he was forced by the 'activities of a hateful enemy' to 'take up the sword in order to preserve the honour of My Monarchy, to protect its reputation, and its position of power, to safeguard its possessions after long years of peace'. Franz Joseph I claimed that he wanted to put an end to 'the incessant challenges of Serbia' and the 'bloody trace of those secret machinations visible from afar'.[68]

Serbia was therefore the aggressor. According to Franz Joseph I, it had 'set in motion and directed a series of assassinations' and had also refused to cease its

---

[65] F. von Liszt, *Das Völkerrecht. Systematisch dargestellt* (11th edn, 1920), at 30, for example, refers to a British 'policy of encircling the German Reich' before the First World War.
[66] Christopher Clark in T. Kößler and C. Clark, 'Dieser Krieg hat das ganze Jahrhundert entstellt. Interview', *Deutschlandfunk* (20 January 2014), available at: https://www.deutschlandfunk.de/interview-mit-christopher-clark-dieser-krieg-hat-das-ganze-100.html (last visited 1 December 2022).
[67] Clark (n. 3), at xxvii.
[68] Franz Joseph I, 'An Meine Völker!', *Wiener Zeitung* (29 July 1914).

'criminal activities'. Vienna therefore saw itself as being in the right to force Serbia to do so. Franz Joseph I referred to war as the *ultima ratio*. In vain, he claimed, his government had 'made one last attempt' to achieve this goal by peaceful means, 'to persuade Serbia to turn back by means of a stern warning'.[69]

The declaration of war was preceded by an Austro-Hungarian ultimatum. On the one hand, the sources provide evidence of the direct involvement of Serbian military officers—but not of Serbian politicians!—in the assassination.[70] On the other hand, it is known that the Viennese foreign minister Count Berchtold— with the German 'blank cheque'—issued an ultimatum to Serbia that was as unacceptable as possible.[71] Furthermore, Berchtold anticipated the possibility of an intervention by Russia in defence of Serbia, and thus the escalation of what was to become a European war.[72] Irrespective of how valid or appropriate one considers the Viennese declaration of war, until 28 July 1914, the discourse on the legitimization of violence was formally and materially entirely within the framework of what had been customary in the nineteenth century.

This changed with the entry of the German Empire into the war, which was preceded first by the partial, then the general mobilization of the Russian army (29/31 July) in response to the Vienna declaration of war. In its war legitimations, the Empire concluded that the mobilization was an imminent Russian attack and declared war on Russia—*before* an actual Russian attack had occurred—on 1 August. The 'localized war' now became the Great War, which, according to historians' estimates, claimed the lives of ten million soldiers and seven million civilians between 1914 and 1918.

How was the German entry into the war justified? The German declaration of war of 1 August emphasized that Russia had pre-empted all efforts at negotiation by mobilizing its armed forces, which posed a grave and immediate danger to Germany.[73] Had the German government failed to prevent this danger, it would have put the security and existence of Germany itself at risk. The *Kaiserreich* thus argued in terms of pre-emptive self-defence, i.e. against an *imminent* attack. This argument was still to change. Previously, in his balcony speeches of 31 July and 1 August, Wilhelm II had portrayed Russia as the aggressor and tried to legitimize the German violence as a 'just defence': 'They are putting the sword in our hand' ('*Man drückt uns das Schwert in die Hand.*')[74]

---

[69] Ibid.
[70] Krumeich (n. 64), at 74 ff.
[71] Clark (n. 3).
[72] Krumeich (n. 64), at 75 ff.
[73] 'German Declaration of War (1 August 1914)', in J.B. Scott (ed.), *Diplomatic Documents Relating to the Outbreak of the European War* (1916), at 1377.
[74] Wilhelm II, 'Erste Balkonrede Kaiser Wilhelms II., Berlin, 31. Juli 1914', *Kriegs-Rundschau. Zeitgenössische Zusammenstellung der für den Weltkrieg wichtigen Ereignisse, Urkunden, Kundgebungen, Schlacht- und Zeitberichte*, vol. 1 (1914/15) 37.

The German justifications thus corresponded—at first glance—entirely to Europe's normative frame of reference and to both of the analytical categories of 'order-related' and 'ontological' narratives of war justifications proposed by Jochen von Bernstorff.[75] On the one hand, the German war justifications addressed the defence of the nation (ontological argument), for example when the Kaiser declared that he 'no longer thought in terms of parties or confessions; today we are all German brothers and only German brothers'.[76] On the other hand, however, the legitimations also referred to the international peace order, which was emphasized as worthy of protection (order-related argument). Purely ontological justifications would have sounded quite different!

So was the Empire's entry into the war legitimate from the perspective of the international normative order? At first glance, it seems so. Jochen von Bernstorff, for example, argues that—

> all of those legal restrictions on the right to wage war in 1914, which may have formed part of international legal discourse up until the mid-19th century, had lost most of their regulating impact through an ever wider range of ontological justifications for waging war recognized by Western governments and Western scholars, including a broad notion of the fundamental right to self-preservation and necessity ('*Notstand*').[77]

Accordingly, Bernstorff continues, the portrayal of a German breach of law as a scandal with regard to the *ad bellum* level was primarily an ex post construction in Versailles 1919:

> Hence, in Versailles in 1919, it was not the pre-war *ius ad bellum* regime but, rather, the monstrosity of the overall effects of Germany's move to war, the millions of dead soldiers in poison gas-soaked trenches and the German massacres and destruction in civilian areas that, in retrospect, made the war an aggressive, and, thus, also 'illegal', war in Western public opinion.[78]

This perspective is consistent with the thesis of Oona A. Hathaway and Scott J. Shapiro, that the First World War was the last great war of an 'old world order' in which war was always permitted and which subsequently gave way to a 'new world order' with its ban on war and violence.[79]

---

[75] Bernstorff, 'The Use of Force in International Law before World War I: On Imperial Ordering and the Ontology of the Nation State', 29 *European Journal of International Law* (2018) 233, at 236.
[76] Wilhelm II, 'Zweite Balkonrede des Kaisers, Berlin, 1. August 1914', *Kriegs-Rundschau. Zeitgenössische Zusammenstellung der für den Weltkrieg wichtigen Ereignisse, Urkunden, Kundgebungen, Schlacht- und Zeitberichte*, vol. 1 (1914/15) 43.
[77] Bernstorff (n. 75), at 257.
[78] *Ibid.*
[79] O.A. Hathaway and S.J. Shapiro, *The Internationalists: How a Radical Plan to Outlaw War Remade the World* (2017).

Against the background of the research already presented in this study, however, it becomes clear that the argument of a purely ex post construction of a German breach of law at the *ad bellum* level is not convincing at all. It is true that the field of *ius ad bellum* had changed since 1856 and that it had also expanded.[80] Arguments of honour, national unity, and self-preservation gained importance, as I have shown above.[81] However, what Bernstorff, Hathaway/Shapiro, and others ignore is that a *sole* recourse to ontological arguments was not sufficient under *any* circumstances during the second half of the century. Even primarily ontologically motivated wars such as the Franco-Prussian War *always* required a simultaneous recourse to the accepted norms of the international order. When France declared war on Prussia in 1870 with recourse to '*la défense de son honneur et de ses intérêts compromis*', it was impossible to gain international acceptance with these ontological legitimation narratives. Instead, France was now considered the aggressor in an obvious preventive war.[82]

Even in 1914, no state could afford to justify a war solely by recourse to ontological justifications for war—especially since the efforts to introduce a *ius contra bellum* had steadily increased since 1856/1899/1907. The only exception was an obvious case of self-defence against an attack that had already taken place. Here, however, lay the real problem of German war justifications in August 1914: an attack against German territory had de facto *not* taken place! Germany's political and military elites could therefore only use the *Schlieffen Plan* (see below) on one condition: they had to invent an enemy attack.

This resulted in a self-contradictory change of strategy, as Isabel V. Hull has recently described in detail.[83] On 1 August, in view of the mobilization of the Russian army, the *Kaiserreich* initially argued that a Russian attack was imminent. The German argument for justification was thus initially one of pre-emptive self-defence. However, mobilization constituted neither aggression nor a violation of the law; rather, it was common in many conflicts as a threatening gesture, not least to induce a party to the conflict to resume negotiations.[84] The argument of a pre-emptive war was thus scarcely suitable for generating international legitimacy in 1914.

At the beginning of August, the German leadership therefore decided to change its propaganda strategy. On the initiative of General Moltke the Younger, it invented Russian and French border violations as well as French air attacks on railways near Karlsruhe and Nuremberg. This meant that the argument was no longer one of pre-emptive self-defence, but rather the much stronger one of *actual*

---

[80] I. Brownlie, *International Law and the Use of Force by States* (1963), at 42 ff.
[81] See Chapters 7 and 8.
[82] See Chapter 5.4.
[83] Hull (n. 63).
[84] *Ibid.*, at 195, 198.

self-defence against attacks by Russia and France that had already taken place.[85] Furthermore, the declaration of war on France on 3 August stated that several French aircraft had penetrated Belgian airspace and had thus violated the Belgian neutrality of 1839.[86] The accusations of French and Russian border violations and air strikes were indeed conjured out of thin air. Accordingly, they were not convincing internationally.[87]

The German change of strategy is nevertheless noteworthy here for two reasons. *First*, it points to the fact that the German elites were aware that even a *pre-emptive* defence against a supposedly concrete aggression was a weak argument—not to mention a *preventive* war against an unspecified aggression (see below). *Second*, the change of strategy underlines that the *Kaiserreich's* (legitimation) politics were hostile to international law. To avoid misunderstandings, it was the rule rather than the exception in the nineteenth century for statesmen to wait for their enemies to make their first mistake and then to exploit it as an ostensibly legitimate reason for war. However, inventing an aggression (twice) was new in the nineteenth century.

This addresses the explicit illegality—and in fact the anti-legalism—that was inextricably linked to Germany's entry into the war of 1914. For, as is well known, the war planning of the Great General Staff had been based on the *Schlieffen Plan* since 1905 at the latest.[88] In order to avoid a war on two fronts, France was to be defeated in a quick and decisive offensive, before the bulk of the German army would take action against Russia in the east. To this end, the German army was to bypass the eastern French fortifications at Verdun, Nancy, Epinal, and Belfort by marching through Belgium and Luxembourg. Without any doubt, the Schlieffen Plan, which had been devised for a long time, included a massive breach of law: the violation of Belgian neutrality.

Speaking Right and Wrong: The First World War as another Struggle for Law

In fact, as Isabel V. Hull has pointed out, the First World War began with a breach of law.[89] The violation of the Treaty of London (1839) was the most serious of many errors in the German legitimation strategy. For the German invasion of Belgium also spurred into action the latter's protecting power, Great Britain, which explicitly

---

[85] Ibid., at 198 ff.
[86] 'Plusieurs de ces derniers ont manifestement violé la neutralité de la Belgique en survolant le territoire de ce pays', in K. Kautsky (ed.), *Documents allemands relatifs à l'origine de la guerre: collection complète des documents officiels*, vol. 3 (1922), at 187.
[87] Clark (n. 3); Hull (n. 63).
[88] On this, see Hull (n. 1), at 160; H. Ehlert, M. Epkenhans, and G.P. Groß (eds), *Der Schlieffenplan. Analysen und Dokumente* (2007).
[89] I.V. Hull, *A Scrap of Paper: Breaking and Making International Law during the Great War* (2014), at 16.

referred to the German violation of Belgian neutrality in its declaration of war of 4 August.[90]

The breach of Belgian neutrality was perceived as a massive injustice in British politics and public opinion. Foreign Secretary Edward Grey underlined in his speech in the House of Commons on 3 August that, in addition to friendship with France and British political and economic interests in the Mediterranean, among other things, the German violation of Belgian neutrality was decisive for British entry into the war. Grey described non-intervention against this background as a loss of honour in an international community of law that the British wanted to lead:

> ... if we were to say that all those things matter nothing, were as nothing, and to say we would stand aside, we should, I believe, sacrifice our respect and good name and reputation before the world, and should not escape the most serious and grave economic consequences.[91]

Although long overlooked by researchers after 1919, the First World War thus developed into a struggle for international law.[92]

With the breach of Belgian neutrality, Germany manoeuvred itself into a legitimatory dead end. It was now seen as a nation that could not adhere to the norms and 'civilizational standards' of the international legal community.[93] In a conversation with the British ambassador Edward Goschen, Imperial Chancellor Bethmann Hollweg is said to have described Belgian neutrality as a 'scrap of paper' that was not worth a war between Britain and Germany.[94] Even if it cannot be proven with certainty that Bethmann Hollweg used precisely these words, the 'scrap of paper' became a central reference in British wartime propaganda. However, it was also 'an adequate summary of what the war was actually about'.[95] As at the Hague Peace Conferences, Western European legalism and German anti-legalism were antithetical to each other.

Germany's bad reputation as a lawbreaker was reinforced during the war in view of the German army's massive violations of *ius in bello*: atrocities committed by the German army against Belgian and French civilians with more than 6,000

---

[90] The declaration of war was printed in numerous British newspapers, such as the *Daily Mail* and the *Birmingham Post* of 5 August.
[91] Quoted from Rawlinson, 'The Motif of Sacrifice in the Literature and Culture of the Second World War', in: A. Houen and J.-M. Schramm (eds), *Sacrifice and Modern War Literature: From the Battle of Waterloo to the War on Terror* (2018) 161, at 164.
[92] Hull (n. 89); Diggelmann, 'Beyond the Myth of a Non-relationship: International Law and World War I', 19 *Journal of the History of International Law* (2017) 93; Payk (n. 19); Vec (n. 20).
[93] Welch, 'Images of the Huns: The Portrayal of the German Enemy in British Propaganda in World War I', in: D. Welch (ed.), *Propaganda, Power, and Persuasion. From World War I to Wikileaks* (2013) 37; Hull (n. 89), at 43; Payk (n. 19), at 83 ff.
[94] Hull (n. 89), at 43; Payk (n. 19), at 86.
[95] Payk (n. 19), at 86.

casualties,[96] the destruction of large parts of Louvain, and the use of new weapons technologies that were problematic under international law, such as the flamethrower or poison gas.[97] The British population was outraged. Accordingly, in British propaganda, the German soldiers were called brutal, uncivilized 'Huns'.[98] The distinction between 'civilized' and 'uncivilized' nations that had emerged in the context of imperialism[99] was now having an impact on Europe.

However, even in the First World War, it was not only one side violating the laws of war: the British naval blockade caused more than 300,000 deaths among the German civilian population.[100] Although the German protests about the blockade initially triggered a response in the USA, they were ultimately unable to produce a similar effect to the British war propaganda. For there were material differences:[101] not only was the naval blockade more difficult to judge under international law than Germany's clear violation of the Treaty of 1839. The Empire was now also simply seen as 'despising international law'.[102] Since Germany had blatantly violated the 'civilizational standards of international law', it could now only invoke this very law to a limited extent. The fact that the German protests against the naval blockade had barely any effect was also due to another German breach of law: the unrestricted submarine warfare it had waged since 1 February 1917, which led the USA to enter the war.[103]

Lawyers also intervened in the dispute over the legality of German violence.[104] German legal scholars attempted to present the German breaches of law as legitimate on both the *ad bellum* and the *in bello* levels. Christian Meurer, in his *Der Volkskrieg und das Strafgericht über Löwen* (1914), presented the brutality of German action as a justifiable response to claimed attacks by Belgian *francs-tireurs*. Johannes Kriege and Josef Kohler legitimized the violation of Belgian neutrality as 'self-defence' ('*Notwehr*'),[105] or an 'act of necessity' ('*Notstandshandlung*').[106] In reference to Great Britain, the German lawyer and *Reichstag* member Ernst Müller-Meiningen argued that it was an 'irony of world history' that the state that historically had most often abused international law was now acting as the representative of international law. International law and freedom of nations were now

---

[96] *Ibid.*, at 51–94.
[97] *Ibid.*, at 232; Vec (n. 1); Vec (n. 20).
[98] A. Toppe, *Militär und Kriegsvölkerrecht. Rechtsnorm, Fachdiskurs und Kriegspraxis in Deutschland 1899–1940* (2008), at 82; Welch (n. 93).
[99] See Chapters 6.4 and 7.2.
[100] Moyn, 'Review of Isabel V. Hull, A Scrap of Paper', *The Wall Street Journal* (5 June 2014); Ziemann, 'Review of Hull, Isabel V.: A Scrap of Paper. Breaking and Making International Law During the Great War', *H-Soz-Kult* (21 May 2015).
[101] Payk (n. 19), at 82–99.
[102] *Ibid.*, at 82.
[103] Hull (n. 89), at 215–75; Payk (n. 19), at 94 ff.
[104] Vec (n. 1); Vec (n. 20).
[105] Kohler, 'Notwehr und Neutralität', 8 *Zeitschrift für Völkerrecht* (1914) 576; Hull (n. 89), at 45.
[106] Payk (n. 19), at 82–99.

to be redeemed by 'German culture—by the German essence'.[107] English and US journals such as the *American Journal of International Law*, on the other hand, emphasized the 'sanctity of treaties' and Germany's massive violation of Belgian neutrality.[108]

This battle for international law was thus indeed primarily about the German violation of Belgian neutrality and the rules of *ius in bello*.[109] Yet, the more fundamental question of whether the *ad bellum* justifications of the Empire against France and Russia were appropriate, i.e. whether the Empire was allowed to go to war at all in August 1914, played a lesser role in the debates.

However, this was not—as Jochen von Bernstorff[110] assumes—because there was a *liberum ius ad bellum* in 1914. Rather, the decisive factor was the significantly higher degree of determinacy of the international treaty law of 1839 and the 'sanctity of treaties' based on which the Allied war propaganda could justify portraying German aggression as a scandal. As Marcus M. Payk has aptly argued, by the end of the nineteenth century, positive international law had gained considerable political currency and momentum, particularly in Western European societies.[111] Respect for international law had virtually become 'a quintessence of the liberal conceptions of the world at the end of the 19th century'.[112] Accordingly, it was—

> by no means a mere formality, but indispensable to the existence of the entire international order .... The violation of Belgian neutrality therefore enabled the British government to avoid any further argument about its own, quite varied, interests in entering the war and instead to present intervention not only as justified but also as imperative for overriding reasons.[113]

Payk's finding supports my argument that the Vienna Order's prohibition of war, which had been emerging since the Congress of Vienna in 1814/15, had developed in normatively vague terms, i.e. not yet in the vocabulary of treaty law. To avoid any misunderstandings: this emerging norm *did* result from robust treaty law—the territorial order as enshrined in the Final Act of the Vienna Congress—and was institutionalized in the European Concert.[114] However, a general prohibition of war had not been formulated *expressis verbis* in any international treaty.

---

[107] E. Müller-Meiningen, *Der Weltkrieg 1914–1917 und der 'Zusammenbruch des Völkerrechts'*, vol. 1 (4th edn, 1917), at 1 ff.
[108] 'Editorial: The Hague Conventions and the Neutrality of Belgium and Luxemburg', 9 *American Journal of International Law* (1915) 959; Payk (n. 19), at 88 ff.
[109] Bernstorff (n. 75), at 257.
[110] Bernstorff (n. 75).
[111] Payk (n. 19), at 85.
[112] *Ibid.*
[113] *Ibid.*, at 85 ff.
[114] Chapter 4.

For the war discourse in August 1914, this very vaguely formulated norm was therefore more difficult to grasp than the German violation of Belgian neutrality. Ex post perspectives that conclude a 'free right to wage war' from a lack of a treaty-based prohibition of war ignore the normative complexity of nineteenth-century war discourse, which was also at work in 1914! Quite apart from the fact that the warring parties would have had no reason to go to such enormous lengths to justify themselves in war declarations and colour books if the use of force had in principle been open to any state at any time in 1914. In the historical context of 1914, it was quite logical that British war propaganda referred primarily to the strongest and clearest treaty law available to it. In other words, the First World War was not only a struggle for law, but unquestionably also a struggle for treaty law.

With the Great War, therefore, the dramatically increased role of international law and treaty law can be observed as if under a magnifying glass. Had the German violation of Belgian neutrality occurred fifty years earlier (or later), Marcus M. Payk convincingly argues, it would have been presented using different words and images.[115] In the months after August 1914, however, a key argument of the Allies had been that the war was not a struggle between rival nations, but between two antagonistic conceptions of world order.[116] International law as the language of 'civilization' was decisive for this idea.

'Necessities' of War: Elements of a German 'Special Path'

It should have become clear from the above that the First World War was an important climax in the dispute between liberal and realist conceptions of world order. Great Britain, in particular, referred to international law in this context. The political leadership of the *Kaiserreich* by no means claimed a 'free right to go to war', as bellicist German military and legal writers did.[117] In its declarations of war, however, Germany not only demonstrated knowingly invented breaches of law by France and Russia; it also pleaded for a broad interpretation of the necessity of war that had developed in Germany since the Wars of Unification.

This recourse became particularly clear in Bethmann Hollweg's infamous speech to the *Reichstag* on 4 August, in which the Imperial Chancellor announced:

> Gentlemen, we are now in a state of necessity, and necessity knows no law. Our troops have occupied Luxemburg and perhaps have already entered Belgian

---

[115] Payk, '"What We Seek Is the Reign of Law": The Legalism of the Paris Peace Settlement after the Great War', 29 *European Journal of International Law* (2018) 809, at 812.
[116] Payk (n. 115).
[117] See Chapters 7–9.

territory. Gentlemen, this is a breach of international law. It is true that the French government declared at Brussels that France would respect Belgian neutrality as long as her adversary respected it. We knew, however, that France stood ready for an invasion. France could wait, we could not .... Thus we were forced to ignore the rightful protests of the governments of Luxemburg and Belgium. The wrong—I speak openly—the wrong ['*Unrecht*', HS] we thereby commit we will try to make good as soon as our military aims have been attained. He who is menaced as we are and is fighting for his highest possession can only consider how he is to hack his way through ['*wie er sich durchhaut*'].[118]

Two aspects of Bethmann Hollweg's *Reichtstag* speech of 4 August are particularly noteworthy. *First*, the *Reichskanzler* asserted the danger of imminent French aggression, which Germany had pre-emptively forestalled.[119] However, this was a self-contradiction to the German declaration of war issued the day before. As shown above, Germany had first *pre-emptively* declared war on Russia on 1 August, but in the declaration of war on France on 3 August invented a French aggression and claimed self-defence. In other words: these justifications did not fit together logically.

Second, Bethmann Hollweg openly admitted the German violation of Belgian neutrality, and now justified it again by referring to an 'act of necessity' ('*Notstandshandlung*'): 'Necessity knows no law!' ('*Not kennt kein Gebot!*'). This, too, indicates that the German justifications for war were nothing but fabrications and lies. For the recourse to the weak argument of 'necessity' ('*Notstand*') would not have been necessary if there had been an actual French attack that would have legitimized German 'self-defence'.

This self-contradiction in Bethmann Hollweg's argumentation caught the eye of the *Reichstag* member and nationalist war advocate Müller-Meiningen.[120] According to the German lawyer, Bethmann Hollweg's declaration of 4 August contained 'a certain contradiction, strictly speaking in legal terms'.[121] Müller-Meiningen noted that Bethmann Hollweg had mixed 'self-defence'—that is defence against a 'present illegal attack' ('*gegenwärtigen rechtswidrigen Angriffs*')—with the justification of a German breach of law in Belgium in the sense of a 'state of necessity'.[122] Müller-Meiningen, however, was more than willing to overlook Bethmann Hollweg's self-contradiction. The latter, he claimed, had to be understood psychologically 'and in terms of the concrete situation'.[123] After all, the *Reichskanzler*

---

[118] Bethmann-Hollweg, 'Reichstagsrede vom 4. August 1914', in F. Thimme (ed.), *Bethmann Hollwegs Kriegsreden* (1919) 3, at 10; English Translation in U.S. Government Printing Office, *War Information Series* (1917), at 47.
[119] Hull (n. 63).
[120] Müller-Meiningen (n. 107), at 29 ff.
[121] *Ibid.*
[122] *Ibid.*
[123] *Ibid.*

was speaking 'not as a lawyer, not as a professor of international law, but as a *politician*'.[124] For Müller-Meiningen, the legally nonsensical conflation of self-defence and necessity was politically excusable.[125]

In fact, however, this excuse is not very convincing. For the contradiction in Bethmann Hollweg's speech demonstrates the changing argumentation strategies behind the scenes in German politics. In his *Reichstag* speech, the Chancellor had simply lost track of these false arguments himself. However, Bethmann Hollweg's self-contradictory speech also underlines that the German leadership was prepared to subordinate international law to an extremely broad interpretation of the 'necessity of war'—even at the *ad bellum* level![126] Realist arguments and a primacy of the political—or even a primacy of the military—were thus by no means only prevalent among the military and state-affiliated lawyers, but also guided the actions of the political elites of the Empire in their legitimization of war.

Because the Western Great Powers were more committed to a primacy of international law, the conflict between Kant's ideas and those of the early and late Clausewitz (see above) can also be identified in political practice. The *Kaiser*'s politics of international law again point to the German 'special path' in international law,[127] which was ultimately intended to conceal the real German war motives. However, the German justifications for war were considered completely unacceptable in the international order of justification. As Isabel V. Hull has shown, a specific 'military culture' had developed in the Empire since the precedent of the Franco-Prussian War.[128] Entirely in the spirit of the young Clausewitz, it was based on an existential conception of war oriented towards the destruction of the enemy, if possible, in a decisive battle. The concept promoted a total dissolution of the boundaries of violence.

This existential conception of war was not only present in bellicist realist German literature on international law.[129] Rather, a manifesto of this militaristic thinking had been published by the Great General Staff in 1902 under the title *Kriegsbrauch im Landkrieg*. In a clear analogy to Lueder's use of the 'manners' or 'customs of war' ('*Kriegsmanier*'),[130] it substituted mere 'custom and convention, philanthropy and calculating egoism' for the law of war. However, even for the observance of this wartime custom there was no 'external coercion' ('*äußerer Zwang*'); 'only "the fear of reprisals" was decisive'.[131] 'Humanitarian demands', however, 'i.e. the sparing of

---

[124] '*nicht als Jurist, nicht als Professor des Völkerrechts, sondern als Politiker*', ibid.
[125] *Ibid.*
[126] See also Hull (n. 63), at 202 ff.
[127] For a description of this 'special path', see also Koskenniemi (n. 4), at 210.
[128] Hull (n. 88), Chapter 8.
[129] Chapter 7.
[130] Chapter 7.3.
[131] Großer Generalstab, *Kriegsbrauch im Landkriege* (1902), at 2 ff.

people and property', could only come into play, according to the manifesto, 'to the extent that the nature and purpose of the war permits'.[132]

This German concept of the necessity of war had been invented in the German Wars of Unification; it was perfected in Africa. In 1884, as part of its incipient colonial policy, the German Empire claimed Southwest Africa as a German protectorate. When the Herero revolted in 1904, the German colonial power committed 'the first genocide of the 20th century'.[133] The Germans had tried in vain to defeat the Herero in a decisive battle at the Waterberg on 11 August 1904. When the approximately 60,000 Herero fled to the Omaheke Desert and thus evaded the decisive battle preferred by the Germans, the German troops sealed off the desert, leaving a large part of the Herero population to die of starvation.

This absolute delimitation of colonial from genocidal violence went back to the 'extermination order' ('*Schießbefehl*' or '*Vernichtungsbefehl*') of the commander of the German *Schutztruppe* (African colonial troops), Lothar von Trotha. On 2 October 1904, Trotha had announced:

> The Hereros are German subjects no longer. They have killed, stolen, cut off the ears and other parts of the body of wounded soldiers, and now are too cowardly to want to fight any longer.... The Herero nation must now leave the country. If it refuses, I shall compel it to do so with the 'long tube' [cannon]. Any Herero found inside the German frontier, with or without a gun or cattle, will be executed. I shall spare neither women nor children. I shall give the order to drive them away and fire on them. Such are my words to the Herero people.[134]

Trotha's order was only revised weeks later by the civilian leadership in Berlin. This, however, was also a strategic move. German troops were now needed to supress the Nama uprisings.[135]

Since the Franco-Prussian War and especially the genocide of the Herero and Nama, a primacy of the necessity of war was emerging in German discourse, which was in tension with the primacy of politics.[136] In the end, it gained the upper hand. But why was the German political discourse on the legitimacy of war in 1914 characterized by a primacy of military necessity, when in Berlin it was not a military

---

[132] *Ibid.*, at 1 ff.
[133] Zimmerer, 'The First Genocide of the Twentieth Century. The German War of Destruction in Southwest Africa (1904–1908) and the Global History of Genocide', in D.L. Bergen (ed.), *The Holocaust. Lessons and Legacies* (2008) 34.
[134] Quoted after Zimmerer, 'War, Concentration Camps and Genocide in South-West Africa: The First German Genocide', in J. Zimmerer and J. Zeller (eds), *Genocide in German South-West Africa* (2008) 41, at 42.
[135] Zimmerer (n. 133).
[136] See also Chapter 7.5.

commander like Trotha who ruled, but a civilian *Reichskanzler* like Bethmann Hollweg?

The answer to this question can be found in the structural importance of the military in the political system of the German Empire. It is not without reason that the Great General Staff has been called a 'state within the state' or, by Liebknecht, even the 'state above the state'.[137] The General Staff, which was not provided for in the imperial constitution at all, but to which military planning and, in the event of war, even command authority was subject, repeatedly became an independent political actor in the Empire itself—even in the permanent dispute over competences with the civilian political leadership. Here, too, the intra-*Clausewitzian* dispute between the primacy of politics and the primacy of the military becomes clear once again.[138]

This dispute had already become hostile in the German Wars of Unification. Moltke (the Elder) wanted to continue the war after political victory to achieve the complete destruction of France's military power.[139] Bismarck, on the other hand, in view of the dwindling international acceptance of the war, demanded an end to it[140] and—thanks to an intervention by Wilhelm I—was able to prevail against Moltke.[141] This juxtaposition of politics and the military was pictorially depicted in Anton von Werner's painting *The Proclamation of the German Empire* (18 January 1871), as Andreas observes:

> Politics [Bismarck, HS] and the military [Moltke, HS] on the same level—only subordinate to the Emperor. Therein lies a parable for errors of constitutional construction concerning the primacy of politics in the Empire.[142]

The dualism between the political and the military prevailed in the Empire—and in fact intensified: in 1883, the Great General Staff was granted *Immediatrecht* (the right of direct access to the king). From then on, it was free to advise the Emperor beyond any political control.[143]

Particularly in the Wilhelminian era, the military gained influence in the political sphere. The *Immediatrecht* was extended to almost forty command authorities of the army and navy. This decision resulted in a veritable militarization of

---

[137] Khan, '"Der ewige Friede ist ein Traum, und nicht einmal ein schöner." Anmerkungen zu einem Briefwechsel zwischen Johann Caspar Bluntschli und Helmuth Graf von Moltke', in T. Groh et al. (eds), *Verfassungsrecht, Völkerrecht, Menschenrechte – vom Recht im Zentrum der internationalen Beziehungen. Festschrift für Ulrich Fastenrath zum 70. Geburtstag* (2019) 159, at 170.
[138] See also Chapter 7.5.
[139] A. Dietz, *Das Primat der Politik in kaiserlicher Armee, Reichswehr, Wehrmacht und Bundeswehr. Rechtliche Sicherungen der Entscheidungsgewalt über Krieg und Frieden zwischen Politik und Militär* (2011), at 51 ff.
[140] See also Chapter 4.3.
[141] Dietz (n. 139), at 51 ff.
[142] *Ibid.*, at 47 ff.
[143] *Ibid.*, at 63.

the Emperor's foreign policy advice.[144] The conflict of competences developed in favour of the military. In this respect, the *Kaiserreich* differed decisively from other European states, although armies in all states tended to use unrestricted violence—an important example being the approach of the British army in the Boer Wars. At the same time, however, civilian checks and balances were much more pronounced in France and Great Britain than in the Empire.[145]

Thus, even before the July Crisis in 1914 the primacy of the military had generally prevailed in German planning for a possible war. Manfred Messerschmidt's argument, 'the attitude of the military, especially of the General Staff, did not fundamentally differ from the standards of the political leadership of the German Reich',[146] is most clearly seen in the *Schlieffen Plan*. Although the late Moltke (the Elder) came to the conclusion that Germany could only wage a two-front war against France and Russia in a defensive war,[147] after him a veritable 'ideology of the offensive'[148] prevailed among German officers. This ideology culminated in the megalomaniac *Schlieffen Plan*, which was inseparably linked to the idea of an (illegitimate) preventive war.[149]

Against this background, the path on which the German military—and politicians—found themselves in July 1914 becomes clear. In Moltke (the Younger's) view, there was a window of opportunity for the German army to successfully implement the *Schlieffen Plan* in 1914, which, however, was beginning to close because of Russia's advances in military armament. The state secretary of the *Auswärtige Amt*, Gottlieb von Jagow, reported a conversation with Moltke (the Younger) in the spring of 1914. According to Jagow, Moltke had expressed the view that 'nothing would remain ... but to wage a pre-emptive war to defeat the enemy as long as we could still sustain the war'.[150]

In July 1914, the military was able to assert the preventive logic resulting from the *Schlieffen Plan*. Bethmann Hollweg, who had only known the main features of the Schlieffen Plan since 1912,[151] admitted in a private conversation with the liberal Conrad Haussmann in January 1918:

> Yes, My God, in a certain sense it was a preventive war. But when war was hanging above us, when it had to come in two years even more dangerously and more inescapably, and when the generals said, now it is still possible, without defeat, but not in two years' time.[152]

---

[144] *Ibid.*; C.H. Hermann, *Deutsche Militärgeschichte. Eine Einführung* (3rd edn, 1979), at 265.
[145] Hull (n. 88); Hull (n. 89).
[146] Messerschmidt (n. 1), at 237.
[147] Hull (n. 88), at 161.
[148] J. Snyder, *The Ideology of the Offensive. Military Decision Making and the Disasters of 1914* (1984).
[149] D. Hoffmann, *Der Sprung ins Dunkle oder wie der 1. Weltkrieg entfesselt wurde* (2010).
[150] J. Leonhard, *Die Büchse der Pandora. Geschichte des Ersten Weltkriegs* (2014), at 92 ff.
[151] Hull (n. 63), at 201.
[152] Quoted from Geiss, 'The Outbreak of the First World War and German War Aims', 1 *Journal of Contemporary History* (1966) 75, at 82.

If recent scholarship thus gives the impression that the German declarations of war in August 1914 were—apart from the subsequent violation of Belgian neutrality—legal,[153] this overlooks the fact that the political and military leadership was not reacting to a previous or imminent attack. Their action was in line with the idea of German preventive war. However, as I have demonstrated in Part I of this study, there can be no doubt that preventive war was entirely incompatible with the norms of the Vienna Order! In those cases in which a state did justify a preventive war—in the French declaration of war on Austria in 1792,[154] in the Austrian declaration of war on Sardinia-Piedmont in 1859,[155] or in the French declaration of war on Prussia in 1870[156]—the respective state faced foreign policy isolation. A preventive war was considered aggression.[157] *Realpolitiker* such as Cavour and Bismarck, who were well aware of the normative constraints of the international order, knew this—and for precisely this reason never waged a preventive war.[158]

In 1914, however, the (supposed) preventive war of the *Kaiserreich* was to be disguised by arguments of (pre-emptive or actual) self-defence.[159] Dieter Hoffmann has therefore rightly described the First World War as a 'covert war of aggression' by Germany.[160] At the time of Germany's declaration of war, neither Russia nor France had begun hostilities against Germany (or its ally Austria-Hungary)—and according to historical sources, nor were they planning to.[161] Thus even the German leadership's idea of preventive war had no empirical basis. The historical thesis that Germany was not solely responsible for the outbreak of the war, but nevertheless bore the main responsibility, seems plausible in light of these findings.[162]

9.4 Conclusion: A German *Sonderweg*

Two central findings can be derived from the analysis of the German war discourse of political practice between 1890 and 1914. *First,* the contemporary German discourse on the legitimacy of war was indeed characterized by a 'special path'. Like political and legal theory, military and political practice in Germany was also driven by a primacy of the 'necessity of war'. This anti-legal *Sonderweg* is illustrated

---

[153] Bernstorff (n. 75); Hathaway and Shapiro (n. 79).
[154] Chapter 3.
[155] Chapter 3.3.
[156] Chapter 5.4.
[157] See also Hull (n. 63).
[158] Chapter 5.
[159] Hull (n. 63).
[160] Hoffmann (n. 149).
[161] Ullrich, 'Hegemonialkrieg oder Präventivkrieg? Neues über die Entfesselung des Ersten Weltkriegs, Rezension von Dieter Hoffmann, Der Sprung ins Dunkle oder wie der 1. Weltkrieg entfesselt wurde (2010)', *Neue Gesellschaft/Frankfurter Hefte* (2010) 71.
[162] Krumeich (n. 64); Mombauer (n. 63).

by corresponding statements by political and military leaders throughout the Wilhelmine era. Take, for instance, Wilhelm II at the Hague Conference of 1899 ('And shit on all the resolutions!'), Molke the Elder (peace as 'a dream—and not even a beautiful one'), or Bethmann Hollweg ('scrap of paper'; 'necessity knows no law'). The primacy of the military in political decision-making was a structural problem and distinctive characteristic of the *Kaiserreich*. This problem was not faced by other European Great Powers due to functioning checks and balances.

Second, it has to be noted that with this anti-legalism—and indeed antinomianism—Germany became diplomatically isolated. Germany's hostility to international law finally culminated in the concealment of a war of aggression, which followed the logic of a factually and normatively unfounded 'preventive war' and involved the invention of corresponding justifications for war by German military officers and politicians. The fact that the Empire had taken a 'special path' in its conceptions of war and international order became particularly clear in the counter-normativity of its enemies: during the Great War, the *Kaiserreich* was denied recognition as a 'civilized state'. This deprivation of its status as a full-fledged member of the legal community made cooperation after the war considerably more difficult.

But it is precisely this invention of legitimate reasons for war by the German leadership in the summer of 1914 that refutes the thesis of the 'free right to wage war', also with regard to the July crisis. War still needed justification in terms of the norms of the Vienna Order. The German leadership, which was driven by 'military realism',[163] felt bound by the international norms. It knew that it could not afford to refer to a 'free right to go to war' or to start a war without justification.

In short, the Empire became an exception in the late nineteenth-century discourse on the justification of war and international order. It rejected those international rules which it saw as obstacles to its development of power. However, the German leadership was aware that it had to obey the principles and norms of the international order, at least ostensibly, for its power to be seen as legitimate internationally. The Empire could not escape the factual power of the normative, for a normative order that prohibited aggression had been intact since 1814/15. Even the international exception, the Empire, was aware of this norm. The exception confirmed the rule(s).

[163] Messerschmidt (n. 1).

10
Old Order, New Order
Historiography between Anarchy and Progress

10.1 Introduction: Beyond Black and White

Black and white.
Two halves of a circle.
Contrasting and yet connected.
Beige background.

This briefly describes the motif of Hilma af Klint's oil painting bearing the name *Buddhas standpunkt i jorde livet*. For all those who cannot readily imagine the picture, it can be found on the cover of this book. The painting, completed by the Swedish artist in 1920, is interesting here for three reasons.

First, the world historical context: Hilma af Klint created this painting during the transitional period of interest here from the 'long nineteenth' to the 'short twentieth century'—a time of rationalization and bureaucratization, to use the words of Weber, a time characterized by the 'disenchantment of the world' (*Entzauberung der Welt*).[1] The abstract art that emerged during this period, usually associated with artists such as Wassily Kandinsky, was a counter-movement. It confronted the rational with the irrational, the concrete with the abstract, the sober with the spiritual and mystical. Af Klint's painting emerged at a time of international reorganization after the First World War. For all the legalist ideas and plans, to many the past seemed disturbing, the future unclear, and the present marked by uncertainty. Supposed security at the international level and a deep insecurity in European societies went hand in hand.

Second, the painting is interesting from a biographical perspective. With a penchant for the spiritual, the artist had already produced her first abstract paintings around 1906. According to the latest art historical research, she can therefore be considered the real pioneer of abstract art.[2] After Hilma af Klint's death in 1944, however, her work was buried under a thick layer of oblivion from which it has only gradually begun to emerge since the 1980s,

---

[1] Weber, 'Science as a Vocation [1922]', in H.H. Gerth and C. Wright Mills (eds), *Max Weber: Essays in Sociology* (1946) 129.
[2] J. Voss, *Hilma af Klint: A Biography* (2022).

and especially in the last ten years. Just like Hilma af Klint herself, *Buddha's standpunkt i jorde livet* was long forgotten. Other paintings were shown. Other artists such as Kandinsky were celebrated as pioneers of abstract art. Against the background of the reception of its artist, the oil painting therefore offers a cultural memory analogy to the object of the present work. In this book, I have argued that there was no such thing as a 'free right to go to war' in the nineteenth century, and that instead a complex and sometimes contradictory normative order prohibiting the use of force emerged. Nevertheless, this normative order fell into oblivion, while the thesis of the 'free right to go to war' was to become the prevailing doctrine in the disciplines of international relations, international law, and international history—to this day.[3] Heinrich Rettich's accurate observation in 1888 that only a minority of scholars was asserting the existence of a nineteenth-century 'positive right to go to war' against an academic mainstream, has been turned on its head.[4]

But how could this happen? In this chapter I will provide two answers to this question, in the form of brief sketches rooted in the history of science. Hilma af Klint's *Buddhas standpunkt i jorde livet* can help here in—as one might expect—abstract form, for a *third* aspect that makes the painting so interesting is the motif of the painting itself. As in the juxtaposition of two contrary standpoints, in thinking in black-and-white categories, two 'world views'[5] manifest themselves in the modern historiography of the international order, which repel, but at the same time are mutually dependent. The assertion that there was a *liberum ius ad bellum* before 1920/28/45 paradoxically fits easily into both narratives, which in fact are diametrically opposed. They have already been briefly reconstructed in Chapter 2 of this study with a view to the state of research. To close the circle, the present chapter will now deal with the genesis of these two narratives, which were to become constitutive for the formation of the academic disciplines of International Relations and International Law in the twentieth century: the *realist* narrative of 'anarchy' and the *liberal* narrative of 'progress'.

10.2 Beyond Anarchy and War: The Narrative of Progress

'What we seek is the reign of law, based upon the consent of the governed and sustained by the organized opinion of mankind.' In his 1918 declaration of US war

---

[3] Chapter 2.
[4] Chapter 7.2.
[5] On world views in International Relations, see G. Krell and P. Schlotter, *Weltbilder und Weltordnung. Einführung in die Theorie der internationalen Beziehungen* (5th edn, 2018), at 31–5; and Haas and Nau, 'Political Worldviews in International Relations. The Importance of Ideologies and Foreign Policy Traditions', in P.J. Katzenstein (ed.), *Uncertainty and Its Discontents. Worldviews in World Politics* (2022) 73.

aims, President Woodrow Wilson underlined the great importance that international law had gained during the nineteenth century.[6] As shown in the previous chapter, this also applied to the First World War. It became a struggle for law. However, the Allies' invocation of law also generated public expectations for the period after the war. After the heated disputes on international law, the latter now had to be enforced, in order not to undermine public trust in the law. To achieve this, Germany was to be held accountable for its violations of the law.

Thus, it was even considered whether to bring Kaiser Wilhelm II to trial for the German breaches of law during the war.[7] And the infamous Article 231 of the Treaty of Versailles stated that—

> The Allied and Associated Governments affirm and Germany accepts the responsibility of Germany and her allies for causing all the loss and damage to which the Allied and Associated Governments and their nationals have been subjected as a consequence of the war imposed upon them by the aggression of Germany and her allies.

The Versailles Peace Treaty was morally and legally charged in a way no other peace agreement had ever been before.[8] The idea of an international legal order was by no means abandoned due to the setbacks of the Great War. On the contrary, similar to what happened after the Napoleonic Wars,[9] the collective experience of the First World War provoked intense international deliberation about the possibilities of abolishing war. There was a 'veritable boom in world order designs'.[10] Liberalism, according to the prevailing narrative to this day, experienced its 'first heyday'.[11]

If one believes the popular narratives,[12] the Great War was the true founding moment of the modern discipline of International Relations. In 1919, in the context of the Treaty of Versailles, the first Chair of International Relations was established in Aberystwyth. One of the central themes of this supposedly 'new' discipline was collective peacekeeping and legal pacifism. Marjo Koivisto and Tim Dunne state

---

[6] Quoted from Payk, '"What We Seek Is the Reign of Law": The Legalism of the Paris Peace Settlement after the Great War', 29 *European Journal of International Law* (2018) 809, at 809.

[7] W.A. Schabas, *The Trial of the Kaiser* (2018).

[8] Lesaffer, 'Peace Treaties and the Formation of International Law', in B. Fassbender and A. Peters (eds), *The Oxford Handbook of the History of International Law* (2nd edn, 2014) 71, at 91.

[9] Chapter 4.

[10] J. Steffek and L. Holthaus (eds), *Jenseits der Anarchie. Weltordnungsentwürfe im frühen 20. Jahrhundert* (2014).

[11] N. Deitelhoff and M. Zürn, *Lehrbuch der Internationalen Beziehungen: Per Anhalter durch die IB-Galaxis* (2016), at 25.

[12] Pfaltzgraff, 'World War I and IR Theory', 43 *The Fletcher Forum of World Affairs* (2019) 5; A. Acharya and B. Buzan, *The Making of Global International Relations. Origins and Evolution of IR at its Centenary* (2019), at 82; Booth, 'International Relations: The Story So Far', 33 *International Relations* (2019) 358.

that liberal internationalism 'is the default setting for thinking about the development of international institutions since 1919'.[13]

But why only since 1919?! As the preceding historical discourse analysis should have proven, questions of international order, law, war, peace, and international institutions were already being discussed in the nineteenth century, in astonishing anticipation of the debates that would follow after the Great War. Against the background of the long history of the emergence of the modern discourse on violence and order, the innovations of 1919 are to be deemed less radical than is still assumed today—all was not as new after the Western Front as is generally claimed.

So why is 1919 seen as a turning point in international thought? One answer to this might be the important role of the League of Nations for further historiography. Despite all its weaknesses, the League of Nations (1920) represented an at times underestimated step towards the further institutionalization of the postwar world order.[14] By introducing the cooling-off period, it took up the *ius contra bellum* discourse of the nineteenth century. However, the discourse of a ban on war was not invented in 1919/20. Rather the discourse, which had been started in Vienna in 1814/15, was pursued further at the beginning and in the middle of the twentieth century. The League of Nations thus sent out an important signal.

Parallel to the 'emerging' 'new' discipline of International Relations, liberal legal doctrine in Europe and the USA turned to the idea of a prohibition of war based on positive law. More recently, Oona A. Hathaway and Scott J. Shapiro have reconstructed the development of this discourse in their readable, but historiographically problematic book *The Internationalists* (2017).[15] Hathaway and Shapiro describe how, among others, the (competing) peace activists Salmon Levinson and James T. Shotwell, the US diplomat Sumner Welles, and the British international lawyer Hersch Lauterpacht sought an 'outlawry of war' under treaty law. To achieve this, however, the 'internationalists' did not remain in an academic ivory tower. They practised political consulting. From 1918 at the latest, they persistently influenced public discourse: more than 350,000 copies of Levinson's pamphlet *The Legal Status of War* (1918) were printed—within six months! United States secretary of state Frank Kellogg was familiar with Levinson's *The Outlawry of War* (even if he later downplayed its influence[16]), and the French foreign minister Briand knew

---

[13] Koivisto and Dunne, 'Crisis, What Crisis? Liberal Order Building and World Order Conventions', 38 *Millennium: Journal of International Studies* (2010) 615; see also G. Sluga, *Internationalism in the Age of Nationalism* (2013); and A. Tooze, *The Deluge: The Great War and the Remaking of Global Order* (2015).

[14] Kennedy, 'The Move to Institutions', 8 *Cardozo L. Rev.* (1987) 841; P.O. Cohrs, *The New Atlantic Order. The Transformation of International Politics, 1860–1933* (2022), Chapter 10.

[15] This paragraph is based on Simon, 'Das Alte in der neuen Ordnung', 27 *Rechtsgeschichte - Legal History* (2019) 448.

[16] Kellogg had corresponded with the lawyer, but in 1929 could not (or refused to) remember Salmon Levinson's first name—possibly because he had learned that Levinson, like himself, had been nominated for the Nobel Peace Prize; see O.A. Hathaway and S.J. Shapiro, *The Internationalists: How a Radical Plan to Outlaw War Remade the World* (2017), at 130.

Shotwell's memorandum. Political practice and international legal theory interacted with each other.

A central result of these legal pacifist efforts was the Kellogg-Briand Pact of 1928, which contained the first treaty-based prohibition of war in history.[17] According to Hathaway and Shapiro, the 'radical plan to outlaw war' involved a transformation from an 'old order', which was supposedly characterized by a 'free right to go to war', to a 'new order', in which war was prohibited.[18] Based on the analysis of nineteenth-century political and international legal discourse on war and international order in Part I of this book, I argue that Hathaway and Shapiro's characterization of the 'old order' is historically inaccurate: there was no 'free right to go to war' in political practice.

Nor was the plan developed by Levinson, Shotwell, and others as 'radical' as Hathaway and Shapiro claim. As we have seen in Part I, throughout the nineteenth century, the outlawry of war under positive international law was regularly debated in European international legal theory.[19] However, this Kantian tradition in international legal doctrine in nineteenth-century international legal debate is almost completely ignored by Hathaway and Shapiro—as is Kant, who is only briefly mentioned in his critique of Grotius as a tiresome or 'sorry comforter'.[20] Strangely enough, an analysis of the arguably most important liberal theory of modern *ius contra bellum* and its impact is missing. If one *does* take into account the importance of Kant's work for the nineteenth-century discourse of war and order, however, the dichotomy of 'old' and 'new order' before/after 1920 can hardly be maintained. This deficient treatment of nineteenth-century legal theory and political practice results in a radical teleological history of progress, which does not do justice to the long historical evolution of the modern prohibition of war.

These objections regarding Part I of their book aside, Hathaway and Shapiro offer important insights into how interwar liberal thought continued to engage critically in the discourse of the prohibition of war.[21] This was not a new discourse. But the discourses of the 'long nineteenth century' found their continuation after the First World War. This once again underpinned Kant's dialectic of war and order.[22]

Perhaps the most important liberal legal theorist of that time was Hans Kelsen.[23] During the Second World War—another German war of aggression that had been

---

[17] Ibid.; E. Buchheim, *Der Briand-Kellogg-Pakt von 1928 – Machtpolitik oder Friedensstreben?* (1998); B. Roscher, *Der Briand-Kellogg-Pakt von 1928. Der 'Verzicht auf den Krieg als Mittel nationaler Politik' im völkerrechtlichen Denken der Zwischenkriegszeit* (2004).
[18] Hathaway and Shapiro (n. 16).
[19] Chapters 6, 8, and 9.
[20] Hathaway and Shapiro (n. 16), at 94.
[21] Ibid.
[22] Chapter 3.3.
[23] On Kelsen and international law, see e.g. J. von Bernstorff, *The Public International Law Theory of Hans Kelsen. Believing in Universal Law* (2010).

started with a fabricated reason for war (the Gleiwitz incident as part of the false flag Operation Himmler undertaken by the *Schutzstaffel* [SS])—Kelsen presented his book *Peace through Law* (1944). It was clearly written in the tradition of Kant's project of a complete legalization of national, international, and global relations.[24] For Kelsen, war was 'mass murder' ('*Massenmord*') and 'the greatest disgrace of our culture' ('*die größte Schande unserer Kultur*').[25] It had to be eradicated.[26]

Much like Kant, Kelsen was convinced that real socio-political progress was only possible through an international, ultimately universal organization capable of law enforcement.[27] And much like the nineteenth-century liberals before him,[28] Kelsen adopted important concepts from Kant, such as those of '(legal) peace' and 'cosmopolitan law', as well as Kant's federal model, which, after a long historical process, could finally merge into a 'Permanent League for the Maintenance of Peace'.[29] Kelsen saw the League of Nations as a promising, but not yet sufficient first step. A future international organization, he argued, would have to be less political and more legal—especially in the sense of the idea of arbitration.[30]

However, Kelsen differed from his legal pacifist role model in one important respect: unlike Kant, Kelsen adhered in principle to the idea of 'just war'.[31] In the literature, this has often been interpreted as a self-contradiction vis-à-vis his legal positivism. In fact, however, Kelsen's recourse to 'just war' can be better understood after having analysed the discourses on war in international law in the nineteenth century, which Kelsen was able to build on. For like nineteenth-century liberal scholars, Kelsen conceived 'just war' not as the enforcement of morality— but of law! He thus referred to an international order whose law was already constituted in principle but whose appropriate institutionalization still had to be provided in the future. Kelsen wrote accordingly that only if one was able to see in war, 'just as in reprisal', the reaction of law against injustice, 'can one recognize in it the starting point for a development that will gradually transform it from a means of self-help to a coercive act of central organs of legal protection.'[32] For Kelsen, as

---

[24] Chapter 3.3.
[25] H. Kelsen, *Peace through Law* (1944), at vii.
[26] See also Brock and Simon, 'Die deutsche Sprache des Rechts', in S. Jäger and W. S. Heinz (eds), *Frieden durch Recht: Rechtstraditionen und Verortungen* (2020) 33.
[27] See also Fassbender, 'Friede durch Recht. Hans Kelsen und die Vereinten Nationen', in H. Brunkhorst and R. Voigt (eds), *Rechts-Staat. Staat, internationale Gemeinschaft und Völkerrecht bei Hans Kelsen* (2008) 126, at 127.
[28] Chapter 6.
[29] Zolo, 'Hans Kelsen: International Peace through International Law', 9 *European Journal of International Law* (1998) 306, at 317.
[30] Ibid.
[31] See also Widłak, 'From Vladimiri's Just War to Kelsen's Lawful War: the Universality of the "bellum justum" Doctrine', 53 *Studia Philosophiae Christianae* (2017) 77; Daase and Deitelhoff, 'The Justification and Critique of Coercion as World Order Politics', in L. Brock and H. Simon (eds), *The Justification of War and International Order: From Past to Present* (2021) 489.
[32] 'Nur wenn man im Krieg, ganz ebenso wie in der Repressalie, die Reaktion des Rechts gegen das Unrecht sieht, kann man in ihm den Ansatzpunkt zu einer Entwicklung erkennen, die ihn allmählich aus einem Mittel der Selbsthilfe zu einem Zwangsakt zentraler Rechtsschutzorgane verwandeln wird.' H. Kelsen, *Unrecht und Unrechtsfolge im Völkerrecht* (1932), at 594.

for the liberals in the nineteenth century, the concept of war as a legal remedy was thus a placeholder for the future coercive act of a more sophisticated institutionalized world order. 'Just war' thus in no way contradicted Kelsen's project of positivist legalization of international relations. It was part of this project.

The Kantian idea of achieving peace through law[33] thus proved to be extremely resilient between 1919 and 1945. The United Nations, founded after the Second World War, did not mean a complete victory of legal normativity over power politics, as lawyers such as Kelsen, Schücking, or Wehberg had striven for following Kant. However, it took up the discourse on the legitimacy of war that had been developing since 1814/15 and now standardized its prohibition of war as a general prohibition of violence. Article 2(4) of the UN Charter—the 'basic norm of the international order'[34]—states accordingly:

> All members shall refrain in their international relations from the threat or use of force against the territorial integrity or political independence of any state, or in any other manner inconsistent with the purposes of the United Nations.

This was a remarkable stage victory for legal pacifists and internationalists. In liberal historiographies in particular, the UN Charter is seen as the culmination of the development of *ius contra bellum*: it is, as Lesaffer has characterized it, 'mankind's most ambitious attempt, to date, to ban war. The UN Charter stands at the end of an evolution by which the right of States to use force was progressively limited.'[35] According to Hathaway and Shapiro, the 1928 prohibition of war, an important step towards the UN Charter's prohibition of the use of force, was even 'among of the most transformative events of human history': it 'ultimately made our world far more peaceful'.[36] Kant, it seems, had triumphed over Clausewitz. 'Perpetual peace' became treaty law, the anarchy of international violence was ruled out. In this narrative of legal progress, the ongoing importance of the late nineteenth-century dichotomy between realism and liberalism once again becomes clear.

As I have shown in Part I of this book, the 1928 prohibition of war and the 1945 prohibition of the threat or use of force go back to the Vienna Order's prohibition of war, which became an emerging norm in 1814/15. One could therefore intuitively assume that twentieth-century international lawyers took up the political and normative processes and principles of the nineteenth century.

---

[33] Chapters 3.3.
[34] Dörr, 'Gewalt und Gewaltverbot im modernen Völkerrecht', 43 *Aus Politik und Zeitgeschichte* (2004) 14.
[35] Lesaffer, 'Too Much History: From War as Sanction to the Sanctioning of War', in M. Weller (ed.), *The Oxford Handbook of the Use of Force in International Law* (2015) 35, at 35; critically C. Peevers, *The Politics of Justifying Force. The Suez Crisis, the Iraq War, and International Law* (2013); I. Hurd, *How to Do Things with International Law* (2017); and T.M. Fazal, *Wars of Law: Unintended Consequences in the Regulation of Armed Conflict* (2018).
[36] Hathaway and Shapiro (n. 16), at xiii.

Surprisingly, however, the opposite is the case: liberal lawyers in the interwar period explicitly distanced themselves from the supposedly anarchic international relations of the nineteenth century. As I have already indicated in this book's Introduction, in 1941 Hans Wehberg distinguished himself particularly succinctly not only from Carl Schmitt's idea of *Ius Publicum Europaeum*,[37] but also from the European Concert of Great Powers. The international law of the nineteenth century, according to Wehberg, clearly dissociating from Schmitt, was only 'anarchic law' (*'anarchisches Recht'*) and thus an oxymoron.[38] 'Every state', argued Wehberg, 'could use the *jus belli ac pacis* to unilaterally assert not only its rights but also its political interests, if only it was militarily strong enough.' In other words, according to Wehberg, states in the nineteenth century had a 'free right to wage war', as he stated *expressis verbis*: 'Even at the Hague Peace Conferences this unrestricted right of sovereign states to wage war has not been disputed.'[39] As I have shown in Part II, however, this finding is historically inaccurate.

The reason Wehberg's contribution in Die Friedens-Warte of 1941 is nevertheless remarkable here is because it summarizes in an ideal typical way the objections of liberals in the interwar period to the international order of the nineteenth century: the Concert was too political, the normative order of Vienna too vague, and a compulsory court of arbitration was not in sight. In addition, words of praise for the political character of the Concert came from, of all people, the representative of absolute political decisionism in international relations: Carl Schmitt.

Here, then, a motive for interwar liberals to distance themselves from the supposedly 'anarchic law' of the nineteenth century becomes clear. As Emmanuelle Tourme-Jouannet has rightly observed:

> Through its unparalleled scale, the First World War changed the deal as to the issue of security and at the same time led to some particularly stinging criticism with respect to classical international law. The aspiration to peace became the fundamental provision of the internationalist discourse and it was unanimously celebrated by international lawyers from the end of the war .... Throughout the inter-war years there was an avalanche of studies on the law of peace, as if the doctrinal repetition or incantation could build a rampart against war. In truth, criticism was once again excessive and too prompt to disqualify classical international law. In an over-hasty amalgam, commentators inferred that states legally had the right to trigger any war at any time.[40]

---

[37] See Chapter 2 and below.
[38] Wehberg, 'Ideen und Projekte betr. die Vereinigten Staaten von Europa in den letzten 100 Jahren', 41 Die Friedens-Warte (1941), at 162.
[39] Ibid.
[40] E. Jouannet, *The Liberal-Welfarist Law of Nations* (2012), at 130, see also Chapter 10.3.

Efforts at peace as well as the legalization and institutionalization of the new liberal world order since 1919 from the League of Nations to the United Nations appeared all the more progressive, the more backward and anarchic the period before 1920 was portrayed. Much in this vein, Ian Brownlie characterized the phase after the First World War as a decisive era for the formation of the modern international order.[41] For this (false) claim to appear correct, however, the complex normative order of the nineteenth century had to be ignored or even downplayed.

Wehberg opted for the latter, describing the mediation regulations in the 1856 Treaty of Paris as 'modest' ('*bescheiden*').[42] He also delivered a scathing overall verdict on the international law of the nineteenth century: such a law 'as existed between the European powers before the world war', he argued, could 'not well be called the regulation of a specific order'. Nor, according to Wehberg, under 'the rule of the European Concert in the nineteenth century', could any 'fundamentally significant attempt be detected to eliminate the existing anarchy, not only on a case-by-case basis and not only by a more or less miserable compromise, but once and for all'.[43] According to Wehberg, the nineteenth century was a century of anarchy.

Wehberg, however, was not only concerned with denigrating nineteenth-century international relations as anarchic. He also wanted to emphasize the progressiveness of liberal thought and action in the interwar period. For despite the disappointing efforts of the nineteenth century, between 1919 and 1939, one had—

> at least made the unsuccessful but nevertheless remarkable attempt to eliminate international anarchy, an attempt which, incidentally, failed not least because the European powers as a whole remained among themselves too much and the United States of America did not join the League of Nations.[44]

Wehberg's message was clear: the Paris Order had proved unsuccessful in overcoming international violence. But at least it represented a serious attempt to defeat international anarchy through law—an attempt which had supposedly failed to materialize in the nineteenth century. Wehberg thus constructed the photo-negative of an 'old' and 'new order' that Hathaway and Shapiro erroneously repeat today. Wehberg was not an exception, however. Other liberal legal scholars of the interwar period made very similar statements. Hersch Lauterpacht, for example, convinced the US chief prosecutor at Nuremberg, Robert H. Jackson, that only the prohibition of war in the Kellogg-Briand Pact transformed the 'right to war' into a right against war.[45]

---

[41] I. Brownlie, *International Law and the Use of Force by States* (1963), at 65.
[42] Wehberg (n. 38), at 162; on the treaty, see Chapter 5.2.
[43] Ibid.
[44] Ibid.
[45] Hathaway and Shapiro (n. 16), at 247.

To construct this narrative, a demarcation from the nineteenth century was helpful: reference to the debates and efforts towards pacification through legalization and institutionalization since 1814/15 would have made it much more difficult to present interwar progress as 'radical'. This confirms David Kennedy's finding that liberal lawyers of the 1920s constructed a dark and anarchic image of the nineteenth century in order to portray the League of Nations and its norms as particularly progressive.[46] The incremental legalization of 1920/1928/1945 seemed all the brighter, the darker the preceding era was painted.

The light of progress was dependent on the (supposed) darkness of the past. While liberals continued to work on the further development of the international legal order in the sense of Kant's telos of *ius contra bellum*, they at the same time constructed an anarchic nineteenth century, at the centre of which was the supposed 'free right to wage war' of sovereign states. Paradoxically, then, a realist thesis was to become the midwife of the liberal historiography of the interwar period.

10.3 Beyond Law and Order: Constructing the Narrative of Anarchy

But this is just one piece of the puzzle, just one explanation for the breakthrough of the thesis of the 'free right to go war' after 1920. There is another piece of the puzzle, which leads us back to the *realist* thought on war and peace reconstructed in Part II—and back to Germany.

Since liberals upheld the idea of legal peace despite the world wars, world political events between 1919 and 1945 could by no means be interpreted solely as a history of progress in international law. In fact, as Marcus M. Payk has recently argued, the high expectations of law in Western European societies in 1919 were detrimental to political compromise in the peace settlement.[47] A look at the 1919 peace treaties underlines that law alone could not secure peace.[48] Nor would more law have prevented the First World War.[49] Paradoxically, public trust in international law made trust-building between the enemies of the First World War difficult. Political respect, recognition, and trust-building between the Great Powers and a reintegration of Germany into the international order might have created a better basis for peaceful international relations—along the lines of the Congress of Vienna, for example.

---

[46] Kennedy, 'International Law and the Nineteenth Century: History of an Illusion', 65 *Nordic Journal of International Law* (1996) 385.

[47] M. Payk, *Frieden durch Recht? Der Aufstieg des modernen Völkerrechts und der Friedensschluss nach dem Ersten Weltkrieg* (2018); Payk, '"What We Seek Is the Reign of Law": The Legalism of the Paris Peace Settlement after the Great War', 29 *European Journal of International Law* (2018) 809, at 812.

[48] *Ibid.*

[49] Chimni, 'Peace through Law: Lessons from 1914', in L. Brock and H. Simon (eds), *The Justification of War and International Order: From Past to Present* (2021) 241.

The strict legalism of the 1919/20 negotiations made a diplomatic compromise much more difficult: the Allies were determined to fulfil public expectations and punish Germany under international law. Germany, on the other hand, demanded a 'genuine' legal peace, in the sense of Wilson's fourteen points. Legal pacifist Walther Schücking, as the diplomatic representative of the young German Republic, even criticized the rigid Allied negotiating positions as an expression of a 'might is right' logic.[50] However, the desired effect remained elusive: rather, Schücking simply reaffirmed the Allies' insistence on their formalistic, legalistic positions.

From the German side, on the other hand, the Peace of Versailles was unanimously perceived as a *Diktatfrieden* ('dictated peace'). It challenged the stability of the young Weimar Republic and European peace. In other words, in 1919, international law prevented political compromise. Less law might have meant a better peace agreement. This was also true for the Ottoman Empire, which for its part entered the war on the side of Germany by recourse to an invented argument of self-defence.[51] Under the Treaty of Sèvres, it lost a large part of its territories to the new League of Nations mandate system. In the latter, Europe's imperial rule in Africa and Asia continued by other means.[52] This created the basis for new and partly still unresolved conflicts, for example in the Middle East.[53]

This argument of a 'dictated peace' was honed by realists of various colours. According to them, the international legal regulations between 1919 and 1945 were in no way conducive to international peace or the security of individual states. Realists saw the liberal legalism of the interwar years as no more than pious and utopian idealism. This was very much in line with Moltke's response to Bluntschli: a naïve dream—'and not even a beautiful one'.[54] This critique could be directly linked to the realist war discourse of the late nineteenth century.

Moreover, a direct connection can be reconstructed between the advocates of a 'free right to go to war' in the *Kaiserreich* and those in the interwar period. These linkages have been overlooked in research until now. This is hardly surprising, since the genesis of the thesis of *liberum ius ad bellum* in late nineteenth-century Germany has also been ignored.[55] For even in the few critical studies engaging with

[50] Payk, *Frieden durch Recht* (n. 47), at 409.
[51] Genell and Aksakal, '"Salvation through War?" The Ottoman Search for Sovereignty in 1914', in L. Brock and H. Simon (eds), *The Justification of War and International Order: From Past to Present* (2021) 207.
[52] M. Mazower, *No Enchanted Palace: The End of Empire and the Ideological Origins of the United Nations* (2009).
[53] A. Anghie, *Imperialism, Sovereignty and the Making of International Law* (2004), Chapter 3; N. Tzouvala, *Capitalism As Civilisation. A History of International Law* (2020), Chapter 3.
[54] Chapter 8.2.
[55] Anthony Carty's brilliant article on German legal scholarship might be an exception to the rule here. However, Carty identifies only one proponent of *liberum ius ad bellum* (Rettich) and therefore comes to the wrong conclusion that *liberum ius ad bellum* was a minority opinion in the *Kaiserreich*; see Carty, 'The Evolution of International Legal Scholarship in Germany during the Kaiserreich and the

the historiography of the nineteenth-century use of force, the 'myth of *liberum ius ad bellum*' and/or the 'narrative of indifference' are said to have emerged only as ex post constructions after the First World War. For instance, Emmanuelle Tourme-Jouannet has pointed to the genesis of the narrative 'that states [in the nineteenth century, HS] legally had the right to trigger any war at any time' as an effort of interwar commentators to disqualify international law and legal scholarship before 1920. Much in this vein, Agatha Verdebout has recently argued that it was only 'during the interwar years, that the narrative of indifference first surfaced in scholarship'.[56] However, while the interwar years were indeed decisive for the further consolidation of these narratives,[57] the roots of the latter are not to be found here, but in the complex legal discourse on the use of force in the late nineteenth century: as I have reconstructed in Part II of this book, both narratives—that of '*liberum ius ad bellum*' and that of 'indifference'—were indeed developed by realist legal scholars mainly in the German Empire.

This realist German tradition was taken up by revisionist scholarship in the Weimar Republic. Unsurprisingly, the thesis of *liberum ius ad bellum* was particularly popular among realists of the interwar period. It was now directly linked to the question of German war guilt. In his book *Freies Kriegsführungsrecht und Kriegsschuld* ('Free Right to Go to War and War Guilt'), published in 1931, Hanns Göhler, for example, raised the question of whether waging war had been forbidden in 1914. In line with the thesis of *liberum ius ad bellum*, Göhler came to the conclusion that there had been no prohibition of war under international law in 1914. In his analysis, Göhler positively referred to the protagonists of the bellicist and positivist variants of the thesis of the 'free right to go to war' in the German Empire: Carl Lueder and Heinrich Rettich.

The national conservative lawyer Fritz van Calker was also familiar with Lueder's as well as Rettich's work on the law of war. Unsurprisingly, the realist Calker advocated the thesis of *liberum ius ad bellum*: war was for him 'the violent means of the representation of interests between states'.[58] War was 'neither according to its modern concept nor its historical development' a legal means.[59] Calker made these arguments in his review of a book which I have studied in depth in Part II: Heinrich Rettich's *Recht zum Krieg*. Calker had published his book review in 1889, a year

---

Weimarer Republik (1871–1933)', 50 *German Yearbook of International Law* (2007/2008) 29, at 29; for my discussion of Carty's article, see also Chapter 7.

[56] A. Verdebout, *Rewriting Histories of the Use of Force. The Narrative of 'Indifference'* (2021), at 231; see also Bernstorff, 'The Use of Force in International Law before World War I: On Imperial Ordering and the Ontology of the Nation State', 29 *European Journal of International Law* (2018) 233.
[57] Chapter 8.2.
[58] Calker, 'Rezension von Rettich, Heinrich (1888): Zur Theorie und Geschichte des Rechts zum Kriege. Völkerrechtliche Untersuchungen. Stuttgart: Kohlhammer', 31 *Kritische Vierteljahrsschrift für Gesetzgebung und Rechtswissenschaft* (1889) 592, at 594.
[59] Ibid., at 593.

after the publication of both Rettich's work and Calker's own PhD thesis *Das Recht des Militärs zum administrativen Waffengebrauch* ('The Right of the Military to the Administrative Use of Arms') (1888).

Göhler and Calker are examples of those jurists who made the 'legal' doctrine of the *Clausewitzians* in the German Empire[60] into a foundation for the discourses of the Weimar Republic and ultimately the Third Reich. Calker was not only to become a member of the National socialist Academy for German Law (*Akademie für deutsches Recht*) founded by *Reichsleiter* Hans Frank, but was also the doctoral supervisor and mentor of the German scholar who would play a key role in the manifestation of the thesis of the 'free right to go to war' to this day: Carl Schmitt.

This brings us to the beginning of this book. Schmitt's theoretical engagement with the decision for or against war is, as I have already outlined above,[61] characterized by absolute decisionism. Like his realist predecessors in the nineteenth century, Schmitt saw himself as, to a certain extent, following the tradition of Carl von Clausewitz. Schmitt wrote approvingly of the latter's anti-Napoleonic sentiments that a political thinker was always 'drawn into the enmity of the fighting fronts'.[62] According to Schmitt, this was a fact inherent in the concept of the political, which could not be eliminated or mitigated by correct thinking. Rather, it was increased and intensified by the latter, Schmitt wrote, quoting Jean Nicolas Arthur Rimbaud: '*Le combat spirituel est plus brutal que la bataille des hommes*' ('The spiritual battle is more brutal than the battle of men').[63] Schmitt tried here to use Clausewitz's ('Prussian') military and political theory for his thinking in categories of 'enemy' and 'friend'.

Carl Schmitt, I argue, became the most important and effective representative of the thesis of the 'free right to go to war' in the twentieth century. The 'crown jurist of the Third Reich' turned not only against liberalism and parliamentarism,[64] but also against the cosmopolitan project of international legalization. Schmitt became a direct opponent of Hans Kelsen on the question of the legitimacy of war.[65] Whereas Kelsen had understood 'just war' as a provisional means of decentralized coercion of a legal order yet to be adequately institutionalized,[66] Schmitt saw the enforcement of universal peace through war as a self-contradiction of liberal lawyers. According to Schmitt, liberals justify war as a measure to secure peace, but in the end, it remains just that: war.[67]

---

[60] Chapters 7 and 8.
[61] Chapter 2.2.
[62] Schmitt, 'Clausewitz als politischer Denker. Bemerkungen und Hinweise', 6 *Der Staat* (1967) 479.
[63] *Ibid.*
[64] C. Schmitt, *Die geistesgeschichtliche Lage des heutigen Parlamentarismus* (1924).
[65] For a general account, see D. Diner and M. Stolleis (eds), *Hans Kelsen and Carl Schmitt. A Juxtaposition* (1999).
[66] Chapter 10.2.
[67] C. Schmitt, *Der Begriff des Politischen* (1932); Slomp, 'Carl Schmitt's Five Arguments against the Idea of Just War', 19 *Cambridge Review of International Affairs* (2006) 435.

As I have shown in Part II of this book, this criticism was not completely unjustified. However, any affirmative reference to Schmitt, which unfortunately has become fashionable again across academic disciplines (and beyond), is to be omitted here. It seems to me not only ethically highly questionable but also scientifically unnecessary. *First*, Schmitt's critique of the coercive character of international law was neither new nor was it original. Such a critique (albeit in a reflexive sense) was, as shown above, already voiced in the nineteenth century by critical liberals such as Walther Schücking.[68] Hans Kelsen even called the international legal order a 'coercive order' by definition.[69]

Second, and perhaps even more importantly, a positive reference to Schmitt's critique of liberalism obscures the view of his actual, thoroughly bellicist theorem of realpolitik. Schmitt was a highly reactionary author,[70] not least with regard to the legitimization of war. Behind his critique of the 'turn to the discriminatory concept of war', which the Berlin lawyer associated with the League of Nations and the condemnation of the Empire after the First World War, there was anything but a pacifist attitude.[71] When Schmitt argued against the League of Nations, the Kellogg-Briand Pact, and the 'discriminatory concept of war', he attempted to make war—including war of aggression—justifiable as a political means. At the heart of these considerations, most systematically developed in Schmitt's *Der Nomos der Erde*, was the thesis of *liberum ius ad bellum*.[72]

Carl Schmitt therefore continued the tradition of bellicist realist lawyers that had developed in the context of the German Empire. He pursued the idea of an illiberal power state, which made decisions beyond international norms of law or morality and was allowed to resort to war whenever it appeared necessary for a desired expansion of power in its claimed 'greater space' ('*Großraum*'), a space 'in which extra-regional [foreign] powers may not interfere'.[73] Schmitt derived the concept of *Großraum* from the Monroe Doctrine formulated in 1823.[74] His adaption of the doctrine was intended to grant a new 'Greater German Reich' ('*Großgermanische Reich*') an unlimited right to use force without condemnation or interference from outside.

---

[68] Chapter 6.5.
[69] H. Kelsen, *Peace through Law* (1944).
[70] On the importance of continuing to recall Schmitt's involvement in National Socialism, see recently Weiler, 'Editorial: Cancelling Carl Schmitt?', 32 *European Journal of International Law* (2021) 389, available at: *EJIL Talk!* (13 August 2021): https://www.ejiltalk.org/cancelling-carl-schmitt/ (last visited 1 December 2022).
[71] See, for instance, C. Schmitt, *The Nomos of the Earth in the International Law of the Jus Publicum Europaeum*, translated by G.L. Ulmen (2006 [1950]) 152.
[72] See Chapter 2.2.
[73] C. Schmitt, *Völkerrechtliche Großraumordnung: mit Interventionsverbot für raumfremde Mächte. Ein Beitrag zum Reichsbegriff im Völkerrecht* (1941).
[74] Schmitt, 'Grossraum versus Universalism: the International Legal Struggle over the Monroe Doctrine [1939]', translated by M. Hannah, in S. Legg (ed.), *Spatiality, Sovereignty and Carl Schmitt. Geographies of the Nomos*, 46; on the Monroe Doctrine, see also Chapter 4.3.

It is therefore not surprising that Hitler, too, spoke of the '*Großraum*' and the Monroe Doctrine when rejecting Roosevelt's demand for peace, which the US President had addressed to Hitler and Mussolini on 14 April 1939 after the German military occupation of Czechoslovakia:[75] in a speech of 28 April 1939, Hitler replied to Roosevelt that the latter would certainly invoke the Monroe Doctrine with regard to Latin America and that Germany was now doing the same with regard to Europe, but in any case with regard to the interests of the 'Greater German Reich'.[76] Based on this 'German Monroe Doctrine', Hitler's war of aggression and extermination was now legitimized as a war in the alleged 'German *Großraum*'. Schmitt's ideas on international order not only went hand in hand with the National Socialist *Großraum* policy; he provided direct justifications for Hitler's violence—be it the execution of enemies within ('Night of the Long Knives' of 1923)[77] or aggression against other states.[78]

However, the fact that even Hitler found it necessary to invent a previous Polish attack ('Since 5.45 a.m. we have been returning the fire, and from now on bombs will be met by bombs') to justify his aggression against Poland on 1 September 1939 underlines the fact that the doctrine of *liberum ius ad bellum* had not met with any international acceptance in the Paris Order. It was—and remained—a German *Sonderweg*, which subordinated law to the politics of the sovereign.

It is unsurprising that Schmitt also adhered to the totalitarian interpretation of the tradition of military necessity in his argument that the laws of war could be overridden by sovereign decision in cases of 'emergency'. This is clearly reminiscent of the *Kriegsbrauch im Landkrieg* manifesto of the Great General Staff of 1902.[79] Schmitt thus drew on the bellicose realist tradition of lawyers such as Lueder and Meurer,[80] as well as on the military culture of the *Kaiserreich*.[81] As already emphasized above,[82] Schmitt's continuation of the Empire's *Clausewitzian* school of thought was not motivated by a theory of international law, but by one of power politics through and through. Against this background, Martti Koskenniemi's claim that Carl Schmitt should actually be understood as a representative of political realism is correct.[83] The thesis of *liberum ius ad bellum* assumed central importance in his conception of war.

---

[75] R. Mehring, *Carl Schmitt. Aufstieg und Fall* (2nd edn, 2022), at 400.
[76] Quoted after V. Neumann, *Carl Schmitt als Jurist* (2015), at 457.
[77] Schmitt, 'Der Führer schützt das Recht', 39 *Deutsche Juristen-Zeitung* (1934) 945.
[78] It is controversial in historical research whether Hitler was aware of Carl Schmitt's writing on the Monroe Doctrine and '*Großraum*'. What is certain, however, is that Hans Frank let Schmitt know in a phone call that Hitler attached importance to the originality of his thoughts, and that Schmitt's theory gained popularity through Hitler's speech, Neumann (n. 76), at 457.
[79] Chapter 9.3.
[80] Chapter 7.4.
[81] Chapter 9.
[82] Chapter 2.2.
[83] M. Koskenniemi, *The Gentle Civilizer of Nations. The Rise and Fall of International Law 1870–1960* (2002), at 494.

The fact that Carl Schmitt's narrative of a transformation of early modern war discourse towards *liberum ius ad bellum* is still widely disseminated today—not least in the form of the significant influence of Schmittian '*Großraum*' thinking on Russia[84] and China, 200 years after the birth of the original Monroe Doctrine in 1823—is highly problematic in several ways. This narrative is not only historically wrong, but also motivated by realpolitik and anti-legalism. It should therefore be urgently dispensed with.

10.4 Two Halves of a Whole: The Discursive Robustness of a Myth

In the interwar period, liberal and realist positions went head-to-head in the legal discourse on war (legitimacy) and peace. A closer analysis shows that both liberal and realist authors drew on the theoretical debate of the late nineteenth century to discredit the opposing position. The dispute was therefore not new. It was only continued in a modified form.

The fact that realists such as Calker or Schmitt continued to refer to the thesis of *liberum ius ad bellum* is hardly surprising. For them, international relations were shaped by power political interests. At best, war could be hedged—and thus re-legitimized. *Ius in bello* stabilized the 'free right to go to war' in realist notions of anarchy and 'greater space'. However, it could also be arbitrarily restricted and pushed aside, in line with the military primacy of the necessity of war. This realist tradition was continued by conservative reactionary thinkers such as Carl Schmitt in the Weimar Republic. The thesis of *liberum ius ad bellum* therefore continued to exist in the sense of its black-and-white dichotomy of friend vs foe.

What is more surprising, however, is that in the interwar period liberals, too, claimed that there had been a *liberum ius ad bellum* in the nineteenth century. Yet this recourse was made for a completely contrary motive. Liberal international lawyers were concerned with developing a narrative of progress that necessitated a demarcation of 'backward' and 'progressive' in the sense of the figurative dichotomy between black and white of Hilma af Klint's *Buddhas standpunkt i jorde livet*: the darker the supposed 'anarchy' appeared before 1920, the brighter progress could shine after 1920. Liberals thus used the realist thesis of the 'free right to go to war' in the nineteenth century and the narrative of anarchy based on it to give credence to their own 'belief in progress'.[85]

---

[84] Mälksoo and Simon, 'Aggression and the "Civilizational Turn" in Russian Politics of International Law: An Interview with Lauri Mälksoo', *Völkerrechtsblog* (25 February 2022), available at: https://voelkerrechtsblog.org/de/aggression-and-the-civilizational-turn-in-russian-politics-of-international-law/ (last visited 1 December 2022).

[85] For a critical account on progress in international law, see Altwicker and Diggelmann, 'How is Progress Constructed in International Legal Scholarship?', 25 *European Journal of International Law* (2014) 425.

In doing so, however, they ultimately strengthened a false discourse of memory. Because liberals in the interwar period did not object to the historically inaccurate assertion of a nineteenth-century *liberum ius ad bellum*, the long liberal tradition of efforts towards *ius contra bellum* in the previous century was ignored. The 'first heyday'[86] of liberalism is therefore still located in the interwar period. When Martti Koskenniemi writes of the renaissance of 'just war' after 1919, arguing that this 'new just war' was distinguished by the fact that it emerged in a completely secular environment, 'with the significant twist that the power to decide where justice lay was now arrogated to the League Council',[87] the latter is not wrong in principle. But it also undercuts the efforts of the liberal legal doctrine in the nineteenth century to link 'just war' with positive law and thus to secularize it. For 'just war' was part of the liberal discourse on the legitimacy of war throughout the entire nineteenth century!

Liberals thus ultimately denied their own long tradition of thinking about *ius contra bellum* since the first half of the nineteenth century. This negligent disregard of the modern discourse of war legitimization and the normative order of the nineteenth century clearly favoured the rise of the myth of the 'free right to go to war'. This was all the truer since, despite liberal optimism about progress, the increased regulation and institutionalization of international relations after 1919 and the prohibition of war in the Kellogg-Briand Pact failed to prevent renewed violence: neither Japan's invasion of Manchuria (1931–32) or the Second Sino-Japanese War (1937–45), nor the failure to appease Hitler and, associated with it, the Second World War and the Holocaust. It is true that the United Nations' prohibition of the use of force further legalized and institutionalized the discourse on the legitimacy of war. Furthermore, the democratic German and Japanese successor states adopted a ban on the preparation and conduct of wars of aggression in their constitutions (Article 26 of the German Basic Law) and a renunciation of war (Article 9 of the Japanese Constitution). Moreover, large parts of German international law doctrine after 1945 were oriented towards liberal legalism.[88]

Against the backdrop of the global bloc formation of the Cold War and the global 'balance of terror', however, realism began its triumphal march in the political and academic study of international relations and their history. Despite increasing global interdependence,[89] realist thought on the balance of power became central. This was accompanied by a theoretical narrowing across disciplines: the importance of the scientific paradigm of peace and international order dramatically

---

[86] Deitelhoff and Zürn (n. 11), at 25.
[87] Koskenniemi (n. 83), at 425.
[88] F. Lange, *Praxisorientierung und Gemeinschaftskonzeption. Hermann Mosler als Wegbereiter der westdeutschen Völkerrechtswissenschaft nach 1945* (2017); see also Brock and Simon, 'Die deutsche Sprache des Rechts', in S. Jäger and W. S. Heinz (eds), *Frieden durch Recht: Rechtstraditionen und Verortungen* (2020) 33.
[89] R.O. Keohane and J.S. Nye, *Power and Interdependence. World Politics in Transition* (1977).

declined. As already mentioned above,[90] E.H. Carr (1939) formulated a harsh critique of the 'idealists' of the interwar period in his *The Twenty Years' Crisis*. Hans J. Morgenthau, in turn, made Carr's book known in the USA and established realism there as the leading school of thought in modern international relations.[91] It was now less Kant than Thucydides, Machiavelli, Hobbes, and Clausewitz who were perceived as authorities on international relations. Clausewitz, it seemed, had triumphed over Kant.

While the balancing of power and morality certainly played an important role in the thinking of Morgenthau—an international legal scholar by training[92]—a 'denormativization' (*Entnormativierung*)[93] of realist theory occurred after him, particularly in Kenneth Waltz's structural realism. Realist theory now turned primarily to performing a balancing act between the global rival powers, the USA and the USSR.

This increasing dominance of realist thinking after 1945 was also conducive to the further spread of the myth of the 'free right to go to war'. Now, no straw man of realism is to built here: this is a rich tradition with different and sometimes contradictory strands. Important classical realists such as Morgenthau had quite an ambivalent view on the relationship between power and norms. While Morgenthau conducted a 'hidden dialogue' with Carl Schmitt,[94] he was at the same time shaped not only by German but also by Anglo-American legal influences.[95] However, it was not least through the enthusiastic and affirmative reception of Carl Schmitt that the German tradition of realpolitik was able to attain significance in the realist theory of international relations.[96]

According to Isabel V. Hull, the *Machtstaat* of the German Empire now became a model state for realist theory formation.[97] Even if this assessment could be considered exaggerated, Martti Koskenniemi has rightly noted that Schmittian perspectives on politics and law were to become 'absolutely central' to realism in international relations theory.[98] This remains true today. The reception of and

---

[90] Chapter 8.2.
[91] W.E. Scheuerman, *Hans Morgenthau: Realism and Beyond* (2009).
[92] O. Jütersonke, *Morgenthau, Law and Realism* (2010).
[93] Daase and Deitelhoff, 'Jenseits der Anarchie: Widerstand und Herrschaft im internationalen System', 56 *Politische Vierteljahresschrift* (2015) 299.
[94] Scheuerman (n. 91).
[95] For the various influences, see for example Koskenniemi (n. 83), at Chapter 6; Scheuermann (n. 91); Jütersonke (n. 92); Reichwein, 'Rethinking Morgenthau in the German Context', *International Relations Online Working Papers Series* (2011); C. Rohde and J. Troy (eds), *Macht, Recht, Demokratie. Zum Staatsverständnis Hans J. Morgenthaus* (2015).
[96] On the nineteenth-century roots of the dialogue between German and US realists, see M. Specter, *The Atlantic Realists: Empire and International Political Thought Between Germany and the United States* (2022).
[97] I.V. Hull, *A Scrap of Paper: Breaking and Making International Law during the Great War* (2014), at 14.
[98] Koskenniemi (n. 83), at 494.

fascination with Schmitt continues unabated.[99] Schmitt's thesis of the emergence of a non-discriminatory concept of war resulting in *liberum ius ad bellum* has been widely received—across disciplines.

As a result, the thesis of the 'free right to go to war' continued to prevail after 1945 in International Relations, International History, and the History of International Law. The author of the German-language standard book on the history of international law, Wilhelm Grewe,[100] referred frequently and positively to Carl Schmitt's *Großraumlehre*. Schmitt had a strong influence on Grewe.[101] Grewe thus also disseminated Carl Schmitt's central theses at the same time—and with this the *Clausewitzian* tradition of the German Empire. This already becomes clear from Grewe's approach of writing the history of international law as a history of hegemonic powers and assigning them corresponding epochs.

Furthermore, Grewe also took from Schmitt the idea of a transformation of the early modern discourse on war towards a 'non-discriminatory concept of war'. Wilhelm Grewe was thus to become one of the main proponents of the myth of *liberum ius ad bellum*.[102] His *Epochs of International Law*, much of which he wrote during the Third Reich, and which was first published in 1984 and translated into English by Michael Byers in 2000, remains today one of the most important reference works on the history of international law. As Jürgen Habermas has rightly observed in a comment on Matthew Specter's *The Atlantic Realists*, in post-war Germany, Wilhelm Grewe 'played a role similar to that of Morgenthau in the USA'.[103] But also Habermas (like so many others), as a leading liberal intellectual, fell for the realist narrative of Schmitt and Grewe when he assumed that the 'free right to go to war' was the structural core of classic international law.[104]

And yet, early on, there was also criticism of the new dominance of (neo-) realism in the scholarly study of war justifications. Here, German historian Konrad Repgen deserves particular mention as a pioneer of research on war justifications beyond the realist paradigm. Around the same time as Grewe's *Epochs* was first published,[105] Repgen had criticized realist approaches as unhistorical in a programmatic essay on the scholarly study of war manifestos in the early modern period. Repgen did this—as he states in his essay—in a dialogue with an American colleague. When, at the end of the winter of 1984, Repgen reports, he—

---

[99] But there are also more recent critical discussions of Schmitt: see Teschke, 'Carl Schmitt's Concepts of War: A Categorical Failure', in J. Meierhenrich and O. Simons (eds), *The Oxford Handbook of Carl Schmitt* (2016) 367; Weiler (n. 70).

[100] Hueck, 'Völkerrechtsgeschichte: Hauptrichtungen, Tendenzen, Perspektiven', in W. Loth and J. Osterhammel (eds), *Internationale Geschichte. Themen - Ergebnisse - Aussichten* (2000) 267.

[101] Fassbender, 'Stories of War and Peace: On Writing the History of International Law in the "Third Reich" and After', 13 *European Journal of International Law* (2002) 479, at 511 ff.

[102] Chapter 2.2.

[103] See 'Reviews' available at: https://www.sup.org/books/title/?id=28906 (last visited 1 December 2022).

[104] J. Habermas, *The Divided West*, edited and translated by C. Cronin (2006), at 118.

[105] W.G. Grewe, *The Epochs of International Law*, translated and revised by M. Byers (2000), at 209.

had already spent a considerable part of his research leave for a year, weeks and weeks, in the [Bavarian, HS] State Library in Munich, searching rather in vain (and therefore, as I openly confess, sometimes close to despair) for texts of early modern war manifestos from all over Europe, I met an American colleague.[106]

It is worth quoting this dialogue (as reported by Repgen) in its entirety.[107] Repgen recalls that when his US colleague heard what he was looking for,

> he asked me, with the benevolent sad look of a neurologist: 'What on earth do you want to do with these texts?'
> I replied: 'Read them.'
> US colleague: 'But these texts contain nothing but lies.'
> I replied: 'It is for exactly that reason that I want to study them.'[108]

The American colleague mentioned here argued entirely in the spirit of realism: legitimations of war are propaganda without normative meaning.[109] Repgen's counterargument was groundbreaking. He continued:

> And besides: they are not just lies, but they are all pleas, and these use, I suspect, a quite manageable number of arguments, of justifications. If this proves to be correct, then we should be able to generate a fairly complete compilation of these arguments. This way we could advance our understanding of the onset of wars in Europe from the fall of Constantinople to the French Revolution. Nobody can force us to continue to look at international relations as an issue of the balance of power, ... which has been the dominant approach for the past 250 years. Presumably we would learn more by looking into the specific reasons given by the war parties to legitimize their use of force. We would thus be able to construct a pattern which would enable us to discover and describe the particular as it relates to the general without resorting to whatever is fashionable at a certain time.[110]

Repgen clearly opposed ahistorical neo-realist notions of balance of power. Paul W. Schroeder would later do the same when confronting Kenneth Waltz's theory with historical complexity.[111] Repgen's 1985 essay was thus in several respects a genuinely pioneering analysis of war justifications.[112] It is unclear, however, why

---

[106] K. Repgen, *Kriegslegitimationen in Alteuropa. Entwurf einer historischen Typologie* (1985), at 19 ff.
[107] Simon and Brock, 'The Justification of War and International Order: From Past to Present', in L. Brock and H. Simon (eds), *The Justification of War and International Order: From Past to Present* (2021) 3, at 10 ff.
[108] Repgen (n. 106), at 19 ff.
[109] See also Chapter 3.
[110] Repgen (n. 106), at 19 ff.
[111] Schroeder, 'Historical Reality vs. Neo-Realist Theory', 19 *International Security* (1994) 108.
[112] See also Simon and Brock (n. 107), at 11 ff.

Repgen did not continue his work on war manifestos—even though he had collected quite a respectable amount of historical material. Repgen's work was later continued by Anuschka Tischer,[113] among others. In any case, back in 1985, Repgen was unable to break the dominance of realism in the academic treatment of war discourses.

Only after the end of the Cold War and the peaceful reunification of Germany, which realist approaches were unable to adequately explain,[114] did this dominance decline in favour of new liberal as well as constructivist approaches in international relations. The context around 1990 would thus also have been well suited to deconstructing the myth of the 'free right to go to war'. Paradoxically, however, exactly the opposite happened. The myth was perpetuated in liberal and critical historiographies: Martti Koskenniemi, for example, confirmed the thesis of the 'free right to go to war' in his much-acclaimed article 'The Politics of International Law' in the founding issue of the *European Journal of International Law* in 1990. Koskenniemi wrote: 'The legal scholarship of the 19th century ... [i]n particular ... renounced theories of the just war: war now became one political procedure among others'.[115]

The myth of the 'free right to go to war' thus remained unchallenged at the end of the Cold War—despite the 'historiographical turn in international law' triggered, at least to some extent, by Koskenniemi's *Gentle Civilizer* (2002). The fact that the myth lives on to this day is, in my opinion, primarily due to the importance of liberal narratives of progress, which despite all critical tendencies in the (history of) international relations and international law still run deep in both disciplines. Even leading liberal intellectuals such as Jürgen Habermas,[116] Michael Walzer,[117] Mary Kaldor,[118] and Ernst-Otto Czempiel,[119] or leading critical authors such as Martti Koskenniemi[120] or Antony Anghie,[121] have not challenged the realist thesis of *liberum ius ad bellum*. Yet particularly interesting in this context is the teleological foreshortening recently made by Oona A. Hathaway and Scott J. Shapiro to serve

---

[113] A. Tischer, *Offizielle Kriegsbegründungen in der Frühen Neuzeit. Herrscherkommunikation in Europa zwischen Souveränität und korporativem Selbstverständnis* (2012); see also Tischer, 'Princes' Justifications of War in Early Modern Europe: the Constitution of an International Community by Communication', in L. Brock and H. Simon (eds), *The Justification of War and International Order: From Past to Present* (2021) 65.
[114] Deitelhoff and Zürn (n. 11), Chapter 6.
[115] Koskenniemi, 'The Politics of International Law', 1 *European Journal of International Law* (1990) 4, at 6.
[116] Habermas (n. 104), at 117 ff.
[117] Walzer, 'The Triumph of Just War Theory (and the Dangers of Success)', 69 *Social Research* (2002) 925, at 927.
[118] M. Kaldor, *New and Old Wars. Organized Violence in a Global Era* (3rd edn, 2012), at 19.
[119] E.-O. Czempiel, *Friedensstrategien. Eine systematische Darstellung außenpolitischer Theorien von Machiavelli bis Madariaga* (2nd edn, 1998), at 89; B. Heuser, *War: A Genealogy of Western Ideas and Practices* (2022), at 189 ff.
[120] Koskenniemi (n. 115), at 6.
[121] Anghie, 'Wo der Imperialismus noch wirkt', *Frankfurter Rundschau* (27 January 2018).

the narrative of progress.[122] Their juxtaposition of the 'old' and 'new order' makes for an exciting read. But it is unsubstantiated and fails to take historical complexity into account. In their teleology, liberals ultimately support Carl Schmitt's realist narrative of *liberum ius ad bellum*—just as their predecessors did in the interwar period.

In view of the historical complexity of the nineteenth-century normative order regulating the use of force, however, this narrative of progress is just as unconvincing as that of anarchy. The programme of the Enlightenment was the disenchantment of the world (understood as the dissolution of myths through science), but an absolute, i.e. uncritical belief in the 'rule of reason' leads to exactly the opposite: 'enlightenment reverts to mythology' ('*Aufklärung schlägt in Mythologie zurück*'), as Theodor W. Adorno and Max Horkheimer formulated it.[123] Belief in 'radical' progress is historically unconvincing: it does not enlighten but in fact helps to create myths.

10.5 Conclusion: Towards a New Historiography of War and International Order

To conclude the present chapter: I have argued that after its emergence in the German *Kaiserreich*, the strengthening of the myth of *liberum ius ad bellum* in the twentieth century can be traced back to a multitude of intertwined political and scientific circumstances that defy simple black-and-white dichotomies. In today's historiography of international order, this myth, the genesis of which can now be explained, is still omnipresent, as identified in the Introduction of this study. For to this day, textbooks on the history and theory of international law and international relations state that sovereign states had a 'free right to go to war' (*liberum ius ad bellum*) in the nineteenth century.[124] The historiography of the modern international order to date has strictly followed this assertion. Epochs and caesurae have been determined in accordance with it. In turn, continuities have been overlooked, dissenting voices have been marginalized, silenced, and forgotten.

It is therefore by no means an exaggeration to describe the thesis of *liberum ius ad bellum* as almost constitutive of the historiography of the modern international order. In light of the findings in Part I of this book, however, conventional historiography of the genesis of the modern international order governing the use of force is not convincing. It is therefore in need of revision. After the rediscovery

---

[122] Hathaway and Shapiro (n. 16).
[123] M. Horkheimer and T.W. Adorno, *Dialektik der Aufklärung. Philosophische Fragmente* (2015 [1944]), at 6.
[124] Introduction and Chapter 2.

of Hilma af Klint, the art historian Julia Voss wrote an article for the *Frankfurter Allgemeine Zeitung* calling for art history to be rewritten.[125] In a certain analogy to Voss, a similar demand can also be made here. The history of the modern international order, especially in respect of its dialectical relationship to the justification of war,[126] must be rewritten. If the present study has contributed to this endeavour, then it has achieved its goal.

---

[125] Voss, 'Die Kunstgeschichte muss umgeschrieben werden', *Frankfurter Allgemeine Zeitung* (24 February 2013).
[126] See also Simon and Brock (n. 107), at 10 ff.

CONCLUSION

11
War, Normativity, and the Birth of Modern International Order

Was there a 'free right to go to war' in the nineteenth century? This question is still predominantly answered in the affirmative in research today—even though it is rarely asked explicitly. In the present study, therefore, before answering it, the question had to be formulated as such.

To do this, however, the thesis of *liberum ius ad bellum* first had to be reconstructed. The thesis is based on the narrative of a transformation of the European discourse on the legitimacy of war. According to this narrative—made prominent in particular by Carl Schmitt[1] and Wilhelm G. Grewe[2]—the medieval doctrine of 'just war' (*bellum iustum*) was abandoned in the course of the early modern period. In the nineteenth century at the latest, the 'heyday of state sovereignty', every state was always entitled to go to war in the absence of a prohibition of war. Accordingly, war required no justification, but was 'merely the continuation of politics by other means', in the sense of Carl von Clausewitz. Nineteenth-century international relations are therefore said to have been characterized by anarchy in the all-important field of the use of force.

This widespread and, at first glance, conclusive narrative is countered in the present study by a simple but momentous observation: the history of war is at the same time a history of its justification and critique. References to 'just causes' are not only to be found in international relations 'again' since 1918, after they were supposedly gradually eradicated since the early modern period and especially in the nineteenth century; rather, arguments of *bellum iustum* can be identified throughout history. This fundamental finding of the need for justification remains unchanged to this day. States—like all political actors—are 'justifying beings'[3] and this also applies to violence.

How can this be explained? From a realist point of view, the justification of war is at best political propaganda without normative meaning.[4] It is 'cheap talk'[5] or

---

[1] C. Schmitt, *The Nomos of the Earth in the International Law of the Jus Publicum Europaeum*, translated by G.L. Ulmen (1950).
[2] W.G. Grewe, *The Epochs of International Law*, translated and revised by M. Byers (2000), at 209.
[3] R. Forst, *Normativity and Power. Analyzing Social Orders of Justification* (2017), at 15.
[4] Grewe (n. 2), at 623.
[5] Goldsmith and Posner, 'Moral and Legal Rhetoric in International Relations: A Rational Choice Perspective', 108 *John M. Olin Program in Law and Economics Working Paper* (2000), at 21.

'cheating'[6] which is not to be trusted. There is no doubt that justifications of war are usually also used to conceal the political motives of a use of force. However, this is not the end of the story, but rather its beginning. Even when Hitler declared on 1 September 1939 that 'since 5:45 a.m. we have been returning the fire', this was an attempt to justify the German war of aggression as self-defence. Irrespective of the fact that Hitler had planned his war of aggression and extermination long in advance, this justification communicatively confirmed the ban on aggressive war that had been developing in Europe since 1814/15 and was regulated under treaty law in 1928.

In other words, regardless of 'real' or 'hidden' political motives behind war justifications, states usually refer to international norms in their attempts to legitimize violence. They do so in order to portray their own violence as 'internationally appropriate behaviour'.[7] By having recourse to norms, states are thus, according to Lothar Brock, seeking 'to make something available to themselves, the value of which for them is its unavailability'.[8] Even if a state is referring to a norm for reasons of power politics, it must still fundamentally recognize the normativity of this norm and the discursive effect it has in the international 'communication community'.[9] Otherwise, recourse to it would simply be politically pointless. The communicative practice of legitimizing war is undoubtedly always political—but not only: rather, it takes place in the nexus between power and normativity.[10]

This makes it clear, however, that discourses on the legitimation of war do not refer to anarchy, but to order in international relations. International justifications and critiques of violence can thus be understood as communicative practices of formation, enforcement, and questioning[11] of international norms and thus of 'normative orders'.[12] In this context, the discourse of the legitimation of war and the formation of the international order as an 'order of justification'[13] are historically co-constitutive. Just as the discourse on the legitimacy of international violence

---

[6] C. Schmitt, *Der Begriff des Politischen* (1932), at 55.

[7] Finnemore and Sikkink, 'International Norm Dynamics and Political Change', 52 *International Organization* (1998) 887, at 891; Jepperson, Wendt and Katzenstein, 'Norms, Identity, and Culture in National Security', in P.J. Katzenstein (ed.), *The Culture of National Security: Norms and Identity in World Politics* (1995) 33, at 54.

[8] Brock, 'Frieden durch Recht?', in P. Becker, R. Braun, and D. Deiseroth (eds): *Frieden durch Recht* (2010) 15, at 31.

[9] A. Tischer, *Offizielle Kriegsbegründungen in der Frühen Neuzeit. Herrscherkommunikation in Europa zwischen Souveränität und korporativem Selbstverständnis* (2012); see also Tischer, 'Princes' Justifications of War in Early Modern Europe: the Constitution of an International Community by Communication', in L. Brock and H. Simon (eds), *The Justification of War and International Order: From Past to Present* (2021) 65.

[10] Forst (n. 3); see also Chapter 2.

[11] On contestation, see A. Wiener, *The Invisible Constitution of Politics. Contested Norms and International Encounters* (2008).

[12] N. Deitelhoff, *Überzeugung in der Politik. Grundzüge einer Diskurstheorie internationalen Regierens* (2006); R. Forst and K. Günther (eds), *Die Herausbildung normativer Ordnungen. Interdisziplinäre Perspektiven* (2011); R. Forst and K. Günther (eds), *Normative Ordnungen* (2021).

[13] Forst (n. 3).

shapes the international order of legitimate reasons for violence, this normative order shapes what is sayable in practices of justifying war.

The historical continuity of this co-constitution of 'the justification of war and international order', which Lothar Brock and I have already analysed in an edited volume under this title elsewhere,[14] has been the decisive factor in this study for testing the empirical validity of the 'free right to wage war' with the help of a genealogy of modern war justifications. The focus of the analysis—based on a critical examination of the Eurocentric thesis of *liberum ius ad bellum*—has been on the discourse of the European Great Powers as well as the theory of international law of the 'long nineteenth century' (1789–1918). Both theory and practice were deeply enmeshed in imperialism, nationalism, and racism (see below). As could be shown in Part I of the book, the principle that had been valid since European antiquity was also adhered to in the nineteenth century: war was always considered legitimate if it was either to sanction a breach of law that had been committed or was in self-defence.

This fundamental principle did not change in the transition from the early modern period to the nineteenth century. A transformation of the discourse of war justification from 'just war' to the 'free right to go to war', as claimed by authors as different as Carl Schmitt[15] and Michael Walzer,[16] did *not* take place. Contrary to what is asserted in research to this day, the doctrine of 'just war' by no means enjoyed a shadowy existence in the discourse of the nineteenth century.[17] Rather, the historical analysis of war legitimation reveals a continuity of the doctrine of *bellum iustum* that cannot be seriously disputed: states continued to refer to 'just causes' to justify their international violence. The doctrine of 'just war' was not outlawed in the Vienna Order—indeed, it was highly compatible with it.

In the absence of a prohibition of war under treaty law, the majority of nineteenth-century liberal lawyers also continued to appeal to the doctrine of 'just war'—even if they increasingly endeavoured to transform the doctrine into positive law. These attempts to modify the law by liberal lawyers confirm another fundamental feature of the modern discourse on the legitimacy of war: the continuity of the need to justify war by no means implies that everything in it has always remained the same. In the sense of Koselleck's 'structures of repetition' ('*Wiederholungsstrukturen*'),[18] the discourse on the justification of war and the international order has consolidated historically and yet is dynamic at the same time: it continues to develop in the historical process. For even if political actors refer to an

---

[14] L. Brock and H. Simon (eds), *The Justification of War and International Order: From Past to Present* (2021).
[15] Schmitt (n. 1).
[16] Walzer, 'The Triumph of Just War Theory (and the Dangers of Success)', 69 *Social Research* (2002) 925, at 927.
[17] As argued by Grewe (n. 2), at 623; S.C. Neff, *War and the Law of Nations: A General History* (2005), at 62; see also I. Brownlie, *International Law and the Use of Force by States* (1963), at 27.
[18] Koselleck, 'Wiederholungsstrukturen in Sprache und Geschichte', 57 *Saeculum* 1.

existing normative order in their justifications of war, they are at the same time endeavouring to shape this order, e.g. through reinterpretations of existing norms or the formulation of alternative normative claims. In their recourse to the existing norms, the actors legitimizing violence thus always also create something new.[19] Old and new world views, normative convictions, and discursive continuities and innovations go hand in hand here.

This can be observed particularly clearly in the formation of the international order related to the genealogy of war legitimations as a narrowing of the range of legitimate reasons for war: in the early modern period, the international order was barely institutionalized. At the same time, however, there was a particularly large number of different reasons for justifying violence that vied with each other for discursive acceptance in the communication community of princes.[20] In contrast, as I have argued, the dispute, both theoretical and in political practice, over legitimate international violence in the context of the French Revolution and the Coalition Wars triggered the quest for a stronger institutionalization of the European discourse on the legitimacy of war.

My argument is that it was during the revolutionary era that the modern discourse on the legitimacy of war started to emerge in the face of the danger of popular war. Immanuel Kant and Carl von Clausewitz provided probably the most innovative—and at the same time mutually contradictory—responses to this challenge. They established a bifurcation of the modern discourse on the legitimacy of war between primacies of international law (Kant) and political means (Clausewitz).[21]

After the victory over Napoléon, the international order of justification developed in the direction of Kant's theories. This was reflected in a considerable narrowing of the range of legitimate reasons for violence in the Vienna Order from 1814/15 onwards both in political practice and legal theory. Throughout the nineteenth century, liberal lawyers referred to Kant's project of 'perpetual peace' to discuss the necessity and possibility of a legal prohibition of war. This proves that Carl Schmitt's claim that Kant's 'influence on areas of international law ... became evident only in the 20th century' was completely wrong.[22] In political practice, since 1814/15, war was only considered legitimate if it could be justified as a contribution

---

[19] Brock and Simon, 'Justifications of the Use of Force as Constitutive Elements of World Order. Points of Departure, Arrivals, and Moving Destinations', in L. Brock and H. Simon (eds), *The Justification of War and International Order: From Past to Present* (2021) 503; Brock and Simon, 'Discourses of Power and Normativity: Ordering the International via War Justifications', *Völkerrechtsblog* (04 June 2021), available at: https://voelkerrechtsblog.org/de/discourses-of-power-and-normativity/ (last visited 1 December 2022); see also, for an affirmative account, Wouter Werner's review, Werner, 'Rethinking the Justification of War. A Case Study of the Fight Against the LRA', *Völkerrechtsblog* (04 June 2021), available at: https://voelkerrechtsblog.org/de/rethinking-the-justification-of-war/ (last visited 1 December 2022).
[20] Tischer (n. 9).
[21] Chapter 3.3.
[22] Schmitt (n. 1), at 168.

to the general peace of Europe or as self-defence. This international order, with the Concert of Europe as its central institution, was built on a vague normative vocabulary. However, the justifications for violence in the context of measures short of war and '(humanitarian) intervention' in the first half of the century confirmed the validity of its norms,[23] as did the justifications presented for wars between the Great Powers in the middle of the century.[24]

As other studies as well as several chapters in this book prove, violence was not only justified within Europe. Rather, violence of the European Great Powers towards non-European peoples was also legitimized—the latter also being systematically discriminated against by European international law which classified them as 'semi-' or 'uncivilized' peoples.[25] This also manifests the highly paradoxical character of the Vienna Order: peace, trust, and solidarity between the Great Powers in Europe went hand in hand with coercion and violence against medium-sized and smaller powers, as well as with imperialism and colonialism. For some nineteenth-century pacifists, the Vienna Order was thus both a cause of and an end to violence.

The fact that the Vienna Order did indeed also have violence-limiting effects within Europe can be seen in the case of preventive violence, which was perceived as aggression. This becomes clear in the analysis of the justification discourse of the Italian and German Wars of Unification (Austrian and French declarations of war) as well as in the First World War (Germany's declaration of war). Even *Realpolitiker* such as Bismarck, Cavour, or Napoléon III were aware that preventive violence had *never* been accepted as legitimate in the international (communication) community and would therefore meet with resistance from the Concert.[26] In the First World War, Germany even invented French aggression in order not to have to legitimize its own aggression as preventive war. As is well known, this attempt backfired.[27]

The impression that the international norms of the Vienna Order narrowed down the acceptable reasons to justify the use of force in international relations is largely confirmed by nineteenth-century legal doctrine.[28] And the further revaluation of positive law at the end of the nineteenth century at the Hague Peace Conferences also supports the finding that modern *ius contra bellum* did not emerge only in the twentieth century. Rather, the prohibition of war became an emerging norm in the context of the European Concert in 'Vienna 1814/15'. There was no place for a 'free right to go to war' in this emerging normative order of

---

[23] Chapter 4.
[24] Chapter 5.
[25] Chapter 5; see also A. Anghie, *Imperialism, Sovereignty and the Making of International Law* (2004), Chapter 1; Benton, 'Protection Emergencies: Justifying Measures Short of War in the British Empire', in L. Brock and H. Simon (eds), *The Justification of War and International Order: From Past to Present* (2021) 167; N. Tzouvala, *Capitalism As Civilisation. A History of International Law* (2020).
[26] Chapter 5.
[27] Chapter 9.
[28] Chapters 4, 6, and 8.

modernity. This 'right of the strongest' would have fundamentally contradicted the justification practice of the contemporaries and its underlying normativity.

Yet it would be an abridgement of the historical complexity of war discourses to reduce them solely to the dichotomy between power and law. For this would underestimate the diversity of normative claims in the history of war justifications, which, in addition to constricting, also allows for the expansion of justifications of violence in existing normative orders. Genealogical discourse research as it is understood here is rather a form of discourse analysis in the context of conflicts: as the historical analysis of war justifications has shown, the meaning and authority of norms is always contested.[29] A war discourse is thus at the same time always a 'struggle over the possibility of structuring, or even dominating, the store of justifications on which others can draw',[30] or in the words of Rudolf von Jhering: a 'struggle for law'.[31] In this process, actors justifying violence benefit, on the one hand, from the 'indeterminacy'[32] of norms and the accompanying scope for interpretation. And on the other hand, they benefit from the diversity of moral, legal, ethical, religious, technical, and other 'norms ... without binding rules of collision in the case of conflicts of norms'.[33]

This historically constant and highly dynamic multinormativity of war discourses offers politicians the opportunity to play off different normative claims against each other and to circumvent norms without having to question their discursive authority in recourse to political arguments. From the perspective of a Kantian legal pacifism, this pitting of different norms against each other is highly problematic. It enables political actors to bypass international law to a certain extent in their war justifications. At the end of the supposedly 'positivist nineteenth century', this was still possible through recourse to the argument of humanity, religion, and national self-determination. And even in the UN Charter, to date the high point of the legal limitation of the use of force,[34] natural law lives on in Article 51, which states that '[n]othing in the present Charter shall impair the inherent right of individual or collective self-defence'. The debates on the relationship between

---

[29] Wiener (n. 11).

[30] Forst (n. 3), at 63.

[31] R. von Jhering, *The Struggle for Law*, translated by J.J. Lalor (1997 [1915]), at 1; see also Cotterrell, 'The Struggle for Law: Some Dilemmas of Cultural Legality', 4 *International Journal of Law in Context* (2009) 373; and J. von Bernstorff and P. Dann (eds), *The Battle for International Law: South-North Perspectives on the Decolonization Era* (2019).

[32] M. Koskenniemi, *From Apology to Utopia. The Structure of International Legal Argument. Reissue with a New Epilogue* (2005).

[33] Vec, 'Multinormativität in der Rechtsgeschichte', in Berlin-Brandenburgische Akademie der Wissenschaften (vormals Preußische Akademie der Wissenschaften) *Jahrbuch 2008* (2009) 155, at 162–5.

[34] See also Lesaffer, 'Too Much History: From War as Sanction to the Sanctioning of War', in M. Weller (ed.), *The Oxford Handbook of the Use of Force in International Law* (2015) 35, at 35; critically C. Peevers, *The Politics of Justifying Force. The Suez Crisis, the Iraq War, and International Law* (2013); I. Hurd, *How to Do Things with International Law* (2017).

the UN Charter and natural law continue to this day,[35] as has been the subject of particularly controversial discussion in the case of NATO's military intervention in Kosovo in 1999.[36]

The United Nations Charter is accompanied by both a narrowing and an expansion of the practice of justifying war: as Tanisha M. Fazal has shown, there have been only two formal declarations of war between states in thirty-six interstate military conflicts since 1945.[37] This empirical finding underlines that the positive law's narrowing of the range of legitimate reasons for war has a direct influence on the justification practice of states. However, this does *not* mean that the world has become less violent, nor that supposedly 'new' forms of violence are no longer justified. Rather, this finding points to the fact that since 1945, violence has rarely been formally legitimized *as* war, but rather, for example, as police action, or intervention to protect human rights.[38] These strategies to circumvent the concept of war also existed in the nineteenth century: where war seemed illegitimate under international law, intervention could sometimes be justified by reference to religion, national honour, self-determination, and humanity. So even though these are not new strategies, they have not lost their importance since then.

The Russian war of aggression against Ukraine confirms this in a particularly dramatic way today. Not only is the war euphemistically called a 'special operation' by the Russian state, but its accurate designation as 'war' is usually prosecuted in Russia with massive prison sentences of up to fifteen years. Russia's contemptuous treatment of basic international norms point to the Kremlin's *Großraum* thinking. Exactly 200 years after the Monroe Doctrine (1823), Russia claims absolute power of disposal over the states in what it defines as its 'territorial backyard': to Russia's leadership, Ukraine is part of a common geopolitical family—the '*Russkiy mir*'.[39] In view of this political decisionism and Russia's contemptuous treatment of

---

[35] Brown, 'Justified: Just War and the Ethics of Violence and World Order', in L. Brock and H. Simon (eds), *The Justification of War and International Order: From Past to Present* (2021) 435; for a contrasting view, see Marauhn, 'How Many Deaths Can Article 2(4) UN Charter Die?', in L. Brock and H. Simon (eds), *The Justification of War and International Order: From Past to Present* (2021) 449.

[36] *The Independent International Commission for Kosovo* found that the intervention was 'illegal, but legitimate', see *The Kosovo Report: Conflict, International Response, Lessons Learned* (2000), at 4; see also Habermas, 'Bestiality and Humanity: A War on the Border between Legality and Morality', 6 *Constellations* (1999) 263; for a critical account see Brock, 'Normative Integration und kollektive Handlungskompetenz auf internationaler Ebene', 6 *Zeitschrift für Internationale Beziehungen* (1999) 323; see also Chinkin, 'The Legality of Nato's Action in the Former Republic of Yugoslavia (FRY) under International Law', 49 *The International and Comparative Law Quarterly* (2000) 910.

[37] T.M. Fazal, *Wars of Law: Unintended Consequences in the Regulation of Armed Conflict* (2018).

[38] *Ibid.*; Brock (n. 8); T. Hippler and M. Vec (eds), *Paradoxes of Peace in Nineteenth Century Europe* (2015).

[39] Mälksoo and Simon, 'Aggression and the "Civilizational Turn" in Russian Politics of International Law: An Interview with Lauri Mälksoo', *Völkerrechtsblog* (25 February 2022), available at: https://voelkerrechtsblog.org/de/aggression-and-the-civilizational-turn-in-russian-politics-of-international-law/ (last visited 1 December 2022); Kotova and Tzouvala, 'In Defense of Comparisons: Russia and the Transmutations of Imperialism in International Law', 116 *American Journal of International Law* (2022) 710.

international norms, it may hardly come as a surprise that the political doctrine of Carl Schmitt has become particularly important in the international thought of influential Russian scholars such as Alexsandr Dugin and Alexsandr Panarin.[40]

Nevertheless, besides the importance of *Großraum* thinking, even Moscow cannot avoid justifying its violence internationally. What is striking about these justifications is that they are also characterized by multinormativity. Russia refers to international law when it is useful, e.g. to prior Western violations of international law (Kosovo 1999; Iraq 2003; Libya 2011), and ignores it when it runs counter to its own justification strategy.[41] Russia's attempts to justify what is unmistakably aggression are too weak to generate broad international legitimacy.[42] Putin, to refer to Thomas Franck's famous formula here,[43] has not killed Article 2(4) of the UN Charter after all. However, important states such as India, South Africa, Brazil, and Mexico (not to mention China) did not join the Western sanctions policy against Russia in 2022. Thus, the multinormative arguments seem to catch on, at least partially.

This points to the fact that multinormativity in the discourse on the justification of war is multifaceted and ambivalent. For it can tempt political actors to circumvent the law. St Petersburg, for example, succeeded in 1877 in justifying a war against the Ottoman Empire that violated international law by referring to morality and religion.[44] But multinormativity has also been helpful to condemn war. At the end of the nineteenth century, liberal lawyers such as Walther Schücking resorted to moral arguments in order to construct a positive legal prohibition of war *de lege ferenda*.[45] Even Kant, as the forefather of modern legal pacifism, derived his plea for the legalization of human relations from a non-legal sphere: reason. In normative terms, too, the historicizing analysis of multinormativity thus eludes simple black-and-white dichotomies.

This addresses the final finding of this work, that of the emergence of the myth of the 'free right to go to war': for the historiography of the international order to date is still characterized by black-and-white thinking.[46] The latter is based on two central narratives that resulted in the historical complexity of the nineteenth-century

---

[40] Auer, 'Carl Schmitt in the Kremlin: the Ukraine Crisis and the Return of Geopolitics', 91 *International Affairs* (2015) 953.

[41] Mälksoo, 'The Annexation of Crimea and Balance of Power in International Law', 30 *European Journal of International Law* (2019) 303; Robinson and Antonov, 'In the Name of State Sovereignty? The Justification of War in Russian History and the Present', in L. Brock and H. Simon (eds), *The Justification of War and International Order: From Past to Present* (2021) 395.

[42] A total of 141 states condemned the Russian war of aggression in the UN General Assembly at the beginning of March 2022, and 143 states declared the annexations of the Ukrainian regions of Luhansk, Donetsk, Zaporizhzhya, and Kherson invalid in October 2022; see also Brock and Simon, 'Ist das Völkerrecht am Ende?', *Frankfurter Rundschau* (28 November 2022).

[43] Franck, 'Who Killed Article 2(4)? or: Changing Norms Governing the Use of Force by States', 64 *American Journal of International Law* (1970) 809.

[44] Chapter 6.4.

[45] Chapter 6.4.

[46] Chapter 10.

international normative order largely being forgotten in the twentieth century. *First*, a liberal narrative of progress that highlights legal progress after the First World War by disregarding the normative order of the nineteenth century. *Second*, a realist narrative of anarchy that rejects the idea of normative progress in international relations in favour of total political decisionism. Paradoxically, these two—mutually exclusive—narratives both underpin the prevailing doctrine that there was a 'free right to go to war' before 1920. They fit together like two halves of a whole to construct the image that, when it comes to the use of force in international relations, the nineteenth century was a century of anarchy (as I have tried to illustrate with Hilma af Klint's 1920 *Buddhas standpunkt i jorde livet* as the cover image of this book). The myth of *liberum ius ad bellum* has survived to this day not least because it corresponds to the memory agendas of both realism *and* liberalism.

In order to trace—and deconstruct—this myth, it was therefore necessary to depart from well-trodden methodological paths. It was particularly important to link the discourses of legal and political theory with those of political practice. Only with this connection of nineteenth-theory theory and practice could the emerging normative order regulating the use of force be reconstructed (Part I). Moreover, only with a deeper analysis of the legal discourses of the nineteenth century could the beginnings of the thesis of the 'free right to wage war' be located among realist lawyers in the German Empire (Part II).

To recapitulate once again: the 'free right to go to war', which to this day enjoys great popularity in the public, political, and scientific discourses, never actually existed. It is an invention of realist legal scholars at the end of the nineteenth century and therefore represents a myth in the History of International Relations and International Law. War remained in need of justification throughout the nineteenth century. The latter, in turn, was neither an era of international anarchy nor a photonegative of the modern international order—but the era of its birth.

Select Bibliography

Note: Sources (1.) as well as Literature before 1920 (2.) are complete. Under 'Literature after 1920' (3.), I have listed a selection of the research literature cited in this book.

1. Sources

1.1 Source Editions

C. Abel, *Letters on International Relations before and during the War of 1870*, vol. 2 (1871).
L.K. Aegidi and A. Klauhold (ed.), *Das Staatsarchiv. Sammlung der officiellen Actenstücke*, vol. 6 (1864).
Foreign Office (ed.), *British and Foreign State Papers*, vol. 57: 1866–1867 (1871).
W.G. Grewe (ed.), *Fontes Historiae Iuris Gentium (FHIG), Sources Relating to the History of the Law of Nations*, vol. 2: 1493–1815 (1988).
W.G. Grewe (ed.), *Fontes Historiae Iuris Gentium (FHIG), Sources Relating to the History of the Law of Nations*, vol. 3/1: 1815–1945 (1992).
O.A. Hathaway et al., *War Manifestos Database* (2017), available online at https://documents.law.yale.edu/manifestos (last visited 1 December 2022).
E. Hertslet, (ed.), *The Map of Europe by Treaty*, vol. 2 (1875).
E. Hertslet, (ed.), *The Map of Europe by Treaty*, vol. 4 (1891).
J. von Jasmund (ed.), *Aktenstücke zur orientalischen Frage*, vol. 2. (1855).
K. Kautsky, *Documents allemands relatifs à l'origine de la guerre: collection complète des documents officiels*, vol. 4 (1922).
J.L. Klüber (ed.), *Akten des Wiener Kongresses in den Jahren 1814 und 1815*. 8 vols (1815–19).
H. Kohl, (ed.), *Die politischen Reden des Fuersten Bismarck* (1893).
W. Schüßler (ed.), *Bismarck: Die gesammelten Werke*, vol. 10 (1928).

1.2 Declarations and Justifications of War (in chronological order)

Cloots, 'Discours prononcé à la barre de l'Assemblée nationale le 12 avril 1792, l'an IV de la liberté, par Anarcharsis Cloots, Orateur du genre humain', in M. Duval (ed.), *Écrits révolutionnaires 1790–1794* (1979) 338.
Déclaration de guerre de la France au roi de Bohême et de Hongrie (20 April 1792).
Decree of the French National Assembly (21 April 1792).
Franz II, *Contre-Declaration de la Cour de Vienne au Sujet de l'Agression de la France* (5 July 1792).
Franz II, *Manifeste de François II, empereur très chrétien, roi de Bohême et de Hongrie; fait à Vienne et envoyé à tous les rois de l'Europe, sur l'attaque de la Turquie contre l'Empire, sur l'invasion prochaine des troupes françoise; sur la levée de 700 mille hommes de troupes dans ses états, et sur la déclaration de guerre de la France contre l'Angleterre et la Hollande* (30 January 1793).
Decree of the National Convention . . . declaring that the French Republic is at war with Spain (1793), in Hathaway et al. (eds), *War Manifesto Database* (2017), available at https://documents.law.yale.edu/manifestos (last visited 1 December 2022).

George III, 'Message from George III (12 February 1793)', in R. Coupland (ed.), *The War Speeches of William Pitt the Younger* (1915) 52.

Pitt, 'The French Declaration of War (12 February 1793)', in R. Coupland (ed.), *The War Speeches of William Pitt the Younger* (1915) 52.

'Decree of the French National Convention declaring William Pitt an "Enemy of Mankind" (7 August 1793)', in W.G. Grewe (ed.), *Fontes Historiae Iuris Gentium (FHIG), Sources Relating to the History of the Law of Nations*, vol. 2: 1493–1815 (1988) 661.

Friedrich Wilhelm III, 'Manifest des Königs von Preußen Friedrich Wilhelm III. zur Begründung der Kriegserklärung an Frankreich vom 9. Oktober 1806', in P.A.G. Meyer (ed.), *Corpus Juris Confoederationis Germanicae oder Staatsacten für Geschichte und öffentliches Recht des Deutschen Bunds* (3rd edn, 1858) 150.

D.J.A.C., *El tirano de la Europa, Napoleon primero: manifiesto que á todos los pueblos del mundo y principalmente á los españoles* (1808).

Hardenberg, 'Kriegserklärung an Frankreich, 16. März 1813', in P.A.G. Meyer (ed.), *Corpus Juris Confoederations Germanicae oder Staatsacten für Geschichte und öffentliches Recht des Deutschen Bundes* (3rd edn., 1858) 163.

Friedrich Wilhelm III, 'An mein Volk. Se. Majeſtät der König haben mit Sr. Majeſtät dem Kaiser aller Reußen ein Off- und Defensiv-Bündniß abgeschlossen', *Schlesische privilegirte Zeitung* (20 March 1813) 593 ff.

'Austro-Prusso-Russian Circular Dispatch (8 December 1820)', in W.G. Grewe (ed.), *Fontes Historiae Iuris Gentium (FHIG), Sources Relating to the History of the Law of Nations*, vol. 3/1: 1815–1945 (1992) 113.

'Greek Declaration of Independence (1822)', in Hathaway et al., *War Manifesto Database* (2017), available at: https://documents.law.yale.edu/manifestos (last visited 1 December 2022).

'Manifesto of the Ottoman Porte – Issued in the beginning of January, after the Departure of the Ambassadors (within the Annual Register) (1828)', in Hathaway et al. (eds), *War Manifesto Database* (2017), available at: https://documents.law.yale.edu/manifestos (last visited 1 December 2022).

Manifesto of 23 March 1848 to Venice, in Venice governo provvisorio, *Raccolta per ordine cronologico di tutti gli atti, decreti, nomine ecc. del governo prov. della Repubblica veneta (di Venezia)* (1848).

'Turkish Declaration of War against Russia (4 October 1853)', in E. Hertslet (ed.), *The Map of Europe by Treaty*, vol. 2 (1875) 1171.

'Russian Declaration of War against Turkey (20 October/1 November 1853)', in E. Hertslet (ed.), *The Map of Europe by Treaty*, vol. 2 (1875) 1177.

Westminster, 'War Declaration', *The London Gazette* (28 March 1854).

'Austrian Declaration of War against Sardinia (28 April 1859)', in E. Hertslet (ed.), *The Map of Europe by Treaty*, vol. 2 (1875) 1362.

'Sardinian Declaration of War against Austria (29 April 1859)', in E. Hertslet (ed.), *The Map of Europe by Treaty*, vol. 2 (1875) 1365.

'French Declaration of War against Austria (3 May 1859)', in E. Hertslet (ed.), *The Map of Europe by Treaty*, vol. 2 (1875) 1368.

'French Declaration of War (19 July 1870)', in M. Schilling (ed.), *Quellenbuch zur Geschichte der Neuzeit. Für d. oberen Klassen höherer Lehranst* (1884) 464 ff.

'Bismarck's Declaration of War', in C. Abel (ed.), *Letters on International Relations before and during the War of 1870*, vol. 2 (1871) 430.

'Alexander Gortschakow (19 November 1876)', in E. Hertslet (ed.), *The Map of Europe by Treaty*, vol. 4: 1875–1891 (1891) 2523.

'Alexander II's Declaration of War (24 April 1877)', in E. Hertslet (ed.), *The Map of Europe by Treaty*, vol. 4: 1875–1891 (1891) 2599.
'Alexander Gortschakow (9 April 1878)', in E. Hertslet (ed.), *The Map of Europe by Treaty*, vol. 4: 1875–1891 (1891) 2712.
Franz Joseph I, 'An Meine Völker!', *Wiener Zeitung* (29 July 1914).
Wilhelm II, 'Erste Balkonrede Kaiser Wilhelms II., Berlin (31 July 1914)', *Kriegs-Rundschau. Zeitgenössische Zusammenstellung der für den Weltkrieg wichtigen Ereignisse, Urkunden, Kundgebungen, Schlacht- und Zeitberichte*, vol. 1 (1914/15) 37.
Wilhelm II, 'Zweite Balkonrede des Kaisers, Berlin (1 August 1914)', *Kriegs-Rundschau. Zeitgenössische Zusammenstellung der für den Weltkrieg wichtigen Ereignisse, Urkunden, Kundgebungen, Schlacht- und Zeitberichte*, vol. 1 (1914/15) 43.
'German Declaration of War (1 August 1914)', in J.B. Scott (ed.), *Diplomatic Documents Relating to the Outbreak of the European War* (1916) 1377.
'British Declaration of War (4 August 1914)', *Birmingham Post* (5 August 1914).

1.3 (Peace) Treaties (in chronological order)

Traité De Paix Entre La France Et Les Puissances Alliées, Conclu A Paris, Le 30 Mai 1814, Et Traités Et Conventions signés Dans La Même Ville Le 20 Novembre 1815 (1815).
'Constitution of the Germanic Confederation (8 June 1815)', in W.G. Grewe (ed.), *Fontes Historiae Iuris Gentium (FHIG), Sources Relating to the History of the Law of Nations*, vol. 3/1: 1815–1945 (1992) 174.
'Final Act of the Congress of Vienna (9 June 1815)', in W.G. Grewe (ed.), *Fontes Historiae Iuris Gentium (FHIG), Sources Relating to the History of the Law of Nations*, vol. 3/1: 1815–1945 (1992) 3.
'The "Holy Alliance" (14/26 September 1815)', in W.G. Grewe (ed.), *Fontes Historiae Iuris Gentium (FHIG), Sources Relating to the History of the Law of Nations*, vol. 3/1: 1815–1945 (1992) 107.
'Quadripartite Alliance of the Great Powers (20 November 1815)', in W.G. Grewe (ed.), *Fontes Historiae Iuris Gentium (FHIG), Sources Relating to the History of the Law of Nations*, vol. 3/1: 1815–1945 (1992) 100.
'Protocol of the French Accession to the Quadripartite Alliance/Aix-la-Chapelle (15 November 1818)', in W.G. Grewe (ed.), *Fontes Historiae Iuris Gentium (FHIG), Sources Relating to the History of the Law of Nations*, vol. 3/1: 1815–1945 (1992) 104.
'Final Act of the Ministerial Conference Concerning the Organization of the German Confederation (15 May 1820)', in W.G. Grewe (ed.), *Fontes Historiae Iuris Gentium (FHIG), Sources Relating to the History of the Law of Nations*, vol. 3/1: 1815–1945 (1992) 178.
'The Congress of Troppau (19 November 1820)', in W.G. Grewe (ed.), *Fontes Historiae Iuris Gentium (FHIG), Sources Relating to the History of the Law of Nations*, vol. 3/1: 1815–1945 (1992) 110.
'Treaty between Great Britain, France, and Turkey. Military Aid to Turkey, 12 March 1854', in E. Hertslet (ed.), *The Map of Europe by Treaty*, vol. 2 (1875) 1181.
'Peace Treaty Concerning the Termination of the Crimean War/Paris (30 March 1856)', in W.G. Grewe (ed.), *Fontes Historiae Iuris Gentium (FHIG), Sources Relating to the History of the Law of Nations*, vol. 3/1: 1815–1945 (1992) 19.
'Prusso-Austrian Peace Treaty with Denmark (30 October 1864)', in W.G. Grewe (ed.), *Fontes Historiae Iuris Gentium (FHIG), Sources Relating to the History of the Law of Nations*, vol. 3/1: 1815–1945 (1992) 63.

'Treaty on the Neutralization of Luxemburg and its Sovereignty/London (11 May 1867)', in W.G. Grewe (ed.), *Fontes Historiae Iuris Gentium (FHIG), Sources Relating to the History of the Law of Nations*, vol. 3/1: 1815-1945 (1992) 169.

'Peace Treaty Concerning the Settlement of the Oriental Question (Act of the Congress of Berlin) (13 July 1878)', *Fontes Historiae Iuris Gentium (FHIG), Sources Relating to the History of the Law of Nations*, vol. 3/1: 1815-1945 (1992) 38.

1.4 Other Sources (Documents and Letters)

'Bluntschli's Reply to Count von Moltke (Christmas 1880)', in T.E. Holland (ed.), *Letters to 'The Times' Upon War and Neutrality (1881-1909): With Some Commentary* (1909) 26.

Bunsen, 'The Chevalier Bunsen to Viscount Palmerston, 28 November 1847', in Foreign Office (ed.), *British and Foreign State Papers*, vol. 57: 1866-1867 (1871) 949.

'Call for the Congress', in G. Spiller (ed.). *Papers on Inter-racial Problems Communicated to the First Universal Races Congress* (1911).

Castlereagh, 'Castlereagh to Liverpool. (No. 44)', in C.K. Webster (ed.), *British Diplomacy 1813-1815. Select Documents Dealing With the Reconstruction of Europe* (1921) 278.

'Castlereagh to Cathcart (No. 65.) Foreign Office, September 1813', in C.K. Webster, *British Diplomacy, 1813-1815: Select Documents Dealing with the Reconstruction of Europe* (1921) 19.

Castlereagh, 'Extracts from a Speech of Castlereagh in the House of Commons, March 20th, 1815', in C.K. Webster (ed.), *British Diplomacy 1813-1815. Select Documents Dealing With the Reconstruction of Europe* (1921) 396.

Castlereagh, 'Lord Castlereagh's Confidential State Paper of May 5th, 1820', in A.W. Ward and G.P. Gooch (eds), *The Cambridge History of British Foreign Policy, 1783-1919*, vol. 2 (1923) 621.

Cavour to Vittorio Emanuele II, 24 July 1858, in C.B. conte di Cavour, *Il carteggio Cavour-Nigra dal 1858 al 1861: Plombières*, vol. 1 (1926) 112.

'Extract from an Official Communication made to the Russian Ambassador at London, on the 19 January, 1805', in House of Commons (UK) (ed.), *Miscellaneous Papers. Also, Treaties with Foreign Powers* (1814-1815).

Gladstone, 'The Bulgarian Horrors and the Question of the East (1876)', in W.D. Handcock and G.M. Young (eds), *English Historical Documents 1874-1914* (2nd edn, 1996) 351.

Großer Generalstab, *Kriegsbrauch im Landkriege* (1902).

Kriegs-Rundschau. Zeitgenössische Zusammenstellung der für den Weltkrieg wichtigen Ereignisse, Urkunden, Kundgebungen, Schlacht- und Zeitberichte, vol. 1 (1914/15).

Leuchtènberg, 'Lettre de S. Â: î. le Nicolas de Leuchtènberg à M. de Martens', 13 *Revue de droit international et de législation comparée* (1881) 307.

Martens, 'Lettre de M. de Martens à S. Â: î. le Duc Nicolas de Leuchtènberg', 13 *Revue de droit international et de législation comparée* (1881) 309.

'Moltke to Bluntschli (11 December 1880)', in T.E. Holland (ed.), *Letters to 'The Times' Upon War and Neutrality (1881-1909): With Some Commentary* (1909) 24.

Report by Reuß to Bismarck 12 September 1870, in H.G. Linke (ed.), *Quellen zu den deutsch-russischen Beziehungen. 1801-1917* (2001) 146.

Statuts votés par la Conférence Juridique internationale de Gand, le 10 Septembre 1873 (1877).

U.S. Government Printing Office, *War Information Series* (1917).

2. Literature until 1920

Adler, 'Kriegsritualmordschablone, Flottenrüstungen - Interventionspolitik, relativ gerechter casus belli - Emancipation des Mannes', 8 *Die Waffen nieder!* (1899) 414.

N. Angell, *The Great Illusion. A Study of the Relation of Military Power in Nations to Their Economic and Social Advantage* (3rd edn, 1911).
D. Anzilotti, *Corso di diritto internazionale* (1915).
Bassano, 'Bericht des französischen Außenministers Herzog Bassano an den Kaiser von Frankreich und König von Italien Napoleon bezüglich der Kriegserklärung Österreichs an Frankreich (20 August 1813)', in P.A.G. Meyer (ed.), *Corpus Juris Confoederationis Germanicae oder Staatsacten für Geschichte und öffentliches Recht des Deutschen Bunds* (3rd edn, 1858) 191.
L. Bara, *La science de la paix: programme: mémoire couronné, à Paris, en 1849, par le congrès des sociétés anglo-américains des Amis de la paix* (1872).
V. Benedetti, *Le Comte: Ma Mission en Prusse* (1871).
Bentham, 'Critical Examination of the Declaration of Rights', in J. Bowring (ed.), *The Works of Jeremy Bentham* (1843) 496.
Berner, 'Intervention', in J.C. Bluntschli and C.L.T. Brater (eds), *Deutsches Staats-Wörterbuch*, vol. 5 (1860) 341.
O.E.L. Bismarck, *Gedanken und Erinnerungen* (1959 [1890]).
J.C. Bluntschli and C.L.T. Brater (eds), *Deutsches Staats-Wörterbuch* (1857).
J.C. Bluntschli, *Das moderne Völkerrecht in dem Kriege 1870. Rede zum Geburtsfeste des höchstseligen Grossherzogs Karl Friedrich von Baden und zur akademischen Preisvertheilung am 22. November 1870* (1870).
Bluntschli, 'Arische Völker und arische Rechte', in J.C. Bluntschli and C.L.T. Brater (eds), *Deutsches Staats-Wörterbuch*, vol. 2 (1857).
J.C. Bluntschli, *Das moderne Völkerrecht der civilisierten Staaten als Rechtsbuch dargestellt* (2nd edn, 1872).
J.C. Bluntschli, *Allgemeine Staatslehre* (6th edn, 1886).
A. del Bon, *Istituzioni del diritto pubblico internazionale* (1868).
H. Bonfils, *Lehrbuch des Völkerrechts für Studium und Praxis, durchgesehen und ergänzt von Paul Fauchille* (3rd edn, 1904).
J. Bowring (ed.), *The Works of Jeremy Bentham* (1843).
G. Büchmann, *Geflügelte Worte. Der Citatenschatz des Deutschen Volkes* (1882).
A. von Bulmerincq, *Das Völkerrecht oder das internationale Recht: Systematisch dargestellt* (2nd edn, 1889).
Calker, 'Rezension von Rettich, Heinrich (1888): Zur Theorie und Geschichte des. Rechts zum Kriege. Völkerrechtliche Untersuchungen. Stuttgart: Kohlhammer', 31 *Kritische Vierteljahrsschrift für Gesetzgebung und Rechtswissenschaft* (1889) 592.
C. Calvo, *Dictionnaire de Droit International Public et Privé* (1885).
C. von Clausewitz, *On War*, edited and translated by M. Howard and P. Paret (1976 [1832]).
C. von Clausewitz, 'Vom Kriege', in M. von Clausewitz (ed.), *Hinterlassene Werke über Krieg und Kriegsführung des Generals von Clausewitz* (1832).
Clausewitz, 'Bekenntnisschrift von 1812', *Carl von Clausewitz. Ausgewählte militärische Schriften* (1981) 140.
R. Coupland (ed.), *The War Speeches of William Pitt the Younger: Selected by R. Coupland* (1915).
L.M. Drago, *Cobro Coercitivo de Deudas Públicas* (1906).
'Editorial: The Hague Conventions and the Neutrality of Belgium and Luxemburg', 9 *American Journal of International Law* (1915) 959.
Fallati, 'Die Genesis der Völkergesellschaft. Ein Beitrag zur Revision der Völkerrechtswissenschaft', 1 *Zeitschrift für die gesamte Staatswissenschaft* (1844) 160.
Fichte, 'Anhang zu den Reden an die deutsche Nation, geschrieben im Jahre 1806', in J.H. Fichte (ed.), *Johann Gottlieb Fichte's sämmtliche Werke* (1846) 259.
P. Fiore, *Trattato di diritto internazionale pubblico* (2nd edn, 1879).

R.R. Foulke, *A Treatise on International Law. With an Introductory Essay on the Definition and Nature of the Laws of Human Conduct* (1920).
Fried, 'Herr von Stengel und die Friedenskonferenz', 1 *Die Friedens-Warte* (1899) 53.
Fried, 'Prof. Dr. von Liszt über die Friedensidee', 3 *Die Friedens-Warte* (1901) 17.
C. von Gareis, *Institutionen des Völkerrechts* (1888).
F.H. Geffcken, *Zur Geschichte des Orientalischen Krieges* (1881).
Geffcken, Comments in A.W. Heffter, *Das Europäische Völkerrecht der Gegenwart auf den bisherigen Grundlagen* (8th edn, 1888).
F. von Gentz, *Kleinere Schriften* (1839).
Gentz, 'Ueber de Pradt's Gemälde von Europa nach dem Kongreß von Aachen', in G. Schlesier (ed.), *Kleinere Schriften* (1839) 88.
George III, 'Message from George III', in R. Coupland (ed.), *The War Speeches of William Pitt the Younger* (1915) 52.
F.W. Ghillany, *Diplomatisches Handbuch Sammlungen der wichtigsten europäischen Friedensschlüsse, Congreßacten und sonstigen Staatsurkunden vom Westphälischen Frieden bis auf die neueste Zeit; mit kurzen geschichtlichen Einleitungen*, vol. 7: Friede zu Zürich zwischen Österreich und Frankreich, 10. November 1859 (Der französisch-sardinisch-österreichische Krieg vom Jahr 1859) (1868).
Gladstone, 'The Bulgarian Horrors and the Question of the East (1876)', in W.D. Handcock and G.M. Young (eds), *English Historical Documents 1874–1914* (2nd edn, 1996) 351.
Gundermann, 'Bentham', in J.C. Bluntschli and C.L.T. Brater (eds), *Deutsches Staats-Wörterbuch* (1857) 42.
W.E. Hall, *A Treatise on International Law* (1890).
Hamann, 'Zur Literatur über die Friedensfrage. Rezension zu Die Grundlagen des revolutionären Pazifismus by Alfred H. Fried; Der kranke Krieg by Fried; Weltstaat und Friedensproblem by Karl von Stengel', 4 *Zeitschrift für Politik* (1911) 391.
J. von Hartmann, *Militärische Notwendigkeit und Humanität* (1878).
A.W. Heffter, *Das europäische Völkerrecht der Gegenwart* (1844).
P. Heilborn, *Grundbegriffe des Völkerrechts* (1912).
J.A. Freiherr von Helfert, *Fünfzig Jahre nach dem Wiener Congresse von 1814–15. Mit besonderem Hinblick auf die neuesten österreichischen Zustände* (1865).
Hicks, 'Weltstaat und Friedensproblem. By Karl von Stengel. Berlin: Reichl & Co. 1909. pp. xiii, 145', 5 *American Journal of International Law* (1911) 1128.
F. von Holtzendorff, *Die Idee des ewigen Völkerfriedens* (1882).
F. von Holtzendorff (ed.), *Handbuch des Völkerrechts* (1889).
Hubrich, 'Georg Friedrich von Martens und die moderne Völkerrechtswissenschaft', 7 *Zeitschrift für Politik* (1914) 362.
Hufeland, 'Flucht nach Schlesien 1813–1814', in W.V. Brunn (ed.), *Selbstbiographie von Christoph Wilhelm Hufeland* (1937).
R. von Jhering, *The Struggle for Law*, translated by J.J. Lalor (1997 [1915]).
K. von Kaltenborn-Stachau, *Kritik des Völkerrechts nach dem jetzigen Standpunkte der Wissenschaft* (1847).
Kant, 'Idea for a Universal History from a Cosmopolitan Point of View (1784)', in I. Kant, *On History*, edited and translated by L.W. Beck (1963) 11.
Kant, 'Toward Perpetual Peace. A Philosophical Sketch (1795)', in I. Kant, *Toward Perpetual Peace and Other Writings on Politics, Peace, and History*, edited by P. Kleingeld (2006) 67.
E. Kaufmann, *Das Wesen des Völkerrechts und die clausula rebus sic stantibus. Rechtsphilosophische Studie zum Rechts-, Staats- und Vertragsbegriffe* (1911).
B. Kiessling, *Ewiger Krieg* (1885).

J.L. Klüber, *Uebersicht der diplomatischen Verhandlungen des Wiener Congresses* (1816).
J.L. Klüber, *Europäisches Völkerrecht* (1821).
J.L. Klüber, *Pragmatische Geschichte der nationalen und politischen Wiedergeburt Griechenlands, bis zu dem Regierungsantritt des Königs Otto* (1835).
G. Koeppen and G.A. Zimmermann, *Bismarck: Seine Zeit und sein Wirken* (1899)
Kohler, 'Notwehr und Neutralität', 8 *Zeitschrift für Völkerrecht* (1914) 576.
A. Lasson, *Princip und Zukunft des Völkerrechts* (1871).
T.J. Lawrence, *The Principles of International Law* (2nd edn, 1895).
W. Liebknecht, *Die Emser Depesche oder wie Kriege gemacht werden* (1891).
Z. von Lingenthal and K. Salomo, *Vierzig Bücher vom Staate. Regierungslehre* (1826).
Z. von Lingenthal and K. Salomo, *Vierzig Bücher vom Staate. Regierungslehre* (1841).
F. von Liszt, *Das Völkerrecht. Systematisch dargestellt* (11th edn, 1920).
Lorimer, 'Proposition d'un congrès international basé sur le principe de facto', 3 *Revue de Droit Internationale et de Législation Comparée* (1871) 1.
J. Lorimer, *The Institutes of the Law of Nations. A Treatise of the Jural Relations of Separate Political Communities*, vol. 1 (1883).
C. Lucas, *Necessité d'un Congrès Scientifique International relatif à la Civilisation de la Guerre et à la Codification du Droit des Gens* (1873).
C. Lucas, *Civilisation de la guerre: Observations sur les lois de la guerre et l'arbitrage international, à l'occasion de la lettre de m. le comte de Moltke à m. le professeur Bluntschli* (1873).
Lueder, 'Krieg und Kriegsrecht im Allgemeinen', in F. von Holtzendorff (ed.), *Handbuch des Völkerrechts. Auf Grundlage europ. Staatspraxis*, vol. 4 (1889) 169.
H.S. Maine, *International Law: The Whewell Lectures* (1887).
Marx, 'Declaration of War. – On the History of the Eastern Question', *New-York Daily Tribune* (15 April 1854).
F.F. Martens, *Völkerrecht: Das internationale Recht der civilisirten Nationen*, vol. 1 (1883).
F.F. Martens, *Völkerrecht: Das internationale Recht der civilisirten Nationen*, vol. 2 (1886).
G.F. von Martens, *Einleitung in das positive Europäische Völkerrecht auf Verträge und Herkommen gegründet* (1796).
G.F. von Martens, *Précis du droit des gens moderne de l'Europe fondé sur les traités et l'usage: Pour servir d'introduction à un cours politique et diplomatique* (3rd edn, 1821).
W. Menzel, *Der Deutsche Krieg im Jahr 1866*, vol. 1 (1867).
A. Mérignhac, *Traité de droit public international* (1912).
C. Meurer, *Völkerrechtliche Schiedsgerichte: ein populärwissenschaftlicher Vortrag* (1890).
R. von Mohl, *Die Geschichte und Literatur der Staatswissenschaften: In Monographien dargestellt* (1858).
R. von Mohl, *Encyklopädie der Staatswissenschaften* (1859).
R. von Mohl, *Staatsrecht, Völkerrecht und Politik*, vol. 1: Staatsrecht und Völkerrecht (1860).
H. von Moltke (ed.), *Gesammelte Schriften und Denkwürdigkeiten*, vol. 5 (1892).
J.B. Moore, *A Digest of International Law, as Embodied in Diplomatic Discussions, Treaties*, vol. 7 (1906).
W. Müller, *Politische Geschichte der Gegenwart* (1886).
E. Müller-Meiningen, *Der Weltkrieg 1914–1917 und der 'Zusammenbruch des Völkerrechts'*, vol. 1 (4th edn, 1917).
Muret, 'L'affaire des princes possessionnés d'Alsace et les origines du conflit entre la Révolution et l'Empire', 1 *Revue d'Histoire Moderne & Contemporaine Année* (1899) 433.
L. Neumann, *Grundriss des heutigen europäischen Völkerrechtes* (1877).

L. Nelson, *Die Rechtswissenschaft ohne Recht. Kritische Betrachtungen über die Grundlagen des Staats- und Völkerrechts, insbesondere über die Lehre von der Souveränität* (1917).

J. Novicow, *Der ewige Krieg. Antwort auf die Schrift 'Der Ewige Friede' des Herrn Professor Karl Feiherr von Stengel. Aus dem französischen Manuskript übersetzt von Alfred Hermann Fried* (1899).

E. Nys, *Études de droit international et de droit politique* (1896).

D.H.L. von Ompteda, *Litteratur des gesammten sowohl natürlichen als positiven Völkerrechts* (1785).

H.B. Oppenheim, *System des Völkerrechts* (1845).

Oppenheim, 'Die Zukunft des Völkerrechts', in *Festschrift für Karl Binding* (1911) 141.

L.F.L. Oppenheim, *International Law. A Treatise* (3rd edn, 1920).

J. Pétion, *Discours sur la réunion d'Avignon à la France* (1790).

Pfau, 'Preußische Ethik', in L. Pfau (ed.), *Politisches und Polemisches aus den nachgelassenen Schriften, mit einem Vorwort von Dr. Ernst Ziel* (1895) 275.

C. Phillipson, *International Law and the Great War* (1915).

P.-J. Proudhon, *La guerre et la paix. Recherches sur le principe et la constitution du droit des gens* (1863).

K.T. Pütter, *Beiträge zur Völkerrechts-Geschichte und Wissenschaft* (1843).

G. Ratzenhofer, *Die Staatswehr* (1881).

P. Resch, *Das Völkerrecht der heutigen Staatenwelt Europäischer Gesittung. Für Studierende und Gebildete aller Stände* (2nd edn, 1890).

H. Rettich, *Zur Theorie und Geschichte des Rechts zum Kriege. Völkerrechtliche Untersuchungen* (1888).

A. Rivier, *Lehrbuch des Völkerrechts* (1889).

A.L. von Rochau, *Grundsätze der Realpolitik, angewendet auf die staatlichen Zustände Deutschlands* (1859).

Rohland, 'Völkerrecht während der Regierungszeit Kaiser Wilhelms II', *Festschrift der Rundschau für den deutschen Juristenstand* (1913) 257.

Rolin-Jacquemyns, 'Note sur la théorie du droit d'intervention', 8 *Revue de Droit Internationale et de Législation Comparée* (1876) 673.

Rolin-Jaequemyns, 'De la nécessité d'organiser une institution scientifique permanente pour favoriser l'étude et le progrès du droit international', 5 *Revue de Droit Internationale et de Législation Comparée* (1873) 463.

H. von Rotteck, *Das Recht der Einmischung in die inneren Angelegenheiten eines fremden Staates* (1845).

Rougier, 'La Théorie de l'intervention d'humanité', 17 *Revue Génerale de Droit International Public* (1910) 468.

Rousseau, 'The Social Contract [1762]', in J.J. Rousseau, *The Basic Political Writings of Jean-Jacques Rousseau*, edited by D.A. Cress (2nd edn, 2012) 141.

J.J.O.A. Rühle von Lilienstern, *Handbuch für den Offizier zur Belehrung im Frieden und zum Gebrauch im Felde* (1818).

Rühs, 'Über die Forderungen Hamburgs an Frankreich', in F. Rühs (ed.), *Zeitschrift für die neueste Geschichte, die Staaten und Völkerkunde* (1815) 314.

W. Rüstow, *Die Feldherrnkunst des neunzehnten Jahrhunderts. Zum Selbststudium und für den Unterricht an höheren Militärschulen* (1857).

C. Sarolea, *German Problems and Personalities* (1917).

H.G. Scheidemantel, *Das Staatsrecht nach der Vernunft und den Sitten der vornehmsten Völker betrachtet* (1771).

J. Scherr, *Menschliche Tragikkomädien* (1884).

J. von Schmelzing, *Systematischer Grundriss des praktischen europäischen Völkerrecht, Dritter Theil* (1820).
W. Schücking, *Die Organisation der Welt* (1909).
W. Schücking, *Neue Ziele der staatlichen Entwicklung. Eine politische Studie* (1913).
M. von Seydel, *Grundzüge einer allgemeinen Staatslehre* (1873).
K. von Stengel, *Weltstaat und Friedensproblem* (1909).
F. Stier-Somlo (ed.), *Handbuch des Völkerrechts* (1912).
L. Strisower, *Krieg und Völkerrechtsordnung* (1919).
B. von Suttner, *Memoiren* (1909).
H. von Treitschke, *Treitschke. His Doctrine of German Destiny and of International Relations* (1914).
H. von Treitschke, *Politics*, vol. 1 (1916).
Treuenpreuss, 'Queen Augusta and the Red Cross', *The International Review* (1876) 492.
Ullmann, 'Völkerrecht', in E. von Ullmann (ed.), *Handbuch des Öffentlichen Rechts* (2nd edn, 1898).
V. Veit, *Geschichte des Völkerbundgedankens in Deutschland: ein geistesgeschichtlicher Versuch* (1920).
Warnkönig, 'Die gegenwärtige Aufgabe der Rechtsphilosophie nach den Bedürfnissen des Lebens und der Wissenschaft', 7 *Zeitschrift für die gesamte Staatswissenschaft / Journal of Institutional and Theoretical Economics* (1851) 662.
G. Washington, *The Proclamation of Neutrality 1793. A Proclamation* (1897).
C.K. Webster, *The Congress of Vienna. 1814–1815: Publ. for Hist. Sect. of the Foreign Office* (1919).
J. Westlake, *International Law* (2nd edn, 1910).
H. Wheaton, *Elements of Internatnional Law* [1836], edited, with Notes, by R.H. Dana (1866).
G.G. Wilson and G.F. Tucker, *International Law* (5th edn, 1909).
T.D. Woolsey, *Introduction to the Study of International Law: Designed as an Aid in Teaching, and in Historical Studies* (1897).
Woolsey, 'Retaliation and Punishment', in J.B. Scott, *International Law, Public Law and Jurisprudence* (1917) 167.
Zorn, 'Politik als Staatskunst. Ihr Begriff und Wesen', in W. Rothschild (ed.), *Handbuch der Politik*, vol. 1 (1914) 1.

3. Literature after 1920 (Selection)

M. Abbenhuis, *An Age of Neutrals: Great Power Politics, 1815–1914* (2014).
W. Baumgart, *Der Friede von Paris 1856: Studien zum Verhältnis von Kriegführung, Politik und Friedensbewahrung* (1972).
Bélissa, 'War and Diplomacy (1792–95)', in D. Andress (ed.), *The Oxford Handbook of the French Revolution* (2015) 418.
Benton, 'Protection Emergencies: Justifying Measures Short of War in the British Empire', in L. Brock and H. Simon (eds), *The Justification of War and International Order: From Past to Present* (2021) 167.
Benvenisti and Lustig, 'Monopolizing War: Codifying the Laws of War to Reassert Governmental Authority, 1856–1874', 31 *European Journal of International Law* (2020) 127.

Bernstorff, 'The Use of Force in International Law before World War I: On Imperial Ordering and the Ontology of the Nation-State', 29 *European Journal of International Law* (2018) 233.

Brock, 'Frieden durch Recht?', in P. Becker, R. Braun, and D. Deiseroth (eds): *Frieden durch Recht* (2010) 15.

Brock and Simon, 'Die Selbstbehauptung und Selbstgefährdung des Friedens als Herrschaft des Rechts', 59 *Politische Vierteljahresschrift* (2018) 269.

L. Brock and H. Simon (eds), *The Justification of War and International Order: From Past to Present* (2021).

I. Brownlie, *International Law and the Use of Force by States* (1963).

B. Buzan and G. Lawson, *The Global Transformation: History, Modernity and the Making of International Relations* (2015).

Carty, 'The Evolution of International Legal Scholarship in Germany during the Kaiserreich and the Weimarer Republik (1871-1933)', 50 *German Yearbook of International Law* (2007) 29.

Chimni, 'Peace through Law: Lessons from 1914', in L. Brock and H. Simon (eds), *The Justification of War and International Order: From Past to Present* (2021) 241.

S.E. Cooper, *Patriotic Pacifism: Waging War on War in Europe, 1815-1914* (1991).

Daase and Deitelhoff, 'The Justification and Critique of Coercion as World Order Politics', in L. Brock and H. Simon (eds), *The Justification of War and International Order: From Past to Present* (2021) 489.

J. Dülffer, *Regeln gegen den Krieg? Die Haager Friedenskonferenzen von 1899 und 1907 in der internationalen Politik* (1981).

Eberl, 'Kant's Rejection of Just War: International Order between Democratic Constitutionalism and Revolutionary Violence', in L. Brock and H. Simon (eds), *The Justification of War and International Order: From Past to Present* (2021).

R.J. Evans, *The Pursuit of Power: Europe, 1815-1914* (2017).

Faber, 'Realpolitik als Ideologie. Die Bedeutung des Jahres 1866 für das politische Denken in Deutschland', 203 *Historische Zeitschrift* (1966) 1.

R. Forst, *Normativity and Power. Analyzing Social Orders of Justification* (2017).

R. Forst and K. Günther, *Normative Ordnungen* (2021).

M. Foucault, *Society Must Be Defended: Lectures at the Collège de France, 1975-76* (2004).

W.G. Grewe, *The Epochs of International Law*, translated and revised by M. Byers (2000).

H. Göhler, *Freies Kriegsführungsrecht und Kriegsschuld* (1931).

J. Habermas, *The Divided West*, edited and translated by C. Cronin (2006).

M. Horkheimer and T.W. Adorno, *Dialektik der Aufklärung. Philosophische Fragmente* (2015 [1944]).

O.A. Hathaway et al., 'War Manifestos', 85 *University of Chicago Law Review* (2018) 1139.

O.A. Hathaway and S. Shapiro, *The Internationalists: How a Radical Plan to Outlaw War Remade the World* (2017).

T. Hippler and M. Vec (eds), *Paradoxes of Peace in Nineteenth Century Europe* (2015).

I.V. Hull, *Absolute Destruction: Military Culture and the Practices of War in Imperial Germany* (2004).

Hull, 'The Great War and International Law: German Justifications of "Preemptive Self-Defense"', in L. Brock and H. Simon (eds), *The Justification of War and International Order: From Past to Present* (2021) 183.

Jahn, 'Kant, Mill, and Illiberal Legacies in International Affairs', 59 *International Organization* (2005) 177.

H. Kelsen, *Peace through Law* (1944).

Kennedy, 'International Law and the Nineteenth Century: History of an Illusion', 65 *Nordic Journal of International Law* (1996) 385.
E.J. Kolla, *Sovereignty, International Law and the French Revolution* (2017).
R. Koselleck, *Kritik und Krise: Eine Studie zur Pathogenese der bürgerlichen Welt* (13th edn, 2017).
M. Koskenniemi, *The Gentle Civilizer of Nations: The Rise and Fall of International Law, 1870–1960* (2002).
M. Koskenniemi, *To the Uttermost Parts of the Earth. Legal Imagination and International Power, 1300–1870* (2021).
D. Langewiesche, *Der gewaltsame Lehrer: Europas Kriege in der Moderne* (2019).
R.N. Lebow, *The Tragic Vision of Politics* (2003).
Lesaffer, 'Too much History. From War as Sanction to the Sanctioning of War', in M. Weller (ed.), *The Oxford Handbook of the Use of Force in International Law* (2015) 35.
Lesaffer, 'Aggression before Versailles', 29 *European Journal of International Law* (2018) 773.
Mallavarapu, 'Imperialism, International Law, and War: Enduring Legacies and Curious Entanglements', in L. Brock and H. Simon (eds), *The Justification of War and International Order: From Past to Present* (2021) 45.
Messerschmidt, 'Völkerrecht und "Kriegsnotwendigkeit" in der deutschen militärischen Tradition seit den Einigungskriegen', 6 *German Studies Review* (1983) 237.
J. Mitzen, *Power in Concert: The Nineteenth-Century Origins of Global Governance* (2013).
Münkler, 'Instrumentelle und existentielle Auffassung vom Krieg bei Carl von Clausewitz', 16 *Leviathan* (1988) 235.
S.C. Neff, *War and the Law of Nations: A General History* (2005).
S.C. Neff, *Justice among Nations: A History of International Law* (2014).
L. Nuzzo and M. Vec (eds), *Constructing International Law: The Birth of a Discipline* (2012).
M.E. O'Connell, *The Power and Purpose of International Law: Insights from the Theory and Practice of Enforcement* (2008).
M.M. Payk, *Frieden durch Recht? Der Aufstieg des modernen Völkerrechts und der Friedensschluss nach dem Ersten Weltkrieg* (2018).
K. Repgen, *Kriegslegitimationen in Alteuropa. Entwurf einer historischen Typologie* (1985).
C. Schmitt, *The Nomos of the Earth in the International Law of the Jus Publicum Europaeum*, translated by G.L. Ulmen (1950).
P.W. Schroeder, *The Transformation of European Politics, 1763–1848* (1994).
M. Schulz, *Normen und Praxis: Das europäische Konzert der Großmächte als Sicherheitsrat, 1815–1860* (2009).
Simon, 'Über das "freie Recht zum Krieg" in Politik und Völkerrecht des 19. Jahrhunderts', Research Paper/Max Planck Institute for European Legal History (2012).
Simon, 'The Myth of *Liberum Ius ad Bellum*. Justifying War in 19th-Century Legal Theory and Political Practice', 29 *European Journal of International Law* (2018) 113.
Simon, 'Anarchy over Law? Towards a Genealogy of Modern War Justifications (1789–1918)', in L. Brock and H. Simon (eds), *The Justification of War and International Order: From Past to Present* (2021) 147.
Steiger, 'Das Völkerrecht und der Wandel der Internationalen Beziehungen um 1800', in A. Klinger, H.-W. Hahn, and G. Schmidt (eds), *Das Jahr 1806 im europäischen Kontext: Balance, Hegemonie und politische Kulturen* (2008) 23.
M. Stolleis, *Public Law in Germany, 1800–1914* (2001).
B. Teschke, *The Myth of 1648: Class, Geopolitics, and the Making of Modern International Relations* (2003).

Teschke, 'Carl Schmitt's Concepts of War: A Categorical Failure', in J. Meierhenrich and O. Simons (eds), *The Oxford Handbook of Carl Schmitt* (2016) 367.

A. Tischer, *Offizielle Kriegsbegründungen in der Frühen Neuzeit: Herrscherkommunikation in Europa zwischen Souveränität und korporativem Selbstverständnis* (2012).

Tischer, 'Princes' Justifications of War in Early Modern Europe: the Constitution of an International Community by Communication', in L. Brock and H. Simon (eds), *The Justification of War and International Order: From Past to Present* (2021) 65.

Vec, 'Multinormativität in der Rechtsgeschichte', *Jahrbuch 2008/Berlin-Brandenburgische Akademie der Wissenschaften (vormals Preußische Akademie der Wissenschaften)* (2009) 155.

Vec, 'Sources of International Law in the Nineteenth-Century European Tradition: The Myth of Positivism', in S. Besson and J. d'Aspremont (eds), *The Oxford Handbook of the Sources of International Law* (2017) 121.

Verdebout, 'The Contemporary Discourse on the Use of Force in the Nineteenth Century: A Diachronic and Critical Analysis', 1 *Journal on the Use of Force and International Law* (2014) 223.

A. Verdebout, *Rewriting Histories of the Use of Force. The Narrative of 'Indifference'* (2021).

Walzer, 'The Triumph of Just War Theory (and the Dangers of Success)', 69 *Social Research* (2002) 925.

Wehberg, 'Universales oder Europäisches Völkerrecht? Eine Auseinandersetzung mit Professor Carl Schmitt', 41 *Die Friedens-Warte* (1941) 157.

Wehberg, 'Ideen und Projekte betr. die Vereinigten Staaten von Europa in den letzten 100 Jahren', 41 *Die Friedens-Warte* (1941) 49.

Index

For the benefit of digital users, indexed terms that span two pages (e.g., 52–53) may, on occasion, appear on only one of those pages.

Adorno, Theodor W. 354
Africa 144, 231, 325–31, 343
aggression
  concept/definition of 66, 84, 118–21
  nineteenth century prohibition of 110, 121, 123, 147, 150–52
Alabama Case 299–300
Alexander I 73–74
Alexander II 163, 229, 230–31
alliance
  anti-Russian (1854) 163
  discourse alliance 52, 135–36
  Dual 307
  Franco-Russian/Triple Entente 307
  Holy 111, 120, 137, 139, 140, 142, 162, 170–71
  Quadruple 114–15, 117–18
Americas 140
anarchy, narrative of 31, 342–48
ancien régime 47–48, 115, 119
Angell, Norman 299, 304
annexation 69–71, 94, 134–36, 179–80, 185, 189, 232–33, 256
Anzilotti, Dionisio 279
Aquinas, Thomas 162
arbitration, international 169–70, 205–6, 213–14, 218, 258, 269, 273, 299–300, 312–16
  see also Alabama Case
Arendt, Hannah 47
Asia 144, 148, 231, 343
Asser, Tobias 206–7
Augustine 23–24, 70
Austria/Austria-Hungary
  and the German *Bund* 119–20
  in Italy 172, 173–78
  as a multi-ethnic state 116
Austro-Prussian War (1866) 186–88
authorization of the use of force 118–19, 141, 149–50

balance of power
  concept/principle of 68, 105, 111, 122, 256, 258
  critique of 352–53
  vs hegemony 73–74, 75
  peace through 90, 159–60, 261–62
  in realist thought 105, 258, 261–62, 349–50, 352–53
Balkan Wars (1912/13) 316–17
Bara, Louis 206–7
barbarity, narrative of 47, 215, 231
de Beauharnais, Nikolaus 293–95
Belgium 189
  Belgian Revolution (1830) 142
  German invasion of (1914) 321–22, 325–27
  neutrality (1839) 141, 190, 321, 325–26
belligerent equality 26
Benjamin, Walter 55, 97–98
Bentham, Jeremy 86–89
Berlin Conference (1884/85) 231
von Bethmann Hollweg, Theobald 322, 325–27, 328–29, 330
von Bismarck, Otto 181–98
  and international norms 182, 188, 197
  and realpolitik 181–82
Bluntschli, Johann Caspar
  and antisemitism 227
  and Eurocentrism 233
  on the Franco-Prussian War (1870/71) 195–96, 203–5, 223–28
  on international legal progress 204, 215–19, 221–22, 235, 291
  on the justice/legality of war 208, 209–10, 212–13
  vs Moltke 285–89, 290–92
  on the Ottoman Empire 163–65
  vs realists 221–22, 223–24, 263, 275, 295
Bonaparte, Napoléon 63, 72–75, 81–85, 106–8, 114
Bonfils, Henry 207–8, 209, 210, 211–12, 224, 266
border violations 320–21
Brissot, Jacques Pierre 68, 69, 71–72, 77
British Empire 144, 161
  see also Great Britain
Brussels Declaration (1874) 202, 307, 310
Brussels Peace Congress (1848) 169–70
von Bulmerincq, August 210, 251–52

von Bülow, Bernhard 260, 312–13
Burke, Edmund 79

von Calker, Fritz 344–45, 348
Callwell, Charles Edward 232
Calvo, Carlos 208
capitalism 165
Carr, E.H. 284, 349–50
Castlereagh, Viscount 114, 134–36, 137, 138, 139–42
di Cavour, Camillo Benso 173–78
change, historical 53–56, 63–64, 162, 361
Charter of the United Nations (1945)
  and humanitarian intervention 57
  the prohibition of the use of force in the 32–33, 51, 121, 315, 339
  self-defence according to the 364–66
  see also prohibition of the use of force
China 148, 164–65, 348, 366
Christianity 145, 158–59, 229
civilization
  civilizing mission 162, 220–22, 227–29, 230–31, 271–72
  and international law 35, 90, 110, 131, 207, 213, 229, 231, 322–222, 325
  narrative of 38–39, 41–42, 90, 147–48, 149–50, 165–66, 195, 227
  and war 41–42, 143–48, 292–93, 310–11
classism 227, 236, 237–38, 254
von Clausewitz, Carl
  Clausewitzians (lawyers) 264–76, 283–95, 345
  on war and politics 32, 43–44, 99–106, 251, 253, 259–61, 264–66, 280
Cloots, Anacharsis 69–70
coercion 109–10, 133–50, 213, 268, 269, 327–28, 345
coexistence 76, 80–81, 90
Cold War
  end of 111, 353–54
  global bloc formation in the 349–50
  theory of international relations during 349–50
colonialism/imperialism
  colonial power 270, 328
  colonial warfare 26–27, 232, 328
  critique of 220–21, 233–34
  and humanitarian intervention 143–44, 227
  and international law 41–42, 165–67, 231–33
  see also British Empire; genocide; German Empire; postcolonialism; TWAIL
'communication community' (A. Tischer) 15, 52–53, 55–56, 60, 118–19, 159–60
Concert of the Great Powers, *see* European Concert of the Great Powers

conference/congress, concept of 54, 109
  'permanenter Staatencongress' (I. Kant) 118, 219
congresses (in chronological order)
  Congress of Westphalia (1645–48) 163, 168
  Congress of Vienna (1814/15) 18, 34, 43, 57, 109–10, 111–33, 134–36, *see also* Final Act of the Congress of Vienna (1815)
  Congress of Aix-la-Chapelle (Aachen) (1818) 117–18, 132
  Congress of Troppau (1820) 138
  Congress of Laibach (1821) 139
  Congress of Verona (1822) 139
  Congress of Paris (1856) 163, 168–70, 199–200, *see also* Treaty of Paris (1856)
  Congress of Berlin (1878) 231, 308
conquest
  definition of 66, 134–36
  prohibition of 70, 121, 131, 134–36
  right to 32, 33, 66, 134–36
  self-defence as 71
constitution
  European Concert as 133
  Final Act of Vienna as 132
  French 66, 68
  and intervention 90, 130–31, 137, 138
  making force 70–71
constructivism 31–35, 49–53
continuity, historical 11–12, 53–56, 209–10, 211, 236, 361
Crimean War (1853–56) 154–71
  see also Treaty of Paris (1856)
critical theory 32, 46–49, 354
customary international law (CIL), *see* international law

Dano-Prussian War (1864) 183–85
declarations/justifications of war (in chronological order)
  Anacharsis Cloots on German princes (12 April 1792) 69–70
  France on Austria (20 April 1792) 67
  France on Austria (21 April 1792) 67–68
  Austria on France (5 July 1792) 78
  Austria on France (30 January 1793) 78
  George III on France (12 February 1793) 79–80
  Pitt on France (12 February 1793) 79
  France on Spain (9 March 1793) 68
  France on Pitt (7 August 1793) 71
  Prussia on France (9 October 1806) 80
  Spain (Junta) on France (September/October 1808) 81
  Prussia on France (16 March 1813) 82–83

INDEX 383

Prussia on France (20 March 1813) 82
Austria, Prussia, and Russia (8 December 1820) 139
Greece on the Ottoman Empire (27 January 1822) 145
Ottoman Empire on Russia (January 1828) 147
Sardinia-Piedmont on Austria (23 March 1848) 172
Ottoman Empire on Russia (4 October 1853) 158–59
Russia on the Ottoman Empire (20 October/ 1 November 1853)
Great Britian on Russia (27 March 1854) 160–61
Austria on Sardinia (28 April 1859) 174–75
Sardinia on Austria (29 April 1859) 176–77
France on Austria (3 May 1859) 178
France on Prussia (19 July 1870) 192
Bismarck on France (19 July 1870) 194
Gorchakov on the Ottoman Empire (19 November 1876) 229
Russia on the Ottoman Empire (24 April 1877) 229
Gorchakov on the Ottoman Empire (9 April 1878) 229
Japan on Russia (4 February 1904) 315
Austria on Serbia (29 July 1914) 317
Wilhelm II on Russia (31 July 1914) 318
Wilhelm II on Russia (1 August 1914) 319
German Empire on Russia (1 August 1914) 318–19, 326
Great Britain on Germany (4 August 1914) 321–22
democracy
  democratic peace 226
  democratic wars 98–99, 366
  German 253–54
Denmark 183–85
  see also Dano-Prussian War (1864)
diplomacy 57–60, 87–88, 109, 110, 116–18, 136–37
  diplomatic negotiations 116–18, 136–37, 138
  diplomatic two-class society 117
  and the 'free right to go to war' 251–52
  see also conference/congress; European Concert of the Great Powers; mediation; multilateralism; neutrality
disarmament 87–88, 169–70, 273, 300, 304, 308, 309–10, 311
discourse
  analysis 9–17, 39–46
  discourse alliance 52, 135–36
  discursive authority 38–57

discursive power 38–57
  theory 49–53
  transformation of war discourse 23–25, 36–38, 47–48, 53–56, 348
  war discourse 13–14, 52, 65–67, 108, 200, 209, 306–7, 325, 343, 364
Drago, Luis María 315
Dunant, Henry 179

early modernity 22, 24, 32, 53–54, 70, 91–92, 96
  see also modernity; postmodernity
East India Company 16–17, 221
Eastern Question
  definition of 136
  and the European war discourse 162
  and humanitarian intervention 144–45
  and international law 154–71
'Ems Dispatch' 190
enemy image 160, 199
enforcement, *see* international law
England, *see* British Empire; Great Britain
English School 212
Enlightenment 69–70, 86, 91, 99, 113–14, 210, 220, 255–56, 354
  dialectic of 354
  ethics 28, 29–30, 37, 56–57, 289–90
  see also law; morality; multinormativity
Europe
  Eurocentrism 26–27, 165, 201, 233, 361
  European war discourse 3, 7, 11, 18, 22
  and the Ottoman Empire 136, 154–71
European Concert of the Great Powers
  and Bismarck 198
  end of 316
  genesis of 111–33
  and Italy 180
  and Kant 219
  and mediation 157, 317
  as a 'nineteenth-century Security Council' (M. Schulz) 54
  and the Ottoman Empire 227–28
  as a '*permanenter Staatencongress*' (I. Kant) 118, 219
  and Prussia 162–63
  and Russia 159
  and the use of force 118–21, 133–50, 151–52, 183–84, 324
  and Wilhelm II 242
exception
  German Empire as an 282–83, 304–5, 332
  to the prohibition of the use of force 94, 139–40, 142–43, 150, 161, 187, 320
  state of 268
  see also prohibition of war/the use of force

fear in international relations 261–62
feminism/anti-feminism 206–7, 227, 237–38
Final Act of the Congress of Vienna (1815) 43, 113, 117, 121, 122, 132, 136, 139–40, 152, 171–72, 186–87, 324
Fiore, Pasquale 214–15, 217
First Geneva Convention (1864) 202
First World War 316–31
force, *see* war
foreign policy 65–66, 106, 169, 182–83, 189–90, 197, 228, 329–30, 331
Foucault, Michel 9–10, 199
France
   and the Concert of Europe 117–18, 156
   and the Ottoman Empire 146, 156
   and Prussia 188–98
   Revolutionary 64–85
   and Sardinia-Piedmont 173
Franco-Prussian War (1870/71) 188–98
   as a historical caesura 19, 201
Frankfurt School, *see* critical theory
Franz Joseph I 174–77, 178, 194, 200, 317–18
'free right to go to war', *see* liberum ius ad bellum
French Revolution (1789–1799) 63–64
   French Revolutionary Wars 64–85
Fried, Alfred H. 235, 301, 304
Friedrich II '*der Große*' 82, 224, 251, 256
Friedrich Wilhelm III 82, 84–85

Garibaldi, Giuseppe 179–80
Geffcken, Friedrich Heinrich 159, 169, 267
genocide 328–29
Gentili, Alberico 26
Gentz, Friedrich von 113–14
Germany
   and the French Revolution 76–81
   German Confederation (1815–1866) 115, 119–20, 173–74, 181, 182, 183, 184
   German Empire (1871–1918) 282–83, 304–5, 332
   German realism 241–43
   German *Sonderweg* ('special path') 282–83, 304–5, 331–32
   see also Austria; liberum ius ad bellum; Machtstaat; military; Prussia
Gladstone, William 170, 228–29
globalization 26–27, 41–42, 97, 114, 349–50
   global bloc formation 349–50
Goffman, Erving 59–60
Gorchakov, Alexander 229
Great Britain
   and the Concert of Europe 114, 140
   and the French Revolution 79–80
   and the German Empire 316–17
   vs the Holy Alliance 140

   and humanitarian intervention 144, 146
   and the Ottoman Empire 146, 162
   see also British Empire; colonialism/imperialism
Greek War of Independence (1821–32) 145–47
Grewe, Wilhelm G. 28, 31, 65, 120–21, 247–48, 351
Grey, Edward 322
Großer Generalstab (Great General Staff) 271, 286, 287, 316–17, 321, 327–28, 329, 347
   see also military; Moltke (the Elder); Moltke (the Younger)
Grotius, Hugo 16–17, 212, 221

Habermas, Jürgen 32–33, 150
Hague Convention II (1907) 310, 315
Hague Convention III (1907) 315
Hague Peace Conferences (1899/1907) 308–11
Heffter, August Wilhelm 124–26, 127, 128–29, 147, 170–71, 245
Hegel, Georg Friedrich Wilhelm 58, 97, 125, 245, 251, 255–56, 261, 290–91
Heilborn, Paul 276–77
Herero 328–29
historicism 216, 253–64, 273
Hitler, Adolf 347
Hobbes, Thomas 27, 30, 93, 105, 212, 248–49, 261–62
von Holtzendorff, Franz 219–20, 222, 303
   on Kant 222
Holy Alliance, *see* alliance
honour 68, 71, 82, 84–85, 122, 175, 176, 189, 191–92, 195, 210, 223–24, 229, 254–55, 259–60, 268–69, 287–88, 313, 317
Horkheimer, Max 354
human rights 106–7, 149–50, 165, 219, 365
'humanitarian intervention', *see* intervention

imperialism, *see* colonialism/imperialism
India 146, 161, 366
Institut de Droit International 207, 216, 226, 285–86
International History/IH (academic discipline) 40, 256, 333–34, 351
international humanitarian law (IHL), *see* ius in bello
international institution 57, 118–19, 218, 335–36
international law
   anti-legalism 301–2, 312–16
   circumvention of 232
   codification of 87–88, 169–70
   and colonialism, *see* colonialism/imperialism
   concept of 87
   customary 140, 318
   'deniers of' 304

dynastic 68
enforcement of 31, 48–49, 104, 266, 338
historiography of 37, 39–46, 87, 354–55
legalistic avoidance of 311
modern 26, 64–65, 87
natural law 23, 29–30, 37, 43–44, 87, 90–91, 96, 103–4, 107, 122, 143, 148–49, 151–52, 187–88, 230–31, 237, 248, 310–11, 364–65
peace through 34, 92–99, 112–18, 203–20, 261–62, 275, 290–93, 308, 336–38, 339, 340
and politics 16, 35, 49–53, 107, 178, 226, 229–31, 238, 242, 297–98, 353
positivism in 28–30, 86–87, 89, 92, 128–30, 212, 243–53, 276–79
as progress 31–35
sources of 8, 85, 86–99, 128–30, 212, 243–53, 276–79
theory of 86–99, 128–30, 243–53
and war 31–35, 92–99, 125, 201–3, 221–22, 271–72
see also international institution; international order/global order
International Law/IL (academic discipline) 40–41, 45, 89–90, 124–25, 236, 353–54
History of 17, 21, 28, 40–41, 45, 151, 201, 242, 253–54, 351
international order
birth of modern 53–56, 111–33
co-constitution of war justifications and 10–11, 49–53, 320
concept of 10–11
historiography of 37, 39–46, 87, 354–55
normativity of 10, 49–53
war and 31–35, 46–49, 92–99, 125, 201–3, 221–22, 271–72
international relations
early modern 47–48
historiography of 37, 39–46, 87, 354–55
legalization of 35, 41
modern 53–56, 111–33
theory of, *see* constructivism; critical theory; liberalism; realism
see also international order
International Relations/IR (academic discipline) 39–40, 45, 283–95, 335–37, 353–54
'First Great Debate' in 283–95
see also constructivism; critical theory; liberalism; realism
intervention
and Africa 143–44
and the Eastern Question 144–45, 165–67, 227–31
and the European Concert 136–41
'humanitarian intervention' 143–47, 165–67, 227–31

legal debate on 141–43
liberal interventionism 143–47, 165–67, 227–31
non-intervention 70, 139–41, 143–47, 188, 189, 322
and Russia 166, 227–31
see also European Concert of the Great Powers
Islam 73, 157–58, 159–60, 227, 292–93
Italy
Austrian rule in 116, 137–38, 173–74
Italian Question 173, 177
Italian Wars of Independence (1848–1849/1859/1866) 171–80
Sardinian rule in 179–80
see also Cavour; Sardinia-Piedmont
ius ad bellum 3, 29, 43
and *ius in bello* 246, 348
see also liberum ius ad bellum
ius contra bellum, *see* prohibition of war/the use of force
ius in bello
codification of 179, 202
critique of focus on 288, 291, 296, 311, 314
and *ius ad bellum* 246, 348
myth of modern 25–27, 251
and the 'necessity of war' 103, 268–69, 306–7, 322–23, 324
suspending 270

Japan 148, 164–65, 315, 349
Jhering, Rudolf von 42, 55, 224–25
July Crisis (1914) 317–21
July Revolution (1830) 141
juridification/legalization, international 26–27, 35, 41, 56–57, 87–88, 92–99, 169–70
'reflexive legalization' (L. Brock and H. Simon) 98, 233–36
'semi-legalization of war' 207, 246
just war (*bellum iustum*)
concept of 23–25
criteria of 23–25
critique of 92–93, 96, 277, 299–300
and the French Revolution 107
historiography of 23–25, 36, 349, 353, 359, 361
and international law 125, 127, 151, 197, 202–3, 220, 236, 277, 298
just cause 23–24
and Kant 92–93, 96, 98
and Kelsen 338–39, 345
and neutrality 24, 42–43
and the nineteenth century 125, 127, 128, 135, 151–52, 174–75, 197, 202–3, 208, 220, 236, 277, 298
and Schmitt 25–26, 299–300, 345
unjust enemy 24, 26, 71, 81, 84, 98–99

justification
  narrative of 52, 53, 65–66
  order of 52, 92–93, 150–51, 199
  of war, concept 38–57
  of war and international order, dialectic of 38–57
  of war, research on 13–17
  see also declarations/justifications of war

von Kaltenborn-Stachau, Carl 126–27, 128–29, 130, 132–33
Kant, Immanuel
  vs the 'free right to go to war' 34, 99
  in the historiography of international order 35, 337–39
  on just war 92–93, 96, 98, 212
  on law and peace 35, 92–99
  nineteenth-century scholars' reception of 129–30, 211–13, 215, 217–18, 219–22, 234–35, 237, 271–72, 273–74, 283, 290–91
  on the '*permanenten Staatencongress*' 118, 219
  on self-defence 94
Kaufmann, Erich 269
Kellogg-Briand Pact (Pact of Paris) (1928) 32–33, 151, 205–6, 237, 337, 341, 346, 349
Kelsen, Hans
  on just war 338–39
  on Kant 337–39
  on law and peace 337–38
  on objectivity and science 16–17, 97–98
af-Klint, Hilma 333–34
Klüber, Johann Ludwig 117, 122, 123–25, 128, 130–32
Koselleck, Reinhart 11–12, 63, 84, 361–62
Kriege, Johannes 314–15, 323–24

Lammasch, Heinrich 220
Lasson, Adolf 261–64
Latin America 347
Lauterpacht, Hersch 120–21, 336–37, 341
law, *see* international law
law of armed conflict, see *ius in bello*
Lawrence, Thomas Joseph 278
league of nations (theoretical concept) 95, 132
  see also Kant
League of Nations (1920) 64–65, 132, 168, 299–300, 314, 336, 338, 341, 342, 343, 346
legal pacifism, *see* pacifism
legalization, *see* juridification/legalization
liberalism
  critique of 31, 258, 280–81, 283–95, 345
  as a discriminatory project 226
  and the European Concert 132–33, 219
  and imperialism 165–67, 231–33
  on legal progress 31–35, 349
  liberal international order 131
  liberal interventionism 143–47, 165–67, 227–31
  on peace through law 92–99, 233–36
  pre-March 117
  vs realism 283–95
  and realpolitik 254
  see also Bluntschli; Habermas; international law; juridification/legalization; Kant; Kelsen; Schücking; Wehberg
liberum ius ad bellum ('free right to go to war')
  definition of 3–8, 30
  genesis of 241–64
  narrative of 4–5, 23–31, 344–45, 354–55
  and neutrality 25–26
  varieties of 276–77, 278–79
  see also Germany; Lueder; Machtstaat; military; politics; power; realism; realpolitik; Rettich; sovereignty
Lieber, Francis 205, 221–22
von Liszt, Franz 149, 163, 167–68, 211, 276, 304
London Protocols (1850/52) 184, 185
Lorimer, James 116, 208, 218–19, 227
Lucas, Charles 213–14, 290–92
Lueder, Carl
  as a *Clausewitzian* 264–71
  vs liberalism 266, 275, 295–98
  on military authors 267, 295
  against perpetual peace 275, 295–96
  on the 'necessity of war'/military necessity/*Kriegsraison* 268–69, 270–71
  on war 264–73, 276–79, 295–96
Luxembourg 325–26

Machiavelli, Niccolò 31, 32, 69–70, 96, 251, 262–63
Machtstaat 36, 106, 251, 253–64, 303, 350–51
  see also realism
Mancini, Pasquale Stanislao 215, 222–23
mandate system 343
von Martens, Fedor Fedorovich
  at the Hague (1899) 310–11
  on intervention 148
  Martens Clause, myth of 310–11
  on Moltke (the Elder) 293–95
  vs realists 244–45
  on the Russo-Turkish War (1877/78) 229–31
  on war 209
von Martens, Georg Friedrich 89–92
  and the French Revolution 91
  on positive/natural law 90–91
  on self-defence 91–92
Marx, Karl 93–94, 156–57

measures short of war, *see* war
media 155, 157, 193
mediation
  in the Crimean War (1853-56) 157
  and the European Concert 122, 131-32
  failed 171
  and the German Empire 242, 273
  in the Greek War of Independence (1821-32) 146
  and international law 279
  in the Luxembourg Crisis (1867) 190
  as a pacifist demand 205-6
  in the Second Italian War of Independence (1859) 174-75
  in the Treaty of Paris (1856) 168-70, 177-78, 199-200, 273, 341
Merlin de Douai, Philippe Antoine 68-69, 72, 223
von Metternich, Clemens Wenzel Lothar 114, 116, 119-20, 138-39, 140-41, 173-74
Meurer, Christian 271-74, 280-81, 289, 323-24, 347
military
  antimilitarism 233-36, 289-90, 291, 298-301
  culture 12-13, 27, 254, 267-71, 327, 347
  'emasculation' 272, 302
  vs law 271, 285-89, 293-95
  literature 99-106, 209, 267, 268, 271, 280, 284-89
  militarism 84, 202, 242-43, 255, 259-60, 282, 291, 298, 303-5, 316, 327-28, 329-30
  necessity 27, 267-71, 296, 297, 305, 328-29, 347
  'spirit' 291
  see also Clausewitz; Großer Generalstab; intervention; war
modernity
  modern international law 26, 64-65, 87
  modern international order 53-56, 111-33, 363-64
  modern international relations 53-56, 111-33
  modern prohibition of war 92-99, 110, 121, 337
  modern war discourse, birth of 53-56, 63-64, 68, 128-29
  modern warfare 130-31, 155
  and peace 92-99, 233-36
  and pre-modernity 53-54, 63-64
  and trust 47, 261-62
  and war 47, 99-106
Mohl, Robert von 124-25, 126
von Moltke, Helmuth (the Elder) 128-29, 186, 196, 255, 275, 285-95, 329-30
von Moltke, Helmuth (the Younger) 320-21, 330

Monroe Doctrine (1823) 346-48, 365-66
morality
  immoral realism 257-60, 261-64, 295-96
  and international law 56-57, 90, 92-99, 122, 128, 130, 149, 151-52, 158-59, 208, 221-22, 235, 237, 254-55, 296-98, 335
  and international order 117
  and the justification of war 51-52, 56-57, 60, 366
  'moral positivity' (H. Rettich) 249
  moralizing 245, 250
  and politics 49-50, 56-57, 92-99, 211, 242-43, 249, 254-55, 257-60, 261-64, 295-98, 350
  and sovereignty 144-45, 149, 242-43, 249, 254-55, 257-60, 261-64, 295-96
  of war 60, 125, 211-12, 213, 216, 221-22, 224-25, 228-29, 257-60, 261-64, 290-95, 296-98
  see also ethics; international law; intervention; just war; multinormativity; politics
Morgenthau, Hans J. 49-50, 257, 349-51
Morocco Crises (1905/11) 316-17
Moynier, Gustave 204
multilateralism 54, 95, 113-14, 117-18, 133, 139-40
multinormativity 8, 10-11, 56-57, 72, 162, 165-66, 212, 224-25, 364-66
  see also ethics; international law; morality; politics

Napoleón I 63, 72-75, 76-77, 81-85
Napoleón III 170-71
Napoleonic Wars 37, 80, 15-6, 172, 184-5, 507
nationality, principle of 170-71
natural law, *see* international law; multinormativity
navy 232, 329-30
necessities of war, *see* military
Nelson, Leonard 301
neutrality
  as an 'abnormality' (J. Lorimer) 208
  Belgian 141, 190, 321, 325-26
  as betrayal 80, 120
  of the Black Sea 229
  and the European Concert 42-43
  and just war 24, 42-43
  and *liberum ius ad bellum* 25-26, 42-43, 120-21, 251-52
  and Luxembourg 190
  and Prussia 162-63
  scientific 221
  Switzerland's perpetual 120
  see also Alabama Case

Nicholas I 156
Nicholas II 300, 309, 311, 313
non-intervention, *see* intervention
normativity/norms
    in International History 40
    of international order 10, 49–53
    in International Relations 21, 38–57
    normative order/order of justification 10–11, 19, 49
    permissive effects of 311
    and power 134–36
    'unavailability of norms' (L. Brock) 51, 200, 237, 360
    see also international order; multinormativity; politics
Novicow, Jacques 298–301

occupation 70–71, 81, 131–32, 158, 159–60, 232–33, 347
Oppenheim, Heinrich Bernhard 127, 130–31, 132–33, 219
Oppenheim, Lassa 122, 232–33, 278
order, *see* international order; Paris Order (1919/20–39); Treaty of Paris (1856); Vienna Order (1814/15–1914)
othering 147, 148, 152, 159–60, 228
Ottoman Empire
    Egypt 73
    and the European Concert 54, 146, 152, 162
    and European scholars 148, 163–65, 230–31
    and the First World War 343
    and the Greek War of Independence (1821–32) 145
    and international law 158–59, 162, 165–67
    and intervention 144–45, 146, 148, 159–60, 228–31
    and Russia 147, 156, 157, 228–31
    see also Eastern Question
Oxford Manual (1880) 202, 285–86, 288, 291, 293–94, 295

pacifism
    anarchy vs 301–2
    and the French Revolution 67
    and Kant 93–94, 99
    legal 93–94, 99, 220, 235–36, 297, 301–2
    and liberal scholars 220, 235–36, 297, 301–2
    and militarism 202, 282, 301–2
    as a 'mistaken belief' (W.G. Grewe) 31
Palmerston, Viscount 160, 183
Paris Order (1919/20–39) 341, 347
Paris Peace Conference (1919/20)
parliamentary debates 65–67, 79–80, 169–70, 181–82, 184, 189, 325–26

peace
    activists 336–37
    advocates of peace vs realism 233–36, 289–92, 298–301
    anarchy vs 301–2, 312
    through balance of power 90, 159–60, 261–62
    and coercion 109–10, 133–50, 152
    and colonialism 110, 152, 231–33
    democratic 226
    dictated 343
    as a dream ('and not even a beautiful dream') 275, 286, 289, 331–32, 343
    and the European Concert 112–18, 130–52, 169, 171, 175, 188, 317
    European peace project 219–20
    as 'feminine' 302
    general/European 137–38, 139–40, 142–43, 153–54, 161, 180, 188, 194, 198–200, 229
    'Hundred Years' Peace', thesis of 54–55, 150–52
    institutionalization of 130–33
    through law 34, 92–99, 112–18, 203–20, 261–62, 274, 275, 290–93, 308, 336–38, 339, 340
    movements 169–70
    as a norm 153–54, 175, 182, 187, 198–200
    organizing 217–20
    peacekeeping 120–21, 335–36
    perpetual 92–99, 131, 151–52, 219, 283, 286, 339
    through polemics 298–301
    and power 261–62
    reflexive 233–36
    and revolution 141
    societies 169–70
    treaties, analysis of 38
    war and 41–42, 55, 70, 127, 136–41, 220–33, 290–93, 345
    see also arbitration; diplomacy; Hague Peace Conferences (1899/1907); mediation; pacifism
peace treaties (in chronological order)
    Peace of Westphalia (1648), *see* Congress of Westphalia (1645–48)
    Peace of Utrecht (1713) 75
    Peace of Basel (1795) 80, 93–94, 101
    Peace of Tilsit (1807) 74, 80–81
    First Peace of Paris (1814) 115
    Peace of Vienna (1814/15), *see* Congress of Vienna (1814/15)
    Second Peace of Paris (1856), *see* Congress of Paris (1856); Treaty of Paris (1856)
    Peace of Villafranca (1859) 179, 192
    Peace of Zurich (1859) 179
    Peace of Versailles (1919), *see* Paris Order (1919/20–1939); Treaty of Versailles (1919)

Pétion de Villeneuve, Jérôme 69
Pfau, Ludwig 289–90
Pitt, William 71, 79–80, 84, 112–14
Poland 73–74, 80–81, 94, 116, 134, 138, 181, 184, 347
　Partitions of (1772/93/95) 80–81
　Polish-Saxon Question 116, 134
politics
　and international law 16, 35, 49–53, 107, 178, 226, 229–31, 238, 242, 297–98, 353
　and morality 49–50, 56–57, 92–99, 211, 242–43, 249, 254–55, 257–60, 261–64, 295–98, 350
　politicization/depoliticization 16, 56–57, 160, 199, 224, 228, 235, 237, 250
　and scientific objectivity 16–17, 97–98, 250
　see also multinormativity; power; realpolitik
positivism in international law, see international law
possession 68–69, 78, 112–13, 132, 174–75, 253, 299, 317, 325–26
postcolonialism 220–33
　see also colonialism/imperialism
postmodernity, see modernity
power, political
　asymmetries 50
　concept/theory of 38–57, 254–60, 261–64
　discursive power 38–57
　in the justification of war 49–50, 57–60, 96
　and norms 55, 134–36, 225
　see also balance of power; discourse; Machtstaat; normativity/norms; realism; realpolitik
practice, political/state 6–7, 16–17, 28–29, 89–90, 91–92, 123, 127, 141, 210, 216
　see also theory and practice
pre-emptive war (preemption) 318, 320–21, 326, 330, 331
preventive war (prevention) 67, 105, 176, 194, 196, 197, 200, 256, 320, 321, 330–31, 332
progress, narrative of 31–35, 334–42
prohibition of war/the use of force
　as an emerging norm 18, 123, 151, 324, 339
　under the Kellogg-Briand Pact (1928) 33, 336–37, 339, 341
　in the 'long nineteenth century' (1789–1918) 18, 86, 92–99, 110, 121, 122–28, 147, 150–52, 237, 277, 315, 324–25, 339
　modern 92–99, 110, 121, 337
　UN Charter's 33, 51, 315, 339, 349
propaganda, political 51–52, 84–85, 155, 156, 230–31, 320–21, 322–23, 324, 352, 359–60
　justifications of war as 51–52
　justifications of war as 'not only' 51–52, 352
protectorate 231

Prussia
　and Clausewitz 102
　and the Crimean War (1853–56) 162–63
　and the European Concert 116, 134
　and France 188–98
　and the hegemony in Germany 181–98, 223–25, 254
　in the Napoleonic Wars 73–74, 76–81
　'Prussian Ethics' (L. Pfau) 289–90
　'Prussification' ('*Verpreußung*') (W. Schücking) 233
public opinion 162–63, 193
　see also communication community; media
Pütter, Karl Theodor 89–90, 250–51

racism 227, 236, 237–38, 254, 361
　see also colonialism/imperialism
raison d'état 24–25
Ranke, Leopold von 254–57
realism
　vs advocates of peace 233–36, 289–92, 298–301
　vs constructivism 51–52
　critique of 283–95, 352
　'denormativization of' (C. Daase and N. Deitelhoff) 350
　German 241–43
　immoral 257–60, 261–64, 295–96
　vs liberalism 283–95
　'military realism' (J. von Hartmann) 271, 306–7, 332, 347
　political 31
　structural/neo- 350, 352
　as a substitute religion 30–31
　triumph of 349–50
　varieties of 276–79
　see also balance of power; Carr; Clausewitz; Clausewitzians (lawyers); liberum ius ad bellum; Machtstaat; Morgenthau; politics; power; realpolitik; Treitschke
realpolitik 30, 37, 172, 179–80, 181–83, 185, 191, 197, 198–200, 209, 255, 346, 348
　'age of' 153–54, 198
　and law 225
　and liberal scholars 254
　and principles 179–80, 200
　see also Bismarck; Cavour; Gorchakov
regulation, see ius ad bellum; *ius in bello*; juridification/legalization
religion
　and the French Revolution 107–8
　and international law 37, 128, 137, 148, 158–62, 310–11
　and intervention 149, 152
　of the nation 83–84

religion (*cont.*)
  overcoming of 37, 252
  and politics 156
  in war justifications 82, 107–8, 178, 229, 253
  see also Christianity; ethics; Islam; just war; morality; multinormativity
  repetition structures ('*Wiederholungsstrukturen*') (R. Koselleck) 11–12, 361–62
Repgen, Konrad 14–15, 51, 351–53
reprisal 43–44, 91–92, 127, 157, 158, 327–28, 338–39
Rettich, Heinrich 243–53, 263–64, 267, 277, 344–45
de Robespierre, Maximilien 70
von Rochau, August Ludwig 225, 226
Rolin-Jaecquemyns, Gustave 147–48, 207
Root, Elihu 315
Rotteck, Hermann von 143
Rougier, Antoine 144–45, 147–48, 149–50
Rousseau, Jean-Jacques 69–71
Rühle von Lilienstein, August Otto 104, 267
Russia
  in the Crimean War (1853–56) 157–62
  and France 156, 157
  and international law 228–31, 293–95
  and Napoléon I 73–74
  and the Ottoman Empire 145–46, 148, 154, 157–65, 228–31, 293–95
  and Prussia 116
  and religion 156
  Russian aggression against Ukraine (2014/22) 35, 365–66
  and the Treaty of Paris (1856) 228–31

sanction 23–24, 67, 81, 126, 127, 209, 265–66, 283, 299–300
  economic 33
  war 126, 127, 283, 299–300
Sardinia-Piedmont
  in the Crimean War (1853–56) 163
  and the European Concert 163–64
  rule in Italy 179–80
  and the Unification of Italy 172, 173–78, 179–80
  see also Cavour
Saripolos, Nikolaos J. 292–93
von Savigny, Friedrich Carl 215, 216, 222–23
Schlieffen Plan 321, 330
Schmitt, Carl 25–31, 251, 268, 340, 345–48, 350–51
  thesis of a transformation of the European war discourse 23–25
  see also Calker; Germany; Hitler; Lueder; Machtstaat; realism; realpolitik; Treitschke; war

Schroeder, Paul W. 18, 111, 153–54, 352–53
Schücking, Walther 233–36, 273, 297, 304–5, 339, 346
  on Bluntschli 233
  as a diplomat 343
  on Eurocentrism 233
  as an exception in German legal discourse 236
  against German realism/anti-legalism 233
  on the Hague Peace Conferences (1899/1907) 234
  and legal pacifism 235
  on liberal scholars 233
  on Lueder 296, 297, 304
  on the peace movements 235
  on perpetual peace 234–35
  on '*Prussification*' of German legal scholars 233
  see also Fried; Kant; Kelsen; pacifism; Suttner; Wehberg
Second Schleswig War, *see* Dano-Prussian War
Second World War 33, 337–38, 339, 349
security
  of the army 288
  collective 54, 119–20
  council 54, 133
  international 182, 333, 340
  and just war 123–24
  national 72, 79–80, 105, 107–8, 158–59, 192, 193, 194, 223, 318, 343
  and violence 300–1
  see also balance of power; European Concert of the Great Powers; peace
self-defence
  concept of 51
  as a justification of the use of force 51, 53–54, 57, 121
  Kant on 94
  Martens on 91–92
  and the Revolutionary Wars 71, 78, 79–80
  in the Vienna Order (1814/15–1914) 121, 126
  see also aggression; pre-emptive war (preemption); preventive war (prevention)
self-determination 65, 170–71, 173, 193–94, 199, 222, 226
  see also sovereignty/popular sovereignty
self-preservation of a state 121, 199, 210, 319, 320
small war, *see* war
sovereignty
  as the basis of *liberum ius ad bellum* 28, 30–31, 250, 253, 267–71, 304
  concept/theory of 26, 30–31
  -free space (*terra nullius*) 231
  and international law 258, 304, 307, 312, 316

vs intervention 141–47, 157, 158, 165, 166–67, 169, 229
modern 27, 119
popular 65–72, 170–72, 173–74, 219, 227, 229
semi- 144–45
Spain 81, 116, 137–38, 139, 142, 167–68, 192, 195–96
von Stengel, Karl Michael Joseph Leopold 273–76, 298–301
Strisower, Leo 142–43, 211–12
von Suttner, Bertha 235, 302, 311, 312–13, 314

theory and practice 13–17, 45, 48, 68–69, 111, 113–14, 282, 367
Third World Approaches to International Law (TWAIL) 220–33
transformation of war discourse, narrative of 23–25
see also Schmitt
Treaty of Küçük Kaynarca (1774) 145–46, 157
Treaty of Paris (1856)
 as an international suborder 19, 162–65
 and mediation 168–70
 as 'modest' regulation (H. Wehberg) 341
 as the 'most important document of the Ius publicum Europaeum' since 1814/15 (W. Baumgart) 163
 and Ottoman submission to European international law 165–67
Treaty of Versailles (1919) 64–65, 235–36, 335–36
von Treitschke, Heinrich Gotthard 257–60
von Trotha, Lothar 328–29
trust in international relations/law 47, 49, 95, 109, 113, 122, 205, 334–35, 342
 via diplomacy 309
 distrust 258–59, 261–62, 293, 304
 as taboo 262–63

Ullmann, Emanuel 276–77
ultimatum 157–58, 174–75, 185, 315, 318
UN Charter, *see* Charter of the United Nations (1945)
United Kingdom, *see* Great Britain
United Nations (UN) 339
 see also Charter of the United Nations (1945)
United States of America (USA)
 Civil War 205
 and the First World War 323
 and the French Revolution 80
 and imperialism 231
 and international law 167–68
 and intervention 140
 and the League of Nations 341
 and peace movements 169, 205

unjust enemy, *see* just war
use of force, *see* war

de Vattel, Emer 25–26, 28, 80, 96, 98–99
Vienna Order (1814/15–1914) 55, 109–10, 121, 122, 123, 133, 150–52, 162, 187–88, 306–7, 324, 331, 332, 339
 see also Congress of Vienna
violence, *see* intervention; peace; war
de Vitoria, Francisco 23–24
Vittorio Emanuele II 172, 176–77

war
 'cabinet war' 84, 101, 186, 198–99, 253
 definition/changing character of 209
 discourse of 13–14, 52, 65–67, 108, 200, 209, 306–7, 325, 343, 364
 guerrilla 46, 81, 203–4
 and masculinity 272, 302
 manifestos, *see* declarations/justifications of war
 measures short of 18, 43–44, 127
 non-discriminatory concept of (C. Schmitt) 25–31, 47–48, 57, 59–60, 66, 250, 351
 and order, dialectic of 46–49
 and peace 41–42, 55, 70, 127, 136–41, 220–33, 290–93, 345
 pre-emptive 318, 320–21, 326, 330, 331
 preventive 67, 105, 176, 194, 196, 197, 200, 256, 320, 321, 330–31, 332
 prohibition of, *see* prohibition of war/the use of force
 as sanction 126
 small 137, 232
 trauma of 130–33
 as unilateral use of force 122–23, 126, 137, 139–40, 182, 194, 195, 210, 221, 271–72, 299–300
 see also declarations/justifications of war; intervention; just war; liberum ius ad bellum; peace; prohibition of war/the use of force
Wehberg, Hans
 on 'a century of anarchy' 5, 31–33, 297–98, 340
 on the European Concert 340
 on German anti-legalism 297–98
 and Kant 339
 on organizing peace 218, 233–34
 on the Paris Order (1919/20–39) 341
 on Schmitt 340
 on the Treaty of Paris (1856) 341
 see also Schücking

Westlake, John 206–7, 222–23, 232–33, 278–79, 296
Wheaton, Henry 124–25, 148
Wilhelm I 157–97, 223–24, 241, 242, 329
Wilhelm II 242–43, 312–13, 316–17, 318, 331–32, 335

World War I, *see* First World War
World War II, *see* Second World War

Zachariä, Karl Salomo 130–31, 132–33, 213
Zorn, Albert 305
Zorn, Philipp 269–70, 302, 304–5, 312